ANNUAL REVIEW
OF NURSING RESEARCH

Volume 27, 2009

SERIES EDITOR

Annual Review of Nursing Research

Volume 27, 2009

Advancing Nursing Science in Tobacco Control

CHRISTINE E. KASPER, PhD, RN, FAAN
Series Editor

LINDA SARNA, RN, DNSc, FAAN
STELLA AGUINAGA BIALOUS, RN, DrPH, FAAN
Volume Editors

SPRINGER PUBLISHING COMPANY
New York

To purchase copies of other volumes of the *Annual Review of Nursing Research* at 10% off the list price, go to www.springerpub.com/ARNR

Copyright © 2009 Springer Publishing Company, LLC.

Springer Publishing Company, LLC
11 West 42nd Street
New York, NY 10036
www.springerpub.com

Acquisitions Editor: Allan Graubard
Project Manager: Julia Rosen
Composition: Apex CoVantage, LLC

09   10   11   12/   5   4   3   2   1

ISBN 978-0-8261-1757-1
eBook ISBN 978-0-8261-1758-8
ISSN 0739-6686
Online ISSN 1944-4028

Printed in the United States of America by Hamilton Printing Company

The author and the publisher of this Work have made every effort to use sources believed to be reliable to provide information that is accurate and compatible with the standards generally accepted at the time of publication. Because medical science is continually advancing, our knowledge base continues to expand. Therefore, as new information becomes available, changes in procedures become necessary. We recommend that the reader always consult current research and specific institutional policies before performing any clinical procedure. The author and publisher shall not be liable for any special, consequential, or exemplary damages resulting, in whole or in part, from the readers' use of, or reliance on, the information contained in this book. The publisher has no responsibility for the persistence or accuracy of URLs for external or third-party Internet Web sites referred to in this publication and does not guarantee that any content on such Web sites is, or will remain, accurate or appropriate.

Contents

Contributors

Karen Ahijevych, PhD, RN, FAAN
The Ohio State University
College of Nursing

Jeannette O. Andrews, PhD,
APRN, BC
Associate Dean for Research
and Evaluation
Director, Center for Community
Health Partnerships
College of Nursing
Medical University of South
Carolina

Kristin B. Ashford, PhD, ARNP
Assistant Professor and NIH/
BIRCWH Scholar
University of Kentucky College
of Nursing

Heibatollah Baghi, PhD
Department of Global and
Community Health
College of Health and Human
Services
Associate Professor
George Mason University

Cathy J. Baker, PhD, CNS
Case Western Reserve University
School of Nursing

Sharon Bennett, MSN, FNP
Assistant Professor, DNP,
APRN-BC
Medical College of Georgia
School of Nursing, Augusta,
Georgia

Stella Aguinaga Bialous, RN, DrPH,
FAAN
Tobacco Policy International

Susan W. Blaakman, MS,
APRN, BC
Research/Senior Associate &
Doctoral Candidate

Joan L. Bottorff, PhD, RN,
FCAHS
Professor
School of Nursing
University of British Columbia
Okanagan, Kelowna, British
Columbia, Canada

Maria Britain, MS
Informatics
Indianapolis, Indiana

Kristine K. Browning, PhD, CNP
The Ohio State University College
of Public Health

Mary E. Cooley, PhD, RN
Nurse Scientist
The Phyllis F. Cantor Center
Research in Nursing and Patient
    Care Services
Dana-Farber Cancer Institute and
    College of Nursing and Health
    Sciences
University of Massachusetts–Boston

Geoff Cox, PharmD
Director of Pharmacy Services
Georgetown University Hospital
Washington, DC

**Erika Sivarajan Froelicher, PhD,
RN, FAAN**
Professor
School of Nursing
University of California–San
    Francisco

**Kathleen F. Gaffney, PhD, RN,
CS-F/PNP**
Professor
School of Nursing
College of Health and Human
    Services
George Mason University

Mary Beth Ginn, MSN, FNP
Nurse Practitioner
Novant Health, Salem Family
    Practice
Winston-Salem, North Carolina

Ellen J. Hahn, DNS, RN
Professor and Director, Tobacco
    Policy Research Program
University of Kentucky College
    of Nursing

**Janie Heath, PhD, APRN-BC,
FAAN**
Associate Dean Academic Affairs
    and E. Louise Grant Endowed
    Chair in Nursing
Medical College of Georgia

Rebecca Lundin, MPH
Doctoral Student
Department of Society, Human
    Development and Health
Harvard School of Public Health

**Ruth E. Malone, RN, PhD,
FAAN**
Professor and Vice Chair
Department of Social & Behavioral
    Sciences
School of Nursing
University of California–San
    Francisco

**Anna M. Mcdaniel, DNS, RN,
FAAN**
Indiana University Schools
    of Nursing

Stephanie Barclay McKeown, MA
Doctoral Student
Faculty of Education
University of British Columbia,
    Vancouver, British Columbia

**Gretchen A. McNally, PhD,
CNP**
The Ohio State University
Comprehensive Cancer Center

Lyndsay Murray, BSN
Staff Nurse
Department of Nursing
Brigham and Women's Hospital

Kathleen A. O'Connell, PhD, RN, FAAN
Isabel Maitland Stewart Professor of Nursing Education
Teachers College Columbia University
New York, New York

Ayako Okada
University of California – San Francisco

Chizimuzo T. C. Okoli, PhD, MPH, RN
Research Associate-Tobacco
British Columbia Centre of Excellence for Women's Health

Mary Kay Rayens, PhD
Professor
University of Kentucky College of Nursing and College of Public Health

Virginia Hill Rice, PhD, RN, CNS, FAAN
Professor
Wayne State University
College of Nursing &
Karmanos Cancer Institute

S. Lee Ridner, PhD, ARNP
Assistant Professor
University of Louisville School of Nursing

Linda Sarna, RN, DNSc, FAAN
Professor and Lulu Wolf Hassenplug Endowed Chair
School of Nursing
University of California–Los Angeles

Annette S. H. Schultz, PhD, RN
Assistant Professor
Psychosocial Oncology and Cancer Nursing Research Group
Faculty of Nursing, University of Manitoba
Winnipeg, Manitoba, Canada

Daryl L. Sharp, PhD, APRN, BC
Associate Professor of Clinical Nursing
Director, Doctor of Nursing Practice Program

Sarah E. Sheehan, MLS, MEd
Liaison Librarian
College of Health and Human Services
George Mason University

Kawkab Shishani
Hashemite University, Zarqa, Jordan

Min Sohn
Inha University, Incheon, South Korea

Ashley W. Stevenson, BA
Research Assistant, Georgia Prevention Institute
Department of Pediatrics
School of Medicine
Medical College of Georgia

Renee M. Stratton, MS
Indiana University Schools of Nursing

Martha S. Tingen, PhD, APRN, BC
Professor, Georgia Prevention Institute
Department of Pediatrics
School of Medicine
Medical College of Georgia

Mary Ellen Wewers, PhD, MPH
The Ohio State University College
    of Public Health

Sara Young, MD, MS
Assistant Professor
Medical College of Georgia School
    of Medicine and

Department of Family Medicine
Augusta, Georgia

**Nancy L. York, PhD, RN,
    CNE**
Assistant Professor
School of Nursing
University of Nevada–Las Vegas

Preface

The learned of the day must direct the people to acquire those branches of knowledge which are of use, that both the learned themselves and the generality of mankind may derive benefits therefrom. Such academic pursuits as begin and end in words alone have never been and will never be of any worth.

—(Bahá'u'lláh, Taherzadeh, & Universal House of Justice Research Department, 1994)

While engaged in the pursuit of research, we often forget its true purpose; which is to advance science in order to alleviate human suffering. The use of tobacco and its associated products have for the last few centuries resulted in addiction, illness, suffering, and death. As recently as 25 years ago public tobacco use was a pervasive part of society. Health care providers and especially nurses witnessed firsthand the devastation of tobacco addictions. Nurses and others began the long road of creating a unique body of research devoted to determining effective methods of tobacco control and cessation, educating the public, and knowledgeably applying their findings to public policy. Their efforts have been heroic and the results of their efforts to change social behavior utterly amazing. We owe them much.

This issue of the *Annual Review of Nursing Research* clearly demonstrates the importance of nursing research and interdisciplinary collaboration to conduct targeted research, which truly benefits society. While nursing research was advancing health care in the realm of tobacco control, once again while caring for others we neglected ourselves. Tobacco addiction in the nursing population was recognized, researched, and continues to be targeted by organizations such as Tobacco Free Nurses.

The following compilation demonstrates how nursing research can forge interdisciplinary and global collaborations to forward cutting-edge investigations and change behavior. Those presented here are indeed impressive. The authors lead by Drs. Linda P. Sarna and Stella Aguinaga Bialous, both distinguished researchers and pioneers in the field of tobacco control, are to be congratulated for their outstanding achievement in bringing together a volume that should lay the groundwork for research in this field for years to come.

On another note, this issue, the 27th edition of the *Annual Review of Nursing Research*, has a new editorial team to carry it forward. Recently, the new Editorial Board reviewed the entire corpus of ARNR since its inception and marveling at its scope. Each issue ably and creatively lead by Dr. Joyce Fitzpatrick, an internationally known nursing leader and researcher, presented a body of work that often became the next hot topic in health care. We are all indebted to Dr. Fitzpatrick and her Editorial Board for steadily advancing the discipline of nursing science by providing it with the international visibility it so well deserves. Let us continue to pursue and develop nursing science that matters to our patients and society and "not those which begin with words and end with words"(Bahá'u'lláh, Taherzadeh, & Universal House of Justice Research Department, 1994).

Christine E. Kasper, PhD, RN, FAAN
Series Editor

ACKNOWLEDGMENT

The views expressed in this article are those of the author and do not necessarily reflect those of the Department of Veterans Affairs, or the Uniformed Services University of the Health Sciences. There is no conflict of interest in this publication.

REFERENCE

Bahá'u'lláh, H., Taherzadeh, & Universal House of Justice Research Department. (1994). *Tablets of Bahá'u'lláh, revealed after the Kitáb-i-Aqdas*. Willamette, IL: Bahá'í Pub.

ANNUAL REVIEW
OF NURSING RESEARCH

Volume 27, 2009

PART I

Building the State
of the Science

Chapter 1

Why Nursing Research in Tobacco Control?

Linda Sarna and Stella Aguinaga Bialous

ABSTRACT

Tobacco use is an epidemic of overwhelming proportions affecting survival, causing millions of deaths every year, causing untold human suffering worldwide, and contributing to escalating health care costs. Nursing research is vital to advancing knowledge in the field and to the translation of science to evidence-based practice. As the largest group of health care professionals (17 million worldwide), nurses have the capacity for an enormous impact on this leading cause of preventable death. This chapter thus provides a historical overview of the tobacco epidemic, health risks of smoking and benefits of quitting, nicotine addiction, and recommendations of evidence-based tobacco dependence treatment as a backdrop for understanding the importance and need for nursing scholarship. Also examined are nursing science efforts and leadership in removing two barriers to mounting programs of nursing research in tobacco control: (1) lack of nursing education and training in tobacco control, and (2) limited research funding and mentorship. The chapter also addresses the issue of smoking in the profession as it impacts nurses' health, clinical practice, and, potentially, scholarship efforts.

Keywords: nurses; tobacco; smoking; research

3

DOI: 10.1891/0739-6686.27.3

The devastating health consequences of tobacco use became rampant in the second half of the 20th century. The evolution of changes in tobacco use prevalence, advances in scientific understanding of the health consequences, as well as data about nursing and tobacco use provide a backdrop for the emergence of nursing scholarship in the field (Table 1.1). An estimated 100 million people died from tobacco use in the 20th century and, if changes are not made, one billion people are projected to die in the 21st century (World Health Organization [WHO], 2008). Half of all smokers are projected to die of a tobacco-related cause (Doll, Peto, Boreham, Sutherland, 2004). Approximately 443,000 deaths each year in the United States are due to smoking or exposure to secondhand smoke (Centers for Disease Control and Prevention [CDC, 2008a]). Those exposed to secondhand smoke, especially children, have serious health consequences, including 49,000 annual deaths (CDC, 2008c). The wide-ranging health effects of tobacco use and exposure to secondhand smoke are well documented and continue to expand (Table 1.2). Annually, smoking is attributed to causing $96 billion in direct medical costs and $97 billion in lost productivity, the cost equivalent of $10.46 per pack of cigarettes (CDC, 2008a). Unlike other large scale epidemics, the health consequences of the tobacco epidemic have been attributed to the business tactics and strategies of the tobacco industry (U.S. Department of Health and Human Services [USDHHS], 2008; WHO, 2008). If the 17.2 million nurses worldwide (WHO, 2009) are provided with the knowledge and skills to intervene, this would result in outreach to millions of smokers.

This chapter sets the stage for understanding the evolution and importance of nursing science in the field by providing a brief historical overview of the tobacco epidemic and emerging science, describing changing trends in tobacco use, reviewing health risks of smoking and benefits of quitting, reviewing concepts in nicotine addiction and evidence-based recommendations for tobacco dependence treatment. Also highlighted are nursing science efforts and leadership in addressing two barriers to mounting programs of nursing research in tobacco control: (1) lack of nursing education and training in tobacco control, and (2) limited research funding and mentorship. Finally, the chapter addresses the issue of smoking in the profession as it influences nurses' health, interventions with patients, and, potentially, scholarship efforts.

EVOLUTION OF THE TOBACCO EPIDEMIC

Knowledge about the health effects and disease burden of tobacco use became apparent in the later half of the 20th century, termed by Brandt as "the cigarette century" (2007). The 50-year prospective findings from the British doctor's study that followed 34,000 physicians confirmed that over half of all smokers die prematurely

TABLE 1.1   Evolution of the Tobacco Epidemic and Scientific Understanding About the Health Impact From a Nursing Perspective

Date	Milestone	Comment
Last 19th century	Invention of a machine for mass production of cigarettes	Previously hand rolled
1920s to 1930s	Cigarette advertising campaigns, first campaigns targeting women	Nurses and physicians were used as smoking role models.
1939	First reports of association of smoking and lung cancer by Dr. Ochsner and Dr. Debakey.	Previously, lung cancer was a rare cancer.
1940s	Increases in smoking among men during World War II.	Free cigarettes sent to American troops until the Gulf War.
1950	Link between smoking and lung cancer confirmed.	Same issue of JAMA featured cigarette advertisements; tobacco advertisements also ran in nursing journals.
1950s	Beginning of filtered cigarettes as a marketing tool as an image of safety. Lung cancer becomes the leading cause of cancer death among men.	Filtered cigarettes increased 10% to 90% in the 1970s.
1960	Smoking linked to increased heart disease in the Framingham study.	
1964	First Surgeon General's Report on smoking and health	The causal link between smoking and lung cancer was established; half of adult men smoked.
1968	Virginia Slims campaign	Women were aggressively targeted by the tobacco industry.
1969	U.S. Surgeon General's Report confirms link between maternal smoking and low birth weight infants.	Smoking among pregnant women was still acceptable.

(Continued)

TABLE 1.1   Evolution of the Tobacco Epidemic and Scientific Understanding About the Health Impact From a Nursing Perspective (*Continued*)

Date	Milestone	Comment
1970s	Cigarette advertisements banned on television.	Eliminated in response to vigorous health advertisement campaigns.
1970s	Over one third of women smoke	Smoking rates among female RNs (38.9%) higher than among women in the general public. Initiation of the Nurses' Health Study
1972	Marlboro becomes leading cigarette in the world.	
1980	First Surgeon General Report focused on women and tobacco	Prior reports were primarily based on data from male smokers; smoking may actually be worse for women due to reproductive impact.
1981	Surgeon General Koop takes on tobacco.	Excise tax on cigarettes raised, warning labels on cigarettes include women.
1984	Nicotine gum available	First nicotine replacement medication
1985	Lung cancer surpasses breast cancer as the leading of cancer death among women.	Remains the leading cause of cancer death among U.S. women.
1988	Surgeon General report on addictive nature of nicotine in cigarettes. Framingham heart study confirms increased risk of stroke associated with smoking.	
1990	Smoking banned on domestic airplanes in the United States.	
1990s	Smoking among RNs decline (18.3%) Formation of International Network of Women Against Tobacco (INWAT) that included many nurses.	
1992	*Tobacco Control*, first peer-reviewed journal on tobacco control	Now edited by a nurse, Dr. Ruth Malone.

(Continued)

TABLE 1.1   Evolution of the Tobacco Epidemic and Scientific Understanding About the Health Impact From a Nursing Perspective (*Continued*)

Date	Milestone	Comment
1993	U.S. Environmental Protection Agency Report on health risks of secondhand smoke.	Secondhand smoke declared a Class-A carcinogen.
1994	U.S. hospitals accredited by the Joint Commission required to become smoke free.	
1994	Tobacco industry executives declare that cigarettes were "not addictive" in testimony to Congress.	FDA declares cigarettes "drug delivery devices."
1994	Society for Research on Nicotine and Tobacco established	Scientific venue for scientists in tobacco control.
1995	International Council of Nurses published a position statement on tobacco.	
1996	First U.S. Public Health Service *Smoking Cessation Clinical Practice Guideline*	First research-based guide for smoking cessation, a nurse scientist was included in the panel.
1996	President Clinton publishes the FDA Tobacco Rule, granting the agency regulatory authority over tobacco products.	Tobacco companies went to Court and in 1998 a Court of Appeals agrees that the FDA has no jurisdiction over tobacco under existing law, confirmed in 2000 by the Supreme Court.
1998	Master settlement agreement between tobacco companies and U.S. attorney generals from 46 states	
1998	World Health Organization Tobacco Free Initiative launched	
1999	Tobacco companies sued by U.S. Department of Justice for "fraud and deceit," including through funding of research to delay or mislead public awareness about the harms of smoking.	In 2009 a Court of Appeal confirmed Judge Kessler's final opinion that tobacco companies conspired to fraud the American public.
2000	Continued decline in smoking among RNs (14.8%)	

(*Continued*)

TABLE 1.1   Evolution of the Tobacco Epidemic and Scientific Understanding About the Health Impact From a Nursing Perspective (*Continued*)

Date	Milestone	Comment
2000	Second PHS *Tobacco Dependence Clinical Practice Guideline*	Updated guideline expanding FDA-approved medications, a nurse scientist was included in the panel, confirms the role of all health care professions in helping smokers quit.
2003	Launch of the Tobacco Free Nurses initiative, the first ever national program to address smoking among nurses.	
2004	World Health Organization publishes *Code of Practice on Tobacco Control for Health Professional Organizations*	Encourages all health care professionals to be smoke free, be vigorously involved in tobacco control, refrain from accepting funds from the tobacco industry.
2004	First ever nursing leadership conference focused on tobacco control.	A gathering of researchers and clinicians representing 20 nursing organizations to stimulate interest in tobacco control as critical to the nursing agenda.
2004	Formation of the Nightingales	A nurse-led advocacy group to fight "big tobacco."
2004	Availability of the national telephone quitline, 1-800 QUIT-NOW	Available for free to all smokers in the United States (depending upon state, availability in different languages).
2005	First ever invitational conference focused on nursing research and tobacco dependence as a preconference to the National Conference on Tobacco Or Health.	Recommendations were made for a strategic plan for increasing nursing research in the field.
2005	World Health Organization Framework Convention on Tobacco Control	Uses international law to reduce tobacco use.
2008	Publication of third issue of clinical practice guideline: *Treating Tobacco Use and Dependence Clinical Practice Guideline: 2008 Update*	Includes most recent data on effective treatments, two nurse scientists were involved in the panel.

(*Continued*)

TABLE 1.1   Evolution of the Tobacco Epidemic and Scientific Understanding About the Health Impact From a Nursing Perspective (*Continued*)

Date	Milestone	Comment
2008	WHO MPOWER report, comprehensive report on the global status of tobacco use and tobacco control policies.	
2009	Preconference Workshop on Nurses and Tobacco Control, 14th World Conference on Tobacco Or Health, Mumbai, India	Focused on advancing a global partnership of nurses interested in tobacco control with a focus on enhancing nursing research.
2009	352 municipalities smoke free in addition to 18 state bans (100% smoke free apply to all workplaces restaurants and bars, with no size exemptions or designated smoking areas).	
2009	Legislation to increase federal excise taxes on tobacco products to enhance the State Children's Health Insurance Program (SCHIP) signed into law.	Tobacco tax increase will expand health care coverage for children.
2009	Family Smoking Prevention and Tobacco Control Act (H.R. 1256)	Gives the FDA authority to regulate the manufacturing, marketing, and sales of tobacco products.

Note. Adapted from *The Cigarette Century: The Rise, Fall, and Deadly Persistence of the Product That Defined America*, by A. Brandt, 2007, Cambridge: Basic Books; "Tobacco: An Emerging Topic in Nursing Research," by L. Sarna & L. Lillington, 2002, *Nursing Research, 51*(4), 245–253; "Strategies to implement tobacco control policy and advocacy initiatives," by L. Sarna, S. Bialous, E. Barbeau, & D. McLellan, 2006, *Critical Care Nursing Clinics of North America, 18*(1), xiii, 113–22. "Trends in Smoking in the Nurses' Health Study (1976–2003)," by L. Sarna, S. A. Bialous, M. E. Wewers, M. E. Cooley, J. H. Jun, & D. Feskanich, 2008, *Nursing Research 57*(6), 374–382; *The Tobacco Atlas*, 3rd ed., by O. Shafey, M. Eriksen, H. Ross, & J. Mackay, 2009, Atlanta, GA: American Cancer Society and World Lung Foundation; *WHO Report on the Tobacco Epidemic, 2008: The MPOWER package*, by WHO, 2008.
FDA = Federal Food and Drug Administration.

TABLE 1.2 Overview of Health Effects of Tobacco Use and Exposure to Secondhand Smoke

Health effects on unborn babies and infants	Increased risk of pregnancy complications, premature delivery, low birth weight infants, stillbirth, and sudden infant death syndrome (SIDS).
	Nicotine is vasoconstricting and may decrease the amount of oxygen available to the fetus.
	Nicotine also may reduce the amount of blood in the fetal cardiovascular system.
	Nicotine found in breast milk.
	Smoking during pregnancy reduces babies' lung function.
Health effects on children, and adolescents	Children and adolescents who smoke are less physically fit and have more respiratory illnesses than their nonsmoking peers.
	Smoking by children and adolescents hastens the onset of lung function decline during late adolescence and early childhood.
	Smoking by children and adolescents is related to impaired lung growth, chronic coughing, and wheezing.
Health effects of exposure to second-hand smoke on infants and children	Health effects of exposure to secondhand smoke: low birth weight or small for gestational age, SIDS, acute lower respiratory tract infections, asthma induction and exacerbation, chronic respiratory symptoms, middle ear infections.
	Suggestive evidence of exposure of secondhand smoke linked with spontaneous abortion, adverse impact on cognition and behavior, respiratory effects, exacerbation of cystic fibrosis, decreased pulmonary function.

Health effects on adults	Cancers: oral cavity, pharynx, larynx, esophagus, lung, bladder, stomach, cervix, kidney, pancreas, and acute myeloid leukemia.
	Cardiovascular: coronary heart disease, stroke, congestive heart failure, abdominal aortic aneurysm. Contributes to the development of atherosclerosis, associated with sudden cardiac death.
	Respiratory: chronic obstructive pulmonary disease (COPD), faster decline in lung function, pneumonia. Related to chronic coughing and wheezing. Increased incidence of upper and lower respiratory track infections.
	Reproductive: increased risk for female infertility and pregnancy complications such as placenta previa and placental abruption, premature rupture of membranes. May be associated with erectile dysfunction.
	Other: periodontitis, reduced bone density, increased risk for hip fractures, nuclear cataracts of the lens of the eye and age-related macular degeneration, lower survival rate and higher risk for postsurgery complications, higher incidence of peptic ulcers secondary to *Heliobacter pylori* bacterium infection.
Exposure to secondhand smoke	Eye and nasal irritation, lung cancer, nasal sinus cancer, increased heart disease mortality, acute and chronic heart disease morbidity. Suggestive evidence of an association with cervical cancer.

Note. From "Strategic Directions for Nursing Research in Tobacco Dependence," by L. Sarna & S. A. Bialous, 2006, *Nursing Research*, 55(Suppl. 4), S1–S9.

from a tobacco-related cause, particularly heart disease and a variety of cancers (Doll, Peto, Boreham, & Sutherland, 2004). Nurses contributed to the knowledge about the risks of tobacco use among women and the benefits of quitting through participation in the Nurses' Health Study, launched in 1976 (Kenfield, Stampfer, Rosner, & Colditz, 2008; Sarna et al., 2008b).

Cigarette smoking is the leading cause of preventable death in the United States (CDC, 2002a). The proportion of tobacco-related deaths due to various causes in the United States are displayed in Figure 1.1 (USDHHS, 2004). World-wide, the distribution of deaths, approximately five million each year (WHO, 2008), is slightly different with the majority of tobacco-related deaths due to a variety of cancers (34%), followed by cardiovascular disease (29%), and respiratory disease (29%; Shafey, Eriksen, Ross, & Mackay, 2009). It is projected that the majority of tobacco-caused deaths (>80%) in the 21st century will occur in low- and middle-income countries, including the deaths of over 100 million Chinese men if current trends remain (WHO, 2008).

The tobacco epidemic can be viewed in four stages that demonstrate the relationship between patterns of consumption of smoking and the delayed health impact, 2 to 3 decades after widespread uptake in tobacco use (Lopez, Collishaw, & Piha, 1994). In Stage 1 there is a steep increase in smoking, usually among men and a slight increase in male deaths caused by smoking. In Stage 2 there is a dramatic increase in female smokers and continued increase in male smokers, with increasing tobacco-related deaths among men, but only subtle increases among women. In Stage 3, there is a slow decline in smoking among males and smoking plateaus among females; tobacco-related deaths among men accelerate and deaths among women begin to climb. Finally, in Stage 4, as smoking among men and women continue to decline; male deaths from tobacco decline while female tobacco-related deaths continue to increase (Lopez et al., 1994). Using this model for identifying consumption and smoking attributable mortality in different parts of the world: sub-Saharan Africa is in the 1st stage; China, Latin America, Southeast Asia are in the 2nd stage; Eastern Europe is in the 3rd stage; and the United States, Canada, United Kingdom, Western Europe, and Australia are in the 4th stage of the epidemic.

Tobacco use has been described as a "social phenomenon" (USDHHS, 2008, p. iii), resulting from mass media marketing of tobacco products. It also is a social justice issue where the most vulnerable, especially women and children and those with the least resources, are at the highest risk (WHO, 2008). There is no such thing as a safe cigarette. So-called light cigarettes have been shown to be harmful (USDHHS, 2004), Americans and even nurses were unaware of the risks and thought they were safer (Borelli & Novak, 2007). Given the profound impact of tobacco to health, there is no question that nursing research is important and necessary.

Even though tobacco use has been identified as the greatest public health threat of the 20th century, the number of nursing researchers in this field is rela-

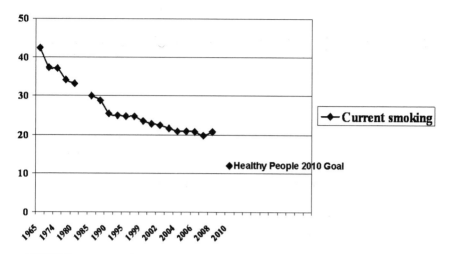

FIGURE 1.1   Prevalence of current smoking among adults aged 18 years and over: United States, 1965–2007. From "Early Release of Selected Estimates Based on Data from the January–June 2008 National Health Interview Survey: Current Smoking," by National Center for Health Statistics, 2008.

tively limited. Overcoming multiple barriers and challenges, nurse scientists in tobacco control are making important contributions to the field. These researchers are using a variety of methods of inquiry and conceptual models. They are addressing all aspects of tobacco control including primary prevention, initiation of smoking, genetic, biological, behavioral, and social aspects of addiction, methods of quitting, exposure to secondhand smoke, cultural and social influences of tobacco use, impact of the tobacco industry, and impact of policy on tobacco control, among others. Nursing research in tobacco control fits with the National Institute of Nursing Research's (NINR) 2006–2009 strategic plan that lists "promoting health and preventing disease" as one of four key crosscutting areas of research emphasis (National Institutes of Health, 2009). As nursing research supported by NINR develops knowledge to "prevent disease and disability" and builds the scientific foundation for clinical practice, research in tobacco control is especially important to guide nursing care.

CHANGES IN TOBACCO USE

There are a variety of tobacco products, including cigarettes, smokeless tobacco (i.e., moist and dry snuff, spit/chewing tobacco), cigars, pipes, and others (e.g., bidis, kreteks, water pipes). As 96% of tobacco products consumed worldwide are cigarettes (Shafey et al., 2009), the majority of research on health effects and quitting focuses on cigarette smoking. As a result, changing trends in cigarette smoking are the focus of this discussion. Smoking prevalence in the United States has declined since the 1960s (CDC, 2009). When the first Surgeon General Report linking smoking to health consequences was released in 1964 (U.S. Department of Health, Education, and Welfare [USDHEW], 1964), over half of adult men smoked and smoking was entrenched in all areas of society. Cigarettes were widely advertised in print and electronic media by celebrities, cartoon characters such as the Flintstones were seen smoking, and airplanes were filled with secondhand smoke (Brandt, 2007). About 40% of pregnant White women and 33% of pregnant Black women smoked in 1967 (USDHHS, 2001). Smoking was part of everyday life in hospitals where patients and health care providers smoked. Even now almost one of every five persons aged 18 and older in the United States smokes (CDC, 2008a).

US Trends

Increasing public awareness through public health and media efforts (USDHHS, 2008) have made a difference in smoking prevalence. Although continued declines in smoking (as displayed in Figure 1.2), and impressive public health efforts, policies, and legislation to confront tobacco use in the last decades are encouraging, the change in the prevalence of smokers has been relatively flat in the past several years (CDC, 2007b). Now, the majority of Americans are *never* smokers (51.6% men, 63.3% of women) National Center for Health Statistics [NCHS], 2008 and the number of *ever* smokers who quit smoking is increasing (52.1%, 47.3 million; CDC, 2008a). However, tobacco use is increasing and quitting tobacco use is still rare in many parts of the world (WHO, 2008).

There are important differences in smoking prevalence by sex and age in the United States (NCHS, 2008). More men than women smoke but that gap is narrowing. In the United States, smoking is highest among those aged 18 to 44 years of age (28.6% of men and 21.1% of women, the critical years of reproduction and when small children are commonly at risk for exposure to secondhand smoke). Smoking use declines with age among 45 to 65-year-olds, but the difference is not dramatic (24.5% of men and 19.5% of women). Older adults, aged 65 years and older, have the lowest prevalence of smoking with rates less than half that of smokers in the 45 to 65 year group (10.7% of men and 8.7% of women). After a lifetime of smoking, this is a time when older adults may be experiencing the comorbities of tobacco use. Over a third of adults with a smoking-related chronic illness (36.9%) are current smokers, including 49.1% with emphysema, 29.3% with coronary heart disease, and 20.9% with lung cancer (CDC, 2007b).

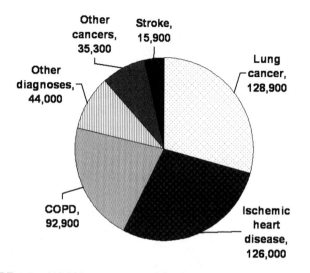

FIGURE 1.2   443,000 average annual deaths attributable to cigarette smoking: United States, 2000–2004. From "Smoking-attributable mortality, years of potential life lost, and productivity losses—United States, 2000–2004" by CDC. *Morbidity and Mortality Weekly Report,* 57(45): 1226–1228.

Smoking in the United States also differs by race–ethnicity and education. In 2006, smoking was highest among American Indian/Alaskan Natives (32.4%), followed by non-Hispanic Blacks (23.0%), non-Hispanic Whites (21.9%), Hispanics (15.2%), and Asians (10.4%; CDC, 2007b). Smoking is inversely related to years of formal education (26.7% for those with no high school diploma, compared with 9.6% for those with an undergraduate degree; CDC, 2007b). Twenty percent of high school students are current smokers, pointing to the need for strengthening prevention measures among adolescents and youth (CDC, 2008b). These statistics demonstrate that there are important disparities in tobacco use and that most population subgroups have not met the 2010 Healthy People objective for ≤12% smoking among the general population (USDHHS, 2009).

Global Trends

There are more than one billion male tobacco users in the world, with 28% of the 2008 estimates of overall consumption of tobacco coming from three countries: China (>311,203,200), India (>229,392,700), and Indonesia (>53,392,700;

Shafey et al., 2009). Similar to the smoking rate of U.S. men in the mid-20th century, over half of all Chinese men smoke. Twelve percent of women smoke throughout the world (250 million), with the greatest number of female smokers in the United States (>23,671,800), although other forms of tobacco use are more prevalent among women in certain countries (Shafey et al., 2009). Smoking is declining among women in developed countries, but is increasing in developing countries, especially those in Central and Eastern Europe (WHO, 2008). Worldwide, the poor will experience the greatest economic burden from tobacco use, will be more likely to die prematurely, and will have the fewest resources to quit (WHO, 2008). Women and children worldwide (especially China) are more likely to suffer the health impact of exposure to secondhand smoke.

CONCEPTS IN NICOTINE ADDICTION

Unlike other diseases, the root cause of tobacco-related disease is well established. Smoking is not a habit. The nicotine in cigarettes is addictive; so addictive that challenges in quitting have been compared to withdrawal from heroin. The understanding of the addiction continues to evolve, including genetic pathways and the pharmacogenetics of nicotine treatment (Thomas et al., 2009). Similar to other addictions, addiction to tobacco use is defined as "compulsive drug use, with loss of control, the development of dependence, continued use despite negative consequences, and specific withdrawal symptoms when the drug is removed" (Fiore et al., 2008). Tobacco dependence can include any form of tobacco (e.g., cigarettes, spit–chewing tobacco, pipes, cigars). In the U.S. Public Health Service *Treating Tobacco Use and Dependence Guideline: 2008 Update* (*Guideline*; Fiore et al., 2008), tobacco use is viewed as a "chronic relapsing condition" where relapse after quitting is common. Awareness of this was further heightened when President Barack Obama openly acknowledged his struggles with nicotine addiction and cessation (ABC News White House Team, 2009).

Withdrawal symptoms occur within the first days–weeks after stopping tobacco use (e.g., irritability, difficulty concentrating, depressed mood, sleep disturbance; Bialous & Sarna, 2004). These symptoms of nicotine withdrawal are associated with increased risk for relapse. Although the symptoms dissipate over time, craving for a cigarette can continue for years (Ferguson & Shiffman, 2009). Even light smokers (i.e., smoke fewer than 10 cigarettes per day or do not smoke every day) still have challenges in quitting (USDHHS, 2004).

Evidence-Based Tobacco Dependence Treatment

Quitting smoking is one of the most cost-effective strategies for improving public health (Coffield et al., 2001). Some of the established health benefits of smoking cessation are listed in Table 1.3. The majority of smokers (70%) do want to quit (CDC, 2002b) and 40% of all smokers make an attempt to quit each year (CDC, 2007a). Based on an extensive research review, the *Guideline* expanded and refined the recommendations for treatment of nicotine dependence (Fiore et al., 2008). The most effective strategies for treatment of tobacco use, including the strength of the evidence as evaluated by the *Guideline* panel, is displayed in Table 1.4. Similar to treatment for other addictions, both the physiological and behavioral aspects of tobacco dependence must be addressed. Advances in the science of nicotine addiction led to the development of medications that directly replace nicotine in the system during quitting. More recently, non-nicotine medications that block the pleasurable aspects of smoking by blocking or neutralizing the effects of the drug at a neural receptor site are now available. As a review and to aid with interpretation of the literature for those not familiar with tobacco research, common definitions used in the literature to describe smoking status, quitting, and nicotine addiction are provided in Table 1.5.

TABLE 1.3   Examples of Health Benefits of Quitting

Medical Conditions	Improvement After Quitting
Cardiovascular disease	
Coronary artery disease	Risk is cut by half 12 months after quitting; nearly the same as a never smoker 15 years after quitting
Peripheral vascular disease	Declines after quitting
Cancers	
Mouth, throat, esophagus	Risk reduced by 50% after 5–15 years of quitting
Larynx	Reduced risk
Lung	Risk drops by half after 10 years of quitting
Cervical cancer	Risk reduce a few years after quitting
Pulmonary disease	
Chronic obstructive pulmonary disease	Risk for death reduced after quitting
Low birth weight baby	Risk drops to normal if pregnant women quit in first trimester

Note. As described in the *Health Consequences of Smoking: A Report of the Surgeon General*, by U.S. Department of Health and Human Services, 2004, Atlanta, GA.

TABLE 1.4 Updated Recommendations for Treatment of Tobacco Dependence Based on Evidence in the 2008 PHS *Guideline*

Key Components	2008 Recommendations	Strength of Evidence
Screening and assessment	All patients should be asked if they use tobacco and have their tobacco use status documented on a regular basis (e.g., chart stickers, computer prompts).	A
Counseling and behavioral therapies	Providing smokers with practical counseling (problem-solving skills/skills training) and providing support and encouragement as part of treatment are effective in helping smokers quit. Tailored print and web-based materials appear to be effective.	B
Smokers unwilling to make a quit attempt	Motivational intervention techniques are successful in increasing likelihood of quit attempts.	B
Medications[a]	Clinicians should encourage all patients attempting to quit to use effective medications for tobacco dependence treatment, except where contraindicated (i.e., pregnant women, smokeless tobacco users, light smokers, adolescents).	A
Combination medications	Consider use of combination of medications. Effective medications are long-term (>14 weeks) nicotine patch + other NRT (gum + spray), nicotine patch + inhaler, and nicotine patch + buproprion SR.	A
Combining counseling and medications	Combination of counseling and medications is more effective than either alone and both should be offered to patients trying to quit smoking. Multiple counseling sessions are most effective in achieving abstinence.	A
Special populations	Recommended interventions are effective with variety of populations and are recommended for all tobacco users, except when contraindicated (e.g., pregnant women) or when effectiveness has not been demonstrated (e.g., smokeless tobacco users, light smokers, adolescents).	B

Light smokers	Should be encouraged to quit and supported with counseling interventions.	B
Children and adolescents	Adolescents should be provided with counseling interventions	B
	To protect children from secondhand smoke, clinicians should ask parents about tobacco use and offer them cessation advice and assistance.	B
Noncigarette tobacco users	Should be identified, strongly urged to quit, and provided counseling interventions.	A
Cost-effective tobacco dependence interventions	Sufficient resources should be allocated for systems support to ensure the delivery of effective tobacco use treatments.	C
Tobacco dependence treatment as part of assessing health care quality	Should be included in standard measures of overall health care quality, including measures of outcome (e.g., use of treatments, abstinence rates).	C
Providing smoking cessation treatments as a covered benefit	Treatments (medications and counseling) shown to be effective should be included in covered services in public and private health benefit plans as it increases the proportion of smokers who use cessation services and who quit.	A

Note. As described in *Treating Tobacco Use and Dependence: 2008 Update, Clinical Practice Guideline*, 2008, by M. Fiore, C. R. Jaen, T. B. Baker, W. C. Bailey, N. L. Benowitz, S. J. Curry, et al., 2008, Rockville, MD: U.S. Department of Health and Human Services.

[a]Varenicline (strength of evidence = A) and nicotine lozenge (strength of evidence = B) were added to the listing of approved medications (i.e., nicotine gum, nicotine patch, nicotine nasal spray, buproprion SR).

TABLE 1.5 Common Terms and Concepts Used in Tobacco Control Research Studies

Terms	Definitions
Smoking status	
Ever smoker	Smoked more than 100 cigarettes in their lifetime.
Current smoker	Smoked 100 or more cigarettes in their lifetime and now smoke every day or some days.
Light smoker	Smokes fewer than 10 cigarettes per day or who may not smoke daily.
Biochemical confirmation of smoking status	Use of biological samples (i.e., blood, saliva, urine, expired air) to confirm the presence–absence of tobacco-related compounds (e.g., cotinine) to confirm self-report of smoking.
Quitting smoking	
Quit attempt	Purposefully not smoking for at least 24 hours.
Point prevalence	A term for evaluating not smoking (even a single puff in the previous) within a specific time period (e.g., 7 days) prior to follow-up.
Continuous abstinence	No tobacco use during a period of time (i.e., 6 months).
Long-term abstinence	Not smoking for at least 5 months after treatment.
Relapse	Return to regular tobacco use after a period of quitting: may last for months to years.
Slip	Also known as lapse. A brief period of smoking during the quitting process.

Level of addiction

Smoking within the first 30 minutes of awakening	A screening question that can be used as an indicator of addiction.

Research analysis—strategies

Intent-to-treat	Analysis where all tobacco users who are lost to follow-up are counted as smokers.
Bogus pipeline	Smokers are told that their smoking status is being monitored by another means in order to improve the accuracy of self-reported smoking status.

Note. As defined by *Treating Tobacco Use and Dependence: 2008 Update, Clinical Practice Guideline*, 2008, by M. Fiore, C. R. Jaen, T. B. Baker, W. C. Bailey, N. L. Benowitz, S. J. Curry, et al., 2008, Rockville, MD: U.S. Department of Health and Human Services.; "Cigarette Smoking Among Adults—United States, 2007," by CDC, 2008, *Morbidity and Mortality Weekly Report*, 57(45), 1221–1226.

BARRIERS TO NURSING SCHOLARSHIP
IN TOBACCO CONTROL

As nursing research in a wide variety of areas for tobacco control is emerging, barriers remain. Two of these factors impact nursing practice and scholarship: (1) limited nursing education and training in tobacco control, and (2) limited research funding and mentorship.

Limited Education and Training

In order to increase the number of nursing scientists in tobacco control, nursing students need exposure to the health impact, key concepts, and methods of inquiry as part of their education (Sarna, Bialous, Rice, & Wewers, 2009b). Similar to other health care disciplines (e.g., Ferry, Grissino, & Rufola, 1999), data from a survey of nursing educators in 385 baccalaureate and 246 graduate programs suggest that the coverage of tobacco control content in graduate and undergraduate nursing programs, especially content related to clinical intervention, is inadequate (Wewers, Kidd, Armbruster, & Sarna, 2004). As a result, nurses do not receive adequate education for the delivery of interventions to help smokers quit. Model curricula and educational resources are now available to enhance nursing education in tobacco control (Sarna et al., 2009b). If students are not aware of the importance and current state of the knowledge in this line of research, they will not have the impetus or basic knowledge for pursuing a program of research. Similar results in the lack of tobacco control content for nursing programs have been found in international surveys of nursing programs (e.g., CDC, 2005; Sarna Bialous, Barbeau, & McLellan, 2006b; Warren, Jones, Chauvin, & Peruga, 2008). Pre- and postdoctoral training opportunities are urgently needed to continue building the critical mass of nurse researchers in the field (Wewers, Sarna, & Rice, 2006).

This lack of basic knowledge influences awareness, the ability to intervene with patients, and ultimately the value of the topic as a legitimate area for nursing inquiry. For example, in a national survey of members with the Oncology Nursing Society (ONS), 53% of the respondents reported lacking the skills to help patients quit (Sarna et al., 2000). Further, only 10% had heard of the evidence-based practice guideline for tobacco dependence treatment. Although the evidence of the importance and efficacy of nursing interventions in tobacco cessation are convincing (Rice & Stead, 2008), much more research is needed. The results of a meta-analysis of 31 randomized clinical trials demonstrate that nursing intervention, as compared to usual care, increased 5-month quit rates by 28% (Rice & Stead, 2008). Additionally, the expectations for intervention with smokers are changing with the Joint Commission and other agencies requiring the identification and treatment of tobacco use as core quality measures (Williams, Schmaltz, Morton, Koss, & Loeb, 2005). The Joint Commission cites the importance of nursing intervention in improving delivery of smoking cessation interventions to patients with heart failure, heart attack, and pneumonia (Williams, Morton, et al., 2005; Williams, Schmaltz, et al., 2005).

Limited Research, Research Funding, and Mentorship

Given the enormity of the health burden, it might be expected that research in tobacco control among all health researchers would be substantial. In fact, research in the area of tobacco is relatively small in comparison to research on other topics affecting public health, albeit to a less extreme level. For example, in a PubMed search of keywords in 2008, tobacco was listed 58,750 times as compared to 2,172,278 for cancer, 1,481,519 for cardiovascular disease, and 287,129 for hypertension (Shafey et al., 2009). Not surprisingly, nursing publications in tobacco also are relatively modest. Using tobacco as a keyword for a search on PubMed of nursing journals in 2008, only 77 articles were identified compared to 1,346 for cancer, 1,011 for cardiovascular disease, and 158 for hypertension. Using "smoking" or "tobacco" as keywords in a PubMed search of nursing journals published in English from 1950 to 2009, there is an escalation of articles over the past 70 years that is promising: 1950–1959 (0), 1960–1969 (n = 52), 1970–1979 (n = 198), 1980–1989 (n = 461), 1990–1999 (n = 846), 2000–2009 (n = 1563). The first published article in the nursing literature located in this search was published in *Nursing Times* in 1962 on the dangers of smoking (Anderson, 1962) and the first publication in the *American Journal of Nursing* was a "Stop Smoking Program" (James, 1964). When the search was further delimited to "clinical trial" or "randomized controlled trial," the results indicate the exponential growth in experimental studies as well: 1970–1979 (n = 1), 1980–1989 (n = 9), 1990–1999 (n = 34), and 2000–2009 (118). The first study with an experimental design focused on group versus individual preoperative teaching, with smoking history included as a classification variable, was published in 1972 (Lindeman, 1972).

In a 48-year review of data-based articles related to tobacco use in the journal *Nursing Research* (Sarna & Lillington, 2002), it was demonstrated that studies focusing on tobacco control were limited with most studies published in the past decade. Tobacco use was rarely included in the description of sample characteristics. The first mention of smoking as a variable influencing outcomes was in 1961 in a description of methods where smoking was not recommended prior to evaluation of temperature (Sellars & Yoder, 1961). However, the growing number of citations on the *library tab* of the Tobacco Free Nurses (TFN) Web site (www.tobaccofreenurses.org) indicates that nursing publications and research are increasing (Wells, Sarna, & Bialous, 2006).

Efforts are being made to increase the profile of nursing scholarship in tobacco control. A special focus of the TFN initiative was to increase the importance and visibility of tobacco control to the nursing scientific community. An invitational national conference was convened by the authors in 2005 to address the issue of nursing research in tobacco dependence (Sarna & Bialous, 2006a).

Nurse researchers, although small in number, also have been recognized for their efforts from the tobacco control community. For example, Ruth Malone, is the editor of the premier journal, *Tobacco Control*. She is also the founder of the Nightingales (Schwarz, 2004), an advocacy group of nurses committed to taking on "Big Tobacco." Both Malone and one of the authors (Aguinaga Bialous) have received the Sybil G. Jacobs Adult Award for Outstanding Use of Tobacco Industry Documents from the American Legacy Foundation recognizing their extraordinary contributions to public health with the innovative use and application of tobacco industry documents in research, policy, and advocacy. Ellen Hahn received the American Public Health Association's John D. Slade Memorial Advocacy Award recognizing her leadership and scholarship in challenging the tobacco control policies in Kentucky. Nurse scientists Mary Ellen Wewers and Erika S. Froelicher both served on the *Guideline* panel Nurse scientists (Fiore et al., 2008); Dr. Wewers has served on all three panels (1996, 2000, and 2008). Several nursing organizations helped craft the *Code of Practice on Tobacco Control for Health Professional Organizations* at a 2004 meeting organized by the WHO (2004). Additionally, TFN was recognized by the WHO as an exemplar for health care professions on World No Tobacco Day (WHO Tobacco Free Initiative, 2005). These are just a few examples of the recognition that nurses have received in the tobacco control community.

Limited Funding for Tobacco Research as a Public Health Priority

In order to accelerate research in tobacco control, adequate funding is imperative and tobacco-related research in all dimensions has been seriously underfunded given the public health impact of tobacco use. One of the issues that may be influencing the paucity of nurse-led studies in the field may be the lack of value or priority placed on such research by the nursing community of scholars. This is troubling. For example, although tobacco use is related to 30% of all cancer deaths, and health promotion and tobacco control are included in the ONS's priorities (Berger, 2009), a survey of the membership in 2008 (including the general membership, advanced practice nurses, and doctorally prepared nurses, n = 713) placed tobacco use as a focus of research as 64th in 70 overall, and 10th out of 11 areas (Doorenbos et al., 2008). This and similar surveys are used to direct priority setting and research funding.

The need for increased funding for tobacco-related research is essential, but will involve collaboration of multiple scientific and professional groups, including nursing voices (Gritz, Sarna, Dresler, & Healton, 2007). Considering the negative impact of tobacco as a measure of deaths per dollar spent, the comparative expenditure of tobacco research by the National Institutes of Health is very low with estimates of $1,224 per death for tobacco as compared to $257,763 per tuberculosis, $241,262 per HIV/AIDs, $16,260 per hypertension, and $2,885 for cardiovascular disease (Shafey et al., 2009). Even in the area of cancer, funding for tobacco-related cancers is far lower compared to other cancers (e.g., $548.7 million on breast cancer as compared to $273.5 million on lung cancer research). This lack of funding hinders training opportunities as well (Wewers et al., 2006). As a result, fewer researchers may pursue or be adequately trained for a career in tobacco-related research.

Although funding may be limited, nurse scientists are cautioned from accepting funding from the tobacco industry. Due to conflict of interest and the strong history of corruption of science by the tobacco industry, acceptance of funding by researchers from the tobacco industry is not recommended by the WHO *Code of Practice* and funding of such researchers is prohibited by some funders (e.g., American Cancer Society, American Legacy Foundation, Cancer Research UK, National Cancer Institute of Canada).

SMOKING AMONG NURSES

Similar to changes in tobacco use among adults in the United States (Figure 1.1), there have been profound changes in smoking prevalence among nurses (Table 1.1). Mirroring changes in the general population, smoking among female nurses has declined but is still a public health concern, as nurses who smoke are less likely to engage in smoking cessation interventions, as discussed below. Smoking is also a concern for the health of nursing professionals. In our analysis of data (1976–2003) from the Nurses' Health Study, we found that smoking rates in all birth cohorts declined with 79% of ever smokers in the study having quit smoking; highest smoking prevalence at the end of the study was among birth cohorts born in 1940–1944 (Sarna et al., 2008b). Of concern, the lowest prevalence of former smokers at the end of the study was in the youngest birth cohort, born in 1960–1964. In addition to the increased morbidity and mortality of smokers, quality of life of nurses who were current smokers was significantly lower than among former or never smokers (Sarna et al., 2008a). According to the most recent data from our analysis of the Current Population Survey-Tobacco Use Supplement (2006/2007), smoking rates among registered nurses is 10.7% and 20.7% among licensed practical nurses. By comparison, 2.3% of physicians smoke (Sarna, Bialous, Yang, & Wewers, n.d.).

Researchers may question why smoking among nurses should be addressed when discussing nursing research in tobacco control. Even after the Surgeon General Report, in the 1970s and 1980s, smoking was part of the culture of the nursing profession, with smokers often beginning to smoke in nursing school

(Bialous, Sarna, Wewers, Froelicher, & Danao, 2004). Even well-known nursing leaders were smokers. Although smoking has declined, it continues to negatively affect the workplace (Sarna, Bialous, Wewers, Froelicher, & Danao, 2005), and workplace routine (Sarna et al., 2009). Has smoking among nursing professionals influenced interest in nursing science in tobacco control? The authors are unable to determine the if delayed response of nurse scholars to the mounting scientific evidence of the harms of tobacco use was related to the cohort affected by the high rates of smoking among nurses in the 1970s. On one hand, experience with nicotine addiction may inform the researcher. For example, Malone (2007) describes her struggles with nicotine addiction and how her research of industry documents had greater meaning because of her personal struggle. On the other hand, nurses who never smoked may not be aware of smoking as an addiction. Whether or not nurses are nonsmoking role models, a growing body of literature supports the negative relationship between smoking among health care professionals, including nurses, and interventions with patients and attitudes toward tobacco control resulting in recommendations that health care providers who smoke quit (Fiore et al., 2008; WHO, 2004, 2008).

International Smoking Patterns Among Nurses

Smoking patterns among nurses vary worldwide. In many countries, smoking is still permitted in hospitals and in clinics and the prevalence of current smoking among health care professionals in some countries is 40 to 50% (Shafey et al., 2009). In several countries in the world where smoking is very low among women, smoking is low among nurses too (Shafey et al., 2009), but, similar to smoking in the United States in the 1970s, there are countries where smoking among nurses or students nurses is higher than smoking among women in general (Smith 2007; Smith & Leggat, 2007). However, in countries such as China, where nurses smoke at low rates and physicians have high rates of smoking (anywhere form 30% to 50%; Jiang et al., 2007; Shaffey et al., 2009), nurses may be well positioned for the delivery of interventions in tobacco control (Chan, Sarna, & Danao, 2008).

CONCLUSION

In conclusion, the health impact of the tobacco epidemic continues to evolve and will persist through the 21st century. Nursing research in all phases of tobacco control, from primary prevention, tobacco dependence treatment, efforts to reduce exposure to secondhand smoke, and to providing the foundation for health care policy is needed. Scholarship in the area of tobacco is one the most important ways that nurse scientists can contribute to health and well-being of society and ameliorate suffering. Research contributions by nursing scholars have been recognized and valued but more attention is needed to increase the next cadre of nurse researchers in the field. This can be achieved by increasing tobacco control content in nursing education and other training opportunities in the United States and internationally, and by increasing funding opportunities and mentors. Given its importance to public health and to nursing care, established nursing scientists in other fields should consider expanding their own areas of scholarship to include consideration of tobacco use as a variable impacting health outcomes and symptom management.

REFERENCES

ABC News White House Team. (2009). *Political punch: President Obama signs tobacco bill*. Retrieved August 3, 2009, from http://blogs.abcnews.com/politicalpunch/2009/06/presi dent-obama-invoked-own-struggle-with-cigarettes-as-he-signs-tobacco-bill.html

Anderson, J. (1962). The dangers of smoking. *Nursing Times, 58*, 424–426.

Berger, A. (2009). *Oncology nursing society 2009–2013 research agenda*. Retrieved from http://www.ons.org/research/information/documents/pdfs/2009-2013ONSResearch Agenda.pdf

Bialous, S. A., & Sarna, L. (2004). Sparing a few minutes for tobacco cessation: If only half of all nurses helped one patient per month quit smoking, more than 12 million smokers would overcome their addictions every year. *American Journal of Nursing, 104*(12), 54–60.

Bialous, S., Sarna, L., Wewers, M. E., Froelicher, E. S., & Danao, L. (2004). Nurses' perspectives of smoking initiation, addiction, and cessation. *Nursing Research, 53*(6), 387–395.

Borrelli, B., & Novak, S. P. (2007). Nurses' knowledge about the risk of light cigarettes and other tobacco "harm reduction" strategies. *Nicotine & Tobacco Research, 9*(6), 653–661.

Brandt, A. (2007). *The cigarette century: The rise, fall, and deadly persistence of the product that defined America*. Cambridge: Basic Books.

Centers for Disease Control and Prevention (CDC). (2002a). Annual smoking-attributable mortality, years of potential life lost, and economic costs—United States, 1995–1999. *Morbidity and Mortality Weekly Report, 51*(14), 300–303.

Centers for Disease Control and Prevention. (2002b). Cigarette smoking among adults— United States, 2000. *Morbidity and Mortality Weekly Report, 51*(29), 642–645.

Centers for Disease Control and Prevention. (2005). Tobacco use and cessation counseling—Global health professionals survey pilot study, 10 countries, 2005. *Morbidity and Mortality Report, 54*(2), 505–509.

Centers for Disease Control and Prevention. (2007a). *Best practices for comprehensive tobacco control programs—2007*. Atlanta, GA: U.S. Department of Health and Human Services, National Center for Chronic Disease Prevention and Health Promotion, Office on Smoking and Health.

Centers for Disease Control and Prevention. (2007b). Cigarette smoking among adults— United States, 2006. *Morbidity and Mortality Weekly Report, 56*(44), 1157–1161.

Centers for Disease Control and Prevention. (2008a). Cigarette smoking among adults— United States, 2007. *Morbidity and Mortality Weekly Report, 57*(45), 1221–1226.

28 ANNUAL REVIEW OF NURSING RESEARCH

Centers for Disease Control and Prevention. (2008b). Cigarette smoking among high school students—United States, 1991–2007. *Morbidity and Mortality Weekly Report, 57*(25), 689–691.

Centers for Disease Control and Prevention. (2008c). Smoking-attributable mortality, years of potential life lost, and productivity losses—United States, 2000–2004. *Morbidity and Mortality Weekly Report, 57*(45): 1226–1228.

Centers for Disease Prevention and Control. (2009). Trends in current cigarette smoking among high school students and adults, United States, 1965–2007. Retrieved from http://www.cdc.gov/tobacco/data_statistics/tables/trends/cig_smoking/

Chan, S. S., Sarna, L., Danao, L. L. (2008). Are nurses prepared to curb the tobacco epidemic in China? A questionnaire survey of schools of nursing. *International Journal of Nursing Studies, 45*(5), 706–713.

Coffield, A. B., Maciosek, M. V., McGinnis, J. M., Harris, J. R., Caldwell, M. B., Teutsch, S. M., et al. (2001). Priorities among recommended clinical preventive services. *American Journal of Preventive Medicine, 21*(1), 1–9.

Doll, R., Peto, R., Boreham, J., & Sutherland, I. (2004). Mortality in relation to smoking: 50 years' observation on male British doctors. *British Medical Journal, 328*(7455), 1519–1527.

Doorenbos, A., Berger, A., Brohard-Holbert, C., Eaton, L., Kozachik, S., LoBiondo-Wood, G., et al. (2008). 2008 ONS research priorities survey. *Oncology Nursing Forum, 35*(6), E100–E107.

Ferguson, S., & Shiffman, S. (2009). The relevance and treatment of cue-induced cravings in tobacco dependence. *Journal of Substance Abuse Treatment, 36*(3), 235–243.

Ferry, L. H., Grissino, L. M., & Rufola, P. S. (1999). Tobacco dependence curricula in US undergraduate medical education. *Journal of the American Medical Association, 282*(9), 825–829.

Fiore, M. C., Bailey, W. C., Cohen, S. J., Dorfman, S. F., Goldstein, M. G., Gritz, E. R., et al. (1996). *Smoking cessation clinical practice guideline no. 18.* Rockville, MD: U.S. Department of Health & Human Services, Public Health Service, Agency for Health Care Policy and Research.

Fiore, M., Jaen, C. R., Baker, T. B., Bailey, W. C., Benowitz, N. L., Curry, S. J., et al. (2008). *Treating tobacco use and dependence: 2008 update, clinical practice guideline.* Rockville, MD: U.S. Department of Health and Human Services.

Gritz, E., Sarna, L., Dresler, C., & Healton, C. (2007). Building a united front: Aligning the agendas for tobacco control, lung cancer research, and policy. *Cancer Epidemiology and Biomarkers, 16*(5), 859–863.

James, G. (1964). A "stop smoking" program. *American Journal of Nursing, 64,* 122–125.

Jiang, Y., Ong, M., Tong, E. K., Yang, Y., Nan, Y., Gan, Q., et al. (2007). Chinese physicians and their smoking knowledge, attitudes, and practices. *American Journal of Preventive Medicine, 33*(1), 15–22.

Kenfield, S., Stampfer, M. J., Rosner, B. A., & Colditz, G. A. (2008). Smoking and smoking cessation in relation to mortality in women. *Journal of the American Medical Association, 299,* 2037–2047.

Lindeman, C. A. (1972). Nursing intervention with the presurgical patient: Effectiveness and efficacy of group and individual preoperative teaching. *Nursing Research, 21*(3), 196–209.

Lopez, A. D., Collishaw, N. E., & Piha, T. (1994). A descriptive model of the cigarette epidemic in developed countries. *Tobacco Control, 3,* 242–247.

Malone, R. E. (2007). Taking action: The Nightingales take on big tobacco. In D. Mason, J. K. Leavit, & M. W. Chaffee (Eds.), *Policy & politics in nursing and health care* (pp. 109–119). St. Louis, MO: Saunders Elsevier.

National Center for Health Statistics. (2008). Early release of selected estimates based on data from the January–June 2008 national health interview survey: Current smoking. *National Health Interview Survey.* Retrieved August 1, 2009, from http://www.cdc.gov/ nchs/data/nhis/earlyrelease/200812_08.pdf

National Institutes of Health. (2009). NINR strategic plan: An overview. In *The NIH almanac, national institute of nursing research.* Bethesda, MD. Retrieved from http://www. nih.gov/about/almanac/organization/NINR.htm

Rice, V. H., & Stead, L. F. (2008, January 23). Nursing interventions for smoking cessation. *Cochrane Database Systematic Review,* (1), CD001188.

Sarna, L., & Bialous, S. A. (2006a). Strategic directions for nursing research in tobacco dependence. *Nursing Research, 55*(Suppl. 4), S1–S9.

Sarna, L., Bialous, S., Barbeau, E., & McLellan, D. (2006b). Strategies to implement tobacco control policy and advocacy initiatives. *Critical Care Nursing Clinics of North America, 18*(1), 113–122, xiii.

Sarna, L., Bialous, S. A., Cooley, M. E., Jun, H. J., & Feskanich, D. (2008a). Impact of smoking and smoking cessation on quality of life in women in the nurses' health study. *Quality of Life Research, 17*(10), 1217–1227.

Sarna, L., Bialous, S. A., Rice, V. H., & Wewers, M. E. (2009b). Promoting tobacco dependence treatment in nursing education. *Drug and Alcohol Review, 28.*

Sarna, L., Bialous, S., Wells, M., Kotlerman, J., Froelicher, E. S., & Wewers, M. E. (2009a). Do you need to smoke to get a break? *American Journal of Preventive Medicine, 37*(2S), S165–S171.

Sarna, L., Bialous, S. A., Sinha, K., Yang, Q., & Wewers, M.E. (n.d.). *Trends in smoking prevalence among healthcare providers.* Tobacco use supplement: Current population survey 2003–2006/2007.

Sarna, L., Bialous, S. A., Wewers, M. E., Cooley, M. E., Jun, J. H., & Feskanich, D. (2008b). Trends in smoking in the nurses' health study (1976–2003). *Nursing Research 57*(6), 374–382.

Sarna, L., Bialous, S. A., Wewers, M. E., Froelicher, E. S., & Danao, L. D. (2005). Nurses, smoking, and the workplace. *Research in Nursing and Health, 28*(1), 79–90.

Sarna, L., Brown, J. K., Lillington, L., Rose, M., Wewers, M. E., & Brecht M. L. (2000). Tobacco interventions by oncology nurses in clinical practice: Report from a national survey. *Cancer, 89*(4), 881–889.

Sarna, L., Danao, L. L., Chan, S. S., Shin, S. R., Baldago, L. A., Endo, E., et al. (2006c). Tobacco control curricular content in baccalaureate nursing programs in four Asian nations. *Nursing Outlook, 54*(6), 334–344.

Sarna, L., & Lillington, L. (2002). Tobacco: An emerging topic in nursing research. *Nursing Research, 51*(4), 245–253.

Schwarz, T. (2004). Nightingales vs. big tobacco: Nurses confront the nation's greatest public health threat. *American Journal of Nursing, 104*(6), 27.

Sellars, J., & Yoder, A. (1961). A comparative study of temperature readings. *Nursing Research, 10,* 43–45.

Shafey, O., Eriksen, M., Ross, H., & Mackay, J. (2009). *The tobacco atlas* (3rd ed.). Atlanta, GA: American Cancer Society and World Lung Foundation.

Smith, D. (2007). A systematic review of tobacco smoking among nursing students. *Nurse Education in Practice, 7*(5), 239–302.

Smith, D., & Leggat, P. A. (2007). An international review of tobacco smoking research in the nursing profession, 1976–2006. *Journal of Research in Nursing, 12,* 165–181.

Thomas, P. D., Mi, H., Swan, G. E., Lerman, C., Benowitz, N., Tyndale, R. F., et al. (2009). A systems biology network model for genetic association studies of nicotine addiction and treatment. Pharmacogenetics and Genomics, 19(7), 538–551.

U.S. Department of Health and Human Services (USDHHS). (2001). *Women and smoking: A report of the surgeon general.* Rockville, MD: Public Health Service, Office of the Surgeon General.

U.S. Department of Health and Human Services. (2004). *The health consequences of smoking: A report of the surgeon general.* Atlanta, GA: Department of Health and Human Services, Centers for Disease Control and Prevention, National Center for Chronic Disease Prevention and Health Promotion, Office on Smoking and Health.

U.S. Department of Health and Human Services. (2009). *Healthy people 2010.* Retrieved from http://www.healthypeople.gov

U.S. Department of Health and Human Services. (2008). *The role of the media in promoting and reducing tobacco use* (Monograph 19). Bethesda, MD: National Institutes of Health.

U.S. Department of Health, Education, and Welfare (USDHEW). (1964). *Smoking and health: Report of the advisory committee to the surgeon general of the public health service.* Washington, DC: U.S. Department of Health, Education, and Welfare, Public Health Service. Publication No 1103, 386.

Warren, C. W., Jones, N. R., Chauvin, J., Peruga, A., & GTSS Collaborative Group. (2008). Tobacco use and cessation counseling: Cross-country. Data from the global health professionals student survey (GGPSS), 2005–2007. *Tobacco Control, 17*(4), 238–247.

Wells, M., Sarna, L., & Bialous, S. A. (2006). Nursing research in smoking cessation: A listing of the literature, 1996–2005. *Nursing Research, 55*(Suppl. 4), S16–S28.

Wewers, M., Kidd, K., Armbruster, D., & Sarna, L. (2004). Tobacco dependence curricula in U.S. baccalaureate and graduate nursing education. *Nursing Outlook, 52*(2), 95–101.

Wewers, M. E., Sarna, L., & Rice, V. H. (2006). Nursing research and treatment of tobacco dependence: State of the science. *Nursing Research, 55*(Suppl. 4), S11–S15.

Williams, S. C., Morton, D. J., Jay, K., Koss, R., Shroeder, S. A., & Loeb, J. M. (2005). Smoking cessation counseling in U.S. hospitals: A comparison of high and low performers. *Journal of Clinical Outcomes Management, 12*(7), 1–8.

Williams, S. C., Schmaltz, S. P., Morton, D. J., Koss, R. G., & Loeb, J. M. (2005). Quality of care in U.S. hospitals as reflected by standardized measures, 2002–2004. *New England Journal of Medicine, 353*(3), 255–264.

World Health Organization (WHO). (2004). *WHO informal meeting of health professional organizations and tobacco control* [Press release]. Retrieved August 1, 2009, from http://www.who.int/tobacco/communications/events/30jan_2004/en/index.html

World Health Organization. (2008). *WHO report on the tobacco epidemic, 2008: The MPOWER package.* Retrieved from http://www.who.int/tobacco/mpower/en/

World Health Organization (2009). *Global atlas of the health workforce*. Retrieved from http://apps.who.int/globalatlas/dataQuery/reportData.asp?rptType=1

World Health Organization. (2009). *Global health atlas*. Retrieved from http://apps.who.int/globalatlas/default.asp

World Health Organization Tobacco Free Initiative. (2005). *The role of health professionals in tobacco control, world no tobacco day—May 31*. Geneva, Switzerland: World Health Organization.

Chapter 2

Theories Used in Nursing Research on Smoking Cessation

Kathleen A. O'Connell

ABSTRACT

Theories tell how and why things work; how and why one variable is related to another. Research findings that are theory based can be placed in a framework that advances science further than findings that are unconnected to formal theory. However, much of the research in smoking cessation is atheoretical. This review of nursing research on smoking cessation published from 1989 through 2008 revealed that nearly half of the studies were based on explicit formal theories. The transtheoretical model and self-efficacy theory were the most frequently used explicit theories with most theories emanating from psychology. Five nursing theories were identified in this review. Studies that used implicit rather than explicit theories dealt with five major concepts: nicotine dependence, social support, high-risk situations, mood–affect, and the influence of clinical diagnosis. Largely missing from this set of studies were investigations based on biobehavioral models, including genetics and neuroscience. The relevance of the theories and concepts identified in this review to current clinical guidelines on smoking cessation is discussed. With their grounding in theory and their expert knowledge of clinical issues, nurses are in an excellent position to develop theories that will help researchers in every discipline make sense of smoking cessation.

DOI: 10.1891/0739-6686.27.33

Keywords: smoking cessation; theoretical frameworks;
transtheoretical model; self-efficacy theory; nursing theory

THEORIES USED IN NURSING RESEARCH ON SMOKING CESSATION

The purpose of this chapter is to identify the theories, theoretical frameworks, and conceptual models used in nursing research on smoking cessation. A theory has been defined as an abstract generalization that offers a systematic explanation of how variables are interrelated (Polit & Beck, 2008). Theories tell how and why things work; how and why one variable is related to another. Using formal theories, theoretical frameworks, or models (I'll use the terms interchangeably) allows you to take advantage of the thinking, the logic, and often the prior research of those who invent, espouse, and use the theories. Research findings that are theory based can be placed in a framework that advances science further than findings that are unconnected to formal theory.

Theories and Smoking Cessation

All research is guided by explicit or implicit theories. An explicit theory is one that the author acknowledges and describes. In this chapter, explicit theories are formal and have been developed and described previously. Implicit theories are informal and usually not described by the researcher. Implicit theories used in particular studies can be deduced from the variables chosen and from the relationships that are tested. Even though much smoking cessation research (done by both nurses and nonnurses) appears atheoretical, implicit theories are used to choose which of dozens of plausible variables should be selected for study. Sometimes the use of an implicit theory is necessary because no formal theory has yet been elaborated. Sometimes investigators are unaware of relevant formal theories. And sometimes investigators prefer the freedom to choose the variables they want to study without the constraints of formal theories. But when no formal theories are used, investigators rely on often unarticulated notions about which variables are important and that should be related. The problem with implicit theories is that they are easy to misunderstand and misinterpret. Sometimes the logic is problematic. Often, implicit theories are based on the implicit theories prior researchers assumed to be important but these implicit frameworks are not clearly articulated by either the prior or the current researcher. Although investigations that use implicit theories can make important contributions to the literature, they are more likely to stand as individual findings waiting to be incorporated into a systematic way of understanding the phenomena.

Using a formal, explicit theory offers no guarantee of success, however. Factors influencing smoking cessation include a large array of variables at many levels of analysis: societal norms, community, family, individual, intraindividual, physiological, and molecular. No useful theory can manage all these levels. A theory is a map of the important features of a particular phenomenon. If your city map included every feature of the environment, it would be as big as your city and therefore useless. A useful map has the features you're interested in, at the right scale, and leaves out all the other details. Likewise, researchers must select theories that include only the variables that are crucial to explaining the phenomenon of interest. For a description of how a theory was selected, see the article by Froelicher and Kozuki (2002) who described their process of selecting and rejecting theories for an intervention study.

Testing Versus Using Theory

Research can employ theory in two different ways. You can test a theory and you can use a theory. You test a theory when your research is designed to see if the map is accurate. You test whether the relationships the theory posits actually hold true in the empirical world and sometimes you test the assumptions of the theory. When you use a theory, on the other hand, you are setting out to determine whether the theory does an adequate job of explaining a phenomenon of interest. In my own work on reversal theory and smoking (e.g., O'Connell, Gerkovich, & Cook, 1995), I did not want to test whether people reverse back and forth between metamotivational states as the theory posits. I assumed that such reversals happen. Instead, I wanted to use the theory to determine if specific metamotivational states could explain why people lapsed during highly tempting situations.

Intervention researchers in smoking cessation face the daunting task of testing a new intervention while attempting to address all the variables outside of the intervention that are thought to have an effect on success. Because no single theory has been developed that comprises all these factors, theory-based interventions often use more than one theory (e.g., Andrews, Felton, Wewers, Waller, & Tingen, 2007; Hilberink, Jacobs, Schlosser, Grol, & de Vries, 2006; Rowe & Clark, 1999). Noninterventional investigations about smoking and smoking cessation may be able to use more focused theories because researchers are not responsible for getting people to quit smoking but rather for trying to explain the relationships among variables (e.g., Bursey & Craig, 2000; Reynolds, Neidig, & Wewers, 2004).

METHOD

For purposes of this review, a literature search of the online version of *Index Medicus (Medline)* for articles appearing during the 20-year period of 1989 through 2008 that had the term *smoking cessation* in the abstract or title and with the limits on the search of English, nursing journals, and research (of various types) yielded a total of 345 articles. The list of articles was reviewed and articles were excluded if they were research reviews, if they concerned nurses' attitudes about smoking or smoking cessation or nurses' plans to institute cessation programs. Also excluded were studies that primarily reported smoking prevalence rather than focusing on cessation behaviors or intentions. In order to focus on nursing research we limited the search to nursing publications. Most such journals have the term *nursing* in the title and publish research by or for nurses, but several journals (e.g., *Patient Education and Counseling, Journal of School Health*) include other disciplines besides nursing. The author list was reviewed for articles in these multidisciplinary journals and if any authors were nurses, the article was included in the analysis; if no nurse authors were identified, the article was excluded. After exclusions, a set of 137 articles were included in the analyses. This review excluded studies by nurse investigators published in nonnursing journals.

Each article was reviewed to determine whether the study was based on one or more formal theories. Table 2.1 lists the formal theories used and brief explanations of the theories along with citations to the relevant articles. Articles are listed in the table more than once if they reported using more than one of the formal theories. For articles that didn't use a formal theory, the concepts under study were reviewed to determine possible implicit theories. Concepts used by more than one study and possible implicit theories based on those concepts are listed in Table 2.2, along with the citations to the relevant articles. Articles are listed in the table more than once if they reported using more than one of the concepts listed on Table 2.1. However, Tables 2.1 and 2.2 are mutually exclusive. Articles using both formal theories and additional concepts not included in those theories are only listed in Table 2.1.

FINDINGS

The 137 studies included descriptive, qualitative, and correlational research as well as experimental studies. A total of 65 (47%) studies used one or more formal theories. Table 2.1 lists the 23 theories used in the studies, brief synopses of the theories, and articles that used these theories. Five of the theories are nursing theories and 18 are nonnursing theories. Two of the nursing theories are considered grand theories: the Roy adaptation model (Roy & Andrews, 1999) and the Orem self-care deficit theory (Orem, 1995), while transition theory (Meleis, 1997; Meleis, Sawyer, Im, Messias, & Schumacher, 2000), the interaction model of client behavior (Cox, 1982) and Mercer's stages of becoming a mother (Mercer & Mercer, 2004) are considered middle-range theories (McEwen & Wills, 2007). Among the nonnursing theories, reversal theory (Apter, 1982, 1989), Smuts holistic theory (cited in Lindberg, Hunter, & Kruszewski, 1990), and Lewin's field theory (Chaney & Hough, 2005), would be considered grand theories, while the remaining would be considered middle-range theories.

TABLE 2.1 Formal Theories Guiding Nursing Research About Smoking Cessation

Named Theoretical Frameworks	Description of Theory–Model	Studies Using Theory–Model
1a. Transtheoretical model (Prochaska & DiClemente, 1983; Prochaska et al., 1994) This group of studies focused on stages of change only.	Individuals are characterized at different stages of readiness for behavior change. The stages are: • Precontemplation • Contemplation • Preparation • Action • Maintenance	Andrews, Felton, Wewers, Waller, & Humbles, 2005 Attrebring et al., 2004 Chalmers et al., 2004 Clarke & Aish, 2002 DeJong, Veltman, DeJong, & Veltman, 2004 Efraimsson, Hillervik, & Ehrenberg, 2008 Hilberink et al., 2006 Hokanson, Anderson, Hennrikus, Lando, & Kendall, 2006 Jonsdottir, Jonsdottir, Geirsdottir, Sveinsdottir, & Sigurdardottir, 2004 Koivula & Paunonen, 1998 Reeve, Calabro, & Adams-McNeill, 2000 Rowe & Clark, 1999 Sharp & Tishelman, 2005 Shuster, Utz, & Merwin, 1996 Wilson, Fitzsimons, Bradbury, & Stuart Elborn, 2008
1b. Transtheoretical model This group of studies used both stages and processes of change	Individuals at each stage are hypothesized to use different processes of change. Ten different processes are identified.	Andersen & Keller, 2002 Andrews et al., 2007 Scheibmeir, O'Connell, Aaronson, & Gajewski, 2005 Ward, 2001 Webb, 2008

(Continued)

37

TABLE 2.1 Formal Theories Guiding Nursing Research About Smoking Cessation (*Continued*)

Named Theoretical Frameworks	Description of Theory–Model	Studies Using Theory–Model
1c. Transtheoretical model This group of studies used stages and processes of change and decisional balance	Individuals at each stage vary in their decisional balance, for example, perceptions of the pros and cons of smoking and quitting.	Chouinard & Robichaud-Ekstrand, 2005 Fritz, Hardin, Gore, & Bram, 2008 Ham, 2007 Ham & Lee, 2007 Keller & McGowan, 2001 Kelley, Thomas, & Friedmann, 2000 Kim, 2006 Macnee & McCabe, 2004 Macnee & Talsma, 1995b Ridner & Hahn, 2005
2. Self-efficacy theory (Bandura, 1977, 1997)	Part of social cognitive theory, but also considered a theory unto itself. Self-efficacy is the extent to which one sees oneself as capable of performing a specific behavior. Sources of self-efficacy are: • vicarious experience (modeling) • mastery experiences • persuasion • physiological arousal recognition and control.	Andrews et al., 2005 Andrews et al., 2007 Buchanan & Likness, 2008 Chen & Yeh, 2006 Condon, 1997 Fritz et al., 2008 Ham & Lee, 2007 Froelicher & Christopherson, 2000 Gaffney & Henry, 2007 Gulick & Escobar-Florez, 1995 Haddock & Burrows, 1997 Ham, 2007 Hilberink et al., 2006

		Hokanson et al., 2006 Johnson, Budz, Mackay, & Miller, 1999 Kim, 2008 Kim, 2006 Kowalski, 1997 Martin, Froelicher, & Miller, 2000 Wang, Harrell, & Funk, 2008
3. Health belief model (Becker & Maiman, 1975; Janz & Becker, 1984)	Performing a health behavior is a function of the degree of the perceived threat, measured as perceived severity of the illness to be prevented and perceived susceptibility to the illness; perceived benefits of the behavior; perceived barriers to the behavior; and the existence of a cue to action.	Clark, Haverty, & Kendall, 1990 Conrad, Campbell, Edington, Faust, & Vilnius, 1996 Haddock & Burrows, 1997 Hilberink et al., 2006 Marshall, 1990 Rowe & Clark, 1999
4. Expected utility theory (Keeney, 1982)	Expectations of the risks and trade-offs to health both for making the behavior change and for not making the change.	Clarke & Aish, 2002 Price, 1992
5a. Theory of reasoned action (TRA; Ajzen & Fishbein, 1980)	Behavior is predicted by intention to carry out the behavior. Intention is a function of the attitudes toward the behavior and the subjective norms with respect to the behavior.	Clarke & Aish, 2002 Gulick & Escobar-Florez, 1995 Haddock & Burrows, 1997
5b. Theory of planned behavior (TPB; Ajzen, 1991)	Theory of planned behavior adds the element of perceived behavioral control to the theory of reasoned action.	Bursey & Craig, 2000 Hilberink et al., 2006 Kim, 2008 Wilson et al., 2008 Winkelstein & Feldman, 1993

(Continued)

TABLE 2.1 Formal Theories Guiding Nursing Research About Smoking Cessation (*Continued*)

Named Theoretical Frameworks	Description of Theory–Model	Studies Using Theory–Model
6. Relapse prevention model (Marlatt, 1985)	Relapse prevention is promoted by avoiding high-risk situations and by effective coping responses and confidence in coping ability when presented with high-risk situations. Decreased confidence and ineffective coping leads to initial lapses; internal and stable attributions and guilt for the lapse lead to further use and relapse.	Froelicher & Christopherson, 2000 Gaffney & Henry, 2007 Gaffney, Henry, Douglas, & Goldberg, 2008 Johnson, Ratner, Bottorff, Hall, & Dahinten, 2000 Lillington, Royce, Novak, Ruvalcaba, & Chlebowski, 1995
7. Reversal theory (Apter, 1982, 1989)	Individuals are inherently inconsistent; they reverse back and forth between opposing states of mind. Motivations differ depending on the state of mind.	Burris & O'Connell, 2003 Cook, Gerkovich, O'Connell, & Potocky, 1995 O'Connell et al., 1995
8. Health locus of control (Wallston, 2001; Wallston, Wallston, & DeVellis, 1978)	The causes for health and illness are attributed to internal, powerful others, and chance factors.	Leong, Molassiotis, & Marsh, 2004
9. Social stress model of substance abuse (Lindenberg, Reiskin, & Gendrop, 1994)	Engaging in drug abuse is a function of stress, social networks, social competence, and resources.	Jesse, Graham, & Swanson, 2005
10. Illness representation model (Leventhal, Leventhal, & Cameron, 2001)	Health and illness behaviors are influenced by the individual's perceptions of the cause, consequences, timelines, and duration of the illness in question.	Reynolds et al., 2004

11. Smuts holistic theory cited in Lindberg et al. (1990)	Biophysical, cognitive, psychological, and social systems interrelate with each other.	Kowalski, 1997
12. Lewin's field theory with emphasis on change (Chaney & Hough, 2005)	Driving forces (hopes and emotional investments) and restraining forces (past and future elements inhibiting event) affect group change.	Chaney & Sheriff, 2008
13. Integrated change model (I-change; encompasses theory of planned behavior, self-efficacy, transtheoretical model, health belief model, goal setting and task performance (Locke & Lathan, 1990), and implementation intentions (Gollwitzer, 1999)	Behavior change involves three phases: premotivational, motivational, and postmotivational. Four types of factors determine phase: behavioral, psychological, biological, and sociocultural.	Hilberink et al., 2006
14. Jessor's problem behavior theory (Jessor, Donavan, & Costa, 1992)	Adolescents' cognitions, attitudes, and expectations of social behaviors influence the adoption and continuation of problem behaviors such as smoking.	Albrecht et al., 2006
15. Cognitive behavior theory (Beck, Wright, Newman, & Sliese, 1993)	Strategies to decrease self-defeating behavior, alter maladaptive perceptions, set goals, control urges, and garner social support are crucial to behavior change.	Albrecht et al., 2006
16. Self-determination theory (Ryan & Deci, 2000)	Intrinsic motivation and autonomy are crucial for behavior change.	Bottorff et al., 2004
17. Theory of behavior modification (Green & Kreuter, 1991)	Behavior change is affected by predisposing factors, such as attitudes, enabling factors, and reinforcing factors.	Koivula & Paunonen, 1998

(Continued)

41

TABLE 2.1 Formal Theories Guiding Nursing Research About Smoking Cessation (*Continued*)

Named Theoretical Frameworks	Description of Theory–Model	Studies Using Theory–Model
18. Transactional model of stress (Lazarus, 1966)	Reactions to stressors are determined by cognitive appraisals of the stressor. Primary appraisal involves evaluating whether an event is a threat; secondary appraisal involves evaluation of resources for coping with the event.	Macnee & Talsma, 1995a
Nursing Theories		
1. Mercer's stages of becoming a mother (Mercer & Mercer, 2004)	Four stages: (1) commitment, attachment, and preparation (pregnancy); (2) acquaintance, learning, and physical restoration (2 to 6 weeks postpartum); (3) moving toward a new normal (2 weeks to 4 months); (4) achievement of maternal identity (around 4 months).	Gaffney & Henry, 2007 Gaffney et al., 2008
2. Orem self-care deficit theory (Orem, 1995)	People maintain life and well-being by caring for themselves. Comprises three theories: self-care deficits, self-care, nursing systems.	Utz, Shuster, Merwin, & Williams, 1994

Model	Description	Reference
3. Roy adaptation model (Roy & Andrews, 1999)	A person is an adaptive system with input (focal, residual, and contextual stimuli), control processes (regulator and cognator), effectors (physiologic, self-concept, role function, and interdependence), and output (adaptive and ineffective responses).	Villareal, 2003
4. Interaction model of client behavior (Cox, 1982)	Health outcomes are influenced by elements of client's singularity (e.g., previous experience, intrinsic motivation, affective responses) and the client–provider relationship (e.g., affective support, decisional support, professional competence).	Rice et al., 1994
5. Meleis transition theory (Meleis, 1997; Meleis et al., 2000)	A transition is a change in health status, role relationships, expectations, or abilities. Transitions may involve perceptions of disconnectedness, temporary loss of familiar reference points, new needs, or unmet needs and vulnerability to risks.	Sharp & Tishelman, 2005

TABLE 2.2 Frequently Used Concepts and Possible Implicit Theories in Smoking Cessation Studies Not Using Formal Theories

Major Concepts	Possible Implicit Theories	Studies Using Concepts
1. Nicotine Dependence		
1a. Nicotine dependence	There are racial differences in dependence.	Ahijevych & Gillespie, 1997, Huang, Lin, & Wang, 2006
	Smoking to cope with stress leads to increased dependence.	Ahijevych & Wewers, 1993
	Secondhand smoke leads to nicotine dependence. Dependence influences quitting.	Okoli, Browning, Rayens, & Hahn, 2008, Green & Clarke, 2005
1b. Nicotine replacement therapy or pharmacotherapy	Because nicotine is addictive, success at quitting is increased by using pharmacotherapy to replace nicotine or to mimic its effects.	Browning, Ahijevych, Ross, & Wewers, 2000Challis & Surgenor, 2004
		Chou, Chen, Lee, Ku, & Lu, 2004
		Jonsdottir & Jonsdottir, 2001
		Kupezc & Prochazka, 1996
		Mahrer-Imhof, Froelicher, Li, Parker, & Benowitz, 2002
		Reilly, Murphy, & Alderton, 2006
		Tonstad, 2006
		Van Dongen, Kriz, Fox, & Haque, 1999
		Wakefield, Olver, Whitford, & Rosenfeld, 2004
		Wewers, Neidig, & Kihm, 2000
2. Social Support		
2a. Support from nurses	Support for cessation from nurses including interventions by nurses improves quit rates.	Browning et al., 2000
		Challis & Surgenor, 2004
		Clark, Rowe, & Jones, 1993
		Gebauer, Kwo, Haynes, & Wewers, 1998
		Gies, Buchman, Robinson, & Smolen, 2008
		Grossman, Donaldson, Belton, & Oliver, 2008

		Jiang, Sit, & Wong, 2007
		Jonsdottir & Jonsdottir, 2001
		McDaniel, 1999
		Racelis, Lombardo, & Verdin, 1998
		Wewers et al., 1994
		Wewers, Jenkins, & Mignery, 1997
2b. Other health care provider support	Support for cessation from health care providers improves quit rates.	de Vries, Bakker, Mullen, & van Breukelen, 2006
		Echer & Barreto, 2008
		Helyer et al., 1998
		McLeod et al., 2004
2c. Partner–family support	Partner and family support helps improve quit rates.	Echer & Barreto, 2008
		Holmes, 2001
		McLeod et al., 2004
		Winkelstein, Tarzian, & Wood, 1997
2d. Support groups and peer support	Peer support helps quit rates.	Albrecht, Payne, Stone, & Reynolds, 1998
		Echer & Barreto, 2008
		Helyer et al., 1998
		Huang, 2005
		Reilly et al., 2006
		Van Dongen et al., 1999

(Continued)

45

TABLE 2.2 Frequently Used Concepts and Possible Implicit Theories in Smoking Cessation Studies Not Using Formal Theories (*Continued*)

Major Concepts	Possible Implicit Theories	Studies Using Concepts
3. High-risk Situations		
3a. Strategies for coping with cravings	Use of coping strategies during high-risk situations improves success at quitting.	Browning et al., 2000 Clark et al., 1993 Cobb, Bott, & O'Connell, 1997 Griebel, Wewers, & Baker, 1998 Helyer et al., 1998 Huang, 2005 Jannone & O'Connell, 2007 Jonsdottir & Jonsdottir, 2001 O'Connell et al., 1998 O'Connell et al., 2006 Stanislaw & Wewers, 1994 Steuer & Wewers, 1989 Van Dongen et al., 1999 Wewers et al., 1994 Wewers et al., 2000
3b. Environmental cues, including partner or family smoking	Smoking cues engender cravings and lead to lapses during cessation.	Lemola & Grob, 2008 McLeod et al., 2004 Miller, Ratner, & Johnson, 2003 Snyder, McDevitt, & Painter, 2008
4. Affect–Mood		
4a. Anxiety and psychiatric symptoms	Anxiety and psychiatric symptoms increase relapse.	Chou et al., 2004

4b. Stress	Stress increases smoking.	Mackey, McKinney, & Tavakoli, 2008 Snyder et al., 2008
	Stress increases relapse.	Cummins, Trotter, Moussa, & Turham, 2005 Miller et al., 2003
	Interventions to reduce stress will prevent relapse.	Helyer et al., 1998 Wynd, 1992 Wynd, 2005
5. Influence of Diagnosis		
5a. Diabetes	Severity of diabetes affects willingness to quit.	Haire-Joshu et al., 1995
5b. Heart	Gender and age affects likelihood of continued smoking.	Conn, Taylor, & Abele, 1991
5c. Lung disease	Feedback on decline in lung function increases likelihood of quitting. Lung cancer diagnosis affects willingness to quit.	Wells & de Lusignan, 2003 Sarna, 1995 Wewers et al., 1997
5d. Pregnancy	Pregnancy affects willingness to quit. Age and socioeconomic status affect pregnant smokers' willingness to quit.	Edwards & Sims-Jones, 1998 Allnutt & Reid, 1999 Pletsch & Johnson, 1996 Tod, 2003
5e. Mental illness	Serious mental illness makes cessation more difficult.	Snyder et al., 2008

The most frequently cited theory was the transtheoretical model (TTM; Prochaska et al., 1994), which was used in 30 of the studies. As is often the case, some investigators used only parts of major theories. This phenomenon was especially true of the TTM with 50% of the studies using only the stages of change portion of the model, while others added processes of change and still others used the full model, which includes decisional balance (measures of the perceived pros and cons to smoking) as a factor. Self-efficacy theory (Bandura, 1997), the second most popular theory, was used in 20 reports.

Theories generally under the category of expected utility theories were frequently mentioned. These include the health belief model (six times) along with the theory of reasoned action and its close cousin the theory of planned behavior (used eight times collectively). Two studies reported using another more general expected utility model. Marlatt and Gordon's (1985) relapse prevention model was used five times. All other theories, including the nursing theories, were used in only one study or by a single group of investigators in two or three studies.

Table 2.2 lists the major concepts measured or operationalized in the articles that did not report using formal theories. Also listed are possible implicit theories used in the articles along with citations to the 55 relevant articles. Five major classes of concepts were identified: (1) nicotine dependence, (2) social support, (3) high-risk situations, (4) affect–mood, and (5) influence of diagnosis.

Nicotine Dependence

Of the 16 studies that used concepts of nicotine dependence, some studied the concept directly (e.g., Ahijevych & Gillespie, 1997), but most used it in relation to supplying nicotine replacement therapy to smokers in the interventions tested. Research on withdrawal symptoms were included in this category.

Social Support

The most frequently used concept (26 studies) was the concept of social support, including family and partner support, peer support, nurse, and other health care provider support. In some cases, clinicians provided brief support interventions (e.g., McDaniel, 1999). In other studies clinician support was more intense (e.g., Wewers, Bowen, Stanislaw, & Desimone, 1994).

High-Risk Situations

The third major set of concepts centered on resisting smoking in high-risk situations characterized by increased craving or increased probability of lapsing (19 studies). Fifteen of the articles focused on specific strat-egies for coping, while four focused on the triggers for high-risk situations, such as smoking cues.

Affect–Mood

The fourth class of concepts was related to affective symptoms other than withdrawal symptoms such as anxiety and stress as they relate to quitting and relapse (eight studies), with some reporting on interventions to reduce stress (e.g., Helyer, Brehm, Gentry, & Pittman, 1998; Wynd, 2005).

Influence of Diagnosis

The influence of the clinical diagnoses of the smoker constituted the fifth major concept (10 studies). Some studies posited that clients with specific diagnoses would be more likely to quit, such as those with declines in lung function (Wells & de Lusignan, 2003) or those who were pregnant (Edwards & Sims-Jones, 1998). However, other studies showed that diagnoses seem to complicate quitting (e.g., Haire-Joshu, Ziff, & Houston, 1995; Sarna, 1995).

The remaining 17 studies in the data set neither used a formal theory nor one of the five concepts in Table 2.2. These studies concerned a disparate group of concepts that were unique or idiosyncratic in this data set. Some referred to characteristics of interventions studied (e.g., Dino et al., 2001; Higgs, Edwards, Harbin, & Higgs, 2000), while others referred to individual differences among the participants in the samples (e.g., Stewart et al., 1996; Wynd, 2006)

DISCUSSION

This review revealed that a sizable number (nearly half) of nursing research studies on smoking cessation are based at least in part on formal theories. Some reports use only parts of these theories. For instance, many use only the stages of change concept in the transtheoretical model with little attention to the processes of change or to the balance of pros and cons that characterize different stages. This partial use of theories may be necessary in some investigations, especially when the theory is complex and not primarily focused on behavior change. But in the case of the TTM, which is focused on behavior change, it is possible that researchers were only superficially aware of the model and tended to focus on its easiest-to-understand feature, the stages of change. Nevertheless, using formal theories or parts of them grounds a study in the logic of the theory and connects it to other studies that are grounded in the same logic. Results of such investigations can be used to support or refute the premises of such theories and enable subsequent researchers to judge the usefulness of these systems of thought.

The use of nursing theories in smoking cessation research was relatively rare. This is understandable because nursing theories are usually grand theories that do not lend themselves to the specific issue of smoking cessation or of behavior change. Nevertheless, it is possible that nursing theories may be able to explain some phenomena in smoking. For instance, Gaffney and Henry (2007) used Mercer's theory of becoming a mother (Mercer & Mercer, 2004) to explain the smoking behavior of pregnant and postpartum women. Many women quit smoking when they get pregnant, remaining smoke free for many months, but the majority of them relapse shortly after delivery. Gaffney and Henry sought to use the stages of becoming a mother to explain this phenomenon (2007).

Of the 23 formal theories identified in this review, 17 were used in single studies or by a single group of authors. Thus, except for the mainstream psychological theories represented by the TTM and self-efficacy theory, it does not appear that there is much spread of the theories to other researchers. The reasons for this insularity of theory use are unclear. Because smoking cessation research is a multidisciplinary phenomenon, nurse researchers are required to be familiar with a wide array of disciplinary approaches and probably tend to look outside of nursing literature for ideas about smoking. Moreover, it is only in the last few years that research on smoking cessation has become more common in nursing. In a previous review of research on smoking published between 1981 and 1987 (O'Connell, 1990), I found only 23 studies published in nursing journals, an average of 3.3 studies per year, compared to the average of 6.8 studies per year for the 20 years reviewed in this chapter.

Implicit theories were used in 53% of the studies reviewed in this chapter. The problem with implicit theories is that the exact postulates of the theories remain unclear and the hypotheses derived from them vary according to the investigators' understanding of the concept. Moreover, an in-depth understanding of the concepts under investigation is often precluded by the failure to elaborate and use more formal theories. For instance, if we posit that the implicit theory behind nicotine replacement therapy is: *Because nicotine is addictive, success at quitting is increased by using pharmacotherapy to replace nicotine or to mimic its effects*, how does this implicit theory help us guide the use of the therapy? Why is the recommended therapy time limited? Using the methadone treatment model for heroin addiction, shouldn't we give the smoker supplemental nicotine for a longer period of time than the 6 to 12 weeks that is recommended for nicotine replacement therapy? Does the addiction go away? How should patients deal with coming off nicotine replacement therapy? Obviously, a more elaborated theory of nicotine dependence and its treatment is needed. Sometimes research using implicit theory is useful; nicotine replacement therapy has been shown to be so valuable that it has become a standard of care in clinical guidelines. But our understanding of the reason it works, for whom it works, and why it frequently fails is hampered by the lack of a formal theory about the role of replacement in nicotine dependence. Genetic and neuroscience models (e.g., Portugal & Gould, 2008; Stevens et al., 2008) appear underutilized in the research reviewed here and may be useful in contributing to a theory of nicotine dependence.

For some investigations, no formal theories appear appropriate. Such studies might be termed atheoretical or pretheoretical. My own work on coping strategies (O'Connell et al., 1998; O'Connell, Hosein, & Schwartz, 2006) is an example of pretheoretical research. These studies were carried out in hopes of differentiating effective from ineffective strategies, a finding that could have led to a theory of coping with temptations similar to the stress coping theory proposed by Lazarus and Folkman (1984), which differentiated problem-focused and emotion-focused coping. However, the results of my studies gave little indication that strategies were differentially effective or differentially appropriate—one seemed to be as good as another. I regard these findings as contributing to a theoretical framework that has yet to be developed.

The TTM was the most frequently used theory in this group of studies. Indeed, the TTM is widely used in addiction research. However, a number of authors have questioned the utility of the stage concept of the TTM (e.g., Balmford, Borland, & Burney, 2008; West, 2005), suggesting that stages are neither useful nor predictive. Although proponents of the model have vociferously defended it (Prochaska, 2006), the most recent clinical guideline for smoking cessation (Fiore et al., 2008) does not specifically recommend using the model to guide interventions. The guideline suggests that clinicians offer every tobacco user at least a brief intervention without mention of matching the intervention to stage of change.

The guideline (Fiore et al., 2008) does recommend social support, nicotine replacement therapies, and training in problem solving and coping skills, concepts (not theories) that were frequently used in the nursing research studies reviewed here. The interest of nurse researchers in social support is evident in this review, which identified 26 studies as using this concept. Social support might be a particularly fruitful avenue for theory development by nurse researchers, but it is clear that the theory must go beyond the implicit theory that interventions delivered by nurses are especially effective. What is it about the nurses' activities that increase effectiveness? Is it specific knowledge of the client? Is it clinical expertise? Is it accessibility? A theory about social support in behavior change is clearly needed.

Limitations

This review has several limitations. First, the research published by nurses in nonnursing journals is not reviewed. The difficulty of identifying such research and in determining who is a nurse in nonnursing publications is the main reason for this exclusion. Nevertheless, most veteran nurse researchers tend to publish their work both inside and outside of nursing. While all their work is not represented, it is fair to conclude that some of the work has been considered here. Secondly, my literature search method and exclusion procedure may have missed important studies that should be in the sample. Third, the studies that were categorized as using formal theories may also have used additional implicit theories. I preferred to keep the studies where only implicit theories were used separate to make interpretation easier. For instance, implicit theories concerning affective symptoms, such as depression, were used in some theory-based studies, but such studies were not included in Table 2.2. This practice reduced the number of studies in each category of implicit theories. Finally, recognition and interpretation of implicit theories depended on my judgment, which may have been faulty. (But misinterpretation is the problem with implicit theories!)

SUMMARY

This review has shown that nursing research on smoking cessation during the last 20 years is frequently guided by formal theories. Although I have not done a similar review of nonnursing research, I suspect that nursing research on smoking cessation may use formal theories more frequently than nonnursing research on smoking cessation. Nursing education may emphasize theory more than many disciplines, leading nurses to at least acknowledge the need for theory in their investigations. For instance, in their nursing research methods text, Polit and Beck (2008) devote an entire chapter to theory, while nonnursing research methods texts such as those by Locke, Silverman and Spirduso (2004) and by Cherulnik (2001) appear to exclude it from consideration. The TTM and self-efficacy theory were the dominant formal theories used in research on smoking cessation. Implicit theories tended to center around issues with nicotine dependence and social support. Largely missing from this set of studies were investigations based on biobehavioral models, including genetics and neuroscience.

IMPLICATIONS FOR FUTURE
RESEARCH AND POLICY

Future nursing research in smoking cessation should be grounded in well-articulated theories. Coherent stories are crucial to policy. Few policy makers can convert a plethora of scientific findings into the focused messages that are needed to lobby for changes in smoking-related laws and health care policies. Well-articulated theories tend to organize findings in a way that tells a coherent story about a phenomenon and can be much more understandable and interpretable to policy makers than disparate empirical findings.

Theories used in the sample of studies reviewed here tend to be those generated by psychologists. However, nurses who are experts in smoking cessation have a valuable perspective, especially with respect to patient populations who need to quit smoking. In addition, school nurses and community health nurses may have important contributions to make in understanding community and environmental variables affecting smoking uptake and relapse. Isn't it time that nurse experts generate well-articulated theories for psychologists (and other disciplines) to use? With their grounding in theory and their expert knowledge of clinical issues, nurses are in an excellent position to develop theories—to draw the maps—that will help researchers in every discipline make sense of smoking cessation.

ACKNOWLEDGMENT

I am grateful to Kimberly Glazier for her excellent assistance with the literature search, locating sources, and constructing the bibliographic database for this chapter.

REFERENCES

Ahijevych, K., & Gillespie, J. (1997). Nicotine dependence and smoking topography among black and white women. *Research in Nursing & Health, 20,* 505–514.

Ahijevych, K., & Wewers, M. E. (1993). Factors associated with nicotine dependence among African American women cigarette smokers. *Research in Nursing & Health, 16,* 283–292.

Ajzen, I. (1991). The theory of planned behavior. *Organizational Behavior and Human Decision Processes, 50,* 179–211.

Ajzen, I., & Fishbein, M. (1980). *Understanding attitudes and predicting social behavior.* Englewood Cliffs, NJ: Prentice Hall.

Albrecht, S. A., Caruthers, D., Patrick, T., Reynolds, M., Salamie, D., Higgins, L. W., et al. (2006). A randomized controlled trial of a smoking cessation intervention for pregnant adolescents. *Nursing Research, 55,* 402–410.

Albrecht, S. A., Payne, L., Stone, C. A., & Reynolds, M. D. (1998). A preliminary study of the use of peer support in smoking cessation programs for pregnant adolescents. *Journal of the American Academy of Nurse Practitioners, 10,* 119–125.

Allnutt, J., & Reid, P. (1999). Identification of target groups for cessation of smoking programmes in pregnancy. *Birth Issues, 8,* 106–112.

Andersen, S., & Keller, C. (2002). Examination of the transtheoretical model in current smokers. *Western Journal of Nursing Research, 24,* 282–294.

Andrews, J. O., Felton, G., Wewers, M. E., Waller, J., & Humbles, P. (2005). Sister to sister: A pilot study to assist African American women in subsidized housing to quit smoking. *Southern Online Journal of Nursing Research, 6,* 23.

Andrews, J. O., Felton, G., Wewers, M. E., Waller, J., & Tingen, M. (2007). The effect of a multi-component smoking cessation intervention in African American women residing in public housing. *Research in Nursing & Health, 30,* 45–60.

Apter, M. J. (1982). *The experience of motivation: The theory of psychological reversals.* London: Academic Press.

Apter, M. J. (1989). *Reversal theory: Motivation, emotion, and personality.* London: Routledge.

Attebring, M. F., Hartford, M., Hjalmarson, A., Caidahl, K., Karlsson, T., & Herlitz, J. (2004). Smoking habits and predictors of continued smoking in patients with acute coronary syndromes. *Journal of Advanced Nursing, 46,* 614–623.

Balmford, J., Borland, R., & Burney, S. (2008). Is contemplation a separate stage of change to precontemplation? *International Journal of Behavioral Medicine, 15,* 141–148.

Bandura, A. (1977). Self-efficacy: Toward a unifying theory of behavior change. *Psychological Review, 84,* 191–215.

Bandura, A. (1997). *Self-efficacy: The exercise of control.* New York: W.H. Freeman & Co.

Beck, A., Wright, F., Newman, C., & Sliese, B. (1993). *Cognitive therapy of substance abuse.* New York: Guilford Press.

Becker, M. H., & Maiman, L. A. (1975). Sociobehavioral determinants of compliance with health and medical care recommendations. *Medical Care, 13,* 10–24.

Bottorff, J. L., Johnson, J. L., Moffat, B., Fofonoff, D., Budz, B., Groening, M., et al. (2004). Synchronizing clinician engagement and client motivation in telephone counseling. *Qualitative Health Research, 14,* 462–477.

Browning, K. K., Ahijevych, K. L., Ross, P., Jr., & Wewers, M. E. (2000). Implementing the agency for health care policy and research's smoking cessation guideline in a lung cancer surgery clinic. *Oncology Nursing Forum, 27,* 1248–1254.

Buchanan, L., & Likness, S. (2008). Evidence-based practice to assist women in hospital settings to quit smoking and reduce cardiovascular disease risk. *Journal of Cardiovascular Nursing, 23,* 397–406.

Burris, R. F., & O'Connell, K. A. (2003). Reversal theory states and cigarette availability predict lapses during smoking cessation among adolescents. *Research in Nursing & Health, 26,* 263–272.

Bursey, M., & Craig, D. (2000). Attitudes, subjective norm, perceived behavioral control, and intentions related to adult smoking cessation after coronary artery bypass graft surgery. *Public Health Nursing, 17,* 460–467.

Challis, S., & Surgenor, S. (2004). Helping patients with Crohn's disease to stop smoking. *Professional Nurse, 19,* 386–389.

Chalmers, K., Gupton, A., Katz, A., Hack, T., Hildes-Ripstein, E., Brown, J., et al. (2004). The description and evaluation of a longitudinal pilot study of a smoking relapse/reduction intervention for perinatal women. *Journal of Advanced Nursing, 45,* 162–171.

Chaney, S. E., & Hough, L. (2005). Lewin's field theory with emphasis on change. In S. M. Ziegler (Ed.), *Theory-directed nursing practice* (2nd ed.). New York: Springer Publishing.

Chaney, S. E., & Sheriff, S. (2008). Weight gain among women during smoking cessation: Testing the effects of a multifaceted program. *American Association of Occupational Health Nurses Journal, 56,* 99–105.

Chen, H. H., & Yeh, M. L. (2006). Developing and evaluating a smoking cessation program combined with an internet-assisted instruction program for adolescents with smoking. *Patient Education & Counseling, 61,* 411–418.

Cherulnik, P. D. (2001). *Methods for behavioral research: A systematic approach.* Thousand Oaks, CA: Sage Publications.

Chou, K. R., Chen, R., Lee, J. F., Ku, C. H., & Lu, R. B. (2004). The effectiveness of nicotine-patch therapy for smoking cessation in patients with schizophrenia. *International Journal of Nursing Studies, 41,* 321–330.

Chouinard, M.C., & Robichaud-Ekstrand, S. (2005). The effectiveness of a nursing inpatient smoking cessation program in individuals with cardiovascular disease. *Nursing Research, 54*, 243–254.

Clark, J.M., Haverty, S., & Kendall, S. (1990). Helping people to stop smoking: A study of the nurse's role. *Journal of Advanced Nursing, 15*, 357–363.

Clark, J.M., Rowe, K., & Jones, K. (1993). Evaluating the effectiveness of the coronary care nurses' role in smoking cessation. *Journal of Clinical Nursing, 2*, 313–322.

Clarke, K.E., & Aish, A. (2002). An exploration of health beliefs and attitudes of smokers with vascular disease who participate in or decline a smoking cessation program. *Journal of Vascular Nursing, 20*, 96–105.

Cobb, A.K., Bott, M.J., & O'Connell, K.A. (1997). A qualitative/interpretive taxonomy of stop smoking strategies (QU/ITS). *Western Journal of Nursing Research, 19*, 702–725.

Condon, C. (1997). Long term effects of smoking cessation program for cardiac patients. *Kansas Nurse, 72*, 1–2.

Conn, V.S., Taylor, S.G., & Abele, P.B. (1991). Myocardial infarction survivors: Age and gender differences in physical health, psychosocial state and regimen adherence. *Journal of Advanced Nursing, 16*, 1026–1034.

Conrad, K.M., Campbell, R.T., Edington, D.W., Faust, H.S., & Vilnius, D. (1996). The worksite environment as a cue to smoking reduction. *Research in Nursing & Health, 19*, 21–31.

Cook, M.R., Gerkovich, M.M., O'Connell, K.A., & Potocky, M. (1995). Reversal theory constructs and cigarette availability predict lapse early in smoking cessation. *Research in Nursing & Health, 18*, 217–224.

Cox, C.L. (1982). An interaction model of client health behavior: Theoretical prescription for nursing. *Advances in Nursing Science, 5*, 41–56.

Cummins, D., Trotter, G., Moussa, M., & Turham, G. (2005). Smoking cessation for clients who are HIV-positive. *Nursing Standard, 20*, 41–47.

DeJong, S.R., Veltman, R.H., DeJong, S.R., & Veltman, R.H. (2004). The effectiveness of a CNS-led community-based COPD screening and intervention program. *Clinical Nurse Specialist, 18*, 72–79.

de Vries, H., Bakker, M., Mullen, P.D., & van Breukelen, G. (2006). The effects of smoking cessation counseling by midwives on Dutch pregnant women and their partners. *Patient Education & Counseling, 63*, 177–187.

Dino, G.A., Horn, K.A., Goldcamp, J., Maniar, S.D., Fernandes, A., & Massey, C.J. (2001). Statewide demonstration of Not On Tobacco: A gender-sensitive teen smoking cessation program. *Journal of School Nursing, 17*, 90–97.

Echer, I.C., & Barreto, S.S.M. (2008). Determination and support as successful factors for smoking cessation. *Revista Latino-Americana de Enfermagem, 16*, 445–451.

Edwards, N., & Sims-Jones, N. (1998). Smoking and smoking relapse during pregnancy and postpartum: Results of a qualitative study. *Birth, 25*, 94–100.

Efraimsson, E.O., Hillervik, C., & Ehrenberg, A. (2008). Effects of COPD self-care management education at a nurse-led primary health care clinic. *Scandinavian Journal of Caring Sciences, 22*, 178–185.

Fiore, M.C., Jaen, C.R., Baker, T.B., Bailey, W.C., Benowitz, N.L., Curry, S.J., et al. (2008). *Treating tobacco use and dependence: 2008 update, clinical practice guideline.* Rockville, MD: U.S. Department of Health and Human Services.

Fritz, D. J., Hardin, S. B., Gore, P. A., Jr., & Bram, D. (2008). A computerized smoking cessation intervention for high school smokers. *Pediatric Nursing, 34*, 13–17.

Froelicher, E. S., & Christopherson, D. J. (2000). Women's initiative for nonsmoking (WINS) I: Design and methods. *Heart & Lung, 29*, 429–437.

Froelicher, E. S., & Kozuki, Y. (2002). Theoretical applications of smoking cessation interventions to individuals with medical conditions: Women's initiative for nonsmoking (WINS) III. *International Journal of Nursing Studies, 39*, 1–15.

Gaffney, K. F., & Henry, L. L. (2007). Identifying risk factors for postpartum tobacco use. *Journal of Nursing Scholarship, 39*, 126–132.

Gaffney, K. F., Henry, L. L., Douglas, C. Y., & Goldberg, P. A. (2008). Tobacco use triggers for mothers of infants: Implications for pediatric nursing practice. *Pediatric Nursing, 34*, 253–258.

Gebauer, C., Kwo, C. Y., Haynes, E. F., & Wewers, M. E. (1998). A nurse-managed smoking cessation intervention during pregnancy. *Journal of Obstetric, Gynecologic, & Neonatal Nursing, 27*, 47–53.

Gies, C. E., Buchman, D., Robinson, J., & Smolen, D. (2008). Effect of an inpatient nurse-directed smoking cessation program. *Western Journal of Nursing Research, 30*, 6–19.

Gollwitzer, P. M. (1999). Implementation intentions: Strong effects of simple plans. *American Psychologist, 54*, 493–503.

Green, L. W., & Kreuter, M. W. (1991). *Health promotion planning: An educational and environmental approach* (2nd ed.). Toronto, Ontario, Canada: Mayfield.

Green, M. A., & Clarke, D. E. (2005). Smoking reduction & cessation: A hospital based survey of outpatients' attitudes. *Journal of Psychosocial Nursing & Mental Health Services, 43*, 18–25.

Griebel, B., Wewers, M. E., & Baker, C. A. (1998). The effectiveness of a nurse-managed minimal smoking-cessation intervention among hospitalized patients with cancer. *Oncology Nursing Forum, 25*, 897–902.

Grossman, J., Donaldson, S., Belton, L., & Oliver, R. H. (2008). 5 A's smoking cessation with recovering women in treatment. *Journal of Addictions Nursing, 19*, 1–8.

Gulick, E. E., & Escobar-Florez, L. (1995). Reliability and validity of the smoking and women questionnaire among three ethnic groups. *Public Health Nursing, 12*, 117–126.

Haddock, J., & Burrows, C. (1997). The role of the nurse in health promotion: An evaluation of a smoking cessation programme in surgical pre-admission clinics. *Journal of Advanced Nursing, 26*, 1098–1110.

Haire-Joshu, D., Ziff, S., & Houston, C. (1995). The feasibility of recruiting hospitalized patients with diabetes for a smoking cessation program. *Diabetes Educator, 21*, 214–218.

Ham, O. K. (2007). Stages and processes of smoking cessation among adolescents. *Western Journal of Nursing Research, 29*, 301–321.

Ham, O. K., & Lee, Y. J. (2007). Use of the transtheoretical model to predict stages of smoking cessation in Korean adolescents. *Journal of School Health, 77*, 319–326.

Helyer, A. J., Brehm, W. T., Gentry, N. O., & Pittman, T. A. (1998). Effectiveness of a worksite smoking cessation program in the military. Program evaluation. *American Association of Occupational Health Nurse Journal, 46*, 238–245.

Higgs, P. E., Edwards, D., Harbin, R. E., & Higgs, P. C. (2000). Evaluation of a self-directed smoking prevention and cessation program. *Pediatric Nursing, 26*, 150–153.

Hilberink, S. R., Jacobs, J. E., Schlosser, M., Grol, R. P. T. M., & de Vries, H. (2006). Characteristics of patients with COPD in three motivational stages related to smoking cessation. *Patient Education & Counseling, 61*, 449–457.

Hokanson, J. M., Anderson, R. L., Hennrikus, D. J., Lando, H. A., & Kendall, D. M. (2006). Integrated tobacco cessation counseling in a diabetes self-management training program: A randomized trial of diabetes and reduction of tobacco. *Diabetes Educator, 32*, 562–570.

Holmes, C. (2001). Partner involvement in smoking cessation. *British Journal of Midwifery, 9*, 357–361.

Huang, C. L. (2005). Evaluating the program of a smoking cessation support group for adult smokers: A longitudinal pilot study. *Journal of Nursing Research, 13*, 197–205.

Huang, C. L., Lin, H. H., & Wang, H. H. (2006). Psychometric evaluation of the Chinese version of the Fagerstrom tolerance questionnaire as a measure of cigarette dependence. *Journal of Advanced Nursing, 55*, 596–603.

Jannone, L., & O'Connell, K. A. (2007). Coping strategies used by adolescents during smoking cessation. *Journal of School Nursing, 23*, 177–184.

Janz, N. K., & Becker, M. H. (1984). The health belief model: A decade later. *Health Education Quarterly, 11*, 1–47.

Jesse, D. E., Graham, M., & Swanson, M. (2006). Psychosocial and spiritual factors associated with smoking and substance use during pregnancy in African American and white low-income women. *Journal of Obstetric, Gynecologic, & Neonatal Nursing, 35*(1), 68–77.

Jessor, R., Donavan, J. E., & Costa, F. M. (1992). *Beyond adolescence: Problem behavior and young adult development.* Cambridge, UK: Cambridge University Press.

Jiang, X., Sit, J. W., & Wong, T. K. (2007). A nurse-led cardiac rehabilitation programme improves health behaviours and cardiac physiological risk parameters: Evidence from Chengdu, China. *Journal of Clinical Nursing, 16*, 1886–1897.

Johnson, J. L., Budz, B., Mackay, M., & Miller, C. (1999). Evaluation of a nurse-delivered smoking cessation intervention for hospitalized patients with cardiac disease. *Heart & Lung, 28*, 55–64.

Johnson, J. L., Ratner, P. A., Bottorff, J. L., Hall, W., & Dahinten, S. (2000). Preventing smoking relapse in postpartum women. *Nursing Research, 49*, 44–52.

Jonsdottir, D., & Jonsdottir, H. (2001). Does physical exercise in addition to a multicomponent smoking cessation program increase abstinence rate and suppress weight gain? An intervention study. *Scandinavian Journal of Caring Sciences, 15*, 275–282.

Jonsdottir, H., Jonsdottir, R., Geirsdottir, T., Sveinsdottir, K. S., & Sigurdardottir, T. (2004). Multicomponent individualized smoking cessation intervention for patients with lung disease. *Journal of Advanced Nursing, 48*, 594–604.

Keeney, R. L. (1982). Decision analysis: An overview. *Operations Research, 30*, 803–838.

Keller, C. S., & McGowan, N. (2001). Examination of the processes of change, decisional balance, self-efficacy for smoking and the stages of change in Mexican American women. *Southern Online Journal of Nursing Research, 2*, 1–31.

Kelley, F. J., Thomas, S. A., & Friedmann, E. (2000). Smoking patterns, health behaviors, and health-risk behaviors of college women. *Clinical Excellence for Nurse Practitioners, 4*, 302–308.

Kim, S. S. (2008). Predictors of short-term smoking cessation among Korean American men. *Public Health Nursing, 25*, 516–525.

Kim, Y.H. (2006). Adolescents' smoking behavior and its relationships with psychological constructs based on transtheoretical model: A cross-sectional survey. *International Journal of Nursing Studies, 43*, 439–446.

Koivula, M., & Paunonen, M. (1998). Smoking habits among Finnish middle-aged men: Experiences and attitudes. *Journal of Advanced Nursing, 27*, 327–334.

Kowalski, S.D. (1997). Self-esteem and self-efficacy as predictors of success in smoking cessation. *Journal of Holistic Nursing, 15*, 128–142.

Kupezc, D., & Prochazka, A. (1996). A comparison of nicotine delivery systems in a multimodal smoking cessation program. *Nurse Practitioner, 21*, 73–84.

Lazarus, R.S. (1966). *Psychological stress and the coping process.* New York: McGraw-Hill.

Lazarus, R.S., & Folkman, S. (1984). *Stress, appraisal, and coping.* New York: Springer Publishing.

Lemola, S., & Grob, A. (2008). Smoking cessation during pregnancy and relapse after childbirth: The impact of the grandmother's smoking status. *Maternal & Child Health Journal, 12*, 525–533.

Leong, J., Molassiotis, A., & Marsh, H. (2004). Adherence to health recommendations after a cardiac rehabilitation programme in post-myocardial infarction patients: The role of health beliefs, locus of control and psychological status. *Clinical Effectiveness in Nursing, 8*, 26–38.

Leventhal, H., Leventhal, E.A., & Cameron, L. (2001). Representations, procedures, and affect in illness self-regulation: A perceptual-cognitive model. In A. Baum, T.A. Revenson & J.E. Singer (Eds.), *Handbook of Health Psychology.* Mahwah, NJ: Lawrence Erlbaum Associates.

Lillington, L., Royce, J., Novak, D., Ruvalcaba, M., & Chlebowski, R. (1995). Evaluation of a smoking cessation program for pregnant minority women. *Cancer Practice, 3*, 157–163.

Lindberg, J.B., Hunter, M.L., & Kruszewski, A.Z. (1990). *Introduction to nursing: Concepts, issues, & opportunities.* Philadelphia, PA: J.B. Lippincott.

Lindenberg, C.S., Reiskin, H.K., & Gendrop, S.C. (1994). The social stress model of substance abuse among childbearing-age women: A review of the literature. *Journal of Drug Education, 24*, 253–268.

Locke, E.A., & Lathan, J.P. (1990). *A theory of goal-setting and task performance.* Englewood Cliffs, NJ: Prentice-Hall.

Locke, L.F., Silverman, S.J., & Spirduso, W.W. (2004). *Reading and understanding research* (2nd ed.). Thousand Oaks, CA: Sage Publications.

Mackey, M.C., McKinney, S.H., & Tavakoli, A. (2008). Factors related to smoking in college women. *Journal of Community Health Nursing, 25*, 106–121.

Macnee, C.L., & McCabe, S. (2004). The transtheoretical model of behavior change and smokers in southern Appalachia. *Nursing Research, 53*, 243–250.

Macnee, C.L., & Talsma, A. (1995a). Development and testing of the barriers to cessation scale. *Nursing Research, 44*, 214–219.

Macnee, C.L., & Talsma, A. (1995b). Predictors of progress in smoking cessation. *Public Health Nursing, 12*, 242–248.

Mahrer-Imhof, R., Froelicher, E.S., Li, W., Parker, K.M., & Benowitz, N. (2002). Women's initiative for nonsmoking (WINS V): Under-use of nicotine replacement therapy. *Heart & Lung, 31*, 368–373.

Marlatt, G. A. (1985). Relapse prevention: Theoretical rationale and overview of the model. In G. A. Marlatt & J. R. Gordon (Eds.), *Relapse prevention* (pp. 3–70). New York: Guilford.

Marlatt, G. A., & Gordon, J. R. (1985). *Relapse prevention: Maintenance strategies in the treatment of addictive behaviors.* New York: Guilford Press.

Marshall, P. (1990). "Just one more . . . !" A study into the smoking attitudes and behaviour of patients following first myocardial infarction. *International Journal of Nursing Studies, 27*, 375–387.

Martin, K., Froelicher, E. S., & Miller, N. H. (2000). Women's initiative for nonsmoking (WINS) II: The intervention. *Heart & Lung, 29*, 438–445.

McDaniel, A. M. (1999). Assessing the feasibility of a clinical practice guideline for inpatient smoking cessation intervention. *Clinical Nurse Specialist, 13*, 228–235.

McEwen, M., & Wills, E. M. (2007). *Theoretical basis for nursing* (2nd ed.). Philadelphia, PA: Lippincott, Williams & Wilkins.

McLeod, D., Pullon, S., Benn, C., Cookson, T., Dowell, A., Viccars, A., et al. (2004). Can support and education for smoking cessation and reduction be provided effectively by midwives within primary maternity care? *Midwifery, 20*, 37–50.

Meleis, A. I. (1997). *Theoretical nursing: Development and progress* (3rd ed.). Philadelphia, PA: Lippincott.

Meleis, A. I., Sawyer, L. M., Im, E., Messias, D. K. H., & Schumacher, K. (2000). Experiencing transitions: An emerging middle-range theory. *Advances in Nursing Science, 23*, 12–28.

Mercer, R. T., & Mercer, R. T. (2004). Becoming a mother versus maternal role attainment. *Journal of Nursing Scholarship, 36*, 226–232.

Miller, C. E., Ratner, P. A., & Johnson, J. L. (2003). Reducing cardiovascular risk: Identifying predictors of smoking relapse. *Canadian Journal of Cardiovascular Nursing, 13*, 7–12.

O'Connell, K. A. (1990). Smoking cessation: Research on relapse crises. In J. J. Fitzpatrick, R. L. Taunton, & J. Q. Benoliel (Eds.), *Annual review of nursing research* (Vol. 8). New York: Springer Publishing.

O'Connell, K. A., Gerkovich, M. M., & Cook, M. R. (1995). Reversal theory's mastery and sympathy states in smoking cessation. *Image—The Journal of Nursing Scholarship, 27*, 311–316.

O'Connell, K. A., Gerkovich, M. M., Cook, M. R., Shiffman, S., Hickcox, M., & Kakolewski, K. E. (1998). Coping in real time: Using ecological momentary assessment techniques to assess coping with the urge to smoke. *Research In Nursing and Health, 21*, 487–497.

O'Connell, K. A., Hosein, V. L., & Schwartz, J. E. (2006). Thinking and/or doing as strategies for resisting smoking. *Research in Nursing & Health, 29*, 533–542.

Okoli, C. T. C., Browning, S., Rayens, M. K., & Hahn, E. J. (2008). Secondhand tobacco smoke exposure, nicotine dependence, and smoking cessation. *Public Health Nursing, 25*, 46–56.

Orem, D. (1995). *Nursing: Concepts of practice* (5th ed.). St. Louis, MO: Mosby.

Pletsch, P. K., & Johnson, M. K. (1996). The cigarette smoking experience of pregnant Latinas in the United States. *Health Care for Women International, 17*, 549–562.

Polit, D. F., & Beck, C. T. (2008). *Nursing research: Generating and assessing evidence for nursing practice.* Philadelphia: Lippincott, Williams & Wilkins.

Portugal, G. S., & Gould, T. J. (2008). Genetic variability in nicotinic acetylcholine receptors and nicotine addiction: Converging evidence from human and animal research. *Behavioural Brain Research, 193*, 1–16.

Price, J. (1992). Patients' decision making concerning smoking behaviour following myocardial infarction. *Heart & Lung, 21*, 292.

Prochaska, J. O. (2006). Moving beyond the transtheoretical model. *Addiction, 101*, 768–774.

Prochaska, J. O., & DiClemente, C. C. (1983). Stages and processes of self-change smoking: Toward an integrative model of change. *Journal of Consulting and Clinical Psychology, 51*, 390–395.

Prochaska, J. O., Velicer, W. F., Rossi, J. S., Goldstein, M. G., Marcus, B. H., Rakowski, W., et al. (1994). Stages of change and decisional balance for twelve problem behaviors. *Health Psychology, 13*, 39–46.

Racelis, M. C., Lombardo, K., & Verdin, J. (1998). Impact of telephone reinforcement of risk reduction education on patient compliance. *Journal of Vascular Nursing, 16*, 16–20.

Reeve, K., Calabro, K., & Adams-McNeill, J. (2000). Tobacco cessation intervention in a nurse practitioner managed clinic. *Journal of the American Academy of Nurse Practitioners, 12*, 163–169.

Reilly, P., Murphy, L., & Alderton, D. (2006). Challenging the smoking culture within a mental health service supportively. *International Journal of Mental Health Nursing, 15*, 272–278.

Reynolds, N. R., Neidig, J. L., & Wewers, M. E. (2004). Illness representation and smoking behavior: A focus group study of HIV-positive men. *Journal of the Association of Nurses in AIDS Care, 15*, 37–47.

Rice, V. H., Fox, D. H., Lepczyk, M., Sieggreen, M., Mullin, M., Jarosz, P., et al. (1994). A comparison of nursing interventions for smoking cessation in adults with cardiovascular health problems. *Heart & Lung, 23*, 473–486.

Ridner, S. L., & Hahn, E. J. (2005). The pros and cons of cessation in college-age smokers. *Clinical Excellence for Nurse Practitioners, 9*, 81–87.

Rowe, K., & Clark, J. M. (1999). Evaluating the effectiveness of a smoking cessation intervention designed for nurses. *International Journal of Nursing Studies, 36*, 301–311.

Roy, C., & Andrews, H. A. (1999). *The Roy adaptation model* (2nd ed.). Stamford, CT: Appleton & Lange.

Ryan, R., & Deci, E. L. (2000). Self-determination theory and the facilitation of intrinsic motivation, social development, and well-being. *American Psychologist, 55*, 68–78.

Sarna, L. (1995). Smoking behaviors of women after diagnosis with lung cancer. *Image— The Journal of Nursing Scholarship, 27*, 35–41.

Scheibmeir, M. S., O'Connell, K. A., Aaronson, L. S., & Gajewski, B. (2005). Smoking cessation strategy use among pregnant ex-smokers. *Western Journal of Nursing Research, 27*, 411–436.

Sharp, L., & Tishelman, C. (2005). Smoking cessation for patients with head and neck cancer: A qualitative study of patients' and nurses' experiences in a nurse-led intervention. *Cancer Nursing, 28*, 226–235.

Shuster, G. F., 3rd, Utz, S. W., & Merwin, E. (1996). Implementation and outcomes of a community-based self-help smoking cessation program. *Journal of Community Health Nursing, 13*, 187–198.

Snyder, M., McDevitt, J., & Painter, S. (2008). Smoking cessation and serious mental illness. *Archives of Psychiatric Nursing, 22*, 297–304.

Stanislaw, A. E., & Wewers, M. E. (1994). A smoking cessation intervention with hospitalized surgical cancer patients: A pilot study. *Cancer Nursing, 17*, 81–86.

Steuer, J. D., & Wewers, M. E. (1989). Cigarette craving and subsequent coping responses among smoking cessation clinic participants. *Oncology Nursing Forum, 16*, 193–198.

Stevens, V. L., Bierut, L. J., Talbot, J. T., Wang, J. C., Sun, J., Hinrichs, A. L., et al. (2008). Nicotinic receptor gene variants influence susceptibility to heavy smoking. *Cancer Epidemiology, Biomarkers & Prevention, 17*, 3517–3525.

Stewart, M. J., Gillis, A., Brosky, G., Johnston, G., Kirkland, S., Leigh, G., et al. (1996). Smoking among disadvantaged women: causes and cessation. *Canadian Journal of Nursing Research, 28*, 41–60.

Tod, A. M. (2003). Barriers to smoking cessation in pregnancy: A qualitative study. *British Journal of Community Nursing, 8*, 56–64.

Tonstad, S. (2006). Smoking cessation efficacy and safety of varenicline, an alpha 4-beta 2 nicotinic receptor partial agonist. *Journal of Cardiovascular Nursing, 21*, 433–436.

Utz, S. W., Shuster, G. F., 3rd, Merwin, E., & Williams, B. (1994). A community-based smoking-cessation program: Self-care behaviors and success. *Public Health Nursing, 11*, 291–299.

Van Dongen, C. J., Kriz, P., Fox, K. A., & Haque, I. (1999). A quit smoking group. Pilot study. *Journal of Psychosocial Nursing & Mental Health Services, 37*, 31–36.

Villareal, E. (2003). Using Roy's adaptation model when caring for a group of young women contemplating quitting smoking. *Public Health Nursing, 20*, 377–384.

Wakefield, M., Olver, I., Whitford, H., & Rosenfeld, E. (2004). Motivational interviewing as a smoking cessation intervention for patients with cancer: Randomized controlled trial. *Nursing Research, 53*, 396–405.

Wallston, K. A. (2001). Conceptualization and operationalization of perceived control. In A. Baum, T. A. Revenson, & J. E. Singer (Eds.), *Handbook of health psychology* (pp. 49–48). Mahwah, NJ: Lawrence Erlbaum Associates.

Wallston, K. A., Wallston, B. S., & DeVellis, R. (1978). Development of the multidimensional health locus of control (MHLC) scales. *Health Education Monographs 6*.

Wang, H. L., Harrell, J., & Funk, S. (2008). Factors associated with smoking cessation among male adults with coronary heart disease in Taiwan. *Journal of Nursing Research, 16*, 55–64.

Ward, T. (2001). Using psychological insights to help people quit smoking. *Journal of Advanced Nursing, 34*, 754–759.

Webb, M. S. (2008). Focus groups as an intervention for low-income African American smokers to promote participation in subsequent intervention studies. *Research in Nursing & Health, 31*, 141–151.

Wells, S., & de Lusignan, S. (2003). Health promotion. Does screening for loss of lung function help smokers give up? *British Journal of Nursing, 12*, 744–750.

West, R. (2005). Time for a change: Putting the transtheoretical (stages of change) model to rest. *Addiction, 100*, 1036–1039.

Wewers, M. E., Bowen, J. M., Stanislaw, A. E., & Desimone, V. B. (1994). A nurse-delivered smoking cessation intervention among hospitalized postoperative patients—influence of a smoking-related diagnosis: A pilot study. *Heart & Lung, 23*, 151–156.

Wewers, M.E., Jenkins, L., & Mignery, T. (1997). A nurse-managed smoking cessation intervention during diagnostic testing for lung cancer. *Oncology Nursing Forum, 24,* 1419–1422.

Wewers, M.E., Neidig, J.L., & Kihm, K.E. (2000). The feasibility of a nurse-managed, peer-led tobacco cessation intervention among HIV-positive smokers. *Journal of the Association of Nurses in AIDS Care, 11,* 37–44.

Wilson, J.S., Fitzsimons, D., Bradbury, I., & Stuart Elborn, J. (2008). Does additional support by nurses enhance the effect of a brief smoking cessation intervention in people with moderate to severe chronic obstructive pulmonary disease? A randomised controlled trial. *International Journal of Nursing Studies, 45,* 508–517.

Winkelstein, M.L., & Feldman, R.H. (1993). Psychosocial predictors of consumption of sweets following smoking cessation. *Research in Nursing & Health, 16,* 97–105.

Winkelstein, M.L., Tarzian, A., & Wood, R.A. (1997). Motivation, social support, and knowledge of parents who smoke and who have children with asthma. *Pediatric Nursing, 23,* 576–581.

Wynd, C.A. (1992). Relaxation imagery used for stress reduction in the prevention of smoking relapse. *Journal of Advanced Nursing, 17,* 294–302.

Wynd, C.A. (2005). Guided health imagery for smoking cessation and long-term abstinence. *Journal of Nursing Scholarship, 37,* 245–250.

Wynd, C.A. (2006). Smoking patterns, beliefs, and the practice of healthy behaviors in abstinent, relapsed, and recalcitrant smokers. *Applied Nursing Research, 19,* 197–203.

Chapter 3

The Social and Political Context of the Tobacco Epidemic: Nursing Research and Scholarship on the Tobacco Industry

Ruth E. Malone

ABSTRACT

Context matters in addressing tobacco as a global nursing issue. The tobacco epidemic and its resulting health consequences are in great measure the result of industrial decisions over the past century that included deliberately enhancing the addictiveness of cigarettes, marketing them aggressively to vulnerable groups, hiding or manipulating knowledge about the products' harmfulness, and undermining public health efforts. The efforts of the tobacco industry to perpetuate the idea that smoking is solely a problem of individual behavior, or even a "right," still creates barriers to understanding the larger social and political context within which individuals use and attempt to quit tobacco. Nurses have been among the researchers worldwide who are studying tobacco industry activities and their role in policy and public health. This chapter reviews data sources, methods, and analytic approaches for conducting research using documents from the

DOI: 10.1891/0739-6686.27.63

tobacco industry, and provides an overview of research conducted by nurses on this topic. Much of the nursing research to date on the tobacco industry focuses in four broad areas: (1) tobacco industry influence on policy; (2) tobacco industry strategic responses to public health efforts, including use of front groups and attempts to divide and conquer public health advocates; (3) tobacco industry targeting of marginalized groups; and (4) tobacco industry influence on science. Implications of this work for nursing practice, research, and policy intervention are discussed.

Keywords: tobacco industry; archival research; industry documents; policy; marginalized

The cigarette is the single most deadly consumer product ever made (Centers for Disease Control and Prevention, 2005, 2009; Mokdad, Marks, Stroup, & Gerberding, 2004). As a major global contributor to illness, tobacco is projected to kill more than one billion people during this century if present trends continue (World Health Organization [WHO], 2008). Because nurses work with communities, families, clients, and patients at every life stage, tobacco is an appropriate focus for nursing research.

However, tobacco use does not take place in a vacuum. The activities (or lack thereof) of the tobacco industry in relation to governments and other institutions also affect tobacco use initiation, addiction, and cessation, as well as perceptions about tobacco products and users. These public perceptions (including those of many health professionals) may be among the biggest obstacles to addressing the tobacco epidemic at a systems level.

For example, tobacco addiction is often not regarded as being like other addictions that are identified and treated effectively in hospital settings. In psychiatric hospitals, tobacco use may still be permitted or even encouraged (Ziedonis et al., 2008). While it would be unthinkable to allow a hospitalized diabetic patient to be discharged without teaching them about insulin or other blood sugar control approaches, cigarette smokers are still too often discharged without having been provided with smoking cessation interventions (Nides, Leischow, Sarna, & Evans, 2007; Sarna, Bialous, Wells, & Kotlerman, 2009). This reflects an enduring professional blind spot, despite some very encouraging initiatives by individuals and nursing organizations (Naegle, Baird, & Stein, 2009; Sarna & Bialous, 2006).

This blind spot—which also extends to other arenas involved with tobacco—may be partially attributable to the fact that, despite their deadliness, cigarettes remain aggressively marketed and widely sold, available at virtually every grocery, convenience and liquor store, gas station, many bars, and most chain pharmacies. This contributes to the idea that smoking is normal and will always be with us, when actually the phenomenon of cigarette smoking is relatively recent, a relatively recent, industrially engineered historical construction (Kluger, 1997). As a result, smokers who recognize that smoking is bad for them in a general, abstract way, also note the cigarette's ubiquitous presence, suggesting that it surely cannot be that bad; studies showing that smokers consistently underestimate their risks (Weinstein, 1998; Weinstein, Marcus, & Moser, 2005). By comparison with heavily regulated products, like most prescription drugs and toxic chemicals, cigarettes remain highly visible and attractively positioned in the retail environment.

The cigarette's special position in this regard, including within the context of government policies, and the efforts of the tobacco industry to perpetuate the idea that smoking is solely a problem of individual behavior, a *choice*, or even a *right*, thus still create barriers to understanding the larger social and political context within which individuals use and attempt to quit tobacco.

While a significant portion of tobacco-related research conducted by nurses addresses important individual-level factors, a growing body of research drawing on archival and social science methods has contributed to knowledge about the contexts within which tobacco disease has become a global epidemic and the structural factors that have allowed the epidemic to grow. After a brief overview of research on corporate activities, this chapter will focus on research on the tobacco industry. Two main objectives are (1) to discuss the methods used for research with reference to tobacco industry documents, and (2) to highlight research on the tobacco industry and its activities conducted by nurses.

RESEARCH ON CORPORATE ACTIVITY

A growing body of literature suggests that corporate activities and government policies contribute to disease and must be considered causal factors (Freudenberg, 2005; McDaniel & Malone, 2009; Wiist, 2006). This is particularly true for tobacco: The tobacco industry has long been identified as a "corporate vector" of disease (LeGresley, 1999). Taking an "upstream" (McKinlay & Marceau, 2000) approach to tobacco requires looking beyond individual behavior to the ways in which societal institutions create the conditions favorable for it to continue. For example, governments can encourage or discourage particular behaviors through policy measures such as smoke-free indoor air laws; corporations can use lobbying and corporate contributions to influence policy (Smith, Blackman, & Malone, 2007; Tesler & Malone, 2008). United States nursing emerged within a strong public health tradition dating from the early 1900s, in which social systems and political advocacy were keys to achieving health improvements (Dock, 1907/1985; Lewenson, 2002); therefore, nursing research focusing on such topics is legitimately called *nursing* research.

TOBACCO INDUSTRY RESEARCH: METHODS

Background: Noticing the Tobacco Industry

For many years, the same extraordinary blind spot discussed above allowed most clinical and public health practitioners and researchers, as well as most of the public, to generally ignore the presence of the tobacco industry, as though smoking and its consequences were solely problems created by smokers themselves. However, the disclosure in the 1990s of millions of pages of internal tobacco company documents from the largest U.S.-based tobacco companies (Hurt, Ebbert, Muggli, Lockhart, & Robertson, 2009; Malone & Balbach, 2000; University of California–San Francisco, 2007) as a result of the Master Settlement Agreement (MSA), an agreement resolving multiple state attorneys general lawsuits against the tobacco industry to recover the costs of treating sick smokers, spotlighted the multiple ways in which the tobacco companies first created, and then sustained through deceptive practices an epidemic of tobacco-caused diseases. The tobacco industry documents, which are now archived electronically in a web-hosted, full-text searchable database at the University of California–San Francisco, comprise a vast array of corporate documents, including business plans, marketing documents, public opinion studies, memos of executives, minutes of cross-company organizational meetings, copies of checks, research-related documentation, public relations plans, government relations documents, copies of correspondence from policy makers, consumers, retailers, political allies, and much more. They span decades, with the earliest documents dating to the early 1900s. Furthermore, documents continue to be released in conjunction with ongoing legal cases against the tobacco companies, so the archive includes documents dating into the 2000s.

One oft-asked question is why the tobacco companies agreed to release the documents, given the damaging revelations that they must have suspected would result. While no one except the tobacco company lawyers and executives know the answer, two important considerations inform thinking in this area. First, the tobacco companies were experiencing the worst legal and public relations threats in their history—or at least the worst since the 1950s, when the damaging evidence of the link between cigarettes and lung cancer was highlighted in *Reader's Digest* (Brandt, 2007; Kluger, 1997). The first state legal settlements in the 1990s had involved large payouts, which worried company investors; the specter of dozens of other cases playing out one after another across the country, with unfavorable media coverage, made getting a national settlement of all the remaining cases a priority worth some sacrifice.

Second, the documents were initially to be released to the public only in paper form, at vast warehouse depositories in Minneapolis, Minnesota and Guildford, England. At the time of their release into these archives, which were maintained by industry-contracted personnel, public access was limited, and constituted a time-consuming and laborious process that involved seeking permission to visit, searching separate and inadequate industry-supplied indexes for each company, filling out paper request forms, rummaging through boxes of paper documents, filling out additional requests, and waiting weeks to months for expensive copies of the requested documents to be mailed (Malone & Balbach, 2000). It is likely that, given these circumstances, the industry may have reasoned that few would make the effort and that even for those who did, by the time they found anything of value amidst the mass of material, it would be out of date and of minimal interest.

What the industry may not have anticipated was a happy (for public health) confluence of three events: The National Cancer Institute announced a special request for proposals to conduct research drawing on the documents; the rapid development of technology allowed large archives to be made available on the web in electronic form; and funders provided money for the procurement and scanning of virtually the entire contents of the depositories. Subsequently, additional funding and technological capability made possible the optical character recognition scanning of all documents, so that today one can conduct searches for words used anywhere in the documents.

Methods for Industry Documents Research

Most studies using the tobacco industry documents as data use qualitative, interpretive approaches. While it is theoretically possible to use the documents as quantitative data, their sheer volume, the number of duplicate or near-duplicate documents, and the necessity to interpret the contents of the documents limit somewhat their practical usefulness for quantitative studies. They are also not a complete set of all industry documents, but a large sample obtained in response to specific legal requests, which may not have covered all topics in which a researcher might be potentially interested.

That said, it could be possible to conduct more quantitatively oriented content analyses using selected sets of documents retrieved from the archives. For example, one could find all examples of a certain type of regularly filed report across a time period and conduct a content analysis in which one analyzed the number of times particular types of language appeared. It is also possible to conduct quantitative analyses of other types of industry-related data; for example, one could conduct economic studies drawing on publicly available data in industry reports filed with the Securities and Exchange Commission, public opinion surveys about the industry, or comparative analyses of overall medical costs from tobacco-related illness that are attributable to various companies by market share at given time periods. This chapter, however, focuses primarily on qualitative, interpretive archival research working with the corpus of tobacco industry documents to explore the industry's influence on the social contexts of tobacco use.

Data Sources

As qualitative archival data, the tobacco industry documents offer an unparalleled window into the workings of this vast corporate enterprise, an enterprise that has played a major role in the disease and early deaths of millions. While there are some other smaller collections of corporate documents available (see, for example, http://www.chemicalindustryarchives.org/ and http://dida.library.ucsf.edu/), nothing approaches the volume and coverage of the *Legacy Library* collection (University of California–San Francisco, 2007). For this reason alone, it is a valuable resource for nursing research.

However, it is not the only potential source of data for nursing research on the tobacco industry and the context of tobacco use. Industry annual reports, Web sites, marketing, trade publications, external communications, public opinion polling, media accounts, and interviews with or surveys of the public or targeted groups about the industry and its activities may also be excellent data sources, and all have been used in nursing research in this area. Federal Freedom of Information Act requests, or the state-level equivalent, may result in additional data from government archives. Documenting and analyzing geographic placement of industry advertising, as Hackbarth and colleagues (2001) did with studies of billboards in Chicago, is another way to approach studying the tobacco industry.

Researcher Considerations

Using the industry documents as data requires the researcher to draw on multiple skills that nurses typically have in abundance: For example, the ability to recognize patterns (in this case, not in a patient's symptoms, but in the archival data); to piece together a history and a diagnosis from a set of apparently discongruent symptoms (or in this case, documentary materials); to question assumptions and look for evidence in making a case; and to think like a good detective in asking questions of the patient (in this case, of the data in the archives). This type of research requires good organizational skills and the patience to recognize that one may have to sift through large amounts of material to separate the relevant from the irrelevant or less important documents.

Developing Research Questions

Unlike the research questions or hypotheses associated with most quantitative studies, research questions in this type of archival inquiry are often broad areas of focus. Developing archival research questions is thus dependent on having a familiarity with existing literature in the field, including not only peer reviewed papers but also contemporary news coverage of key policy dynamics, scientific controversies, political issues, and so forth. Informed about the field, one can then begin to ask how the industry developed strategies and responded to events, scientific findings, political situations, and policies. This is part of the contextualization process that is necessary throughout good archival studies. Too narrow a research question may mean that one is able to find limited data. A broader initial approach allows the researcher to take the inquiry in directions that seem most promising in terms of the quality of evidence available.

Sampling

Sampling in archival research varies from research approaches where one determines clearly in advance what to include and exclude as data. Instead, archival research requires scholars to make multiple interpretive decisions throughout the inquiry. For example, while one may begin with a broad area of focus, such as what the industry knew about smoking cessation and when, the volume of the archive necessitates making pragmatic decisions about what to include and what to leave for another research project (searching for "cessation" returns more than 108,000 hits within the *Legacy Library* collection). An advantage of the *Legacy Library* is that it permits refinement of search strategies using Boolean operators (and not, and) and date ranges, which enables the researcher to eliminate some sets of nonrelevant documents.

In general, then, document sampling involves a snowball approach of retrieving documents, examining them for relevance, using them to generate additional search terms, searching again using the new terms, and repeating the process. The researcher should keep a record of searches conducted to minimize duplication of effort and facilitate targeted searching as new clusters of documents are released. The *Legacy Library* Web site has a feature for doing this, as well as tutorials to help researchers get started.

Contextualization

Once one begins to retrieve interesting documents, it is important to try to interpret them within the context within which they were produced. A common error for beginners is to think one can simply string together sets of quotations from documents to tell a story. However, validity and integrity in archival research require the researcher to search for other confirming or disconfirming evidence as the analysis develops, perhaps including searching for media coverage on the topic at the time period in question or interviewing those who may have knowledge of the events. It is also important to place one's interpretation within the overall political and policy contexts of the time: For example, a document showing that a tobacco company knew privately about the deadliness of secondhand smoke long before suggesting on its Web site that consumers attend to the recommendations of "public health authorities" would be an important one, but it would be impossible to know this without reviewing the literature and perhaps earlier versions of the Web site.

Data Management

The *Legacy Library* allows researchers to download documents and their indexing into the Endnote bibliographic software program and to other database management software. This allows the researcher to add his or her own codes/keywords to the reference entry, facilitating later searches and identification of clusters of documents related to similar topics. Selections of material from the searchable PDFs can also be cut and pasted into other documents or programs for analysis.

Data Analysis

Data may be analyzed using several different approaches. Analysis is typically a process of reviewing the documents iteratively to make sense of their content, which may involve identifying multiple instances of a particular phenomenon of interest, ordering the data chronologically, sorting them by company or by persons involved, or other strategies. Most published studies drawing on tobacco industry documents utilize one of two approaches: A chronology, in which events are described in the order in which they occurred, or a thematic approach in which themes or foci of interest are described using examples. Sometimes the two are combined, as in McDaniel and Malone's (2009) analysis of tobacco industry credibility building, which focused on how tobacco companies conceptualized credibility and how these conceptions appeared to change over time.

A key aspect of quality tobacco industry documents research, as for other types of archival studies, is noting gaps in the emerging analysis and considering how to account for them or fill them—perhaps through interviews with public health authorities involved in the events under discussion, or through looking for outside evidence that a plan discussed in the documents was actually implemented. It is occasionally suggested by a peer reviewer that researchers should interview tobacco company executives or employees, and a researcher may choose to attempt to do so. However, given the tobacco industry's long and extremely well-documented history of systematic deception and subterfuge (U.S. District Court for the District of Columbia, 2006), it would be epistemologically dubious to make the assumption that communicating contemporaneously with self-interested individuals about events that occurred years ago (and about which they may now have reason to be less than forthcoming) would result in a more valid or truthful account of events than examining documents prepared at the time of those events by persons who did not expect them to become publicly available.

Limitations

Tobacco industry documents research, like all research, has limitations. It is not possible to claim that one has searched all the documents, and thus it is always at least theoretically possible that new evidence could emerge at a later time that might differently inform one's account. All archival research involves interpretive decision making, and as historians do, it is possible (and valid) to use the same set of materials to develop different arguments about what they mean within a historical context.

NURSING RESEARCH ON THE TOBACCO INDUSTRY

Nurses have been among the most active researchers using these documents as data (see Table 3.1) and have served as industry documents research consultants to the U.S. Justice Department in its successful racketeering lawsuit against the tobacco companies (U.S. District Court for the District of Columbia, 2006), the Centers for Disease Control (CDC), and the World Health Organization (WHO, 2000, 2009). Nursing studies based on archival research using these documents, often supplemented through analyses of secondary data sources such as company annual reports, Web sites, advertising, and other documents, have made important contributions to understanding how tobacco industry activity affects the contexts of tobacco use.

While clinical and epidemiological studies have identified important disparities in tobacco use and tobacco caused disease and death among particular groups (U.S. Department of Health and Human Services, 1998), research using these corporate documents as data has identified deeper contextual causes. If the tobacco industry had not aggressively targeted their marketing to women during the last several decades (Amos & Haglund, 2000), for example, lung cancer would not be the number one cause of cancer mortality among U.S. women today (Jemal et al., 2003).

To date, research by nurses using the tobacco industry documents has primarily focused on four broad areas: (1) tobacco industry influence on policy; (2) tobacco industry strategic responses to public health efforts, including use of front groups and attempts to divide and conquer public health advocates; (3) tobacco industry targeting of marginalized groups; and (4) tobacco industry influence on science. The literature discussed here (Table 3.1) was identified by conducting a

TABLE 3.1 Nursing Research Using Tobacco Industry Documents as a Data Source

Authors, Date	Major Findings—Conclusions
Tobacco Industry Influence on Policy	
Bialous & Glantz, 2002	Demonstrated that the tobacco industry has been involved, both directly and through consultants and allies, for over 20 years in influencing ventilation standards for indoor air quality developed by the American Society of Heating, Refrigeration, and Air Conditioning Engineers. Tobacco companies sought to standardize an "accommodation" framework to allow continued indoor smoking.
Bialous, Mochizuki-Kobayashi, & Stillman, 2006	Revealed that Japan Tobacco and Philip Morris International developed campaigns promoting courtesy and tolerance, and funded scientific research promoting "ventilation" in efforts to thwart development of smoke-free policies.
Bialous & Yach, 2001	Documented how the tobacco industry, through the Cooperation Centre for Scientific Research Relative to Tobacco, played a major role in determining scientific evidence and suggesting the standards that were eventually adopted as international standards for tobacco and tobacco products in several areas, including the measurement of cigarette tar and nicotine yield. Tobacco and tobacco products standards are not adequate to guide tobacco products regulatory policies.
Dearlove et al., 2002	Demonstrated how the tobacco industry used the *accommodation* message to mount an aggressive and effective worldwide campaign to recruit or create hospitality associations, such as restaurant associations, to serve as the tobacco industry's surrogate in fighting against smoke-free environments. Through the myth of lost profits, the tobacco industry fooled the hospitality industry into embracing expensive ventilation equipment, while in reality 100% smoke-free laws have been shown to have no effect on business revenues or even to improve them.
Drope et al., 2004	Described how the tobacco industry developed a network of consultants who represented themselves as independent to promote ventilation as a solution to secondhand smoke (SHS) in the USA. In the 1980s, the industry used them in an effort to steer concerns about indoor air quality away from secondhand smoke; by the 1990s, the industry and its consultants were maintaining that adequate ventilation could easily accommodate moderate smoking. The consultants carried the ventilation message to businesses, particularly the hospitality business, and to local, national, and international regulatory and legislative bodies.

MacDonald, Aguinaga, & Glantz, 1997	Described the strategies used by PM and other tobacco companies to promote a California initiative (Proposition 188) preempting local control of tobacco and those used by public health groups to defeat the initiative. Tobacco companies nearly succeeded in passing Proposition 188 by presenting it as a prohealth measure that would prevent children from obtaining cigarettes and provide protection against secondhand smoke. Public health groups defeated it by highlighting tobacco industry backing.
McDaniel & Malone, 2005	Explored Philip Morris's support of U.S. Food and Drug Administration regulation of tobacco products and its relationship to the company's image enhancement strategies. Philip Morris's support for government regulation of tobacco is part of a broader effort to address its negative public image, which has a damaging impact on the company's stock price, political influence, and employee morale. Whereas health advocates frame tobacco use as a public health policy issue, PM's regulatory efforts focus on framing tobacco use as an individual choice by informed adults to use a risky product.
McDaniel, Solomon, & Malone, 2005	Described industry activities aimed at influencing pesticide regulations in cases involving methoprene, the ethylene bisdithiocarbamates, and phosphine. The tobacco industry successfully altered the outcome in two cases by hiring ex-agency scientists to write reports favorable to industry positions regarding pesticide regulations for national (U.S. Environmental Protection Agency) and international (World Health Organization) regulatory bodies. The industry worked to forestall tobacco pesticide regulation by attempting to self-regulate in Europe, and encouraged a pesticide manufacturer to apply for higher tolerance levels in Malaysia and Europe while keeping tobacco industry interest a secret from government regulators.
Wander & Malone, 2006c	Explored Philip Morris's response to shareholder activists' demands that consumers in developing countries be informed about smoking risks. After resisting for 11 years, PM unilaterally reversed direction, and proposed its own labeling initiative. When PM gave in, it exchanged negative publicity for positive public relations and political credibility. Tobacco companies can appear to accommodate public health demands while securing strategic advantages.
Smith, Blackman, & Malone, 2007	Revealed how the tobacco industry successfully exploited complex relationships among the Congress, the Defense Department, commissaries, exchanges and private industry, obstructing efforts to raise cigarette prices in military commissaries for over a decade. High-level military officials were apparently threatened with retaliation from protobacco Congressmen. Against its own best interests, the U.S. military still makes tobacco available to service members at prices below those in the civilian sector.

(Continued)

TABLE 3.1 Nursing Research Using Tobacco Industry Documents as a Data Source (*Continued*)

Authors, Date	Major Findings—Conclusions
Arvey & Malone, 2008	Presented four case studies based on industry documents that illustrate how pressures exerted by multiple political actors, including the tobacco industry, resulted in weakening or rescinding military tobacco control policy initiatives.
Apollonio & Malone, in press	Revealed that "We Card," the most ubiquitous tobacco industry youth smoking prevention program in the United States, which has its retailer materials copied in other countries, was undertaken for two primary purposes: to improve the tobacco industry's image and to undermine and co-opt retailer compliance programs run by law enforcement and state public health departments.

Tobacco Industry Responses to Public Health

Authors, Date	Major Findings—Conclusions
Mandell, Bialous, & Glantz, 2006	Exposed that, even though their own research showed the industry-sponsored programs were ineffective, tobacco companies continued to award grants to schools for Life Skills Training programs as part of a public relations strategy to shift the "youth smoking paradigm" away from programs that highlight the tobacco industry's behavior and toward programs in which the industry could be a partner.
Bialous, Fox, & Glantz, 2001	Described how the tobacco industry filed formal complaints of illegal lobbying activities against state tobacco control initiatives. These complaints had a temporary chilling effect on tobacco control policy interventions. Some self-reported self-censorship in policy activity occurred in 11 of the 17 states (65%).
Malone, 2002b	Described how the tobacco industry engaged in aggressive intelligence gathering about public health groups, used intermediaries to obtain materials under false pretenses, sent public relations spies to organizations' meetings, and covertly taped strategy sessions. Other industry strategies included planning to redirect the funding of tobacco control organizations to other purposes.
Smith & Malone, 2003a	Analyzed implications of Philip Morris Companies, the world's largest and most profitable tobacco seller, changing its corporate name to The Altria Group, showing that these changes have been planned for over a decade and that the company expects to reap specific and substantial rewards from them.
Smith & Malone, 2003c	Reported how in the early 1990s, Philip Morris, faced with increasing pressures generated both externally, from the nonsmokers' rights and public health communities, and internally, from the conflicts among its varied operating companies, seriously considered leaving the tobacco business. Discussions of this option, which occurred at the highest levels of management, focused on the changing social climate regarding tobacco and smoking. This option was rejected in favor of an image enhancement strategy.

74

Smith & Malone, 2004	Analyzed the "Creative Solutions" Benson & Hedges cigarette advertising campaign. Philip Morris developed Creative Solutions to directly confront the successes of the tobacco control movement in establishing new laws and norms that promoted clean indoor air. The campaign's imagery attempted to help smokers and potential smokers overcome the physical and social downsides of smoking by managing risk and resolving internal conflict. The campaign also featured information about the Accommodation Program, Philip Morris's attempt to organize opposition to clean indoor air laws.
Wander & Malone, 2004	Described Philip Morris's response to two cases of threatened academic divestment. In each case, the world's largest tobacco company succeeded in minimizing the impact of divestment activities—in the first, by muting the consequences of a divestment, and in the second, by convincing university decision makers to recommend against tobacco stock divestment. The company exploited university concerns about losing corporate research funding as a key element of its antidivestment strategy.
Smith & Malone, 2007	Assessed industry attempts to organize smokers rights groups (SRGs) and the image of the smoker that underlay these efforts. From the late 1970s through the late 1990s they were active in numerous policy arenas, particularly the defeat of smoke-free laws. Their strategies included asserting their right to smoke and positioning themselves as courteous victims. SRGs' inability to attract members highlights the conflict between the image of the smoker in cigarette ads and that of the smokers' rights advocate.
Wander & Malone, 2006a	Described how when U.S. tobacco control advocates began urging government investment and pension funds to divest from tobacco stocks as a matter of responsible social policy in 1990, Philip Morris led the divestment opposition, insisting that funds had to be managed for the exclusive interest of beneficiaries, not the public at large, and for high share returns above all.
McDaniel, Smith, & Malone, 2006	Analyzed Philip Morris's Project Sunrise, initiated in 1995. This was a long-term plan to address tobacco industry delegitimization and ensure the social acceptability of smoking and of the company itself. Project Sunrise laid out an explicit divide-and-conquer strategy against the tobacco control movement, proposing the establishment of relationships with PM-identified moderate tobacco control individuals and organizations and the marginalization of others. Philip Morris planned to use carefully orchestrated efforts to exploit existing differences of opinion within tobacco control, weakening its opponents by working with them.

(Continued)

TABLE 3.1 Nursing Research Using Tobacco Industry Documents as a Data Source (*Continued*)

Authors, Date	Major Findings—Conclusions
Wander & Malone, 2006b	Examined how, as part of a campaign to restore its credibility as an investment vehicle with public fund managers, PM commissioned a report from the influential investment managers advisors Wilshire Associates. Findings show how Wilshire produced apparently diametrically opposed reports for clients with different interests. It reveals a pattern of potential conflicts of interest among tobacco companies, financial analysis firms, investment authorities, and institutional fund managers.
McDaniel, Intinarelli, & Malone, 2008	Documented a series of cross-company tobacco industry "issues management organizations" that coordinated and implemented common strategies to defeat tobacco control efforts at international, national, and regional levels. The massive scale and scope of this industry effort illustrate how corporate interests, when threatened by the globalization of public health, sidestep competitive concerns to coordinate their activities.
Tesler & Malone, 2008	Explored philanthropy undertaken as part of Philip Morris's PM21 image makeover. Philip Morris explicitly linked philanthropy to government affairs and used contributions as a lobbying tool against public health policies. Through advertising, covertly solicited media coverage, and contributions to legislators' pet causes, Philip Morris improved its image among key voter constituencies, influenced public officials, and divided the public health field as grantees were converted to stakeholders.
Yang & Malone, 2008	Described how, beginning in 1999, Philip Morris sought to become "societally aligned" by identifying expectations of a responsible tobacco company through public opinion research and developing and publicizing programs. Societal alignment was undertaken within the U.S. and globally. Despite PM's claims to be changing however, PM responded to public expectations largely by retooling existing positions and programs, ignoring other expectations that might have interfered with its business goals.
Smith & Malone, 2008	Examined how the language on the PM Web site and in industry documents reveals many contradictions and omissions that may undermine public health messages. Among these are vague and confusing information about addiction, tar, and nicotine, a lack of motivators to quit smoking, and silence about tobacco-related mortality.
Apollonio & Malone, 2008	Described tobacco industry and public health research on the American Legacy Foundation's "truth" campaign. The tobacco industry determined that the most effective advertisements run by Legacy's truth campaign were negative advertisements. Although the tobacco industry's own research suggested that these negative ads identified and effectively reframed the cigarette as a harmful consumer product rather than focusing solely on tobacco companies, Philip Morris accused Legacy of vilifying it.

McDaniel & Malone, 2009	Reported that tobacco companies conceptualized credibility primarily as altering public perception of the industry. *Truth* was largely absent from tobacco industry conceptualizations of credibility. However, industry research found that the public regarded credibility and responsibility differently, expecting these to entail truth telling, advertising reductions, less harmful products, apologies for deception, making amends, or exiting the tobacco business altogether. Overall, industry credibility-building projects failed repeatedly. For public health to address corporate disease promotion effectively, undermining corporate credibility may be strategically important.

Tobacco Industry Targeting of Marginalized Groups

Yerger & Malone, 2002	Described how the tobacco industry established relationships with virtually every African American leadership organization and built longstanding social connections with the community, for three specific business reasons: to increase African American tobacco use, to use African Americans as a frontline force to defend industry policy positions, and to defuse tobacco control efforts.
Smith & Malone, 2003b	Analyzed events surrounding the first time a major tobacco company advertised in gay media. Philip Morris was unprepared for the attention its entry into the gay market received. The company's reaction to this incident demonstrates that its approach to the gay community both parallels and diverges from industry strategies toward other marginalized communities.
Offen, Smith, & Malone, 2003	Examined how PM used the AIDS Coalition to Unleash Power (ACT-UP) yearlong boycott (starting in 1990) of Philip Morris's Marlboro cigarettes and Miller beer, protesting the company's support of Senator Jesse Helms (R-North Carolina), a leading opponent of AIDS funding and civil rights for lesbian, gay, bisexual, and transgender (LGBT) people. Philip Morris used the boycott to its own advantage, exploiting differences within the community and settling the boycott by pledging large donations to combat AIDS. Through corporate philanthropy, Philip Morris gained entrée to the LGBT market without appearing gay friendly.
Apollonio & Malone, 2005	Showed that the tobacco industry has marketed cigarettes to the homeless and seriously mentally ill, part of its downscale market, and developed relationships with homeless shelters and advocacy groups, gaining positive media coverage and political support.

(Continued)

TABLE 3.1 Nursing Research Using Tobacco Industry Documents as a Data Source (*Continued*)

Authors, Date	Major Findings—Conclusions
McDaniel, Solomon, & Malone, 2006	Reviewed history of tobacco industry's efforts to create internal guidelines on the conditions to be met before employee taste testers could evaluate cigarettes made from tobacco treated with experimental pesticides. Highlights ethical issues raised by unregulated industrial research: conflict of interest and lack of informed consent.
Yerger, Przewoznik, & Malone, 2007	Showed how major tobacco companies, which targeted inner cities populated predominantly by low-income African American residents with highly concentrated menthol cigarette marketing, competed against one another in "menthol wars" fought within these urban cores and how the industry's innovative marketing activities contributed to the racialized geography of today's tobacco-related health disparities.
Cataldo & Malone, 2008	Described how tobacco companies, based on extensive marketing research, aggressively targeted older smokers and sought to prevent them from quitting. Through marketing low tar or light cigarettes to older smokers at risk of quitting, the industry contributes to the illusion that such cigarettes are safer, although light cigarettes may make it harder for addicted smokers to quit. Through targeted mailings of coupons and incentives, the industry discourages older smokers from quitting. Through rhetoric aimed at convincing addicted smokers that they alone are responsible for their smoking, the industry contributes to self-blame, a documented barrier to cessation.
Smith & Malone, 2009a	Analyzed internal tobacco industry documents about the Gulf War (1990–1991). Tobacco companies targeted troops with free cigarettes, direct advertising, branded items, ways to communicate with family, and welcome home events. Military authorities sometimes restricted this activity, but frequently enabled it; tobacco companies were regarded as benefactors.
Smith & Malone, 2009b	Described tobacco sponsorship of events targeted to military personnel. More than 1400 events were held between 1980 and 1997. In 1986, the DOD issued a directive forbidding such special promotions; however, with the frequently eager cooperation of military personnel, they continued for more than a decade, apparently ceasing only due to the restrictions of the Master Settlement Agreement. The U.S. military collaborated with the tobacco industry for decades, creating a military culture of smoking.

McDaniel & Malone, in press	Explored how and why PM sought to improve its image among women, while keeping tobacco off their organizational agendas. The company sponsored women's groups and programs, and sought to appeal to women it defined as "active moms." It was more successful in securing women's organizations as allies than active moms. Increasing tobacco's visibility as a global women's health issue may require addressing industry influence.

Tobacco Industry Influence on Science

Hirschhorn, Bialous, & Shatenstein, 2001	Reviewed what is known about the Philip Morris External Research Program (PMERP). The majority of the named grant reviewers have had previous affiliation with the tobacco industry either as reviewers or grantees, but only a minority have done research directly on tobacco or smoking. The programmatic substance of the PMERP could be interpreted as soliciting exculpatory evidence with respect to smoking and exposure to smoke.
Hirschhorn, Bialous, & Shatenstein, 2006	Described how the Philip Morris External Research Program (PMERP) continues a longstanding industry pattern of seeking to fund research to meet public relations goals, rather than funding rigorous peer reviewed scientific studies. Over half PMERP participants had previously received or applied for tobacco company funding. One internal document indicated PMERP's objectives included gaining credibility and goodwill, and finding young scientists.
Yach & Bialous, 2001	Discussed the need for policy makers to be prepared for new and continuing challenges posed by the tobacco industry, because, despite the industry's claims, there is little evidence of fundamental change in its objectives.
Hirschhorn & Bialous, 2001	Described the tobacco industry's development of a well-coordinated, multipronged strategy to create doubt about research on exposure to SHS by trying to link it to the broader discussion of risk assessment of low doses of a number of toxins whose disease burden may still be a matter of scientific debate, thus trying to make SHS their equivalent; and by attempting, through third party organizations and persons, to impugn agencies using risk assessment to establish SHS was a hazard.

(Continued)

TABLE 3.1 Nursing Research Using Tobacco Industry Documents as a Data Source (*Continued*)

Authors, Date	Major Findings–Conclusions
Other Research	
Malone & Balbach, 2000	Described the industry documents databases and strategies for using them to conduct research.
Offen, Smith, & Malone, 2005	Analyzed tobacco focused boycotts retrieved from internal tobacco industry documents, Web sites and other scholarship on boycotts. Most boycotts targeted the industry itself and were unrelated to tobacco disease, often resulting in settlements that gave the industry marketing and public relations advantages. In contrast, a perimetric boycott (targeting institutions at the perimeter of the core target) of an organization that was taking tobacco money mobilized its constituency and convinced the organization to end the practice.
Yerger, Daniel, & Malone, 2005a	Reported results of urban African American focus group participants reviewing internal tobacco industry documents. Their responses suggested that such documents may be useful in efforts to socially denormalize tobacco use, promote critical reflection about community targeting, and mobilize individuals toward quitting.
Balbach, Smith, & Malone, 2006b	Analyzed trial testimony of tobacco industry executives to determine how they used the concepts of information and choice. Executives deployed the concept of information as a mechanism that shifted to consumers full moral responsibility for the harms caused by tobacco products. The industry's role was characterized as that of impartial supplier of value-free information, without regard to its quality, accuracy, and truthfulness.

McDaniel & Malone, 2007	Examined how the U.S. tobacco industry markets cigarettes as "natural" and American smokers' views of the naturalness (or unnaturalness) of cigarettes. Tobacco company market research revealed that smokers initially had difficulty interpreting the term natural in relation to cigarettes; however, after discussion of cigarette ingredients, smokers viewed natural cigarettes as healthier. Companies regarded implied health benefits as a key selling point, but hesitated to use "natural" in marketing because doing so might raise doubts about the composition of their highly profitable regular brands.
Smith, Thomson, Offen, & Malone, 2008	Reported findings from focus groups with LGBT individuals in four U.S. cities who viewed industry documents and explored perceptions of tobacco industry targeting. Participants often responded positively to tobacco company targeting; targeting connoted community visibility, legitimacy, and economic viability. Participants did not view tobacco as a gay health issue.
Froelicher et al., in press	Described results of a randomized clinical trial of a smoking cessation intervention for inner city African Americans, incorporating tobacco industry documents as part of a social justice-focused intervention, and community participatory aspects of project.

Note. PM = Philip Morris; SHS = secondhand smoke.

search for articles published by nurses and their colleagues known by the author to be active in tobacco industry documents analyses. Much of this research has been published in public health and multidisciplinary journals and may not be readily identifiable as nursing research. A much more extensive literature by scholars from many other disciplines covers other topics related to tobacco industry activities and is not discussed here, but can be located by searching "tobacco industry" as a keyword. Examples from the four areas are reviewed here representatively; see Table 3.1 for more comprehensive listing.

Tobacco Industry Influence on Policy

The tobacco industry has worked tirelessly to influence or thwart public health policies in multiple arenas. Nursing research showed that the industry has influenced national policy standards for ventilation in public and private buildings in order to avoid smoking bans (Bialous & Glantz, 2002), and has tried in multiple ways to undermine efforts to achieve smoke-free policies at the national and international levels (Bialous, Mochizuki-Kobayashi, & Stillman, 2006; Dearlove, Bialous, & Glantz, 2002; Drope, Bialous, & Glantz, 2004; Smith & Malone, 2007). Tobacco companies have also exerted undue influence over international standard setting for tobacco and tobacco products (Bialous & Yach, 2001), and worked covertly to influence national and international pesticide regulations, since tobacco is a heavily pesticide-dependent crop (McDaniel, Solomon, & Malone, 2005). Working with their powerful political allies in Congress, the tobacco industry has repeatedly thwarted stronger tobacco control policies within the U.S. military, even when those have been initiated at the Defense Department level (Arvey & Malone, 2008; Smith et al., 2007; Smith & Malone, 2009a, 2009b). Recently, Philip Morris, the nation's largest tobacco company, has touted its support for the newly passed Food and Drug Administration regulation of tobacco products (Family Smoking Prevention and Control Act, 2009). However, McDaniel and Malone (2005) showed that this was long planned as a strategic move, aimed at shoring up its damaged public reputation to ensure it could continue to do business.

Tobacco Industry Responses to Public Health Efforts

Nurses have been among the most active researchers exploring how tobacco companies have responded to public health efforts at local, national, and international levels. While one would expect any company to actively market its products and oppose regulations that might hamper its ability to sell them, analyses of tobacco industry documents reveal that tobacco companies go further: They actively conduct surveillance of public health and tobacco control groups and individuals and seek to "divide and conquer" their opponents, whom they regard as the "antitobacco industry" (Malone, 2002b; McDaniel, Intinarelli, & Malone, 2008). In the 1990s, Philip Morris developed a long-term (10–20 year) plan aimed at "creating schisms" among its opponents by working to establish partnerships with some of them (McDaniel, Smith, & Malone, 2006), and there is evidence to suggest that the plan has been carried out successfully.

Tobacco companies have also created and supported so-called smoker's rights groups, which have fought tobacco control regulations, often without revealing their tobacco company backing (Smith & Malone, 2007). These groups are created to give the impression of grassroots community opposition to public health measures. Perhaps because most smokers want to quit (Fiore et al., 2008), most of these groups were not very effective long-term. However, in the short-term they were successful in creating an impression in the media that there was controversy over tobacco control policies.

The industry has also worked to create additional burdens for local, state, and national public health programs; for example, by using public records acts to make unreasonable and excessive demands for copies of documents, taxing the limited staff resources of such programs (Aguinaga & Glantz, 1995), or by accusing tobacco control programs of engaging in illegal lobbying, discouraging legal policy advocacy by tobacco control programs and requiring them to use their resources to defend themselves (Bialous, Fox, & Glantz, 2001).

Tobacco Industry Targeting of Marginalized Groups

Nursing's traditional concern with social justice and the health of marginalized groups is reflected in several studies of the tobacco industry's targeting of marginalized populations, including the ways in which groups are characterized for marketing purposes and how best to appeal to them. Studies of tobacco industry documents related to the African American community reveal the intensive marketing of menthol cigarettes to geographically dense communities of African Americans in inner cities, for example. Companies developed innovative marketing methods for reaching poor inner city areas, including mobile van programs that distributed free cigarettes while playing music (Yerger, Przewoznik, & Malone, 2007). For decades, tobacco companies created and sustained social and economic ties to African American leadership groups for the purposes of marketing, establishing policy allies, and buying silence on tobacco and disease issues (Yerger & Malone, 2002). Similar strategies have been used with women's groups (McDaniel & Malone, 2009b).

Other marginalized groups have also been targeted. Older smokers, for example, begin to worry about their health as they age. Such smokers, nursing research shows, were targeted with marketing and promotion efforts aimed at discouraging quitting, including sending discount coupons near New Year's Day when many people resolve to try to quit. They were also targeted with marketing suggesting that "light" cigarettes might be a safer alternative, while the industry's own research had showed they were not (Cataldo & Malone, 2008).

Those enlisting in the military tend to skew African American and are often young people away from home for the first time. Tobacco companies view the military as a key market for recruiting new young smokers, and for many years they aggressively promoted their products on military bases (Smith & Malone, 2009a, 2009b). Tobacco companies have also targeted the most marginalized, including the homeless and mentally ill and their caregivers (Apollonio & Malone, 2005).

Tobacco companies used rhetorical strategies to suggest to the gay community that smoking cigarettes was a *right* that needed to be protected. When threatened with a boycott unrelated to health concerns, Philip Morris provided economic support to a major national gay organization to co-opt opposition, turning the threat into a marketing opportunity (Offen, Smith, & Malone, 2003; Smith & Malone, 2003b). Tobacco industry employees were also exploited, used to taste test experimental pesticide-laden cigarettes without adequate human subjects protections (McDaniel, Solomon, & Malone, 2006). This body of research has been valuable in raising tobacco control as an issue within different marginalized communities and lending support to efforts to establish stronger policies about tobacco among racial–ethnic and other marginalized groups' organizations.

Tobacco Industry Influences on Science

Nursing research and analysis has also explored the industry's (mis)use of scientific risk assessment as a strategy to prevent regulatory measures (Hirschhorn & Bialous, 2001) such as the passage of legislation promoting smoke-free environments. Other research has explored Philip Morris's new research program, initiated after the Master Settlement Agreement of 1998 (Hurt et al., 2009) required the dissolution of previous industry-funded research programs that had been shown to engage in deceptive and misleading practices (Hirschhorn, Bialous, & Shatenstein, 2001, 2006; Yach & Bialous, 2001).

Other Research

Additional nursing studies have used the documents archives to explore more theoretical questions such as how boycotts affect the industry, how the industry utilizes the idea of information for public relations purposes, and how tobacco companies conceive the idea of credibility (Balbach, Smith, & Malone, 2006a; McDaniel & Malone, 2009; Offen, Smith, & Malone, 2005). In addition, some nursing research has explored public perceptions of the industry, using industry documents as focal points for group discussions or as part of a cessation intervention (Froelicher, Doolan, Yerger, McGruder, & Malone, in press; Smith, Thomson, Offen, & Malone, 2008; Yerger, Daniel, & Malone, 2005b). For example, African American smokers shown a set of internal company documents about industry targeting of their community appeared motivated to share the information with others and consider quitting tobacco (Yerger et al., 2005b). However, in a similar study with individuals self-identifying as members of the lesbian, gay, bisexual, and transgender (LGBT) community, targeting was in many cases perceived as a positive sign of social validation and recognition (Smith et al., 2008). There remain many questions yet to be explored using this unprecedented set of archival data.

DISCUSSION

Nurses are increasingly engaged in community- and policy-level activities to improve health and prevent suffering and disease. Traditional tobacco prevention and cessation efforts must be complemented with understanding how the tobacco industry has shaped the very contexts within which these efforts are undertaken. This chapter helps to broaden the scope within which nurses are prepared to intervene as clinicians, community health proponents, policy advocates, researchers, and educators. Nurses have both the numbers and the political power to influence perceptions about tobacco and the tobacco industry, if they organized to address them: They are highly trusted by the public and respected by policy makers for their numbers and political savvy. As a tobacco industry executive once noted, nurses could be "formidable opponents" of the tobacco industry (Malone, 2002a).

While nursing research is often thought of in terms of clinical research, this review shows that nurses are continuing to embrace wider ideas of what constitute legitimate domains for nursing research. Innovative archival research on the tobacco industry can help nurses reframe tobacco as a nursing issue and link corporate practices and government policies to clinical issues. Nurses working on smoking cessation within a particular population group may find it valuable to explore research on industry target marketing practices in order to help their patients contextualize their experience of trying to quit. For example, counseling clients that it is common for the industry to send discount coupons for cigarettes to older smokers around New Year's Day, when many worried smokers resolve to try to quit smoking (Cataldo & Malone, 2008), may help some of them resist such tactics. Nurses working with youth may want to be aware of the tobacco industry's so-called youth smoking prevention programs and discuss their ineffectiveness and true purposes with parent groups. Finally, nurses working in public health and policy arenas can help educate the public about the tobacco industry's ongoing (and increasingly, global) efforts to perpetuate corporate disease promotion.

REFERENCES

Aguinaga, S., & Glantz, S. A. (1995). The use of the public records acts to disrupt tobacco control. *Tobacco Control, 4,* 222–230.

Amos, A., & Haglund, M. (2000). From social taboo to "torch of freedom": The marketing of cigarettes to women. *Tobacco Control, 9*(1), 3–8.

Apollonio, D., & Malone, R. E. (2005). Marketing to the marginalized: Tobacco industry targeting of the homeless and mentally ill. *Tobacco Control, 14*(6), 409–415.

Apollonio, D. E., & Malone, R. E. (2008). Turning negative into positive: Public health mass media campaigns and negative advertising. *Health Education Research, 24*(3), 483–495.

Apollonio, D. E., & Malone, R. E. (in press). The we card program: Tobacco industry "youth smoking prevention" as industry self-preservation. *American Journal of Public Health.*

Arvey, S., & Malone, R. E. (2008). Advance and retreat: Tobacco control policy in the U.S. military. *Military Medicine, 173,* 985–991.

Balbach, E. D., Smith, E. A., & Malone, R. E. (2006b). How the health belief model helps the tobacco industry: Individuals, choice, and "information." *Tobacco Control, 15*(Suppl. 4), iv37–iv43.

Bialous, S. A., Fox, B. J., & Glantz, S. A. (2001). Tobacco industry allegations of "illegal lobbying" and state tobacco control. *American Journal of Public Health, 91*(1), 62–67.

Bialous, S. A., & Glantz, S. A. (2002). ASHRAE Standard 62: Tobacco industry's influence over national ventilation standards. *Tobacco Control, 11*(4), 315–328.

Bialous, S. A., Mochizuki-Kobayashi, Y., & Stillman, F. (2006). Courtesy and the challenges of implementing smoke-free policies in Japan. *Nicotine and Tobacco Research, 8*(2), 203–216.

Bialous, S. A., & Yach, D. (2001). Whose standard is it, anyway? How the tobacco industry determines the international organization for standardization (ISO) standards for tobacco and tobacco products. *Tobacco Control, 10*(2), 96–104.

Brandt, A. M. (2007). *The cigarette century: The rise, fall, and deadly persistence of the product that defined America.* New York: Basic Books.

Cataldo, J., & Malone, R. E. (2008). False promises: The tobacco industry, low-tar cigarettes, and older smokers. *Journal of the American Geriatrics Society, 56,* 1716–1723.

Centers for Disease Control and Prevention. (2005). Annual smoking-attributable mortality, years of potential life lost, and productivity losses—United States, 1997–2001. *Morbidity and Mortality Weekly Report, 54,* 625–628.

Centers for Disease Control and Prevention. (2009). *Tobacco use: Targeting the nation's leading killer.* Retrieved from http://www.cdc.gov/nccdphp/publications/aag/osh.htm

Dearlove, J. V., Bialous, S. A., & Glantz, S. A. (2002). Tobacco industry manipulation of the hospitality industry to maintain smoking in public places. *Tobacco Control, 11*(2), 94–104.

Dock, L. L. (1907/1985). Some urgent social claims. In J. W. James (Ed.), *The Lavinia dock reader.* New York: Garland.

Drope, J., Bialous, S. A., & Glantz, S. A. (2004). Tobacco industry efforts to present ventilation as an alternative to smoke-free environments in North America. *Tobacco Control, 13*(Suppl. 1), i41–i47.

Family Smoking Prevention and Control Act. (2009). Retrieved from http://www.thomas.gov/cgi-bin/bdquery/z?d111:HR01256:|/bss/111search.html

Fiore, M. C., Jaen, C. R., Baker, T. B., Bailey, W. C., Benowitz, N. L., Curry, S. J., et al. (2008). *Treating tobacco use and dependence: 2008 update, clinical practice guideline.* Rockville, MD: U.S. Department of Health and Human Services. Public Health Service.

Freudenberg, N. (2005). Public health advocacy to change corporate practices: Implications for health education practice and research. *Health Education and Behavior, 32*(3), 298–319.

Froelicher, E. S., Doolan, D., Yerger, V. B., McGruder, C. O., & Malone, R. E. (in press). Combining community participatory research with a randomized clinical trial: Lessons learned from the Protecting the 'Hood Against Tobacco' (PHAT) study. *Heart & Lung.*

Hackbarth, D. P., Schnopp-Wyatt, D., Katz, D., Williams, J., Silvestri, B., & Pfleger, M. (2001). Collaborative research and action to control the geographic placement of outdoor advertising of alcohol and tobacco products in Chicago. *Public Health Reports, 116*(6), 558–567.

Hirschhorn, N., & Bialous, S. A. (2001). Second hand smoke and risk assessment: What was in it for the tobacco industry? *Tobacco Control, 10*(4), 375–382.

Hirschhorn, N., Bialous, S. A., & Shatenstein, S. (2001). Philip Morris' new scientific initiative: An analysis. *Tobacco Control, 10,* 247–252.

Hirschhorn, N., Bialous, S. A., & Shatenstein, S. (2006). The Philip Morris external research program: Results from the first round of projects. *Tobacco Control, 15*(3), 267–269.

Hurt, R. D., Ebbert, J. O., Muggli, M. E., Lockhart, N. J., & Robertson, C. R. (2009). Open doorway to truth: Legacy of the Minnesota tobacco trial. *Mayo Clinic Proceedings, 84*(5), 446–456.

Jemal, A., Murray, T., Samuels, A., Ghafoor, A., Ward, E., & Thun, M. J. (2003). Cancer statistics, 2003. *CA: Cancer Journal for Clinicians, 53*(1), 5–26.

Kluger, R. (1997). *Ashes to ashes: America's hundred-year cigarette war, the public health, and the unabashed triumph of Philip Morris.* New York: Vintage Books.

LeGresley, V. E. (1999, April). A 'vector analysis' of the tobacco epidemic. *Bulletin von Medicus Mundi Schweiz, 72.* Retrieved from http://www.medicusmundi.ch/mms/services/bulletin/bulletin199901/kap199901/199903legresley.html

Lewenson, S. B. (2002). Pride in our past: Nursing's political roots. In D. J. Mason & J. K. Leavitt (Eds.), *Policy and politics in nursing and health care* (3rd ed., pp. 19–30). Philadelphia, PA: W.B. Saunders.

MacDonald, H., Aguinaga, S., & Glantz, S. A. (1997). The defeat of Philip Morris' 'California uniform tobacco control act.' *American Journal of Public Health, 87*(12), 1989–1996.

Malone, R. E. (2002a). Nursing, our public deaths, and the tobacco industry. *American Journal of Critical Care, 11*(2), 102–105.

Malone, R. E. (2002b). Tobacco industry surveillance of public health groups: The case of STAT and INFACT. *American Journal of Public Health, 92*(6), 955–960.

Malone, R. E., & Balbach, E. D. (2000). Tobacco industry documents: Treasure trove or quagmire? *Tobacco Control, 9,* 334–338.

Mandell, L., Bialous, S. A., & Glantz, S. (2006). Avoiding 'truth': Tobacco industry promotion of life skills training. *Journal of Adolescent Health, 39*(6), 868–879.

McDaniel, P. A., Intinarelli, G., & Malone, R. E. (2008). Tobacco industry issues management organizations: Creating a global corporate network to undermine public health. *BioMed Central Globalization and Health, 4*(2). Retrieved from http://www.globalizationandhealth.com/content/4/1/2

McDaniel, P. A., & Malone, R. E. (2005). Understanding Philip Morris's pursuit of US government regulation of tobacco. *Tobacco Control, 14*(3), 193–200.

McDaniel, P. A., & Malone, R. E. (2007). 'I always thought they were all pure tobacco': American smokers' perceptions of 'natural' cigarettes and tobacco industry marketing strategies. *Tobacco Control, 16,* e7.

McDaniel, P. A., & Malone, R. E. (2009b). Legitimizing disease promotion: The role of corporate credibility. *American Journal of Public Health, 99,* 452–461.

McDaniel, P. A., & Malone, R. E. (2009b). Creating the "desired mindset": Philip Morris's efforts to improve its corporate image among women. *Women and Health, 49,* 441–474.

McDaniel, P. A., Smith, E. A., & Malone, R. E. (2006). Philip Morris's Project Sunrise: Weakening tobacco control by working with it. *Tobacco Control, 15,* 215–223.

McDaniel, P. A., Solomon, G., & Malone, R. E. (2005). The tobacco industry and pesticide regulations: Case studies from tobacco industry archives. *Environmental Health Perspectives, 113*(12), 1659–1665.

McDaniel, P. A., Solomon, G., & Malone, R. E. (2006). Taste-testing pesticide treated tobacco: The ethics of industry experimentation using employees. *American Journal of Public Health, 96,* 37–46.

McKinlay, J., & Marceau, L. (2000). Upstream healthy public policy: Lessons from the battle of tobacco. *International Journal of Health Services, 30*(1), 49–69.

Mokdad, A. H., Marks, J. S., Stroup, D. F., & Gerberding, J. L. (2004). Actual causes of death in the United States, 2000. *Journal of the American Medical Association, 291*(10), 1238–1245.

Naegle, M., Baird, C., & Stein, K. F. (2009). Psychiatric nurses as champions for smoking cessation. *Journal of the American Psychiatric Nurses Association, 15*(1), 21–23.

Nides, M., Leischow, S., Sarna, L., & Evans, S. E. (2007). Maximizing smoking cessation in clinical practice: pharmacologic and behavioral interventions. *Preventive Cardiology, 10*(2, Suppl. 1), 23–30.

Offen, N., Smith, E. A., & Malone, R. E. (2003). From adversary to target market: The ACT-UP boycott of Philip Morris. *Tobacco Control, 12*(2), 203–207.

Offen, N., Smith, E. A., & Malone, R. E. (2005). The perimetric boycott: A tool for tobacco control advocacy. *Tobacco Control, 14,* 272–277.

Sarna, L., & Bialous, S. A. (2006). Strategic directions for nursing research in tobacco dependence. *Nursing Research, 55*(Suppl. 4), S1–S9.

Sarna, L., Bialous, S. A., Wells, M. J., & Kotlerman, J. (2009). Smoking among psychiatric nurses: Does it hinder tobacco dependence treatment? *Journal of the American Psychiatric Nurses Association, 15*(1), 59–67.

Smith, E. A., Blackman, V., & Malone, R. E. (2007). Death at a discount: How the tobacco industry thwarted tobacco control policies in U.S. military commissaries. *Tobacco Control, 16,* 38–46.

Smith, E. A., & Malone, R. E. (2003a). 'Altria' means tobacco: Philip Morris's identity crisis. *American Journal of Public Health, 93*, 553–556.

Smith, E. A., & Malone, R. E. (2003b). The outing of Philip Morris: Advertising tobacco to gay men. *American Journal of Public Health, 93*, 988–993.

Smith, E. A., & Malone, R. E. (2003c). Thinking the 'unthinkable': Why Philip Morris considered quitting. *Tobacco Control, 12*, 208–213.

Smith, E. A., & Malone, R. E. (2004). "Creative Solutions": Selling cigarettes in a smoke-free world. *Tobacco Control, 13*(1), 57–63.

Smith, E. A., & Malone, R. E. (2007). 'We will speak as the smoker': The tobacco industry's smokers' rights groups. *European Journal of Public Health, 17*(3), 306–313.

Smith, E. A., & Malone, R. E. (2008). Philip Morris's health information web site appears responsible but undermines public health. *Public Health Nursing, 25*(6), 554–564.

Smith, E. A., & Malone, R. E. (2009a). 'Everywhere the soldier will be': Wartime tobacco promotion in the U.S. military. *American Journal of Public Health.* epub ahead of print, http://www.ajph.org/cgi/reprint/AJPH.2008.152983v1?view=long&pmid= 19608945

Smith, E. A., & Malone, R. E. (2009b). Tobacco promotion to military personnel: "The plums are here to be plucked." *Military Medicine, 174*, 8, 797–806.

Smith, E. A., Thomson, K., Offen, N., & Malone, R. E. (2008). "If you know you exist, it's just marketing poison": Meanings of tobacco industry targeting in the LGBT community. *American Journal of Public Health, 98*(6), 996–1003.

Tesler, L., & Malone, R. E. (2008). Corporate philanthropy, lobbying and public health policy. *American Journal of Public Health, 98*(12), 2123–2133.

University of California–San Francisco. (2007). *Legacy tobacco documents library.* Retrieved from http://legacy.library.ucsf.edu

U.S. Department of Health and Human Services. (1998). *Tobacco use among U.S. racial/ ethnic minority groups: A report of the surgeon general.* Washington, DC: Centers for Disease Control and Prevention, Office on Smoking and Health.

U.S. District Court for the District of Columbia. (2006). *Final opinion in United States of America v. Philip Morris et al.* Retrieved December 11, 2008, from http://www.tobacco lawcenter.org/doj-litigation.html

Wander, N., & Malone, R. E. (2004). Selling off or selling out? Medical schools and ethical leadership in tobacco stock divestment. *Academic Medicine, 79*(11), 1017–1026.

Wander, N., & Malone, R. E. (2006a). Fiscal vs. social responsibility: How Philip Morris shaped the public funds divestment debate. *Tobacco Control, 15*, 231–241.

Wander, N., & Malone, R. E. (2006b). Keeping public institutions invested in tobacco. *Journal of Business Ethics, 73*(2), 161–176.

Wander, N., & Malone, R. E. (2006c). Making big tobacco give in: You lose, they win. *American Journal of Public Health, 96*(11), 2048–2054.

Weinstein, N. D. (1998). Accuracy of smokers' risk perceptions. *Annals of Behavioral Medicine, 20*(2), 135–140.

Weinstein, N. D., Marcus, S. E., & Moser, R. P. (2005). Smokers' unrealistic optimism about their risk. *Tobacco Control, 14*(1), 55–59.

Wiist, W. H. (2006). Public health and the anticorporate movement: Rationale and recommendations. *American Journal of Public Health, 96*(8), 1370–1375.

World Health Organization. (2000). *Tobacco company strategies to undermine tobacco control activities at the world health organization: Report of the committee of experts on tobacco industry documents*. Geneva, Switzerland: World Health Organization. http://www. who.int/tobacco/media/en/who_inquiry.pdf

World Health Organization. (2008). *Tobacco free initiative*. Retrieved from http://www. who.int/tobacco/en/

World Health Organization. (2009). *Tobacco industry interference with tobacco control*. http://www.who.int/tobacco/resources/publications/9789241597340.pdf

Yach, D., & Bialous, S. A. (2001). Junking science to promote tobacco. *American Journal of Public Health, 91*(11), 1745–1748.

Yang, J. S., & Malone, R. E. (2008). 'Working to shape what society's expectations of us should be': Philip Morris's societal alignment strategy. *Tobacco Control, 17,* 391–398.

Yerger, V., Daniel, M., & Malone, R. E. (2005a). Taking it to the streets: African American young adults respond to internal tobacco industry documents about targeting. *Nicotine and Tobacco Research, 7,* 163–172.

Yerger, V. B., Daniel, M. R., & Malone, R. E. (2005b). Taking it to the streets: Responses of African American young adults to internal tobacco industry documents. *Nicotine and Tobacco Research, 7*(1), 163–172.

Yerger, V. B., & Malone, R. E. (2002). African American leadership groups: Smoking with the enemy. *Tobacco Control, 11,* 336–345.

Yerger, V. B., Przewoznik, J., & Malone, R. E. (2007). Racialized geography, corporate activity, and health disparities: Tobacco industry targeting of inner cities. *Journal of Health Care for the Poor and Underserved, 18,* 10–38.

Ziedonis, D., Hitsman, B., Beckham, J. C., Zvolensky, M., Adler, L. E., Audrain-McGovern, J., et al. (2008). Tobacco use and cessation in psychiatric disorders: National institute of mental health report. *Nicotine and Tobacco Research, 10*(12), 1691–1715.

Chapter 4

Monitoring the Tobacco Epidemic With National, Regional, and International Databases and Systematic Reviews: Evidence for Nursing Research and Clinical Decision Making

Virginia Hill Rice

ABSTRACT

Tobacco use (primarily cigarette smoking) continues to be the most preventable health risk in the United States and the second greatest health threat around the world. In 2020 the global burden is expected to exceed nine million deaths annually. Nursing, with the largest numbers of health care professionals has an opportunity to make a significant reduction in tobacco use through its research and client-focused care. This chapter addresses why and how monitoring the tobacco epidemic with population-based databases

DOI: 10.1891/0739-6686.27.91

and meta-analyses is important for nurse researchers and for evidence-based nursing practice. Population-based surveys permit an examination of trends in tobacco use and the progress in tobacco control with some confidence across time, places (i.e., states, nations, communities, etc.), and large numbers of participants. Included in this review are a description of the numerous national and international databases and other resources that nurse researchers can use to build the science of tobacco use. Additionally, research reviews and meta-analyses are described as other vehicles for providing a basis for making evidence-based decisions about nursing intervention. Nurse scientists have an obligation to use and evaluate these diverse resources to determine the gaps in knowledge, provide a foundation for clinical practice, and identify the needs and directions for future research in the field.

Keywords: nursing research; tobacco use; databases; meta-analysis; evidence-based practice

In the 20th century the tobacco use epidemic killed 100 million people worldwide; in the 21st century it could kill one billion if not stopped (World Health Organization (WHO) Report on the Global Tobacco Epidemic, 2008). Tobacco use (primarily cigarette smoking) continues to be the most preventable health risk in the United States (Centers for Disease Control and Prevention[CDC], 2008) and the second greatest health threat around the world (WHO Tobacco Free Initiative, 2008). The global burden of deaths from smoking, which lags behind trends in cigarette consumption by 30 to 60 years, is increasing ever more rapidly in the economically developing rather than developed countries. In 2020 the global burden is expected to exceed nine million deaths annually with seven million of these occurring in the economically developing countries (Abdullah & Husten, 2004). Nursing, with the largest numbers of health care professionals in the United States and around the world, has an opportunity and an obligation to make a significant reduction in tobacco use risk through its research and client-focused care.

This chapter addresses why and how monitoring the tobacco epidemic through population-based databases and meta-analyses are important for nurse researchers and for evidence-based nursing practice. The first part will focus on large-scale national and international databases and other resources that nurse researchers can use to build the nursing science of tobacco use. The latter part will discuss reviews, including meta-analyses that nurse clinicians can utilize for evidence-based decision making relative to client care.

Advantages and Limitations of Tobacco Control Databases

Population-based studies and surveys permit nurses to review the trends in tobacco use and the progress in tobacco control with some confidence across time, places (i.e., states, nations, communities, etc.), and large numbers of participants. Such studies can also be used to identify health disparities, examine racial, ethnic, gender, and geographic differences, establish a framework for evidence-based health policies, and allow for trend analyses (Jones & Mark, 2005). Meta-analysis, the merging of findings from many small and individualized studies that have examined the same phenomenon, such as testing the efficacy of nursing interventions to increase tobacco cessation (Rice & Stead, 2008), provide a statistical estimation of a population-based effect. Meta-analysis can provide a sense of unity of knowledge within a given topical area (Burns & Grove, 2007).

Zeni and Kogan (2007) point out the advantages of large population-based databases versus individual studies with convenience sampling. The former, if weighted appropriately, permits generalizability of the findings based on a representative sample and an adequate sample size. Population-based surveys in most cases are more cost- and time-efficient if steps are taken for meticulous instrument development, data collection, and data management. Studies with population-based data provide an opportunity for researchers to collaborate within and across disciplines. For example, a team of scientists examining Behavioral Risk Factor Survey data (http://www.cdc.gov/HealthyYouth/yrbs/index.htm) could include nurse investigators, epidemiologists, health policy analysts, sociologists, demographers, and many other public health researchers depending on the question(s) being asked. If a survey is completed on a regularly scheduled basis (e.g., annually or biannually), as is true of most national and international population-based studies, it is possible to look at trends across selected years and decades. The time frame for clustering smaller sample-based studies is less consistent and predictable.

However there are limitations to the use of tobacco control databases. Sample-based studies tend to have more depth of knowledge of a phenomenon, such as tobacco use, because the study measures can be tailored to the characteristics of the participants (e.g., rural youth) and allow for qualitative data to expand descriptions. This is less true with large population-based samples of thousands of individuals where mostly quantitative data are sought. A major concern for both population- and sample-based studies is that the information given is usually self-reported and, therefore, may lack reliability. In addition, participants may choose to give socially desirable responses. This is a particular worry as more and more of the world defines and labels tobacco use as a bad behavior. Another concern is the lack of consistency in the definition of terms across studies.

Since the 1950s many national and international surveillance systems based on population-based surveys have been implemented to monitor tobacco use on a regular basis. Understanding, documenting, and quantifying the characteristics of tobacco users and potential users has been fundamental to the tobacco control effort (Delnevo & Bauer, 2009).

National and Regional Tobacco Use Databases for Monitoring and Surveillance

Table 4.1 identifies key national and regional surveillance and evaluation systems of tobacco use, their source and year of initiation, the participants, methodology, tobacco use variables, and nature of data collected. In addition, a contact web address is provided for the reader. An overview of these selected databases is provided below.

American Cancer Society Cancer Prevention Study (ACS CPS)

The ACS CPS I survey was developed in 1959 to evaluate factors and behaviors that increased or decreased risk for cancer. Data compilations over the years resulted in a series of National Cancer Institute Smoking and Tobacco Control Monographs (http://cancercontrol.cancer.gov/TCRB/monographs/). The ACS CPS II focused on nutrition and health and ACS CPS III is in progress and targeting lifestyle, environmental, and genetic factors.

Adult Tobacco Survey (ATS)

In 2002, the CDC and individual state partners developed the focused ATS to survey noninstitutionalized adults, 18 years and older with telephones. Data were collected using random digit dialing and computer-assisted telephone interviews. Nineteen states have participated thus far. This survey is available in Spanish for this rapidly growing population in the United States.

Behavioral Risk Factor Surveillance System (BRFSS)

The BRFSS was first established in 1984 by the CDC as a state-based system of health surveys that collects information on health risk behaviors, preventive health practices, and health care access primarily related to chronic disease and injury. For many states, the BRFSS was the only available source of timely and accurate information on tobacco use and health behaviors. The survey brings data together monthly from all 50 states, the District of Columbia, Puerto Rico, the U.S. Virgin Islands, and Guam; it is the largest telephone health survey in the world. States use BRFSS data to identify emerging health problems, establish and track health objectives, and develop and evaluate public health policies and legislative programs. A major limitation is that those without a telephone are not eligible for participation. The emergence of unlisted cellular telephones may pose an additional barrier.

TABLE 4.1 National Tobacco Control Databases

Name	Source	Participants	Methodology	Tobacco Use Variables	Data Collected
American Cancer Society Prevention studies (ACS CPS)					
ACS CPS I Cancer Prevention study (CPS)-1 (1959–1972)	American Cancer Society (ACS) Cancer Prevention Study (CPS-1) http://www.cancer.org/docroot/RES/content/RES_6_2_Study_Overviews.asp http://www.cancer.org/docroot/RES/content/RES_6_4x_Cancer_Prevention_Study_CPS_I.asp	Approximately one million adult men and women from 25 states enrolled 1959–1960, and followed through September 1972.	Prospective cancer mortality study. Convenience sampling and enrollment by family households. Prospective cohort study Mortality was assessed at 1, 3, 5, and 11 years. There was an 88% retention rate.	Baseline questionnaire includes: body size, personal and family health history, demographics, diet, alcohol, *tobacco use*, and physical activity. Assessed mortality and continuing smoking status biennially.	Eight follow-ups until 1972. Deaths confirmed by state health departments

(*Continued*)

TABLE 4.1   National Tobacco Control Databases (Continued)

Name	Source	Participants	Methodology	Tobacco Use Variables	Data Collected
ACS CPS II (Nutrition & health) 1982–2006	American Cancer Society (ACS) Cancer Prevention Study (CPS II) http://www.cancer.org/docroot/res/content/res_6_2_study_overviews.asp	In 1982, 1.2 million adults in 50 states, D.C., and Puerto Rico were recruited by the ACS to participate in a 12-year prospective mortality study.	Longitudinal prospective cohort study.	Over 488,000 deaths have occurred in this cohort from 1982 to 2006.	Vital status linkage with the National Death Index. Cause of death has been documented for 99% of all deaths. Mortality follow-up of the CPS-II baseline cohort is complete through 2006. Data are in National Cancer Institute, Smoking and Tobacco Control Monograph Series (1–19) 1991–2008.
ACS CPS III (Lifestyle, behavioral, environmental and genetic factors)	American Cancer Society Cancer Prevention Study-3 (CPS-3) is currently being established to replace the older cohort of CPS-II because of changes over time in the causes of cancer within populations and in our understanding of cancer etiology. Like CPS-II, the CPS-3 cohort is designed to be a long-term resource to examine the relationship between cancer incidence and mortality, and a wide range of exposures, including tobacco.	CPS-3 will recruit 500,000 between 30 and 65 years including large numbers of nonwhite and Hispanic participants with respect to age, ethnicity, and geography.	Like CPS-II, CPS-3 cohort is designed to be a long-term resource to examine the relationship between cancer incidence and mortality, and a wide range of exposures, including tobacco.	Will assess lifestyle factors such as diet, use of alcohol and *tobacco*, occupation, medical history, and family cancer history in relation to cancer mortality.	In progress

Survey	Source	Recruits/Description	Sampling Method	Questions	Frequency/Notes
General Population State Adult Tobacco Survey (ATS) and Hispanic/Latino Adult Tobacco Survey (H/L ATS)	Centers for Disease Control and Prevention and state partners (CDC) http://www.cdc.gov/tobacco/data_statistics/state_data/index.htm http://www.cdc.gov/Tobacco/data_statistics/surveys/hispanic_latino_ats_guide/sect_a/ind	Recruits noninstitutional adults 18 years and older with telephone. (Available in English and Spanish)	Uses ongoing Random digit dialing with computer-assisted-telephone-interviewing. Has proportional weighting to achieve a representative sample.	There are 9 questions on cigarette smoking (Q2–Q10) and 11 on Cessation (Q11–Q21). Current smoker has smoked at least 100 cigarettes in their lifetime and was smoking every day or some days at the time of survey.	Ongoing Nineteen states have participated.
Behavior risk factor surveillance system (BRFSS) In use since 1984	Centers for Disease Control and Prevention (CDC) www.cdc.gov/brfss www.cdc.gov/brfss/technical_infodata/survey-data.htm	State-based system of health surveys of more than 350,000 adults on health risk behaviors, preventive health practices, and health care access related to chronic disease and injury.	Disproportionate stratified random sampling based on high and low population density by state is used to arrive at sample for telephone interviews.	Section 11 Questions: 11.1 Have you smoked at least 100 cigarettes in your entire life? 11.2 Do you now smoke cigarettes every day, some days, or not at all? 11.3 During the past 12 months, have you stopped smoking for one day or longer because you were trying to quit smoking? 11.4 How long has it been since you last smoked cigarettes regularly? 11.5 Do you currently use chewing tobacco, snuff, or snus every day, some days, or not at all?	Annual The BRFSS questionnaire was designed by state and CDC staffs. It has three parts: the core component consisting of the fixed core, rotating core, and emerging core; the optional modules; and the state-added questions. Note: All health departments must ask core component questions without modification, however many use other modules as well.

(Continued)

TABLE 4.1 National Tobacco Control Databases (*Continued*)

Name	Source	Participants	Methodology	Tobacco Use Variables	Data Collected
Health information national trends survey (HINTS) In use since 2003	National Cancer Institute in 2003 http://hints.cancer.gov/questions/section.jsp?section=Tobacco+Use	Noninstitutionalized adults, 18 years and older. In 2003, 6,369 participated.	Uses ongoing Random digit dialing with computer-assisted-telephone-interviewing. Has proportional weighting to achieve a representative sample. Minorities are oversampled and sample weights are used for analyses.	Tobacco use questions on 2003, 2005, and 2007 are: *Have you smoked at least 100 cigarettes in your entire life? Do you now smoke cigarettes? On the average, how many cigarettes do you now smoke a day? On how many of the past 30 days, did you smoke a cigarette? On the average, when you smoked during the past 30 days, about how many cigarettes did you smoke a day?*	Biannually Assessed for cancer-relevant knowledge, attitudes, and behaviors and cigarette use, number of cigarettes smoked, quit attempts, attitudes toward use of potential reduced exposure products (PREPS).
Monitoring the future surveys (MTFS) In use since 1991	NIH National Institute of Drug Abuse & Institute for Social Research at the University of Michigan. http://monitoringthefuture.org/ http://www.monitoringthefuture.org/data/08data.html#2008data-cigs http://www.icpsr.umich.edu/SAMHDA/	Each year, approximately 50,000 eighth, 10th, and 12th grade students are surveyed (12th graders have been since 1975, and 8th and 10th graders since 1991) plus randomly selected follow-up surveys mailed to a sample of each graduating class for a number of years after initial participation.	Data collection in 420 public and private schools, high schools/middle schools for representative cross section at each grade level. Uses multistage random sampling by geographic area, with probability proportionate selection of classes within schools.	Data collected on use of 16 substances including *cigarettes and smokeless tobacco.* Two Questions asked of all are: "Have you ever smoked cigarettes?" and "How frequently have you smoked cigarettes during the past 30 days?" Smokeless use questions as well.	Annually The 2008 rates of 30 day cigarette smoking were 7%, 12%, and 20% in grades 8, 10, and 12, respectively. These are the lowest levels since the early 1990s. Smokeless use has leveled off and access to all tobacco remains high.

National health interview survey (NHIS) In use since 1957	National Center for Health Statistics (NCHS) of the Centers for Disease Control and Prevention (CDC) Administered by the U.S. Census Bureau http://www.cdc.gov/nchs/about/major/nhis/quest_data_related_1997_forward.htm http://www.cdc.gov/nchs/about/major/nhis/tobacco/nhis_quest_pdf.htm	Is a nationwide in-person survey of 40,000 households, or about 100,000 persons in the civilian noninstitutionalized population. It oversamples African-American and Hispanic respondents.	Sampling plan follows a multistage probability design that permits representative sampling of households and noninstitutional group quarters.	Has core set of basic health and demographic questions and 64 *Tobacco use questions* One or more sets of supplemental questions on specific health topics, including cancer (i.e., Cancer Control Supplement) are added every 3 to 5 years.	Annually Questionnaires, datasets, and related documentation 1997–2009 are available at the Web site.
National survey on drug use and health (NSDUH) In use since 1971	Substance Abuse and Mental Health Services Administration (SAMHSA), (parts of U.S. Public Health Service) and the DHHS. Authorized by Section 505 of the Public Health Service Act, which requires annual surveys on the level and patterns of substance abuse. Research Triangle Institute (since 1988) http://www.oas.samhsa.gov/NSDUH/Methods.cfm http://www.oas.samhsa.gov/NSDUH/2k7NSDUH/2k7results.cfm#Ch3	NSDUH provides yearly national and state-level data on the use of alcohol, tobacco, illicit and nonmedical prescription drugs by a civilian, noninstitutionalized population aged 12 or older.	Uses a sampling plan that follows a multistage probability design that permits representative sampling of households and noninstitutional units by states. Interviewers attempt to immediately conduct the NSDUH interview with each selected person in the household.	NSDUH 2005 Questionnaire 25 Questions re: cigarettes 25 Questions re: snuff 25 Questions re: cigars	Annually

TABLE 4.1 National Tobacco Control Databases (*Continued*)

Name	Source	Participants	Methodology	Tobacco Use Variables	Data Collected
Smoking attributable mortality, morbidity, and economic costs (SAMMEC) In use since 1985	CDC Online versions of adult and maternal and child health SAMMEC available at http://apps.nccd.cdc.gov/sammec/	Calculates state and national-level smoking-attributable deaths and years of life lost by adults and infants in United States from existing databases.	Data from: a. Smoking prevalence of NHIS, BRFSS b. Relative risk of death (CPS-II) c. Deaths from smoking-related diseases (NCHS & death certificates) d. Data from medical expenditures panel and NHIS to estimate costs.	It calculates medical costs and loss of productivity for adults and loss of potential life for infants.	Annually Reports outcomes for health and economics: (a) Smoking attributable fractions (SAF); (b) Smoking attributable mortality (SAM); (c) Smoking attributable years of potential life lost (YPLL); (d) Smoking attributable fractions of expenditures (SAFE); (e) Smoking attributable healthcare expenditures (SAE); (f) smoking attributable productivity losses (SAPL)
State tobacco activities tracking & evaluation (STATE) In use since 1995	CDC and the National Center for Chronic Disease Prevention and Health Promotion http://www2a.cdc.gov/nccdphp/osh/state/	An electronic data warehouse containing up-to-date and historical state-level information on tobacco use prevention and control.	Developed to integrate survey data (including BRFSS, TUS CPS, etc.) for a comprehensive summary of tobacco use.	STATE system presently offers the ability to generate or build reports on tobacco use behaviors, demographics, economics, environment, funding, health consequences and costs, and legislation.	Ongoing Across state comparisons, trends, and tobacco control highlights can be detailed.

Survey	Source	Sample/Population	Methodology	Measures	Frequency/Use
Tobacco use supplement (TUS)–Current population survey (CPS) In use since 1992	National Cancer Institute and U.S. Census Bureau http://riskfactor.gov/studies/tus-cps/	Representative sampling of U.S. households for those 15 years and older. Sample sizes range from 2,100 for D.C. to 18,700 for California.	Multistage random sampling of 240,000; 70% respond on telephone survey and 30% in person. Most are self-reports but 20% are proxy.	Measured are current smoking history, quit attempts, intentions to quit, medical–dental advice to quit for all forms of tobacco. Questions vary depending upon survey focus. In depth questions about tobacco cessation in 2002/2003. Also assesses work place and public smoking attitudes and polices.	Triennially Data can be used to (a) monitor control progress, (b) conduct tobacco-related research, and (c) evaluate tobacco control programs.
Youth risk behavior surveillance system (YRBSS) In use since 1991	CDC and Prevention http://www.cdc.gov/HealthyYouth/yrbs/index.htm	The YRBSS monitors priority health-risk behaviors and the prevalence of obesity and asthma among youth and young adults.	A three-stage cluster sample design produces a nationally representative sample of public and private school students in at least one of the grades 9–12 in the 50 states and the District of Columbia. African American and Hispanic students are oversampled.	Students complete a self-administered national questionnaire contained 98 questions that assess demographics, six categories of health-risk behaviors including smoking.	Biannually during the spring semester.

(Continued)

Health Information National Trends Survey (HINTS)

In 2003 the National Cancer Institute (NCI) initiated HINTS to assess nonin-stitutional adults, 18 years and older, using random digit dialing and computer-assisted telephone interviews methodology. The survey focuses on cancer-relevant knowledge, attitudes, beliefs, and on tobacco use behaviors including cigarette use, numbers of cigarettes smoked, quit attempts, and attitudes toward use of alterna-tive tobacco products such as potentially reduced exposure products (i.e. PREPS).

Monitoring the Future (MTF)

The MTF is an ongoing study of the behaviors, attitudes, and values, including to-bacco use, of secondary school students, college students, and young adults. Each year, approximately 50,000 eighth, 10th, and 12th grade students are surveyed (12th graders since 1975, and 8th and 10th graders since 1991). In addition, annual follow-up questionnaires are mailed to a sample of each graduating class for a number of years after their initial participation. The MTF survey has been funded under a series of investigator-initiated competing research grants from the National Institute on Drug Abuse (NIDA) and is being conducted by the Survey Research Center in the Institute for Social Research at the University of Michigan.

National Health and Nutrition Examination Survey (NHANES)

The NHANES program was developed by the National Center for Health Statis-tics (NCHS) at the CDC. Its purpose is to assess the health and nutritional status of adults and children, including tobacco use. The survey is unique in that it combines interviews and physical examinations. The NHANES program began in the early 1960s and has been conducted as a series of surveys focusing on different popula-tion groups or health topics. In 1999, the survey became an ongoing program that has a changing focus on a variety of health and nutritional measurements to meet emerging needs. It examines a nationally representative sample of about 5,000 per-sons each year and oversamples those 60 and older, including African-Americans and Hispanic-Americans. For researchers throughout the world, NHANES survey data are available on the Internet and on easy-to-use CD-ROMs.

National Health Interview Survey (NHIS)

The oldest of the U.S. databases is the NHIS. It is the principal source of informa-tion on the health of the civilian noninstitutionalized population and is one of the major data collection programs of the National Center for Health Statistics. The NHIS data are used widely throughout the Department of Health and Hu-man Services (DHHS) to monitor trends in illness and disability and to track progress toward achieving national health objectives like those of the Healthy People 2010 (http://www.healthy people.gov/Document/), including tobacco use and cessation. Public health researchers also use these data for epidemiologic and policy analysis of such timely issues as exposure to secondhand smoke. A multistage random sampling design is used to achieve a representative sample with oversampling of African Americans, Hispanics, and Asians. While the NHIS has been conducted continuously since 1957, the content of the survey has been modified and updated about every 10 to 15 years.

National Survey on Drug Use and Health (NSDUH)

The NSDUH began in 1971 to provide yearly national and state-level data on the use of alcohol, tobacco, and illicit and nonmedical prescription drugs (Section 505 of the Public Health Service Act requires this annual survey). Other health-related questions have been added from year to year, including questions about mental health. The Substance Abuse and Mental Health Services Administration, an agency of the U.S. Public Health Service, and a part of the DHHS, sponsors the NSDUH.

National Youth Tobacco Survey (NYTS)

Developed in 1999, the NYTS was designed to provide a baseline for comparing progress toward meeting the Healthy People 2010 goals for reducing tobacco use among youth (middle and high school students). Items measured as part of the NYTS survey included correlates of tobacco use such as demographics, access to tobacco, exposure to secondhand smoke, and factors that encourage–discourage smoking. The study design makes it possible to include enough African American, Hispanic, and Asian American youth to produce nationally representative estimates for these populations as well as for White youth. Follow-up assessment is every 2 years.

Smoking-Attributable Mortality, Morbidity, and Economic Costs (SAMMEC)

Since 1987 SAMMEC has been used by the CDC to estimate the health effects of tobacco use on the national, state, and large adult populations in the United States and it offers specific data on maternal and child health. The SAMMEC online version was released in 2002.

State Tobacco Activities Tracking & Evaluation System (STATE)

The STATE system, in use since 1995, is an electronic data warehouse containing up-to-date and historical state-level information on tobacco use prevention and control. The CDC and the National Center for Chronic Disease Prevention and Health Promotion developed it to integrate survey data (including BRFSS, TUS CPS, etc.) for a comprehensive summary of tobacco use.

Tobacco Use Supplement (TUS)-Current Population Survey (CPS)

The TUS-CPS is a National Cancer Institute sponsored survey of tobacco use and policy information that has been administered every 3 years as part of the CPS since 1992. It is a key source of national and state level data on smoking and other tobacco use in the U.S. household by those 15 years and older. State sample sizes range from 2,100 for the District of Columbia to 18,700 for California.

Youth Risk Behavior Surveillance System (YRBSS)

The YRBSS has monitored priority health-risk behaviors (e.g., smoking) and the prevalence of obesity and asthma among the young and young adults since 1991. Forty-eight states, 6 U.S. territories, 2 tribal governments, and 22 of the largest urban school districts in the United States (through a cooperative agreement with the Division of Adolescent and School Health and the CDC) administer the survey to scientifically defined samples of high school student in the spring or fall of odd numbered years. Some sites administer the YRBSS to middle school students as well. An advantage to reaching the younger students is that the law requires that all youth be in school prior to the age of 16; those 16 years and older may not be in school so can miss being monitored. A Guide to Conducting Your Own Youth Risk Behavior Survey is available (http://www.cdc.gov/yrbss).

Other National Tobacco Use Resources

A variety of other resources on tobacco use are available to nurse researchers at the national level. These include the *Morbidity & Mortality Weekly Reports*, the U.S. Surgeon General Reports, and Database 2010. Each is described briefly below.

The CDC prepares the *Morbidity & Mortality Weekly Reports*; it has been published since 1952 and it is freely available. It is often called "the voice of CDC" and is the agency's primary vehicle for scientific publication of public health information and recommendations. Its readership consists of physicians, nurses, public health practitioners, epidemiologists and other scientists, researchers, and educators. Data in the weekly *Morbidity & Mortality Weekly Reports* are provisional, based on weekly reports to the CDC by state health departments. The reporting week concludes at close of business on Friday; compiled data on a national basis are officially released to the public the succeeding Friday. See http://www.cdc.gov/mmwr/about.html

The U.S. Surgeon General Reports have focused the nation's attention on many important public health issues over the years including tobacco use. Since the first report on Smoking and Health in 1964, there have been 34 other reports focused on tobacco use along with numerous articles and briefs. These reports summarize the evidence about tobacco risks, the benefits of cessation, and other topics.

The most recent report is Children and Secondhand Smoke Exposure (2007). To-bacco use has been the topic of more Surgeon General Reports than any other hu-man health behavior. The reports can be accessed at http://www.surgeongeneral. gov/library/reports/index.html

DATA2010 is an interactive database system developed by staff of the Divi-sion of Health Promotion Statistics at the National Center for Health Statistics, and contains the most recent monitoring data for tracking the Healthy People 2010 agenda. The Healthy People 2010 (first released in 2000) has 467 objectives that identify specific measures to monitor health in the first decade of the 21st cen-tury (http://www.healthypeople.gov/Document/). Each objective includes a state-ment of intent, a baseline value for the measure to be tracked, and a target to be achieved by the year 2010. Objectives may include more than one measure; each is shown separately in the database. Data for the population-based objectives may be presented separately for select populations, such as racial, gender, educational attainment, or income groups. The objectives are organized into 28 focal areas, each representing an important public health issue; focus 27 is for tobacco use. The midcourse review of progress toward the Healthy People 2010 tobacco use goals can be found at http://www.healthypeople.gov/data/midcourse

International Tobacco Use Databases and Monitoring and Surveillance Systems

International databases available for research are listed in Table 4.2 and sum-marized below.

Global Tobacco Surveillance System (GTSS)

On the international scene, the WHO, the CDC, and the Canadian Public Health Association (CPHA) developed the GTSS in 1999. The purpose of the GTSS is to enhance the capacity of countries to design, implement, and evaluate their own national tobacco action plans and to monitor key articles of the WHO Framework Convention on Tobacco Control (WHO FCTC). The GTSS components include the Global Healthcare Professional Students Survey (GHPSS), the Global Youth Tobacco Survey (GYTS), the Global School Personnel Survey (GSPS), and the Global Adult Tobacco Survey (GATS) added in 2007. The GHPSS focuses on third year college students pursuing degrees in dentistry, medicine, nursing, and/or phar-macology. The GYTS questions youth ages 13 to 15 in their schools on tobacco use and the GSPS surveys the teachers and administrators of the same GYTS schools. The GATS is a global household survey that tracks prevalence (cigarette smok-ing and other tobacco use), exposure to risk, secondhand smoke, cessation, risk perceptions, knowledge and attitudes, and exposure to media as well as price

TABLE 4.2 International Tobacco Control Databases and Resources

Name	Source	Participants	Methodology	Tobacco Use Variables	Data Collected
Global Tobacco Surveillance System (GTSS)					
Global adult tobacco survey (GATS) In use since 2007 In pilot testing	World Health Organization (WHO), Centers for Disease Control and Prevention (CDC) http://www.cdc.gov/tobacco/global/gats/questionnaire/index.htm	Adults (15 + years)	Uses a nationally representative household survey Samples for the GATS are selected using a multistage, geographically clustered design to ensure adequate coverage of the entire target population while simultaneously minimizing data collection costs.	47 core items that assess: smoking and smokeless tobacco products use, secondhand tobacco smoke exposure, cessation, knowledge, attitudes, and risk perceptions. In addition, it assesses media exposure and economics	Data will be collected from 16 low- and middle-income countries which include more than half of the world's smokers: Bangladesh, Brazil, China, Egypt, India, Indonesia, Mexico, Pakistan, Philippines, Poland, Russian Federation, Thailand, Turkey, Ukraine, Uruguay and Vietnam.
Global healthcare professional student survey (GHPSS) In use since 2004	WHO, CDC Canadian Public Health Association (CPHA) http://www.cdc.gov/tobacco/global/ghpss/ghpss_results.htm	School-based survey of third year students pursuing advanced degrees in dentistry, medicine, nursing, and pharmacy	Multistage sample design with schools selected proportional to enrollment size or classrooms are chosen randomly within selected schools or there is a census of schools and students in countries with few health professional schools.	45 core country-approved questions on demographics, prevalence of cigarette smoking and other tobacco use, knowledge and attitudes about tobacco use, exposure to secondhand smoke and desire to quit. Training is given for patient counseling on smoking cessation techniques.	Students from Albania (dental, medical, nursing, and pharmacy), Argentina (medical), Bangladesh (ental) Croatia (medical), Egypt (medical), Federation of Bosnia and Herzegovina (nursing), India (dental), the Philippines (pharmacy), the Republic of Serbia (dental, medical, and pharmacy), and Uganda (medical and nursing).

Global school personnel survey (GSPS) In use since 2000	WHO & CDC http://www.cdc.gov/tobacco/Global/gsps/intro.htm	School Personnel *All schools selected for GYTS (below) are eligible. All school personnel are eligible.	GSPS questionnaires are distributed to all personnel of schools selected for the GYTS described below.	GSPS Core Questionnaire components are: demographics, tobacco use prevalence, knowledge and attitudes, school policy and school curriculum	Includes all countries selected for GYTS (see below)
Global youth tobacco survey (GYTS) In use since 1999	WHO & CDC http://www.cdc.gov/tobacco/global/gyts/results.htm	Tracks tobacco use of school-based youth (13–15 years) across countries using a common methodology and core questionnaire.	Methodology can include: public and private schools, multistage sample design with schools selected proportional to enrollment size; classrooms chosen randomly within selected schools; and/or all students in selected classes eligible for participation. Countries may add questions to the questionnaire. Computer scanable answer sheets Country-level data with regional-level stratification possible	56 Core Items that assess: knowledge and attitudes of young people toward cigarette smoking, prevalence of cigarette smoking and other tobacco use among young people, role of the media and advertising in young people's use of cigarettes, access to cigarettes, tobacco-related school curriculum, environmental tobacco smoke, cessation of cigarette smoking	1999–2004 Fact Sheets available for Regional Offices African Region Eastern Mediterranean Region European Region (EURO) Western Pacific Region (WPRO) Pan American Health Organization South-East Asia Regional Office

(Continued)

TABLE 4.2 International Tobacco Control Databases and Resources (*Continued*)

Name	Source	Participants	Methodology	Tobacco Use Variables	Data Collected
Tobacco control country profiles (2003) Country data now available through MPOWER at WHO	American Cancer Society, WHO, and International Union Against Cancer jointly publish this edition of the monograph. The WHO & CDC, and World Bank Group provided, in kind, data, and personnel resources in support of this project. http://www.who.int/tobacco/global_data/country_profiles/en/index.html	A national system for the epidemiological surveillance of tobacco consumption and the social, economic, and health indicators and a global system to regularly collect and disseminate information on tobacco production, and the activities of the tobacco industry that have an impact on national tobacco control activities.	The data are compiled from numerous national and international sources, including databases maintained by WHO TFI Geneva, WHO Regional Offices, United Nations Statistics Division (UNSD), World Bank Group, national government agencies, such as the United States Department of Agriculture (USDA), national Ministries of Health and statistical offices, and nongovernmental institutions, such as academic researchers, public health organizations, and tobacco control advocates.	Profiles organize each country into five categories: 1. Sociodemographic situation 2. Smoking prevalence (i.e., cigarettes) 3. Tobacco economy 4. Smoking-related disease impact 5. Tobacco control regulations	Regional summaries available at: African Region Region of the Americas Eastern Mediterranean Region European Region South-East Asia Region Western Pacific Region Most nations have collected some tobacco use prevalence data of their own.

World Health Organization Statistical Information System (WHOSIS) In use since 1990	An interactive database bringing together core health statistics for the 193 WHO member states. http://www.who.int/whosis/en/ Data are published annually in the World Health Statistics Report released in May. http://www.who.int/whosis/whostat/2009/en/index.html	Adults and youth who provided information for primary other databases.	Secondary data analyses. Data are collected from other surveys, publications, and databases.	It has more than 100 indicators, which can be accessed by way of quick search, by major categories, or through user-defined tables. Includes demographics, SES, health inequities, health expenditures, mortality–morbidity, infectious diseases, health services, health workforce, and risk factors including tobacco use.	*World Health Statistics 2009* contains annual compilation of data from its 193 member states, and includes a summary of progress toward meeting the health-related Millennium Development Goals (MDGs) and targets. It is a midcourse review.

109

taxation issues for adults 15 years and older. The surveillance surveys are managed through six WHO Regional Offices (African [AFRO], Eastern Mediterranean [EMRO], European Region [EURO], Western Pacific Region [WPRO], Pan American Health Organization [PAHO], and South-East Asia [SEARO]).

Tobacco Control Country Profiles (TCCP)

The WHO and the ACS first compiled the TCCP in 2000. In addition to survey data from the GTSS measures above, the 2003 edition provided information on tobacco production, trade, consumption, legislation, and disease burden for 196 countries and territories worldwide. Collectively these country pictures present a composite of the status of the tobacco pandemic in the early 21st century. They also illustrate the strength of the current system of global tobacco surveillance and the future challenges that must be confronted to improve the system. Updated country data are now part of the MPOWER system through the WHO.

WHO Statistical Information System (WHOSIS)

The WHOSIS is an interactive database that brings together core health statistics from 193 WHO member states. It monitors more than 70 health indicators including current tobacco use by youth (13–15 years) and by adults (>15 years). These data also are published annually in the World Health Statistics Report released in May each year.

Other International Tobacco Use Resources

The WHO Report on the Global Tobacco Epidemic (2008) is the first in a series of WHO reports that will track the status of the tobacco epidemic and the impact of interventions implemented to stop it. The report provides a roadmap of six tobacco control policies related to the WHO FCTC (in the form of the MPOWER package) to reverse the devastating global tobacco epidemic. The report is available in six languages at http://www.who.int/tobacco/mpower/gtcr_download/en/index.html

The Global Information System on Tobacco Control (GISTOC) is in development. Its purpose is to promote and facilitate the exchange of standardized global tobacco data through online database systems, and to assess progress toward the adoption of effective national tobacco control measures. The progress of GISTOC system can be monitored on the WHO Web site (http://www.who.int/tobacco/global_data/en/index.html). The future challenge of global tobacco surveillance is to further design, refine, and implement systems that provide more accurate, timely, reliable, and readily analyzable information on the key indices of the tobacco problem for nurses and other health workers in countries and regions worldwide.

RESEARCH REVIEWS

In addition to large population-based surveys for describing, detailing, and tracking the phenomenon of tobacco use, research reviews can be useful for evidence-based nursing practice. Examples of reviews can include a time-ordered listing of the current tobacco use literature (Wells, Sarna, Bialous, & Aguinaga, 2006), a narrative literature review (Schultz, 2003), and a structured meta-analysis (Rice, 1999; Rice & Stead, 2008). There are some important differences among these three. The first is the purpose of the review. Wells and her colleagues (2006) maintain an ongoing list of publications related to nursing and tobacco use on the Tobacco Free Nurses Web site (http://www.tobaccofreenurses.org/) to document nursing publications in the field, including articles focused on smoking cessation and articles involving nurses (as investigators, interventionists, or study participants). Data based articles are identified and it only contains English language publications. The ongoing list contains articles published since 1996. As of 2008, there are 150 articles listed.

The narrative review by Schultz (2003) reported on activities of two groups of nurses (nursing governance bodies & nurse scientists) relative to tobacco use reduction and the identification of the gaps. It looked at (a) nurses' personal use of tobacco, (b) nurse-delivered smoking cessation interventions, (c) dissemination of the clinical guidelines through the nursing literature and basic nursing education, and (d) nurses' engagement in tobacco reduction. This review addressed a wide range of topics and the sources of the studies, and the searching strategies are not specified.

The purpose of the Rice and Stead (2008) meta-analysis or systematic review was to examine and summarize randomized clinical trials conducted over a specified period of time in which nurses provided smoking cessation intervention. In the research literature a systematic review has been described as a concise scientific investigation, with preplanned methods that summarize, appraise, synthesize, and communicate the results of many primary studies (Cook, Mulrow, & Hayes, 1997). In the Rice review the sources and search strategies for locating the studies are explicitly stated and the criteria for selection of the studies were uniformly applied and critical appraisal was rigorous (Leonard & Wynd, 2008). As with traditional narrative reviews of the literature, systematic reviews are retrospective. The quality and usefulness of the final systematic review is determined by the extent and rigor with which it was conducted and the efforts of the reviewer to minimize bias and error (Evans, 2001). Systematic reviews, often, but not always, use statistical techniques as it did in the Rice review to combine valid studies, or at the very least uses grading (A, B, or C) of the levels of evidence. After reviewing 42 clinical trials published between 1987 and 2008, Rice, Weglicki, Templin, Jamil, & Hammad (2010) found that smokers given advice by a nursing professional had an increased likelihood of quitting by approximately 50% compared with smokers without nursing intervention. The evidence of an effect was weaker when the interventions were brief and provided by nurses whose main role was not health promotion or smoking cessation.

There are almost 100 Cochrane Database Systematic Reviews (http://www. cochrane.org/reviews/en/topics/94_reviews.html) related to some aspect of tobacco use over the past 12 years; 46 have focused on interventions for cessation. There has been one Cochrane review each for interventions by nurses (Rice & Stead, 2008), physicians (Stead, Bergson, & Lancaster, 2008) and dentists (Carr & Ebbert, 2006). In addition, there are meta-analyses published in other journals including comparisons of nurses with those in other disciplines (e.g., Gorin & Heck, 2004). While many reviews are based on an explicit quantitative meta-analysis of available data, there are also qualitative reviews that adhere to standards for gathering, analyzing, and reporting their evidence (Evans & Pearson, 2001). Systematic reviews can be an invaluable resource for nurse clinicians, consumers, researchers, and policy makers.

CONCLUSION

In summary, there are numerous national, international, and regional database resources and meta-analytic and research summaries available to assist nurses in the conduct of nursing research and in the provision of evidence-based care. Nurses have an obligation to use and evaluate these resources to determine the gaps in the knowledge and the direction for future research. They must help to generate the questions used in these large surveys to have population-based answers to their unique tobacco use questions. For example, there are no national or international tobacco use surveys that ask questions about water pipe smoking, a rapidly growing form of tobacco use in the United States (American Lung Association, 2007; Rice et al., 2006) and around the world (Knishkowy & Amitai, 2005). Nurses also need to participate in the ongoing evaluation of tobacco cessation and prevention interventions through clinical practice and primary and secondary research. It is essential that nursing's contribution to the tobacco use science be considered in the updating of the *Treating Tobacco Use and Dependence Clinical Practice Guideline Updates* (http://www.ahrq.gov/clinic/tobacco/tobaqrg.htm) and that the unique contribution of nursing be recognized. Nurses must implement the current standard; every patient is to be evaluated for tobacco use and the appropriate intervention initiated. Given the fact that nurses are the most numerous health professionals in the field, there is a golden opportunity for them to become experts in this knowledge, add to the science, provide evidence-based nursing care, and to make a significant impact on reducing the tobacco use burden of the future.

REFERENCES

Abdullah, A., & Husten, C. (2004). Promotion of smoking cessation in developing countries: A framework for urgent public health interventions. *Thorax, 59*(7), 623–630.

American Lung Association [ALA]. (2007). *Tobacco policy trend alert. An emerging deadly trend: Waterpipe tobacco use.* Available from http://slati.lungusa.org/alerts/Trend%20 Alert_Waterpipes.pdf

Burns, N., & Grove, S. (2007). *The practice of nursing research: Conduct, critique, & utilization* (5th ed.). New York: W. B. Saunders Company.

Carr, A. B., & Ebbert, J. O. (2006). Interventions for tobacco cessation in the dental setting. *Cochrane Database of Systematic Reviews,* (1), CD005084. doi: 10.1002/14651858. CD005084.pub2

Centers for Disease Control and Prevention. (2008). Cigarette smoking among adults— United States, 2007. *Morbidity and Mortality Weekly Report, 57*(45), 1221–1226.

Cook, D., Mulrow, C., & Hayes, B. (1997). Systematic reviews: Synthesis of best evidence for clinical decisions. *Annals of Internal Medicine, 126*(5), 376–380.

Delnevo, C. & Bauer, U. (2009). Monitoring the tobacco use epidemic. The host: Data sources and methodological challenges. *Preventive Medicine, 48*(Suppl. 1), S16–S23.

Evans, D. (2001). Systematic reviews of nursing research. *Intensive and Critical Care Nursing, 17,* 51–57.

Evans, D., & Pearson, A. (2001). Systematic reviews: Gatekeepers of nursing knowledge. *Journal of Clinical Nursing, 10*(5), 593–599.

Gorin, S., & Heck, J. E. (2004). Meta-analysis of the efficacy of tobacco counseling by health care providers. *Cancer Epidemiology, Biomarkers & Prevention, 13*(12), 2012–2022.

Jones, C. B., & Mark, B. A. (2005). The intersection of nursing and health services research: Overview of an agenda setting conference. *Nursing Outlook, 53*(6), 270–273.

Knishkowy, B., & Amitai, Y. (2005). Water-pipe (narghile) smoking: An emerging health risk behavior. *Pediatrics, 116*(1), e113–e119.

Leonard, E. E., & Wynd, C. (2008). Meta-analysis as a tool for evidence-based practice: An example using Rice meta-analysis of smoking cessation interventions. *Applied Nursing Research, 21*(1), 40–44.

Rice, V. H. (1999). Nursing intervention and smoking cessation: A meta-analysis. *Heart & Lung, 28*(6), 438–454.

Rice, V. H., & Stead, L. F. (2008). Nursing interventions for smoking cessation. *Cochrane Database of Systematic Reviews,* (1), CD001188. doi: 10.1002/14651858.CD001188. pub3

Rice, V. H., Weglicki, L. S., Templin, T., Hamad, A., Jamil, H., & Kulwicki, A. (2006). Predictors of Arab American adolescent tobacco use. *Merrill-Palmer Quarterly, 52*(2), 327–342.

Rice, V. H., Weglicki, L. S., Templin, T., Jamil, H., & Hammad, A. (2010). Intervention effects on tobacco use in Arab and non-Arab adolescents. *Addictive Behaviors, 35,* 45–48.

Schultz, A. (2003). Nursing and tobacco reduction: A review of the literature. *International Journal of Nursing Studies, 40,* 571–586.

Stead, L. F., Bergson, G., & Lancaster, T. (2008). Physician advice for smoking cessation. *Cochrane Database of Systematic Reviews,* (2), CD000165. doi: 10.1002/14651858. CD000165.pub3

U.S. Department of Health and Human Services. (1964). *Smoking and health: Report of the advisory committee of the surgeon general of the public health service.* Washington, DC: Department of Health Education and Welfare, Public Health Service.

U.S. Department of Health and Human Services. (2007). *Children and secondhand smoke exposure: Excerpts from the health consequences of involuntary exposure to tobacco smoke: A Report of the Surgeon General.* Washington, DC: Author.

Wells, M., Sarna, L. & Bialous, S. A., & Aguinaga, S. (2006). Nursing research in smoking cessation: A listing of the literature, 1996–2005. *Nursing Research, 55*(4, Suppl. 1), S16–S28.

WHO Tobacco Free Initiative (2008). *WHO report on the global tobacco epidemic, 2008—The MPOWER package.* Geneva, Switzerland. World Health Organization. Retrieved from http://www.who.int/gov/tobacco/mpower/en/

Zeni, M., & Kogan, B. (2007). Existing population-based health databases: Useful sources for nursing research. *Nursing Outlook, 55*(1), 20–30.

Chapter 5

Nurses' Use of Qualitative Research Approaches to Investigate Tobacco Use and Control

Annette S. H. Schultz, Joan L. Bottorff,
and Stephanie Barclay McKeown

ABSTRACT

Qualitative research methods are increasingly used by nurse scientists to explore a wide variety of topics relevant to practice and/or health policy issues. The purpose of this chapter is to review the contributions of nurse scientists to the field of tobacco control through the use of qualitative research methods. A systematic literature search strategy was used to identify 51 articles published between 1980 and 2008. The majority (84%) of reviewed articles were authored by North American nurse scientists. Cessation was the most commonly (85%) studied aspect of tobacco control. Six qualitative research approaches were used: qualitative descriptive (55%), narrative analysis (8%), phenomenology (6%), grounded theory (14%), ethnography (12%), and case study (6%). Qualitative descriptive methods were primarily one-off studies to address practical problems or issues encountered in practice, and often validated current understandings related to tobacco. Researchers who used other types of qualitative methods and who conducted qualitative studies as part of programs of research were more likely to

DOI: 10.1891/0739-6686.27.115

make more substantive contributions to the evolving field of tobacco control. These contributions related to how smoking intertwines with personal and social identities, the influence of social context on tobacco use, and nurses' involvement in tobacco control (both of their own tobacco use and in assisting others). Nurse scientists interested in exploring tobacco-related issues are encouraged to consider the full range of qualitative research approaches. Qualitative research methods contribute to our understanding of tobacco use arising from nursing practice, health care and policy, along with the field of tobacco control in general.

Keywords: nursing research; qualitative methods; smoking; tobacco cessation and prevention

Nurses have been leaders in the development and use of qualitative research methods to examine a wide range of health-related topics (Hutchinson, 2001; Sandelowski, 2004; Thorne, Reimer Kirkham, & MacDonald-Emes, 1997). Therefore, it is not surprising that nurses have used qualitative approaches to investigate tobacco-related topics. Such studies generate evidence relevant to practice and/or health policy issues by exploring various standpoints or the social context of those being influenced by, required to deliver, or make decisions about health care services. This chapter reviews the contributions of nurse scientists' investigations of tobacco use and control issues through the use of qualitative methods.

The term *qualitative research* encompasses a variety of methods that share some common attributes (Creswell, 2007; Denzin & Lincoln, 2005). Qualitative research methods are used to study phenomena in the natural world; involve the use of interactive data collection procedures; focus on making sense of, describing, or interpreting personal experience from the perspective and worldview of those being researched; and include an inductive approach to generating evidence. Differences in qualitative approaches lay in how evidence is generated and what is accepted as evidence. Table 5.1 presents characteristics of six qualitative research approaches: qualitative description, narrative inquiry, phenomenology, grounded theory, ethnography, and case study. While there are other qualitative research approaches, these represent the most frequently used methods (Creswell, 2007; Sandelowski, 2000).

This chapter begins with details of our search strategy along with exclusion criteria. General description of the articles reviewed is followed by findings for each of the qualitative designs highlighting nurses' contributions. A discussion of key issues and implications for future research and health policy completes the chapter.

TABLE 5.1 Comparing Characteristics of Six Qualitative Approaches Used in Nursing Research on Tobacco

	Qualitative Description	Narrative Inquiry	Phenomenology	Grounded Theory	Ethnography	Case Study
Aim	Comprehensive and straightforward account of an event or experience.	Describe how individuals understand and make sense of life experiences.	Construct an evocative description of the nature of lived experience.	Data generated theory development.	Provide rich insights into the culture, perspectives, and practices of particular groups.	Capture an understanding of the inner workings and complexities for a case or cases.
Type of Problem	Useful for practice or policy questions; an accurate portrayal of events and meanings participants attribute provides practical guidance.	Useful for understanding phenomena through the meanings people assign to them.	Useful for exploring the meaning and significance of lived experiences.	Useful for explaining social processes common to individuals who have similar experiences.	Useful for exploring social practices and behaviors within a particular setting or group.	Useful for providing an in-depth understanding of a case or a comparison of several cases.
Unit of Analysis	One or more individuals	Stories of experiences	Meaning structures of human experience or themes	Experiences of the process under study	An identified group	A case may involve an individual, several individuals, a program, an event, or an activity.

(Continued)

TABLE 5.1 Comparing Characteristics of Six Qualitative Approaches Used in Nursing Research on Tobacco (*Continued*)

	Qualitative Description	Narrative Inquiry	Phenomenology	Grounded Theory	Ethnography	Case Study
Data Collection Forms	Interview data or observation data directed toward discovering the who, what, and where.	Journals, field notes, diaries, interviews, personal documents, and artifacts	In-depth interviews, observations, personal experiences, and experiential descriptions in biographies, poetry, and art	Interviews, observations, documents, audiovisual materials	Participant observations, interviews, document analysis, photographs	Observations, interviews, documents, and tangible artifacts
Analysis Strategy	Descriptive summaries of the data content and themes generated from the data; minimal interpretation.	Examine stories individuals' use regarding an experience; the words used to identify the structure and form of narratives, the positioning of the storyteller, and sequencing of events.	Deep questioning of experience, identifying thematic aspects of experience, exploration of existential themes of lived space, lived body, lived time, and lived relations	Analysis occurs simultaneously with data collection; data coded into categories for the purpose of comparison; constant comparison used to identify relationships and properties.	Inductive, thematic analysis of data to identify key issues and themes that capture meanings and functions of human behavior; reflexivity is a central element.	Description of the case can be conducted or a description of detailed aspects of the case can be explored through an analysis of identified aspects.

Interpretation

A straight descriptive summary of inductively generated patterns and/or themes.	Interpret stories to identify meanings of experiences to individuals.	Reflection, writing and rewriting to make explicit lived experiences in ways that reveal the what and how of a phenomena.	A core category is identified to integrate the conceptual categories, and provide a foundation for a theory that offers fresh insights into and interpretations of social processes.	Interpretations are made based on the shared values, behaviors, beliefs, and language of a group.	The significance of the case—what lessons were learned?

METHODS

The systematic literature review involved an initial search of literature to retrieve relevant articles. The search included several data bases: PubMed, CINAHL, Scopus, EMBASE, and Web of Science. Since qualitative methods began to be used by nurse scientists during the 1980s (Hutchinson, 2001), we limited the search to publications between 1980 and December 2008. The search was limited to peer-reviewed articles in English and included the following terms found as either a key word or in the subject heading: tobacco, secondhand smoke, smoking, smoke, smoking cessation, tobacco use cessation, tobacco use disorder, and tobacco smoke pollution. Results from these terms were then combined with: nursing research, clinical nursing research, nursing education research, nursing administration research, nursing qualitative research, and nursing. Finally, these results were combined with a search using terms reflecting qualitative research methods: phenomenology, ethnography, focus groups, narrative, discourse analysis, grounded theory, and case study. This search resulted in the retrieval of 111 articles.

Abstracts of the articles retrieved were reviewed against four inclusion–exclusion criteria. (1) Since the focus of this chapter is to discuss nurses' contribution to tobacco control science, we only included articles with nurses as first authors. This criterion excluded 41 articles. (2) Papers were included if they had a primary focus on tobacco control topics. Four articles were excluded because they focused on another health issue and only had a minor mention of tobacco control or use. (3) Papers were excluded if they did not report research findings. Six papers were excluded because they focused on methodological discussions rather than reporting research findings. (4) Nine papers were excluded based on one of three methodological subcriteria; poorly developed methods ($n = 3$; i.e., limited details were provided about study design), study not solely qualitative (mixed methods approach; $n = 4$), or the article reported on a program evaluation ($n = 2$). Since the focus of this chapter is qualitative research, these methodological subcriteria filtered out those articles reporting on alternate research approaches. At the end of this second step we were left with 51 articles.

The 51 articles retained were then reviewed using a data extraction tool. The tool was collaboratively developed by the three authors and drew on processes used in earlier literature reviews conducted by the first two authors. The articles were reviewed by at least one of the authors. Data retrieved from the articles was managed and analyzed using Microsoft ACCESS.

RESULTS

A list of articles included in this review is presented in Table 5.2. The majority of articles (76%; $n = 39$) were published between 2003 and 2008. Nursing journals published about two thirds of the articles and most were authored by North American nurse scientists (84%); 49% from the United States (n = 25) and 35% from Canada (n = 18). Of the 51 articles reviewed 84% (n = 43) reported on studies investigating aspects of cessation. Five articles focused on prevention and in three articles protection issues were explored. Other issues studied were tobacco control policies (n = 2) and denormalization of tobacco use (n = 1). The qualitative descriptive method was the most common approach used in the reviewed articles (55%). Other qualitative approaches included: narrative analysis (8%), phenomenology (6%), grounded theory (14%), ethnography (12%), case study (6%). In the following sections the use of each of these methods by nurse scientists is described.

Qualitative Descriptive

Twenty-eight studies using the qualitative descriptive approach were retrieved. The aim of this approach is to provide comprehensive, straightforward accounts of events or phenomenon from the research participants' viewpoint (Milne & Oberle, 2005; Sandelowski, 2000). A variety of sampling and data collection strategies can be used to obtain information from participants. Data analysis focuses on summarizing the content of the data to depict the situation–experience being studied with minimal interpretation in comparison to other qualitative methods. This approach is useful to address practice or policy-related questions and when practical solutions or directions for practice are sought.

In this group of qualitative studies, the majority focused on cessation (85%; n = 23); one studied protection, two focused on prevention, one investigated denormalization and one studied tobacco control policies. Data collection in two thirds of the articles involved focus groups (n = 17) and in 41% interviews (n = 11). Multiple data collection procedures were used in 12 studies; 8 of these used a questionnaire and either a focus group or an interview. Sample size varied: Studies that involved interviews ranged between 6 and 26 participants and those that involved focus groups ranged from 13 to 75 study participants. The qualitative descriptive studies can be grouped into five types based on focus and potential contribution.

Experiences With Tobacco Use Among Diverse Ethnic Groups

Eight studies focused on describing the tobacco-related needs within diverse ethnic groups including Korean male smokers (Kim & Nam, 2005; Kim, Son, & Nam, 2005), Arab adolescent male smokers (Kulwicki & Hill Rice, 2003), Iranian male nurses who were smokers (Nikbakht Nasrabadi, Parsayekta, & Emami, 2004), Appalachian former and current smokers (Ahijevych et al., 2003), Brazilian former smokers (Echer & Barreto, 2008), Ojibwa elders (Struthers & Hodge, 2004), and Maori women who were former and current smokers (Fernandez & Wilson, 2008). While

TABLE 5.2 Type of Qualitative Method, Focus, Country, and Population of Articles Reviewed

Method Lead Author (Year)	n	Focus	Country	Population
Qualitative Descriptive	28			
Echer, I. C. (2008)		Cessation	Brazil	Adults 24–62 years; former smokers of mixed gender
Fernandez, C. (2008)		Cessation	New Zealand	Maori adult woman 28–45 years; former smokers
Kulbok, P. A. (2008)		Prevention	USA	Adolescent 16–17 years; never smokers; mixed gender
Snyder, M. (2008)		Cessation	USA	Adults 24–54 years with a serious mental illness; smokers; mixed gender
Schofield, I. (2007)		Cessation	UK	Adults 51–79 years with chronic obstructive pulmonary disease; former and current smokers; mixed gender
Treacy, M. P. (2007)		Cessation	UK	Adolescents 11–16 years; mixed smoking status and gender
Yousey, Y. (2007)		Protection	USA	Families with children younger than 5 years; mixed smoking status and gender
Staten, R. R. (2006)		Cessation	USA	College students 18–24 years; mixed smoking status and gender
Green, M. A. (2005)		Cessation	Canada	Adults 21–73 years with a mental illness; former and current smokers; mixed gender
Kim, S. S. (2005a)		Cessation	USA	Korean American adult men 22–49 years; former and current smokers

Kim, S. S. (2005b)	Tobacco Control Policy	USA	Korean American adult men 22–49 years; former and current smokers
Sarna, L. (2005)	Cessation	USA	Nurses 30–70 years; former and current smokers; mixed gender
Bialous, S. A. (2004)	Cessation	USA	Nurses 30–70 years; former and current smokers; mixed gender
Nikbakht Nasrabadi, A. (2004)	Cessation	Iran	Iranian male nursing students 18–29 years; current smokers
Pletsch, P. K. (2004)	Cessation	USA	Postpartum women in their 20s; former and recent relapsed smokers
Reynolds, N. R. (2004)	Cessation	USA	Adult HIV-positive men; former and current smokers
Struthers, R. (2004)	Prevention	USA	Ojibwa adult healers; mixed smoking status
Denham, S. A. (2004)	Cessation	USA	Appalachian adolescent females; mixed smoking status
Ahijevych, K. (2003)	Cessation	USA	Appalachian adult former and current smokers; mixed gender
Aquilino, M. L. (2003)	Cessation	USA	Female health providers working with women, infants or children; mixed smoking status
Kulwicki, A. (2003)	Cessation	USA	Arab American adolescent smokers; mixed gender
Pletsch, P. K. (2003)	Cessation	USA	African American prenatal women in their 20s; former and current smokers
McCarty, M. C. (2001)	Cessation	USA	Acute care hospital nurses
McFeely, S. (2001)	Cessation	UK	Adolescents

(Continued)

TABLE 5.2 Type of Qualitative Method, Focus, Country, and Population of Articles Reviewed (*Continued*)

Method Lead Author (Year)	n	Focus	Country	Population
Malone, R. E. (2001)		Denormalization	USA	African American adolescents; mixed smoking status and gender
Edwards, N. (1998)		Cessation	Canada	Postpartum women; recent relapsed smokers
Pletsch, P. K. (1996)		Cessation	USA	Pregnant American Latino women 14–24 years; current smokers
Puskar, M. (1995)		Cessation	USA	Women 23–44 year; former smokers
Narrative Inquiry	4			
Irwin, L. G. (2005)		Cessation	Canada	Postpartum women 18–39 years; recently relapsed smokers
Johnson, J. L. (2003b)		Cessation	Canada	Adolescent former and current smokers; mixed gender
Moffat, B. M. (2001)		Cessation	Canada	Adolescent girls; current smokers
Bottorff, J. L. (2000)		Cessation	Canada	Postpartum women 18–39 years; recently relapsed smokers
Phenomenological	3			
Jonsdottir, R. (2007)		Cessation	Iceland	Women 47–65 years with chronic obstructive pulmonary disease; current smoker
DiNapoli, P. P. (2004)		Cessation	USA	Adolescent girls; current smoker

Author	N	Focus	Country	Sample
Heath, J. (2004)		Cessation	USA	Nurse practitioners; current smokers; mixed gender
Grounded Theory	7			
Bottorff, J. L. (2006a)		Cessation	Canada	New parent couples; mixed smoking status
Bottorff, J. L. (2005)		Cessation	Canada	New parent couples; mixed smoking status
Bottorff, J. L. (2004a)		Cessation	Canada	Surgical adult smokers; mixed gender
Johnson, J. L. (2004)		Cessation	Canada	Adolescent former and current smokers; mixed gender
Small, S. P. (2002)		Cessation/Prevention	Canada	Parents and their adolescents; nonsmoking adults and smoking adolescents; mixed gender
Dunn, D. A. (2001)		Prevention	Canada	Adolescent girls; never smokers
Brown, J. (1996)		Cessation	USA	Adult 60–78 years; former smokers; mixed gender
Ethnographic Research	6			
Bottorff, J. L. (2006b)		Cessation/Protection	Canada	New fathers; current smokers
Schultz, A. S. H. (2006)		Cessation/Protection	Canada	Hospital settings and nurses; mixed smoking status and gender

(Continued)

TABLE 5.2 Type of Qualitative Method, Focus, Country, and Population of Articles Reviewed (*Continued*)

Method Lead Author (Year)	n	Focus	Country	Population
Bottorff, J. L. (2004b)		Prevention	Canada	Adolescent; experimenter, former and current smokers; mixed gender
Chalmers, K. (2003)		Cessation	Canada	Student nurse; mixed smoking status and gender
Johnson, J. L. (2003a)		Cessation	Canada	Adolescent smokers; mixed gender
Seguire, M. (2000)		Cessation	Canada	Female adolescent; former and current smokers
Case Studies	3			
Bonnette, M. L. (2008)		Cessation	USA	Adults 35–68 years; former smokers; mixed gender
Hahn, E. J. (2007)		Tobacco Control Policy	USA	Adults involved in adolescent tobacco use and laws; mixed gender
Whyte, R. E. (2006)		Cessation	UK	Nurses

these studies revealed perspectives unique to the group studied, the information reported tended to reflect perspectives concerning tobacco that was similar to the general population. For example, the two studies that focused on Aboriginal peoples (Fernandez & Wilson, 2008; Struthers & Hodge, 2004) provided unique findings regarding how language and worldviews influenced tobacco use and control issues. In other studies, the importance of including family and peers in cessation programs was identified. In the study of 22 Korean male immigrant smokers, participants reported that they believed immigrants were being targeted by the tobacco industry and that accessible cessation programs would be a better strategy to reduce tobacco use rather than an increase in taxes (Kim & Nam, 2005).

Experiences of Women During Pregnancy

Five studies focused on cessation issues related to women who were pregnant. Evidence from three of the studies suggests that expectations of people in the women's lives and environmental stress influenced decisions related to tobacco use, stopping and relapsing (Edwards & Sims-Jones, 1998; Pletsch & Johnson, 1996; Pletsch, Morgan, & Pieper, 2003). In another article, Pletsch and Kratz's (2004) study of 15 women smokers reported that smoking cessation during pregnancy was experienced as easy by most participants due to an aversion to the taste of cigarettes and smell of tobacco smoke, although the majority relapsed postpartum. Finally, Aquilino, Goody, and Lowe's (2003) study with health providers confirmed commonly reported barriers to providing cessation support to patients.

Experiences of Adolescents

Youth under the age of 19 years were the focus of five qualitative descriptive studies. Tobacco cessation was the focus of three studies (Denham, Meyer, & Toborg, 2004; McFeely, 2001; Treacy et al., 2007). One of the three explored the experiences of Appalachian females living in tobacco growing communities (Denham et al., 2004). In the only longitudinal study, Treacy and colleagues (2007) examined changes in youths' thoughts about smoking over a 4-year time period. In a study with nonsmoking youth, Kulbok and colleagues (2008) explored gender differences concerning decisions to remain smoke free and found more similarities than differences. Finally, Malone, Yerger, and Pearson (2001) described African American youths' perceptions of risk related to cigar smoking.

Experiences of Diverse Clinical Populations

Seven studies focused on smokers from different clinical populations. Individuals with mental illness were involved in two of these studies. Based on data collected from three focus groups with patients with mental illnesses ($n = 21$), Green and Clarke (2005) reported that most wanted to stop smoking but had limited knowledge of programs and no developed plans to quit. Snyder, McDevitt, and

Painter (2008) conducted four focus groups to describe the central role of smoking in the everyday life of the 25 individuals with mental illness who participated, and the personal, social, and environmental factors that influenced their tobacco use. Cessation experiences with HIV patients (Reynolds, Neidig, & Wewers, 2004) and older adults with chronic obstructive pulmonary disease (Schofield, Kerr, & Tolson, 2007) were also studied; findings from these studies provide insight into unique needs of these patient groups and a foundation for future research. Puskar (1995) was the oldest qualitative study reviewed. At the time of publication Puskar's study revealed novel insights into adults' experiences with cessation and her suggestion to frame cessation as part of a larger commitment to health continues to be relevant. Staten and Ridner's (2007) findings from interviews with 19 college-age men and women suggest that cessation messages for college students are ineffective because they are not relevant to their world. Unfortunately, there was no exploration of gender influences in this study. Finally, the only study that involved families focused on family efforts to protect children from secondhand smoke (Yousey, 2007).

Nurses' Experiences

Three studies investigated nurses' experiences: One focused on nurses' integration of cessation support during hospitalization (McCarty, Zander, Hennrikus, & Lando, 2001) and the other two explored nurses' attitudes toward their own smoking and stopping (Bialous, Sarna, Wewers, Froelicher, & Danao, 2004; Sarna, Bialous, Wewers, Froelicher, & Danao, 2005). McCarty and colleagues' (2001) findings confirmed nurses believe hospitalization is a useful time to address tobacco use with patients interested in stopping or with a smoking-related illness. However, these nurses lacked education and resources and felt unprepared. Bialous and colleagues (2004) studied nurses that were either former or current smokers. The findings suggest nurses' knowledge and experiences with smoking and quitting was similar to the general public. Sarna and colleagues' (2005) findings revealed how smoking was not simply a personal decision; rather smoking at work for nurses was affected by ward routines, staff breaks, nurses' ability to cope with stress, and workplace relations. Findings from these two studies reinforce the need for work-based strategies and programs to support cessation efforts by nurses.

Narrative Inquiry

Narrative inquiry was used in four studies led by Canadian nurse scientists (Bottorff, Johnson, Irwin, & Ratner, 2000; Irwin, Johnson, & Bottorff, 2005; Johnson, Lovato, et al., 2003b; Moffat & Johnson, 2001). This qualitative approach takes advantage of people's propensity to narrate or tell stories about their experiences in daily life. Stories are representative of an individual's process of reflecting on and talking about the experience, which underlies the meaning made of the experience along with shaping imaged possibilities related to the experience. These personal accounts provide a useful way to understand how individuals make sense of their experiences. The way individuals situate themselves in the stories reflects the identities they take on and preserve over time. As such, narrative inquiry is particularly useful in exploring the realms of meaning, language used, and identity. A variety of strategies have been developed to elicit and analyze participant narratives (Lieblich, Tuval-Mashiach, & Zilber, 1998; Mathieson & Barrie, 1998; Mishler, 1996; Riessman, 1993; Sandelowski, 1991), and the usefulness of this research approach in understanding health and illness experience has been demonstrated by nurses as well as those outside of nursing (e.g., Abma, 1998; Frank, 1995; Sandelowski, Holditch-Davis, & Harris, 1990).

The narrative inquiry studies identified in this review examined women's narratives of postpartum smoking relapse to understand the ways women accounted for their relapse (Bottorff et al., 2000), adolescent narratives of smoking to understand smoking identities (Johnson et al., 2003b), and adolescent girls' narratives of smoking to explore the meaning of nicotine addiction (Moffat & Johnson, 2001). In the fourth study, Irwin and colleagues (2005) used discourse analysis methods to examine social discourses influencing mothers' narratives of smoking and mothering practices. The four studies each contribute to a more complex understanding of smoking and quitting, and challenge our reliance on cognitive approaches to behavior change when assisting smokers with tobacco reduction or cessation.

Postpartum Relapse Narratives

The storylines of postpartum smoking relapse from interviews with 27 women (i.e., controlling one's smoking, being vulnerable to smoking, nostalgia for one's former self, smoking for relief, and never really having quit) provide new evidence regarding the complexities inherent in experiences of smoking relapse among postpartum women (Bottorff et al., 2000). The authors argue that the findings are not consistent with commonly used theories of relapse (e.g., Martlatt, 1985) and behavior change (e.g., Prochaska & DiClemente, 1983), and point to limitations of some explanations of postpartum relapse (McBride, Pirie, & Curry, 1992; Stotts, DiClemente, Carbonari, & Mullen, 1996). The research findings provide direction for theory development and have been incorporated into recommendations for strengthening smoking cessation interventions for postpartum women (e.g., Mullen, 2004).

Adolescent Narratives of Smoking

The two narrative studies focused on adolescent smoking. Both provide detailed descriptions of youth smoking and are part of the growing interest in studying social identity perspective to explore youth smoking. Johnson et al., (2003b) report seven smoking-related identities among the 35 adolescents interviewed (i.e., confident nonsmoker, vulnerable smoker, ardent smoking, accepting nonsmoker, in-control smoker, confirmed smoker, the contrite smoker). Moffat and Johnson (2001) describe the meaning nicotine addiction had for 12 adolescent girls with recent experiences of smoking; narratives represented identities of invincibility, giving in, and unanticipated addiction. Each study discusses how these identities influence decisions about smoking. Beyond providing nuanced understanding of the multiple meanings youth have of smoking, findings offer insights into why existing tobacco control initiatives have low participation and success rates among youth. In addition, the findings suggest new directions for intervening with youth that are congruent with youths' experiences. For example, Johnson and colleagues (2003b) recommend that since adolescent identities are in the process of developing, helping youth to develop identities in relation to tobacco that "resonate with resistance" may be appropriate for this age group. Finally, these narrative studies have provided a foundation for future research. Okoli, Richardson, Ratner, and Johnson's (2008) recent cross-sectional survey study supports the use of self-reported identities in conjunction with existing taxonomies of smoking behavior when conducting research focused on youth smoking.

Narratives of Mothers Who Smoke

Irwin and colleagues' (2005) examination of women's stories of smoking focused on the influence of social discourses that stigmatize smoking among mothers. Their findings describe how women preserved their image as good mothers. The narrative strategies used included positioning themselves as knowledgeable about the health risks of smoking and secondhand smoke, openly sharing their guilt for transgressions in exposing their children to secondhand smoke, describing the extraordinary efforts they were willing to undertake to protect their children from secondhand smoke, constructing smoking as a way to be a better mother, and taking an antismoking stance by disapproving of smoking especially among children and youth. These findings help us understand the bind that women are in when it comes to smoking and fulfilling the social requirements of motherhood and provide a foundation for women-centered approaches to supporting tobacco reduction among mothers.

Phenomenology

Three phenomenological studies were identified, two led by nurses in the United States (DiNapoli, 2004; Heath, Andrews, Kelley, & Sorrell, 2004) and the other by a nurse scientist in Iceland (Jonsdottir & Jonsdottir, 2007). Although several approaches to conducting phenomenological research exist, all start at the point of everyday lived experience or experience as we live through it in actions, relations, and situations. Findings are typically presented as rich descriptions that are grounded in the everyday and reverberate with our own ordinary experiences of life (van Manen, 1997). Phenomenological studies do not produce proscriptive models or directions for practice but rather invite reflection and open up possibilities for being more thoughtful and tactful in relational situations (van Manen, 2007).

Lived Experiences of Smokers

Two of the studies focus on the lived experiences of smokers. DiNapoli (2004) studied the lived experience of adolescents' relationship with tobacco, and Jonsdottir and Jonsdottir (2007) examined women with advanced chronic obstructive pulmonary disease who repeatedly experienced smoking relapses. Heath et al. (2004), on the other hand, focused on tobacco dependent nurses' experiences with health promotion and disease prevention practices. Although the researchers indicated they used phenomenological methods, it was not consistently clear what approach to phenomenology was used. The exception to this was Jonsdottir and Jonsdottir (2007) who used an interpretive phenomenological approach drawing on Heideggerian phenomenology (Leonard, 1994; Plager, 1994). The identified themes attempt to capture aspects of lived experiences. For example, Heath et al. (2004) depict the everyday lived experiences of tobacco-dependent nurses through the following themes "Living as an insider in the world of tobacco addiction," "The outside-in view of living with a tobacco addition," and "Caught in the middle of the tobacco addiction." The three studies represent attempts to describe the everyday lived experiences of different groups of smokers. Although they fall short of the goal of phenomenology to gain a deeper understanding of the nature or meaning of everyday experience, the findings draw attention to some of the challenges of individual smokers that warrant further study.

Grounded Theory

Grounded theory was used in seven studies; all but one (Brown, 1996) was led by Canadian nurses. This qualitative approach, initially developed by two sociologists (Glaser & Strauss, 1967), focuses on generating theory from data; it involves both inductive and deductive thinking. Researchers using grounded theory aim to describe basic social processes that account for variations over time in the phenomena under study. These studies involve simultaneous data collection and analysis, a process that directs theoretical sampling and increasingly focused data collection (e.g., semistructured interviews, observations). Constant comparative analysis is a hallmark of grounded theory. When done well, findings have the "grab of description and voice, and the elegance and power of theory" (Schreiber, 2001, p. 213). Grounded theory is particularly useful in developing new ways to view phenomena, and subsequently, directing related practice and research issues. Nurses have made important contributions to the development of grounded theory methods (Hutchinson, 1986; Strauss & Corbin, 1998).

The grounded theory studies included in this review focused on a variety of topics related to experiences of smoking including the process adolescents undergo in controlling their tobacco use (Johnson, Kalaw, Lovato, Baillie, & Chambers, 2004), the processes that nonsmoking females undertake to remain smoke free (Dunn & Johnson, 2001), and the process of quitting smoking for older adults (Brown, 1996). Interactions related to tobacco use were the focus of the four remaining studies and included studies examining nonsmoking parents' interactions with smoking adolescents (Small, Brennan-Hunter, Best, & Solberg, 2002), couple interactions related to tobacco use (Bottorff et al., 2005; Bottorff, Oliffe, et al., 2006b), and interaction dynamics during telephone support for smoking cessation (Bottorff et al., 2004a). With one exception (Bottorff et al., 2004a), the primary data collection method was interviews with samples that ranged from 17 to 35 participants. The study by Bottorff et al. (2004a), was conducted within a clinical trial of a tailored nurse-administered smoking cessation intervention for surgical patients. The trial included a telephone counseling component and produced a data set of over 350 tape recorded telephone support calls that were used to examine the interactive dynamics of telephone support over time.

Adolescent Processes Concerning Tobacco Use and Nonuse

These grounded theory studies produced a number of potentially useful theories. For example, Johnson et al. (2004), drawing from adolescent perspectives on quitting smoking, propose a theory of regaining control that reconceptualizes youth quit attempts as natural cycles reflective of efforts to control smoking. Based on this model, they recommend that tobacco reduction interventions be targeted toward enhancing or supporting youth's natural propensities to control their tobacco use; a marked departure from current youth smoking cessation programs. Interestingly, the findings from this study have informed other adolescent smoking cessation studies, including the development of a new measure of adolescent smoking cessation (Falkin, Fryer, & Mahadeo, 2007; McVea, Miller, Creswell, McEntarrfer, & Coleman, 2009; Myers, MacPheson, Jones, & Aarons, 2007).

Exploring Processes Between Tobacco Use and Couple Dynamics

Bottorff led two grounded theory studies of couple interactions related to tobacco use. The approach taken in this research is a marked departure from studying smoking as an individual behavior. In these studies, researchers explored how smoking behaviors were situated in and shaped by couple dynamics and relationships prior to pregnancy (Bottorff et al., 2005), and during pregnancy (Bottorff et al., 2006a). Three tobacco-related interaction patterns were identified: disengaged, conflictual, and accommodating. These patterns open up new ways to understand smoking behavior and the role intimate partners play in tobacco use decisions, and provide a rationale for investigating the influence of social context on smoking.

From these two studies the concept of "compelled tobacco reduction" was proposed as a way to understand the effects of pressure from others to stop smoking that women experience as well as to explain shifts in tobacco-related interaction patterns during pregnancy. The concept deepened our understanding of how tension and conflict related to smoking is experienced by some women during childbearing years. As part of a program of research, these grounded theory studies have contributed to the development of new approaches to supporting women's tobacco reduction in pregnancy and postpartum, and examine the influence of gender on tobacco use. Evidence from these studies has informed a new information booklet to help women understand the influence of relationship dynamics on their efforts to reduce or quit smoking during pregnancy (Bottorff, Carey, Poole, Greaves, & Urquhart, 2008).

Ethnography

Six studies reviewed used ethnographic research methods; all led by Canadian nurses. Ethnography has a long history in both social and cultural anthropology and in sociology. It has been used to study a broad range of issues and topics focused on taken-for-granted dimensions of the everyday. Many different approaches to conducting ethnographic research exist, but typically this inquiry recognizes meaning as socially constructed, which is present in patterns of behavior, interactions, and implicit assumptions shared by a particular group in a specified social system (Creswell, 2007; Miller, Hengst, & Wang, 2003; Roper & Shapira, 2000). Ethnographic research aims to portray the dynamic cultural structures and meanings from the perspective of participants and the interpretive social science lens of the researcher.

The Culture of Tobacco Use: From Adolescents and Novice Nursing Students

Two studies explored tobacco use among adolescents through their use of language and dialogue patterns to construct experiences of tobacco dependence (Johnson, Bottorff, et al., 2003a) and nicotine addiction (Bottorff et al., 2004b). Ethnographic approaches were also used to study the experiences of smoking among female adolescents (Seguire & Chalmers, 2000) and student nurses' constructions of their role in addressing tobacco use (Chalmers, Seguire, & Brown, 2003). Although the latter studies were less clear in their ethnographic focus, the studies by Johnson et al. (2003a) and Bottorff et al. (2004b) stated the underlying assumption was that young people share a dynamic culture characterized by shared meanings, language, and socially patterned behaviors. The findings from these two studies describe adolescent cultural knowledge and beliefs related to tobacco dependence and nicotine addiction and provide additional evidence that adolescent experiences are qualitatively different from other age groups. Importantly, Johnson et al.'s (2003a) model of emerging tobacco dependence from adolescent perspectives offers a novel framework useful for research and interventions with youth. This framework extends conceptualizations of nicotine dependence to include other "needs" for smoking that may be precursors to nicotine addiction. The qualitative evidence from the Johnson et al. (2003a) and Bottorff et al. (2004b) studies have provided the foundation for the development of a new measure of emerging tobacco dependence with items that hold relevance to youth (Johnson et al., 2005; Richardson et al, 2007). This new assessment tool may be useful in alerting teens to emerging dependence and tailoring cessation interventions for them.

Two Alternate Cultures: Masculinity and Nurses' Workplace

In the remaining two studies, different ethnographic approaches were used. A study conducted by Bottorff, Oliffe, Kalaw, Carey, and Mroz, (2006b) explores smoking from the perspective of new fathers. In this study, the focus was how discourses reflecting socially accepted ideals related to masculinity and fatherhood influenced men's smoking patterns. In the other study, Schultz, Bottorff, and Johnson (2006) used ethnographic methods to study hospital workplace culture relevant to the integration of cessation interventions by registered nurses. This study provides a practical example of how triangulation of diverse data collection approaches (observation, interviews, and document collection) contributes to understanding a particular group's culture. Detailed descriptions of the hospital setting, tobacco control strategies and policies, and the activities of and discourse among nurses involved in the study contributed to a clearer understanding of the complex challenges nurses face in integrating tobacco dependence interventions in their practice.

Case Study

There were three articles that reported on qualitative case studies; all conducted by U.S. nurse scientists. This qualitative approach focuses on capturing the complexities involved in a single case, and draws on naturalistic, holistic, ethnographic, phenomenological, and biological research methods (Stake, 1995). Accordingly there are many ways to conduct case studies, which can draw on a variety of data sources including field work, verbal reports, observations, documents, or any combination of these (Stake, 1995; Yin, 2003). This diversity is reflected in the tobacco control case studies included in this review.

Hahn et al. (2007) examined the implementation and enforcement of the purchase, use, and possession *tobacco laws directed toward youth* in four Kentucky communities. The communities were selected on the basis of variations in enforcement and illegal sales, and to represent different regions of the state. Analysis of semistructured interviews with 44 key informants representing each of the communities resulted in the identification of similarities as well as differences among the communities. Bonnette's (2008) case study explored the effects of ATENS (auricular transcutaneous electrical neuro-stimulation) in combination with other types of *smoking cessation support interventions* with six smokers. Within case analyses of interview data were used to identify themes related to each stage of the addiction treatment process. Given the purpose was to explore the effects of ATENS on smoking cessation, data collection during the cessation process rather than one year following treatment would have allowed for a wider variety of data to be used and a more nuanced understanding. Whyte, Watson, and McIntosh's (2006) case study explored the *health education practices* of 12 nurses in three hospitals in Scotland using nonparticipant observations, semistructured interviews, and recordings of nurse–patient interactions. In this study each case represented one nurse and the patients he or she cared for. The researchers explored interactions within each case, and conducted a cross-case analysis using an analytical framework that reflected elements of health education practice. Although in each of these case studies recommendations are made for the study settings and for further research, there is a general lack of attention to the complexities that characterize the use of case studies, and little attention to generation of hypotheses or theoretical insights. Case studies are a valuable approach to examining topics in relation to tobacco control that to date remains largely untapped by nurses.

DISCUSSION

Over the last decade, an increase in nurse-led qualitative research studies in the field of tobacco use and control is evident. This shift in approach by nurse scientists suggests a growing interest in the social context surrounding tobacco use issues and in exploring relevant emic perspectives (Creswell, 2007; Sandelowski, 2004). There are examples where knowledge generated has begun to challenge practice and policy arenas in the tobacco control field, and to provide direction for future research.

With few exceptions the majority of reviewed qualitative studies appear to be one-off studies conducted to address practical problems or issues encountered in practice. Of the articles reviewed, 60% reported using either a qualitative descriptive or case study method. Many of these studies were small scale, conducted at a single location with small samples. There was also no obvious methodological stance or social theory perspective, which then resulted in minimal theoretical development. Although the pragmatic value of these qualitative research studies cannot be underestimated, their contribution to advancing the field of tobacco control is less clear. The findings are limited to summaries of the data and at best confirm results of similar research. However, when nurse scientists used qualitative approaches with recognized theoretical underpinnings of the methods (e.g., grounded theory, ethnography etc.) there was a greater likelihood of substantive contributions to knowledge. Based on this review of qualitative studies, theoretically driven qualitative methods tend to be underutilized by nurse scientists investigating tobacco control issues.

The predominance of studies investigating tobacco cessation issues is noteworthy. Of the articles reviewed, 84% focused on a variety of cessation issues that spanned diverse ages, ethnic groups, and patient populations, in addition to nurses' own experiences with smoking and stopping. This focus may reflect nurses' frequent contact with smokers and an interest in individualizing tobacco-related interventions. Others dimensions of tobacco control may also benefit from attention by nurses who are skilled in qualitative research methods.

There are three areas where nurses are making important contributions to the field of tobacco control. The first area is in relation to smoking identity. Findings from several studies revealed how smoking becomes part of a person's identity both personally and socially. These studies highlight the importance of identity for understanding smoking behaviors and to guiding intervention and program development. Social context of tobacco use is the second area where nurses have contributed. While several studies acknowledged the influence that family members and friends can have on decisions related to smoking, stopping, and relapse, some nurses have taken advantage of qualitative methods to examine the social context of smoking in more depth. These studies focus on the influence of gender, diversity, place, and intimate relationships issues. Evidence generated from these studies challenge assumptions that tobacco use decisions solely reside within the individual and demonstrate how social context plays a role. The third area of nurse scientists' contribution has focused on nurses' involvement in tobacco. Studies investigating cessation issues for nurses and their workplace have deepened our understanding of the challenges nurses face in addressing their own tobacco dependence along with how organizational structures limit the legitimization of cessation support and nurses' ability to effectively address patients' tobacco use.

Evident in this review are developing programs of qualitative research in tobacco control. For example, programs of research related to adolescent smoking, and smoking in pregnancy and postpartum by Canadian teams have produced a number of qualitative studies. Different qualitative approaches have been used to build a comprehensive knowledge base on which the development of new measures, interventions, or policy directions has been developed. The use of sequential qualitative studies allowed for the exploration of issues uncovered in previous studies. There is some evidence that these programs of research led by nurses have impacted the tobacco control field (Bottorff et al., 2009; Falkin et al., 2007; McVea et al., 2009; Mullen, 2004; Myers et al., 2007; Richardson et al., 2007).

IMPLICATIONS FOR FUTURE
RESEARCH AND POLICY

Nurse scientists have made important contributions to the field of tobacco control using qualitative research approaches. While qualitative descriptive studies demonstrate utility in addressing practical questions, we suggest nurse scientists interested in exploring tobacco-related issues consider the full range of qualitative research approaches. There is much to be gained from all of the qualitative research methods in addressing questions related to tobacco use arising from nursing practice and the field of tobacco control in general. Alternatively, the value of using mixed methods research designs has been demonstrated and has the potential to generate evidence relevant to practice and policy arenas along with challenging theoretical assumptions (Creswell, 2003; Morse, 2003; Tashakkori & Teddlie, 1998). While an examination of studies involving mixed methods was beyond the scope of this review, a small number of nurse researchers have begun to publish studies that used this approach (Duffy, Reeves, Hermann, Karvonen, & Smith, 2008; Stoltz & Sanders, 2000; Thompson, Parahoo, & Blair, 2007; Thompson, Parahoo, McCurry, O'Doherty, & Doherty, 2004).

Notable in this review is the strong focus on cessation, which reflects an obvious interest to nurses. Since tobacco-related illnesses dominant the health of people globally and nurses have the most amount of contact with people within the context of health care, nurses have the potential to be leaders in smoking cessation (International Council of Nurses, 1999; Sarna & Bialous, 2006; Schultz, 2003). As Rice and Stead (2004) note, we have evidence that direct patient care nurses can effectively support cessation; however, achieving a practice standard where every patient's tobacco use is addressed has not been realized. Qualitative research has a role to play in generating evidence specific to building and expanding theories related to cessation and the enhancement of delivering cessation interventions.

Qualitative research approaches can also generate valuable insights about populations where tobacco use rates are high. Reasons for starting and continuing to smoke vary among these populations (Doolan & Froelicher, 2006; Greaves et al., 2006); moreover, there is emerging evidence that suggests individual behavioral perspectives are inadequate when it comes to investigating tobacco use and control issues in these populations (Appollonio & Malone, 2005; Kim et al., 2005b). Novel evidence concerning tobacco use generated through qualitative research approaches could be instrumental in the development of appropriate strategies to reduce tobacco use, including approaches to address social–environmental determinants of smoking (New South Wales Government: Department of Health, 2003; Whitehead & Dahlgren, 2007).

CONCLUSION

In this chapter, we reviewed the contributions of nurse scientists to the field of tobacco control through the use of qualitative research approaches. Nurses have made some important contributions to the field of tobacco control and their work provides useful models for others considering the use of qualitative methods to investigate tobacco related topics. Capturing perspectives of those effected by and delivering tobacco control strategies is a prominent benefit demonstrated in the knowledge generated through qualitative research methods. Nurses have been identified as leaders in tobacco control practice and policy; we believe that qualitative research has an essential role in sustaining and strengthening our influence in combating the health consequences of tobacco use and exposure to tobacco smoke.

ACKNOWLEDGMENTS

We acknowledge the valuable assistance provided by Christine Shaw-Daigle, Librarian, St. Boniface Research Centre and Julia Oosterveen, Project Manager, Cancer Nursing Research Group, University of Manitoba.

REFERENCES

Ahijevych, K., Kuun, P., Christman, S., Wood, T., Browning, K., & Wewers, M. E. (2003). Beliefs about tobacco among Appalachian current and former users. *Applied Nursing Research, 16*(2), 93–102.

Abma, T. A. (1998). Storytelling as inquiry in a mental hospital. *Qualitative Health Research, 8*, 821–838.

Appollonio, D., & Malone, R. (2005). Marketing to the marginalised: Tobacco industry marketing to the homeless and mentally ill. *Tobacco Control, 14*, 409–415.

Aquilino, M. L., Goody, C. M., & Lowe, J. B. (2003). WIC providers' perspectives on offering smoking cessation interventions. *The American Journal of Maternal Child Nursing, 28*(5), 326–332.

Bialous, S. A., Sarna, L., Wewers, M. E., Froelicher, E. S., & Danao, L. (2004). Nurses' perspectives of smoking initiation, addiction, and cessation. *Nursing Research, 53*(6), 387–395.

Bonnette, M. L. (2008). Auricular transcutaneous electrical neuro-stimulation, addiction education, behavioral training, coaching support and the nicotine addiction treatment process. *Journal of Addictions Nursing, 19*(3), 130–140.

Bottorff, J. L., Carey, J., Poole, N., Greaves, L., & Urquhart, C. (2008). *Couples and smoking: What you need to know when you are pregnant.* Jointly published by the British Columbia Centre of Excellence for Women's Health, the Institute for Health Living and Chronic Disease Prevention, University of British Columbia Okanagan, and NEXUS, University of British Columbia Vancouver. Retrieved October 19, 2009, from www.facet.ubc.ca and www.hcip-bc.org.

Bottorff, J.L., Johnson, J.L., Irwin, L.G., & Ratner, P.A. (2000). Narratives of smoking relapse: The stories of postpartum women. *Research in Nursing & Health, 23*(2), 126–134.

Bottorff, J.L., Johnson, J.L., Moffat, B., Fofonoff, D., Budz, B., & Groening, M. (2004a). Synchronizing clinician engagement and client motivation in telephone counseling. *Qualitative Health Research, 14*(4), 462–477.

Bottorff, J.L., Johnson, J.L., Moffat, B., Grewal, J., Ratner, P.A., & Kalaw, C. (2004b). Adolescent constructions of nicotine addiction. *The Canadian Journal of Nursing Research, 36*(1), 22–39.

Bottorff, J.L., Kalaw, C., Johnson, J.L., Chambers, N., Stewart, M., Greaves, L., et al. (2005). Unraveling smoking ties: How tobacco use is embedded in couple interactions. *Research in Nursing and Health, 28*(4), 316–328.

Bottorff, J.L., Kalaw, C., Johnson, J.L., Stewart, M., Greaves, L., & Carey, J. (2006a). Couple dynamics during women's tobacco reduction in pregnancy and postpartum. *Nicotine and Tobacco Research, 4,* 499–509.

Bottorff, J.L., Oliffe, J., Kalaw, C., Carey, J., & Mroz, L. (2006b). Men's constructions of smoking in the context of women's tobacco reduction during pregnancy and postpartum. *Social Science and Medicine, 62*(12), 3096–3108.

Bottorf, J.L., Poole, N. & the FACET research team (2009). Reducing smoking among mothers: The FACET Program. In *Knowledge to action: A knowledge translation casebook.* Ottowa, ON: Canadian Institutes of Health Research, 35–37.

Brown, J. M. (1996). Redefining smoking and the self as a nonsmoker. *Western Journal of Nursing Research, 18*(4), 414–428.

Chalmers, K., Seguire, M., & Brown, J. (2003). Health promotion and tobacco control: Student nurses' perspectives. *Journal of Nursing Education, 42*(3), 106–112.

Creswell, J. W. (2003). *Research design: Qualitative, quantitative, and mixed methods approaches.* Thousand Oaks, CA: Sage.

Creswell, J. W. (2007). *Qualitative inquiry & research design: Choosing among five approaches.* Thousand Oaks, CA: Sage.

Denham, S. A., Meyer, M. G., & Toborg, M. A. (2004). Tobacco cessation in adolescent females in Appalachian communities. *Family & Community Health, 27*(2), 170–181.

Denzin, N. K., & Lincoln, Y. S. (2005). *The Sage handbook of qualitative research* (3rd ed.). Thousand Oaks, CA: Sage.

DiNapoli, P.P. (2004). The lived experiences of adolescent girls' relationship with tobacco. *Issues in Comprehensive Pediatric Nursing, 27*(1), 19–26.

Doolan, D. M., & Froelicher, E.S. (2006). Efficacy of smoking cessation interventions among special populations: Review of the literature from 2000–2005. *Nursing Research, 55*(4S), S29–S37.

Duffy, S.A., Reeves, P., Hermann, C., Karvonen, C., & Smith, P. (2008). In-hospital smoking cessation programs: What do VA patients and staff want and need? *Applied Nursing Research, 21*(4), 199–206.

Dunn, D. A., & Johnson, J. L. (2001). Choosing to remain smoke-free: The experiences of adolescent girls. *The Journal of Adolescent Health, 29*(4), 289–297.

Echer, I. C., & Barreto, S. S. (2008). Determination and support as successful factors for smoking cessation. *Revista Latino-Americana De Enfermagem, 16*(3), 445–451.

Edwards, N., & Sims-Jones, N. (1998). Smoking and smoking relapse during pregnancy and postpartum: Results of a qualitative study. *Birth, 25*(2), 94–100.

Falkin, G. P., Fryer, C. S., & Mahadeo, M. (2007). Smoking cessation and stress among teenagers. *Qualitative Health Research, 11*, 812–823.

Fernandez, C., & Wilson, D. (2008). Maori women's views on smoking cessation initiatives. *Nursing Praxis in New Zealand, 24*(2), 27–40.

Frank, A. W. (1995). *The wounded storyteller: Body, illness and ethics.* Chicago: University of Chicago Press.

Glaser, B., & Strauss, A. (1967). *The discovery of grounded theory.* Chicago: Aldine.

Greaves, L., Johnson, J., Bottorff, J., Kirkland, S., Jategaonkar, N., McGowan, M., et al. (2006). What are the effects of tobacco policies on vulnerable populations? A better practices review. *Canadian Journal of Public Health, 97*(4), 310–315.

Green, M. A., & Clarke, D. E. (2005). Smoking reduction & cessation: A hospital based survey of outpatients' attitudes. *Journal of Psychosocial Nursing and Mental Health Services, 43*(5), 18–25.

Hahn, E. J., Riker, C., Butler, K. M., Cavendish, S., Lewis, P., Greathouse Maggio, L. W., et al. (2007). Enforcement of tobacco purchase, use, and possession laws in four Kentucky communities. *Policy, Politics & Nursing Practice, 8*(2), 140–147.

Heath, J., Andrews, J., Kelley, F. J., & Sorrell, J. (2004). Caught in the middle: Experiences of tobacco-dependent nurse practitioners. *Journal of the American Academy of Nurse Practitioners, 16*(9), 396–401.

Hutchinson, M. (1986). Grounded theory: The method. In P. Munhall & C. Oiler (Eds.), *Nursing research: A qualitative perspective* (pp. 111–130). Norwalk, CT: Appleton-Century-Crofts.

Hutchinson, S. A. (2001). The development of qualitative health research: Taking stock. *Qualitative Health Research, 11*(4), 505–521.

International Council of Nurses. (1999). *Tobacco use and health: Position statement.* Geneva, Switzerland: Author.

Irwin, L. G., Johnson, J. L., & Bottorff, J. L. (2005). Mothers who smoke: Confessions and justifications. *Health Care for Women International, 26*, 577–590.

Johnson, J. L., Bottorff, J. L., Moffat, B., Ratner, P. A., Shoveller, J. A., & Lovato, C. Y. (2003a). Tobacco dependence: Adolescents' perspectives on the need to smoke. *Social Science & Medicine, 56*(7), 1481–1492.

Johnson, J. L., Kalaw, C., Lovato, C. Y., Baillie, L., & Chambers, N. A. (2004). Crossing the line: Adolescents' experiences of controlling their tobacco use. *Qualitative Health Research, 14*(9), 1276–1291.

Johnson, J. L., Lovato, C. Y., Maggi, S., Ratner, P. A., Shoveller, J., Baillie, L., et al. (2003b). Smoking and adolescence: Narratives of identity. *Research in Nursing & Health, 26*(5), 387–397.

Johnson, J. L., Ratner, P. A., Tucker, R., Bottorff, J. L., Zumbo, B., Prkachin, K., et al. (2005). Development of a multi-dimensional measure of tobacco dependence in adolescence. *Addictive Behavior, 30*(3), 501–515.

Jonsdottir, R., & Jonsdottir, H. (2007). The experience of women with advanced chronic obstructive pulmonary disease of repeatedly relapsing to smoking. *Scandinavian Journal of Caring Sciences, 21*(3), 297–304.

Kim, S. S., & Nam, K. A. (2005a). Korean male smokers' perceptions of tobacco control policies in the United States. *Public Health Nursing, 22*(3), 221–229.

Kim, S. S., Son, H., & Nam, K. A. (2005b). Personal factors influencing Korean American men's smoking behavior: Addiction, health, and age. *Archives of Psychiatric Nursing, 19*(1), 35–41.

Kulbok, P. A., Rhee, H., Botchwey, N., Hinton, I., Bovbjerg, V., & Anderson, N. L. (2008). Factors influencing adolescents' decision not to smoke. *Public Health Nursing, 25*(6), 505–515.

Kulwicki, A., & Hill Rice, V. (2003). Arab American adolescent perceptions and experiences with smoking. *Public Health Nursing, 20*(3), 177–183.

Leonard, V. W. (1994). A Heideggerian phenomenological perspective on the concept of person. In P. Benner (Ed), *Interpretive phenomenology: Embodiment, caring, and ethics in health and Illness* (pp. 43–63). Thousand Oaks, CA: Sage.

Lieblich, A., Tuval-Mashiach, R., & Zilber, T. (1998). *Narrative research: Reading, analysis, and interpretation.* Thousand Oaks, CA: Sage.

Malone, R. E., Yerger, V., & Pearson, C. (2001). Cigar risk perceptions in focus groups of urban African American youth. *Journal of Substance Abuse, 13*(4), 549–561.

Martlatt, G. A. (1985). Relapse prevention: Theoretical rationale and overview of the model. In G. A. Marlatt & J. R. Gordon (Eds.), *Relapse prevention: Maintenance and strategies in the treatment of addictive behaviors* (pp. 3–70). New York: Guilford Press.

Mathieson, C. M. & Barrie, C. M. (1998). Probing the prime narrative: Illness, interviewing, and identity. *Qualitative Health Research, 8,* 581–601.

McBride, C. M., Pirie, P. L. & Curry, S. J. (1992). Postpartum relapse to smoking: A prospective study. *Health Education Research, 7,* 381–390.

McCarty, M. C., Zander, K. M., Hennrikus, D. J., & Lando, H. A. (2001). Barriers among nurses to providing smoking cessation advice to hospitalized smokers. *American Journal of Health Promotion, 16*(2), 85–87.

McFeely, S. (2001). Young people's pathway to smoking cessation. *Nursing Standard, 16*(2), 39–42.

McVea, K. L., Miller, D. L., Creswell, J. W., McEntarrfer, R., & Coleman, M. J. (2009). How adolescents experience smoking cessation. *Qualitative Health Research, 19,* 580–592.

Miller, P. J., Hengst, J. A., & Wang, S. (2003). Ethnographic methods: Applications from developmental cultural psychology. In P. M. Camic, J. E. Rhodes, & L. Yardley (Eds.), *Qualitative research in psychology: Expanding perspectives in methodology and design* (pp. 219–242). Washington, DC: American Psychological Association.

Milne, J., & Oberle, K. (2005). Enhancing rigor in qualitative description: A case study. *Journal of Wound Ostomy & Continence Nursing, 32*(6), 413–420.

Mishler, E. G. (1996). *Research interviewing: Context and narrative.* Cambridge: Harvard University Press.

Moffat, B. M., & Johnson, J. L. (2001). Through the haze of cigarettes: Teenage girls' stories about cigarette addiction. *Qualitative Health Research, 11*(5), 668–681.

Morse, J. M. (2003). Principles of mixed methods and multimethod research design. In A. Tashakkori & C. Teddlie (Eds.), *Handbook of mixed methods in social & behavioral research* (pp. 189–208). Thousand Oaks, CA: Sage.

Mullen, P. D. (2004). How can more smoking suspension during pregnancy become lifelong abstinence? Lessons learned about predictors, interventions, and gaps in our accumulated knowledge. *Nicotine & Tobacco Research, 6*(2), 217–238.

Myers, M. G., MacPheson, L., Jones, L. R., & Aarons, G. A. (2007). Measuring adolescent smoking cessation strategies: Instrument development and initial validation. *Nicotine & Tobacco Research, 9*(11), 1131–1138.

New South Wales Government: Department of Health (2003). *Four steps towards equity: A tool for health promotion practice.* Available from www.health.nsw.gov.au

Nikbakht Nasrabadi, A., Parsayekta, Z., & Emami, A. (2004). Smoking as a symbol of friendship: Qualitative study of smoking behavior and initiation of a group of male nurse students in Iran. *Nursing & Health Sciences, 6*(3), 209–215.

Okoli, C. T. C, Richardson, C. G., Ratner, P. A. & Johnson, J. L. (2008). An examination of the smoking identities and taxonomies of smoking behavior of youth. *Tobacco Control, 17,* 151–158.

Plager, K. A. (1994). Hermeneutic phenomenology: A methodology for family health and health promotion study in nursing. In P. Benner (Ed.), *Interpretive phenomenology: Embodiment, caring, and ethics in health and Illness* (pp. 65–83). Thousand Oaks, CA: Sage.

Pletsch, P. K., & Johnson, M. K. (1996). The cigarette smoking experience of pregnant Latinas in the United States. *Health Care for Women International, 17*(6), 549–562.

Pletsch, P. K., & Kratz, A. T. (2004). Why do women stop smoking during pregnancy? *Health Care for Women International, 25*(7), 671–679.

Pletsch, P. K., Morgan, S., & Pieper, A. F. (2003). Context and beliefs about smoking and smoking cessation. *The American Journal of Maternal Child Nursing, 28*(5), 320–325.

Prochaska, J. O., & DiClemente, C. C. (1983). Stages and processes of self-change of smoking: Toward an integrative model of change. *Journal of Consulting and Clinical Psychology, 51,* 390–395.

Puskar, M. (1995). Smoking cessation in women: Findings from qualitative research. *The Nurse Practitioner, 20*(11), 80.

Reynolds, N. R., Neidig, J. L., & Wewers, M. E. (2004). Illness representation and smoking behavior: A focus group study of HIV-positive men. *The Journal of the Association of Nurses in AIDS Care, 15*(4), 37–47.

Rice, V. H., & Stead, L. F. (2004). Nursing interventions for smoking cessation. *Cochrane Database of Systematic Reviews 2007,* (4), CD001188. doi: 10.1002/14651858.CD001188.pub3

Richardson, C. G., Ratner, P. A., Zumbo, B. D., Bottorff, J. L., Shoveller, J. A., Prkachin, K. M., et al. (2007). Validation of the dimensions of tobacco dependence scale for adolescents. *Addictive Behaviors, 32*(7), 1498–1504.

Riessman, C. K. (1993). *Narrative analysis.* Newbury Park, CA: Sage.

Roper, J. M., & Shapira, J. (2000). *Ethnography in nursing research.* Thousand Oaks, CA: Sage.

Sandelowski, M. (1991). Telling stories: Narrative approaches in qualitative research. *Image: Journal of Nursing Scholarship, 23,* 161–166.

Sandelowski, M. (2000). Whatever happened to qualitative description? *Research in Nursing & Health, 23,* 334–340.

Sandelowski, M. (2004). Using qualitative research. *Qualitative Health Research, 14*(10), 1366–1386.

Sandelowski, M., Holditch-Davis, D., & Harris, B. G. (1990). Living the life: Expectations of infertility. *Sociology of Health and Illness, 12,* 195–215.

Sarna, L., & Bialous, S. A. (2006). Strategic directions for nursing research in tobacco dependence. *Nursing Research, 55*(4S), S1–S9.

Sarna, L., Bialous, S. A., Wewers, M. E., Froelicher, E. S., & Danao, L. (2005). Nurses, smoking, and the workplace. *Research in Nursing & Health, 28*(1), 79–90.

Schofield, I., Kerr, S., & Tolson, D. (2007). An exploration of the smoking-related health beliefs of older people with chronic obstructive pulmonary disease. *Journal of Clinical Nursing, 16*(9), 1726–1735.

Schreiber, R. S. (2001). *Using grounded theory in nursing.* New York: Springer Publishing.

Schultz, A. S. H. (2003). Nursing and tobacco reduction: A review of the literature. *International Journal of Nursing Studies, 40*(6), 571–586.

Schultz, A. S. H., Bottorff, J. L., & Johnson, J. L. (2006). An ethnographic study of tobacco control in hospital settings. *Tobacco Control, 15*(4), 317–322.

Seguire, M., & Chalmers, K. I. (2000). Late adolescent female smoking. *Journal of Advanced Nursing, 31*(6), 1422–1429.

Small, S. P., Brennan-Hunter, A. L., Best, D. G., & Solberg, S. M. (2002). Struggling to understand: The experience of nonsmoking parents with adolescents who smoke. *Qualitative Health Research, 12*(9), 1202–1219.

Snyder, M., McDevitt, J., & Painter, S. (2008). Smoking cessation and serious mental illness. *Archives of Psychiatric Nursing, 22*(5), 297–304.

Stake, R. (1995). *The art of case study research.* Thousand Oaks, CA: Sage.

Staten, R. R., & Ridner, S. L. (2007). College students' perspective on smoking cessation: "If the message doesn't speak to me, I don't hear it." *Issues in Mental Health Nursing, 28*(1), 101–115.

Stoltz, A. D., & Sanders, B. D. (2000). Cigar and marijuana use: Their relationship in teens. *The Journal of School Nursing, 16*(4), 28–35.

Stotts, A., DiClemente, C. C., Carbonari, J. P., & Mullen, P. D. (1996). Pregnancy smoking cessation: A case of mistaken identity. *Addictive Behaviors, 21,* 459–471.

Strauss, A., & Corbin, J. (1998). *Basics of qualitative research: Techniques and procedures for developing grounded theory* (2nd ed.). Thousand Oaks, CA: Sage.

Struthers, R., & Hodge, F. S. (2004). Sacred tobacco use in Ojibwe communities. *Journal of Holistic Nursing: Official Journal of the American Holistic Nurses' Association, 22*(3), 209–225.

Tashakkori, A., & Teddlie, C. (1998). *Mixed methodology: Combining qualitative and quantitative approaches.* Thousand Oaks, CA: Sage.

Thompson, K. A., Parahoo, A. K., & Blair, N. (2007). A nurse-led smoking cessation clinic: Quit rate results and views of participants. *Health Education Journal, 66*(4), 307–322.

Thompson, K. A., Parahoo, K. P., McCurry, N., O'Doherty, E., & Doherty, A. M. (2004). Women's perceptions of support from partners, family members and close friends for smoking cessation during pregnancy: Combining quantitative and qualitative findings. *Health Education Research, 19*(1), 29–39.

Thorne, S., Reimer Kirkham, S., & MacDonald-Emes, J. (1997). Interpretive description: A non-categorical qualitative alternative for developing nursing knowledge. *Research in Nursing & Health, 20*(2), 169–177.

Treacy, M. P., Hyde, A., Boland, J., Whitaker, T., Abaunza, P. S., & Stewart-Knox, B. J. (2007). Children talking: Emerging perspectives and experiences of cigarette smoking. *Qualitative Health Research, 17*(2), 238–249.

Van Manen, M. (1997). *Researching lived experience: Human science for an action sensitive pedagogy.* London: The Althouse Press.

Van Manen, M. (2007). Phenomenology of practice. *Phenomenology & Practice, 1*(1), 11–30.

Whitehead, M., & Dahlgren, G. (2007). *Leveling up (part 1): A discussion paper on concepts and principles for tackling social inequities in health.* WHO Collaborating Centre for Policy Research on Social Determinants of Health, University of Liverpool. Retrieved from http://www.who.int/social_determinants/resources/leveling_up_part1.pdf

Whyte, R. E., Watson, H. E., & McIntosh, J. (2006). Nurses' opportunistic interventions with patients in relation to smoking. *Journal of Advanced Nursing, 55*(5), 568–577.

Yin, R. K. (2003). *Case study research: Design and methods* (3rd ed.). Thousand Oaks, CA: Sage.

Yousey, Y. (2007). Family attitudes about tobacco smoke exposure of young children at home. *The American Journal of Maternal Child Nursing, 32*(3), 178–183.

Chapter 6

Biological Models for Studying and Assessing Tobacco Use

Karen Ahijevych

ABSTRACT

The purpose of this chapter on biological models for studying and assessing tobacco use is to provide an introduction to some of the common concepts and biomarkers in this arena to ultimately inform intervention research by nurse scientists. An overview of selected biomarkers of tobacco exposure in individuals includes exhaled carbon monoxide, cotinine (the proximate metabolite of nicotine), and measurement of an individual's puffing pattern termed smoking topography. Common tobacco contents discussed include tobacco specific nitrosamines (TSNA) and polycyclic aromatic hydrocarbons (PAH) some of which increase disease risk including cancer. Exemplars of additives to cigarettes by the tobacco industry will be described including menthol, one additive marketed by the industry. Genetics and tobacco addiction has emerged as a rapidly expanding field. Illustrative of this area are twin studies, nicotinic receptors, CYP2A6 polymorphisms, and genes that impact dopamine receptors. The cadre of nurse scientists conducting research in this much needed area is small. The opportunity for nurse scientists educated in biological inquiry in tobacco-related research is great. Nurse scientists actively involved in multidisciplinary translational teams to address nicotine addition are needed.

DOI: 10.1891/0739-6686.27.145

Keywords: components of tobacco; biomarkers of tobacco use; smoking
topography; carcinogen markers

Integration of biological models in nursing research that address tobacco use and
resulting exposures is critical to portray a comprehensive scope of the problem
from the individual level to policy formulation. A psychobiophysiological framework is essential in examining nicotine dependence as biomarkers of tobacco exposure that provide data to understand individual variations of smoking behavior
and metabolism of tobacco constituents. While there are hundreds of potential
additives in tobacco products, several exemplars are identified in this chapter to
illustrate modification of the sensory experience of the tobacco user and ultimately their impact on nicotine dependence. Genome-wide association studies
(GWAS) to identify genetic associations with observable traits such as nicotine
dependence in combination with clinical and other phenotype data will advance
our understanding of nicotine dependence, which in turn will lead to improved,
personalized treatment. For example, if individuals are rapid nicotine metabo-
lizer phenotype, they may benefit from increased dosage of nicotine replacement
pharmacotherapy. Nurse researchers with knowledge and basic science skills to
conduct complex multilevel studies regarding biomarkers, genetics, and behavior are critical to more accurately reflect cigarette smoking and appropriate interventions.

Areas of biological inquiry included in this chapter are biomarkers of exposure, selected cigarette additives, and examples of genetics and tobacco addiction.
Selected subtopics for each area, its associated impact, as well as the contribution
to understanding tobacco use exposure are presented in Table 6.1. While there are
4,000 ingredients in a cigarette, those selected represent some of the common constituents. Several of the genetic variations affecting smoking behavior include
nicotinic acetylcholine receptors, dopamine receptor genes, and CYP2A6, the
primary enzyme in nicotine and cotinine metabolism. Research by nurse scientists is included where available. To illustrate, nursing research of biobehavioral aspects of smoking among adolescents (Wood, Wewers, Groner, & Ahijevych, 2004)
presents data regarding biomarkers of tobacco exposure similar to that of adults.
This guides intervention development with adolescents who are sometimes in-
appropriately considered "social" smokers or not nicotine dependent. Findings from
a study of compensation of smoking behaviors among adults are applicable to interventions in that cigarette reduction as a quitting strategy may not be effective when
the smoker is consuming more of the cigarette rod and increasing puff volumes
(Ahijevych, Weed, & Clarke, 2004). The chapter concludes with future directions for research and policy development.

TABLE 6.1 Selected Areas of Biological Inquiry in Tobacco Use

Area	Terminology	Impact	Contributions to Biological Inquiry
Tobacco ingredients and illustrative additives	Nicotine	Psychoactive and reinforcing pharmacological effects impact addiction	Plasma nicotine levels pre- to post-cigarette indicate level of dosing
	Cotinine	Proximate, inactive metabolite of nicotine. Half-life 18 hour (Benowitz et al., 2002)	Provides data on nicotine exposure for past several days
	Ammonia-related compounds	Increases sensory impact and/or delivery of nicotine to smoker (Henningfield et al., 2004)	In cigarette design, can be used to manipulate nicotine transfer steps
	Gamma-valerolactone	Inhibits CYP2A6, which is involved in metabolism of nicotine and could lead to higher nicotine levels (Rabinoff et al., 2007)	Persons with normal CYP2A6 activity may experience decreased nicotine metabolism with gamma-valerolactone.
	Levulinic acid	Enhances binding of nicotine to nicotinic receptors; increases peak plasma levels; desensitizes upper respiratory tract (Rabinoff et al., 2007; Keithly et al., 2005)	Data on additives by cigarette brand are not known. There are complex interactions of cigarette components.
	Menthol	Stimulates cold receptors yielding cooling sensation; complex interaction with nicotine (Rabinoff et al., 2007)	Menthol cigarette preference is available by self-report. Levels of menthol in various cigarette brands are in literature (Kreslake et al., 2008).

(Continued)

TABLE 6.1 Selected Areas of Biological Inquiry in Tobacco Use (*Continued*)

Area	Terminology	Impact	Contributions to Biological Inquiry
Genetics and tobacco addiction	Family-based genetically informative designs include twin studies	Heritable nicotine dependence phenotype impacts initiation and persistent smoking.	Moderate to high genetic influences on nicotine addiction with estimates from 0.30 to 0.70 (Agrawal et al., 2008).
	Variability in genes that encode nicotinic acetylcholine receptors.		
	CHRNA5-A3-B4 region as risk factor for nicotine addiction (Weiss et al., 2008).	Susceptibility and protective haplotypes at this locus are associated with beginning daily smoking before age 16.	Importance of preventing early exposure to tobacco through public health policies.
	Haplotypes are combinations of several polymorphisms.		
	Two independent variants in this CHRNA5-A3-B4 cluster contribute to development of habitual smoking (Bierut et al., 2008)	Variant is common in populations of European and Middle Eastern descent (rare in African, American, and Asian descent).	May be useful in predicting response to pharmacological smoking cessation therapies.
	Single nucleotide polymorphisms (SNPs) in CHRNB3 (Zeiger et al., 2008)	Associated with early subjective responses to tobacco	Two SNPs significantly related to adverse, and negative and positive physical responses.

Nicotine enhances reward functions in mesocorticolimbic dopamine system. Genes encoding dopamine receptors may be involved in nicotine dependence. SNPs of dopamine D$_3$ receptor gene (DRD3)	Dopamine receptors mediate effects of neurotransmitter dopamine. DRD3 is significantly associated with nicotine dependence in White with a specific polymorphism identified. No significant association in African American sample (Huang et al., 2008).	Further elucidation of environmental and lifestyle factors interaction with genetic variability is needed (Chanock & Hunter, 2008). race-specific association of DRD3 and nicotine dependence may lead to future personalized treatment of nicotine dependence.
CYP2A6 is the main enzyme catalyzing nicotine to cotinine. CYP2A6 polymorphisms generate low to high activity.	Proportion of persons who smoked first cigarette of the day within 5 minutes was significantly higher in high-activity CYP2A6 polymorphism group versus low-activity group (Kubota et al., 2006)	More severe nicotine withdrawal among high-activity group. Consider CYP2A6 genotype as one element of novel pharmacogenomic strategy.
Biomarkers of exposure	See Table 6.2	

BIOMARKERS OF EXPOSURE

With each biomarker of tobacco use exposure, a brief description is provided along with several research exemplars. A summary is presented in Table 6.2 that addresses the source of the biomarker, measurement equipment, typical values, half-life where applicable, and interpretation of results.

Bioconfirmation of Tobacco Use

Markers of bioconfirmation of tobacco use have been used to validate nonsmoking status in tobacco cessation treatment. The demand characteristic to self-report successful cessation is a limitation in intervention trials as participants may overreport cessation. In addition, biomarkers such as carbon monoxide (CO) in exhaled air can be used to raise awareness among smokers and create a teachable moment. For research purposes, quantification of exposure is possible with CO levels pre- and post-cigarette, for example. Levels of cotinine, the proximate metabolite of nicotine, can be assessed at baseline prior to a nicotine replacement therapy intervention and then estimate percentage of nicotine replacement via cotinine concentrations while on pharmacotherapy. A higher percentage of replacement may enhance quitting success.

Carbon Monoxide

Carbon monoxide in exhaled air is a common, noninvasive measure of exposure with CO levels at or above 8 ppm considered smoker status. There is a high correlation between exhaled air CO and carboxyhemoglobin ($r = 0.98$; Jarvis, Tunstall-Pedoe, Feyerabend, Vesey, & Saloojee, 1987). Several devices exist to measure CO in exhaled air (Bedfont Mini and Micro-Smokerlyzer, Innovative Marketing, Medford, NJ; Breath CO carbon monoxide monitor, Vitalograph Lenexa, KS). Carbon monoxide is considered a valid measure of smoking status with sensitivity and specificity to tobacco of 90% (Benowitz et al., 2002). The instrument is calibrated with a 50 ppm CO standard and detects CO from 0 to 500 ppm (Bedfont) and 0 to 199 ppm (Vitalograph). The half-life of CO at 4 hours indicates its validity is limited by the individual's time since last cigarette. A common use of CO measures in clinical studies is the increase in CO from pre- to post-cigarette or CO boost in ppm. In a 6-day Clinical Research Center inpatient study of behavioral smoking compensation, participants experienced three conditions: usual number of cigarettes per day (cpd), restricted to 50% of usual and increased to 150% of usual (Ahijevych et al., 2004). Carbon monoxide boost was a dependent variable. There were significantly larger increases in CO post-cigarette in the restricted condition compared to the other two conditions. Thirty-five percent of the

TABLE 6.2 Methods and Measures of Illustrative Techniques to Assess Tobacco Use Exposure

Biomarker	Source	Measurement	Values	Half-Life	Interpretation
Carbon monoxide	Exhaled air	Bedfont Smokerlyzer; Vitalograph CO monitor	0–500 ppm	4 hours	Cigarette combustion generates CO. Directly affected by time since last cigarette. Higher exposure with increased values. Cardiotoxicity
Cotinine	Saliva, plasma, urine	HPLC, GC-MS	<14 ng/ml = nonsmoker 15 ng/ml = smoker	18 hours	Indicates level of cigarette use in the past 4–7 days.
3'-hydroxy-cotinine	Saliva, plasma, urine	HPLC MS/MS	ng/mL	N/A	Ratio of 3-HC to cotinine is phenotypic measure of CYP2A6 activity. Higher ratio associated with increased craving, lower quit rate in NRT patch treatment. (Lerman et al., 2006) NNAL is a carcinogen.
Tobacco specific nitrosamine: NNAL NNAL glucuronide	Urine, blood	High-performance liquid chromatography electrosprayionization tandem mass (Xia et al., 2005).	µg/g; pmol/mg creatinine	N/A in humans	NNAL glucuronide is less harmful form. NNAL gluc:NNAL indicates ability to detoxify carcinogen

(Continued)

TABLE 6.2 Methods and Measures of Illustrative Techniques to Assess Tobacco Use Exposure (*Continued*)

Biomarker	Source	Measurement	Values	Half-Life	Interpretation
Polycyclic aromatic hydrocarbons (PAH)	Urine, feces	Gas chromatography/isotope dilution high-resolution mass spectrometry (Li et al., 2006)	pg/ml; ng/L	12–15 hours	BAP, a PAH, is related to lung cancer. Large size is typically eliminated in feces, while smaller PAHs are in urine. Hydroxypyrene has been used as a marker of general PAH exposure, although the parent compound is not a carcinogen.
Menthol Menthol glucuronide (MG)	Urine	GC-MS	µg/ml	11.7 min (MG) (Ahijevych & Garrett, 2004)	Quantify menthol exposure beyond type of cigarette.
Smoking topography	Puffing behaviors during smoking	CReSS Technology (Borgwaldt Kc Inc.)	Puff volume (ml) Puff duration, inter-puff interval (msec) Flow rate (ml/sec)	N/A	Individual puffing pattern data enhance interpretation of other biomarkers

Note. High performance liquid chromatography = HPLC; gas chromatography mass spectrometry = GC-MS; tandem mass spectrometry = MS-MS; parts per million = ppm; nanograms per milliliter = ng/ml; micrograms per milliliter = mg/ml; milliseconds = msec.

variance in CO increase was accounted for by ethnicity. Being African American was associated with greater CO percentage increases post-cigarette in the restricted condition (Ahijevych et al., 2004).

Cotinine

Cotinine, the metabolite of nicotine, is frequently used to measure nicotine exposure in research because of its longer half-life of 18 hrs compared to that of nicotine at 2 hrs. There is less variability in cotinine throughout the day (Benowitz et al., 2002). The publication by the Society for Research on Nicotine and Tobacco Subcommittee on Biochemical Verification provides an overview of biochemical markers of tobacco cessation (Benowitz et al., 2002).

Cotinine provides more accurate data on tobacco exposure than CO which has a shorter half-life. Recently, Jarvis, Fidler, Mindell, Feyerabend, and West (2008) examined cotinine cut-points to determine smoking status using a large population survey. A cut-point of 12 ng/ml performed best overall with 96.9% specificity and 96.7% sensitivity to discriminate current smokers from nonsmokers. This is slightly lower than the previous cut-point of 15 ng/ml since there have been declines in environmental tobacco exposures. To determine smoking abstinence when the participant is not using nicotine replacement therapy (NRT), cotinine is the measure of choice. However, in the presence of NRT, CO is the best practice to readily assess smoking abstinence.

Beyond confirming smoking abstinence, quantification of cotinine is useful in understanding tobacco exposure. In a sample of 142 African American women, cotinine concentrations averaged 392 ng/ml (med = 384 ng/ml), with average cotinine in menthol smokers at 394 ng/ml compared to nonmenthol smokers at 369 ng/ml (Ahijevych & Wewers, 1994). African American smokers have higher average cotinine levels, although they smoke fewer cigarettes per day on average than White smokers. Perez-Stable, Marin, Marin, Brody, and Benowitz (1990) estimated nicotine exposure was dividing cotinine concentration by number of self-reported cigarettes per day with higher values indicating a maximization of intake with each cigarette. In their African American sample, the cotinine–cigarette value was 37.6 ng/ml/ cigarette on average, which was higher than that reported for Mexican American women. In the previously described compensation study, the cotinine per cigarette ratio in the restricted cpd condition was 31.9 ng/ml/cigarette and significantly higher than in the other two conditions (Ahijevych et al., 2004). These data indicate increased tobacco exposure per cigarette in the restricted condition, which simulates financial constraints of lower cigarette availability. And, finally, Wood et al. (2004) reported baseline plasma cotinine concentrations among adolescent smokers averaged 224 ng/ml (med = 159 ng/ml) and a plasma nicotine boost cpd of 23.4 ng/ml. These levels are higher than previously reported in adolescent samples and indicate considerable tobacco exposure in adolescents beyond that of occasional cigarette smoking.

While nicotine is metabolized to cotinine, cotinine is metabolized to 3'hydroxycotinine (3-HC). The ratio of 3-HC to cotinine is an indicator of the rate of nicotine metabolism. More rapid metabolism of nicotine may result in lower nicotine blood concentrations from NRT and lower smoking cessation rates (Lerman et al., 2006). In a trial of transdermal NRT, odds of abstinence were reduced by almost 30% with each increasing quartile of 3-HC/cotinine ratio, indicative of more rapid nicotine metabolism and lower circulating nicotine concentrations. More severe cravings occurred with higher ratios. This ratio may be useful in screening smokers to determine potential success with a standard dose of transdermal nicotine (Lerman et al., 2006).

Smoking Topography

The way an individual smokes a cigarette is unique to each smoker. Two individuals may smoke the same cigarette brand, but extract different levels of nicotine and carbon monoxide that is related to smoking topography (Ahijevych & Gillespie, 1997). Topography in general refers to variation in terrain. Graphic representation of a puff on the computer screen resembles this variation in peaks and valleys. Figure 6.1 illustrates smoking topography equipment and the graphic of a single puff. Puffing behavior is an important variable to measure when describing tobacco use exposure and includes discrete markers of the volume of each puff (ml), its duration (msec), interpuff interval between puffs (msec), and maximum puff velocity (ml/sec). The number of puffs per cigarette and time to smoke a cigarette are generated to describe the overall puffing pattern for a given cigarette. These variables are obtained using the Clinical Research Support System (CReSS) originally designed by PlowShare Technologies and now available through Borgwaldt Kc Inc. (Richmond, Virginia). Briefly, the cigarette is placed in a small holder and the individual smokes through the mouthpiece. A differential pressure transducer is used to detect measures of flow from two ports that have a short distance between them from which software then creates data for puffing behavior variables. The equipment is available in a desk model for stationary situations and a portable model for use in the natural environment with storage and download capabilities. Reliability and validity of smoking topography variables have been analyzed comparing conventional smoking with the cigarette on the lips and smoking through a topography mouthpiece (Lee, Malson, Waters, Moolchan, & Pickworth, 2003). Reliability was assessed with participants smoking their usual cigarette brand through the topography mouthpiece on four consecutive sessions. Validity was examined when participants smoked their usual cigarette brand on two separate days, once through the mouthpiece and once conventionally (holding the cigarette with their fingers and placing it on their lips). Dependent variables of plasma for nicotine analysis, blood pressure, and heart rate were obtained before smoking a cigarette and 2, 5, 10, 15, 30, and 60 minutes after smoking a single cigarette. Exhaled carbon monoxide (CO) was measured 15, 30, and 60 minutes after the cigarette. Intraclass correlation coefficients were 0.66 for puff volume and 0.75 for puff duration. Within subject differences across the 4 days were small and accounted for less than 7% of variance in any variable. There were no significant differences across time for cardiovascular measures or CO increases postcigarette. Validity was supported with no significant differences within subject across the two conditions.

Topography was employed in a descriptive study of adolescent and tobacco use exposure (Wood et al., 2004) with a reported average puff volume of 42.2 ml and puff duration of 1.16 seconds. Maximum puff duration predicted 11.1% of baseline cotinine concentration in adolescents ($N = 50$). Franken, Pickworth, Epstein, and Moolchan (2006) identified that higher baseline puff volume and cpd predicted being a smoker at 3 months after treatment in adolescent participants in a nicotine replacement therapy (NRT) trial ($N = 66$). Similarly, Strasser, Pickworth, Patterson, and Lerman (2004) identified average puff volume and interpuff interval as significant predictors of abstinence among 113 adults in a NRT trial. Smaller puff volume and longer interpuff interval were associated with greater odds of smoking abstinence. In a study evaluating filter vent blocking, larger puff volume and longer puff duration were positively associated with greater CO boost (Strasser, Ashare, Kozlowski, & Pickworth, 2005). In the previously cited smoking compensation study, puff volume per cigarette was higher in the usual and

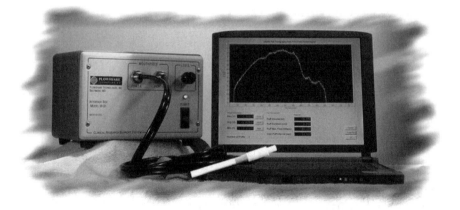

FIGURE 6.1 Smoking topography graphic representation of a puff.

Note. Retrieved from http://www.plowshare.com/products/lab/index.html. Reprinted with permission.

restricted cpd conditions compared to those in the increased cpd condition. In the restricted condition there was a significantly shorter butt length remaining, another compensation behavior of smoking more of the cigarette rod (Ahijevych et al., 2004). Strasser, Malaiyandi, Hoffman, Tyndale, and Lerman (2007) reported an effect of CYP2A6 phenotype (slow, intermediate, and normal nicotine metabolizers) on mean and total puff volume. Slow metabolizers exhibited smaller average puff volumes than normal and intermediate metabolizers indicating puffing compensation for circulating nicotine concentrations. In another exemplar, topography was used to compare puffing behaviors between Marlboro Lights, Marlboro Ultralights, and Marlboro UltraSmooth (MUS), a potential reduced exposure product (PREP; Rees, Wayne, & Connolly, 2008). The MUS was modified incorporating activated carbon in the filter. Puff volume was significantly higher in the PREP condition compared to the other two brands. Therefore, it is unlikely in the short-term that this type of PREP product will reduce exposure among smokers who switch from a conventional brand. In summary, smoking topography variables provide increased understanding of unique behaviors influencing tobacco use exposure.

TOBACCO CONTENTS

Tobacco-specific nitrosamines and polycyclic aromatic hydrocarbons are two components of cigarettes that impact health. Additives to tobacco products affect nicotine delivery and sensory responses, with menthol being an additive that is used by the tobacco industry to promote cigarettes.

Tobacco-Specific Nitrosamines

Tobacco-specific nitrosamines (TSNAs), a group of carcinogens present in tobacco, are formed from tobacco alkaloids during the curing and processing of tobacco. The most carcinogenic of the commonly occurring TSNAs is 4-(methylnitrosamino)-1-(3-pyridyl)-1-butanone (NNK) and is associated with lung and pancreatic cancer and a potential role in oral cancer from smokeless tobacco products (Stepanov & Hecht, 2005). Specific urinary biomarkers of NNK uptake by humans include NNAL (4-(methylnitrosamino)-1-(3-pyridyl)-1-butanol) and NNAL glucuronides, the detoxified form (Hecht, 2002). The ratio of NNAL glucuronide to NNAL is an indicator of increased health risk when NNAL glucuronide is proportionally lower than NNAL, the carcinogen. This ratio can be used to identify slow and rapid glucuronidation phenotypes. Muscat, Djordjevic, Colosimo, Stellman, and Richie (2005) reported a higher proportion of White versus Black women who were categorized as "rapid" glucuronidators. There were higher concentrations of NNAL and cotinine in Black men compared to White men, but no significant differences by NNAL glucuronide: NNAL phenotype. While reducing the number of cpd is one smoking cessation strategy, it was reported that smokers who significantly reduced their number of cigarettes per day experienced a four- to eightfold increased exposure to NNK per cigarette (Hatsukami et al., 2006). Compensatory smoking behaviors countered the harm reduction value of decreasing the number of cpd.

The interaction of menthol cigarettes and TSNA exposure was examined in a sample of 147 participants noting no significant differences in TSNA biomarkers by menthol or nonmenthol cigarette smokers (Muscat et al., 2009). It was noted however that participants with a shorter time to first cigarette had higher TSNA biomarkers. In *in vitro* studies, menthol inhibited the glucuronidation of NNAL and thus might inhibit detoxification of NNAL, a potent lung carcinogen (Muscat et al., 2009). Menthol content of cigarettes has been manipulated by tobacco manufacturers (Kreslake, Wayne, Hillel, & Koh, 2008) and thus varies by cigarette brand. Categorizing participants as menthol and nonmenthol smokers may not capture the variability of menthol exposure. In a 36 hour inpatient research protocol, 24 hour urine samples were collected from 136 participants representing African American and White and menthol and nonmenthol cigarette smokers balanced by race (Ahijevych, Buckley, Weed, Bernert, & Sjodin, 2009). There was a significant positive correlation of total menthol (free + glucuronide forms) to free NNAL ($r = 0.476$, $p < .001$), controlling for race. Men had significantly higher NNAL glucuronide to NNAL ratios than women indicating more detoxification of NNAL among men. Twenty-seven percent of variance in NNAL was explained by total menthol concentration (18.6%) and race (8.4%), $p < .001$. This indicates that higher NNAL is correlated with higher menthol concentrations and African American race. Interestingly, there were no differences in the NNAL glucuronide to NNAL ratio by the type of cigarette (menthol/nonmenthol). Measurement and quantification of menthol exposure is more explanatory of biomarker exposure compared to dichotomous self-reported menthol or nonmenthol cigarette use (Ahijevych et al., 2009).

The TSNA biomarkers have also been used to examine exposure with smokeless tobacco products and sidestream cigarette smoke in the environment. Moist snuff is the leading type of smokeless tobacco in the United States and can lead to nicotine addiction. The Centers for Disease Control and Prevention (CDC) analyzed the top 40 selling moist snuff brands for levels of TSNAs as well as nicotine and pH (Richter, Hodge, Stanfill, Zhang, & Watson, 2008). There was an 18-fold range of carcinogenic TSNAs across the various brands. The current promotion of smokeless tobacco as a harm-reduction product is therefore a concern.

Smokeless tobacco products as a substitute for cigarettes have been receiving more attention by public health and the tobacco industry (Hatsukami, Ebbert, Feuer, Stepanov, & Hecht, 2007). In the public health community some consider this a harm-reduction option, although this is greatly debated. While medicinal nicotine products are potential reduced exposure products (PREPs), smokeless to-bacco products have increasing support as PREPs in areas such as Sweden (Hatsukami et al., 2007). One strategy to assess harm reduction, is to determine the amount of TSNA in these products. The total TSNA ranged from 0.002 mg/g product weight in Nicorette gum to 9.2 mg/g in Skoal Long cut straight (Hatsukami et al., 2007). Levels of total TSNAs were highest in the most popular tobacco products in the United States (Copenhagen and Skoal). While there may be lower toxicant exposure with smokeless tobacco than cigarette smoking, oral tobacco is addictive and not safe (Hatsukami et al., 2007). In the CDC analysis of the 40 top-selling brands of moist snuff, TSNA's ranged from 4.87 mg/g to 90.02 mg/g and flavored low-priced brands were significantly correlated with total TSNAs and carcino-genic TSNAs. Promotion of smokeless tobacco for use in places where smoking is prohibited, as well as a harm-reduction product and the highly flavored smoke-less varieties warrant further study of tobacco constituent exposure (Richter et al., 2008).

Research on tobacco-specific nitrosamines in environmental tobacco or sec-ondhand smoke exposure was identified in the internal tobacco industry documents now available (Schick & Glantz, 2007). The NNK, a highly carcinogenic TSNA, can form in sidestream cigarette smoke after it has been released into the air. Philip Morris conducted these experiments between 1983 and 1997 according to the inter-nal documents. To illustrate, in an enclosed chamber, airborne NNK concentra-tions in sidestream smoke increased by 46% to 205% per hour during the first hour after the cigarettes had been extinguished. NNK formation in aging environmen-tal smoke may contribute to nitrosamine exposure in humans.

Polycyclic Aromatic Hydrocarbons

Polycyclic aromatic hydrocarbons (PAH) are formed during incomplete combus-tion of organic materials and are found in automobile exhaust, wood smoke, grilled food, and cigarette smoke (Li et al., 2006). The PAHs have carcinogenic and muta-genic potential and possess reproductive, developmental, hemato-, cardio-, neuro-, and immunotoxicities (Agency for Toxic Substances and Disease Registry [ATSDR], 1995). Documented toxicity has led to 16 PAHs being included on the Environmental Protection Agency's list of hazardous air pollutants. As an example, the PAH benzo(a)pyrene (BAP) is positively associated with lung cancer (Li et al., 2006).

Phase I metabolism of PAHs yields hydroxylated derivatives (OH-PAH) that have a urinary elimination half-life of 12 to 15 hours. Although its parent compound is not carcinogenic, 1-hydroxypyrene is the most commonly used indicator in bio-monitoring PAH exposure. Larger PAHs such as BAP are excreted primarily in feces, while smaller PAHs are excreted in urine (Li et al., 2006).

Melikian and colleagues (2007) measured mainstream smoke emissions of BAP using each participant's individual smoking topography parameters to generate mainstream smoke via a smoking machine. They identified a higher BAP level in men compared to women (20.5 ng/cigarette vs. 18 ng/ cigarette, respectively), although women's topography pattern yielded significantly higher NNK emissions per cigarette. In the Ahijevych et al. (2009) 36 hour inpatient research study, 10 PAH metabolites were correlated with each other ranging from $r = 0.58$ to 0.90. Nine of 10 PAH's were positively correlated with total menthol concentration, controlling for race. Similar to the relationship with NNAL, total menthol concentration was correlated with nine PAH metabolites, while menthol–nonmenthol cigarette type was not correlated with any PAH metabolites.

Additives

Of the 599 documented cigarette additives, more than 100 have pharmacological actions that maintain or enhance nicotine delivery, mask symptoms and illnesses associated with smoking behaviors, or camouflage the odor of environmental cigarette smoke (Rabinoff, Caskey, Rissling, & Park, 2007). It is not known if such uses were specifically intended for these agents. Few additives were used in cigarettes by the tobacco industry before 1970 in the United States. The most recent public list of additives provided by the industry was in 1994. About 10% of cigarette weight is additives such as sugars, humectants, ammonia compounds, and cocoa (Keithly, Wayne, Cullen, & Connolly, 2005). Additives such as gamma-valerolactone are mild to weak inhibitors of CYP2A6 involved in nicotine metabolism and could slow nicotine degradation, thus maintaining nicotine concentrations (Rabinoff et al., 2007). In adolescent rats, there was enhanced nicotine self-administration with acetaldehyde, a major component of tobacco smoke when cigarette constituents including sugars are burned (Belluzzi, Wang, & Leslie, 2005). The youngest animals responded significantly more for nicotine plus acetaldehyde than for either drug alone or saline. Further testing identified the drug effects were mediated by central, rather than peripheral nicotine receptors. Tobacco industry data generated in 1974 identified that the combination of sugar, sorbitol, and diammonium phosphate increases nicotine and tar levels and number of puffs taken (Rabinoff et al., 2007). The addition of ammonia or ammonia-precursor compounds has an effect in tobacco and tobacco smoke on converting protonated nicotine to unprotonated (free-base) nicotine increasing the transfer of nicotine from the cigarette to mainstream smoke (Henningfield, Pankow, & Garrett, 2004). Further, the tobacco industry documents indicate that boosting free nicotine levels in smoke by base addition leads to a greater impact or "kick" (Henningfield et al., 2004).

In the tobacco industry monograph on additives, levulinic acid is identified as a flavorant because of its sweet caramel taste and body (Leffingwell, Young, &

Bernasek, 1972). However, internal industry projects indicated that levulinic acid was used by manufacturers to improve sensory character of smoke, such as smoothness, to raise nicotine delivery, and to increase nicotine receptor binding (Keithly et al., 2005).

Menthol

Menthol as a tobacco additive is promoted and advertised by the tobacco industry. While overall cigarette sales decreased 22% from 2000 to 2005, menthol cigarette sales remained stable (Kreslake et al., 2008). Properties of menthol include cooling and local anesthesia that may reduce the perception of harshness in cigarette smoking and permit greater inhalation of cigarette smoke (Ahijevych & Garrett, 2004). Transdermal and transbuccal permeability of drugs was increased by menthol, while menthol demonstrated surfactant qualities in lowering surface tension *in vitro* (Zanker, Tolle, Blumel, & Probst, 1980) and reduced cilia beat frequency (Riechelmann, Brommer, Hinni, & Martin, 1997). Celebucki, Wayne, Connolly, Pankow, and Chang (2005) determined menthol content of 48 cigarette subbrands and concluded that menthol per unburned cigarette in milligrams and milligrams of menthol per gram of tobacco filler (mg/g) were significantly greater in cigarettes labeled as ultralight or light. This suggests that menthol may be used to offset reductions in smoke delivery or impact and facilitate compensatory smoking behaviors.

In the Ahijevych et al. (2009) 36 hour inpatient research study, total urinary menthol concentrations in a 24 hour sample were 0.37 ug/ml in nonmenthol smokers with a median of 0.27 ug/ml and maximum of 2.2 ug/ml. In menthol smokers, the average total menthol concentration was 2.56 ug/ml with a median of 1.9 and a maximum of 10.0 ug/ml. Time to first cigarette of the day, an indicator of dependence, was significantly and inversely related to menthol concentration. In addition, menthol concentration explained 18.6% of the variance in NNAL, a carcinogen.

Kreslake and colleagues (2008) analyzed data from tobacco industry documents related to menthol product development and marketing reports. Cigarettes with lower menthol levels appealed to young smokers, while higher menthol levels and stronger perceived menthol sensations were selected by long-term smokers, according to tobacco industry documents. "Mild" descriptors may be used in marketing to indicate menthol level or flavor intensity (Kreslake et al., 2008). Menthol as a percentage of tobacco weight was measured with levels ranging from 0.32% (Newport) to 0.63% (Kool Milds) in cigarettes manufactured in 2007 (Kreslake et al., 2008). Manipulation of sensory elements of cigarettes has been done to promote smoking initiation and dependence. Cigarette additives, such as menthol, should be included in federal regulations of tobacco products.

GENETICS AND TOBACCO ADDICTION

Common complex conditions such as tobacco addiction often represent a gene-environment interaction for their development (Workman & Winkelman, 2008). An imbalance of genetic susceptibility and resistance and environmental susceptibility and resistance would increase personal risk for a specific condition. The substantial impact of genetic factors on smoking behavior has led to molecular genetic research of this complex trait (Sullivan & Kendler, 1999).

Twin Study Design and Genetic Influence

The classical twin study design includes data from monozygotic (MZ, identical) and dizygotic (DZ, fraternal) twin pairs, reared together, to examine the role of genetic and environmental influences on a behavior or outcome (Agrawal & Lynskey, 2008). The MZ twin pairs on average share 100% of genetic influences, while the DZ twin pairs share 50% of their additive genetic influences. Environment is considered to overlap in both types of twin pairs. Heritability was determined to account for 50%–70% of the total variance in persistent smoking (Agrawal & Lynskey, 2008). A genotype by environment interaction was noted in a sample of 14-year-old twins where there was an increase in heritability of experimentation with cigarettes when more time was spent with parents. The reverse occurred with decreased heritability of cigarette experimentation as parental supervision decreased (Dick, Rose, Viken, Kapiro, & Koskenvuo, 2007). Kendler, Schmitt, Aggen, and Prescott (2008) identified a model in an adult male twin study where initiation and early patterns of substance use were strongly influenced by familial and social environmental factors, while later levels of substance use were strongly influenced by genetic factors.

Nicotinic Receptors

Nicotine acts as an antagonist at brain nicotinic receptors with acetylcholine as the neurotransmitter (Berrettini, 2008). Genetic factors that alter susceptibility to nicotine addiction include genes that encode nicotinic acetylcholine receptor (nAChR) proteins (Portugal & Gould, 2008). While nicotine dependence is a complex phenomenon modulated by numerous genes, understanding how nAChR influences nicotine sensitivity may lead to development of more effective treatment of nicotine dependence. Bierut et al. (2008) examined the role of genetic variation in the nicotinic cholinergic receptor cluster (CHRNA5-CHRNA3-CHRNB4) with smoking and identified at least two independent genetic variants in the cluster. One variant common in populations of European and Middle Eastern descent increased the risk of transitioning from nondependent to dependent smoking. This variant was rare in populations of African, American, and Asian descent. Pharmacogenetic response to nicotine is illustrated in these findings, which may be useful in predicting response to medications such as varenicline and nicotine replacement therapy.

Weiss et al. (2008) identified age-dependent nicotine addiction susceptibility and protective haplotypes in the CHRNA5-A3-B4 cluster. Persons who began daily smoking at or before 16 years of age and who possessed a susceptibility variant resulted in a more severe form of adult nicotine dependence, than those who began smoking after 16 years of age. This reinforces the importance of public health policies to prevent early exposure to tobacco.

CYP2A6 Polymorphisms

Nicotine disposition is depicted in Figure 6.2. Approximately 70%–80% of nicotine from cigarette smoking is metabolically inactivated to cotinine and CYP2A6 accounts for about 90% of this conversion (Messina, Tyndale, & Sellers, 1997). Cotinine, in turn, is oxidized to form trans-3'-hydroxycotinine (3-HC), a process almost entirely catalyzed by CYP2A6 (Dempsey et al., 2004). Interindividual variations in nicotine metabolism are at least partially related to CYP2A6 gene polymorphisms (Kubota et al., 2006). Variations of CYP2A6 gene have been grouped as high activity and low activity. Compared to the low-activity group, the high-activity group smoked their first cigarette of the day earlier and experienced more severe withdrawal symptoms in cessation, indicating more marked nicotine addiction. More rapid metabolism of nicotine in the high-activity group may guide individualization of pharmacotherapy including nicotine replacement in smoking cessation.

Dopamine Receptor Genes

Nicotine activates the ascending dopaminergic neurons yielding increased dopamine levels in the nucleus accumbens (Huang, Payne, Ma, & Li, 2008). The dopaminergic reward pathway has been implicated in the development of nicotine addiction and thus study of variations in genes with dopaminergic function are of interest. For example, the gene DRD3 that encodes the D3 receptor and its association with nicotine dependence was examined in the Mid-South Tobacco Family Cohort (Huang et al., 2008). The DRD3 was significantly associated with nicotine dependence in Whites with a likely polymorphism identified. The association was not present in African Americans in the sample.

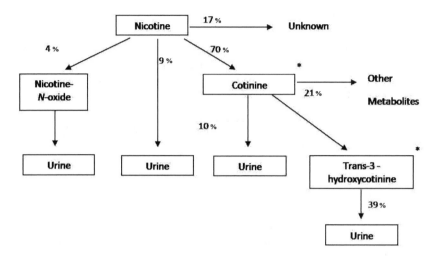

FIGURE 6.2   CYP2A6 action in the disposition of nicotine and cotinine.

*Indicates CYP2A6 activity. Adapted from Benowitz, N. L., Porchet, H., & Jacob, P., III., *Nicotine Psychopharmacology: Molecular, Cellular, and Behavioural Aspects*, Oxford University Press, Oxford, 1990.

FUTURE POLICY ISSUES AND RESEARCH DIRECTION

Key issues in biological research related to tobacco use include surveillance of cigarette smoke constituents over time, integration of genetic and biological factors in treatment of nicotine dependence, and incorporation of biomarkers with intervention research. Expanding the number of nurse scientists educated in tobacco-related research is vital to demonstrate their significant contribution to this multidisciplinary field.

Stellman & Djordjevic (2008) published a report of the Agent Working Group recommending systematic surveillance of mainstream smoke constituents such as PAH, TSNA, total and free-base nicotine, volatile organic compounds, and aromatic amines, as well as cigarette design elements of tobacco blend, additives, and filter ventilation. This is in contrast to the current FTC systematic monitoring of only tar, nicotine, and carbon monoxide in mainstream smoke generated by a smoking machine protocol not reflective of human smoking patterns. Smokeless tobacco products have not been regularly monitored, nor have potential reduced-exposure products (PREPs). The Working Group also recommended population monitoring of smoking topography, emissions of toxic constituents, and biomarkers of exposure. Implementation of these recommendations could provide a scientific basis for more extensive regulatory proposals. Significant progress in this area occurred in June 2009 when Congress passed the Family Smoking Prevention and Tobacco Control Act (H.R. 1256) giving the U.S. Food and Drug Administration (FDA) authority to regulate tobacco products including mandating changes in tobacco products, such as the reduction of harmful ingredients. This is a major step in the effort to begin to address cigarette and smokeless tobacco constituent exposures. Research to determine changes in tobacco use exposures as a result of this legislation over time will be invaluable.

Education of nurse researchers with expertise in tobacco-related biomarkers, genetics, and associated laboratory skills needs to be expanded as there is currently a limited cadre of nurse scientists in this arena. Nurse researchers leading and participating in multidisciplinary teams enrich research design, implementation, and translational application of findings in this significant health risk area of tobacco use. With the funding of 39 Clinical Translational Science Awards (CTSA) in the United States since 2006, multidisciplinary research teams are being facilitated within and across the consortium of centers. The CTSAs can provide an environment and mentorship of nurse scientists in their doctoral and postdoctoral work, and beyond (CTSAweb.org). This is an opportune time to be involved in research that has the potential to impact a serious, far-reaching health issue.

ACKNOWLEDGMENT

Partial funding support was provided by the National Institute of Drug Abuse grants R01 DA017313 and R21 DA024765; NCRR M01-RR00034.

REFERENCES

Agency for Toxic Substances and Disease Registry (ATSDR). (1995). *Toxicological profile for polycyclic aromatic hydrocarbons*. Atlanta, GA: Author.

Agrawal, A., & Lynskey, M. T. (2008). Are there genetic influences on addiction: Evidence from family, adoption and twin studies. *Addiction, 103*, 1069–1081.

Ahijevych, K., Buckley, T., Weed, T., Bernert, J. T., & Sjodin, A. (2009, April). *Relationship of menthol and race with tobacco specific nitrosamine and PAH metabolites*. Proceedings of 2009 Conference of Society for Research on Nicotine and Tobacco, Dublin, Ireland, POS4–69.

Ahijevych, K., & Garrett, B. (2004). Menthol pharmacology and its potential impact on cigarette smoking behavior. *Nicotine & Tobacco Research, 6*, S17–S28.

Ahijevych, K., & Gillespie, J. (1997). Nicotine dependence and smoking topography among black and white women. *Research in Nursing and Health, 20*, 505–514.

Ahijevych, K., Weed, H., & Clarke, J. (2004). Levels of cigarette availability and exposure in black and white women and efficient smokers. *Pharmacology, Biochemistry & Behavior, 77*, 685–693.

Ahijevych, K. L., & Wewers, M. E. (1994). Patterns of cigarette consumption and cotinine levels among African American women smokers. *American Journal of Respiratory & Critical Care Medicine, 150,* 1229–1233.

Belluzzi, J. D., Wang, R., & Leslie, F. M. (2005). Acetaldehyde enhances acquisition of nicotine self-administration in adolescent rats. *Neuropsychopharmacology, 30,* 705–712.

Benowitz, N. L., Jacob, P., III, Ahijevych, K., Jarvis, M. J., Hall, S., LeHouezec, J., et al. (2002). Biochemical verification of tobacco use and cessation. *Nicotine & Tobacco Research, 4,* 149–159.

Benowitz, N. L., Porchet, H., & Jacob, P., III. (1990). Pharmacokinetics, metabolism, and pharmacodynamics of nicotine. In S. Wonnacott, M. A. H. Russell, I. P. Stolerman (Eds.), *Nicotine psychopharmacology: Molecular, cellular, and behavioural aspects.* Oxford: Oxford University Press.

Berrettini, W. (2008). Nicotine addiction: Editorial. *American Journal of Psychiatry, 165,* 1089–1092.

Bierut, L. J., Stitzel, J. A., Wang, J. C., Hinrichs, A. L., Grucza, R. A., Xuei, X., et al. (2008). Variants in nicotinic receptors and risk for nicotine dependence. *American Journal of Psychiatry, 165,* 1163–1171.

Celebucki, C. C., Wayne, G. F., Connolly, G. N., Pankow, J. F., & Chang, E. I. (2005). Characterization of measured menthol in 48 U.S. cigarette sub-brands. *Nicotine & Tobacco Research, 7,* 523–531.

Chanock, S. F., & Hunter, D. J. (2008). When the smoke clears . . . *Nature, 452,* 537–538.

Dempsey, D., Tutka, P., Jacob, P., III, Allen, F., Schoedel, K., Tyndale, R. F. et al. (2004). Nicotine metabolite ratio as an index of cytochrome P450 2A6 metabolic activity. *Clinical Pharmacological Therapeutics, 76,* 64–72.

Dick, D. M., Rose, R. J., Viken, R. J., Kapiro, J., & Koskenvuo, M. (2007). Parental monitoring moderates the importance of genetic and environmental influences on adolescent smoking. *Journal of Abnormal Psychology, 116,* 213–218.

Franken, F. H., Pickworth, W. B., Epstein, D. H., & Moolchan, E. T. (2006). Smoking rates and topography predict adolescent smoking cessation following treatment with nicotine replacement therapy. *Cancer Epidemiology, Biomarkers & Prevention, 15,* 154–157.

Hatsukami, D. K., Ebbert, J. O., Feuer, R. M., Stepanov, I., & Hecht, S. S. (2007). Changing smokeless tobacco products: New tobacco-delivery systems. *American Journal of Preventive Medicine,* S368–S378.

Hatsukami, D. K., Le, C. T., Shang, Y., Joseph, A. M., Mooney, M. E., Carmella, S. G., et al. (2006). Toxicant exposure in cigarette reducers versus light smokers. *Cancer Epidemiology Biomarkers, 15,* 2355–2358.

Hecht, S. S. (2002). Human urinary carcinogen metabolites: Biomarkers for investigating tobacco and cancer. *Carcinogenesis, 23,* 907–922.

Henningfield, J. E., Pankow, J. F., & Garrett, B. E. (2004). Ammonia and other chemical base tobacco additives and cigarette nicotine delivery: Issues and research needs. *Nicotine & Tobacco Research, 6,* 199–205.

Huang, W., Payne, T. J., Ma, J. Z., & Li, M. D. (2008). A functional polymorphism, rs6280, in DRD3 is significantly associated with nicotine dependence in European-American smokers. *American Journal of Medical Genetics Part B, 147B,* 1109–1115.

Jarvis, M. J., Fidler, J., Mindell, J., Feyerabend, C., & West, R. (2008). Assessing smoking status in children, adolescents, and adults: Cotinine cut-points revisited. *Addiction, 103,* 1553–1561.

Jarvis, M. J., Tunstall-Pedoe, H., Feyerabend, C., Vesey, C., & Saloojee, Y. (1987). Comparison of tests used to distinguish smokers from nonsmokers. *American Journal of Public Health, 77,* 1435–1438.

Keithly, L., Wayne, G. F., Cullen, D. M., & Connolly, G. N. (2005). Industry research on the use of and effects of levulinic acid: A case study in cigarette additives. *Nicotine & Tobacco Research, 7,* 761–771.

Kendler, K. S., Schmitt, E., Aggen, S. H., & Prescott, C. A. (2008). Genetic and environmental influences on alcohol, caffeine, cannabis, and nicotine use from early adolescence to middle adulthood. *Archives of General Psychiatry, 65,* 674–682.

Kreslake, J. M., Wayne, G. F., Hillel, R. A., & Koh, H. K. (2008). Tobacco industry control of menthol in cigarettes and targeting of adolescents and young adults. *American Journal of Public Health, 98,* 1–8.

Kubota, T., Nakajima-Tabniguchi, C., Fukuda, T., Funamoto, M., Maeda, M., Tange, E., et al. (2006). CYP2A6 polymorphisms are associated with nicotine dependence and influence withdrawal symptoms in smoking cessation. *The Pharmacogenomics Journal, 6,* 115–119.

Lee, E. M., Malson, J. L., Waters, A. J., Moolchan, E. T., & Pickworth, W. B. (2003). Smoking topography: Reliability and validity in dependent smokers. *Nicotine & Tobacco Research, 5,* 673–679.

Leffingwell, J. C., Young, H. F., & Bernasek, E. (1972). *Tobacco flavoring for smoking products.* Winston-Salem, NC: R.J. Reynolds Tobacco Company.

Lerman, C., Tyndale, R., Patterson, F., Wiley, E. P., Shields, P. G., Pinto, A., et al. (2006). Nicotine metabolite ratio predicts efficacy of transdermal nicotine for smoking cessation. *Clinical Pharmacology and Therapeutics, 79,* 600–608.

Li, Z., Romanoff, L. C., Trinidad, D. A., Hussain, N., Jones, R. S., Porter, E. N., et al. (2006). Measurement of urinary monohydroxy polycyclic aromatic hydrocarbons using automated liquid-liquid extraction and gas chromatography/isotope dilution high-resolution mass spectrometry. *Analytical Chemistry, 78,* 5744–5751.

Melikian, A. A., Djordjevic, M. V., Hosey, J., Zhang, J., Chen, S., Zang, E., et al. (2007). Gender differences relative to smoking behavior and emissions of toxins from mainstream cigarette smoke. *Nicotine & Tobacco Research, 9,* 377–387.

Messina, E. S. Tyndale, R. F., & Sellers, E. M. (1997). A major role for CYP2A6 in nicotine C-oxidation by human liver microsomes. *Journal of Experimental Therapeutics, 282,* 1608–1614.

Muscat, J. E., Chen, G., Knipe, A., Stellman, S. D., Lazarus, P., & Richie, J. P., Jr. (2009). Effects of menthol on tobacco smoke exposure, nicotine dependence, and NNAL glucuronidation. *Cancer Epidemiology Biomarkers and Prevention, 18,* 35–41.

Muscat, J. E., Djordjevic, M. V., Colosimo, S., Stellman, S. D., & Richie, J. P., Jr. (2005). Racial differences in exposure and glucuronidation of the tobacco-specific carcinogen 4-(methylnitrosamino)-1-(3-ypridyl)-1-butanone (NNK). *Cancer, 103,* 1420–1426.

Perez-Stable, E., Marin, B., Marin, G., Brody, D., & Benowitz, N. (1990). Apparent underreporting of cigarette consumption among Mexican American smokers. *American Journal of Public Health, 80,* 1057–1061.

Portugal, G. S., & Gould, T. J. (2008). Genetic variability in nicotinic acetylcholine receptors and nicotine addiction: Converging evidence from human and animal research. *Behavioural Brain Research, 193*, 1–16.

Rabinoff, M., Caskey, N., Rissling, A., & Park, C. (2007). Pharmacological and chemical effects of cigarette additives. *American Journal of Public Health, 97*, 1981–1991.

Rees, V. W., Wayne, G. F., & Connolly, G. N. (2008). Puffing style and human exposure minimally altered switching to a carbon-filtered cigarette. *Cancer Epidemiology, Biomarkers & Prevention, 17*, 2995–3003.

Richter, P., Hodge, K., Stanfill, S., Zhang, L., & Watson, C. (2008). Surveillance of moist snuff: Total nicotine, moisture, pH, un-ionized nicotine, and tobacco-specific nitrosamines. *Nicotine & Tobacco Research, 10*, 1645–1652.

Riechelmann, H., Brommer, C., Hinni, M., & Martin, C. (1997). Response of human ciliated respiratory cells to a mixture of menthol, eucalyptus oil and pine needle oil. *Arzneimittell Forschung, 47*, 1035–1039.

Schick, S. F., & Glantz, S. (2007). Concentrations of the carcinogen 4-(methylnitorsamino)-1-(3-pyridyl)-1-butanone in sidestream cigarette smoke increase after release into indoor air: Results from unpublished tobacco industry research. *Cancer Epidemiology Biomarkers and Prevention, 16*, 1547–1543.

Stellman, S., & Djordjevic, M. V. (2008). Monitoring the tobacco use epidemic II. The agent: Current and emerging tobacco products. *Preventive Medicine.* doi: 10.1016/j.ypme.2008.09.004

Stepanov, I., & Hecht, S. S. (2005). Tobacco-specific nitrosamines and their pyridne-N-glucuronides in the urine of smokers and smokeless tobacco users. *Cancer Epidemiology Biomarkers and Prevention, 14*, 885–891.

Strasser, A. A., Ashare, R. L., Kozlowski, L. T., & Pickworth, W. B. (2005). The effect of filter vent blocking and smoking topography on carbon monoxide levels in smokers. *Pharmacology, Biochemistry & Behavior, 82*, 320–329.

Strasser, A. A., Malaiyandi, V., Hoffman, E., Tyndale, R., & Lerman, C. (2007). An association of CYP2A6 genotype and smoking topography. *Nicotine & Tobacco Research, 9*, 511–518.

Strasser, A. A., Pickworth, W. B., Patterson, F., & Lerman. C. (2004). Smoking topography predicts abstinence following treatment with nicotine replacement therapy. *Cancer Epidemiology, Biomarkers & Prevention, 13*, 1800–1804.

Sullivan, P. F., & Kendler, K. S. (1999). The genetic epidemiology of smoking. *Nicotine & Tobacco Research, 1*, S51–S57.

Weiss, R. B., Baker, T. B., Cannon, D. S., von Niederhausern, A., Dunn, D. M., Matsunami, N., et al. (2008). A candidate gene approach identifies the CHRNA5-A3-B4 region as a risk factor for age-dependent nicotine addiction. *PLoS Genetics, 4*(7), e10000125. doi: 10.1371/journal.pgen.1000125

Wood, T., Wewers, M. E., Groner, J., & Ahijevych, K. (2004). Smoke constituent exposure and smoking topography of adolescent daily cigarette smokers. *Nicotine & Tobacco Research, 6*, 853–862.

Workman, L. M., & Winkelman, C. (2008). Genetic influences in common respiratory disorders. *Critical Care Nursing Clinics of North America, 20*, 171–189.

Xia, Y., McGuffey, J. E., Bhattacharyya, S., Sellergren, B., Yilmaz, E., Wang, L., et al. (2005). Analysis of the tobacco-specific nitrosamine 4-(methylnitrosamino)-1-(3-pyridyl)-1-butanol in urine by extraction on a molecularly imprinted polymer column and liquid chromatography/atmospheric pressure ionization tandem mass spectrometry. *Analytical Chemistry, 77,* 7639–7645.

Zanker, K. S., Tolle, W., Blumel, G., & Probst, J. (1980). Evaluation of surfactant-like effects of commonly used remedies for colds. *Respiration, 39,* 150–157.

Zeiger, J. S., Haberstick, B. C., Schlaepfer, I., Collins, A. C., Corley, R. P., Crowley, T. J., et al. (2008). The neuronal nicotinic receptor subunit genes (CHRNA6 and CHRNB3) are associated with subjective responses to tobacco. *Human Molecular Genetics, 17,* 724–734.

PART II

Nursing Intervention Research and Tobacco Control

Chapter 7

Primary and Secondary Tobacco Prevention in Youth

Martha S. Tingen, Jeannette O. Andrews, and Ashley W. Stevenson

ABSTRACT

The childhood years represent a critical time for tobacco experimentation and addiction. This chapter presents risk factors for youth smoking, state of the science of nurse-led primary and secondary tobacco prevention research in youth, and implications for future research, policy, and practice. Nursing research on both primary and secondary tobacco prevention efforts that are school-based, family-based, and community-based are presented. Interventions, including both state and community approaches, and media and policy endeavors to prevent tobacco use and foster successful cessation are discussed. The nursing profession has made an impact on primary and secondary prevention in youth regarding tobacco; however, much remains to be accomplished. As one of the largest health care professions, nurses should seize the important opportunity of positively impacting the health of children and youth through comprehensive and effective primary and secondary tobacco prevention efforts.

Keywords: family-based; nursing research; school-based; tobacco cessation; tobacco prevention; youth

DOI: 10.1891/0739-6686.27.171

The World Health Organization (WHO) estimates there are nearly one billion smokers worldwide (2008). Tobacco use is responsible for approximately 4.9 million premature deaths annually worldwide and continues to be the leading cause of preventable death in the United States (Ezzati & Lopez, 2003; National Center for Chronic Disease Prevention and Health Promotion [NCCDPHP], 2004a). The childhood years represent a critical period for tobacco experimentation and continued use particularly due to the brain's susceptibility to nicotine addiction at an early age and frequent exposure to secondhand smoke (SHS; Faraday et al., 2003). It is well established that 90% of current adult smokers become addicted before most are legally able to purchase cigarettes (American Cancer Society, 2008). DiFranza and Wellman (2003) identify nicotine dependence as "the most common life-threatening condition that presents in the pediatric population" [p. 261] with nicotine dependence occurring after only a few cigarettes. Despite the reality that youth are more susceptible to nicotine addiction, they (i.e., youth) do not believe this to be self-destructive (Fritz, Wider, Hardin, & Horrocks, 2008b). Even when individuals admit to being regular smokers, they still deny being addicted, a finding that was more frequent in males (Fritz et al., 2008b). Additionally, children exposed to tobacco use in their environment are three times more likely to become smokers themselves (Farkas, Gilpin, White, & Pierce, 2000).

Every day in the United States, about 4,000 children and youth under the age of 18 smoke their first cigarette, and an estimated 1,200 children and youth become daily cigarette smokers (Fiore et al., 2008). Tobacco use among youth has decreased over the last 20 years; however, rates of experimentation and use remain high with incremental increases per year of school (CDC, 2004). Rates of lifetime cigarette use among 8th, 10th, and 12th graders are 20.5%, 31.7%, and 44.7%, respectively (National Institute on Drug Abuse [NIDA], 2008). Of these same groups, 3.1%, 5.9%, and 11.4% smoke on a daily basis (NIDA, 2008).

This chapter provides an overview of risk factors for youth smoking and reviews current nurse-led research focused on primary and secondary prevention strategies for reducing tobacco use in youth. Implications for future research, policy, and nursing practice are also presented.

RISK FACTORS FOR YOUTH SMOKING

There are numerous risk factors for youth smoking and the most comprehensive model for understanding the diverse, yet interrelated influences, is the social–ecological framework (Bronfenbrenner, 1979). This conceptual approach incorporates the influences from the various contexts within which people live, interact, and develop. These individual and environmental influences for taking up tobacco use include: intrapersonal (i.e., self-esteem, knowledge, beliefs, attitudes, etc.); interpersonal (i.e., family and peer relationships and tobacco use of each); organizations (i.e., schools, workplaces, etc.); community (i.e., geographical and societal norms and expectations, policies at the local level); media and the society at large; and policy (smoke-free laws, regulation of tobacco products, laws regarding restriction of sales to minors, etc.) (Bronfenbrenner, 1979; Farrelly, 2009).

Intrapersonal

Intrapersonal influences related to tobacco use include self-esteem, knowledge, beliefs, attitudes, and intentions (Bronfenbrenner, 1979). These intrapersonal influences interact with the social environments of children and youth and often simultaneously influence each other (Bandura, 1977, 1997). Intrapersonal and environmental interaction results in attitudes and normative expectations that combine to form intentions and progress to behavior (Ajzen & Fishbein, 1980; Fishbein & Ajzen, 1975). Intention to smoke, reported to strongly predict subsequent regular use (Conrad, Flay, & Hill, 1992; Flay, Phil, Hu, & Richardson, 1998), is considered to be the best single predictor of an individual behavior (Ajzen & Fishbein, 1980; Conrad et al., 1992; Fishbein & Ajzen, 1975).

Interpersonal

Family and peer relationships and respective tobacco use by each comprise interpersonal influences. The family environment is considered a dynamic process for children where socialization occurs to include observing, evaluating, and often modeling the behaviors of adults in the home (Glass, 1986; Maccoby & Martin, 1983). Children's exposure to socialization factors in the home that promote risk-taking behaviors are associated with early experimentation with tobacco (Jackson & Henriksen, 1997). Some authors have identified and coined the process of children adopting their parents' or guardians' lifestyle behaviors as "inter-generational transmission" (Rimal, 2003; Wickrama, Conger, Wallace, & Elder, 1999). Learning to smoke is a gradual process and comprised of four phases: preparation, onset, experimentation, and regular smoking (Best, Thomson, Santi, Smith, & Brown, 1988; Flay, d'Avenernal, Best, Kersell, & Ryan, 1983). Benchmark studies have shown that parent and home influences are stronger than peer influences in the earliest phases of smoking (den Exter Blokland, Engels, Hale, Meeus, & Willemsen, 2004; Farkas et al., 2000; Fiore et al., 2008; Kodl & Mermelstein, 2004; Komro, McCarty, Forster, Blaine, & Chen, 2003).

Children with at least one parent smoker are two times more likely to have initiated tobacco use and two and a half times more likely to progress beyond initial experimentation (Kodl & Mermelstein, 2004). Additionally, parents who are smokers or who had ever smoked felt less efficacious in their parenting roles and have weaker antismoking beliefs than parents who have never smoked (Kodl & Mermelstein, 2004).

Parental involvement can be a powerful tool in preventing substance abuse among youth, including preventing tobacco use (National Center on Addiction and Substance Abuse, 2004; U.S. Department of Health and Human Services (U.S. DHHS), 2007). Parents can model expectations and provide reinforcement for desired behaviors if they know what behaviors to model and reinforce (Flay, 2000) and these clear, consistent messages and family time may serve as protective factors for tobacco abstinence (Andersen et al., 2002; Barnes, Hoffman, Welte, Farrell, & Dintcheff, 2007; Castrucci, Gerlach, Kaufman, & Orleans, 2002; Distefan, Gilpin, Choi, & Pierce, 1998; Farkas, Distefan, Choi, & Pierce, 1999; Jackson, Henriksen, Dickinson, & Levine, 1997). Although the influence of peers increases as children move into adolescence, the influence of parents may not decrease and parents have a powerful influence on how significantly peers impact their children's behavior (Flay, 2000; Flay et al., 1994; Hu, Flay, Hedeker, Siddiqui, & Day, 1995; Nash, McQueen, & Bray, 2005).

Peers can also be a pivotal influence in regards to tobacco experimentation and initiation and early youth smoking frequently occurs with peers (McVie & Bradshaw, 2005). Children have a higher risk of smoking if their best friends and siblings smoke. If their best friends smoke, the risk is higher than if other friends or peers smoke (Thomas & Perera, 2006). There is a positive relationship between spending unsupervised time with peers and cigarette experimentation (Barnes et al., 2007; Greene & Banerjee, 2009).

Organizations and Community

School systems and workplaces are organizational influences impacting youth's tobacco use. The environmental norms and expectations of what is modeled, permitted, and encouraged play a central role in whether youth participate in tobacco use. Geographical and societal norms and expectancies directly influence youth in their early decision-making years regarding tobacco. Whether the societal norm is "everyone smokes" or "no one smokes" impacts attitudes and beliefs of youth as they are determining what their own behavior will be. Tobacco policies at the local level, school systems, and workplaces all have an influence on youth's tobacco use.

Media and Society

Another important domain of influence or risk factor for tobacco use is the media through mass media and movie depictions (DiFranza & Coleman, 2001; National Center for Health Statistics, 2002). Mass media is targeted at modeling behaviors to youth in an effort to produce a lifestyle that is perceived as the societal norm

(Flay, 2000). This has been reiterated and expanded upon in the recent research of DiFranza and colleagues (2006), who report that tobacco promotions "foster positive attitudes, beliefs, and expectations regarding tobacco use" (p. e1237). The synergy of thinking about and believing favorably about tobacco promotes positive intentions toward its use, thus increasing the probability of initiation (DiFranza et al., 2006). Prediction and causality has been established between tobacco promotion efforts and children and youth's tobacco initiation (DiFranza et al., 2006). Research has shown that exposure to smoking in movies, particularly those R-rated, is linked to increased youth tobacco use (DiFranza & Coleman, 2001; NCCDPHP, 2004b). Training students in media literacy skills may countermand these influences and provide a protective effect against unhealthy attitudes and behaviors learned from the media (Alverman & Hagwood, 2000; Austin & Johnson, 1997).

Policy

State and national norms to include smoke-free laws, regulation of tobacco products, and laws regarding restriction of sales to minors all affect youth tobacco use (CDC, 2007). Smoke-free ordinances in restaurants and child- and youth-oriented establishments provide smoke-free eating and recreational environments for children and youth. Recent passing of the Family Smoking Prevention and Tobacco Control Act for Food and Drug Administration (FDA) regulation of all tobacco products is a positive national step toward potentially thwarting youth's tobacco use (H.R. Rep. No. 1256, 2009).

In summary, the intrapersonal, interpersonal, organizational and community, media and societal, and policy factors that increase risk for tobacco experimentation, initiation, and progressing to regular smoking are numerous. Approaches that are personalized, tailored, and comprehensive are needed to prevent youth from becoming regular tobacco users.

STATE OF THE SCIENCE OF NURSE-LED PRIMARY AND SECONDARY TOBACCO PREVENTION

Youth tobacco use is an area of scientific inquiry that has been largely focused on by many behavioral scientists and geneticists, yet not as extensively by nurse researchers. Most tobacco prevention research has been conducted in school settings, in family or home settings, or population-based studies, such as mass media and countermarketing strategies. The purpose of this review is to examine the current literature of nurse-led primary and secondary tobacco prevention efforts in youth.

Search Terms and Methods

The search engines PubMed and Cumulative Index to Nursing and Allied Health (CINAHL; 1999–2009) were used to identify data-based articles discussed in this chapter. The following search terms were used: tobacco prevention in children and youth, tobacco cessation in children and youth, church-based, faith-based, tobacco control, community tobacco prevention mass media campaigns, and nursing. Inclusion criteria included: data-based articles, nurse-led, tobacco prevention or cessation in youth, and written in English. Those that targeted prevention of SHS exposure only were excluded. Nineteen articles met the inclusion criteria and are included in this review (15 targeting primary prevention and 4 in secondary prevention, i.e., cessation). The following sections are organized as: primary tobacco prevention and secondary tobacco prevention, both specific to the youth population.

Primary Tobacco Prevention

Primary prevention of tobacco use involves efforts aimed at preventing persons, especially youth, from ever trying tobacco. Having the opportunity to provide care to youth through numerous clinical venues and paired with concern about youth's tobacco usage, nurses have contributed to the body of scientific knowledge on youth tobacco prevention through research. Studies conducted by those in the nursing field have taken place in schools, home and family settings, and community settings.

School-Based Studies

The social environment of the school has been the focus of nine articles describing nursing research and tobacco prevention in school settings (Burchfield, Marenco, Dickens, & Willock, 2000; Hahn et al., 2005; Hahn, Hall, Rayens, Myers, & Bonnel, 2007; Kulbok et al., 2008; McGahee, Kemp, & Tingen, 2000; McGahee & Tingen, 2000; Seal, 2006; Smith, Tingen & Waller, 2004; Tingen et al., 2006). Schools provide access and a route for communicating tobacco prevention with a large proportion of youth.

   A descriptive study conducted by Smith and colleagues (2004) evaluated the relationships of self-concept, locus of control, attitudes, normative beliefs, and refusal skills on tobacco initiation in a large sample of 4th and 5th grade youth ($n = 666$) from three rural southern counties in the United States. The students were surveyed on self-concept (home, school, peer), locus of control (internal, external), and tobacco use (yes/no). Of the total sample, 9.2% ($n = 61$) reported tobacco use. Youth who reported any tobacco use had lower home self-concept scores ($OR = 0.93$; 95% $CI = 0.88, 0.99$; $p = .03$) and lower school self-concept scores ($OR = 0.93$; 95% CI $= 0.88, 0.98$; $p = .009$) than those who reported no tobacco use. Locus of control was also significant with those reporting tobacco use having greater external locus of control than those who reported never using tobacco (57.4% vs. 39.7%; $p = .0074$). Kulbok and colleagues (2008) conducted a qualitative study with 39 youth (9th–12th grades) to examine attitudes, beliefs, and norms in nonsmokers. Students completed baseline surveys regarding their personal smoking behaviors as well as demographic questions. Survey completion was immediately followed by group interviews with semistructured questions to assess information on risk and protective factors. A total of eight interviews were held, lasting 60 to 90 minutes per session. Results of the study indicated that parents of African American students were more likely to smoke than parents of White students, but that White students were more likely than African American students to have friends that were smokers. Participants agreed that reasons for not smoking involved issues of concern for good health, high self-confidence, positive self-image, and desire for parents' and friends' approval. Participants had a good understanding of the consequences of abstaining from smoking and felt they had good support for their decisions not to smoke.

A quasiexperimental intervention study using a Solomon-Four group design was conducted with 5th grade elementary students across nine public schools ($n = 361$; McGahee & Tingen, 2000). The study tested the American Cancer Society's tobacco prevention program for 5th grade students: "Do It Yourself—Making Healthy Choices" with the purpose of developing attitudes toward choosing never to smoke and developing refusal skills for smoking experimentation in the children. A doctoral nursing student taught all five sessions to the students. Attitudes, subjective norms, refusal skills, and intention to smoke were measured. Youth in the intervention groups at posttest reported more negative attitudes toward smoking ($F[1,360] = 13.6, p = .001$). Attitudes, refusal skills, and having parents who smoke were significant predictors of the youth's intention to smoke and accounted for 38% of the variance of the final regression model.

The LifeSkills (LS) Training Program uses a developmentally appropriate cognitive behavioral approach and focuses on competency enhancement by teaching and equipping children with life skills to make healthy lifestyle choices (National Health Promotion Associates, Inc., 2003). The LS program material is modified based on grade level and provides information and skill development related to:

1. Self-esteem
2. Decision making
3. Effects of smoking
4. Advertising
5. Dealing with stress
6. Communication skills

7. Social skills

8. Assertiveness (National Health Promotion Associates, Inc., 2003).

It is important to note that in a meta-analysis of school-based tobacco prevention studies that followed their participants for at least 12 months after intervention (Wiehe, Garrison, Christakis, Ebel, & Rivara, 2005), only one study (Botvin, Baker, Dusenby, Botvin, & Diaz, 1995) indicated significance of longterm impact of intervention for smoking prevention (Wiehe et al., 2005). The two following studies by nurse scientists (Seal, 2006; Tingen et al., 2006) included the LS program.

Tingen and colleagues (2006) implemented the 15-session (40 minutes/session) LS program (Botvin, 2000a) across the state of Georgia in 23 public school classrooms with 6th grade students (n = 512). School nurses and counselors were trained on the program prior to implementation and fidelity was maintained across all implementation sites. The study also included a parent–guardian (n = 512; total n = 1024) per child who were mailed tobacco-specific information weekly and concurrently as their child was receiving the classroom intervention. The mailings were tailored based on the parents' self-reported tobacco use. Parents who were smokers were also provided information on the State's toll-free tobacco cessation quitline. Implementation of the LS program resulted in significant positive improvements in the child outcomes: drug knowledge ($p = .0001$), refusal skills ($p = .0036$), attitudes ($p = .0495$), normative expectations ($p = .0001$), assertiveness ($p = .0301$), and anxiety reduction techniques ($p = .0001$). Additionally, all parents consistently reported that smoking was detrimental to themselves, the public, and their children. The self-report results also showed that for children living in homes of parent smokers, there is a 50% chance of becoming a smoker themselves; whereas for those living in homes of nonsmoking parents, 77% remained tobacco free. Twelve percent of the 6th grade sample had smoked a cigarette in the preceding year. This was one of the first studies to examine the effectiveness of a school-based intervention based on parent smoking status and to document that child intervention outcomes are impacted by the smoking status of parents. Impact of the intervention on tobacco use was not assessed.

Similarly, Seal (2006) implemented the LS program with 170 Thai students in grades 7 through 12. Students in the intervention group received the LS program (Botvin, 2000b) that provided information and skills specifically related to drug and tobacco use over 10 class periods. Students in the control group received the traditional school-based tobacco and drug education curriculum. Students receiving the LS program had statistically significant positive effects on tobacco knowledge level ($p = .00$), attitudes ($p = .00$), development of refusal skills ($p = .00$), and decision-making and problem-solving skills ($p = .00$). The reported frequency of tobacco and drug use did decrease in the LS group students, although there were no statistical differences between the two groups (Seal, 2006).

A study by a group of nursing students who worked with community partners, including a group of retired teachers, to implement a school-based intervention named "Tar Wars," aimed to increase knowledge about tobacco's harmful effects (Burchfield et al., 2000). The intervention was delivered to 5th grade students ($n = 585$) in 31 classrooms across 12 schools in Tennessee. The program was 1 to 2 hours per day over 2 days of instruction. The goal of the study was that 80% of the children who received the educational program would be able to identify three positive and three negative effects of tobacco use at posttest. The intervention was successful with students being able to recognize both the positive consequences of not beginning tobacco use (89.3%) as well as the negative effects of tobacco use (91.3%; Burchfield et. al., 2000). Supporting youth in their decisions to not use tobacco, as previously discussed, has been identified as a protective factor against tobacco experimentation and initiation and involving others at a community level enhances this support.

Hahn and colleagues (2005) examined factors associated with tobacco-free policies and tobacco cessation in schools serving children in grades 6 through 12 in Kentucky. A cross-sectional telephone survey was conducted of school administrators ($n = 691$). The survey included the following: smoking policies, provision of tobacco prevention and cessation programs, and schools receiving monies from tobacco companies. Only 20% of the schools surveyed had comprehensive tobacco-free policies. Rural schools were less likely to be tobacco free or provide cessation services (Hahn et al., 2005).

School nurses work with children and youth on a daily basis and have insight into this population's receptivity to antitobacco messages. Thus, school nurses perceptions regarding tobacco companies and tobacco prevention efforts were examined in one study (Reinert, Carver, & Range, 2005). Findings revealed that overall school nurses disapprove of tobacco companies and felt that they targeted minors in their advertising. They also overwhelmingly agreed that school personnel should not be seen smoking by students and that nurses have a responsibility to take part in helping student smokers quit (Reinert et al., 2005).

Family-Based Studies

Drug and tobacco prevention interventions implemented by nurses are not limited to the school environment, but also include family-based approaches (Hahn et al., 2007; Tingen, 2007). Interventions such as the LS training program have both school (i.e., student) and home (i.e., parent) components (Botvin, 1999, 2002). Research using this intervention is ongoing in a randomized control trial (RCT; Tingen, 2007). The RCT is testing the effects of a multicomponent, family approach using both the LS child and LS parent components in combination with culturally tailored cessation for parent smokers for the intervention arm and general health education components for the control arm. The investigation proposes that the family approach (combination of child and parent interventions) will provide personal protective factors for both the child and parent and environmental factors that are health protective for both. These protective factors will serve as moderators of health risk behavior and result in health protective attitudes and expectations that form intentions and progress to health protective behaviors. The investigators anticipate that having a child in a school-based tobacco prevention program may impact the parent toward increased self-efficacy in delivering antitobacco socialization in the home and also may increase smoking cessation self-efficacy for parent smokers. They also theoretically propose that having a parent in the home creating an antitobacco socialization environment may positively impact a child in school-based tobacco prevention toward tobacco abstinence. This theoretical and pragmatic approach has not been previously explored in family-based tobacco control studies.

Another program, Beginning Alcohol and Addictions Basic Education Studies (BABES), also takes this more comprehensive approach including both children (5- and 6-year-olds) and their parents (i.e., school and home environments; Hahn et al., 2007). This research included children from three elementary school and a parent–child (total $n = 252$; 126 parent–child dyads). The study used a three-group, pre-, posttest design to determine the differences in reducing environmental risk factors for alcohol, tobacco, and other drug use (ATOD) between the school-only intervention, the school-home components combined, and a no treatment control group. It was found that when parents in the school–home component group assessed their children's adjustment, they found them less anxious and less withdrawn than did parents in the school-only intervention or no treatment control groups ($t[108] = 2.6, p = .01$). The authors also report that the school–home intervention group had better home life ($t[180] = 2.6, p = .01$) and an improvement in parental depressive symptoms after intervention ($t[102] = 3.6, p = .0005$; Hahn, et al., 2007). These findings add to the body of evidence regarding primary prevention efforts and emphasize the importance of positive home environments and greater parental involvement for healthy, risk protective decisions versus risk-taking decision in children and youth (Hahn et al., 2007; National Center on Addiction and Substance Abuse, 2004; U.S. DHHS, 2007). Thus, interventions targeting both the school and home environments simultaneously for youth are needed and beginning evidence supports they may be much more effective at preventing tobacco and other drug use than school interventions alone.

Community-Based Studies

There were four studies reported in the nursing literature that evaluated a tobacco prevention intervention in community settings (Higgs, Edwards, Harbin, & Higgs,

2000; Reinert, Campbell, Carver, & Range, 2003; Reinert, Carver, Range, & Campbell, 2006; Smith, Tally, Hubbard, & Winn, 2008). Higgs and colleagues (2000) evaluated a youth-directed smoking prevention and cessation program titled Breathe Easy!, an active learning program with a series of instructor-facilitated activities and peer input over ten 45-minute sessions during the summer. The program was delivered at two community sites sponsored by the Job Training Partnership Act (n = 251 intervention subjects) and two additional sites served as the control group (n = 159). The 6-month follow-up posttest data revealed smoking prevalence dropped from 18.7% to 8.9% ($p < .005$) in the intervention group, and from 14.1% to 9.4% in the control group ($p < .012$). However, a considerable limitation included a dropout rate of 42% of the participants prior to the 6-month data collection follow-up (Higgs et al., 2000).

Smith and colleagues (2008) evaluated the effectiveness of a tobacco prevention education outreach, using ToPIC, an interactive program with 201 students attending the Boys and Girls Clubs in five rural counties in a southeastern state of the United States. ToPIC included an educational program based on effects of smoking, facts and myths about smoking, smokeless tobacco use, costs of smoking, advertising awareness, smoke-free environment, and smoke-free advocacy. The interactive program was taught weekly in three class sessions to three different age groups of teens and preteens. A significant increase in knowledge from pre- to posttest was found ($t(200) = -13.65$, $p < .0001$; Smith et al., 2008). Changes in tobacco prevalence were not assessed.

Nurses have also implemented tobacco prevention interventions in churches and other faith-based organizations. A case study of faith-based interventions in Mississippi reported a reduction in smoking behavior and use of tobacco products in general among high school students by 23%–25% (Reinert et al., 2003). Similar to the goal of research regarding school nurses' opinions about tobacco prevention (Reinert et al., 2005), Reinert and her colleagues (2006) sought to discover how religious leaders felt about preventive strategies and their role within the faith community. Surveys and a one-day workshop revealed that, when provided with primary prevention materials, faith leaders felt they could effectively educate others about the material and that interventions would have a positive influence on youth (Reinert et al., 2006). The primary obstacle encountered by faith leaders in providing tobacco prevention education was reportedly lack of resources (Reinert, Carver, Range, & Pike, 2008). The faith-based leaders felt materials were needed for providing education more than any other resources, even over monetary means and volunteer hours (Reinert et al., 2008). These findings provide valuable knowledge that can be infused into future efforts for prevention within these settings that may enhance effectiveness for youth participants.

In summary, there is emerging research in the nursing literature addressing tobacco prevention in youth. This research is yielding promise in the areas of school and family-based interventions to prevent youth from using tobacco products.

However, further research is needed that uses experimental designs with control groups, valid and reliable smoking abstinence measures, and long-term follow-up. Extant literature from other sources reveals that school-based, family-based, community-based, and population-level strategies, although with mixed results, are demonstrating effectiveness in preventing tobacco use.

Secondary Tobacco Prevention

While primary prevention efforts target preventing experimentation and use, secondary prevention is aimed at helping individuals who use tobacco with successful cessation. The evidence-based Treating Tobacco Use and Dependence Guideline (Fiore et al., 2008) includes a combination approach of pharmacotherapy and counseling for achieving successful cessation. However, the guideline's recommendations are for adult populations only. Several medications exist for the treatment of tobacco use, such as varenicline, bupropion, as well as nicotine replacement therapy (e.g., patches, lozenge, gum, nasal spray); however, none of these medications have been approved by the FDA for youth (Fiore et al., 2008). Thus, evidence-based recommendations, which include both pharmacological and counseling components, for youth smokers are lacking.

Because youth users are more vulnerable than adults to the consequences of nicotine and subsequent addiction, it is probable that cessation interventions at the early stages of tobacco addiction would be beneficial in motivating young users to quit, helping them do so successfully, and protecting against the threat of resilient addictive behavior. Secondary prevention is pivotal and has been the focus of nurse scientists in adult populations (e.g., Andrews, Bentley, Crawford, Pretlow, & Tingen, 2007; Andrews, Felton, Wewers, Waller, & Tingen, 2007). However, cessation efforts with youth have received minimal investigation by nurse researchers. This may be partly due to the challenges that cessation efforts with youth pose; specifically, the paucity of pharmacological and established counseling treatments that are approved for youth under 18 years of age. There were only four studies that met the inclusion criteria of cessation interventions in youth reported in the nursing literature. Of these, three were conducted in school settings and one in a community clinical setting.

School-Based Studies

The Computerized Adolescent Smoking Cessation Program (CASCP), developed by Deborah Fritz, a family nurse practitioner, was intended for youth that identify with the first two phases (i.e., precontemplation and contemplation) of quitting smoking (Fritz, Gore, Hardin, & Bram, 2008a). Similar to primary prevention strategies, this program incorporated topics of self-efficacy and confidence to aid in the motivation for quitting, as well as providing factual information on the constructiveness of refraining from tobacco use. The program consisted of four, 30-minute sessions over the course of 4 to 6 weeks. Fritz and her colleagues (2008a) implemented the CASCP with high school students ($n = 121$) and found that youth who received the program attempted cessation more than youth who did not ($F[1,114] = 3.70$, $p = .05$). Many of the students in the intervention demonstrated successful cessation at one-month postintervention survey (23%). Also, students receiving intervention had a greater likelihood of advancement in their stage of change than those students in the control group ($\chi^2[1, n = 98] = 6.65, p = .036$). For those students who did not quit successfully, they were able to reduce their cigarette usage and smoke significantly fewer cigarettes than before (Fritz et al., 2008a). The CASCP was also effective at increasing students' self-efficacy and confidence, as well as positively influencing their perceptions about smoking to be more accurate regarding it being a poor behavior choice (Fritz et al., 2008a). An additional study with CASCP revealed that students perceived the information provided to them on the effects of smoking to be the most effective strategy for their cessation (Fritz et al., 2008b).

Another school-based study conducted by an interprofessional team, including a nurse practitioner, implemented the American Lung Association's Not on Tobacco (N-O-T) in 14- to 19-year-olds ($n = 346$) in an Appalachian state (Dino et al., 2001). The intervention, considered "gender-sensitive," included 10 weekly 60-minute sessions delivered to same-gender groups of 4 to 12 teens, led by a same-gender facilitator. The control group received a brief intervention (BI) reflective of typical content in a school health education class. Specifically, the BI students (both genders together) were provided 5 to 10 minutes of cessation advice and self-help materials. This was followed by an additional 10-minute question and answer session. Results showed that the N-O-T female youth were nearly 4 times more likely to quit smoking at the 6 month follow-up than female youth who received the BI ($Z = 2.03$, $p = .043$). Results for male participants were not statistically significant at this time point. Findings also revealed that N-O-T was more effective than the BI in assisting both male and female youth with cigarette reduction ($Z = 2.09$, $p = .037$).

Community-Based Studies

Finding effective youth smoking cessation strategies may involve extending research into other areas of the community rather than schools alone. Prenatal clinics were used to recruit young pregnant female smokers and provide them with cessation intervention (Albrecht, Stone, Payne, & Reynolds, 1998). The interventions, Teen FreshStart (TFS) and Teen FreshStart Plus Buddy (TFSB), were implemented with young mothers, ages 12 to 20, and included information regarding tobacco use and its effects on the baby, as well as raising awareness of individual smoking behavior. The difference between the two programs involved a peer-support component (TFSB) in which the youth goes through the program with a nonsmoking peer (i.e., a buddy) for encouragement. Upon completion of the programs, the youth in TFSB were more likely to make successful quit attempts than the youth in the TFS (Albrecht et al., 1998), a finding similar to primary prevention efforts, where support from parents and peers was a major component in youth's decision making regarding choosing not to smoke.

In summary, there is a paucity of nurse-led youth cessation interventions in the literature, and research for this population remains a priority (Fiore et al., 2008). A recent national survey of youth tobacco cessation programs showed a lack of programs in communities most in need, especially in those where youth smoking prevalence is increasing (Fiore et al., 2008). To provide evidence for practice, RCTs should be conducted with rigorous design and fidelity of the intervention, and a minimum of 6-month follow-up of smoking status that is biochemically validated.

IMPLICATIONS FOR FUTURE RESEARCH, POLICY, AND PRACTICE

While nursing professionals have contributed to primary and secondary prevention efforts of youth tobacco use, much remains to be accomplished to prevent the numerous adverse health effects from tobacco use and secondhand smoke exposure in this population. State and national goals related to percentages of youth using tobacco as well as decreases in tobacco-related morbidity and mortality and health disparities can be achieved with focused, concerted, and sustained efforts. Nurses and nurse scientists can be pivotal leaders in making substantial contributions toward this important public health concern. Endeavors should focus on *research, policy, and practice* with the CDC's Best Practices for Comprehensive Tobacco Control Programs (2007) serving as the blueprint to be followed. The five "overarching components" for effective tobacco control as identified by the Best Practices include:

1. State and community interventions
2. Health communication interventions
3. Cessation interventions
4. Surveillance and evaluation
5. Administration and management

The Best Practices presents a well-designed roadmap with state-specific targets, and identifies the needed monetary appropriations for each of the five categories to foster success for comprehensive tobacco control programs, including the youth population (CDC, 2007).

State and Community Interventions

State and community interventions incorporate evidence-based programs and policies within organizations and systems such as schools, communities, and networks, all with the goal of fostering tobacco-free behavior (CDC, 2007). *Research efforts* should include involving communities and collaborating with them through community-based participatory research (CBPR). The CBPR is defined by the Office of Behavioral Social Sciences Research, National Institutes of Health (2009) as "an orientation to public health research that requires a collaborative approach to involve participants throughout all stages of research projects." Community members can and often are eager to share their goals for having tobacco-free youth and what needs to occur to accomplish these goals. Nurse researchers can lead the way in this approach as they possess skills in networking, group facilitation, and developing and maintaining trusting relationships, all key ingredients in CBPR.

Effective sociocultural and tailored interventions, developed collaboratively using CBPR, are needed to prevent experimentation and initiation of tobacco use and to promote healthy behavior in all youth (Tingen et al., 2009). Based on Thomas, Baker, and Lorenzetti's (2007) systematic review of family-based interventions, those including multicomponent strategies (e.g., education and counseling, printed activity guides, parenting tip sheets, child newsletters and incentives) are more likely to be successful in promoting abstinence among youth.

The best age of intervening in youth is also a significant area of research in meeting youth prevention goals. In the preschool and early school years, children are assimilating their experiences that affect their self-esteem, what they come to believe as social norms for their family and community, and the important roles and influences of both parents and peers. In a systematic review by Petrie and colleagues (2007), the strongest and most rigorous work with family interventions have been conducted with elementary school-age children and in the early adolescent years, with evidence of effectiveness of parenting programs targeted to tobacco prevention. These authors' concluded that the most effective interventions in reducing tobacco use emphasized the development of social skills and personal responsibility among youth along with active parental involvement (Petrie, Bunn, & Byrne, 2007).

In summary, interventions with youth should include novel strategies that are technologically infused, incorporate parent involvement, and peer approaches that have both school- and home-based components (Kulbok et al., 2008; Petrie et al., 2007; Thomas et al., 2007; Tingen et al., 2006). Additionally, differences among ethnicities and disparities of tobacco use among youth must be explored (Hahn et al., 2007). Future research should also incorporate biochemical validation of self-report measures for both children and their parents (Hahn et al., 2000; Tingen et al., 2006).

Media and Policy Efforts

Population-based efforts that are multifocused and inclusive of age restrictions for tobacco purchase, tobacco-free public places, and various mass media communications are often combined to create strategies to prevent tobacco use in youth (Sowden & Stead, 2003). Sowden and Stead, based on their systematic review, recommend building upon elements of existing programs, targeting appropriate messages guided by theoretical constructs, and ensuring the reach of the intended audience in the provision of population-based prevention programs. Strategies such as tobacco advertising restrictions, limiting youth access, and increasing the cost of cigarettes and tobacco products, are in general effective deterrents to youth smoking (Lantz et al., 2000). Farrelly, Niederdeppe, and Yarsevich's (2003) review of the evidence of mass media prevention campaigns show success as well.

Health communication interventions (CDC, 2007) can support local and statewide ordinances for tobacco-free campuses and all youth environments. Health communication interventions can assist with these important media messages and may lend to adherence to the law regarding underage purchases. For example, messages about the importance of tobacco-free environments are critically needed to ensure avoidance of SHS exposure in youth. Making tobacco products more costly and placing more stringent consequences on vendors who sell tobacco products to minors are preventive efforts for youth access (Task Force on Community Preventive Services, 2001). However, to address complex changes in social norms and behavior, youth may require a wealth of messages from varied and diverse sources (in schools or community settings) along with countermarketing messages in the media to be the most effective (Farrelly et al., 2003). The nursing profession can lead the way related to *policy* through research evaluating the impact of media programs and policy measures, as well as through lobbying and advocacy, for example, serving as expert witnesses regarding the health consequences of tobacco use and SHS exposure.

Cessation Interventions

Cessation interventions for adults include a wide range of activities: system, policy, and population-based measures (CDC, 2007). Nurses, who comprise and *practice* as one of the largest workforces in the health care arena, have a responsibility to help any and all individuals with tobacco cessation through implementation of the specific strategies outlined in the Guideline (Andrews, Heath, Barone, & Tingen, 2008). Helping adults quit smoking also positively impacts youth as this is an opportunity to foster smoke-free home environments. Numerous childhood illnesses and well-baby checkups position parents for "teachable moments" related to the importance of their own cessation and avoiding SHS exposure in their children.

A large concern of youth smokers wanting to quit is having someone to guide them with both emotional and cognitive strategies involved with controlling cravings for cigarettes, as well as how to overcome environmental stimuli that prompt smoking behaviors (Staten & Ridner, 2006). Because youth tobacco users are more vulnerable than adults to the consequences of nicotine and subsequent addiction, it is probable that cessation interventions at the early stages of addiction would be beneficial in this population (DiFranza & Wellman, 2003). Additionally, due to the paucity of pharmacological treatments that are approved for youth less than 18 years of age, nurse scientists could make substantial contributions in advancing knowledge related to this area of treatment.

Surveillance and Evaluation

Surveillance and evaluation includes a standardized process for monitoring "tobacco-related attitudes, behaviors, and health outcomes at regular intervals" (CDC, 2007, p. 9). Nurse researchers can use these data to assess objectives and performance indicator outcomes and benchmarks of a successful tobacco control program or initiative.

Administration and Management

Administration and management of a tobacco control program is essential for providing program oversight, fiscal supervision, and technical training and assistance, from the state-specific to the local community-level (CDC, 2007). Nurse scientists could, for example, pursue research to provide evidence as to the best management strategies to decrease tobacco use among youth.

SUMMARY

In summary, as this review demonstrates, there are a vast number of factors influencing youth tobacco use and cessation. Although nursing scientists have made some impact on scholarship related to primary and secondary tobacco prevention in youth, much remains to be accomplished. RCTs in both primary and secondary prevention are needed and all efforts should be comprehensive and multicomponent. Nurse scientists should engage community environments such as schools, churches, youth organizations, and public housing neighborhoods where often large numbers of youth are in need of being reached. The CDC's Best Practices for Comprehensive Tobacco Control Programs (2007) should serve as the umbrella framework for all efforts moving forward. With focused and sustained endeavors of rigorous research, policy initiatives, and diligent practice, nursing can help achieve smoke-free environments, decrease risk factors and enhance protective factors in youth, develop and implement effective interventions that prevent initiation and foster successful cessation, and prevent numerous adverse health outcomes in this vulnerable population and the future of America: the youth.

REFERENCES

Ajzen, I., & Fishbein, M. (1980). *Understanding attitudes and predicting social behavior*. Englewood Cliffs, NJ: Prentice Hall.

Albrecht, S., Stone, C. A., Payne, L., & Reynolds, M. D. (1998). A preliminary study of the use of peer support in smoking cessation programs for pregnant adolescents. *Journal of the American Academy of Nurse Practitioners, 10*(3), 119–125.

Alverman, D. E., & Hagwood, M. C. (2000). Critical media literacy: Research, theory and practice in "new times." *Journal of Educational Research, 93*, 193–205.

American Cancer Society, Inc. (2008). *Cancer prevention and early detection: Facts & Figures*. Atlanta, GA: Author.

Andersen, M. R., Leroux, B. G., Marek, P. M., Peterson, A. V., Kealey, K. A., Bricker, J., et al. (2002). Mothers' attitudes and concerns about their children smoking: Do they influence kids? *Preventive Medicine, 34*, 198–206.

Andrews, J. O., Bentley, G., Crawford, S., Pretlow, L., & Tingen, M. S. (2007). Using community-based participatory research to develop a culturally sensitive smoking cessation intervention with public housing neighborhoods. *Ethnicity and Disease, 17*(2), 331–337.

Andrews, J. O., Felton, G., Wewers, M. E., Waller, J., & Tingen, M. (2007). The effect of a multi-component smoking cessation intervention in African American women residing in public housing. *Research in Nursing & Health, 30*(1), 45–60.

Andrews, J. O., Heath, J., Barone, C. P., & Tingen, M. S. (2008). Time to quit? New strategies for tobacco-dependent patients. *The Nurse Practitioner, 33*(11), 34–42.

Austin, E. W., & Johnson, K. K. (1997). Immediate and delayed effects of media literacy training on third graders' decision making for alcohol. *Health Communication, 9*, 323–349.

Bandura A. (1977). *Social Learning Theory*. Englewood Cliffs, NJ: Prentice Hall.

Bandura A. (1997). *Self-efficacy: The exercise of control*. New York: Freeman.

Barnes, G. M., Hoffman, J. H., Welte, J. W., Farrell, M. P., & Dintcheff, B. A. (2007). Adolescents time use: Effects on substance use, delinquency, and sexual activity. *Journal of Youth and Adolescence, 36*, 697–710.

Best, J. A., Thomson, S. J., Santi, S. M., Smith, E. A., & Brown, K. S. (1988). Preventing cigarette smoking among school children. *Annual Review of Public Health, 9,* 161–201.

Botvin, G. J. (1999). *LifeSkills training student guide—Level 1* (Elementary School). White Plains, NY: Princeton Health Press, Inc.

Botvin, G. J. (2000a). *LifeSkills training student guide—Level 1* (Middle School). White Plains, NY: Princeton Health Press, Inc.

Botvin, G. J. (2000b). *LifeSkills training student guide—Level 3* (Middle School). White Plains, NY: Princeton Health Press, Inc.

Botvin, G. J. (2002). *LifeSkills training parent guide.* White Plains, NY: Princeton Health Press, Inc.

Botvin, G. J., Baker, E., Dusenbury, L. Botvin, E. M., & Diaz, T. (1995). Long-term follow-up results of a randomized drug abuse prevention trial in a white middle-class population. *Journal of the American Medical Association, 272,* 1106–1112.

Bronfenbrenner, U. (1979). *The ecology of human development.* Cambridge, MA: Harvard University Press.

Burchfield, J., Marenco, A., Dickens, D., & Willock, K. M. (2000). An anti-smoking project instituted by senior nursing students in a rural community. *Issues in Comprehensive Pediatric Nursing, 23,* 155–164.

Castrucci, B. C., Gerlach, K. K., Kaufman, N. J., & Orleans, C. T. (2002). The association among adolescents' tobacco use, their beliefs and attitudes, and friends' and parents' opinions of smoking. *Maternal Child Health Journal, 6*(3), 159–167.

Centers for Disease Control and Prevention (CDC). (2004). Surveillance summaries: Youth risk behavior surveillance—United States, 2003. *Morbidity and Mortality Weekly Report, 53,* SS-2.

Centers for Disease Control and Prevention. (2007). *Best practices for comprehensive tobacco control programs—2007.* Atlanta, GA. U.S. Department of Health and Human Services, Centers for Disease Control and Prevention, National Center for Chronic Disease Prevention and Health Promotion, Office on Smoking and Health.

Conrad, K. M., Flay, B. R., & Hill, D. (1992). Why children start smoking cigarettes: Predictors of onset. *British Journal of Addiction, 87,* 1711–1724.

Den Exter Blokland, E. A., Engels, R. C., Hale, W. W., Meeus, W., & Willemsen, M. C. (2004). Lifetime parental smoking history and cessation and early adolescent smoking behavior. *Preventative Medicine, 38*(3), 359–368.

DiFranza, J. R., & Coleman, M. (2001). Sources of tobacco for youths in communities with vigorous enforcement of youth access laws. *Tobacco Control, 10,* 323–328.

DiFranza, J. R., & Wellman, R. J. (2003). Preventing cancer by controlling youth tobacco use. *Seminars in Oncology Nursing, 19*(4), 261–267.

DiFranza, J. R., Wellman, R. J., Sargent, J. D., Weitzman, M., Hipple, B. J., & Winickoff, J. P. (2006). Tobacco promotion and the initiation of tobacco use: Assessing the evidence for causality. *Pediatrics, 117*(6), e1237–e1248.

Dino, G. A., Horn, K. A., Goldcamp, J., Maniar, S. D., Fernandes, A., & Massey, C. J. (2001). Statewide demonstration of not on tobacco: A gender sensitive teen smoking cessation program. *Journal of School Nursing, 17*(2), 90–97.

Distefan, J. M., Gilpin, E. A., Choi, W. S., & Pierce, J. P. (1998). Parental influences predict adolescent smoking in the United States, 1989–1993. *Journal of Adolescent Health, 22,* 466–474.

Ezzati, M., & Lopez, A. (2003). Estimates of global mortality attributable to smoking in 2000. *Lancet, 362,* 847–852.

Faraday, M. M., Elliott, B. M., Phillips, J. M., & Grunberg, N. E. (2003). *Adolescent nicotine exposure results in sensitization to nicotine in adulthood.* PA1-4, Society for Research on Nicotine and Tobacco, 9th Annual Meeting, New Orleans, LA.

Farkas, A. J., Distefan, J. M., Choi, W. S., & Pierce, J. P. (1999). Does parental smoking cessation discourage adolescent smoking? *Preventive Medicine, 28,* 213–218.

Farkas, A. J., Gilpin, E. A., White, M. M., & Pierce J. P. (2000). Association between household and workplace smoking restrictions and adolescent smoking. *Journal of the American Medical Association, 284,* 717–722.

Farrelly, M. C. (2009). Monitoring the tobacco use epidemic V. The environment: Factors that influence tobacco use. *Preventive Medicine, 48,* S35–S43.

Farrelly, M. C., Niederdeppe, J., & Yarsevich, J. (2003). Youth tobacco prevention mass media campaigns: past, present, and future directions. *Tobacco Control, 12,* i35–i45.

Fiore, M. C., Jaen, C. R., Baker, T. B., Bailey, W. C., Benowitz, N. L., Curry, S. J., et al. (2008). *Treating tobacco use and dependence: 2008 update: Quick reference guide for clinicians.* Rockville, MD: U.S. Department of Health and Human Services. Public Health Service.

Fishbein, M., & Ajzen, I. (1975). *Belief, attitude, intention, and behavior: An introduction to theory and research.* Reading, MA: Addison Wesley.

Flay, B. R. (2000). Approaches to substance use prevention utilizing school curriculum plus social environment change. *Addictive Behavior, 25*(6), 861–885.

Flay, B. R. d'Avenernal, J. R., Best, J. A., Kersell, M. W., & Ryan, K. B. (1983). Cigarette smoking: Why young people do it and ways of preventing it. In P. McGrath & P. Firestone (Eds.), *Pediatric and adolescent behavioral medicine* (pp. 132–183). New York: Spring Verlag.

Flay, B. R., Hu, B., Siddiqui, O., Day, L. E., Hedeker, D., Petraitis, J., et al. (1994). Differential influence of parental smoking and friends' smoking on adolescent initiation of smoking and escalation of smoking. *Journal of Health and Social Behavior, 35,* 248–265.

Flay, B. R., Phil, D., Hu, F. B., & Richardson, J. (1998). Psychosocial predictors of different stages of cigarette smoking among high school students. *Preventive Medicine, 27,* 9–18.

Fritz, D. J., Gore, P. A., Hardin, S. B., & Bram, D. (2008a). A computerized smoking cessation intervention for high school smokers. *Pediatric Nursing, 34*(1), 13–17.

Fritz, D. J., Wider, L. C., Hardin, S. B., & Horrocks, M. (2008b). Program strategies for adolescent smoking cessation. *The Journal of School Nursing, 24*(1), 21–27.

Glass, J. (1986). Attitude similarity in three-generation families: Socialization, status inheritance, or reciprocal influence? *American Sociological Review, 51,* 685–698.

Greene, K., & Banerjee, S. C. (2009). Examining unsupervised time with peers and the role of association with delinquent peers on adolescent smoking. *Nicotine & Tobacco Research, 11*(4), 371–380.

Hahn, E. J., Hall, L. A., Rayens, M. K., Burt, A. V., Corley, D., & Sheffel, K. L. (2000). Kindergarten children's knowledge and perceptions about alcohol, tobacco, and other drugs. *Journal of School Health, 70*(2), 51–55.

Hahn, E. J., Hall, L. A., Rayens, M. K., Myers, A. V., & Bonnel, G. (2007). School- and home-based drug prevention: Environmental, parent, and child risk reduction. *Drugs: education, prevention, and policy, 14*(4), 319–331.

Hahn, E. J., Rayens, M. K., Rasnake, R., York, N., Okoli, C. T. C., & Riker, C. A. (2005). School tobacco policies in a tobacco-growing state. *Journal of School Health, 75*(6), 219–225.

Higgs, P. E., Edwards, D., Harbin, R. E., & Higgs, P. C. (2000). Evaluation of a self-directed smoking prevention and cessation program. *Pediatric Nursing, 26*(2), 150–155.

H.R.1256—111th Congress, Session 1. (2009). *Family smoking prevention and tobacco control act.* Retrieved July 14, 2009, from www.tobaccolawcenter.org/documents/FDA-tobacco-regulation-final-bill.pdf

Hu, F. B., Flay, B. R., Hedeker, D., Siddiqui, O., & Day, L. E. (1995). The influences of friends' and parental smoking on adolescent smoking behavior: The effects of time and prior smoking. *Journal of Applied Social Psychology, 25,* 2018–2047.

Jackson, C., & Henriksen, L. (1997). Do as I say: Parent smoking, antismoking socialization, and smoking onset among children. *Addictive Behavior, 22*(1), 107–114.

Jackson, C., Henriksen, L., Dickinson, D., & Levine, D. W. (1997). The early use of alcohol and tobacco: Its relation to children's competence and parents' behavior. *American Journal of Public Health, 87,* 359–364.

Kodl, M. M., & Mermelstein, R. (2004). Beyond modeling: Parenting practices, parental smoking history, and adolescent cigarette smoking. *Addictive Behavior, 29*(1), 17–32.

Komro, K. A., McCarty, M. C., Forster, J. L., Blaine, T. M., & Chen, V. (2003). Parental, family, and home characteristics associated with cigarette smoking among adolescents. *American Journal of Health Promotion, 17*(5), 291–299.

Kulbok, P. A., Rhee, H., Botchwey, N., Hinton, I., Bovbjerg, V., & Anderson, N. L. R. (2008). Factors influencing adolescents' decision not to smoke. *Public Health Nursing, 25*(6), 505–515.

Lantz, P. M., Jacobson, P. D., Warner, K. E., Wasserman, J., Pollack, H. A., Berson, J., et al. (2000). Investing in youth tobacco control: A review of smoking prevention and control strategies. *Tobacco Control, 9,* 47–63.

Maccoby, E. E., & Martin, J. A. (1983). Socialization in the context of the family: Parent-child interaction. *Socialization, Personality, and Social Development,* 1–101.

McGahee, T. W., Kemp, V., & Tingen, M. S. (2000). A theoretical model for smoking prevention studies in preteen children. *Pediatric Nursing, 26*(2), 135–141.

McGahee, T. W., & Tingen, M. S. (2000). The effects of a smoking prevention curriculum on fifth-grade children's attitudes, subjective norms, and refusal skills. *Southern Online Journal of Nursing Research, 1*(2). Retrieved from www.snrs.org

McVie, S., & Bradshaw, P. (2005). *Adolescent smoking, drinking, and drug use.* Retrieved from http://www.law.ed.ac.uk/cls/esytc/findings/digest7.pdf

Nash, S. G., McQueen, A., & Bray, J. H. (2005) Pathways to adolescent alcohol use: Family environment, peer influence, and parental expectations. *Journal of Adolescent Health, 37,* 19–28.

National Center for Chronic Disease Prevention and Health Promotion. (2004a). *The health consequences of smoking: A report of the Surgeon General, 2004.* Retrieved August 18, 2004, http://www.thriveri.org/documents/4g_health_consequences_smoking.pdf

National Center for Health Statistics. (2002). *Healthy people 2002: Trends in racial and ethnic specific area for health status indicators.* Retrieved January 11, 2004, from http://www.cdc.gov/nchs

National Center on Addiction and Substance Abuse. (2004). *Columbia University: National survey of American attitudes on substance abuse VI: Teens.* Retrieved October 2004, from http://www.casacolumbia.org/absolutenm/articlefiles/379-2001%20National%20 Survey%20VI.pdf

National Health Promotion Associates, Inc. (2003). *LifeSkills training products and services* (pp. 1–11). New York: Author.

National Institute on Drug Abuse. (2008). *NIDA infofacts: High school and youth trends.* U.S. Department of Health and Human Services: National Institutes of Health. Retrieved June 8, 2009, from http://www.nida.nih.gov/Infofacts/HSYouthtrends.html

Office of Behavioral Social Sciences Research NIH. (2009, August 10). *American Sociological Association 104th Annual Meeting Special Session on CBPR.* Retrieved on June 19, 2009, from http://obssr.od.nih.gov/scientific_areas/methodology/community_based_participatory_research/CBPR_ASA.aspx

Petrie, J., Bunn, F., & Byrne, G. (2007). Parenting programmes for preventing tobacco, alcohol, or drugs misuse in children <18: A systematic review. *Health Education Research, 22*(2), 177–191.

Reinert, B., Campbell, C., Carver, V., & Range, L. M. (2003). Joys and tribulations of faith-based youth tobacco use prevention: A case study in Mississippi. *Health Promotion Practice, 4*(3), 228–235.

Reinert, B., Carver, V., & Range, L. M. (2005). School nurses' opinions about the prevention of tobacco use. *Journal of Community Health Nursing, 22*(4), 205–211.

Reinert, B., Carver, V., Range, L., & Campbell, C. (2006). Faith-based leaders' opinions before and after a youth tobacco prevention workshop. *Journal of Cultural Diversity, 13*(4), 177–180.

Reinert, B., Carver, V., Range, L., & Pike, C. (2008). Church leaders' tobacco opinions: Send materials, not money. *Journal of Cultural Diversity, 15*(2), 81–85.

Rimal, R. N. (2003). Intergenerational transmission of health: The role of intrapersonal, interpersonal, and communicative factors. *Health Education Behavior, 30*(1), 10–28.

Seal, N. (2006). Preventing tobacco and drug use among Thai high school students through life skills training. *Nursing and Health Sciences, 8,* 164–168.

Smith, T. M., Talley, B., Hubbard, M., & Winn, C. (2008). Evaluation of a tobacco prevention program for children: ToPIC. *Journal of Community Health Nursing, 25*(4), 218–228.

Smith, T. M., Tingen, M. S., & Waller, J. (2004). The influence of self-concept and locus of control on rural preadolescent tobacco use. *Southern Online Journal of Nursing Research, 5*(5), 1–23.

Sowden, A. J., & Stead, L. F. (2003). Community interventions for preventing smoking in young people. *Cochrane Database of Systematic Reviews,* (1), CD001291.

Staten, R. R. & Ridner, S. L. (2006). College students' perspective on smoking cessation: "If the message doesn't speak to me, I don't hear it." *Issues in Mental Health Nursing, 28,* 101–115.

Task Force on Community Preventive Services. (2001). Recommendations regarding interventions to reduce tobacco use and exposure to environmental tobacco smoke. *American Journal of Preventive Medicine, 20*(2), 10–15.

Thomas, R. E., Baker, P., & Lorenzetti, D. (2007, January 24). Family-based programmes for preventing smoking by children and adolescents. *Cochrane Database System Review,* (1), CD004493.

Thomas, R. E., & Perara, R. (2006). School-based programmes for preventing smoking. *Cochrane Database of Systematic Reviews*, (3), CD001293.

Tingen, M. S. (2007). *The impact of a tobacco control intervention in African-American families.* Grant No. 1R01CA118066. Augusta, GA: Medical College of Georgia.

Tingen, M. S., Andrews, J. O., Heath, J., Humphries, M. C., Reimche, D. L., Cartee, S. G., et al. (2009). *Higher rates of smoking experimentation among U.S. rural youth compared to state and national norms.* Proceeding of the 2009 Joint Conference of SRNT (Society for Research on Nicotine and Tobacco) and SRNT-Europe, POS5-73, 154 Dublin, Ireland.

Tingen, M. S., Waller, J. L., Smith, T. M., Baker, R. R., Reyes, J., & Treiber, F. A. (2006). Tobacco prevention in children and cessation in family members. *Journal of the American Academy of Nurse Practitioners*, 18, 169–179.

U.S. Department of Health and Human Services. (2007). *Children and secondhand smoke exposure: Excerpts from the health consequences of involuntary exposure to tobacco smoke: A report of the surgeon general—2006.* Atlanta, GA: U.S. Department of Health and Human Services, Centers for Disease Control and Prevention, Coordinating Center for Health Promotion, National Center for Chronic Disease Prevention and Health Promotion, Office on Smoking and Health.

Wickrama, K. A., Conger, R. D., Wallace, L. E., & Elder, G. H. (1999). The intergenerational transmission of health-risk behaviors: Adolescent lifestyles and gender moderating effects. *Journal of Health and Social Behavior*, 40(3), 258–272.

Wiehe, S. E., Garrison, M. M., Christakis, D. A., Ebel, B. E., & Rivara, F. P. (2005). A systematic review of school-based smoking prevention trials with long-term follow-up. *Journal of Adolescent Health*, 36, 162–169.

World Health Organization. (2008). *WHO report on the global tobacco epidemic, 2008: The MPOWER package.* Geneva, Switzerland: WHO.

Chapter 8

Two Decades of Nurse-Led Research on Smoking During Pregnancy and Postpartum: Concept Development to Intervention Trials

Kathleen F. Gaffney, Heibatollah Baghi, and Sarah E. Sheehan

ABSTRACT

Tobacco use during pregnancy and postpartum is a leading cause of preventable morbidities for women and their infants. Over the past two decades, nursing research has addressed this recalcitrant clinical problem from a variety of conceptual and methodological perspectives. The 64 published studies (1988–2009) that met inclusion criteria for this systematic review represent the full research trajectory from concept development to intervention testing. Meta-analysis demonstrated an overall significant trend in nursing intervention efficacy (OR = 1.14, 95% CI = 1.08–1.2) for studies that examined

DOI: 10.1891/0739-6686.27.195

comparable prenatal and postpartum smoking cessation outcomes. Implications for future nursing research and evidence-based policy are presented.

Keywords: smoking; pregnancy; postpartum; nursing; research; intervention; relapse; cessation

The health consequences of smoking during pregnancy and postpartum are severe and preventable. Tobacco-related morbidities during pregnancy include placental complications, premature delivery, and fetal growth restriction (Cnattingius, 2004; Martin et al., 2003). Infants and young children who are exposed to secondary tobacco smoke have a disproportionately high incidence of low birth weight, sudden infant death syndrome, ear infections, respiratory infections, asthma exacerbations, and behavioral disorders compared to those not so exposed (Button, Thapar, & McGuffin, 2005; National Institute on Drug Abuse [NIDA], 2009; U.S. Department of Health and Human Services [U. S. DHHS], 2006). Despite recent advances in reducing the prevalence of smoking during pregnancy, 13% of pregnant women continue to smoke and those who quit experience postpartum relapse rates of 60% to 70% during the first few months postpartum (Allen, Dietz, Tong, England, & Prince, 2008; Coleman & Joyce, 2003).

This review synthesizes nurse-led research of prenatal and postpartum tobacco use. The presentation is organized around a research trajectory that begins with concept development and extends to theory-driven intervention trials. Preliminary efficacy of tested interventions is reported. It is anticipated that findings from this review will inform future smoking cessation research and health care policy.

METHODOLOGY

A search of nurse-led research on smoking during pregnancy and postpartum was conducted using CINAHL, Medline, and PsycINFO databases as well as the Tobacco Free Nurses (www.tobaccofreenurses.org) library. Combinations of the following key words aided the search: prenatal, pregnancy, postpartum, tobacco, smoking, relapse, cessation, and intervention. Hand searches of bibliographies supplemented electronic searches. Inclusion criteria were: (a) publication in a peer-reviewed journal between 1988 and March 2009, (b) written in English language, (c) nurse-led research, and (c) focus on smoking during pregnancy and/or postpartum.

RESULTS

Using these search methods, a total of 64 studies were found that met the inclusion criteria. Each was classified into one of six categories: (1) concept development/

qualitative approaches (n = 12), (2) concept development/formative descriptive approaches (n = 11), (3) theoretically derived conceptual models (n = 3), (4) identification of correlates and predictors (n = 14), (5) preliminary intervention studies (n = 14), and (6) tests of intervention efficacy (n = 10).

Concept Development

Qualitative Approaches

Four major concepts related to prenatal and postpartum smoking were developed from the qualitative studies that met inclusion criteria for this review: barriers to cessation, cultural influences on tobacco use, sensory aversions to cigarettes, and partner support for cessation efforts.

Barriers. Barriers to cessation were prominent in the findings of four studies. Based on interview data, Tod (2003) used the following labels to describe three perceived barriers to cessation during pregnancy: (a) lack of will power makes failure to quit a self-fulfilling prophecy; (b) smoking helps in coping with stressors of caring for children and financial concerns, and (c) partner smoking has a negative influence on quit efforts. Her findings overlap with those of an earlier study with postpartum women (Edwards & Sims-Jones, 1998) that identified stressful events including caring for a baby, relationship problems, and having a partner who smokes as critical barriers to continued smoking cessation after delivery.

Bottorff, Johnson, Irwin, and Ratner (2000) used narrative research methods to explore postpartum smoking relapse prevention. In their study, two comparable barriers to continued cessation were found among the story lines emerged from mapping of each participant's relapse trajectory: (a) being vulnerable to smoking (issues of addiction and feeling smoking was out of their control) and (b) smoking for relief (from stress). Building on the concept that stress associated with infant care may be a unique barrier to continued smoking cessation for postpartum women, Gaffney, Beckwitt, and Friesen (2008a) explored the early maternal experiences of women who intended to remain smoke free following delivery. Participants reported that infant irritability, especially inconsolable infant crying, triggered both thoughts of smoking and smoking behavior. Four major themes emerged related to infant crying as a perceived barrier to continued smoking cessation: (a) not knowing what to do (to soothe their babies), (b) seeking renewal (after dealing with frustration of inconsolable crying), (c) seeking relief (from the tension they were feeling), and (d) evaluating self (feeling bad about self as mother).

Cultural Influences. Pletsch led two qualitative studies that used thematic content analysis techniques to develop the concept of cultural influence on perinatal tobacco use. Findings from the first study, based on focus group discussions with pregnant Latina smokers, revealed that family involvement in the context of smoking behavior was found to be a powerful and unique factor that influenced smoking behavior for this group (Pletsch & Johnson, 1996). In the second study (Pletsch, Morgan, & Pieper, 2003), the context of smoking and beliefs that African American women hold about tobacco use during pregnancy and postpartum were explored. Two major themes emerged: (a) living a stressful life and (b) personal accountability for smoking cessation. It is particularly noteworthy that the sources of stress described by the women in this study were most often out of their control in contrast to their beliefs that smoking cessation is centered on personal characteristics such as personal determination.

Sensory Aversions. Pletsch and Kratz (2004) examined the concept of sensory aversions to cigarettes during pregnancy and postpartum in a longitudinal descriptive study with women from diverse racial and ethnic backgrounds. They found that most of the women in their study experienced an aversion to the taste or smell of cigarette smoke while pregnant and that this aversion was no longer present by 3 months postpartum. Coincidently, most women also had returned to smoking by this time. The researchers describe this finding as having a good conceptual fit with the notion that olfactory and gustatory aversions to smoking during pregnancy may be an extrinsic motivation for smoking cessation that is temporary.

Partner Support. The concept of partner support for prenatal and postpartum smoking cessation was the major focus for five studies that met the inclusion criteria for this review. Based on interview data, Thompson, Parahoo, McCurry, and O'Doherty (2004) found that pregnant women in their study perceived minimal partner support for their cessation efforts. Examples of this low level support were often expressed as "token gestures" such as smoking outside or putting the windows down in the car when smoking. The women reported that the assistance by partners in their smoking cessation efforts was negligible. Further, they believed that their partners would be unwilling to participate in any smoking cessation interventions that were provided as part of prenatal care.

Bottorff and her colleagues conducted four studies that expand our understanding of the concept of partner support for smoking cessation. In one of these studies, (Bottorff et al., 2005a), dyad case studies were developed from interview data using the family case summary approach developed by Knafl and Ayres (1996). This approach led to the identification of interactive routines related to regulation of smoking, practices related to acquisition, use and handling of tobacco, communication about tobacco and responding to slips and lapses. Based on findings, the researchers recommended the use of interaction models related to smoking, recognizing the critical role of partner influence on a woman's smoking behavior. The concept of partner support was then further developed in a study comprised of interviews with women and their partners that were conducted after delivery and again 3 to 6 months postpartum (Bottorff et al., 2006a). Findings from these data demonstrated that a woman's tobacco reduction altered a couple's established tobacco-related routines and that the intensity of the impact upon couple dynamics varied depending on their previous interaction patterns with respect to tobacco.

To further explore the concept of partner support, a next study was comprised of interviews with fathers during the first 6 weeks following the birth of their infants and again at 16 to 24 weeks postpartum (Bottorff, Oliffe, Kalaw, Carey, & Mroz, 2006b). Four themes emerged as the men described their own smoking during this time of transition: (a) expressing masculinity through smoking, (b) reconciling smoking as a family man (i.e., helps in role of father and partner helping with stress management), (c) losing the freedom to smoke, and (d) resisting a smokeless life. Most recently, Bottorff, Radsma, Kelly, and Oliffe (2009) used narrative methods to further develop the concept of partner support by exploring partners' own approaches to reducing or quitting smoking during the first 6 months postpartum. Four storylines were identified: (a) quitting cold turkey (impulsive decision to quit), (b) planned reduction (based on careful stepwise process), (c) baby as patch (the need to smoke is replaced by having the baby, growing sense of what if means to be a "good" father), and (d) forced reduction (demands by partner).

Formative Descriptive Approaches

This section describes formative nurse-led research published during the past two decades that has used a variety of quantitative methods to advance concept development in the study of prenatal and postpartum tobacco use.

Teen Pregnancy. In a study with pregnant teenager smokers, Albrecht, Higgins, and Lebow (2000) explored the concept of knowledge of the detrimental effects of smoking on health. They found that adolescents who quit smoking had significantly higher knowledge scores than those who did not ($F = 5.78$, $df = 69$, $p = .03$). In a later exploratory study, the concepts of connectedness with family and school and religiosity were explored as potential protective factors against health risk behaviors among pregnant adolescents (Albrecht, Reynolds, Cornelius, Heidinger, & Armfield, 2002). Religiosity, operationally defined with a summary measure of a subjects' religious beliefs, was found to be negatively correlated with cigarette use ($N = 53$, $r = -0.302$, $p < .05$). However, multiple linear regression analysis adjusted for age and race, found no predictive effect on smoking behavior. The study's small sample size may have precluded the detection of a significant effect.

Spirituality. Later, an exploratory study of spirituality and religiosity among pregnant Appalachian women (Jesse & Reed, 2004), demonstrated negative relationships with frequency of smoking ($N = 120$, $r = -.25$ and $-.24$, respectively; $p < .01$). A similar exploratory study with urban pregnant women (Jesse, Graham, & Swanson, 2006) found that no association between spirituality and smoking but a negative relationship with religiosity ($N = 130$, $OR = 0.87$, $95\% \ CI = 0.76-1.00$, $p = .05$).

Measurement. Three formative descriptive studies contributed to future re-search of concept development by publishing "lessons learned" regarding measurement strategies. The importance of measuring nicotine dependence was the focus of one study (Albrecht et al., 1999). In this research ($N = 94$), teenagers who had smoked 10 or more cigarettes per day prior to pregnancy frequently reported severe symptoms of withdrawal when they attempted to quit during pregnancy: craving for cigarettes (79%), irritability (60%), nervousness (55%), and difficulty concentrating (49%). Another study compared measures of self-report and exhaled carbon monoxide (CO) to saliva cotinine levels using a sample of 109 pregnant teens (Albrecht, Reynolds, Salamie, & Payne, 1999). Results indicated that when compared to saliva cotinine, self-report was a stronger indicator of continued smoking (specificity = 86.5%) but CO was a better indicator of smoking cessation (sensitivity = 93.5%). The authors recommended the combination of measures as an inexpensive method for assessing the smoking status of pregnant adolescents. The third measurement study compared self-reported smoking status with urinary cotinine levels using a sample of 94 pregnant women (Britton, Brinthaupt, Stehle, & James, 2004). A 16.6% discordant rate between self-report and urinary cotinine assays was found ($\chi^2 = 27.80$, $df = 1$, $p < .001$). These findings are considered preliminary and interpreted with caution as the subsample of self-reported nonsmokers was small ($n = 24$).

Outcomes. Two innovative preliminary descriptive studies explored potential outcomes of smoking during pregnancy and postpartum. Gennaro, Dunphy, Dowd, Fehder, and Douglas (2001) led formative research to identify the relationship between smoking and immune status of women up to 4 months postpartum ($N = 142$). The relatively small number who smoked ($n = 55$) and inconsistent smoking patterns may have contributed to the unanticipated finding of no significant relationship. Sherman, Young, Sherman, Collazo, and Bernert (2002) explored the effect of prenatal smoke exposure on newborn heart rate ($N = 130$). They found that newborns with cotinine levels above 6.0 ng/ml were significantly different from those with lower levels in maximum heart rate, range of heart rate, and variance of heart rate. The researchers suggest that infants with higher levels of cotinine may be at greater risk for SIDS and apparent life-threatening events due to an inability to maximize cardiac output. Consequently, they recommend large-scale replication studies to validate study findings.

Nurse-Led Reviews. Two previous nurse-led reviews of formative descriptive studies of prenatal and postpartum research met the criteria for this study. Zimmer (2000) conducted an integrative review of nine interdisciplinary studies that explored contributing factors that lead to postpartum smoking relapse. Two factors were identified: (a) the association with other smokers and (b) choosing not to breastfeed. Gage, Everett, and Bullock (2007) used a systematic process of synthesizing and analyzing interdisciplinary studies of the role of male partners in prenatal smoking. The 18 studies in their review were focused primarily on women's perceptions of their partners' support of their cessation efforts. The authors concluded that data also are needed that address the role that smoking plays for men as they experience the transition to fatherhood.

Theoretically Derived Conceptual Models

Building upon previous research that suggests that conceptual models are useful for the general population of smokers do not fit the context and experience of prenatal and postpartum women, Pletsch (2006) proposed a conceptual model based on motivational theory (Deci & Ryan, 1985, 2002) and an adaptation of the stepped-care and matching model (Abrams et al., 1996). Her innovative, blended model is tailored to meet the unique needs of women as they progress through the third trimester of pregnancy and into the early postpartum months. Four key elements of her model are designed for integration into clinical research and practice: assessment, development of a risk profile, triaging to intervention intensity based on this risk profile, and matching intervention strategies to risk assessment and a woman's own intervention priorities. The model is currently being evaluated and refined for use in clinical trials.

Gantt (2001) proposed a model specifically for postpartum smoking-avoidance interventions. Her model, adapted from Ajzen's (1988) theory of planned behavior, proposes that examining postpartum smoking avoidance within the theory's constructs will advance our knowledge of perceived benefits and drawbacks of smoking (attitude), the influence of others (subjective norm), and the perceived difficulty of remaining abstinent (perceived behavioral control).

Another proposed conceptual model for studies of postpartum smoking takes into account the context-specific variables that influence a women's progression through the early months of motherhood while simultaneously trying to remain smoke free (Gaffney, 2006). The model is based on two dynamic and theoretically derived processes: smoking abstinence self-efficacy (Marlatt, 1985; 1996) and becoming a mother (Mercer, 2004). Use of this blended model is predicted to advance our understanding of postpartum smoking by identifying the unique barriers and facilitators for relapse prevention experienced during the first few months after delivery.

Identification of Correlates and Predictors

Over the past two decades, nurse researchers have contributed to the development of effective intervention strategies by conducting studies of the underlying correlates and predictors of smoking during pregnancy and postpartum. As displayed in Table 8.1, their studies have focused on the nature of the relationship between tobacco use and a diverse array of prenatal and postpartum characteristics and experiences. While Table 8.1 provides information about primary outcomes of each study, a few observations are offered here about the overall contributions of this subset of studies.

Stressors

It is noteworthy that the studies led by McFarlane (1996) and Bullock, Mears, Woodcock, and Record (2001) both confirm the relationship between smoking and life stressors, including family and financial problems that overlap with findings from the formative studies cited in this review. While these associations are also well established for individuals in the general population, the investigations led by McFarlane and Bullock underscore the statistically and clinically significant link between smoking and the unique stressor of physical abuse while pregnant. Specifically, their findings support the use of the Abuse Assessment Screen (Parker & McFarlane, 1991) or a comparable measure of abuse in future clinical trials of smoking cessation during pregnancy.

Sensory Aversions

Findings by Pletsch and her colleagues (2008) that pregnant women report aversions to the smell and taste of cigarettes during the first trimester of pregnancy confirms the same findings from their earlier qualitative work (Pletsch & Kratz, 2004). The validation of an association between tobacco-related olfactory and gustatory changes and smoking cessation during pregnancy led to a recommendation for sensory aversion assessments in future intervention trials for prenatal smoking cessation.

Breastfeeding

The association between smoking and early termination of breastfeeding was explored by two research teams (Hill & Aldag, 1996; Ratner, Johnson, & Bottorff, 1999). Together, their findings confirm a positive association. A conclusion from both studies was that the early termination is preceded in a temporal order by the perception of insufficient milk. The latter is viewed as a measurable predictor of the early termination.

Infant Obesity

The examination of the association between smoking during pregnancy and later infant obesity by Sowan and Stember (2000) is considered highly innovative. While a positive association was found, the underpinnings of the relationship are not clear. The obesity pattern of the prenatally smoke-exposed infants was found to be similar to that of babies who had been formula-fed. As the authors

TABLE 8.1 Nurse-Led Studies of the Correlates and Predictors of Prenatal and Postpartum Tobacco Use, 1988–2009 ($N = 14$)

First Author Year	Design Sample	Correlates/Predictors of Tobacco Use	Findings
McFarlane 1996	Prospective cohort ($n = 1203$ pg women)	Physical abuse during pregnancy	African American: 34% not abused, smoked; 50% were abused, smoked; $\chi^2 = 8.21^{**}$ White: 46% not abused, smoked; 60% were abused, smoked; $\chi^2 = 5.22^{**}$
Hill 1996	Correlational ($n = 550$ mothers of infants)	Early weaning (<8 wks)	Mothers of term and LBW infants less likely breastfeed 8 wks pp if they were smokers versus nonsmokers: $\chi^2 = 12.87^{***}$ and $\chi^2 = 28.84^{**}$
Ratner 1999	Secondary analysis ($n = 228$ mothers of infants)	Early weaning (<26 wks)	Women who returned to daily smoking 4 times more likely to wean early than those who had not $\chi^2 = 19.6^{***}$
Albrecht 2000	Longitudinal correlational ($n = 71$ pg teens)	Knowledge of detrimental effects of smoking on women and fetus	Teenagers who quit smoking demonstrated greater knowledge than those who did not, $F = 5.78^{*}$
Sowan 2000	Prospective cohort ($n = 630$ mothers and infants)	Infant obesity	Prenatally smoke-exposed infants more likely to be obese at 14 months than nonsmoke-affected infants, $t = -2.29^{*}$
Albrecht 2001	Comparative correlation ($n = 123$ pg teens)	Racial group	Whites had higher daily level of nicotine intake than Blacks, $t = 2.78^{**}$ and greater nicotine dependence, $t = 4.07^{**}$
Bullock 2001	Retrospective comparative ($n = 299$ pp women)	Stressors during pregnancy	Problems with partner or children ($\chi^2 = 45.14^{***}$) and abuse during pregnancy ($\chi^2 = 16.92^{***}$) distinguished groups of smokers from nonsmokers

(Continued)

TABLE 8.1 Nurse-Led Studies of the Correlates and Predictors of Prenatal and Postpartum Tobacco Use, 1988–2009 (N = 14) (*Continued*)

First Author Year	Design Sample	Correlates/Predictors of Tobacco Use	Findings
Albrecht 2002	Descriptive (n = 142 pg teen smokers)	Social environmental variables from Jessor's problem-behavior theory	Compatibility of parent and peer attitudes (OR = 1.54,* CI 1.0–2.3) and alcohol intake prior to pg (OR = 5.46,* CI 1.2–25.0) predicted long-term smoking abstinence
Fisher 2005	Correlational (n = 1613 pg women)	Ethnicity	Greater smoking prevalence among Jewish than Arab women: 17 versus 3% OR = 7.5,*** CI = 4.2–13.4
Scheibmeir 2005	Cross-sectional (n = 201 pg ex-smokers)	Motivation to quit Intention to remain smoke free Stage of change Nicotine addiction	Motivation to quit smoking was the only significant predictor of smoking cessation strategies: 44% of variance in experiential processes; 31% of variance in behavioral processes
Kulwicki 2007	Cross-sectional (n = 823 pg Arab Americans)	Ethnicity	6.3% of Arab Americans smoked during pg
Gaffney 2007	Correlational (n = 133 pp women who quit smoking)	Factors associated with becoming a mother	After controlling for known smoking predictors: prenatal intention to not smoke after delivery, thinking about smoking in response to baby crying, confidence to not smoke in response to baby crying added to prediction of self-confidence to not smoke, R^2 change = .135.***

| Gaffney 2008 | Secondary analysis ($n = 130$ pp women who quit smoking) | Factors associated with becoming a mother | Groups formed based on intention to not smoke pp and smoking by 2 wk pp differed on: baby's crying triggered thoughts of smoking ($\chi^2 = 7.18^*$); confidence to not smoke in response infant crying, $F = 6.9^{**}$ |
| Pletsch 2008 | Correlational ($n = 209$ pg smokers) | Olfactory and gustatory aversions to cigarettes | Cigarettes smelled and tasted different (63% and 53%); for women with an olfactory changes, 78% reported smoking less ($OR = 2.08^*$, $CI = 1.02–4.23^*$) |

Note. pg = pregnancy; pp = postpartum; wks = weeks; lbw = low birth weight; OR = odds ratio; CI = 95% confidence interval.
$^*p < .05.$ $^{**}p < .01.$ $^{***}p < .001.$

point out, nicotine acts as an appetite suppressant. When nicotine is removed, infants may experience increased appetite and withdrawal symptoms that lead to overfeeding. Further study will clarify the nature of the relationship.

Racial–Ethnic Differences

Four research teams whose work is cited in this section addressed the issue of racial and ethnic group differences in relation to perinatal tobacco use (Albrecht, Taylor, Braxter, & Reynolds, 2001; Fisher et al., 2005; Heaman & Chalmers, 2005; Kulwicki, Smiley, & Devine, 2007). Together, their significant findings of differences among groups underscore the necessity of tailoring intervention strategies to the unique meanings of tobacco use for culturally diverse subpopulations of pregnant and postpartum smokers.

Preliminary Intervention Studies

Studies that were included in this section were those that tested the feasibility and acceptability of intervention strategies and research methods for investigations of prenatal and postpartum smoking cessation. Also included here were studies that assessed the role of health care providers in implementing planned interventions.

Feasibility and Acceptability

Among the pilot studies that met the inclusion criteria was an investigation of a community-based smoking intervention (Chalmers et al., 2004). Evaluative data from 42 participants demonstrated differential acceptability of the planned intervention strategies. Specifically, the investigators found that home visits and resource materials were perceived as helpful, but support groups and telephone helplines were not. Moore, Elmore, Ketner, Wagoner, and Walsh (1995) reported success with the use of telephone calls delivered 2 to 4 days per week from 27 to 37 weeks gestation, as evidenced by a self-reported decrease in smoking by 62% of their sample ($N = 130$).

A preliminary study ($N = 62$) of a relapse prevention intervention delivered during postpartum hospitalization assessed a strategy comprised of a brief counseling session that included the identification of stressors and coping strategies. No preliminary efficacy was found, as 52% of the sample relapsed within 2 weeks of delivery, underscoring the importance of refining the intervention (Suplee, 2005). In another pilot project, Buchanan (2005) demonstrated the use of the U.S. DHHS Clinical Practice Guideline for Treating Tobacco Use and Dependence (2000) in helping pregnant women decrease their smoking ($N = 48$). While women in the intervention group did smoke fewer cigarettes per day at delivery and 2 weeks after delivery than a control group, the rate of relapse by 2 weeks postdelivery was high.

Based on the pilot study, spending more time and resources on the implementation of the practice guidelines throughout the first 6 weeks following delivery was identified as a needed modification for a future clinical trial.

Recruitment

Sheahan and Wilson (1997) conducted a pilot study to evaluate recruitment strategies for enrolling 20 pregnant smokers and their male partners in a home-based couples smoking cessation program. Despite the offer of 10 weeks of free nicotine patches for partners and multiple approaches to enroll 200 eligible subjects, only 7 couples participated and only 3 of those completed the program. This difficult experience led researchers to suggest that an underlying dynamic process around smoking seemed to be operating through the couples' communication, decision making, and positive or negative cooperative behavior. As a result, the pregnant women they interviewed most often expressed a feeling of vulnerability and an unwillingness to urge a partner's cooperation in a smoking cessation program.

Retention

While Sheahan and Wilson (1997) tested the feasibility of recruitment strategies, Albrecht, Higgins, and Stone (1999) conducted a preliminary test of intervention completion. Specifically, the decision making of pregnant adolescents ($N = 53$) regarding the completion of a smoking cessation program was examined using the perspectives of problem behavior theory (Jessor, Donovan, & Costa, 1991) and information processing theory (Simon, 1986) to guide study design and interpretation. Adolescents who completed the cessation program were found to be younger than those participants who decided not to complete the intervention ($p = .01$). Researchers raised the question of whether longer duration of smoking, rather than age-related decision making may explain this finding. More Blacks than Whites decided to complete the intervention ($p = .05$), yet nicotine dependence was also a potential confounder as Black teenagers in the study smoked fewer cigarettes per day. Parental disapproval of teen smoking was also found to be significantly related to completion of the program ($p = .01$).

In another pilot study for the same smoking cessation intervention project for pregnant adolescents, Albrecht, Payne, Stone, and Reynolds (1998) explored the use of peer support in achieving teen smoking cessation. Using a randomized, three-group, controlled design ($N = 84$), they found that smoking cessation and reduction were better in the peer-supported group than either of the comparison groups. This finding supported the design of a large-scale clinical trial, sufficiently powered to test the effect of the peer support. The preliminary study experience also prompted more intensive efforts with a larger sample to retain subjects over a year as the preliminary study illustrated that many of the pregnant adolescents who met the inclusion criteria had transient living conditions that made it difficult to retain them in a longitudinal study.

Intervention Delivery

Several studies examined factors associated with the delivery of smoking cessation interventions to pregnant and postpartum women by health care providers. A survey of smoking cessation practices by midwives (N = 425) found that most respondents used minimal interventions such as advice and education, but few applied more skilled and time-intensive approaches such as counseling about methods for quitting (Cooke, Mattick, & Barclay, 1996). The subjects reported that time constraints and their own perceived lack of ability due to inadequate training for smoking cessation counseling were a substantial barriers to implementing interventions. Dunkley (1997) explored whether a brief, booklet-based training program focused on the stages of change for addictive behavior would help midwives (N = 26) support pregnant women quit smoking (N = 94). No significant difference between quit rates for intervention and control groups was found. A later study comprised of both midwives and doctors found that midwives implemented interventions more often than the doctors (58% vs. 22%, N = 182), but were less likely to offer advice to quit, preferring to suggest that smokers cut down on their tobacco use (Cooke, Mattick, & Walsh, 2001). The midwives also reported insufficient time and training acted as substantial barriers to their smoking education efforts. Another study (N = 78) found that while most (71%) midwives reported that they had not advised any pregnant women to give up smoking in the previous 7 days, 73% reported that helping pregnant women quit smoking was one of the most important things a midwife can do. This paradoxical finding led researchers to conclude that inadequate training in smoking cessation strategies was a barrier to implementation (Condliffe, McEwen, & West, 2005). Focus group interviews (N = 25) were used in another pilot study to examine the perspectives of nurses, dieticians, and social workers about providing smoking cessation interventions (Aquilino, Goody, & Lowe, 2003). Participants reported that prenatal clinic appointments offer insufficient time for smoking cessation counseling and that other health promotion topics are of greater priority than smoking issues. The participants did report having consistently assess for maternal smoking status at each visit, but voiced the notion that it might be unrealistic to provide more in-depth smoking cessation activities due to time constraints. Using a different approach, Semenic and Edwards (2006) recommended simple changes to prenatal health care records that may lead to increased prenatal counseling for pregnant smokers. Using a content analysis approach to the examination of prenatal records, they found that most records lacked prompts to support evidence-based recommended practices for effective screening and treatment of maternal tobacco dependence. Together, these studies point to time constraints, provider education deficits, and health system changes as areas in need for enhancement of smoking cessation intervention delivery.

Tests of Intervention Efficacy

Table 8.2 is a summary of the key components of nurse-led tests of intervention efficacy that met the inclusion criteria for this review, including their use of a conceptual framework, research design, sample sizes, intervention strategies, and primary tobacco-related outcomes. Together these studies demonstrate that prenatal and postpartum counseling on smoking cessation has been the most frequent intervention strategy for nurse-led interventions to address perinatal tobacco use.

Eight of the 10 studies in this subset were tests of theory-derived interventions. Two theories that were foundational for several of these studies are frequently used in interdisciplinary tobacco use research, namely, the relapse prevention model (Marlatt, 1985, 1996) and the transtheoretical model (Prochaska & Velicer, 1997). In addition, Albrecht and her research team (2006) derived their intervention from two theories with a good conceptual fit for their target population of pregnant adolescents that is, cognitive behavioral theory (Beck, Wright, Newman, & Sliese, 1993) and Jessor's problem behavior theory (1991). Based on findings from their earlier studies about the relationship between stress and tobacco use, Bullock and her colleagues (2008b) selected the social stress model of substance abuse (Rhodes & Jason, 1990) to guide their intervention design and testing.

A meta-analysis was conducted to examine intervention efficacy across studies represented in this review. This statistical technique provides the power to detect and integrate treatment effect across multiple studies that use comparable outcome variables. Depending on the study's design and statistical procedures, many effect size indices may be used, including odds ratios (Borenstein, Hedges, Higgins, & Rothstein, 2002; Schulze, 2004). Six studies in this review reported odds ratios for 13 comparable study outcomes regarding prenatal and postpartum smoking cessation. Figure 8.1 displays the meta-analysis findings of intervention efficacy based on the odds ratios (OR) and 95% confidence intervals (CI) for each of these individual outcomes as well as the average effect across studies. As depicted, odds ratios greater than one indicate positive efficacy for the intervention groups compared to the control groups. It is noteworthy that when the odds ratios for all of the represented outcomes are averaged, the effect size ($OR = 1.14$, 95% CI = 1.08–1.2.) demonstrates a significant trend in favor of intervention efficacy.

IMPLICATIONS

Future Nursing Research in Prenatal and Postpartum Smoking Cessation

The body of nursing science represented by the 64 studies of smoking during pregnancy and postpartum in this review (1988–2009) form a strong base for future advancements in research that will lead to cessation interventions with long-term

TABLE 8.2 Nurse-Led Intervention Trials of Prenatal and Postpartum Smoking Cessation, 1988–2009 (N = 10)

First Author Year	Conceptual Framework	Design Sample Size	Intervention Strategies	Primary Outcome(s)
O'Connor 1992	NR	2-grp RCT INT (n = 115) CTL (n = 109)	20-minute nurse-delivered prenatal counseling with telephone follow-up	Cessation rates for smokers 36 wk pg: INT = 13%, CTL = 6%, χ^2 = 2.69, NS 6 wk pp: INT = 14%, CTL = 5%, χ^2 = 4.12*
Lillington 1995	Relapse prevention	2-grp pretest-posttest Smokers: INT (n = 79) CTL (n = 146) Ex-smokers: INT (n = 76) CTL (n = 254)	15-minute prenatal counseling by health educator and self-help guide incorporating behavioral change strategies	Cessation rates for smokers 9 mo pg: INT = 43%, CTL = 25%, χ^2 = 8.08** 6 wk pp: INT = 25%, CTL = 12%, χ^2 = 6.17** Relapse rates for ex-smokers 9 mo pg: INT = 5%, CTL = 11%, NS 6 wk pp: INT = 21%, CTL = 38%, χ^2 = 7.83**
Gebauer 1998	NR	2-group comparison INT (n = 84) CTL (n = 94)	15-minute nurse-delivered prenatal counseling, printed material, one follow-up telephone call	Smoking abstinence 6–12 wk postintervention: INT = 15%, CTL = 0%, χ^2 = 15.7***
Johnson 2000	Relapse Prevention	2-group RCT INT (n = 125) CTL (n = 126)	Nurse-delivered pp counseling, 8 telephone calls, printed materials	At 6 mo pp Continuous abstinence: INT = 38%, CTL = 27%, χ^2 = 2.8, NS Daily smoking: INT = 34%, CTL = 48%, χ^2 = 4.6*
Ratner 2000	Relapse Prevention	RCT, 2-grp INT (n = 119) CTL (n = 119)	Follow up for Johnson et al. (2000)	At 12 mo pp Continuous abstinence: INT = 21%, CTL = 19%, χ^2 = 0.1, NS Daily smoking: INT = 41%, CTL = 50%, χ^2 = 1.7, NS

Source	Theoretical framework	Design (sample)	Intervention	Outcomes
Valanis 2001	Transtheoretical model	Prospective cohort: CTL (n = 1024) INT (n=2055)	Motivational interviews during pg, pp, well child visits, stage-specific cessation messages	At 12 mo pp Sustained smoking abstinence: INT = 18%; CTL = 15%; χ^2 = 6.2*
Pletsch 2002	Transtheoretical model	2-grp RCT INT (n = 31) CTL (n = 43)	Nurse-delivered stage-matched prenatal counseling, videos, two home visits	Becoming a nonsmoker: t = .80, NS Reducing secondary smoke exposure: t = .67, NS
Britton 2006	Transtheoretical model	2-grp pre- and posttest: INT (n = 101) CTL (n = 93)	Nurse-managed prenatal counseling, materials: *Smoke Free Baby and Me*	At 6 wk pp, Smoking cessation INT = 37%, CTL = 17%, χ^2 = 4.37*
Albrecht 2006	Cognitive behavioral theory Problem behavior theory	3-grp, RCT *Teen Fresh Start* (n = 32), *Teen Fresh Start-Buddy* (n = 38), UC (n = 41)	Nurse-delivered 8 week group program using peer buddy and peer coleader with cessation strategies tailored to pregnant teens	Smoking behavior 8 wk postintervention: TFS-B > UC, β = 1.32** 12 wk postintervention: OR = .6, NS
Bullock 2008	Social stress model of substance abuse	4-grp RCT CTL (n = 171) Booklet (n = 179) Social support (n = 176) Combined (n = 170)	Nurse-delivered weekly telephone individualized social support (*Baby Beep program*) and 8 mailed smoking cessation booklets	Point prevalence abstinence group differences Late pregnancy: χ^2 = 1.33, NS 6 wks pp: χ^2 = 1.39, NS

Note. NR= not reported; RCT = randomized controlled trial; INT = intervention; CTL = Control; pg = pregnancy; pp = postpartum; wk = weeks; mo = months; OR = odds ratio; NS = nonsignificant.
*p = <.05. **p = <.01. ***p = <.001.

Author/Year	Outcome	Odds ratio	Lower limit	Upper limit
01. O'Connor/1992	Quit smoking (36 wk pg)	2.240	0.851	5.897
02. O'Connor/1992	Quit smoking (6 wk pp)	2.660	1.032	6.855
03. Lillington/1995	Smokers: Quit rate (9 mo pg)	1.750	1.195	2.562
04. Lillington/1995	Smokers: Quit rate (6 wk pp)	2.170	1.207	3.901
05. Lillington/1995	Ex-smoker: Relapse (9 mo pg)	1.060	0.992	1.132
06. Lillington/1995	Ex-smoker: Relapse (6 wk pp)	1.280	1.100	1.490
07. Johnson/2000	Continuous abstinence (6 mo pp)	1.630	0.958	2.774
08. Johnson/2000	Daily smoking (6 mo pp)	1.800	1.082	2.995
09. Ratner/2000	Continuous abstinence (12 mo pp)	1.170	0.618	2.214
10. Ratner/2000	Daily smoking (12 mo pp)	1.450	0.868	2.423
11. Valanis/2001	Sustained abstinence (12 mo pp)	2.352	1.277	4.331
12. Albrecht/2006	Smoking (8 wk post-intervention)	3.730	1.001	13.896
13. Albrecht/2006	Smoking (12 wk post-intervention)	0.599	0.163	2.203
		1.144	1.080	1.212

Odds ratio and 95% CI

0.01   0.1   1   10   100

Favors CTL   Favors INT

FIGURE 8.1 Estimates of intervention efficacy for selected nurse-led trials, prenatal and postpartum smoking cessation, 1988–2009.

Note. pg = pregnancy; pp = postpartum; *CTL* = control; *INT* = intervention.

effectiveness. Together, they shed light on the intrinsic and extrinsic barriers to quitting that may be evaluated as mediators in future intervention designs, including issues of addiction and feeling helpless to control smoking, unique cultural influences based on racial or ethnic background, temporal changes in sensory responses to tobacco throughout pregnancy, and stressors unique to the transition to motherhood.

The extensive, in-depth work of Bottorff and her research team (2005a, 2005b, 2006a, 2006b) sheds a new light on the complex issues associated with partner support that pregnant women face when attempting to be smoke free. The program of research led by Albrecht is a model for future investigators in terms of concept development, variable testing, and intervention trials. While the range of studies by this nurse scientist offers value for all who study perinatal tobacco use, it holds particular value for researchers who study the unique developmental characteristics of pregnant teenage smokers.

The preliminary intervention studies and tests of intervention efficacy cited in this review lay the groundwork for future study protocols and research methods. The recent study by Bullock and her colleagues (2009) is exemplary in describing recruitment and retention strategies for an area of research that has been fraught with high attrition rates. The meta-analysis findings from the intervention trials depicted in Figure 8.1 argue for replication and extension studies in which interventions are administered over longer periods of time than the first few weeks postpartum. The present review did not include studies on maternal and infant exposure to secondhand smoke, as this growing body of nursing research was beyond the scope of our inclusion criteria.

Evidence-Based Policy for Prenatal and Postpartum Smoking Cessation

In addition to the insights that this body of science offers for future research, implications for evidence-based policy may be drawn from the collection. For instance, future federally funded clinical practice guidelines for addressing tobacco use and dependence may be strengthened by the addition of assessment and action protocols tailored to the specific stressors experienced by women who progress through the developmental stages of pregnancy and postpartum, including the issues of partner support, postpartum depression, and infant irritability.

In addition, funding of large-scale clinical trials to examine the long-term efficacy of interventions that provide nursing support for prenatal and postpartum smoking cessation is warranted. Such an initiative would be most valuable if directed toward pregnant women at high social risk and provided intervention support from early pregnancy when sensory changes in smoking occur until the end of the first year postpartum when the tumultuous events associated with the transition to motherhood have subsided.

The samples of pregnant and postpartum women in this review were typically individuals living with high levels of social stress, sometimes even physical abuse. Policies are needed that ensure that these stressors are assessed and addressed. Bullock and colleagues (2008) point out that cessation interventions are likely to be ineffective until these stressors are addressed because smoking offers a readily available coping mechanism. Finally, health policy regarding smoking cessation should require comprehensive assessments of a wide range of social, emotional, environmental, and behavioral factors associated with prenatal and postpartum smoking along with guidelines for tailored long-term interventions that meet the unique needs of this special population of smokers.

REFERENCES

Abrams, D. B., Orleans, C. T., Niaura, R. S., Goldstein, M. G., Prochaska, J. O., & Velicer, W. (1996). Integrating individual and public health perspectives for treatment of tobacco dependence under managed health care: A combined stepped-care and matching model. *Annals of Behavioral Medicine*, 18, 290–304.

Ajzen, I. (1988). *Attitudes, personality, and behavior*. Chicago, IL: Dorsey Press.

Albrecht, S. A., Caruthers, D., Patrick, T., Reynolds, M., Salamie, D., Higgins, L. W., et al. (2006). A randomized controlled trial of a smoking cessation intervention for pregnant adolescents. *Nursing Research*, 55(6), 402–410.

Albrecht, S. A., Cornelius, M. D., Braxter, B., Reynolds, M. D., Stone, C., & Cassidy, B. (1999). An assessment of nicotine dependence among pregnant adolescents. *Journal of Substance Abuse Treatment*, 16(4), 337–343.

Albrecht, S. A., Higgins, L. W., & Lebow, H. (2000). Knowledge about the deleterious effects of smoking and its relationship to smoking cessation among pregnant adolescents. *Adolescence*, 35(140), 709–716.

Albrecht, S. A., Higgins, L. W., & Stone, C. (1999). Factors relating to pregnant adolescents' decisions to complete a smoking cessation intervention. *Journal of Pediatric Nursing*, 14(5), 322–328.

Albrecht, S., Payne, L., Stone, C. A., & Reynolds, M. D. (1998). A preliminary study of the use of peer support in smoking cessation programs for pregnant adolescents. *Journal of the American Academy of Nurse Practitioners*, 10(3), 119–125.

Albrecht, S. A., Reynolds, M. D., Cornelius, M. D., Heidinger, J., & Armfield, C. (2002). Connectedness of pregnant adolescents who smoke. *Journal of Child & Adolescent Psychiatric Nursing*, 15(1), 16–23.

Albrecht, S. A., Reynolds, M. D., Salamie, D., & Payne, L. (1999). A comparison of saliva cotinine, carbon monoxide levels, and self-report as indicators of smoking cessation in the pregnant adolescent. *Journal of Addictions Nursing*, 11(3), 93–101.

Albrecht, S. A., Taylor, M. V., Braxter, B. J., & Reynolds, M. D. (2001). A descriptive study of smoking patterns among two racial groups of pregnant adolescents *Journal of Addictions Nursing*, 13(1), 19–30.

Allen, A. M., Dietz, P. M., Tong, V. T., England, L. J., & Prince, C. B. (2008). Prenatal smoking prevalence ascertained from two population-based data sources: Birth certificates and PRAMS questionnaires, 2004. *Public Health Reports, 123*(5), 586–592.

Aquilino, M. L., Goody, C. M., & Lowe, J. B. (2003). WIC providers' perspectives on offering smoking cessation interventions. *The American Journal of Maternal Child Nursing, 28*(5), 326–332.

Beck, A., Wright, F., Newman, C., & Sliese, B. (1993). *Cognitive therapy of substance abuse.* New York, NY: Guilford Press.

Borenstein, M., Hedges, L., Higgins, J., & Rothstein, H. (2002). *Comprehensive meta-analysis* (Version 2.0) [Computer Software]. Englewood, NJ: Biostat.

Bottorff, J. L., Johnson, J. L., Irwin, L. G., & Ratner, P. A. (2000). Narratives of smoking relapse: The stories of postpartum women. *Research in Nursing & Health, 23,* 126–134.

Bottorff, J. L., Kalaw, C., Johnson, J. L., Chambers, M. S., Greaves, L., & Kelly, M. (2005a). Unraveling smoking ties: How tobacco use is embedded in couple interactions. *Research in Nursing & Health, 28,* 316–328.

Bottorff, J. L., Kalaw, C., Johnson, J. L., Stewart, M., & Greaves, L. (2005b). Tobacco use in intimate spaces: Issues in the study of couple dynamics. *Qualitative Health Research, 15*(4), 564–577.

Bottorff, J. L., Kalaw, C., Johnson, J. L., Stewart, M., Greaves, L., & Carey, J. (2006a). Couple dynamics during women's tobacco reduction in pregnancy and postpartum. *Nicotine & Tobacco Research, 8*(4), 499–509.

Bottorff, J. L., Oliffe, J., Kalaw, C., Carey, J., & Mroz, L. (2006b). Men's constructions of smoking in the context of women's tobacco reduction during pregnancy and postpartum. *Social Science & Medicine, 62*(12), 3096–3108.

Bottorff, J. L., Radsma, J., Kelly, M., & Oliffe, J. L. (2009). Fathers' narratives of reducing and quitting smoking. *Sociology of Health & Illness, 31*(2), 185–200.

Britton, G. R. A., Brinthaupt, J., Stehle, J. M., & James, G. D. (2004). Comparison of self-reported smoking and urinary cotinine levels in a rural pregnant population. *Journal of Obstetric, Gynecologic and Neonatal Nursing, 33*(3), 306–311.

Britton, G. R. A., Brinthaupt, J., Stehle, J. M., & James, G. D. (2006). The effectiveness of a nurse-managed perinatal smoking cessation program implemented in a rural county. *Nicotine & Tobacco Research, 8*(1), 13–28.

Buchanan, L. (2005). Implementing a smoking cessation program for pregnant women based on current clinical practice guidelines. *Journal of the American Academy of Nurse Practitioners, 14*(6), 243–250.

Bullock, L., Everett, K. D., Mullen, P. D., Geden, E., Longo, D. R., & Madsen, R. (2008). Baby BEEP: A randomized controlled trial of nurses' individualized social support for poor rural pregnant smokers. *Maternal Child Health Journal, 13*(3), 395–406.

Bullock, L. F. C., Mears, J. L. C., Woodcock, C., & Record, R. (2001). Retrospective study of the association of stress and smoking during pregnancy in rural women. *Addictive Behaviors, 26,* 405–413.

Button, T. M., Thapar, A., & McGuffin, P. (2005). Relationship between antisocial behavior, attention-deficit hyperactivity disorder and maternal prenatal smoking. *British Journal of Psychiatry, 187,* 155–160.

Chalmers, K., Gupton, A., Katz, A., Hack, T., Hildes-Ripstein, E., Brown, J., et al. (2004). The description and evaluation of a longitudinal pilot study of a smoking relapse/reduction intervention for perinatal women. *Journal of Advanced Nursing, 45*(2), 162–171.

Cnattingius, S. (2004). The epidemiology of smoking during pregnancy: Smoking prevalence, maternal characteristics, and pregnancy outcomes. *Nicotine and Tobacco Research, 6*(Suppl. 2), S125–S140.

Coleman, G. J., & Joyce, T. (2003). Trends in smoking before, during, and after pregnancy in ten states. *American Journal of Preventive Medicine, 24*(1), 29–35.

Condliffe, L., McEwen, A., & West, R. (2005). The attitude of maternity staff to, and smoking cessation interventions with, childbearing women in London. *Midwifery, 21*(3), 233–240.

Cooke, M., Mattick, R., & Barclay, L. (1996). Predictors of brief smoking intervention in a midwifery setting. *Addiction, 91*(11), 1715–1725.

Cooke, M., Mattick, R. P., & Walsh, R. A. (2001). Differential uptake of a smoking cessation programme disseminated to doctors and midwives in antenatal clinics. *Addiction, 96*(3), 495–505.

Deci, E. L., & Ryan, R. M. (2002). *Handbook of self-determination research.* Rochester, NY: University of Rochester Press.

Deci, E.L., & Ryan, R.M. (1985). *Intrinsic motivation and self-determination in human behavior.* New York, NY: Plenum Press.

Dunkley, J. (1997). Training midwives to help pregnant women stop smoking. *Nursing Times, 93*(5), 64–66.

Edwards, N., & Sims-Jones, N. (1998). Smoking and smoking relapse during pregnancy and postpartum: Results of a qualitative study. *Birth, 25*(2), 94–100.

Fisher, N., Amitai, Y., Haringman, M., Meiraz, H., Baram, N., & Leventhal, A. (2005). The prevalence of smoking among pregnant and postpartum women in Israel: A national survey and review. *Health Policy, 73*, 1–9.

Gaffney, K. F. (2006). Postpartum smoking relapse and becoming a mother. *Journal of Nursing Scholarship, 38*(1), 26–30.

Gaffney, K. F., Beckwitt, A. E., & Friesen, M. A. (2008a). Mothers' reflections about infant irritability and postpartum tobacco use. *Birth: Issues in Perinatal Care, 35*(1), 66–72.

Gaffney, K. F., & Henry, L.L. (2007). Identifying risk factors for postpartum tobacco use. *Journal of Nursing Scholarship, 39*(2), 126–132.

Gaffney, K. F., Henry, L. L., Douglas, C. Y., Goldberg, P. A. (2008b). Tobacco use triggers for mothers of infants: Implications for pediatric nursing practice. *Pediatric Nursing, 34*(3), 253–258.

Gage, J.D., Everett, K.D., & Bullock, L. (2007). A review of research literature addressing male partners and smoking during pregnancy. *Journal of Obstetric and Gynecologic & Neonatal Nursing, 36*(6), 574–580.

Gantt, C. J.(2001). The theory of planned behavior and postpartum smoking relapse. *Journal of Nursing Scholarship, 33*(4), 337–341.

Gebauer, C., Kwo, C., Haynes, E. F., & Wewers, M. E. (1998). A nurse-managed smoking cessation intervention during pregnancy. *Journal of Obstetric, Gynecologic, & Neonatal Nursing, 27*(1), 47–53.

Gennaro, S., Dunphy, P., Dowd, M., Fehder, W., & Douglas, S. D. (2001). Postpartum smoking behaviors and immune response in mothers of term and preterm infants. *Research in Nursing and Health, 24*(1), 9–17.

Heaman, M. I., & Chalmers, K. (2005). Prevalence and correlates of smoking during pregnancy: A comparison of aboriginal and non-aboriginal women in Manitoba. *Birth, 32*(4), 299–305.

Hill, P. D., & Aldag, J. C. (1996). Smoking and breastfeeding status. *Research in Nursing & Health, 19,* 125–132.

Jesse, D. E., Graham, M., & Swanson, M. (2006). Psychosocial and spiritual factors associated with smoking and substance use during pregnancy in African American and white low-income women. *Journal of Obstetric, Gynecologic, & Neonatal Nursing, 35*(1), 68–77.

Jesse, D. E., & Reed, P. G. (2004). Effects of spirituality and psychosocial well-being on health risk behaviors in Appalachian pregnant women. *Journal of Obstetric, Gynecologic, & Neonatal Nursing, 33*(6), 739–747.

Jessor, R., Donovan, J., & Costa, F. (1991). *Beyond adolescence: Problem behavior and young adult development.* Cambridge, UK: Cambridge University Press.

Johnson, J. L., Ratner, P. A., Bottorff, J. L., Hall, W., & Dahinten, S. (2000). Preventing smoking relapse in postpartum women. *Nursing Research, 49*(1), 44–52.

Knafl, K., & Ayres, L. (1996). Managing large qualitative data sets in family research. *Journal of Family Nursing, 2*(4), 350–365.

Kulwicki, A., Smiley, K., & Devine, S. (2007). Smoking behavior in pregnant Arab Americans. *The American Journal of Maternal Child Nursing, 32*(6), 363–367.

Lillington, L., Royce, J., Novak, D., Rubalcaba, M., & Chelbowski, R. (1995). Evaluation of a smoking cessation program for pregnant minority women. *Cancer Practice: A Multidisciplinary Journal of Cancer Care, 3*(3), 157–163.

Marlatt, G. A. (1985). Relapse prevention: Theoretical rationale and overview of the model. In G. A. Marlatt & J. R. Gordon (Eds.), *Relapse prevention: Maintenance strategies in the treatment of addictive behaviors* (pp. 3–70). New York: Guilford.

Marlatt, G. A. (1996). Taxonomy of high-risk situations for alcohol relapse: Evolution and development of a cognitive-behavioral model. *Addiction, 91,* 537–549.

Martin, J. A., Hamilton, B. E., Sutton, P. D., Ventura, S. J., Menacker, F., & Munson, M. L. (2003). Births: Final data for 2002. *National Vital Statistics Report, 52.* Hyattsville, MD: Center for Health Statistics.

McFarlane, J., Parker, B., & Soeken, K. (1996). Physical abuse, smoking, and substance use during pregnancy: Prevalence, interrelationships, and effects on birth weight. *Journal of Obstetric, Gynecologic & Neonatal Nursing, 25*(4), 313–320.

Mercer, R. T. (2004). Becoming a mother versus maternal role attainment. *Journal of Nursing Scholarship, 36,* 226–232.

Moore, M. L., Elmore, T., Ketner, M., Wagoner, S., & Walsh, K. (1995). Reduction and cessation of smoking in pregnant women: The effect of a telephone intervention. *Journal of Perinatal Education, 4*(1), 35–39.

National Institute on Drug Abuse. (2009, March 4). Combination of genes and prenatal exposure to smoking increases teens' risk of disruptive behavior. *NIH News.* Retrieved March 5, 2009, from http://www.nih.gov/news/health/mar2009/nida-04.htm

O'Connor, A. M., Davies, B. L., Dulberg, C. S., Buhler, P. L., Nadon, C., McBride, B. H., et al. (1992). Effectiveness of a pregnancy smoking cessation program. *Journal of Obstetric, Gynecologic, & Neonatal Nursing, 21*(5), 385–392.

Parker, B., & McFarlane, J. (1991). Nursing assessment of the battered pregnant woman. *American Journal of Maternal Child Nursing, 16,* 161–164.

Pletsch, P. K. (2002). Reduction of primary and secondary smoke exposure for low-income black pregnant women. *Nursing Clinics of North America, 37*, 315–329.

Pletsch, P.K. (2006). A model for postpartum smoking resumption prevention for women who stop smoking while pregnant. *Journal of Obstetric, Gynecologic, & Neonatal Nursing, 35*(2), 215–222.

Pletsch, P. K., & Johnson, M. K. (1996). The cigarette smoking experience of pregnant Latinas in the United States. *Health Care for Women International, 17*, 549–562.

Pletsch, P.K., & Kratz, A. T. (2004). Why do women stop smoking during pregnancy? Cigarettes taste and smell bad. *Health Care of Women International, 25*, 671–679.

Pletsch, P. K., Morgan, S., & Pieper, A. F. (2003). Contexts and beliefs about smoking and smoking cessation. *Journal of Obstetric, Gynecologic, & Neonatal Nursing, 28*(5), 320–325.

Pletsch, P.K., Pollak, K.L., Peterson, B.L., Park, J., Oncken, C. A., Swamy, G.K., et al. (2008). Olfactory and gustatory sensory changes to tobacco smoke in pregnant smokers. *Research in Nursing & Health, 31*, 31–41.

Prochaska, J. O., & Velicer, W. F. (1997). The transtheoretical model of health behavior change. *American Journal of Health Promotion, 12*, 38–48.

Ratner, P. A., Johnson, J. L., & Bottorff, J. L. (1999). Smoking relapse and early weaning among postpartum women: Is there an association. *Birth, 26*(2), 76–82.

Ratner, P. A., Johnson, J. L., Bottorff, J. L., Dahinten, S., & Hall, W. (2000). Twelve-month follow-up of a smoking relapse prevention intervention for postpartum women. *Addictive Behaviors, 25*(1), 81–92.

Rhodes, J. E., & Jason, L. A. (1990). A social stress model of substance abuse. *Journal of Consulting and Clinical Psychology, 58*(4), 395–401.

Scheibmeir, M. S., O'Connell, K. A., Aaronson, L. S., & Gajewski, B. (2005). Smoking cessation strategy use among pregnant ex-smokers. *Western Journal of Nursing Research, 27*(4), 411–427.

Schulze, R. (2004). *Meta-Analysis: A Comparison of Approaches*. Hogrefe & Huber: Cambridge, MA.

Semenic, S., & Edwards, N. (2006). Do Canadian prenatal records support evidence-based practices to reduce maternal smoking? *Journal of Obstetrics and Gynaecology Canada, 28*(5), 368–372.

Sheahan, S. L., & Wilson, S. M. (1997). Smoking cessation for pregnant women and their partners: A pilot study. *Journal of the American Academy of Nurse Practitioners, 9*(7), 323–326.

Sherman, J., Young, A, Sherman, M. P., Collazo, C., & Bernert, J. T. (2002). Prenatal smoking and alterations in newborn heart rate during transition. *Journal of Obstetric, Gynecologic, & Neonatal Nursing, 31*(6), 680–687.

Simon, H. A. (1986). Alternative visions of rationality. In H. Arkes & K. Hammond (Eds.), *Judgment and decision making* (pp. 91–113). Cambridge: Cambridge University Press.

Sowan, N. A. & Stember, M. L. (2000). Effect of maternal prenatal smoking on infant growth and development of obesity. *Journal of Perinatal Education, 9*(3), 22–29.

Suplee, P.D. (2005). The importance of providing smoking relapse counseling during the postpartum hospitalization. *Journal of Obstetric, Gynecologic & Neonatal Nursing, 34*(6), 703–712.

Thompson, K. A., Parahoo, K. P., McCurry, N., & O'Doherty, A. M. (2004). Women's perceptions of support from partners, family members and close friends for smoking cessation during pregnancy—combining quantitative and qualitative findings. *Health Education Research, 19*(1), 29–39.

Tod, A. M. (2003). Barriers to smoking cessation in pregnancy: A qualitative study. *British Journal of Community Nursing, 8*(2), 56–64.

U.S. Department of Health and Human Services. (2000). *Clinical practice guideline: Treating tobacco use and dependence.* Rockville, MD: U.S. Public Health Service.

U.S. Department of Health and Human Services. (2006). *The health consequences of involuntary exposure to tobacco smoke: A report of the surgeon general.* Rockville, MD: Centers for Disease Control and Prevention, National Center for Chronic Disease Prevention and Health Promotion, Office of Smoking and Health.

Valanis, B., Lichtenstein, E., Mullooly, J. P., Labuhn, K., Brody, K., Severson, H. H., et al. (2001). Maternal smoking cessation and relapse prevention during health care visits. *American Journal of Preventive Medicine, 20*(1), 1–8.

Zimmer, B. A. (2000). Smoking relapse during postpartum. *The Online Journal of Knowledge Synthesis for Nursing, 7*(6), 7.

Chapter 9

Nursing Interventions in Tobacco-Dependent Patients With Cardiovascular Diseases

Kawkab Shishani, Min Sohn, Ayako Okada,
and Erika Sivarajan Froelicher

ABSTRACT

Smoking is a well-established risk factor for cardiovascular disease (CVD). This chapter provides an overview of a program of nursing research relevant to tobacco use in patients with CVD. The Women's Initiative for Nonsmoking (WINS) provides a rich demonstration of a key randomized clinical trial (RCT) on the efficacy of smoking cessation in women. The National Institutes of Health priority for data mining of existing RCTs is demonstrated in the numerous presentations of findings from secondary papers from WINS that answer additional research questions relevant to smoking cessation, including the influence of depression on smoking, myths about and underuse of nicotine replacement therapy. The methodological and logistical challenges inherent in tobacco intervention studies are presented, including a discussion of research needed in the measurement of withdrawal symptoms. Additionally, the role and contributions of nurses serving on the federal guideline development process are highlighted. International

DOI: 10.1891/0739-6686.27.221

research activities of the coauthors from Jordan and Korea are also presented, including a discussion of the need for research in waterpipe use.

Keywords: cardiovascular diseases; smoking cessation studies; nurses; international; guideline; waterpipe

Smoking is a well-established risk factor for cardiovascular disease (CVD), as well as a prognostic factor after a cardiac event (Ockene & Miller, 1997; U.S. Department of Health and Human Services [DHHS], 2004). Cigarette smoking is the most important preventable cause of premature death in the United States. It accounts for nearly 440,000 deaths each year, of which more than 135,000 are due to smoking related cardiovascular diseases. Cigarette smokers are 2 to 3 times more likely to die from CVD than nonsmokers (American Heart Association [AHA], 2009). The pathophysiologies of the effects of smoking on CVD are clearly delineated in the 2004 Surgeon General's Report (U.S. DHHS, 2004; pp. 363–491) and go beyond the content of this chapter.

As many as 30% of all CVD deaths in the United States each year are attributable to cigarette smoking, with the risk being strongly dose-related (Ockene & Miller, 1997). Smoking nearly doubles the risk of ischemic stroke and acts synergistically with other risk factors, substantially increasing the risk of CVD (Ockene & Miller, 1997). Smokers are also at increased risk for peripheral arterial disease. Furthermore, patients with CVD experience as much as a 50% reduction in risk of reinfarction, sudden cardiac death, and total mortality if they quit smoking after the initial infarction (Ockene & Miller, 1997; Sparrow & Dawber, 1978). Patients with CVD who smoke are more likely to be hospitalized for recurrent episodes of CVD events (Mohiuddin et al., 2007). The health benefits start almost immediately after quitting and within a few years of quitting the risk of stroke and CVD are similar to nonsmokers. In a systematic review of smoking cessation interventions in patients with CVD, the total reduction in mortality rate was 36% (RR, 0.64; 95% CI, 0.58–0.71) and in nonfatal recurrent infarctions was 32% (0.68, 95%; CI, 0.57–0.82) (Critchley & Capewell, 2003). Since the evidence for the benefit of smoking cessation interventions is so strong, the Joint Commission on Accreditation of Healthcare Organization (see The Joint Commission, 2009 at http://www.jointcommission.org/) requires hospitals seeking accreditation to collect data on smoking cessation counseling for patients with acute myocardial infarction (AMI), heart failure, and community acquired pneumonia. Policies for these interventions are expected to become standard for quality nursing care.

Offering smoking cessation interventions to smokers with CVD is an urgent priority. This chapter provides an overview of nursing research in populations with CVD who are tobacco users. A summary of the Women's Initiative for Nonsmoking (WINS) findings is provided along with the challenges and barriers encountered with this type of research, including measurement of withdrawal symptoms. As CVD is an important international health problem, nursing research in tobacco control in this area is also explored. Gaps in the literature and implications for future research will be identified.

HOSPITALIZATION PROVIDES A WINDOW OF OPPORTUNITY

Patients who are hospitalized for CVD, have a window of opportunity for smoking cessation due to their vulnerable health situation and being in a setting where smoking is not allowed (Narsavage & Idemoto, 2003). Additionally, behavior change is easier when the individual is in a new environment and has experienced a frightening event such an admission to the hospital for an AMI. Under such circumstances the patients may be more willing to quit. Health care providers can capture these moments to do a thorough assessment and provide an individualized quit plan. This in itself could motivate the patient to not restart smoking once he or she is discharged to their home. For example, a 60 minute inpatient customized counseling session and telephone follow-up over 6 months yielded a 41.5% quit rate compared to counseling alone (30.2% quit rate) and 20% with no intervention (usual care) confirmed by biochemical marker (Taylor, Houston-Miller, Killen, & DeBusk, 1990). In addition, identification of the patients' self-efficacy to quit can indicate the expected quit rate (Sivarajan Froelicher et al., 2004). Once behavioral outcomes are achieved, it is important to sustain total abstinence, not even a puff. Numerous reports show that patients who relapse after discharge report higher depressive symptoms (OR, 2.40; 95% CI, 1.48, 3.78; Thorndike et al., 2008).

Male and female CVD patients who attend an outpatient clinic or a private doctor's office also benefit from smoking cessation counseling. The CVD risk reduction programs at primary care outpatient clinics demonstrate significant reduction in: smoking rates, systolic blood pressure, diastolic blood pressure, and dyslipidemia (low-density lipoprotein cholesterol; McPherson, Swenson, Pine, & Leimer, 2002).

MAJOR CONTRIBUTIONS TO NURSING SCIENCE

Rice and Stead (2008) conducted an extensive review on all nursing intervention for smoking cessation studies using the Cochrane Connection and concluded that nursing interventions increased the chance of staying quit when compared to usual care. However, they did not separately report on smoking cessation studies in populations with CVD specifically, nor did they separately report the disease specific efficacies.

Controlled Study of Earlier Cardiac Rehabilitation (CSECR)

The CSECR was a nurse-led Randomized Controlled Trial (RCT) that tested an education counseling and behavioral interventions program compared to exercise alone or a control group provided lessons for subsequent risk factor reduction behavioral research (Sivarajan et al., 1981, 1983). This study did not detect a significant treatment effect with respect to smoking cessation outcomes in patients with AMI. Clearly, while multifactorial risk reduction is the preferred approach in patient management during their cardiac rehabilitation treatment, studies of earlier cardiac rehabilitation using multifactorial interventions identified a very complex challenge due to the uneven distribution of the various risk factors in any given RCT, making it difficult to demonstrate efficacy for any particular risk factor intervention. Thus, for research purposes, efforts to test individual risk factor changes is preferable (Newton, Sivarajan Froelicher, & Clarke, 1985; Sivarajan et al., 1981, 1983).

Women's Initiative for Nonsmoking (WINS)

The WINS study builds on prior research by the Stanford University group (Taylor et al., 1990, 1996; Taylor, Houston-Miller, Haskell, & DeBusk, 1988) that included nurse-managed interventions. The behavioral intervention program consisted of physician advice to all patients, followed by random allocation to usual care or special nurse-managed intervention. Quit rates were measured at 12 month follow-up.

The earliest studies by the Stanford group were conducted in the 1970s and in Health Maintenance Organizations (HMO), where cost saving through prevention is a primary institutional objective, and where higher cessation rates are expected in this setting than in other hospitals nationally. Furthermore their first study included only men, precluding inferences to women patients (Taylor et al., 1990). Their subsequent study (Taylor et al., 1996) included a small number of women and failed to provide gender-specific outcomes data, again precluding treatment implications. These earlier studies led to the need to specifically study women cardiac patients.

The Stanford group's initial 26% effect size (Taylor et al., 1990) has, to date, never been duplicated. The most likely reasons for this large effect size are that the study was conducted in an HMO, at a time when smoking rates were much higher, the sample were all patients with a diagnosis of an AMI who might have been highly motivated to quit. In addition, societal changes in smoking prevalence and quitting since the 1990s may contribute to duplication of results of 26% quit rates at 12 months, from the 1980s, no longer feasible.

The WINS adopted the Stanford model and modified it to the unique needs of women, with the messages focused on matters identified as being important to women (such as avoiding weight gain, reducing wrinkles, stress reduction, etc.). This adaptation advanced the smoking cessation studies in three major ways: (1) for the first time, a study about smoking cessation outcomes focused on women with CVD, (2) the sample included patients with multiple CVD diagnoses, and (3) the sample was obtained from public, private, and governmental hospitals. Additionally, it included more than the usual 12 month follow-up. This study was a collaboration between University of California–San Francisco and Stanford University and exemplified multidisciplinary collaborative research. This RCT was designed to test the efficacy of a smoking cessation intervention in terms of relapse to short-term (6 and 12 months), and long-term (24 and 30 months) smoking and allowed for an additional analysis to evaluate time to continuous smoking. The WINS tested an intervention tailored specifically to women who were admitted to one of 12 hospitals in the San Francisco Bay area with diagnoses of CVD.

The WINS had three main objectives. One of the objectives was to test the efficacy of smoking cessation interventions at 6 and 12 months. This short-term duration has been customarily used to assess efficacy; however, consistent with public health principles the important question that remained to be answered was whether smoking cessation can be sustained permanently and for this reason, the second objective was to assess smoking cessation efficacy also at 24 and 30 months. Additionally, it was of interest to identify predictors of successful long-term abstinence or, alternatively, to identify relapse. Thus, a third objective was to estimate predictors of relapse.

The WINS education counseling and behavioral skill building intervention was guided by social learning theory and addiction theory and consisted of an initial bedside intervention during hospitalization. Women in the intervention group who relapsed and met the criteria for nicotine replacement therapy (NRT) were offered this medication; follow-up interventions consisted of five brief telephone counseling sessions at 2, 7, 21, 28, and 90 days. Women in both the usual group and the intervention group were followed up for assessment of smoking status at 6, 12, 24, and 30 months.

WINS Findings

The trial yielded four particularly important findings. (a) The women assigned to the intervention group were statistically significantly more likely to remain nonsmokers for a longer period of time than those in the usual group (Wilxocan statistic $p = .03$) as evaluated by a survival analysis according to the risk difference between the usual group and the intervention group. (b) Both groups had higher nonsmoking point prevalence at 6, 12, 24, and 30 months when compared to rates reported in other recent trials. (c) Although the protocol included NRT for all eligible intervention group participants who resumed smoking, few reported using it. Conversely, a small number (6% NRT gum and 11% NRT patch) of participants in the usual care group obtained NRT from their personal physician or when it became available over the counter. The underuse of NRT by women in the intervention group was an important finding and included the issues of and the reluctance by women to use NRT even when an NRT was indicated (Mahrer-Imhof, Froelicher, Li, Parker, & Benowitz, 2002). NRT was recommended during the hospital interventions and during the 90 days of outpatient phase. Of the 142 patients in the intervention group, 89.4% met the criteria for NRT use. However, during the follow-up assessment it became apparent that the actual reported NRT use ranged from 9% to 22% (Mahrer-Imhof et al., 2002). (d) Survival analysis indicated that continuous nonsmoking rates at 6 and 12 months remained relatively unchanged at 24 and 30 months, supporting the view that 12 months is an adequate follow-up period (Sivarajan Froelicher et al., 2004). The high confirmed smoking cessation rate in the usual care group (40.8%, 41.6%, 46.2%, and 50.0% at 6, 12, 24, and 30 months) versus the intervention group (51.5%, 47.6%, 48.5% and 50.0%) was unexpected (Sivarajan Froelicher et al., 2004), because the usual care group in most smoking trials have consistently shown lower sustained cessation rates than those noted in WINS ranging from 21% to 40% (Hajek, Taylor, & Mills, 2002; Ockene et al., 1992; Sivarajan Froelicher et al., 2004; Taylor et al., 1996).

Several explanations for these findings are plausible. First, because of societal trends since the 1980s, the effect size of smoking cessation interventions had decreased from 26% to 7% (Hajek et al., 2002); WINS effect size was 6%. As previously noted, the report of an effect size of 26% was from a study done with men who were hospitalized in an HMO for treatment of an AMI at a time when hospitals had few, if any no smoking policies and when the prevalence of smoking was higher than they are today (Taylor et al., 1990). More recent studies in samples of men and women have been published since the introduction of no smoking policies in hospitals beyond HMOs. Such changes in social norms may have influenced the smaller effect size found in the WINS. Second, the systematic identification of smokers, the brief intervention with a physician's advice, and the written materials provided to women in the usual care group, together with the consent procedures and the process of data collection for the trial, may have had an impact beyond that which would have resulted with routine hospital care particularly considering that these study groups consisted in large part of older women with limited social and financial resources. Third, the fact that the use of NRT was actually slightly higher in the usual care group (23%) than in the intervention group (20%) suggests that the patients in the usual care group may inadvertently have been encouraged to stop smoking more aggressively by their physicians during their participation in the WINS trial than in the past. Fourth, a sample size of 130 per group was planned in order to provide 80% power to detect a difference of 45% cessation under the usual group versus a 62% rate in the intervention group. These assumed rates were based on results from similar studies in men (Sivarajan Froelicher et al., 2004). We did achieve our planned sample size, however, only after more than doubling the number of enrollment sites from 5 to 12 and by extending the recruitment period by one year.

Additional WINS Finding

WINS' findings confirmed that in women with CVD, a relapse to smoking continues to be a serious challenge for health care professionals. Furthermore, WINS showed that predictors of relapse included low self-efficacy (<70%) and living with a smoker (Li & Froelicher, 2004). Numerous other studies (e.g., Taylor et al., 1988, 1990, 1996) and WINS confirmed the importance of measuring smoking cessation self-efficacy in nursing research. Additionally, the evaluation of health service utilizations and costs for women smokers with CVD in WINS revealed that a high proportion of women had physician visits (94%), emergency room visits (39%), and hospital admissions (36%) during 6 months of index hospitalizations (Froelicher, Sohn, Max, & Bacchetti, 2004b).

The findings also documented use of preventive home care services (26%); cardiac rehabilitation programs 19%, and physical therapy 14% (Froelicher et al., 2004b). This usage decreased over the course of the study follow-up period. One noticeable finding was that despite the high CVD risk factor presence and the many comorbidities in this population only a mere 19% were referred to a cardiac rehabilitation programs for multifactorial risk reduction (Froelicher et al., 2004b).

Although the WINS intervention protocol, designed in 1995, was a state-of-the-art behavioral intervention that was validated by the U.S. Public Health Service Guideline (Fiore et al., 1996), 6 months after the start of the WINS study, new advances in treatment for nicotine dependence emerged. These advances included the recommendations for use of pharmacological therapies such as NRT, even after an AMI and the use of bupropion as a smoking cessation medication. Such pharmacological interventions appear important in supporting women in smoking cessation efforts (Fiore et al., 2000).

Considerations for planning future interventions must include all of the evidence-based strategies delineated in the *Treating Tobacco Use and Dependence: 2008 Clinical Practice Guideline 2008 Update* published by the Public Health Service (Fiore et al., 2008). These strategies will add to the proven benefits and efficacy of multimodal strategies, including behavioral counseling and the use of pharmacotherapy, and follow-up for at least four to eight encounters (Fiore et al., 2008).

Challenges Identified in the WINS Study

Similar to other RCTs, WINS encountered numerous challenges and barriers that provide important lessons for subsequent research. Challenges, discussed below, were in the logistics as well as methodological domains.

Despite investigators' best efforts in the planning stages, the greatest challenge was obtaining participants in sufficient numbers for adequate power to test the study hypotheses. This required an extension from 5 study sites to 12 and an extension in the time line for recruitment from the originally planned 18 months to 30 months to obtain the necessary sample of women smokers.

The effects of temporal changes during a longitudinal follow-up study were evaluated. Investigators implementing a study protocol over several years must be mindful of how to handle temporal changes once the study is in progress. During the enrollment period, three major advancements in smoking cessation came about resulting in temporal changes for which accommodations needed to be made: (1) the publication of the first federal smoking cessation guideline (*Guideline*, Fiore et al., 1996) occurred 6 months after the start of the enrollment; (2) availability of over the counter purchase of NRT products; and (3) the release of off-label use of bupropion as a smoking cessation medication. How these three challenges were addressed is discussed next.

The release of the *Guideline* (Fiore et al., 1996) provided a cautionary statement contraindicating NRT within 6 months of an acute cardiac event. Since our protocol had included the use of NRT for patients who met predefined criteria, maintaining our protocol presented the investigators with the question of whether to eliminate the NRT from the WINS protocol or to continue to offer it as a choice to the subjects who met the criteria. A consultation with the coinvestigator, with expertise in nicotine pharmacology, resulted in the decision to continue the use of NRT, following precautionary statements. Before offering NRT to any patient who met the criteria for NRT use, the patients' primary physician, usually a cardiologist, was consulted and provided with the documentation demonstrating the favorable risk benefit ratio of using NRT compared to the nicotine absorption in an active smoker with heart disease (Benowitz, Hukkanen, & Jacob, 2009). The low proportion of women in WINS who used NRT (Mahrer-Imhof et al., 2002) was previously addressed. One wonders whether the contraindications in the *Guideline* resulted in the nurse cessation interventionists exercising unnecessary reluctance in the NRT component of the intervention. Even though we required a physician prescription for the NRT while patients were in the hospital, despite the NRT being available to obtain over the counter, the *Guideline* cautionary statement regarding NRT for patients with CVD was a barrier.

When NRT became available over the counter (OTC) we added a variable in the data collection form of the intervention and control groups at 6, 12, 24, and 30 months; this allowed us to evaluate the extent to which over-the-counter NRTs were a potential confounder.

When bupropion was being used off label more frequently in clinical practice as a smoking cessation aid, near the end of our study a question was added to all data collection forms at 6, 12, 24, and 30 months inquiring about the use of bupropion use in both groups.

Another challenge was the under use of NRT. Underutilization of NRT as an initial adjuvant to behavioral therapy in the intervention group may account for a small effect size. It is not clear to what extent the women's perception of NRT and their lack of understanding about its safety and positive risk-to-benefit ratio may have influenced their acceptance of our recommendation that they use it (Mahrer-Imhof et al., 2002). Moreover, it is likely that NRT use is a confounder by indication in WINS. That is, rather than offering NRT as an aid to smoking cessation from the beginning of the intervention, NRT was offered by WINS nurses and accepted by the subjects only to women who relapsed to smoking. It is therefore likely that, in this study, use of NRT was a predictor of relapse rather than a predictor of smoking cessation; thus, a confounder by indication.

The short hospital stay for some participants may have reduced the duration of the planned personal intervention. While five scheduled telephone follow-up interventions in the outpatients phase of the study were scheduled at 2, 7, 21, 28, and 90 days after discharge from the hospital, these telephone contacts were based upon prior assumptions about the physiology of withdrawal. Both the number and the timing of contacts may not have been optimal for every woman participating in this trial.

The measurement of addiction with dependence measures was challenging. This chapter addresses the measurement of withdrawal symptoms in a separate section. When assessing patients for smoking history and smoking patterns, a useful adjunct to such an interview is the use of any one of a number of instruments to assess the degree of tobacco dependence in the smoker. The oldest and best known of these measures is the Fagerstrom Dependency Scale (Fagerstrom, 1978). For WINS we used the slightly modified Fagerstrom questionnaire, the Stanford Dependency instrument (SDI). Dependency assessments are useful in determining the severity of addiction in order to provide a commensurate intensity of intervention in the form of education and counseling, and pharmacological support.

Additional challenges consisting of logistical or a methodological nature in the WINS trial included: (1) difficulties in recruiting older women, with low social, financial, and transportation support; (2) fear by some women about traveling to the research site unescorted; and (3) multiple health problems in addition to CVD. As a result, even the most motivated participants had difficulty adhering to all study long-term follow up (Froelicher, 1996; Taylor-Piliae & Froelicher, 2007). Adherence to National Institutes of Health requirements for Data Safety and Monitoring became mandatory after the completion of WINS. However, we developed directions for how to optimally institute such requirements for clinical nursing studies (Artinian, Froelicher, & Vander Wal, 2004).

Awareness of these challenges is necessary for new investigators planning such studies. For example alternative resources such as taxi fares or sufficient nurses for home visits may be needed in order to make it easier to facilitate participants' adherence to the follow-up plans. When a study protocol has specified a clear intervention period, this may not be an optimum time frame for all study subjects and may not reflect clinical practice. For example, a number of study subjects who relapsed after the initial 30-day intervention period would call and require a booster dose of intervention. Neither study design nor Committee on Human Research had provisions for attending individualized requests and such subjects were referred back to the primary care doctors in the intervention group.

Psychometric Measures of the WINS Study

Since earlier studies on hospitalized populations with cardiac disease had not used any psychometric measurements aside from the outcome measure of self-reported, biochemically verified, smoking status it was important to evaluate the reliability and validity of health and psychosocial measures that were used in WINS (Froelicher, Li, Mahrer-Imhof, Christopherson, & Stewart, 2004a).

We examined these using baseline measures from our cross-sectional study, nested within the RCT trial (Froelicher et al., 2004a). Measures included the perceived stress scale, a depression screener (Burnam, Wells, Leake, & Landsverk, 1988), self-efficacy, the sense of mastery scale, and measures of health-related quality of life from the medical outcome study. The 277 women smokers ranged in age from 34 to 86 years (mean 61 ± 10.1). Variability in floor/ceiling effects skewness, range mean and SD indicate that most measures had sufficient variability to predict and detect both positive and negative changes over the time. This internal consistency reliability ranged from .63 to .86. Preliminary evidence of construct validity was found that most of the hypotheses were confirmed. These measures generally performed well and showed promise for advancing our understanding of smokers in this population (Froelicher et al., 2004a) However, when we evaluated the predictive property of these health and psychosocial measures only self-efficacy was repeatedly found to be statistically significantly predictive of smoking cessation at 6, 12, 24, and 30 months (Li & Froelicher, 2008; Sivarajan Froelicher et al., 2004).

Contrary to Cohen and Lichtenstein (1990), the stress scale was unable to predict smoking outcomes in WINS; despite "stress" being the most frequently cited reason for relapse to smoking in these women. Similarly, the Burman depression scale did not offer any predictive value. In future smoking cessation research we would recommend a different instrument for screening of depression, such as the PHQ 9 or the Beck Depression Inventory (BDI; Lichtman et al., 2008). The importance of measuring depression cannot be overestimated given the findings of the association between depression and tobacco use (Strong et al., 2009; Thorndike & Rigotti, 2009). Thus, a greater emphasis must be placed on the effects of depression on smoking as well as the possible increase in depression that might be associated with smoking cessation.

One of the most critical challenges was how to define what constitutes smoking cessation while complying to intention to treat analysis. The methodology for quantification of smoking cessation status across published studies is inconsistent. In WINS we compared three different smoking cessation definitions (Oka, Katapodi, Lim, Bacchetti, & Froelicher, 2006) using the labels naïve (self-reported smoking "not even a puff" was the most liberal or naïve definition); the optimistic definition treating missing values on smoking status as missing and not as "smoker"; and the pessimistic (or the most conservative classification) with 7-day point prevalence verified with saliva cotinine. The pessimistic definition yields a greater number of smokers than the naïve or optimistic definition (Oka et al., 2006). The classification of smoking status is also relevant to time to continuous smoking (necessary for survival analysis). While many studies have used the naïve classification for their reports, a higher standard for measurement is usually demanded of RCTs, namely cotinine verification of smoking status, in which an unknown value is assumed to be "a smoker." However, in a population of CVD patients who are often older, sicker, and have many comorbidities, an unknown value may really constitute the inability to provide a cotinine sample due to illness, lack of transportation, or other circumstances; and therefore, the assumption of a person being a smoker when the data is not available would be erroneous. For this reason we opted to use the "optimistic" classification, which treats a missing data point as missing rather than assuming that the status is "smoker."

Secondary Analysis of WINS

In a secondary analysis of WINS data, Doolan, Stotts, Benowitz, Covinsky, and Froelicher (2008) dispelled the commonly held belief that smokers of advanced ages would not benefit from smoking cessation interventions (Doolan & Froelicher, 2006; Doolan et al., 2008). The current research of practices for older adults and smoking cessation interventions were examined. For almost 17 years the health care literature has mandated that people of all ages be provided with smoking cessation interventions (Doolan & Froelicher, 2006). However, in clinical practice, smoking cessation interventions are rarely offered to older adults (Doolan & Froelicher, 2006). In the WINS study, older women (age greater or equal to 62) as compared to younger women quit in higher proportions at both 6 months

(52.1% vs. 40.6%) and 12 months (52.0% vs. 38.1%) follow-up, a difference that was statistically significant ($p = .04$; Doolan et al., 2008). These findings provide strong support that older adults can quit smoking and should be offered smoking cessation interventions (Doolan et al., 2008).

MEASUREMENT OF WITHDRAWAL SYMPTOMS

Physiological and psychological aspects of nicotine withdrawal symptoms play an important role in relapse to smoking (Shiffman, West, & Gilbert, 2004). Prompted by our experience in WINS, a discussion of the measurement of withdrawal symptoms with valid and reliable tobacco withdrawal symptoms instruments is relevant. There are eight commonly used instruments for measuring tobacco withdrawal: (1) Fagerstrom Dependence on Tobacco Scale (FDT); (2) Stanford Dependency Index (SDI; a slightly modified version of the FDT); (3) Minnesota Withdrawal Scale (MWS; Hughes, Benowitz, Hatsukami, Mermelstein, & Shiffman, 2004; Piper et al., 2008); (4) Wisconsin Smoking Withdrawal Scale (WSWS; Welsch et al., 1999); (5) Shiffman-Jarvik Smoking Withdrawal Scale (S-JSWS; Shiffman & Jarvik, 1976); (6) Smoker Complaint Scale (SCS; Schneider & Jarvik, 1984); (7) Mood and Physical Symptoms Scale (West & Hajek, 2004; West, Hajek, & Belcher, 1989a, 1989b; West & Russell, 1985a, 1985b); and, (8) Cigarette Withdrawal Scale (CWS; Etter, Le Houezec, Huguelet, & Etter, 2009; Piper et al., 2008).

Of those instruments, the MWS is the most widely used and is translated into several languages. The WSWS was developed based on a literature review (Patten & Martin, 1996) and current theoretical grounds. To assess the symptoms that cause significant discomfort or impair the smoker's social and occupational function and cause relapse and considering the overall scale reliability and validity, the WSWS is more appropriate for the changes of smoking status and after the person quits smoking. Even considering the balance between accuracy and feasibility for implementation in the clinical context the WSWS was more appropriate than the MWS as a predictor instrument. The numbers of subscales are reasonable, based on the guidance that no subscale was reduced to fewer than three items to preserve adequate psychometric properties (Nunnally & Bernstein, 1994). Even though WSWS was better in assessing withdrawal symptoms than the MWS, the MWS may be more useful for cross-cultural studies. The MWS has been translated into Chinese (Taiwanese), Czech, Danish, Dutch, French, Korean, Norwegian, and Swedish (Hughes et al., 2004). Therefore, using the MWS provides opportunities for comparing results with other cross-cultural research findings than the WSWS.

Nursing research has the potential to provide essential information to guide symptom management in patients who quit smoking, in smoking cessation interventions, supporting patients who are not able to quit, or supporting patients during abstinence while hospitalized.

NURSE PARTICIPATION ON THE GUIDELINE PANEL

The published findings from WINS earned one of the authors (ESF) an appointment to the U.S. Public Health Services panel developing an update of the clinical practice guideline on tobacco dependence treatment (Fiore et al., 2008). The specific charge of the guideline panel under the leadership of Michel C. Fiore, MD was to provide the newest information updates for evidence-based practice. The committee included two nurse panel members (the author and Dr. Mary Ellen Wewers) and Ernestine Murray, RN, MS, Project Officer at AHRQ, and an avid spokesperson for nursing.

The *Guideline* (Fiore et al., 2008) highlighted 10 key recommendations for practice; illustrating for nurses and other clinicians the vast knowledge that exists with respect to who, when, where, what, how, and how much as well as dosage of intervention on tobacco dependence treatment and illustrates how these reviews can serve nurses, educators, practitioners, and scientists in their work. The overarching goal of the recommendations are that clinicians strongly recommend the use of effective tobacco dependence counseling and medication treatments for their patients who use tobacco, and that the health care system, insurers, and purchasers assist clinicians in making such effective treatments are available. Two types of counseling and behavioral therapies result in higher quit rates: (1) providing smokers with practical counseling such as problem-solving skills and skills training, and (2) providing support and encouragement as part of the treatment. These types of counseling elements should be included in smoking cessation interventions.

INTERNATIONAL NURSING RESEARCH
RELATED TO SMOKING CESSATION

Smoking rates have declined since the 1970s in the United States; while internationally many countries have alarming prevalence of smoking (World Health Organization [WHO], 2008). Particularly parts of Asia (Korea, China, India) and the Middle Eastern region continue to experience high smoking prevalences and in some instances these continue to be on the rise. Similar trends are observed with CVD (Reddy & Yusuf, 1998).

Research is needed to both assess these population's knowledge, attitudes, and beliefs about tobacco use as well as to continue to inform the development of experimental studies on cessation interventions. Research in Korea and Jordan provide two examples of baseline data that will guide pilot testing of smoking cessation interventions (Shishani, Nawafleh, & Sivarajan Froelicher, 2008; Sohn et al., 2007, 2008).

Korea

A particularly high smoking rate and lack of research in smoking cessation among Korean men with CVDs has been noticed. South Korean men have one of the highest rate of smoking in the world (57%); and CVD is the second most common causes of death among South Korean men (Sohn et al., 2007). A cross-sectional descriptive study with Korean men hospitalized for CVDs was conducted to explore their knowledge, attitudes, and smoking behavior and determine needs for smoking cessation (Sohn et al., 2007). This study of 97 men, who were all smokers, revealed that 65% of the men were addicted to nicotine based on the Fagerstrom score; 22% were smoking during their hospitalization despite a hospital no smoking policy; 78% believed that smoking cessation avoids or decreases the chance of developing heart disease; 93% reported their intention to quit; and 74% had moderate to high confidence about quitting in the month after hospital discharge (Sohn et al., 2008). Although the participants were highly motivated to quit smoking, they did not actively seek a proven smoking cessation method. Among men who wanted to quit smoking after discharge, 88% said that they would attempt to quit by themselves without help by health professionals. No one reported that he would attend an educational or smoking cessation program and only 4% were willing to try NRTs in the future. However, 51% were willing to participate in a formal, educational, smoking-cessation program, if such programs were available during their hospitalization (Sohn et al., 2007, 2008). These data indicate that hospital-based smoking cessation interventions are needed in Korea and would be well received. Korean men hospitalized with CVDs were motivated to quit smoking to improve their health, but need education and behavioral interventions to realize their goal.

Jordan

In 2007, a survey of 918 health professionals (nurses and physicians) from 10 major hospitals in Jordan was conducted by nurse researchers (Shishani et al., 2008). Data were collected using the Global Professional Health Survey (GHPS, 2004) instrument developed jointly by the WHO, CDC, and the Canadian Public Health Association (CPHA; Costa e Silva et al., 2005). The GHPS, a 66-item survey questionnaire, was used to collect data on tobacco use and cessation counseling from health care professional students. The GHPS is a valid and reliable measurement tool. Participants consisted of 72.7% nurses and 27.3% physicians, most of the sample were men (66.3%). The overall smoking rate was 39.0% (50.6% in men and 14.9% in women), with the proportion of smokers higher among physicians (n = 113, 46.9%) compared to nurses (n = 230, 36.1%). Additionally, quit rates through assessment of "former smoker" status was higher in physicians (12.4%) than nurses (9.8%). Furthermore, there was interest by nurses and physicians to quit smoking; 53.8 % said they wanted to quit smoking, in a third of the smokers, 60.6% had made previous quit attempts that lasted more than 2 days. However, reported sustained quit rates were only 11%, clearly identifying unmet needs suggested by the high relapse rate (Shishani, Nawafleh, Jarrah, & Sivarajan Froelicher, 2009). A statistically significant interaction was identified between profession and gender, suggesting that gender specific results need to be presented in future studies.

When participants were asked about the addictive properties of tobacco: 31.5% stated cigarettes are addictive; 7.6% stated that *argileh* is addictive, and 40.4% stated that both are addictive; while 20.5% of health care professionals (HCP) endorsed that none were addictive. Among the nurses, 26.6% said that smoking is not harmful, and 17.3% believed that there were no benefits when quit smoking, and that 27.4% of participants stated that the harmful effects of smoking were not discussed during their undergraduate studies. This demonstrates that there is a need to conduct research on the best strategies to promote education about the addictive properties and the harmful health impact of tobacco use to this group of health care professionals.

Overall, 47.8% of HCP responded that they should have an active role in advising patients to quit smoking. Nurses, who never smoked or were former smokers (64%), were significantly more willing to advise their patients to quit smoking than were current smokers (36.0%; p = .00), and the majority (76.7%) believed that HCP advice increased patients' chance to quit. More than two thirds stated that HCPs serve as role models for their patients and the public (Shishani et al., 2009).

Twenty-two percent of respondents said they were not taught about recording patients' smoking history. Thirty percent of participants have not heard about NRT and 32.9% of HCPs stated that they had received some formal training in smoking cessation approaches to use with patients (Shishani et al., 2008).

The encouraging finding from our earlier report (Shishani et al., 2008) was the considerable interest expressed by HCPs who were smokers and nonsmokers about the need of specific training on smoking cessation techniques (Shishani et al., 2009). A high proportion (73.5%) responded that they needed training in smoking cessation. Therefore, interventions to teach nurses and physicians about effective smoking cessation techniques are likely to be most productive (NIH State-of-the-Science Panel, 2006).

Waterpipe Use

Another future area for international nursing research includes the risks of the waterpipe and interventions to promote cessation of waterpipe use. Waterpipe (also known as argeela, nargile, narghile, nargilehb, argeela, argileh, hubbly-bubbly, shisha, sheesha, and hookah), is a form of tobacco use that is a popular and commonly shared social practice in Eastern Mediterranean Region (EMR; Maziak, Ward, & Eissenberg, 2007), but is a relatively new phenomenon outside EMR. For example, the practice of waterpipe use has become particularly worrisome as it is adopted by college students and near college campuses as a popular pastime among youth in the United States (Primack, Walsh, Bryce, & Eissenberg, 2009). Additional research is needed to assess the consequences of this expansion; if this growing trend continues, the long-term health consequences are likely to further compound the harmful effects of smoking on CVD. For this reason, researchers need to be vigilant and begin longitudinal studies to capture the outcomes of waterpipe exposure with a long latency period now. Such research is likely to be most fruitful in countries where waterpipe smoking has been prevalent for a number of decades (WHO Study Group on Tobacco Product Regulation, 2005).

Of concern and of interest for nurse researchers, is the misconception that waterpipe has fewer adverse health effects than cigarettes (Maziak et al., 2007) and how these misconceptions influence cessation interventions for waterpipe users. Additionally, it is a social activity and it is considered to be appealing (Maziak, Ward, Afifi Soweid, & Eissenberg, 2004). However, waterpipe smoking produces large amounts of chemicals known to be hazardous to health, including as a risk factor for CVD. Shihadeh and Saleh (2005) showed that the ratio of carbon monoxide to nicotine was 50:1, as compared to 16:1 for cigarettes. Other harmful cardiovascular effects of waterpipe use include the elevations in heart rate and systolic, diastolic, and mean arterial blood pressure (Shafagoj & Mohammed, 2002). Another case-control study of patients with recently diagnosed CVD found higher rates among those who had ever engaged in water pipe smoking (Jabbour, El-Roueiheb, & Sibai, 2003). Exposure to waterpipe smoke also poses a health risk for nonsmokers and this can be of particular concern for children if their parents use a waterpipe at home.

SUMMARY

CVD is projected to be the leading cause of death and disability among women until at least 2030 (AHA, 2009). Smoking is clearly one of the most preventable risk factors for this epidemic. As this chapter indicates, there is growing amount of nursing research in the area of smoking cessation focused on patients with CVD. There is some evidence from the WINS and other studies that a planned approach to smoking cessation that includes follow-up contact calls offering relapse prevention may lengthen the time to relapse or improve cessation rates. The combination of such a program and pharmacological therapy may be especially important in helping patients who relapse and those who have not succeeded in quitting smoking in the past. A plan for discharge from the hospital should include active involvement of the patient's family in maintaining a smoke-free environment, and the patient's referral to cardiac rehabilitation programs and community resources, such as the programs offered by the American Lung Association, the American Cancer Society, and Nicotine Anonymous groups, among others. These resources are especially important when clinics, office practice staff, and cardiac rehabilitation programs offer systematic smoking cessation interventions. If these services are unavailable then the nurses are urged to advice the patients on the use of a telephone quitline, a free, nationally available resource. Results about low NRT use in WINS suggest that future research concerning myths about NRT pertaining to women is needed. Nurses can help patients dispel these myths and help prevent smoking relapse. Refusal to use NRT was further substantiated in a combined community-based RCT study in a African American sample (Yerger, Wertz, McGruder, Froelicher, & Malone, 2008). A qualitative study would be a suitable approach to gain insight into this challenge. Additionally, continued efforts are needed in the conceptualization and measurement of withdrawal symptoms to guide symptom management during quit attempts and enforced abstinence during hospitalization.

It is of interest that the evidence base for smoking cessation interventions is one of the most detailed and elaborate on the what, when, how, and by whom of smoking cessation should be delivered (Fiore et al., 2008). Yet, few nurses actually have enacted their role as smoking cessation experts in clinical settings. The authors know of no other domains of nursing with as high a degree of science to guide practice. Nevertheless, a great proportion of nurses miss the opportunity to intervene effectively with patients who are smokers. What remains to be seen is the active engagement and enforcement of the *Guideline* in all health care settings.

The successful strategies used to increase smoking cessation in the United States and bring down the smoking rates need to be expanded to developing countries. There is an obligation to disseminate the successes of smoking cessations discussed above to nurses globally (Shishani et al., 2008, 2009). As reviewed here, the evidence indicates that international nursing research efforts have much to offer.

REFERENCES

American Heart Association. (2009). *2009 Heart and stroke statistical update*. American Stroke Association, American Heart Association. Retrieved July 15, 2009, from http://www.americanheart.org/presenter.jhtml?identifier=3000090

Artinian, N.T., Froelicher, E.S., & Vander Wal, J.S. (2004). Data and safety monitoring during randomized controlled trials of nursing interventions. *Nursing Research, 53*(6), 414–418.

Benowitz, N.L., Hukkanen, J., & Jacob, P., (2009). Nicotine chemistry, metabolism, kinetics and biomarkers. *Handbook Experimental Pharmacology, 192,* 29–60.

Burnam, M., Wells, K., Leake, B., & Landsverk, J. (1988). Development of a brief screening instrument for detecting depressive disorders. *Medical Care, 26*(8), 775–789.

Cohen, S., & Lichtenstein, E. (1990). Perceived stress, quitting smoking, and smoking relapse. *Health Psychology, 9*(4), 466–478.

Costa e Silva, V., Chauvin, J., Jones, N. R., Warren, W., Asma, S., & Pechacek, T. (2005). Tobacco use and cessation counseling—Global health professionals survey pilot study, 10 countries, *Morbidity and Mortality Weekly Report, 54*(20), 505–509.

Critchley, J.A., & Capewell, S. (2003). Mortality risk reduction associated with smoking cessation in patients with coronary heart disease: A systematic review. *Journal of the American Medical Association, 290*(1), 86–97.

Doolan, D.M., & Froelicher, E.S. (2006). Efficacy of smoking cessation intervention among special populations: Review of the literature from 2000 to 2005. *Nursing Research, 55*(4 Suppl.), S29–S37.

Doolan, D.M., Stotts, N.A., Benowitz, N.L., Covinsky, K.E., & Froelicher, E.S. (2008). The women's initiative for nonsmoking (WINS) XI: Age-related differences in smoking cessation responses among women with cardiovascular disease. *American Journal Geriatric Cardiology, 17*(1), 37–47.

Etter, J.F., Le Houezec, J., Huguelet, P., & Etter, M. (2009). Testing the cigarette dependence scale in 4 samples of daily smokers: Psychiatric clinics, smoking cessation clinics, a smoking cessation website and in the general population. *Addictive Behaviors, 34*(5), 446–450.

Fagerstrom, K. (1978). Measuring degree of physical dependence to tobacco smoking with reference to individualization of treatment. *Addictive Behaviors, 3*(3–4), 235–241.

Fiore, M., Bailey, W., Cohen, S., Dorfman, S., Goldstein, M., Gritz, E., et al. (1996). *Smoking cessation: Clinical practice guideline No. 18* (AHCPR Publication No. 96-0692). Rockville, MD: U.S. Department of Health and Human Services, Public Health Service, Agency for Health Care Policy and Research.

Fiore, M., Bailey, W., Cohen, S., Dorfman, S., Goldstein, M., Gritz, E., et al. (2000). *Treating tobacco use and dependence: Clinical practice guideline No. 18* (AHCPR Publication No. 96-0692). Rockville, MD: U.S. Department of Health and Human Services, Public Health Service, Agency for Health Care Policy and Research.

Fiore, M., Jaen, C. R., Baker T. B., Benowitz, N. L., Curry, S.J., Dorfman S. F., et al. (2008). *Treating tobacco use and dependence: Clinical practice guideline, 2008 update.* Washington, DC: U.S. Department of Health and Human Services, Government Printing Office.

Froelicher, E.S. (1996). Tracing patients with myocardial infarction for a 10-year follow-up study. *Nursing Research, 45*(6), 341–344.

Froelicher, E.S., Li, W.W., Mahrer-Imhof, R., Christopherson, D., & Stewart, A.L. (2004a). Women's initiative for non-smoking (WINS) VI: Reliability and validity of health and psychosocial measures in women smokers with cardiovascular disease. *Heart & Lung, 33*(3), 162–175.

Froelicher, E. S., Sohn, M., Max, W., & Bacchetti, P. (2004b). Women's initiative for nonsmoking-VII: Evaluation of health service utilization and costs among women smokers with cardiovascular disease. *Journal of Cardiopulmonary Rehabilitation, 24*(4), 218–228.

Hajek, P., Taylor, T. Z., & Mills, P. (2002). Brief intervention during hospital admission to help patients to give up smoking after myocardial infarction and bypass surgery: Randomised controlled trial. *British Medical Journal, 324*(7329), 87–89.

Hughes, J. R., Benowitz, N., Hatsukami, D., Mermelstein, R. J., & Shiffman, S. (2004). Clarification of SRNT workgroup guidelines for measures in clinical trials of smoking cessation therapies. *Nicotine & Tobacco Research, 6*(5), 863–864.

Jabbour, S., El-Roueiheb, Z., & Sibai, A. M. (2003). Narghile (water-pipe) smoking and incident coronary heart disease: A case-control study [Abstract]. *Annals of Epidemiology, 13,* 570.

Li, W. W., & Froelicher, E. S. (2008). Predictors of smoking relapse in women with cardio-vascular disease in a 30-month study: Extended analysis. *Heart & Lung, 37*(6), 455–465.

Lichtman, J. H., Bigger, J. T., Jr., Blumenthal, J. A., Frasure-Smith, N., Kaufmann, P. G., Lesperance, F., et al. (2008). Depression and coronary heart disease: Recommendations for screening, referral, and treatment: A science advisory from the American heart association prevention committee of the council on cardiovascular nursing, council on clinical cardiology, council on epidemiology and prevention, and interdisciplinary council on quality of care and outcomes research: Endorsed by the American psychiatric association. *Circulation, 118*(17), 1768–1775.

Mahrer-Imhof, R., Froelicher, E. S., Li, W. W., Parker, K. M., & Benowitz, N. (2002). Women's initiative for nonsmoking (WINS V): Under-use of nicotine replacement therapy. *Heart & Lung, 31*(5), 368–373.

Maziak, W., Ward, K. D., Afifi Soweid, R. A., & Eissenberg, T. (2004). Tobacco smoking using a waterpipe: A re-emerging strain in a global epidemic. *Tobacco Control, 13*(4), 327–333.

Maziak, W., Ward, K. D., & Eissenberg, T. (2007). Interventions for waterpipe smoking cessation. *Cochrane Database Systematic Review,* (4), CD005549.

McPherson, C. P., Swenson, K. K., Pine, D. A., & Leimer, L. (2002). A nurse-based pilot program to reduce cardiovascular risk factors in a primary care setting. *American Journal of Managed Care, 8*(6), 543–555.

Mohiuddin, S. M., Mooss, A. N., Hunter, C. B., Grollmes, T. L., Cloutier, D. A., & Hilleman, D. E. (2007). Intensive smoking cessation intervention reduces mortality in high-risk smokers with cardiovascular disease. *Chest, 131*(2), 446–452.

Narsavage, G., & Idemoto, B. (2003). Smoking cessation interventions for hospitalized patients with cardio-pulmonary disorders. *Online Journal of Issues in Nursing, 8*(2). Retrieved from http://www.nursingworld.org/MainMenuCategories/ANAMarketplace/ANAPeriodicals/OJIN/TableofContents/

Newton, K., Sivarajan Froelicher, E., & Clarke, J. (1985). Patient perceptions of risk factor changes and cardiac rehabilitation outcomes after myocardial infarction. *Journal of Cardiac Rehabilitation, 5,* 159–168.

NIH State-of-the-Science Panel. (2006). National institutes of health state-of-the-science conference statement: Tobacco use: prevention, cessation, and control. *Annals of Internal Medicine, 145*(11), 839–844.

Nunnally, J., & Bernstein, I. (1994). *Psychometric theory* (3rd ed.). New York: McGraw-Hill.

Ockene, I. S., & Miller, N. H. (1997). Cigarette smoking, cardiovascular disease, and stroke: A statement for healthcare professionals from the American heart association. American heart association task force on risk reduction. *Circulation, 96*(9), 3243–3247.

Ockene, J., Kristeller, J. L., Goldberg, R., Ockene, I., Merriam, P., Barrett, S., et al. (1992). Smoking cessation and severity of disease: The coronary artery smoking intervention study. *Health Psychology, 11*(2), 119–126.

Oka, R. K., Katapodi, M. C., Lim, J. W., Bacchetti, P., & Froelicher, E. S. (2006). Quantifying smoking cessation outcomes: From the women's initiative for nonsmoking study (X): Methodological implications. *Nursing Research, 55*(4), 292–297.

Patten, C. A., & Martin, J. E. (1996). Measuring tobacco withdrawal: A review of self-report questionnaires. *Journal of Substance Abuse, 8*(1), 93–113.

Piper, M. E., McCarthy, D. E., Bolt, D. M., Smith, S. S., Lerman, C., Benowitz, N., et al. (2008). Assessing dimensions of nicotine dependence: An evaluation of the nicotine dependence syndrome scale (NDSS) and the Wisconsin inventory of smoking dependence motives (WISDM). *Nicotine & Tobacco Research, 10*(6), 1009–1020.

Primack, B. A., Walsh, M., Bryce, C., & Eissenberg, T. (2009). Water-pipe tobacco smoking among middle and high school students in Arizona. *Pediatrics, 123*(2), e282–e288.

Reddy, K. S., & Yusuf, S. (1998). Emerging epidemic of cardiovascular disease in developing countries. *Circulation, 97*(6), 596–601.

Rice, V. H., & Stead, L. F. (2008). Nursing interventions for smoking cessation. *Cochrane Database Systematic Review,* (1), CD001188.

Schneider, N. G., & Jarvik, M. E. (1984). Time course of smoking withdrawal symptoms as a function of nicotine replacement. *Psychopharmacology* (Berlin), *82*(1–2), 143–144.

Shafagoj, Y. A., & Mohammed, F. I. (2002). Levels of maximum end-expiratory carbon monoxide and certain cardiovascular parameters following hubble-bubble smoking. *Saudi Medical Journal, 23*(8), 953–958.

Shiffman, S. M., & Jarvik, M. E. (1976). Smoking withdrawal symptoms in two weeks of abstinence. *Psychopharmacology* (Berlin), *50*(1), 35–39.

Shiffman, S., West, R., & Gilbert, D. (2004). Recommendation for the assessment of tobacco craving and withdrawal in smoking cessation trials. *Nicotine & Tobacco Research, 6*(4), 599–614.

Shihadeh, A., & Saleh, R. (2005). Polycyclic aromatic hydrocarbons, carbon monoxide, "tar," and nicotine in the mainstream smoke aerosol of the narghile water pipe. *Food Chemistry and Toxicology, 43*(5), 655–661.

Shishani, K., Nawafleh, H., Jarrah, S., & Sivarajan Froelicher, E. (2009). *Smoking practices among Jordanian nurses and physicians.* Manuscript submitted for publication.

Shishani, K., Nawafleh, H., & Sivarajan Froelicher, E. (2008). Jordanian nurses' and physicians' learning needs for promoting smoking cessation. *Progress in Cardiovascular Nursing, 23*(2), 79–83.

Sivarajan, E. S., Bruce, R. A., Almes, M. J., Green, B., Belanger, L., Lindskog, B. D., et al. (1981). In-hospital exercise after myocardial infarction does not improve treadmill performance. *New England Journal of Medicine, 305*(7), 357–362.

Sivarajan, E. S., Newton, K. M., Almes, M. J., Kempf, T. M., Mansfield, L. W., & Bruce, R. A. (1983). Limited effects of outpatient teaching and counseling after myocardial infarction: A controlled study. *Heart & Lung, 12*(1), 65–73.

Sivarajan Froelicher, E. S., Miller, N. H., Christopherson, D. J., Martin, K., Parker, K. M., Amonetti, M., et al. (2004). High rates of sustained smoking cessation in women hospitalized with cardiovascular disease: The women's initiative for nonsmoking (WINS). *Circulation, 109*(5), 587–593.

Sohn, M., Benowitz, N., Stotts, N., Christopherson, D., Kim, K. S., Jang, Y. S., et al. (2008). Smoking behavior in men hospitalized with cardiovascular disease in Korea: A cross-sectional descriptive study. *Heart & Lung, 37*(5), 366–379.

Sohn, M., Stotts, N. A., Benowitz, N., Christopherson, D., Kim, K. S., Jang, Y. S., et al. (2007). Beliefs about health, smoking, and future smoking cessation among South Korean men hospitalized for cardiovascular disease. *Heart & Lung, 36*(5), 339–347.

Sparrow, D., & Dawber, T. R. (1978). The influence of cigarette smoking on prognosis after a first myocardial infarction. A report from the Framingham study. *Journal of Chronic Disease, 31*(6–7), 425–432.

Strong, D. R., Kahler, C. W., Leventhal, A. M., Abrantes, A. M., Lloyd-Richardson, E., Niaura, R., et al. (2009, July 2). Impact of bupropion and cognitive-behavioral treatment for depression on positive affect, negative affect, and urges to smoke during cessation treatment. *Nicotine & Tobacco Research*. [Epub ahead of print]

Taylor, C. B., Houston-Miller, N., Haskell, W. L., & DeBusk, R. F. (1988). Smoking cessation after acute myocardial infarction: The effects of exercise training. *Addictive Behaviors, 13*(4), 331–335.

Taylor, C. B., Houston-Miller, N., Killen, J. D., & DeBusk, R. F. (1990). Smoking cessation after acute myocardial infarction: Effects of a nurse-managed intervention. *Annals of Internal Medicine, 113*(2), 118–123.

Taylor, C. B., Miller, N. H., Herman, S., Smith, P. M., Sobel, D., Fisher, L., et al. (1996). A nurse-managed smoking cessation program for hospitalized smokers. *American Journal of Public Health, 86*(11), 1557–1560.

Taylor-Piliae, R. E., & Froelicher, E. S. (2007). Methods to optimize recruitment and retention to an exercise study in Chinese immigrants. *Nursing Research, 56*(2), 132–136.

Thorndike, A. N., Regan, S., McKool, K., Pasternak, R. C., Swartz, S., Torres-Finnerty, N., et al. (2008). Depressive symptoms and smoking cessation after hospitalization for cardiovascular disease. *Archives of Internal Medicine, 168*(2), 186–191.

Thorndike, A. N., & Rigotti, N. A. (2009, June 20). A tragic triad: Coronary artery disease, nicotine addiction, and depression. *Current Opinion in Cardiology*. [Epub ahead of print]

U.S. Department of Health and Human Services. (2004). *Cardiovascular diseases: The health consequences of smoking: A report of the Surgeon General* (Chap. 3, pp. 363–491). Atlanta, GA: U.S. Department of Health and Human Services, Centers for Disease Control and Prevention, National Center for Chronic Disease Prevention and Health Promotion, Office on Smoking and Health.

Welsch, S. K., Smith, S. S., Wetter, D. W., Jorenby, D. E., Fiore, M. C., & Baker, T. B. (1999). Development and validation of the Wisconsin smoking withdrawal scale. *Experimental Clinical Psychopharmacology, 7*(4), 354–361.

West, R., & Hajek, P. (2004). Evaluation of the mood and physical symptoms scale (MPSS) to assess cigarette withdrawal. *Psychopharmacology* (Berlin), *177*(1–2), 195–199.

West, R., Hajek, P., & Belcher, M. (1989a). Time course of cigarette withdrawal symptoms while using nicotine gum. *Psychopharmacology* (Berlin), 99(1), 143–145.

West, R. J., Hajek, P., & Belcher, M. (1989b). Severity of withdrawal symptoms as a predictor of outcome of an attempt to quit smoking. *Psychology & Medicine, 19*(4), 981–985.

West, R. J., & Russell, M. A. (1985a). Effects of withdrawal from long-term nicotine gum use. *Psychology & Medicine, 15*(4), 891–893.

West, R. J., & Russell, M. A. (1985b). Pre-abstinence smoke intake and smoking motivation as predictors of severity of cigarette withdrawal symptoms. *Psychopharmacology* (Berlin), 87(3), 334–336.

World Health Organization. (2004). *WHO/CDC global health professional survey.* Retrieved July 8, 2009, from http://www.who.int/tobacco/surveillance/ghps/en/index.html

World Health Organization. (2008). *WHO report on the global tobacco epidemic, 2008.* The MPOWER package. Geneva, World Health Organization. Retrieved July 28, 2009, from http://www.who.int/tobacco/mpower/mpower_report_full_2008.pdf

World Health Organization Study Group on Tobacco Product Regulation. (2005). *Advisory note: Waterpipe tobacco smoking: Health effects, research needs, and recommended actions by regulators.* Retrieved July 15, 2009, from http://www.who.int/tobacco/global_interaction/tobreg/Waterpipe%20recommendation_Final.pdf

Yerger, V. B., Wertz, M., McGruder, C., Froelicher, E. S., & Malone, R. E. (2008). Nicotine replacement therapy: Perceptions of African-American smokers seeking to quit. *Journal of the National Medical Association, 100*(2), 230–236.

Chapter 10

Smoking Cessation Interventions in Cancer Care: Opportunities for Oncology Nurses and Nurse Scientists

Mary E. Cooley, Rebecca Lundin, and Lyndsay Murray

ABSTRACT

Smoking cessation is essential after the diagnosis of cancer to improve clinical outcomes. The purpose of this chapter is to provide a systematic review of research on smoking cessation in the context of cancer care with an emphasis on nursing contributions to the field. Data sources included research reports of smoking cessation interventions conducted in people with cancer. Nineteen primary studies were reviewed. High intensity interventions, targeting multiple behaviors, and/or using a multicomponent intervention that included pharmacotherapy, behavioral counseling, and social support were characteristics of the most successful treatments for tobacco dependence. The majority of interventions were conducted in adults with smoking-related malignancies during acute phases of illness. The most striking finding was that more than one half of the studies tested the efficacy of nurse-delivered interventions. Conceptual and methodological issues that can

DOI: 10.1891/0739-6686.27.243

be improved in future studies include: using theoretical frameworks to specify how the intervention will affect outcomes, ensuring adequate sample sizes, using biochemical verification to monitor smoking outcomes, and using standardized outcome measures of abstinence. Although effective interventions are available for healthy populations, further research is needed to determine if tailored cessation interventions are needed for patients with cancer. To provide optimal quality care it is imperative that delivery of evidence-based smoking cessation interventions be integrated into the cancer treatment trajectory. Multiple barriers, including patient and nurse attitudes toward smoking and lack of knowledge related to tobacco treatment, prevent translating evidence-based tobacco dependence treatment into clinical practice. Further nursing research is needed to address these barriers.

Keywords: smoking cessation, tobacco dependence treatment, nursing interventions, oncology nursing

Smoking cessation is one of the most important interventions to prevent cancer and is also essential after the diagnosis of cancer to improve clinical outcomes. A growing body of literature identifies the devastating effects associated with continued tobacco use after the diagnosis of cancer, which include lower survival, recurrent disease, decreased efficacy of cancer treatment, increased treatment-related complications, increased physical symptoms, and reductions in quality of life (Fox, Rosenzweig, & Ostroff, 2004; Gritz, Dresler, & Sarna, 2005; Jensen, Jensen, & Grau, 2007; Videtic et al., 2003).

The purpose of this chapter is to provide a systematic review of current research on smoking cessation in the context of cancer care with a special emphasis on nursing contributions to the field. The first part of the chapter provides background information on the prevalence of smoking among cancer patients and potential challenges associated with preventing smoking relapse. The second part of the chapter presents the methods that were used to conduct this systematic review. Subsequently, the results of the review are presented with a focus on the effectiveness of smoking cessation interventions for people with cancer, conceptual and methodological issues associated with smoking cessation studies in cancer care, and predictors of continued smoking among people with cancer. Finally, the discussion addresses the unique contributions of nursing, lessons learned from previous studies, and identifies directions for future research.

BACKGROUND

Smoking Prevalence Rates in Cancer Patients

Smoking prevalence rates at the time of diagnosis have been estimated to vary from 45% to 75% (Cox, Africano, Tercyak, & Taylor, 2003). Through a systematic review of studies, Cox and colleagues determined that 14% to 58% of patients who smoked at diagnosis continue to smoke after cancer treatment. The large variation in smoking prevalence rates may be related to a time lag when the various studies were done, as smoking prevalence rates have decreased among the general U.S. population, differences in methodologies used to measure smoking among the studies (e.g., self-report vs. biochemical verification), and/or the fact that many of the studies describing smoking behaviors in cancer patients have been conducted among heterogeneous groups of cancer patients (Cooley et al., 2007; Cox et al., 2003; Centers for Disease Control and Prevention, 2007).

Little information is available on how smoking rates vary among cancer sites and whether cancer site, stage, and type of cancer treatment influence cessation rates (Cox et al., 2003). Some recent studies, however, have examined the frequency of smoking among more homogeneous groups of patients. For example, two recent studies (Cooley et al., 2009; Walker et al., 2006) examined smoking behaviors after curative surgery for early stage lung cancer and found that the frequency of smoking at the time of diagnosis was 37% and that by 2 months after surgery 42% of smokers relapsed back to smoking. Another study examined smoking behaviors in adults who were childhood cancer survivors and found that 28% of the sample reported ever smoking and 17% continued to smoke (Emmons et al., 2003). Taken together, the studies examining smoking behaviors among cancer patients identify that smoking rates are as high if not higher than the general population. Given the profound effect that continued smoking has on decreasing the effectiveness of cancer treatment, smoking cessation interventions are critical in this patient population.

Challenges Associated With Smoking Cessation After the Diagnosis of Cancer

Although the diagnosis of cancer provides a unique opportunity for health care providers to enhance health promoting behaviors such as smoking cessation, it may be difficult for many patients to quit and stay quit because of the highly addictive nature of nicotine. It is important for both nurses and patients to recognize that tobacco dependence is a chronic illness that often requires repeated cessation attempts in order to be successful (Steinberg, Schmelzer, Richardson, & Foulds, 2008).

It often takes smokers many quit attempts before they are successful (Fiore et al., 2008). Moreover, cancer patients often face challenges associated with maintaining abstinence (Gritz et al., 2006). One common challenge is that many cancer patients may experience increased psychological distress including depression, anxiety, or increased stress, which often makes quitting smoking more difficult especially if the underlying condition is not recognized and treated. An additional consideration is there may be smokers within their social support network making long-term abstinence difficult. They may be highly addicted to nicotine and thus may experience severe withdrawal symptoms, if pharmacological cessation aides are not adequately utilized.

Guilt and shame over continued smoking are common and underscore the complex nature of addressing tobacco treatment within this subgroup of patients (Chapple, Ziebland, & McPherson, 2004). Several studies have identified that lung cancer patients often feel stigmatized because lung cancer tends to be associated with previous smoking (Chapple et al., 2004; Wassenaar et al., 2007). A recent study by LoConte, Else-Quest, Eickhoff, Hyde, and Schiller (2008) compared levels of guilt and shame among patients with nonsmall cell lung, prostate, and breast cancer. Results of the study identified that a history of previous smoking was associated with higher levels of guilt and shame among patients with all types of cancer. Thus, this study suggests that guilt and shame may not be a unique issue for patients with smoking-related malignancies but may also be an issue for smokers with other types of cancer. This finding is significant because it underscores that nurses must approach smokers with cancer with sensitivity and compassion when discussing smoking status and actively engage in efforts to minimize and diminish stigma associated with continued smoking after the diagnosis of cancer.

In order to optimize clinical outcomes, smoking cessation must be a critical component of the cancer care continuum from prevention of cancer through diagnosis, treatment, survivorship, and palliative care (Cooley, Sipples, Murphy, & Sarna, 2008). Many opportunities exist for oncology nurses to address smoking cessation for both cancer patients and their families. Effective smoking cessation interventions are available (Fiore et al., 2008). Moreover, it takes more than will power alone to achieve long-term cessation. The use of pharmacological cessation aides combined with behavioral counseling doubles the chances of successfully achieving long-term cessation (Fiore et al., 2008). However, most studies demonstrating effectiveness of treatment have been conducted within the general population and few studies have been conducted among cancer patients and their families (Gritz et al., 2005). A clear understanding of the current state of the science related to smoking cessation interventions in cancer care is necessary in order to provide optimal care and enhance long-term smoking cessation outcomes.

METHODS

The following section provides an overview of the methods that were used to conduct a systematic review of studies examining smoking cessation within the context of cancer care. We choose to focus on the entire spectrum of care so that we could identify whether smoking cessation interventions were conducted during and postcancer treatment and whether studies considered contextual factors associated with quitting and relapse such as smoking within the social network.

Ganong's framework (1987) was used to guide this systematic literature review. This framework directs researchers to pose research questions to focus the review. Subsequently, search criteria are defined and explicit inclusion criteria are developed to guide the literature search. Once the relevant studies have been selected, the researchers examine the characteristics of the studies, identify relevant research findings, and interpret the results. The research questions included: (1) What is the current state of the science regarding the effectiveness of smoking cessation interventions in the context of cancer care? (2) What conceptual and methodological issues need to be addressed in future studies? (3) What are the predictors of continued smoking after the diagnosis of cancer? An article was included if it was found to be an empirical study with a smoking cessation intervention focus in the context of cancer care, directed toward patients or their social networks. Results were limited to English language papers. We searched the National Center for Biotechnology Information (NCBI) PubMed for empirical studies from January 1980 to April 2009. The search terms "cancer screening," "cancer patients," "patients with cancer," "cancer survivors," "smoking cessation intervention," "smoking cessation program," "smoking abstinence intervention," "smoking abstinence program," "smoking intervention," and "tobacco intervention." The bibliographies of identified articles were searched for additional studies.

Twenty-one articles met the inclusion criteria and are included in Table 10.1. Nineteen are primary intervention studies and are used as the n for the analysis; one of the articles reported long-term follow up on the intervention and another was a secondary analysis of the parent study (Cox, McLaughlin, Rai, Steen, & Hudson, 2005; Emmons et al., 2009). Once all of the relevant studies were identified, we gathered information on the theoretical framework, design, sample, type of intervention, measure used to evaluate smoking status, and selected findings.

Each article was assigned a quality rating using the Oncology Nursing Society's (ONS) evidence rating system (Ropka & Spencer-Cisek, 2001; Table 10.2). Studies were graded by two of the authors. Disagreements in ratings were discussed by the two graders to achieve consensus and a third grader was used to resolve any questions. Content analysis was then used to synthesize research findings. Studies were considered to be level 2 if the sample size was greater than 100, was a multisite trial, and a randomized clinical trial. The following section will discuss the results of the review.

TABLE 10.1 Studies Evaluating Smoking Cessation Interventions in Cancer Care (n = 21)

Investigator	Conceptual Framework	Design	Sample	Intervention	Level of Training of Interventionist	Selected Findings	ONS Rating
Duffy et al., 2006	Cognitive behavioral therapy (CBT)	RCT	Head and neck cancer n = 184 ≥18 years of age	Targeting multiple risk factors (smoking, alcohol abuse, depression) Encouragement and support Advice/strategies for quitting NRT, buproprion, or antidepressants as needed	Nurses with CBT training Psychiatrist supervision	Self-reported smoking abstinence at 6 months was 47% in the intervention versus 31% in the usual care group ($p < .05$)	2
Emmons et al., 2005[a]	Social ecological model and principles of motivational interviewing	RCT	Cancer ≥5 year survival <21 years old at diagnosis n = 796 ≥18 years old	Encouragement and support Smoking cessation materials Personalized messages and strategies for quitting NRT Peer support	Trained childhood cancer survivors	7-day pp at 8 and 12 months was16.8% in the intervention versus 8.5% control group at 8 months and 15% versus 9% at 12 months ($p < .01$) Bogus pipeline procedure for verification	2
Emmons et al., 2009[a]	Social ecological model and principles of motivational interviewing	RCT	Cancer ≥5 year survival <21 years old at diagnosis n = 796 ≥18 years old	Encouragement and support Smoking cessation materials Personalized messages and strategies for quitting NRT	Trained childhood cancer survivors	7-day pp at 8 and 12 months and then 2 to 6 years postbaseline. Quit rates at long-term follow-up were 20.6% in intervention versus 17.6% in the control group ($p < .0003$)	2

Gritz et al., 1993	Stages of change model	RCT	Head and neck cancer n = 186	Encouragement and support Smoking cessation materials Personalized messages and strategies for quitting	Physicians or dentists	Continuous abstinence rates at 12-month follow-up, verified with cotinine, were not significantly different between control group	2
McBride et al., 1999	Motivational interviewing techniques	RCT	Abnormal pap test in prior month, n = 580 ≥18 years old	Encouragement and support Smoking cessation materials Personalized message and strategies to quit smoking	Telephone counselors with 20 hours of training	Self-reported smoking at 6- and 15-month follow-up, no significant difference between usual care and self-help groups	2
Schnoll et al., 2003	AHRQ "5 A's"	RCT	Cancer patients n = 432 ≥19 years old	Brief advice Smoking cessation materials Personalized message and strategies to quit smoking. Follow-up letter NRT	Physicians	Self-reported 7-day pp smoking at 6- and 12-month follow-up was not different between the intervention and usual care groups	2
Wakefield et al., 2004	Trans-theoretical model of change and motivational interviewing	RCT	Cancer diagnosis n = 137	Encouragement and support Smoking cessation materials Personalized message and strategies to quit smoking NRT	Trial coordinator	7-day pp at 3- and 6-month follow-up, verified by salivary cotinine or carbon monoxide, showed no differences found between intervention and control groups	2

(*Continued*)

TABLE 10.1 Studies Evaluating Smoking Cessation Interventions in Cancer Care (n = 21) (*Continued*)

Investigator	Conceptual Framework	Design	Sample	Intervention	Level of Training of Interventionist	Selected findings	ONS Rating
Garces et al., 2004	None	QE	Head and neck cancer versus general population n = 202	Initial consultation Individualized treatment plan Phone follow up at 1,3, and 6 months, letter follow-up at 12 months NRT or bupropion	Tobacco treatment specialist	Self-reported 7-day pp at 6 months was 33% for head and neck cancer patients versus 26% for general population (p = .30)	5
Sanderson Cox et al., 2002	None	QE	Lung cancer versus nonlung cancer patients n = 402	Initial consultation Individualized treatment plan Phone follow up at 1,3, and 6 months, letter follow-up at 12 months NRT or bupropion	Tobacco treatment specialist	Self reported 7-day pp smoking at 6 months showed no significant difference between lung and nonlung cancer patients	5
Browning et al., 2000	AHRQ "4 A's"	QE	Lung cancer n = 25	Encouragement and support Smoking cessation materials Personalized messages and strategies for quitting NRT and bupropion encouraged, not provided	Advanced practice nurse	7-day pp abstinence at 6 months, confirmed with expired CO, was 71% for intervention versus 55% for controls (p = .383)	6
Cox et al., 2005[a]	Health belief model	RCT	Cancer in remission ≥2 years n = 267 12–18 years old	Multiple risk factors (i.e., tobacco, alcohol, diet, exercise) Encouragement and support Personalized messages and strategies for quitting	Physician or nurse practitioner	Self-reported smoking abstinence at 12 months remained consistent in the treatment group while decreasing in the control group (p = .088)	6

250

Study	Theory	Design	Sample	Intervention	Interventionist	Outcomes	
Griebel et al., 1998	None	RCT	Cancer n = 28 ≥19 years old	Encouragement and support Smoking cessation materials Personalized messages and strategies for quitting	Advanced practice nurse trained in tobacco treatment	7-day pp abstinence rates at 6 weeks postintervention, verified with cotinine, were 21% for intervention versus 14% usual care (p = NS)	6
Hollen et al., 1999	Conflict model of decision making, cognitive theory, and holistic concept of health	QE	Cancer diagnosis between birth and 12 years, disease free ≥5 n = 64	Multiple risk factors Encouragement and support Decision making materials Advice/strategies for quality decision making	Trained peers and health care professionals	Self reported smoking behaviors at 1, 6, and 12 months found no significant difference between intervention and control groups (p =.27, .08, and .22, respectively)	6
Hudson et al., 2002[a]	Health belief model	RCT	Cancer in remission ≥2 years n = 267, 12–18 years	Multiple risk factors (i.e., tobacco, alcohol, diet, exercise) Encouragement and support Personalized messages and strategies for quitting	Physician or nurse practitioner	Self-reported smoking at 12 months showed no significant differences between intervention and control group	6
Schilling et al., 1997	Trans-theoretical model of change	QE	Relative of cancer patients n = 125	Encouragement and support Smoking cessation materials Personalized message to quit smoking sent in a letter by mail	Physicians	Self-reported smoking cessation at 6 months was 9% among all relatives	6
Schnoll et al., 2005	Cognitive-social health information-processing model and CBT	RCT	Head, neck, or lung cancer n = 109 Smoking in past 30 days	Encouragement and support Smoking cessation materials Personalized message and advice to quit smoking NRT	Health educators	Self-reported 30-day pp smoking at 1- and 3-month follow-up, showed no differences between the intervention and health education groups	6

(Continued)

TABLE 10.1 Studies Evaluating Smoking Cessation Interventions in Cancer Care (n = 21) (*Continued*)

Investigator	Conceptual Framework	Design	Sample	Intervention	Level of Training of Interventionist	Selected findings	ONS Rating
Sharp et al., 2008	Motivational interviewing and the AHRQ "5 A's"	QE	Head or neck cancer n = 50	Encouragement and support Smoking cessation materials Advice/strategies for quitting NRT	Radiotherapy nurses	Continuous abstinence at 12 months (verified by carbon monoxide) was 51%	6
Smith et al., 2002	Self-efficacy theory and relapse prevention	QE	Hospitalized patients n = 1077 (124 with cancer)	Encouragement and support Smoking cessation materials Advice/strategies for quitting NRT as needed	Physicians, nurses	Self-reported 7-day pp at 12-month follow-up was 43% for general patients and 63% for cancer patients	6
Stanislaw & Wewers, 1994	None	RCT	Surgical oncology patients n = 26	Encouragement and support Smoking cessation and relaxation materials Advice/strategies for quitting	Oncology clinical nurse specialists	Self-reported smoking at 5-week follow-up, verified by salivary cotinine, no difference in smoking between experimental and control groups	6

Wewers et al., 1997	Social learning theory and addiction models	QE	Lung cancer n = 15	Encouragement and support Smoking cessation and relaxation materials Advice/strategies for quitting	Advanced practice nurse	7-day pp smoking at 6-week follow-up, verified by cotinine, showed that 40% of patients were abstinent	6
Wewers et al., 1994	National Cancer Institute's "4 A's"	RCT	Surgical patients n = 80 (30 cancer)	Encouragement and support Smoking cessation and relaxation materials Advice/strategies for quitting	Clinical nurse specialist	7-day pp smoking at 6-week follow-up, verified by cotinine, showed no differences between intervention and control groups	6

Note. Authors in **bold** = tested nurse delivered intervention. Authors in ***bold italics*** = principal investigator is a nurse. RCT = randomized clinical trial, QE = quasiexperimental design, NRT = nicotine replacement therapy, pp = point prevalence, AHRQ = Agency for Healthcare Research and Quality, ONS = Oncology Nursing Society. Of the 21 studies, there are 19 primary studies; one study is a long-term follow-up and two are secondary analyses of the primary study.
[a]Related studies.

TABLE 10.2 Oncology Nursing Society Levels of Evidence Used to Grade the Quality of Smoking Cessation Intervention Studies

ONS Levels of Evidence	Evidence Source
1	Qualitative systematic review (also called integrative review) or quantitative systematic review (also called meta-analysis) or multiple, well-designed, randomized, controlled trials of adequate quality
2	At least one properly designed, randomized, controlled trial of appropriate size (record if multisite and over 100 subjects, but not required)
3	Well-designed trial without randomization (e.g., single group pre/post, cohort, time series, meta-analysis of cohort studies)
4	Well-conducted, qualitative, systematic review of nonexperimental design studies
5	Well-conducted case-control study
6	Poorly controlled study (e.g., randomized controlled trial with major flaws) or uncontrolled studies (e.g., correlational descriptive study, case series)
7	Conflicting evidence with the weight of evidence supporting the recommendation of meta-analysis showing a trend that did not reach statistical significance National Institutes of Health Consensus Reports Published practice guidelines, for example, from professional organizations (e.g., Oncology Nursing Society, American Society of Clinical Oncology), health care organizations (e.g., American Cancer Society), or federal agencies (e.g., National Cancer Institute, Centers for Disease Control)
8	Qualitative designs Case studies; opinions from expert authorities, agencies, or committees

Note. From "Rating the Quality of Evidence for Clinical Practice Guidelines," by D. C. Hadorn, D. Baker, J. S. Hodges, and N. Hicks, 1996, Journal of Clinical Epidemiology, 49, 749–753. Copyright 1996 by Excerpta Medical Inc. Adapted with permission from Oncology Nursing Society Publishing.
[a]Levels of evidence range from the strongest evidence at the top to the weakest level of evidence at the bottom.

RESULTS

Effectiveness of Smoking Cessation Interventions

Only two (2/19) of the studies (11%; Duffy et al., 2006; Emmons et al., 2005) reported statistically significant differences in smoking cessation outcomes between control and intervention groups, which favored the intervention group (Table 10.1). Duffy and colleagues (2006) tested a tailored smoking, alcohol, and depression intervention for head and neck cancer patients, and found that after

6 months, head and neck cancer patients participating in the intervention group had significantly higher quit rates (47%) than those with usual care (31%, $p < .05$), which consisted of brief counseling, referrals, and print information. In the second study, Emmons and colleagues (2005) tested a peer-delivered smoking counseling intervention in childhood cancer survivors, entitled Partnership for Health, which consisted of six telephone calls, tailored materials, and free nicotine replacement and found that the intervention group reported significantly higher quit rates both at 8 (16.8% vs. 8.5%, $p < .01$) and 12 months (15% vs. 9%, $p \leq .01$) as compared to those in the control group, who received a physician's letter and cessation materials (Emmons et al., 2005). The effects of this intervention were found to be sustained at 2 to 6 years postbaseline such that quit rates at long-term follow-up were significantly higher in the peer-based telephone counseling group as compared to the self-help control group (20.6% vs. 17.6%; $p < .0003$; Emmons et al., 2009).

Three additional studies approached statistical significance and will be highlighted. Stanislaw and Wewers (1994) tested the effect of a structured smoking cessation intervention during hospitalization on short-term smoking abstinence in surgical cancer patients. The intervention group received a structured smoking cessation intervention during hospitalization, which consisted of three face-to-face visits, followed by five phone calls after discharge, whereas the control group received usual care. At 5 weeks postdischarge, 75% of the intervention group was abstinent as compared to 43% of the control groups ($p < .10$). The second study, conducted by Hollen, Hobbie, and Finley (1999), examined the effects of a decision-making and risk-reduction program for adolescent cancer survivors on smoking, alcohol, or illicit drug use. The intervention group attended a workshop that provided a health promotion program within the context of social support delivered by peers and health care providers as compared to a control group that did not attend the educational program. The effects of the intervention on smoking behavior were marginal at 6 months such that 16% of the control group were smoking at 6 months as compared to 10% of the intervention group ($p = .08$). The third study was a secondary analysis of a parent study that examined a multicomponent behavioral intervention to promote health behaviors among adolescent cancer survivors (Hudson et al., 2002). Cox and colleagues (2005) examined each of the health behaviors separately rather than using a composite score and found that smoking abstinence at 12 months was maintained in the treatment group while decreasing in the control group ($p = .08$).

Delivery, Types, and Components of Effective Smoking Cessation Interventions

In order to gain a better understanding of the smoking cessation interventions that have been conducted within this population (Table 10.1), a brief overview of the delivery, types, and components of the interventions that enhanced smoking cessation outcomes and the samples that have been targeted in these interventions will be discussed.

Who Delivered the Interventions?

The smoking cessation interventions that were identified through this review were delivered by health care providers (12/19, 65%), tobacco treatment specialists and health educators (5/19, 25%), or peer counselors (2/19, 10%). Advanced practice nurses were among the most common health care provider (8/12, 67%) to deliver the smoking cessation intervention.

What Were the Components of the Interventions?

The type of smoking cessation interventions ranged from brief advice only, to counseling only, pharmacotherapy and counseling, or intensive interventions combining pharmacotherapy and counseling with other modalities (Table 10.1). The two studies that demonstrated significant differences between the groups used a multicomponent intervention that combined evidenced-based smoking cessation treatment with social support provided by peer counselors or treatment of comorbid conditions (depression and alcohol abuse) and cognitive behavioral therapy and medications delivered by advanced practice nurses (Duffy et al., 2006; Emmons et al., 2005).

Emmons and colleagues (2005) identified differences in quit rates depending on the number of counseling calls that each participant received for the 8-month follow-up such that there was an increase of 5% for those who received six calls compared with those who received five calls (29% vs. 24%). Similarly, those who used nicotine replacement treatment as part of the intervention had significantly higher quit rates than those who did not use nicotine replacement treatment ($p < .0001$).

Duffy and colleagues (2006) examined the effectiveness of the combined modality intervention among various subgroups and found that those treated for comorbid smoking and depression had higher smoking cessation rates compared with usual care, those treated for comorbid alcohol and depression had higher smoking and alcohol cessation rates compared with usual care and those treated for all three comorbidities had higher smoking cessation rates compared with usual care. Thus, the findings from this study suggest that using a multicomponent intervention to treat concomitant comorbidities improved smoking cessation rates among patients with cancers of the head and neck.

Who Received the Interventions?

The vast majority of studies (17/19, 89%) were conducted in adults with cancer and the remaining two (2/19, 11%) were conducted in adolescents with cancer (Table 10.1). Of the studies conducted in adults with cancer, 47% (8/17) were conducted in patients with smoking-related malignancies, which included lung or head and neck cancers. The remaining studies were conducted in heterogeneous samples of patients with cancer, or those with other illnesses such as cardiovascular disease, pulmonary disease, and/or those who underwent general surgery.

Interventions were conducted along most aspects of the cancer care continuum including prevention, (e.g., women undergoing cervical cancer screening or family members of cancer patients; 2/19, 11%), diagnosis and treatment (14/19, 74%), and survivorship (3/19, 15%). Besides the intervention by Schilling et al. (1997), which exclusively targeted family members of recently diagnosed cancer patients who smoked, only four other studies addressed smoking among participants' family members (Browning, Ahijevych, & Ross, 2000; Emmons et al., 2005; Sharp, Johansson, Fagerstrom, & Rutqvist, 2008; Wakefield, Olver, Whitford, & Rosenfeld, 2004). In the Wakefield and colleagues' study, patients' family members were made aware of the need to quit in support of the patient's quit attempt, while Emmons and colleagues provided NRT to subjects' partners–spouses who smoked and requested NRT. Although targeting family members was not an explicit goal of the Browning and colleagues' studies or the Sharp and colleagues' studies, family members were able to participate in the intervention if they requested assistance with smoking cessation.

CONCEPTUAL AND METHODOLOGICAL ISSUES

Conceptual Issues

A theoretical framework was used to guide the vast majority of interventions (n = 15/19, 79%; Table 10.1). Combining frameworks was the most common approach (n = 7/15, 47%) followed by the Agency for Healthcare Research and Quality's four or five A's (n = 3/15, 20%), Prochaska's transtheoretical stages of change (n = 2/15, 13%), principles of motivational interviewing (n = 1/15, 7%), cognitive behavioral therapy (n = 1/15, 7%), or the health belief model (n = 1/15, 7%).

Methodological Issues

Quality of the Studies

As Table 10.1 illustrates, only about 40% (n = 7/19, 37%) of the intervention studies were rated as level 2 evidence, which indicates a strong quality of evidence. Methodological limitations that affected the quality of the studies were small sample size and/or weak study designs. Although a substantial proportion used a randomized controlled trial design (n = 12/19, 63%), many were plagued by small sample sizes. The number of participants among the various studies ranged from 13 to 1,077; 37% (7/19) of studies had sample sizes ≤100, 42% (8/19) were >100 and ≤300, and only 21% (4/19) were >300.

Endpoints Used to Measure Tobacco Outcomes

The most common endpoints to measure tobacco outcomes were 7-day point prevalence at 6 ($n = 6/19$, 32%) and 12 ($n = 2/19$, 11%) months and continuous abstinence at 12 months (3/19, 16%). Only 47% of studies confirmed smoking cessation status through the use of cotinine, expired CO levels, or the bogus pipeline technique.

PREDICTORS OF SMOKING CESSATION OUTCOMES

Demographic Variables Associated With Smoking Cessation Outcomes

Gender, age, and educational level were reported to be associated with smoking cessation outcomes among head and neck cancer patients and childhood cancer survivors. Gritz and colleagues (1993) found that males were more likely to continue smoking after head and neck cancer. Similarly, Emmons and colleagues (2003) found that long-term smoking cessation outcomes were lower among male childhood cancer survivors. Both studies identified that age was associated with smoking outcomes. Gritz and colleagues (1993) identified that older participants were more likely to continue smoking compared to those who were younger. Similarly, Emmons and colleagues (2003) found that older age was associated with higher smoking rates among childhood cancer survivors. Socioeconomic status was also found to be associated with higher smoking rates among childhood cancer survivors such that survivors with lower socioeconomic status were more likely to continue smoking as compared to those with a higher socioeconomic status.

Illness-Related Variables Related to Smoking Cessation Outcomes

Type of illness, type of cancer treatment, and length of time since diagnosis also were associated with smoking cessation outcomes. Multiple studies found that patients with smoking-related malignancies (lung or head and neck cancer) were more likely to quit smoking as compared to those with other type of cancers, other types of chronic illness, or those undergoing general surgery. Gritz and colleagues (1993) found that patients with head and neck cancer who underwent surgical procedures were twice as likely to remain abstinent as compared to those who received radiation treatment. One potential reason for this difference may be that the types of surgical procedures used in the head and neck cancer group make smoking more physically difficult. Two studies found that patients with smoking-related malignancies (lung or head and neck cancer) who received smoking cessation interventions within 3 months of their diagnosis were more likely to be abstinent as compared to those who did not receive smoking cessation treatment within 3 months (Cox et al., 2003; Garces et al., 2004).

Psychosocial and Behavioral Factors Associated With Smoking Cessation Outcomes

A variety of psychosocial (depressive symptoms and smoking rates within the social network) and behavioral factors (motivational readiness to change, self-efficacy, level of nicotine dependence, and use of smoking cessation treatments) have been associated with smoking cessation outcomes. A discussion of the influence of these factors on smoking cessation outcomes are summarized in the following section.

Psychosocial Factors

Emmons and colleagues (2003) found that higher depressive symptoms as measured by the Brief Symptom Inventory 18 Severity Index were associated with higher smoking rates among childhood cancer survivors at entry to the Partnership for Health, a smoking cessation intervention for smokers in the childhood cancer survivors study. At 8- and 12-month follow-up, the Brief Symptom Inventory scores were associated with smoking cessation outcomes such that childhood cancer survivors with higher levels of depressive symptoms were less likely to quit smoking. Additionally, Emmons and colleagues (2003) identified that childhood cancer survivors who had smokers within their social network were more likely to be smokers and also more likely to be nicotine dependent. In fact, those with more smokers in their social network were twice as likely to be nicotine dependent as those with few smokers in their social network. This is an important issue as several studies identified that approximately 40%–50% of cancer patients lived with another smoker (Cox et al., 2003; Stanislaw & Wewers, 1994; Wakefield, Olver, Whitford, & Rosenfeld, 2004; Wewers, Jenkins, & Mignery, 1997).

Behavioral Factors

Studies have examined the relationship between motivational readiness to change smoking behavior and cessation outcomes in head and neck, lung cancer and childhood cancer survivors. Gritz and colleagues (1993) found that motivational readiness to change was associated with 12 month continuous abstinence rates among head and neck cancer patients such that 46% of precontemplators were abstinent at 12 months as compared to 59% of contemplators and 89% of those in the action stages of motivational readiness. In another study, Schnoll and colleagues (2003) found that cancer patients with a higher motivational readiness to quit smoking were more likely to be abstinent at 6 (OR = 2.9; 95% CI, 1.04–4.75) and 12 months (OR = 1.76; 95% CI, .94–3.30) after a brief physician initiated quit smoking intervention. Schnoll and colleagues also identified that having tried a group counseling cessation program (OR = 3.48; 95% CI, 1.66–6.98) was associated with smoking cessation outcomes in cancer patients who received a brief physician initiated quit smoking intervention at the 12-month follow-up. Schnoll and colleagues (2005) also examined predictors of smoking cessation among cancer patients who received a cognitive behavioral therapy intervention versus those who received basic health education and found that baseline motivational readiness for change was associated with smoking cessation at 1 month but was no longer significant at 3 months. Similarly, Emmons and colleagues (2005) found that baseline motivational readiness for change did not enter the final multivariate logistic regression model for smoking cessation outcomes in childhood cancer survivors at 8 and 12 months.

Self-efficacy or one's confidence in the ability to quit smoking was associated with enhanced smoking cessation. Emmons and colleagues (2009) identified that childhood cancer survivors with high self-efficacy at baseline were 4 times more likely to quit than those with little or no self-efficacy (OR = 4.32; 95% CI, 2.34–8.06) at 8 and 12 months. Situational self-efficacy or one's confidence in not smoking in a variety of situations was associated with smoking cessation at 2 to 6 years after baseline (Emmons et al., 2009).

Various measures of nicotine dependence level were associated with smoking cessation outcomes such that those with higher levels of nicotine dependence, as measured by smoking the first cigarette within 30 minutes of awakening, high levels of nicotine dependence on the Fagerstrom Nicotine Dependence Questionnaire, or smoking >15 cigarettes per day, were more likely to be smokers at follow-up assessments. One study found that use of pharmacotherapy enhanced smoking cessation outcomes. Emmons and colleagues (2005) found that childhood cancer survivors who used nicotine replacement treatment had significantly higher quit rates at the 12-month assessment as compared to nonusers (p < .0001). At long-term follow up of this study, tests of potential mediation effect on the intervention group determined that use of nicotine replacement treatment was the most significant variable that mediated the outcome of the intervention (Emmons et al., 2009).

DISCUSSION

One of the most remarkable findings of this systematic review is the leading role that nurses have played in delivering smoking cessation interventions in the context of cancer care studies. As Table 10.1 illustrates, more than half of the studies (n = 10/19, 53%) tested the efficacy of nurse-delivered interventions or nurses were the primary author of the published paper. Among the 12 studies that tested smoking cessation interventions delivered by health care providers, more than 2/3 (67%) of these studies used a nurse to deliver the intervention. One of the two studies that showed significant effects in promoting smoking cessation was a nurse-delivered intervention led by a nurse investigator (Duffy et al., 2006). Although this review indicates that studies addressed smoking cessation interventions along the cancer care continuum, the vast majority of interventions were conducted in adults with smoking-related malignancies during acute phases of illness in the treatment setting. Only two of the studies examined in this review were conducted in cancer survivors (Emmons et al., 2005; Hudson et al., 2002) and only one was conducted within adolescents with cancer (Hollen, Hobbie, & Finley, 1999). These two groups of patients are particularly important to target for smoking cessation interventions in order to enhance clinical outcomes and promote long-term health. In particular, childhood cancer survivors are at high risk for late-term medical and psychosocial complications and provision of health promotion lifestyle counseling and regular screening may modify these effects (Nathan et al., 2009). Nathan and colleagues identified that many childhood cancer survivors engage in risky health behaviors (smoking, alcohol use, and physical inactivity) but do not receive adequate risk-based health care to modify their risks. In fact, although 90% of the childhood cancer survivors received medical care, less than 1 in 5 reported a visit in which they discussed ways that they can decrease their risks for development of cancer by altering risk behavior.

Lessons Learned

Taken together, synthesis of these studies provides lessons that can be used by oncology nurses and nurse scientists to create opportunities to advance care for cancer patients and their families and identifies avenues for future research. The three major lessons that may be gleaned from the studies conducted to date are (1) characteristics of successful smoking cessation interventions, (2) conceptual and methodological rigor that can be improved in future studies, and (3) understanding factors that are associated with improved smoking cessation outcomes.

Characteristics of Successful Smoking Cessation Interventions

All together, there were five smoking cessation interventions that had significant or marginally significant differences between the intervention and control group. It appears that the successful smoking cessation interventions within this population were characterized by high intensity interventions, interventions that had at least six sessions, targeted multiple risk behaviors and/or used a multicomponent intervention that included pharmacotherapy, behavioral counseling, and social support. In particular, social support seemed to be an important component of interventions delivered to childhood and adolescent cancer survivors. Many of these findings are consistent with recommendations from the U.S. Public Health Services clinical guideline for tobacco treatment (Fiore et al., 2008). For example, a strong dose-response relationship between treatment intensity and improved clinical outcomes and combining counseling with medication is more effective for smoking cessation than either approach used alone. Among smokers who wish to quit, Hughes (2008) recommends that health care providers take advantage of this window of opportunity and use an intensive approach to optimize chances for successful outcomes. This intensive approach may be especially salient among smokers with cancer, who are often highly motivated to quit and for whom smoking cessation after the diagnosis of cancer is essential to improve clinical outcomes. Future research is needed to assess whether more intensive interventions that routinely target multiple risk factors and use multicomponent interventions are needed to improve smoking cessation outcomes among cancer patients as compared to standard evidence-based smoking cessation interventions.

Need for Conceptual Rigor

Although the majority of studies used a theoretical framework to guide the intervention, few reported testing the theory. Rothman (2004) suggests that in order for us to advance our understanding of health behavior change and to advance innovation, intervention studies provide the opportunity to test theories and that data generated from this exercise can then be used to revise the theory and inform future interventions. One way to accomplish this is by having the theoretical framework specify how the intervention will affect clinical outcomes. Subsequently, a statistical test, called mediation analysis, can be used to test whether the smoking cessation intervention changes the variables they are designed to change, and test the theory regarding tobacco cessation outcomes (Judd & Kenny, 1981; MacKinnon, Taborga, & Morgan-Lopez, 2002). The type of approach discussed above is important for intervention research so that we can begin to understand how these third variables or mediators are related to tobacco use, understand how the smoking cessation program affects these mediating variables, and provide information on how the programs can be improved as well as revise the theory (Lipsey, 1993; MacKinnon et al., 2002). Emmons and colleagues (2003, 2005, 2009) provide an excellent example of how the use of a theoretical framework and mediation analyses can be used to guide the development and testing of smoking cessation interventions and advance knowledge of how, when, and for whom the intervention works.

Need for Methodological Rigor

Methodological issues that can be addressed in future studies are ensuring adequate sample sizes, use of biochemical verification to monitor smoking outcomes, and use of standardized outcome measures of abstinence. Many of the studies examined in this systematic review had small sample sizes, which limits the statistical power to detect intervention effects. Recruitment of smokers with cancer into clinical trials is challenging. Large numbers of patients must be screened in order to identify eligible participants. For example, Martinez and colleagues (2009) reported on the feasibility of enrolling cancer patients into smoking cessation clinical trials and found that out of 14,514 screened patients, 263 (<2%) were eligible; 43 (16%) refused enrollment. Among the eligible patients, 220 (84%) enrolled. This finding underscores the need to conduct multisite studies that keep inclusion criteria broad such that all smokers with cancer are eligible to participate except those at the end of life (De Moor, Elder, & Emmons, 2008).

Less than half of the studies used biochemical verification to determine smoking status. Biochemical verification of smoking status, with blood, salivary or urinary cotinine, or carbon monoxide is currently recommended when testing new interventions in special populations such as patients with smoking related diseases (Society for Research on Nicotine and Tobacco, 2002). It is not entirely clear whether biochemical verification is needed in all populations. For example, interventions that have low demand requirements such as large scale trials that have limited face-to-face contact and studies where data is collected through the mail, telephone, or internet may not need biochemical verification. However, for clinic-based studies, those which use higher intensity interventions and involve special populations, biochemical verification may add more precision in determining smoking cessation outcomes. Cooley and colleagues (2007) reported discrepancies between self-report and biochemical verification of smoking status in women with lung cancer such that current smoking status using biochemical verification was 20% higher than self-report. Potential reasons for this discrepancy may be that continued smoking after the diagnosis of lung cancer is associated with guilt and shame and patients may be reluctant to disclose their smoking status (Chapple et al., 2004). It would be helpful for future studies to report smoking status using both self-report and biochemical verification so that we can clarify the utility of using both of these measures in clinical research.

The use of outcome measures of abstinence varied across the studies examined in this systematic review. The most common measure used was 7-day point prevalence at 6 months. Use of standardized measures across studies is recommended so that smoking cessation outcomes can be compared across various studies using a common metric. The most appropriate abstinence measure will vary depending on the type and purpose of the clinical trial. In general, Hughes and colleagues (2003) recommend that all smoking cessation trials report prolonged abstinence as the primary outcome measure plus 7-day point prevalence as the secondary measure because it can be biochemically confirmed and because it has frequently been used in previous trials and meta-analyses. In trials where smokers are willing to set a quit date, it is recommended that prolonged abstinence measures be reported at 6 and/or 12 months after the quit date, whereas in trials where smokers are not currently trying to quit, it is recommended that a prolonged abstinence measure ≥6-month duration be used and point prevalence rates at 6- and 12-month follow-up after the initiation of the intervention. Improving conceptual and methodological rigor in future studies will help us more clearly understand those interventions that are most useful in this population.

Understanding Factors Associated With Smoking Cessation Outcomes

Understanding factors that are associated with smoking cessation outcomes among cancer patients are important so that future studies can use this information to inform the development of interventions. Potentially helpful targets are interventions that address the large numbers of smokers in the social network, motivational readiness to change smoking behavior, and self-efficacy. Zhou and colleagues (2009) examined factors that were associated with successful quit attempts and found that the use of cessation aides along with avoidance of other smokers were key strategies that quitters used to promote success. Given that many cancer patients, especially those with smoking-related malignancies, have a large number of smokers within their social networks, avoiding smokers is not a reasonable strategy. However, avoiding secondhand smoke is an important issue for patients after the diagnosis of cancer. Sarna and colleagues (2004) identified that lung cancer survivors who were exposed to secondhand smoke were 3 times as likely to report respiratory symptoms. In addition, increased respiratory symptoms were associated with decreased quality of life.

The diagnosis of cancer may be an ideal time to motivate both patients and their family members to initiate health changes such as smoking cessation (Emmons et al., 2005; McBride & Ostroff, 2003). Thus, developing and testing a family-based smoking cessation intervention may be a promising approach to promote behavioral change especially after the diagnosis of cancer. Interventions that target decreased exposure of patients to secondhand smoke are a potential option in the case that family members are not ready to quit smoking. One potential strategy to reduce patient exposure to secondhand smoke may be the use of household smoking bans. Shields (2007) examined the association between household smoking bans and smoking cessation outcomes and found that smokers who reported smoking bans at home or work were more likely to quit smoking within the next 2 years. This is an area that deserves further study in the context of cancer care. Only one of the studies in this systematic review focused specifically on promoting smoking cessation among family members of cancer patients (Schilling et al., 1997). Although four other studies addressed smoking among participants' family members, none of these studies focused on the family as a unit for intervention or actively engaged family members to quit smoking as a primary part of the intervention (Browning et al., 2000; Emmons et al., 2005; Sharp et al., 2008; Wakefield et al., 2004). Future studies are needed to see if a family-based approach to promote smoking cessation is more effective than just targeting individuals with cancer.

It is interesting to note that the association between motivational readiness to change behavior and smoking cessation is mixed among these studies. Some studies indicated that motivational readiness to change was a factor that influenced cessation while other studies found that it wasn't a significant factor. The differences across studies may reflect that motivational readiness to change may be affected by the type of cancer, age of the patient, and length of time since diagnosis. For example, several studies identified that patients with smoking-related malignancies were much more likely to quit smoking as compared to those without smoking related malignancies (Smith, Reilly, Houston Miller, DeBusk, & Taylor, 2002; Wewers, Bowen, Stanislaw, & Desimone, 1994). Similarly, two studies identified that smokers who received smoking cessation interventions within 3 months of their diagnosis were more likely to quit smoking (Garces et al., 2004; Sanderson Cox et al., 2002). Thus, a better understanding of how motivation differs among various groups of cancer patients and how it changes over time would provide information that could be used to enhance and sustain motivation for quit attempts.

Another promising target in smoking cessation research is self-efficacy, which is defined as a person's confidence that they can successfully complete a certain task (Bandura, 1977). Incorporating strategies that increase self-efficacy seem to be important components to enhance smoking abstinence. Types of strategies that can be used to enhance self-efficacy in smoking cessation are use of peers that have been successful at quitting, coaching and practical advice about quitting, and the use of cessation aides to decrease withdrawal symptoms. The two studies in this review that have used peer-counseling focused on adolescent or childhood cancer survivors and these studies had positive or marginally positive results (Emmons et al., 2005; Hollen et al., 1999). Thus, testing the application of peer support and counseling among other populations of patients with cancer or at-risk for cancer is warranted.

Opportunities and Challenges for Oncology Nurses and Nurse Scientists

These findings underscore the enormous impact that nurses can make in advancing knowledge of smoking cessation interventions within the context of cancer care. Many opportunities exist for oncology nurses and nurse scientists to influence tobacco control. However, there are also significant barriers that must be addressed in order for oncology nurses to reach their full potential as leaders in tobacco control. The following section will highlight the opportunities and challenges that oncology nurses and nurse scientists face in addressing smoking cessation, discuss lessons learned from the current state of the science related to smoking cessation intervention in cancer care and suggest future directions for research to advance tobacco control.

There is support from the nursing profession for further research in this area. For example, the Oncology Nursing Society's (ONS, 2006) position paper advocates for the involvement of nurses and nursing science to advance tobacco control. Nurses can participate in promoting tobacco control efforts through multiple channels, which include participating in professional education to enhance knowledge of tobacco treatment, enhancing public education materials, supporting local, state, and national legislative and regulatory efforts related to tobacco control, and furthering nursing research on tobacco prevention and cessation interventions.

As this review demonstrates further research is needed to evaluate the need for tailoring smoking cessation interventions in the context of cancer care, especially using nurses as interventionists. The findings of the efficacy of nurse intervention is further supported by the findings of a meta-analysis demonstrating that nursing interventions are effective to promote smoking cessation (Rice & Stead, 2009).

Relevant to this review are the findings of several studies indicating that attitudes toward providing smoking cessation advice influence nurses' behaviors. Hall and Marteau (2007) compared 152 nurses' reports of giving smoking cessation advice in the context of cervical cancer with their reports of giving advice for cardiovascular disease screening and diabetes care and their beliefs about providing advice in these three contexts. Results from this study revealed that nurses were more likely to give smoking cessation advice and had more positive beliefs about giving advice in the context of cardiovascular and diabetes care compared with cervical cancer screening. In another study, Sarna, Wewers, Brown, Lillington, and Brecht (2001) conducted a national survey with a random sample of oncology nurses and examined factors associated with barriers to providing tobacco treatment. Results from this study identified that nurses with the greatest number of barriers to providing smoking cessation were more likely to be current smokers, younger, less likely to have an advanced degree, to be a nurse practitioner, or to have administrative responsibilities. These two studies highlight potential barriers that must be overcome to increase the frequency with which nurses give smoking cessation advice as part of their practice.

Another significant challenge is the lack of information and skills for nurses to effectively deliver evidence-based tobacco treatment. Sarna and colleagues (2000) assessed the frequency of tobacco interventions among 1508 oncology nurses. Only 10% of the nurses were aware of the evidence-based tobacco treatment guideline (Fiore et al., 2008) published through the U.S. Public Health Service. The majority (64%) assessed and documented tobacco status, however, only 36% provided counseling, 24% recommended nicotine replacement, and 16% taught skills to prevent smoking relapse. Eighty-eight percent of nurses wanted to help their patients but 92% identified that they needed additional training. Evidence exists that nurses can be trained quickly to deliver smoking cessation interventions. For example, Borrelli, Lee, and Novak (2008) examined whether it was possible to change nurse attitudes and counseling behaviors with a one-day training session. Results of this study showed that after the training nurses reported higher levels of self-efficacy to counsel, positive outcome expectancies, optimism that patients would follow their advice, and increased perceived importance of providing advice and increased perceived institutional support. In addition, nurses spent more time counseling smokers and were less likely to selectively counsel patients at 6 months after the training session.

CONCLUSION

As this systematic review reveals, there is a small but growing number of studies that examine smoking cessation interventions focused in the area of cancer care. Findings indicate that nurses have had a major role in the development, testing, and delivery of the smoking cessation interventions. Indeed, more than half of the studies tested the efficacy of nurse-delivered interventions. Moreover, among the 12 studies that tested smoking cessation interventions delivered by health care providers, about two thirds of these studies used a nurse to deliver the intervention. Although these findings are promising, further opportunities exist for nurses to expand their leadership in tobacco control in the context of cancer care. For example, most of the studies conducted to date have focused on adults with smoking-related malignancies receiving treatment in an acute care setting. Studies are needed that target other populations with cancer, including those at high risk for cancer, such as women undergoing cervical cancer screening, childhood cancer survivors, and adolescents with cancer. Further research is also needed on tobacco use of family members of patients diagnosed with cancer. Another area that is important to clarify is the specifics of which components of cessation interventions are most effective or those components that do not work during cancer care. This review demonstrates that, for people with cancer, high intensity interventions, targeting multiple risk behaviors and/or using a multi-component intervention that included pharmacotherapy, behavioral counseling, and social support characterized successful interventions. Using a theoretical framework to specify how the intervention is projected to affect outcomes, ensuring that adequate sample sizes are secured, using biochemical verification to monitor smoking outcomes, and using standardized outcome measures of abstinence are other strategies to advance the science. Finally, in order to improve translation of evidence into practice, research is needed to reduce barriers to nursing intervention.

ACKNOWLEDGMENTS

Funding from the National Cancer Institute 1 K07 CA92696-02 (Principal Investigator Mary E. Cooley; Mentors K. M. Emmons, PhD, Harvard School of Public Health and Dana-Farber Cancer Institute; B. E. Johnson MD, Harvard Medical School and Lowe Center for Thoracic Oncology, Dana-Farber Cancer Institute).

REFERENCES

Bandura, A. (1977). Self-efficacy: Toward a unifying theory of behavioral change. *Psychology Review, 84*(2), 191–215.

Borrelli, B., Lee, C., & Novak, S. (2008). Is provider training effective? Changes in attitudes towards smoking cessation counseling behaviors of home health care nurses. *Preventative Medicine, 46*, 358–363.

Browning, K., Ahijevych, K., & Ross, P. (2000). Implementing the Agency for Health Care policy and research's smoking cessation guideline in a lung cancer surgery clinic. *Oncology Nursing Forum, 27*, 1248–1254.

Chapple, A., Ziebland, S., & McPherson, A. (2004). Stigma, shame, and blame experienced by patients with lung cancer: Qualitative study. *British Medical Journal, 328*(7454), 1470.

Cooley, M. E., Sarna, L., Brown, J. K., Williams, R. D., Chernecky, C., Padilla, G., et al. (2007). Tobacco use in women with lung cancer. *Annals of Behavioral Medicine, 33*(3), 242–250.

Cooley, M.E., Sarna, L., Kotlerman, J., Lukanich, J.M., Jaklitsch, M., Green, S.B., et al. (2009). Smoking cessation is challenging even for patients recovering from lung cancer surgery with curative intent. *Lung Cancer*, March 23, (Epub ahead of press).

Cooley, M.E., Sipples, R.L., Murphy, M., & Sarna, L. (2008). Smoking cessation and lung cancer: Oncology nurses can make a difference. *Seminars Oncology Nursing, 24*(1), 16–26.

Cox, C.L., McLaughlin, R.A., Rai, S.N., Steen, B.D., & Hudson, M.M. (2005). Adolescent survivors: A secondary analysis of a clinical trial targeting behavior change. *Pediatric Blood Cancer, 45*(2), 144–154.

Cox, L.S., Africano, N.L., Tercyak, K.P., & Taylor, K.L. (2003). Nicotine dependence treatment for patients with cancer. *Cancer, 98*(3), 632–644.

De Moor, J.S., Elder, K., Emmons, K. M. (2008). Smoking prevention and cessation interventions for cancer survivors. *Seminars in Oncology Nursing, 24*(3), 180–192.

Duffy, S. A., Ronis, D. L., Valenstein, M., Lambert, M. T., Fowler, K. E., Gregory, L., et al. (2006). A tailored smoking, alcohol, and depression intervention for head and neck cancer patients. *Cancer, Epidemiology, Biomarkers, & Prevention, 15*(11), 2203–2208.

Emmons, K., Butterfield, R., Puleo, E., Park, E., Mertens, A., Gritz, E., et al. (2003). Smoking among participants in the childhood cancer survivors cohort: The partnership for health study. *Journal of Clinical Oncology, 21*(2), 189–196.

Emmons, K. M., Puleo, E., Mertens, A., Gritz, E. R., Diller, L., & Li, F. P. (2009). Long-term smoking cessation outcomes among childhood cancer survivors in the partnership for health study. *Journal of Clinical Oncology, 27*(1), 52–60.

Emmons, K. M., Puleo, E., Park, E., Gritz, E. R., Butterfield, R. M., Weeks, J. C., et al. (2005). Peer-delivered smoking counseling for childhood cancer survivors increases rate of cessation: the partnership for health study. *Journal of Clinical Oncology, 23*(27), 6516–6523.

Fiore, M., Jaen, C., Baker, T., Bailey, W., Benowitz, N., Curry, S., et al. (2008). *Treating tobacco use and dependence: 2008 update. Clinical practice guideline*. Rockville, MD: U.S. Department of Health and Human Services, Public Health Services.

Fox, J. L., Rosenzweig, K. E., & Ostroff, J. S. (2004). The effect of smoking status on survival following radiation therapy for non-small cell lung cancer. *Lung Cancer, 44*(3), 287–293.

Ganong, L. H. (1987). Integrative reviews of nursing research. *Research Nursing Health, 10*(1), 1–11.

Garces, Y., Yang, P., Parkinson, J., Zhao, X., Wampfler, J., Ebbert, J., et al. (2004). The relationship between cigarette smoking and quality of life after lung cancer diagnosis. *Chest, 126*(6), 1733–1741.

Griebel, B., Wewers, M., & Baker, C. (1998). The effectiveness of a nurse managed minimal smoking cessation intervention among hospitalized adults with cancer. *Oncology Nursing Forum, 25*(5), 897–902.

Gritz, E. R., Carr, C. R., Rapkin, D., Abemayor, E., Chang, L. J., Wong, W. K., et al. (1993). Predictors of long-term smoking cessation in head and neck cancer patients. *Cancer Epidemiology, Biomarkers, & Prevention, 2*(3), 261–270.

Gritz, E. R., Dresler, C., & Sarna, L. (2005). Smoking, the missing drug interaction in clinical trials: Ignoring the obvious. *Cancer Epidemiology, Biomarkers, & Prevention, 14*(10), 2287–2293.

Gritz, E. R., Fingeret, M. C., Vidrine, D. J., Lazev, A. B., Mehta, N. V., & Reece, G. P. (2006). Successes and failures of the teachable moment: Smoking cessation in cancer patients. *Cancer, 106*(1), 17–27.

Hall, S., & Marteau, T. (2007). Practice nurses' self-reported opportunistic smoking cessation advice in three contexts. *Nicotine & Tobacco Research, 9*(9), 941–945.

Hollen, P. J., Hobbie, W. L., & Finley, S. M. (1999). Testing the effects of a decision-making and risk-reduction program for cancer-surviving adolescents. *Oncology Nursing Forum, 26*(9), 1475–1486.

Hudson, M. M., Tyc, V. L., Srivastava, D. K., Gattuso, J., Quargnenti, A., Crom, D. B., et al. (2002). Multi-component behavioral intervention to promote health protective behaviors in childhood cancer survivors: the protect study. *Medical Pediatric Oncology, 39*(1), 2–11.

Hughes, J. (2008). An algorithm for choosing among smoking cessation treatments. *Journal of Substance Abuse Treatment, 34*(4), 426–432.

Hughes, J. R., Keely, J. P., Niaura, R. S., Ossip-Klein, D. J., Richmond, R. L., & Swan, G. E. (2003). Measures of abstinence in clinical trials: issues and recommendations. *Nicotine & Tobacco Research, 5*(1), 13–25.

Jensen, K., Jensen, A. B., & Grau, C. (2007). Smoking has a negative impact upon health related quality of life after treatment for head and neck cancer. *Oral Oncology, 43*(2), 187–192.

Judd, C., & Kenny, D. (1981). Process analysis: Estimating mediation in treatment evaluations. *Evaluation Reviews, 5*, 602–619.

Lipsey, M. (1993). *Understanding causes and generalizing about them.* San Francisco: Jossey-Bass.

LoConte, N. K., Else-Quest, N. M., Eickhoff, J., Hyde, J., & Schiller, J. H. (2008). Assessment of guilt and shame in patients with non-small-cell lung cancer compared with patients with breast and prostate cancer. *Clinical Lung Cancer, 9*(3), 171–178.

MacKinnon, D. P., Taborga, M. P., & Morgan-Lopez, A. A. (2002). Mediation designs for tobacco prevention research. *Drug and Alcohol Dependence, 68*(Suppl. 1), S69–S83.

Martinez, E., Tatum, K. L., Weber, D. M., Kuzla, N., Pendley, A., Campbell, K., et al. (2009). Issues related to implementing a smoking cessation clinical trial for cancer patients. *Cancer Causes & Control, 20*(1), 97–104.

McBride, C., & Ostroff, J. (2003). Teachable moments for promoting smoking cessation: The context of cancer care and survivorship. *Cancer Control, 10*, 325–333.

McBride, C. M., Scholes, D., Grothaus, L. C., Curry, S. J., Ludman, E., & Albright, J. (1999). Evaluation of a minimal self-help smoking cessation intervention following cervical cancer screening. *Preventative Medicine, 29*(2), 133–138.

Nathan, P. C., Ford, J. S., Henderson, T. O., Hudson, M. M., Emmons, K. M., Casillas, J. N., et al. (2009). Health behaviors, medical care, and interventions to promote healthy living in the childhood cancer survivor study cohort. *Journal of Clinical Oncology, 27*(14), 2363–2373.

Oncology Nursing Society. (2006). *Nursing leadership in global and domestic tobacco control.* Retrieved from http://www.ons.org/Publications/Positions/GlobalTobaccoUse.shtml

Rice, V. H., & Stead, L. F. (2009). Nursing interventions for smoking cessation. *Cochrane Database of Systematic Reviews,* CD00118 (1).

Centers for Disease Control and Prevention (2006). Cigarette smoking among adults— United States, 2006. *Morbidity and Mortality Weekly Report, 56*(44), 1157–1161.

Ropka, M. E., & Spencer-Cisek, P. (2001). PRISM: Priority symptom management project phase I: Assessment. *Oncology Nursing Forum, 28*(10), 1585–1594.

Rothman, A. J. (2004). "Is there nothing more practical than a good theory?": Why innovations and advances in health behavior change will arise if interventions are used to test and refine theory. *International Journal of Behavioral Nutrition & Physical Activity, 1*(1), 11.

Sanderson Cox, L., Patten, C., Ebbert, J., Drews, A., Croghan, G., & Clark, M. (2002). Tobacco use outcomes among patients with lung cancer treated with nicotine dependence. *Journal of Clinical Oncology, 20*(16), 3461–3469.

Sarna, L. P., Brown, J. K., Lillington, L., Rose, M., Wewers, M. E., & Brecht, M. L. (2000). Tobacco interventions by oncology nurses in clinical practice: report from a national survey. *Cancer, 89*(4), 881–889.

Sarna, L., Evangelista, L., Tashkin, D., Padilla, G., Holmes, C., Brecht, M. L., et al. (2004). Impact of respiratory symptoms and pulmonary function on quality of life of long-term survivors of non-small cell lung cancer. *Chest, 125*(2), 439–445.

Sarna, L., Wewers, M. E., Brown, J. K., Lillington, L., & Brecht, M. L. (2001). Barriers to tobacco cessation in clinical practice: Report from a national survey of oncology nurses. *Nursing Outlook, 49*(4), 166–172.

Schilling, A., Conaway, M. R., Wingate, P. J., Atkins, J. N., Berkowitz, I. M., Clamon, G. H., et al. (1997). Recruiting cancer patients to participate in motivating their relatives to quit smoking. A cancer control study of the cancer and leukemia group B (CALGB 9072). *Cancer, 79*(1), 152–160.

Schnoll, R. A., Rothman, R. V., Wielt, D. B., Lerman, C., Pedri, H., Wang, H., et al. (2005). A randomized pilot study of cognitive-behavioral therapy versus basic health education for smoking cessation among cancer patients. *Annals of Behavioral Medicine, 30*(1), 1–11.

Schnoll, R. A., Zhang, B., Rue, M., Krook, J. E., Spears, W. T., Marcus, A. C., et al. (2003). Brief physician-initiated quit-smoking strategies for clinical oncology settings: A trial coordinated by the eastern cooperative oncology group. *Journal of Clinical Oncology, 21*(2), 355–365.

Sharp, L., Johansson, H., Fagerstrom, K., & Rutqvist, L. E. (2008). Smoking cessation among patients with head and neck cancer: Cancer as a 'teachable moment.' *European Journal of Cancer Care* (England), *17*(2), 114–119.

Shields, M. (2007). Smoking bans: Influence on smoking prevalence. *Health Report, 18*(3), 9–24.

Smith, P. M., Reilly, K. R., Houston Miller, N., DeBusk, R. F., & Taylor, C. B. (2002). Application of a nurse-managed inpatient smoking cessation program. *Nicotine & Tobacco Research, 4*(2), 211–222.

Society for Research on Nicotine and Tobacco Subcommittee on Biochemical Verification. (2002). Biochemical verification of tobacco use and cessation. *Nicotine & Tobacco Research, 4*(2), 149–159.

Stanislaw, A., & Wewers, M. (1994). A smoking cessation intervention with hospitalized surgical cancer patients: A pilot study. *Cancer Nursing, 17*(2), 81–86.

Steinberg, M. B., Schmelzer, A. C., Richardson, D. L., & Foulds, J. (2008). The case for treating tobacco dependence as a chronic disease. *Annals of Internal Medicine, 148*(7), 554–556.

Videtic, G. M., Stitt, L. W., Dar, A. R., Kocha, W. I., Tomiak, A. T., Truong, P. T., et al. (2003). Continued cigarette smoking by patients receiving concurrent chemoradiotherapy for limited-stage small-cell lung cancer is associated with decreased survival. *Journal of Clinical Oncology, 21*(8), 1544–1549.

Wakefield, M., Olver, I., Whitford, H., & Rosenfeld, E. (2004). Motivational interviewing as a smoking cessation intervention for patients with cancer: Randomized control trial. *Nursing Research, 53*(6), 396–405.

Walker, M. S., Vidrine, D. J., Gritz, E. R., Larsen, R. J., Yan, Y., Govindan, R., et al. (2006). Smoking relapse during the first year after treatment for early-stage non-small-cell lung cancer. *Cancer Epidemiology, Biomarkers, & Prevention, 15*(12), 2370–2377.

Wassenaar, T. R., Eickhoff, J. C., Jarzemsky, D. R., Smith, S. S., Larson, M. L., & Schiller, J. H. (2007). Differences in primary care clinicians' approach to non-small cell lung cancer patients compared with breast cancer. *Journal of Thoracic Oncology*, 2(8), 722–728.

Wewers, M. E., Bown, J. M., Stanislaw, A. E., & Desimone, V. B. (1994). A nurse-delivered smoking cessation intervention among hospitalized postoperative patients: Influence of a smoking-related diagnosis: A pilot study. *Heart & Lung*, 23(2), 151–156.

Wewers, M. E., Jenkins, L., & Mignery, T. (1997). A nurse-managed smoking cessation intervention during diagnostic testing for lung cancer. *Oncology Nursing Forum*, 24, 1419–1421.

Zhou, X., Nonnemaker, J., Sherrill, B., Gilsenan, A. W., Coste, F., & West, R. (2009). Attempts to quit smoking and relapse: Factors associated with success or failure from the ATTEMPT cohort study. *Addictive Behavior*, 34(4), 365–373.

Chapter 11

Evidence-Based Smoking Cessation Interventions for Patients With Acute Respiratory Disorders

Janie Heath, Sara Young, Sharon Bennett, Mary Beth Ginn, and Geoffrey Cox

ABSTRACT

Worldwide, tobacco use continues to be the most significant preventable cause of death and hospital admissions, particularly related to respiratory diseases. Acute respiratory illnesses requiring hospitalization provide an opportunity for nurses to intervene and help smokers quit. Of the three top hospital admissions related to respiratory diseases, chronic obstructive pulmonary disease (COPD) is the one that continues to have increased mortality whereas community acquired pneumonia and asthma have decreased over the past 5 years. The course of all three can be caused or exacerbated by continued smoking. This review describes the state of the science of nursing research focused on tobacco cessation interventions for hospitalized patients with COPD, asthma, or community acquired pneumonia. Additionally, we describe two evidence-based, nurse-driven, hospital protocols to treat tobacco dependence that can serve as models of care. Recommendations are made as to how to effectively promote nursing interventions for tobacco cessation in the acute care setting.

DOI: 10.1891/0739-6686.27.273

Keywords: tobacco dependence; tobacco/smoking cessation interventions; COPD; community acquired pneumonia; asthma; nursing

Chronic diseases account for a large proportion of hospital admissions, deaths and disabilities in the United States and other countries (Warren, Jones, Eriksen, & Asma, 2006). Throughout the world, it has been estimated that chronic diseases, particularly respiratory illnesses, are responsible for 50% of all deaths (World Health Organization [WHO], 2008). Despite advances with raising awareness and treating tobacco dependence, death rates from smoking are higher among those suffering from chronic disease (Centers for Disease Control [CDC], 2007; WHO, 2008). With tobacco related health care costs soaring higher than $100 billion per year (CDC, 2008b), regulatory bodies such as the Joint Commission (JC) and Centers for Medicare and Medicaid Services (CMS) have taken significant steps to help address tobacco dependence (Joint Commission, 2003; CMS, 2005). Although research to evaluate tobacco cessation interventions has increased dramatically over the past decade, the effectiveness of nurses to prevent and reduce tobacco related morbidity and mortality among patients suffering from respiratory diseases such as COPD, asthma, and pneumonia has not been established. Thus, this review describes the state of nursing research focused on tobacco cessation interventions for hospitalized patients with COPD, asthma, or community acquired pneumonia. Additionally, we describe two evidence-based, nurse-driven, hospital protocols to treat tobacco dependence and to offer recommendations to effectively promote nursing interventions for tobacco cessation in the acute care setting that can serve as models for translational research.

Epidemiology

Informing a nursing research agenda that targets smoking-induced respiratory diseases requires a basic understanding of the epidemiological impact and the physiological mechanisms that lead to poor clinical outcomes and escalated health care costs. Smoking-related illness accounts for a significant amount of hospitalizations each year. Pneumonia (PNA), Chronic Obstructive Pulmonary Disease (COPD), and asthma account for 1.2 million; 513,000; and 444,000 hospital admissions yearly, respectively (DeFrances, Lucas, Buie, & Golosinskiy, 2008). The average length of stay for a discharged pneumonia patient is 5.1 days, compared with 4.7 days for COPD and 3.1 days for asthma (DeFrances et al., 2008). Hospital admission rates and outcomes among patients with respiratory illness have been repeatedly linked to patient smoking status. For example, as many as 53% of readmitted patients with pneumonia in the United States are current smokers and 31% are former smokers, reinforcing the need for active tobacco cessation efforts among these patients (El Sohl, Brewer, Okada, Bashir, & Gough, 2004). Furthermore, smoking status has been identified as a predictor for intensive care unit (ICU) admission in patients with pneumonia (Marrie & Shariatzadeh, 2007). Given the huge impact of smoking-induced respiratory diseases on hospitalization and mortality, acute care nursing practice standards must reflect efforts to minimize the burden of illness for patients and society with a change from reactive disease management to proactive efforts to reduce tobacco use.

Smoking-related illnesses continue to top the charts as leading causes of death each year. Pneumonia accounts for over 61,500 deaths annually (Kung, Hoyert, Xu, & Murphy, 2008) and approximately 5.4% of hospital inpatient deaths (Kozak, DeFrances, & Hall, 2006). Pneumonia and influenza, ranked as one category by the CDC, is currently the eighth leading cause of death; 97% of the deaths in this group are from pneumonia and 3% are from influenza (Kung et al., 2008). Chronic lower respiratory disease ranks as the fourth leading cause of death in the United States. This category includes chronic bronchitis, emphysema, and asthma as well as various other chronic lower respiratory diseases (Kung et al., 2008). In 2005, COPD was the cause of death in over 126,000 people, with this number rising consistently year over year since 2000 (CDC, 2008a). It is predicted that by 2020, COPD will increase its ranking to become the third most common cause of death worldwide and third in morbidity (Chapman et al., 2006; Mannino, Gagnon, Petty, & Lydick, 2000). Acute care nursing practice standards that include tobacco cessation interventions can make a difference toward reducing mortality and health care costs associated with patients suffering from smoking-induced respiratory diseases.

Quantifying true morbidity and mortality from COPD is complicated by the presence of systemic effects of the disease as well as other comorbidities, potentially leading to underrepresentation of COPD as the primary cause of death (Mannino & Buist, 2007). As such, COPD morbidity and mortality are not only underestimated, COPD is underdiagnosed, undertreated, and underfunded compared to other chronic diseases (Gerhardsson de Verdier, 2008). Asthma, also adversely affected by smoking status and exposure to secondhand smoke, continues to account for significant health care utilization and lost productivity. For the 32.6 million Americans who have asthma, there are over 12.2 million asthma attacks and 1.8 million emergency department visits yearly (CDC, 2006). For the period 2001–2003, the CDC (2007) estimates an average of over 4,200 deaths annually from asthma, the majority of which occur in patients over age 65.

While acute and critical care nurses prioritize standards of care for patients with respiratory diseases to stabilize airway management, interventions must also be directed toward supporting patients' tobacco cessation after discharge. Nurses are well positioned to help reduce smoking-attributable deaths through broad-based public health efforts that reduce smoking prevalence rates. Leading causes of death from smoking-induced respiratory diseases, such as COPD, could become relatively uncommon in future generations if the prevalence of smoking was substantially reduced, especially with increased nursing interventions targeting patients, families, and communities at large.

Pathogenesis of Smoking-Induced Respiratory Disorders

Whether sitting in wheelchairs connected to intravenous fluids outside of hospital smoke-free zones or requesting a cigarette after days of ventilation weaning attempts, the power of nicotine addiction underlies why so many patients struggling to breathe will go to dire extremes to smoke (Benowitz, 2008). Often nicotine is thought of as the contributor of ill health effects from smoking but it is the 4800 toxins and 11 known carcinogens in a single cigarette that are detrimental (National Cancer Institute, 2001).

Tobacco smoke, and the toxins associated with it, triggers an oxidative stress response that leads to the morbidity and mortality outcomes of respiratory disorders such as COPD, asthma, and pneumonia (Munro, 2006). This oxidative response results in an inflammatory and protease-antiprotease imbalance that eventually causes various degrees of airway and alveolar injury (Yanbaeva, Dentener, Creutzberg, Wesseling, & Wouters, 2007). The cycle of lung injury begins when smoke exposes the epithelium to oxidant agents and free radicals that stimulates the release of cytokines. Once the proinflammatory mediators (cytokines) are released, lymphocytes and macrophages release further mediators that result in an influx of neutrophils to the area of lung tissue injury. Proteases, released by neutrophils, contribute further to the injury by degrading elastin and collagen in the alveolar wall (Yanbaeva et al., 2007).

As the cycle of epithelial inflammation continues, gas exchange is impaired from narrowed airways (reactivity and degradation) and obstructed airways (mobilization of secretions). Whether from direct or indirect tobacco smoke, over time these physiological mechanisms can also cause genetic changes leading to lung cancer (Yanbaeva et al., 2007). Progressive airway damage gradually compromises a patient's ability to effectively breathe requiring acute and/or chronic interventions. All health care workers are thus challenged to refocus on more proactive disease management strategies to prevent repeated exacerbation and clinical decline (Gerhardsson de Verdier, 2008; Munro, 2006). Nurses managing the care of patients with smoking-induced respiratory diseases in acute and critical care settings, both diagnostically and therapeutically, must address tobacco use and exposure to secondhand smoke, as a standard of care to prevent readmissions and optimize postdischarge health.

INTEGRATED LITERATURE REVIEW

Methods

The Cochrane Library of Systematic Reviews (May 2009), MEDLINE and CINAHL (1996–May 2009) databases were used to address the research question: What outcomes are associated with nurse-driven tobacco cessation interventions among hospitalized patients with asthma, pneumonia, and COPD? Key search terms were "smoking cessation" combined by Boolean [AND] with each of the following exploded MeSH key word subjects "asthma," "chronic obstructive pulmonary disease," "pneumonia," "nurses," and "hospitalization." The method generated 728 publications and abstracts for initial review. Inclusion criteria were that studies be data-based with adults hospitalized for pneumonia, COPD, and/or asthma as the targeted population, use nurses for tobacco cessation interventions, and be conducted in the United States. Although a couple of international studies were found to be relevant, differences among the health care systems (regulatory bodies such as the Joint Commission) were determined to be too great for inclusion. Other reasons for exclusion were lack of data-based results, conducted in out-patient settings, or studies conducted in pediatric populations hospitalized with respiratory diseases.

Results

We were not able to identify any studies that met all of the inclusion criteria for this integrative review. Although the effectiveness of smoking cessation interventions delivered by nurses has been substantiated (Rice & Stead, 2008), our search did not find research studies specific to U.S. hospitalized tobacco-dependent patients with COPD, asthma, and/or pneumonia conducted by nurses. However, as displayed in Table 11.1, we did identify several systematic reviews of data-based studies focused on smoking cessation interventions in hospitalized patients that included a provider mix (some including nursing delivered interventions) and population mixes (some including patients with respiratory disease).

Studies Focused on Tobacco Use and Patients
With Respiratory Disease

One of these reviews specifically included five studies focused on patients with chronic obstructive pulmonary disease (van der Meer, Wagena, Ostelo, Jacobs, & van Schaych, 2003). This review identified two studies that were considered high quality (i.e., Crowley, Macdonald, & Walter, 1995; Tashkin et al., 2001). Based on these two studies, van der Meer and colleagues (2003) found the combination

TABLE 11.1 Summary of Data-Based Studies Reviewed for Tobacco Cessation Interventions Among Hospitalized Patients

Study	Population	Design	Outcome Measures	Interventions & Findings

Rigotti et al., 2007	33 articles
	
	Patients: Adults
	
	Setting: Hospital
	
	Diagnosis: All diagnoses and a subset of cardio-vascular
		Cochrane systematic review
		
		(randomized or quasirandomized controlled trials)
			Self-report smoking abstinence of at least 6 months duration	Interventionist:
				   Mixed (included physicians, nursing staff, psychologists, smoking cessation counselors of other hospital staff)
				Duration:
				   Mixed (included one hospital contact less than 15 minutes to multiple contacts more than 15 minutes and included no discharge support to postdischarge support of more than 1 month)
				Type:
				   Mixed (included advice to quit, behavioral counseling with or without pharmacotherapy, and discharge follow-up)
				Outcome:
				   Psychosocial intervention with pharmacotherapy and postdischarge follow-up is effective

van der Meer et al., 2003	5 articles
	
	Patients: Adults
	Settings: Hospital (general medical ward and chest unit), outpatient clinics, and home visits
		Cochrane systematic review
		
		(randomized controlled trials)
			Self-report smoking abstinence of at least 6 months duration	Interventionist:
				   Mixed (included physicians, nurses, other medical staff, trained counselors, and technician for home visits)
				Duration:
				   Mixed (included hospital contact with medical staff of unreported duration, 3–8 sessions of higher intensity counseling lasting 15–20 minutes in inpatient setting, 30 minute higher intensity counseling for 1 session with physician in outpatient setting, 10 minute daily home visits by technician for 85 days, and 12 group sessions over 10 weeks)

	Diagnosis: COPD			Type: Mixed (individual and group counseling with and without pharmacotherapy, self-help materials, and contingency contracting) Outcome: Psychosocial intervention with pharmacotherapy and postdischarge follow-up is effective
Wolfenden et al., 2003	10 Cochrane Review articles as focus, total of 61 references Patients: Adults Setting: Any, although focused on hospital-based studies Diagnosis: All diagnoses	Selective literature review (Cochrane review articles, nonrandomized trials, descriptive papers, national clinical guidelines, and review papers)	Self-report smoking abstinence of at least 6 months duration	Interventionist: Mixed (included physicians, nursing staff, psychologists, smoking cessation counselors of other hospital staff) Duration: Mixed (any hospital contact plus follow-up of either less than or greater than 1 month, and heterogeneous outpatient contacts) Type: Mixed (included self-help materials, advice to quit, behavioral counseling with or without pharmacotherapy, discharge follow-up, telephone counseling, and physiological feedback) Outcome: Psychosocial intervention with pharmacotherapy and postdischarge follow-up is effective

(*Continued*)

TABLE 11.1 Summary of Data-Based Studies Reviewed for Tobacco Cessation Interventions Among Hospitalized Patients (*Continued*)

Study	Population	Design	Outcome Measures	Interventions & Findings

Wolfenden et al., 2008	7 Cochrane Review articles and 7 clinical practice guidelines as focus, total of 69 references
	
	Patients: Adults
	
	Setting: Any, although focused on hospital-based studies
	Diagnosis: All diagnoses
		Selective literature review
		
		(Cochrane review articles and clinical practice guidelines)
			Self-report smoking abstinence of at least 6 months duration	Interventionist:
				  Mixed (included physicians, nursing staff, psychologists, smoking cessation counselors of other hospital staff)
				Duration:
				  Mixed (any hospital contact plus follow-up of either less than or greater than 1 month, and heterogeneous outpatient contacts)
				Type:
				  Mixed (included self-help materials, advice to quit, behavioral counseling with or without pharmacotherapy, discharge follow-up, and telephone counseling)
				Outcome:
				  Psychosocial intervention with pharmacotherapy and postdischarge follow-up is effective

of psychosocial intervention with pharmacotherapy is effective compared to no treatment in patients with COPD (R^2 = 1.74, 95% CI, 1.01–3.0). Psychosocial interventions included self-help materials, counseling, and behavioral therapy; pharmacotherapy included either nicotine replacement therapy or bupropion. No evidence was available on the effectiveness of psychosocial interventions alone as compared to no treatment in these studies. Neither of the two high-quality studies reviewed focused on interventions in hospitalized patients with COPD, both were in out-patient settings. With mortality continuing to increase with COPD, finding a gap in the literature with targeted smoking cessation interventions for hospitalized patients with COPD is especially concerning (Gerhardsson de Verdier, 2008; Mannino & Buist, 2007; Wolfenden, Campbell, Wiggers, Walsh, & Bailey, 2008). In addition, no systematic reviews were identified that addressed in-patient or out-patient smoking cessation interventions for patients with asthma or pneumonia.

While international studies were not included in this review, the results of Ong and colleagues (2005) and Jonsdottir and colleagues (2004) also support the value of posthospitalization tobacco cessation interventions among patients with respiratory illnesses. In particular, the quasiexperimental study conducted by nurse researchers in Iceland revealed positive clinical outcomes when intervening with tobacco-dependent patients with respiratory illnesses. Based on the transtheoretical model of change and nicotine replacement therapy, hospitalized COPD and asthma patients (n = 85) received an intervention that included either individualized or group counseling and telephone follow-up at 1 wk and 1, 3, 6, and 12 months. At 12 months postdischarge, 39% of patients self-reported smoking abstinence (Jonsdottir, Jonsdottir, Geirsdottir, Sveinsdottir, & Sigurdardottir, 2004).

*Studies Focused on Tobacco Dependence
in Acute Care Hospital Settings*

The selective and systematic reviews evaluated focused on smoking cessation interventions during hospitalizations were not specific as to diagnosis (Rigotti, Munafo, & Stead, 2007; Wolfenden, Campbell, Walsh, & Wiggers, 2003; Wolfenden et al., 2008). A Cochrane review of both randomized and quasirandomized controlled trials of behavioral counseling and/or pharmacotherapy, with at least 6 months of follow-up, found 33 trials that met inclusion criteria (Rigotti et al., 2007). Counseling interventions, generally provided by a research nurse or trained smoking cessation counselor, were classified into four levels of intervention intensity. Levels of intensity were defined by amount of contact time in hospital, whether postdischarge support was provided, and duration of postdischarge support. Meta-analysis of counseling interventions from 17 trials found "Intensity Level 4" interventions, defined as any hospital contact plus more than one month of postdischarge support, increased rates of smoking cessation (pooled odds ratio, 1.65; 95% CI, 1.44–1.90). Interventions with less postdischarge support did not show benefit.

Studies with pharmacotherapy interventions all had a counseling component. Pooled analysis of five trials adding nicotine replacement therapy to counseling showed a trend toward increased efficacy but was not statistically significant (pooled odds ratio, 1.47; 95% CI, 0.92–2.35). The authors do state that, along with the need to treat acute nicotine withdrawal symptoms, these data supports inclusion of nicotine replacement therapy in smoking cessation interventions for hospitalized patients. The effectiveness of counseling was found across all hospitalized smokers regardless of admission diagnosis and within a subset hospitalized for cardiovascular disease (Rigotti et al., 2007).

Only four studies were identified that enrolled patients specifically admitted with respiratory diagnoses (Rigotti et al., 2007). None of these studies found significant effects for their interventions, and no pooled analysis was done due to heterogeneity of the studies. Although evidence was insufficient to support the efficacy of counseling interventions for smokers hospitalized with a respiratory diagnosis, the authors (Rigotti et al., 2007) indicate that these patients should not be excluded from such interventions as there is strong evidence overall for hospitalized smokers. Rigotti and colleagues (2007) concluded that their evidence supports expansion of the JC/CMS tobacco measure standards to include all hospitalized smokers.

Studies Focused on Effective Hospital Initiated Strategies for Implementing Tobacco Cessation

Although there is insufficient evidence for the specific populations of COPD, asthma, and pneumonia, translation of these findings into clinical practice can be made by advancing nursing research and scholarly approaches to evaluate hospital-initiated cessation interventions in patients with smoking-induced respiratory diseases. Another review identified characteristics that may be critical in a successful inpatient smoking cessation programs (Wolfenden et al., 2003). It suggests that effective hospital-initiated interventions occur in settings that develop systems supporting the effort and include the following: (1) in-hospital advice and counseling lasting more than 20 minutes, (2) use of nicotine replacement therapy, (3) postdischarge support of at least 3 months that may be provided by telephone, and (4) at least five contacts made throughout the intervention.

Literature Review Conclusions

As analyses of studies in Table 11.1 reveal, cessation intervention studies conducted by nurse researchers specific to U.S. hospitalized tobacco-dependent patients with COPD, asthma, and/or pneumonia do not exist. Tobacco cessation interventions are provided by a provider mix of nurses, physicians, and others such as psychologists and counselors. The populations for the cessation intervention studies are often mixed with patients diagnosed with respiratory diseases and/or cardiovascular diseases or the populations are not clearly defined at all. Settings for the tobacco cessation studies are varied as well with the majority occurring in hospital settings while others were conducted in out-patient or community settings. All studies support interventions that include psychosocial, pharmacotherapy and postdischarge follow-up are effective for successful tobacco cessation outcomes.

TRANSLATING EVIDENCE-BASED INTERVENTIONS INTO CLINICAL PRACTICE

Although the U.S. Public Health Service (PHS) clinical practice guideline for smoking cessation has existed since 1996 (Fiore et al., 1996), its recommendations are still not fully integrated into nursing practice. Knowledge of critical components to implement and sustain successful evidence-based tobacco cessation interventions by nurses in acute care settings is needed to optimize clinical outcomes and reduce health care costs related to smoking-induced respiratory diseases. We describe nursing leadership in efforts to translate established tobacco cessation research into clinical practice at two large academic medical centers with similar characteristics and protocols (Table 11.2) that can serve as models.

Georgetown University Medical Center, Washington, DC

Despite a substantial improvement in documentation of tobacco use and providing tobacco cessation advice, in 2005 Georgetown University Medical Center (GUMC) remained well below the 90% benchmark for the Joint Commission's mandate that tobacco cessation education be documented for all patients admitted for pneumonia (PNA), heart failure (HF), and acute myocardial infarction (AMI; Centers for Medicare and Medicaid Services [CMS], 2005). This prompted a nurse-driven initiative to implement a hospital-wide, evidence-based, tobacco cessation protocol (Ginn, Cox, & Heath, 2008). The protocol was based on the U.S. PHS clinical practice guideline, *Treating Tobacco Use and Dependence* (Fiore et al., 2000; updated 2008), and implemented in 2006 with the following components: a revised admission database to better capture smokers and assess smoking status, tobacco cessation orders to support in-patient efforts to quit (Table 11.2), staff education, creation of a standard of care to define tobacco cessation education expectations, and interdisciplinary championing to garner hospital-wide support. The implementation process required a series of approvals from the pharmacy and therapeutics committee, forms committee, as well as the approval of

TABLE 11.2   Comparison of Hospital Characteristics: Size, Designation of Nursing Excellence, Admissions, and Tobacco Cessation Protocols, 2008

Georgetown University Hospital		MCG Health Hospital	
Total beds: 609		Total Beds: 632	
Magnet hospital designation[a] *Since 2004*		Magnet hospital in progress[a]	
Beacon unit designation[b] *Medical ICU, 2005* *Surgical ICU, 2007*		Beacon unit designation in progress[b]	
Admissions (12-month data)		Admissions (12-month data)	
Total	13,062	Total	15,260
Tobacco use (all diagnoses)	2078	Tobacco use (all diagnoses)	892
Pneumonia	291	Pneumonia	878
Chronic obstructive pulmonary disease	409	Chronic obstructive pulmonary disease	1,096
Asthma	1389	Asthma	834
Tobacco cessation protocol (computerized provider standing orders) *Since 2006, includes the following:* —*order for counseling* —*order for referral and/or 1-800-QUIT NOW at discharge* —*order for NRT patch* —*order for NRT gum* —*order for NRT lozenge* —*order for bupropion* —*order for varenicline*		Tobacco cessation protocol (computerized provider standing orders) *Since 2007, includes the following:* —*order for counseling* —*order for referral and/or 1-800-QUIT NOW at discharge* —*order for NRT patch* —*order for NRT gum* —*order for NRT lozenge* —*order for bupropion*	

[a]Recognition by the American Nurses Credentialing Center, a subsidiary of the American Nurses Association, for (hospital-wide) Nursing Excellence.
[b]Recognition by the American Association of Critical-Care Nurses for (unit-based) Critical Care Nursing Excellence.

nursing leadership and physician leaders in cardiology, pulmonary and internal medicine, followed by rigorous staff education at the nurse and physician level (Ginn et al., 2008).

As noted in Figure 11.1, the first quarter following protocol roll-out (Q4 2006), documentation of tobacco cessation advice given to patients admitted with

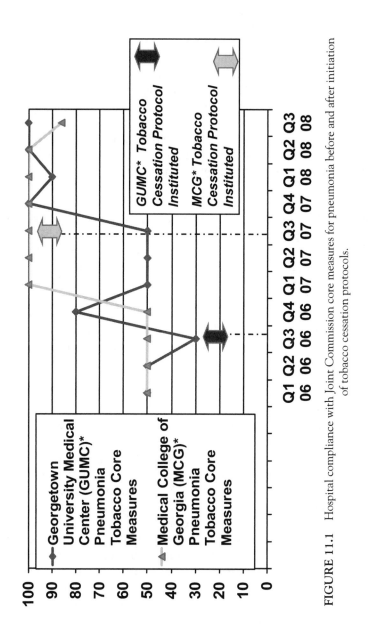

FIGURE 11.1   Hospital compliance with Joint Commission core measures for pneumonia before and after initiation of tobacco cessation protocols.

PNA dramatically improved. Unfortunately, over time, rates dropped, prompting hospital administration to include tobacco cessation education on all discharge paperwork to ensure that 100% of patients received the appropriate advice. More recently the hospital, documented 13,062 admissions for January–December 2008 (Table 11.2); cared for 2,078 smokers and generated 827 in-patient tobacco cessation orders for cessation advice and pharmacotherapy. The majority of pharmacotherapy orders were for 21 mg nicotine replacement therapy (NRT) patches. Services prescribing the highest volumes of tobacco cessation medications were medicine, surgery (general, vascular, and orthopedics) and psychiatry. Although the reason is unknown, data monitoring the prescribing volume for nicotine withdrawal and/or tobacco cessation medications suggest that approximately half of all smokers admitted in 2008 were given pharmacotherapy and the remaining half did not.

The protocol's initial success was likely due to campaigns surrounding its launch and the interdisciplinary support it received, particularly from the pharmacy, and cardiology and pulmonary services. Retrospective analysis affords several key learning points on why protocol adoption has a wax and wane pattern. Continuous education about the Joint Commission core measures and the "how to steps" for providing effective tobacco cessation advice and counseling with house and nursing staff are critical to maintain the protocol's momentum. Dedicated "core measure" nurses with a daily presence on the units performing regular audits and generating real-time performance feedback at the point of care helps to ensure meeting the needs of tobacco-dependent patients are not only positive but valid and reliable.

The Medical College of Georgia Health System, Augusta, GA

Driven by a mission, "to improve health and reduce the burden of illness in society," in August 2006, the Medical College of Georgia (MCG) university campus, Physicians Practice Group, and MCG Health (hospitals and clinics) made an administrative decision to become a tobacco-free campus. Senior leadership from the MCG Enterprise (university campus, PPG, and MCG Health hospitals and clinics) formed service-wide committees with the charge to make implementation recommendations effectively creating a tobacco-free environment within one year (Medical College of Georgia, 2009). After 15 months of committee work, MCG's goal to become tobacco free became a reality on the Great American Smokeout date of November 17, 2007. The Tobacco Cessation Clinic, under the auspices of MCG School of Nursing Faculty Practice Group (NFPG), was approved by the MCG Enterprise to be the exclusive provider of tobacco cessation treatment services for patients, students, and employees. Nurses from the MCG Health Evidence-Based Practice Council helped develop standardized physician orders for tobacco withdrawal/cessation for inpatients, distributed hospital-wide educational materials including toll free numbers to the tobacco quitline and referral cards to the NFPG tobacco cessation program, and revised the patient discharge form to include tobacco cessation counseling (Table 11.2).

Chart audits conducted indicate a steady progress to the current standing of 100% compliance with the Joint Commission mandate for tobacco use identification and tobacco cessation advice for PNA diagnoses in all quarters except one (Quarter 3, 2008, with 86% for PNA) (Figure 11.1). With the exception of the third quarter of 2008, tobacco cessation counseling rates remained the same (100%) for each quarter of 2007 and 2008. During this same time frame, 1243 inpatient tobacco cessation orders were generated for cessation advice and pharmacotherapy (Figure 11.2). The majority of pharmacotherapy orders were for 21 mg NRT patches and services prescribing the highest volumes of nicotine withdrawal and/or tobacco cessation medications were psychiatry, surgery, and medicine. Prescribing volume for tobacco cessation significantly increased throughout the hospital postprotocol with ranges from a 38% increase with OB-GYN patients to 380% with psychiatry patients. However, it is important to note that the psychiatry unit requested additional time to prepare health care providers on managing psychotherapeutic agents while undergoing tobacco cessation, thus the smoke-free policy was not implemented in psychiatry until January 2008.

The MCG audit data reflects that a counseling success rate of 100% has been achieved and sustained at 100% except for one quarter in 2 years (Figure 11.1). There are two predominant factors for this sustained compliance rate. First, all patients are asked on the admission assessment form if "over the last 12 months tobacco was used personally or within the household" and all patients are given the Georgia /Toll Free Quitline number regardless of tobacco use status. Second, MCG Health modified the electronic medical record documentation in January of 2007 to require completion of all fields, such as questions related to tobacco use, prior to moving to the next set of inquiries. Even though education of health care professionals was conducted regarding the 5 As of evidence-based tobacco counseling, documentation of counseling reflects only that some kind of advice or counseling, however brief, was given.

Comparison Analysis

At both academic medical centers, nurse-lead translational research efforts to enhance tobacco cessation interventions have created opportunities to improve clinical outcomes for patients suffering from smoking-induced respiratory diseases. Although admission rates and respiratory disease diagnoses are similar at both GUMC and MCG Health (Table 11.1), there are strikingly different profiles for the number of patients identified with a positive tobacco use history. Six percent of the patients admitted to MCG Health in 2008 were identified as tobacco

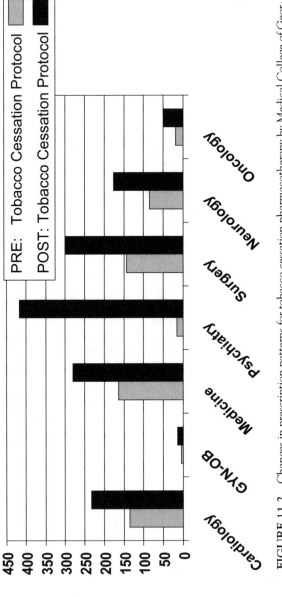

FIGURE 11.2 Changes in prescription patterns for tobacco cessation pharmacotherapy by Medical College of Georgia hospital departments before and after initiation of the 2007 tobacco cessation protocol.

dependent as compared to 16% at GUMC. Both of the hospitals had similar rates for respiratory disease admissions, GUMC had 16% and MCG Health had 18%. Chronic obstructive pulmonary disease (n = 1096; 39% of all respiratory diagnoses) was the leading respiratory diagnosis for MCG Health, whereas asthma was the leading for GUMC (n = 1389; 67%). Both hospitals had similar prescribing patterns with high volume use by medicine and psychiatry for NRT patches being preferred over the oral agents bupropion and varenicline. Although we are unable to determine pharmacological intervention by pulmonology at MCG Health (embedded with medicine), limited use of pharmacological intervention was noted with GUMC pulmonology. Opportunities for closing tobacco cessation practice gaps with a comprehensive plan for proactive disease management with patients admitted with chronic disease exist for both academic medical centers. Dedicated resources are needed to meaningfully evaluate performance measures to ensure effective tobacco cessation interventions, including pharmacotherapy, are implemented and sustained and to determine the impact on clinical outcomes.

IMPLICATIONS FOR RESEARCH, POLICY AND PRACTICE

According to this review, the testing of effective strategies to help hospitalized patients with smoking-induced respiratory diseases quit tobacco use has been neglected in nursing research. Recognizing the challenges in undertaking tobacco cessation interventions in acute care settings, such as large academic medical centers, it is critical for nurses to provide leadership in addressing these barriers. Models of successful nurse-driven tobacco cessation protocols in acute care settings are reported (Balkstra, Fields, & Roesler, 2006; Ginn et al., 2008) but more data-based studies are needed with targeted COPD, asthma, and pneumonia populations. Well-designed cohort or case-control analytic studies provide strong evidence that smoking cessation results in 50% reduction in individual's risk of developing pneumonia (Mandell et al., 2007; Masica, Richter, Convery, & Haydar, 2009; Mitka, 2007). In addition, Bartlett and colleagues (2000) report that approximately 3 million cases of community acquired pneumonia result in 10 million provider visits and 500,000 hospitalizations thus opportunities abound for nurses to intervene through research, policy, and practice.

Future Research

Despite considerable knowledge related to tobacco cessation interventions in inpatient settings (Sarna & Bialous, 2006), this review revealed limited studies focused on patient populations with respiratory diseases and very few nurse-led research studies. Given the tremendous importance of tobacco use in this leading cause of chronic illness, more nursing research is needed to identify the efficacy of different approaches to treat tobacco-dependent patients in COPD, asthma, and pneumonia populations. Similar to other reviews, limitations were found in the varied methods of study designs and identification of specific smoking cessation interventions, such as meeting the Joint Commission core measures for providing tobacco cessation advice to patients with respiratory diseases (Masica, 2009; van der Meer, 2003). Based upon this review and clinical experiences, the following recommendations are offered to guide future nursing research:

Expanding Details in Subject Description

- Provide subanalysis (separate patient categories) when studies include populations of mixed diseases.
- Describe in detail disease specific criteria for inclusion and exclusion; use established diagnostic criteria.

Strengthening Interventions

- Minimize bias by blinding the outcome assessment for the intervention and (whenever possible), blind patients and care providers for the intervention.
- Describe in detail the intensity and duration of the behavioral–psychosocial intervention (number of contacts and length of contacts).
- Describe in detail type of behavioral–psychosocial intervention (e.g., person-to-person contact/group counseling/educational TV, brochures).
- Provide clarity on level of interventionist (e.g., masters-prepared registered nurse, physician, bachelors-prepared respiratory therapist).

Clarifying Measurements

- Provide clarity about the outcome to be measured (e.g., biochemical validation of smoking status; 7-day point prevalence, continuous, or prolonged abstinence) and how assessed (self-report, carbon monoxide or cotinine).
- Provide clarity with timing of measurements; identify starting point and consider use of 6-and 12-month follow-up assessments as "gold standard" to allow for comparisons between studies.
- Include pulmonary function as a relevant secondary outcome measurement when study population has lung disease.

Policy Implications

Hospitals must ensure policies are in place that support and translate the evidence that smoking cessation is the most effective intervention to reduce symptoms and to decrease risk of development and progression of chronic diseases (Srivastava, Currie, & Britton, 2006). In particular, the Joint Commission standards have the potential to have tremendous influence on the quality of outcomes of all patients admitted to the hospital with a tobacco use history, however only tobacco dependence treatment of those with HF, AMI, or PNA are now monitored. In addition, current Joint Commission requirements do not adequately support the U.S. PHS guideline or other scientific recommendations (i.e., Rigotti et al., 2007) for levels of intensity for tobacco cessation intervention (amount of contact time in hospital and postdischarge support) to increase quit rates.

Compliance with the Joint Commission tobacco core measures can be met by hospitals that document asking about tobacco use and providing an educational flyer, but that does not support best practice (Rigotti et al., 2007). Anecdotally nurses know that all too often educational materials end up in the trash or are simply forgotten in the patient's bedside table drawer. Clinically relevant outcome parameters for acute respiratory diseases must continue to be evaluated if evidence-based guidelines are to help change provider behavior and improve health outcomes (Capelastegui et al., 2004; Mandell et al., 2007; Marrie et al., 2000). Considering that Bauer, Brunkhorst, Welte, Gerlach, and Reinhart (2006) found 92% of ICU providers thought protective-lung strategies were being met when in actuality only 4% of the audited charts were in compliance with standards of care, hospitals must ensure gaps are closed to accurately measure quality indicators. Involvement of nursing organizations in acute care, particularly the American Association of Critical-Care Nurses (www.aacn.org), and the American Thoracic Society (www.thoracic.org), among others, can be useful in optimizing nursing research and advocate standardization of care for tobacco-dependent patients. Further, these organizations can (1) support efforts to treat tobacco dependence as a chronic disease, (2) champion specialty nursing organizations/divisions to develop position papers/practice alerts, and (3) initiate accountability for ones' own practice to integrate tobacco cessation as a standard of care. In addition, health care organizations and academic settings need to provide cessation resources, including treatment specialists, education, and evidence-based services for individuals (patients, employees, and students) wanting to quit (Green & Briggs, 2006; Sarnia, Bialous, Barbeau, & McLellan, 2006).

Evidence-Based Practice

While evidence strongly supports that hospital-based smoking cessation interventions initiated by nurses are effective (Rice & Stead, 2008), several studies indicate that lack of education limits the ability of nurses to intervene effectively with tobacco-dependent patients (Heath, Andrews, Thomas, Kelley, & Friedman, 2002; Heath & Crowell, 2007; Hornberger & Edwards, 2004; Wewers, Kidd, Armbruster, & Sarna, 2004). Overcoming barriers, such as lack of education, is important to increase compliance with practice guidelines (Cabana et al., 1999). To further reduce morbidity and mortality related to tobacco use, nurses must know how to effectively intervene with tobacco-dependent patients. This requires going beyond asking the question about tobacco use and just handing patients a tobacco cessation brochure to check off the list for the Joint Commission core measures. It is suggested that all nurses receive education on tobacco use and treatment, and incorporate that knowledge with a framework of research, advocacy, and practice for tobacco control (Bennett, Andrews, & Heath, 2007; Heath & Andrews, 2006). Although the level of intervention intensity and tobacco cessation outcomes have positive correlations, a simple 3-minute intervention can enhance motivation and increase likelihood of a quit attempt (Fiore et al., 2008). In particular, advanced practice nurses can make a difference by translating the latest evidence, evaluating hospital strategies for effectiveness, and providing behavioral and pharmacotherapy interventions for tobacco-dependent patients hospitalized with respiratory diseases.

CONCLUSIONS

Despite the link between mortality and tobacco dependence, as this review demonstrates, there is limited nursing research to improve clinical outcomes and inform policy decisions for patients suffering from respiratory diseases. Hospital admission rates and outcomes among patients with respiratory illnesses have been repeatedly linked to patient smoking status, prompting the Joint Commission to establish core measures requiring tobacco counseling for three medical diagnoses, including pneumonia. The experiences and outcomes of two nurse-led efforts to comply with Joint Commission standards by increasing the delivery of tobacco cessation interventions are encouraging. Additional opportunities to improve efforts to increase provider accountability for integrating tobacco cessation as a standard of care are needed. If progress is to be made toward ending the tobacco problem in the United States, the JC/CMS efforts must be strengthened in hospital settings so that *all* tobacco-dependent patients receive evidence-based assistance that is intense, integrated, and sustained. Furthermore, nurse scientists have an opportunity to examine respiratory disease populations for efficacy of different smoking cessation approaches and cost-effectiveness in promoting cessation, and decreasing length of stay and readmissions. Only when nurse scientists set research agendas targeting proactive disease management treatment for hospitalized tobacco-dependent patients will practice standards and policies drive outcomes to reduce mortality rates and health care costs associated with COPD, asthma, and pneumonia.

ACKNOWLEDGMENT

The authors would like to thank the following for their data management and manuscript support: GUMC colleagues Molly Billingsley, Kierte Amate, Donna Sanford and MCG Health colleagues Carole Ferrang, Deborah Humphry, Ann Marsh, Shirley Williams.

REFERENCES

Balkstra, C., Fields, M., & Roesler, L. (2006). Meeting joint commission on accreditation of healthcare organizations requirements for tobacco cessation: The St. Joseph's/Candler health system approach to success. *Critical Care Nursing Clinics North America, 18*(1), 105–111.

Bartlett, J. G., Dowell, S. F., Mandell, L. A., File, T. M., Jr., Musher, D. M., & Fine, M. J. (2000). Guidelines from the infectious diseases society of America: Practice guidelines for the management of community-acquired pneumonia in adults. *Clinical Infectious Disease, 31*(2), 347–382.

Bauer, M., Brunkhorst, F., Welte, T., Gerlach, H., & Reinhart, K. (2006). Sepsis: Update on pathophysiology, diagnostics and therapy. *Anaesthesist, 55*(8), 835–845.

Bennett, S., Andrews, J., & Heath, J. (2007). Breaking the ties of nicotine dependence. *The Nurse Practitioner, 32*(11), 36–45.

Benowitz, N. L. (2008). Clinical pharmacology of nicotine: Implications for understanding, preventing, and treating tobacco addiction. *Clinical Pharmacology Therapeutics, 83*(4), 531–541.

Cabana, M. D., Rand, C. S., Powe, N. R., Wu, A. W., Wilson, M. H. Abboud, P. C., et al. (1999). Why don't physicians follow clinical practice guidelines? A framework for improvement. *Journal of the American Medical Association, 282*(15), 1458–1465.

Capelastegui, A., Espana, P. P., Quintana, J. M., Gorordo, I., Ortega, M., Itsaso, I., et al. (2004). Improvement of process-of-care and outcomes after implementing a guideline for the management for community-acquired pneumonia: A controlled before-and-after design study. *Clinical Infectious Disease, 39*(7), 955–963.

Centers for Disease Control and Prevention. (2007). National surveillance for asthma: United States 1980–2004. *Morbidity and Mortality Weekly Report, 56*(SS08), 1–14, 18–54.

Centers for Disease Control and Prevention. (2008a). Deaths from chronic obstructive pulmonary disease: United States 2000–2005. *Morbidity and Mortality Weekly Report, 57*(45), 1229–1232.

Centers for Disease Control and Prevention. (2008b). Smoking attributable mortality, years of potential life lost, and productivity losses—United States, 2000–2004. *Morbidity and Mortality Weekly Report, 57*(45), 1226–1228.

Centers for Medicare and Medicaid Services. (2005). Premier hospital quality incentive demonstration. Retrieved on April 26, 2009, from http://www.cms.hhs.gov/HospitalQualityInits/35_HospitalPremier.asp

Chapman, K. R., Mannino, D. M., Soriano, J. B., Vermeire, P. A., Buist, A. S. Thun, M. J. et al. (2006). Epidemiology and costs of chronic obstructive pulmonary disease. *European Respiratory Journal, 27*(1), 188–207.

Crowley, T. J., Macdonald, M. J., & Walter, M. I. (1995). Behavioral anti-smoking trial in chronic obstructive pulmonary disease patients. *Psychopharmacology, 119*(2), 193–204.

DeFrances, C. J., Lucas, C. A., Buie, V. C., & Golosinskiy, A. (2008). *The 2006 national hospital discharge survey*. National health statistics reports; no 5. Hyattsville, MD: National Center for Health Statistics.

El Sohl, A., Brewer, T., Okada, M., Bashir, O., & Gough, M. (2004). Indicators of recurrent hospitalization for pneumonia in the elderly. *Journal of the American Geriatric Society, 52*, 2010–2015.

Fiore, M. C., Bailey, W. C., Cohen, S. J., Dorfman, S. F., Goldstein, M. G., Gritz, E. R., et al. (1996). *Smoking cessation. Clinical practice guideline*. Rockville, MD: U.S. Dept of Health and Human Services, Public Health Service.

Fiore, M. C., Bailey, W. C., Cohen, S. J., Dorfman, S. F., Goldstein, M. G., Gritz, E. R., et al. (2000). *Treating tobacco use and dependence. Clinical practice guideline*. Rockville, MD: U.S. Dept of Health and Human Services, Public Health Service.

Fiore, M. C., Jaen, R. C., Baker, T. B, Bailey, W. C., Benowitz, N. L., Curry, S. J., et al. (2008). *Treating tobacco use and dependence: 2008 update*. Rockville, MD: U.S. Dept of Health and Human Services, Public Health Service.

Gerhardsson de Verdier, M. (2008). The big three concept: A way to tackle the health care crisis. *Proceedings of the American Thoracic Society, 5*(8), 800–805.

Ginn, M. B., Cox, G., & Heath, J. (2008). An evidence-based approach to an in-patient tobacco cessation protocol. *American Association of Critical-Care Nurses Advanced Critical Care, 19*(3), 267–278.

Green, J. S., & Brings, L. (2006). Tobacco cessation in acute and critical care nursing practice: Challenges and approaches. *Critical Care Nursing Clinics North America, 18*(1), 81–93.

Heath, J., & Andrews, J. (2006). Translation of tobacco cessation interventions into clinical practice. *Nursing Research, 55*(4), S44–S50.

Heath, J., Andrews, J., Thomas, S., Kelley, F., & Friedman, E. (2002). Tobacco curriculum in acute care nurse practitioner education. *American Journal of Critical Care, 11*(1), 27–32.

Heath, J., & Crowell, N. (2007). Factors influencing intentions to integrate tobacco education among advanced practice nursing faculty. *Journal of Professional Nursing, 23*(4), 189–200.

Hornberger, C. A., & Edwards, L. C. (2004). Survey of tobacco cessation curricula in Kansas nursing programs. *Nurse Educator, 29*(5), 212–216.

Joint Commission on Accreditation of Healthcare Organizations (2003). *A comprehensive review of development and testing for national implementation of hospital core measures*. Retrieved March 20, 2009, from http://www.jointcommission.org/NR/rdonlyres/48DFC95A-9C05-4A44-AB05-1769D5253014/0/AComprehensiveReviewofDevelopmentforCoreMeasures.pdf

Jonsdottir, H., Jonsdottir, R., Geirsdottir, T., Sveinsdottir, K. S., & Sigurdardottir, T. (2004). Multicomponent individualized smoking cessation intervention for patients with lung disease. *Journal of Advanced Nursing, 48*(6), 594–604.

Kozak, L. J., DeFrances, C. J., & Hall, M. J. (2006). National hospital discharge survey: 2004 annual summary with detailed diagnosis and procedure data. National Center for Health Statistics. *Vital Health Statistics, 13*(162).

Kung, H. S., Hoyert, D. L., Xu, J., & Murphy, S. L. (2008). Deaths: Final data for 2005. *National Vital Statistics Reports: CDC, 56*, 10.

Mandell, L. A., Wunderink, R. G., Anzueto, A., Bartlett, J. G., Campbell, G. D., Dean, N. C., et al. (2007). Infectious diseases society of America/American thoracic society consensus guidelines on the management of community-acquired pneumonia in adults. *Clinical Infectious Diseases, 44*(Suppl. 2), S27–S72.

Mannino, D. M., & Buist, A. S. (2007). Global burden of COPD: Risk factors, prevalence and future trends. *Lancet, 370*(9589), 765–773.

Mannino, D. M., Gagnon, R. C., Petty, T. L., & Lydick, E. (2000). Obstructive lung disease and low lung function in adults in the United States: Data from the national health and nutrition examination survey, 1988–1994. *Archives of Internal Medicine, 160*(11), 1683–1689.

Marrie, T. J., Lau, C. Y., Wheeler, S. L., Wong, C. J., Vandervoot, M. K., & Feagan, B. G. (2000). A controlled trial of a critical pathway for treatment of community-acquired pneumonia. CAPTIAL study investigators. Community-acquired pneumonia intervention trial assessing levofloxacin. *Journal of the American Medical Association, 283*(6), 749–755.

Marrie T. J, & Shariatzadeh R. (2007). Community-acquired pneumonia requiring admission to an intensive care unit. *Medicine, 86*(2), 103–111.

Masica, A. L., Richter, K. M., Convery, P., & Haydar, Z. (2009). Linking joint commission inpatient core measures and national patient safety goals with evidence. *Baylor University Medical Center Proceedings, 22*(2), 103–111.

MCG Tobacco Free Campus Initiative. (2009). Retrieved October 20, 2009, from http://www.mcg.edu/tobaccofree/index.html

Mitka, M. (2007). JCAHO tweaks emergency departments' pneumonia treatment standards. *Journal of the American Medical Association, 297*(16), 1758–1759.

Munro, N. (2006). Weaning smokers from mechanical ventilation. *Critical Care Nursing Clinics North American, 18*(1), 21–28.

National Cancer Institute. (2001). *Risks associated with low machine-measured yields of tar and nicotine* (NIH Publication No. 02-5074). Smoking and Tobacco Control Monograph No. 13. Bethesda, MD: U.S. Department of Health and Human Services, National Institutes of Health, National Cancer Institute.

Rice, V. H. & Stead, L. F. (2008). Nursing interventions for smoking cessation. *Cochrane Database of Systematic Reviews,* (1) CD001188.

Rigotti N., Munafo, M. R., & Stead, L. F. (2007). Interventions for smoking cessation in hospitalized patients. *Cochrane Database of Systematic Reviews,* (I), CD001837.

Sarna, L., & Bialous, S. (2006). Strategic directions for nursing research in tobacco dependence. *Nursing Research, 55*(4), S1–S9.

Srivastava, P., Currie, G. P., & Britton, J. (2006). ABC of chronic pulmonary disease: Smoking cessation. *British Medical Journal, 332*(7553), 1324–1326.

Tashkin, D. P., Kanner, R., Bailey, W., Buist, S., Anderson, P., Nides, M. A. et al. (2001). Smoking cessation in patients with chronic obstructive pulmonary disease: A double-blind, placebo-controlled, randomized trial. *The Lancet, 357*(9268), 1571–1575.

Van der Meer, R. M., Wagena, E., Ostelo, R. W., Jacobs, A. J., & van Schaych, O. P. (2003). Smoking cessation for chronic obstructive pulmonary disease. *Cochrane Database of Systematic Reviews,* (2), CD002999.

Warren, C., Jones, N., Eriksen, M., & Asma, S. (2006). Patterns of global tobacco use in young people and implications for future chronic disease burden in adults. *Lancet, 367*(9512), 749–753.

Wewers, M. E., Kidd, K., Armbruster, D., & Sarna, L. (2004). Tobacco dependence curricula in U.S. baccalaureate and graduate nursing education. *Nursing Outlook, 52*(2), 95–101.

Wolfenden, L., Campbell, E., Walsh, R., & Wiggers, J. (2003). Smoking cessation interventions for inpatients: A selective review with recommendations for hospital-based health professionals. *Drug and Alcohol Review, 22*(4), 437–452.

Wolfenden, L., Campbell, E., Wiggers, J., Walsh, R. A., & Bailey, L. J. (2008). Helping hospital patients quit: What the evidence supports and what guidelines recommend. *Preventive Medicine, 46*(4), 346–57.

World Health Organization. (2008). *WHO report on the global tobacco epidemic, 2008: The MPOWER package*. Geneva, Switzerland: Author.

Yanbaeva, D. G., Dentener, M. A., Creutzberg, E. C., Wesseling, G., & Wouters, E. F. (2007). The systemic effects of smoking. *Chest, 131*, 1557–1566.

Chapter 12

A Review of Research by Nurses Regarding Tobacco Dependence and Mental Health

Daryl L. Sharp and Susan W. Blaakman

ABSTRACT

The prevalence of tobacco use and dependence among those with psychiatric and/or substance use disorders is exceptionally high, contributing to significant morbidity and mortality. The purpose of this review is to discuss the findings conducted by nurses regarding smoking and mental health. A search of the available literature since 1950 resulted in a review of 17 studies authored or coauthored by nurses. Most study designs were descriptive with only one investigator reporting the results of a small clinical trial. In addition to documenting smoking patterns in this population, investigators found that many psychiatric nurses assessed their clients for tobacco use and advised them to stop smoking but few intervened intensively to aid cessation. Psychiatric nurses reported low efficacy for delivering interventions and considerable doubt about their clients' abilities and motivation to stop smoking. Although some desired additional training in tobacco dependence interventions, nurses reported feeling ethically conflicted about, and were inconsistently supportive of, system level interventions such as

DOI: 10.1891/0739-6686.27.297

tobacco free health care settings. It is likely that these findings, as well as the paucity of tobacco dependence studies, reflect the relatively small number of psychiatric nurses conducting research as well as the inattention, until recently, of mental health leaders, policy makers, and funders to the importance of tobacco dependence research in this clinical population. As tobacco dependence treatment for those with mental illnesses and/or addictive disorders becomes more of a public health priority, opportunities abound for nurse researchers to contribute to the growing evidence in this often neglected area.

Keywords: tobacco dependence; mental health; psychiatric disorders; addictive disorders; psychiatric nursing

Smoking rates among persons with mental illnesses and/or addictive disorders are exceptionally high, contributing to significant medical morbidity and mortality in this population, with many unlikely to live until their 50th birthday (Rosenberg, 2009; Ziedonis et al., 2008). It is estimated that approximately 200,000 of the 435,000 annual deaths from smoking in the United States occur among those with mental illnesses and/or substance use disorders (Morris, Waxmonsky, Giese, Graves, & Turnbull, 2007; Schroeder, 2009). Persons with mental illnesses smoke nearly half the cigarettes consumed in the U.S. (Grant, Hasin, Chou, Stinson, & Dawson, 2004; Lasser et al., 2000), spending as much as one third of their monthly public assistance income on cigarettes instead of buying needed food, clothing, and shelter (Steinberg, Williams, & Ziedonis, 2004). Although smoking rates in the general population have declined over the past several decades, the prevalence of tobacco use among individuals with psychiatric illnesses remains more than twice that of the general population (Grant et al., 2004). The mentally ill are dying, on average, 25 years younger than those in the general population with the predominant causes of mortality a function of chronic illnesses, especially infectious, pulmonary, and cardiovascular diseases, as well as diabetes (National Association of State Mental Health Program Directors, 2007). Living with largely preventable comorbid medical diseases, many of which are caused by the harmful health effects of smoking, hinders clients' quality of life and interferes with their ability to maintain employment, integrate into community life, and achieve their recovery goals (NASMHPD, 2007). And yet their smoking epidemic has been described as "hidden and silent" (Schroeder, 2007).

This review describes the challenges of addressing tobacco use in mental health settings and discusses research findings from nurses on smoking and mental health including practice, research, and policy implications.

CONTRIBUTING FACTORS AND CHALLENGES

Smoking rates are highest among those with psychotic and substance use disorders yet tobacco dependence also is highly prevalent for those with anxiety, depressive, and personality disorders (Morris, Waxmonsky, et al., 2007; Williams & Ziedonis, 2004). These high rates are driven by a complex interplay of genetic, biological, psychological, socioeconomic, and cultural factors (Williams & Ziedonis, 2004). There is strong evidence that tobacco use and dependence is heritable, and there is considerable genetic overlap between smoking and depression as well as smoking and alcohol use (Benowitz, 2008a). Nicotine affects several neurotransmitters implicated in mental illness (including dopamine, norepinephrine, acetylcholine, glutamate, serotonin, β-endorphin, & γ-amino butyric acid). Although caution has been advised regarding viewing nicotine dependence as a form of self-medication among the mentally ill (Ziedonis et al., 2008), evidence exists that nicotine is likely to ameliorate symptoms and improve cognition, which may help to explain the high rates of nicotine dependence among those with serious mental illnesses. Nicotine's ability to enhance dopaminergic functioning may diminish some of the negative symptoms associated with traditional antipsychotic medications. Researchers (George et al., 2006; Williams & Ziedonis, 2004) also postulate that nicotine's ability to improve nicotinic acetylcholine receptor functioning may help those with schizophrenia filter out irrelevant stimuli (i.e., improve sensory gating). Nicotine binds with nicotinic receptors and releases many of the same neurotransmitters as are released with antidepressant medications, which also lends support to the neurobiological underpinnings of nicotine dependence in this population (Benowitz, 2008b).

In addition to genetic and biological etiological factors, psychological, environmental, and social factors contribute to high smoking rates among those with psychiatric disorders. Unlike the general population where smoking has become progressively denormalized (Christakis & Fowler, 2008), high prevalence rates among the mentally ill and those with addictive disorders reinforce smoking in this subculture (Schroeder, 2008). Limited educational levels, high unemployment rates and poverty, which predict higher smoking rates in the general population, also contribute to the smoking epidemic among those with these disorders (Fiore et al., 2008; Ziedonis, Williams, & Smelson, 2003).

Unfortunately, psychiatric clinicians have been slower than other health care professionals to intervene with their patients who smoke (Fiore et al., 2008; Williams & Ziedonis, 2004). This response may be related to years of using cigarettes as a form of behavioral reinforcement. Even when treatment facilities are smoke free, staff (often smokers themselves) may accompany clients for cigarette breaks outdoors (Williams, 2008). Clinicians also may seek to avoid depriving already challenged individuals of "their only pleasure" or mistakenly view smoking as "the least of their patients' worries" (Sharp, Blaakman, Cole, & Evinger, 2009). Many clinicians fear that stopping smoking will exacerbate underlying psychiatric disorders, that smoking reduction and/or cessation are not realistic goals for persons with mental illness, or that these individuals are not interested in quitting smoking (Strasser, 2001; Williams, & Ziedonis, 2006; Ziedonis et al., 2003).

On the contrary, research indicates that many persons with mental illness want to quit, often seek information about how, and are capable of reducing and/ or stopping smoking (el-Guebaly, Cathcart, Currie, Brown, & Gloster, 2002; Hall et al., 2006; Sharp, Blaakman, et al., 2009). Studies of smoke-free policies in psychiatric hospital settings have shown that cessation is not only attainable but can have beneficial effects such as reduction in violence and disciplinary action (el-Guebaly et al., 2002) as well as increased staff satisfaction and more staff contact time with patients (Ratschen, Britton, Doody, & McNeill, 2009; Schroeder, 2009).

RESEARCH IN NURSING

The reluctance of practitioners to intervene is mirrored in relatively few studies by nurses focused on generating new knowledge in tobacco dependence treatment among those with psychiatric and/or substance use disorders. A search of the available literature elicited 17 research articles authored or coauthored by nurses.

Methods

Using the key words smoking/smoking cessation, tobacco dependence/tobacco use disorder, psychiatric nursing, nursing research, mental health/mental illness, children/adolescents, and addictions, a literature search was conducted using the entire accessible databases of CINAHL (from 1982), Medline (from 1966), PubMed (from 1950), and PsycInfo (from 1967) in April 2009. Articles from these databases in addition to those located via a hand search of references and of web-based resources (e.g., http://www.tobaccofreenurses.org/) were included for review if they met the criteria of being research focused, authored or coauthored by nurses, and reporting tobacco related data associated with psychiatric patients, nurses and/or settings. Articles were limited to English language, but no year limits were imposed.

Results

Seventeen articles met the inclusion criteria (Table 12.1). The majority of research by nurses in this area has been conducted over the past two decades through descriptive, quantitative survey designs. Six of these studies focused solely on psychiatric nurses–staff, while five surveyed psychiatric patients. Two studies surveyed both nurses and patients. One intervention study was found that met the search criteria. Four additional studies used qualitative or mixed methods designs and/ or analyses.

TABLE 12.1 Summary of Nursing Research Focused on Tobacco-Dependence and Psychiatric-Mental Health/Addictions

Author/Year	Study Design	Participants	Purpose	Findings	Comments
Quantitative studies of psychiatric nurses/staff:					
Dickens et al. (2004)	Descriptive; cross-sectional survey	Clinical staff in United Kingdom psychiatric hospital; (n = 167 RNs, 93 nurse assistants, 8 other health providers; OHPs)	Report smoking behaviors, attitudes, beliefs of RNs and OHPs in order to guide hospital smoking policy	RN smokers more likely to support smoking with patients; less likely to support patients quitting; RNs more likely than OHPs to value smoking with patients	38.9% response rate from nurses (overall 50.3%); 17.4% RNs smokers; 25.1% ex-smokers; RNs most liberal and supported patient choice
Erwin & Biordi (1991)	Descriptive; longitudinal survey before and 1 week/4 weeks after smoke-free policy	Nurses on two psychiatric wards at veterans' center in urban Illinois (n = 29); convenience sample	Examine staff nurse views of implementing smoke-free environment on two inpatient wards	Views/interventions differed by ward; 70%–75% of nurses reported nonsmoking policy success at 1 month	Levine's 4 conservation principles; 50%–77% response rate at 4 weeks; outlined nursing administrative implications

(Continued)

TABLE 12.1 Summary of Nursing Research Focused on Tobacco-Dependence and Psychiatric-Mental Health/Addictions (*Continued*)

Author/Year	Study Design	Participants	Purpose	Findings	Comments
Quantitative studies of psychiatric nurses/staff:					
Hamera et al. (1997)	Descriptive; cross-sectional telephone survey	Nurses on inpatient psychiatric units in midwestern United States (n = 32)	Describe varied implementation of smoking policies on adult inpatient psychiatric units	One unit with ban; 26% smoked in smoking room; 74% smoked outside; 68% no limits on cigs.; 91% offered NRT (gum, patch, smokeless tobacco); 1/3 smoked with NRT; privileges linked to smoking frequency	24% of 44 facilities excluded; 81% urban; 75% private
Sarna et al. (2009)	Descriptive; cross-sectional, secondary analysis of 30-item web-based survey	Self-reported psychiatric nurses from a national survey of >3,000 initial respondents (n = 100)	Describe factors associated with psychiatric nurse tobacco interventions; to test if knowledge of Tobacco Free Nurses (TFN) resource influenced nurse behavior	87% always/usually asked; 70% advised; 74% assessed motivation; 49% assisted; 21% arranged; 49% recommended meds; 20% referred to resources; 8% recommended quitline; 18% aware of TFN & more likely to assess/refer	Grouped by states with high/low smoking prevalence; 20% RN smokers & 92% less likely to "ask" than never smokers; limitations acknowledged

Sharp, Blaak-man, et al. (2009)	Descriptive, cor-relational; national 29-item online survey	E-mail accessible APNA members ($n = 1,365$)	Assess PMH nurses' attitudes and behaviors regarding tobacco dependence interventions with psychiatric patients	91% asked; 85% advised; 61% referred; 29% intensive interventions; likely to refer/intervene if knowledgeable, motivated, confident, rated highly patients' ability/moti-vation to quit smoking and if personal/work priority; nurs-ing curricula lacked tobacco content	31.6% response rate to initial e-mail and two reminders; 6% smoker; 54% former smoker; medium to large effect sizes

Quantitative studies of psychiatric patients:

Byrne et al. (1994)	Descriptive; report of wellness education program for persons with chronic mental illness	Lodging home resi-dents in Ontario, Canada ($n = 9$); 100% men; 25–45 years	Health change via individual, group and environment efforts; smoking reduction 1 of 4 components	60% active in 65% of overall program; one half of smokers participated; 50% interested in cutting down and decreased use	Not clinical trial; used theory; Lung Association used; amount smok-ing reduction not reported
Chou et al. (2004)	Longitudinal clini-cal trial; weekly nurse visits for seven waves of data	Schizophrenic day care patients in Taiwan ($n = 68$); 26 randomized to patch; 42 controls matched by CO; no group differ-ences at baseline	Test effectiveness of 8-week nicotine patch therapy versus control	NRT group had decreased dependence/cigarette use/CO levels at 8 weeks and 3 months; little change in 3 month continuous absti-nence	Controls NRT eli-gible after study; 14 mg tapered to 7 mg after 6 weeks; may be too low

(Continued)

TABLE 12.1 Summary of Nursing Research Focused on Tobacco-Dependence and Psychiatric-Mental Health/Addictions (*Continued*)

Author/Year	Study Design	Participants	Purpose	Findings	Comments
Quantitative studies of psychiatric patients:					
Eastabrook et al. (2003)	Descriptive; client self-report and clinician ratings compared to documented diagnoses	Assertive community treatment (ACT) clients in Ontario, Canada (n = 174)	Part of larger study to estimate prevalence of drug, alcohol and tobacco abuse among ACT clients	9% alcohol & 11% drug abusing; 62% smoked, 48% >25 cigarettes/day; 73% schizophrenic, 15% dual addiction diagnosis	1998–1999 data; randomly selected; 22% refusal rate; clinician ratings correlated with client report; no biological tests
Gerber et al. (2003)	Descriptive; survey interviews; random selection from client list	Persons with serious mental illness (SMI) with ACT services in Ontario, Canada (n = 180)	Compare SMI substance use rates to community population data	63.4% SMI smokers versus 25.9% community; SMI more cigarettes/day (28 vs. 14.6)	Interdisciplinary; RN coauthor
Modrcin-Talbott et al. (1998)	Descriptive; correlational; survey	Adolescent PMH outpatients in Knoxville, TN (n = 77); 12–19 years; 54.5% males; convenience sample	Assess correlates of self-esteem (age, gender, smoking, exercise, anger, depression, parent alcohol use)	Self-esteem lower than nonclinical sample; smokers (66.2%) did not differ on self-esteem; high percentage of smokers	Roy's adaptation model (person, environment, nursing, health); limited sample; smoking false sense self-worth

Murphy et al. (1995)	Descriptive, survey	Patients with chronic mental illness discharged to NJ community (n = 25)	Identify health concerns and health promotion patterns using Healthy People 2000 framework	64% smoked; 36% 2+ ppd; 44% tried to quit; 68% rated smoking harmful; 64% would use cessation program if offered. Smoked more if stressed; 36% lacked coping; 24% used alcohol; 28% used illicit drugs	Small sample; cross-sectional; no diagnosis specific data

Quantitative studies of both psychiatric nurses and patients:

Buchanan et al. (1994)	Descriptive; cross-sectional; 23-item survey; nurse self-report	PMH RNs in Oregon State Hospital (n = 50); 47 women; 20–60+ years	Describe nurse opinions/practices regarding informing patients of smoking health risks	82% provide some smoking information; 51% counsel <25% of patients; mean number of barriers = 3.6; 88% cited patients lacked interest; 40% viewed efforts ineffective; 22% cigarettes as reward	56% nurse response rate overall; 22% smokers; 30% former smokers
	Descriptive; 10-item interview for patients; mostly yes/no; some open responses	Smoking patients from each of five programs (n = 50; 40 men; 17–72 years; 7% random sample	Describe patient experiences with nurse smoking cessation practices	50% counseled by nurse during stay; 80% wanted to quit; 70% 1+ quit attempt; 62% would use nurse support if offered	90% smokers; 10% former smokers (all quit cold turkey); no information about nonparticipants

(Continued)

TABLE 12.1 Summary of Nursing Research Focused on Tobacco-Dependence and Psychiatric-Mental Health/Addictions (*Continued*)

Author/Year	Study Design	Participants	Purpose	Findings	Comments
Quantitative studies of both psychiatric nurses and patients:					
Tilley (1987)	Descriptive; survey;convenience patient sample and matched nurses by age	Patients with anxiety-related diagnoses referred to nurse behavior therapist (n = 40) compared to sample of psychiatric nurses (n = 40) and population data in Scotland	Assess use of alcohol, sedative drugs and tobacco and perceived anxiolytic effectiveness	55% patients & 35% nurses smoked; patients heavier smokers (23% > 200 cigarettes/week); no difference nurses and patients smoking for anxiety/reported effectiveness	Self-report; nurses may underreport own substance use yet reported drinking more than general population
Mixed method and qualitative studies of psychiatric nurses–patients:					
Brimble-combe et al. (2007)	National e-mail consultation survey; qualitative content analysis	PMH nurses/organizations in England (n = 326)	Support PMH nursing holistic care	Health promotion theme, included smoking reduction; training desired	Tobacco dependence not focus
Lawn & Condon (2006)	Grounded theory; in-depth interviews and participant observation	Community and inpatient psychiatric nurses in metropolitan Australia (n=7); part of larger study of 26 multidisciplinary staff	Explore ethical beliefs inhibiting psychiatric nurses support of smoking cessation	Pervasive smoking reinforcement; ethical dilemmas: autonomy versus beneficence/nonmaleficence; no bans; smoking lessens agitation/hinders recovery	RN coauthor; RNs 10+ years; one smoker; three ex-smokers; RN smoking due to role; dialogue/institutional support needed to change culture

Study	Design/Method	Sample	Purpose	Findings	Groups/Comments
Snyder et al. (2008)	Qualitative exploratory/focus groups	Clients of two psychiatric rehab centers in Midwest U.S. (n = 25); 19 men, 6 women; 24–55 years	Identify personal, environmental and social factors that affect smoking cessation in persons with serious mental illness	Personal factors: coping, confidence, quit expectations; reinforcement: environments (smoke free) and social (non-smokers); choice important overall; smoking central in daily life	Two focus groups for quit attempters and two for nonquit attempters; APN-led; some patients declined/anxiety lessened during groups; more research needed
Van Dongen (1999)	Mixed method; 60 minute interviews; convenience sample	Adults receiving long-term supportive care from urban, midwestern U.S. clinic; current or former smokers (n = 36)	Answer: "what do persons with persistent mental illness report regarding the experience and effects of smoking?"	High dependence; Group C healthiest; A 80% SOB sitting/ more medical hospital stays; B more psychiatric symptoms; A > B reasons to quit; 87% began with family/friend and viewed as harmful. Themes: something to do, relax; socialize, addiction; mixed regarding effects on symptoms, thinking & side effects; C many quit attempts & no cessation programs	Three groups: A. smokers wanting to quit (n = 10); B. smokers not wanting to quit (n = 20); C. former smokers with 1+ year abstinence (n = 6)

Note. OHP=other health provider; NRT=nicotine replacement therapy; APNA=American Psychiatric Nurses Association; PMH=psychiatric-mental health; CO=carbon monoxide; ppd=packs per day; RN=registered nurse; APN=advanced practice nurse; TFN=Tobacco Free Nurses; mg=milligram; SOB=shortness of breath; SMI=serious mental illness; ACT=assertive community treatment.

Quantitative Studies of Psychiatric Nurses–Staff

Surveys conducted to date have mostly elicited psychiatric staff attitudes, beliefs, and behaviors with regard to assessing tobacco dependence in their patients, nursing roles in delivering cessation interventions, and implementing smoke-free environments. Although these studies are too few and too varied in design for meta-analyses, overall findings revealed that most psychiatric nurses routinely assess tobacco use and advise their patients to quit (Sarna, Bialous, Wells, & Kotlerman, 2009; Sharp, Blaakman, et al., 2009), yet the delivery of more intensive interventions is lacking. Across these three studies psychiatric nurses tended to rate poorly their ability to effectively assist patients in stopping smoking and rated poorly their patients ability and motivation to quit. These beliefs as well as nurses' knowledge of resources were correlated with nurses' efforts in delivering tobacco dependence interventions.

Three additional studies also examined psychiatric nurses' perspectives regarding implementing smoke-free environment policies in their work settings (Dickens, Stubbs & Haw, 2004; Erwin & Biordi, 1991; Hamera, Williams, Pelan, & Agnew, 1997). While these again are too few to systematically analyze, themes emerged indicating initial resistance to banning smoking in psychiatric settings, varied practices as to how bans are implemented, the use of smoking privileges as a reinforcement for achieving behavior or symptom control, and a relationship between nurse smoking behavior and nurse support of patient smoking, including valuing smoking with patients as therapeutic. With the exception of the study by Sharp, Blaakman, and colleagues (2009) in which 6% of nurses reported current smoking, a relatively high proportion (17%–35%) of psychiatric nurses surveyed identified themselves as current smokers (Buchanan, Huffman, & Barbour, 1994; Dickens et al., 2004) as compared to 11% of registered nurses in national estimates (Sarna et al., 2009).

Quantitative Studies of Psychiatric Patients

Only one nurse-investigator-led clinical trial (Chou, Chen, Lee, Ku, & Lu, 2004) was located in this search. This study recruited a small sample of day care patients with schizophrenia (total $n = 68$) to test the effectiveness of an 8-week trial of 14 mg nicotine patch therapy on smoking abstinence as compared to control. Some favorable group differences were noted in cigarette consumption, reported nicotine dependence, and expired carbon monoxide (CO) levels for the treatment group ($n = 26$) versus controls postintervention, but no differences in 3-month continuous abstinence were found. The researchers hypothesized that the dose of the nicotine patch, which was tapered down to 7 mg after 6 weeks, was possibly inadequate to promote better cessation outcomes. This study may have assisted in exploring interventions with Taiwanese psychiatric patients, but did not add to the general knowledge of treatment considerations for persons with mental illness who are known to require more intensive interventions over time to facilitate and maintain smoking cessation (Steinberg et al., 2006). The remaining quantitative studies surveyed psychiatric patients from various settings and mostly described patients' tobacco and other substance use patterns. Two studies sampled patients receiving Assertive Community Treatment (ACT) in Ontario, Canada (Eastabrook et al., 2003; Gerber, Krupa, Eastabrook, & Gargaro, 2003) and reported high prevalence of smoking rates (62% to 63.4%) and heavy smoking (>25 cigarettes/day) in these persons diagnosed with serious mental illnesses, as compared to the general population, but no higher rates of alcohol or drug abuse. Murphy, Gass-Sternas, and Knight (1995) found similar smoking patterns in a sample (n = 25) of persons with serious mental illnesses discharged to the community in New Jersey, but higher usage rates of other substances. In this sample, 44% reported trying to quit smoking and the majority (>60%) viewed smoking as harmful and desired to use a cessation program if offered.

Although not primarily focused on tobacco dependence, Byrne, Brown, Voorberg, and Schofield (1994) described a wellness education program for a small sample (n = 9) of lodging home residents with serious mental illnesses in Canada that included a smoking reduction program. Half of the smokers participated, expressed interest in quitting and reduced tobacco usage, although smoking rates were not reported. Additionally, in the only study in the sample that centered on adolescent psychiatric patients (Modrcin-Talbott, Pullen, Ehrenberger, Zandstra, & Muenchen, 1998), smoking was evaluated as a correlate of self-esteem among other variables consistent with Roy's Adaptation Model (Roy, 1984). While self-esteem for these adolescents was predictably lower as compared to a nonclinical sample, nonsmokers and smokers did not differ on self-esteem although smoking was prevalent (66.2%) among the participants.

Quantitative Studies of Both Psychiatric Nurses and Patients

Buchanan and colleagues (1994) used surveys differing in length and content to assess psychiatric/mental health (PMH) nurses' practices and patients' experiences regarding smoking cessation. Consistent with other studies most nurses provided low intensity intervention (e.g., gave information about smoking risks), but few provided intensive interventions, rating confidence in their efforts and their patients' potential to quit as low. Over half of these nurses were current or former smokers, and almost one fourth acknowledged using cigarettes to reward positive patient behavior. Only half of the patients in this sample reported being counseled by a nurse during their hospitalization despite the vast majority reporting a desire to quit smoking, at least one quit attempt, and the willingness to accept nurse support if offered. Tilley (1987) examined tobacco use among other substances in a group of patients diagnosed with anxiety disorders and a comparison group of psychiatric nurses matched by age. Patients with anxiety disorders were heavy smokers, drinkers, and sedative users, while the nurses smoked less than patients in this study but drank more alcohol. Both patients and nurses reported smoking to manage anxiety with a small percentage indicating it was effective for this purpose. These studies were conducted 15 to 20 years ago and it is not clear if these results would be replicated today.

Mixed Method and Qualitative Studies of Psychiatric Nurses–Patients

Some qualitative data has been generated from two studies that have used mixed methods, one grounded theory design, and one study that employed exploratory focus groups. Brimblecombe, Tingle, Tunmore, and Murrells (2007) used qualitative content analysis to report data from a national e-mail survey regarding holistic practices in mental health nursing in England. Most nurses supported promoting healthy lifestyles for their patients, including assisting in decreased tobacco and substance use, but also desired more specialty training in order to do so effectively. VanDongen, Kriz, Fox, and Haque (1999) collected both quantitative and qualitative data in hour-long interviews with patients diagnosed with serious mental illnesses who were receiving long-term supportive care from an urban, Midwestern U.S. clinic. Participants were categorized as smokers wanting to quit, smokers not interested in quitting, and former smokers with more than 12 months abstinence from tobacco products. Significant differences were found between the groups regarding physical and mental health symptoms and reasons for quitting. Former smokers were by far the healthiest and reported multiple quit attempts prior to abstinence with family support but no participation in smoking cessation groups.

Lawn and Condon (2006) highlighted the beliefs and ethical dilemmas nurses encounter when addressing patient smoking through a grounded theory approach. Nurses expressed conflicts between supporting patient autonomy and minimizing patient harm when deciding to or not to intervene. Nurses reported reinforcing smoking especially when patients are acutely ill as to not hinder recovery or cause further deprivation. In the only focus group study found (Snyder, McDevitt, & Painter, 2008), outpatients with serious mental illnesses reported many personal, social, and environmental factors as influencing their cigarette consumption. Nonsmoking rules and role models were important for abstinence, as was the ability to choose whether or not to smoke. In this sample of smokers, smoking was described as "central to daily survival" (p. 297).

SUMMARY

Nurse scholars have contributed to our understanding of the scope and significance of tobacco dependence and mental illnesses primarily through descriptive studies. In addition to studies led by nurse investigators, several review papers have helped raise awareness about the clinical importance of addressing tobacco dependence among those with mental illnesses and/or substance use disorders (Cataldo,

2001; Cataldo & Talley, 2001; Doolan & Froelicher, 2006; McCloughen, 2003; Keltner & Grant, 2006). Based on the science to date, nurses who work with psychiatrically ill clients tend to assess tobacco use and advise cessation but are ill equipped to assist their clients to stop smoking despite the presence of efficacious and effective interventions (Currie et al., 2008; Fiore et al., 2008; Foulds, 2006; el-Guebaly et al., 2002; Hitsman, Borrelli, McChargue, Spring, & Niaura, 2003). Although there is some evidence that psychiatric nurses desire more education and training in tobacco dependence interventions, they may be ethically conflicted about and generally less than committed to implementing smoke-free environmental policies. These findings are in contrast to the considerable evidence regarding the positive impact such policies can have in improving clients' and staff members' health (Fiore et al., 2008) and may reflect lack of awareness or understanding among nurses regarding the importance of denormalizing tobacco use among those with mental illnesses and/or substance use disorders (Schroeder, 2008).

Research and Policy Implications

In the United States, advanced practice psychiatric nurses (those most likely to have the knowledge and skills to conduct research) comprise a very small percentage of the total mental health workforce (Hanrahan & Hartley, 2008). Within the specialty, a still smaller subset of psychiatric nurses conduct research with very few focused on tobacco dependence. Additionally, the emphasis in psychiatry and addictions treatment on integrating physical/behavioral health into mainstream treatment is a relatively new phenomenon. Nurses who might initiate such research may also struggle to find funding sources committed to those working on a topic that until recently has not been a psychiatric nursing priority. Another barrier to research is likely linked to the relatively widespread erroneous belief that psychiatrically ill clients are not motivated or able to stop smoking. This may lead psychiatric nurses to think that recruiting participants into studies designed to evaluate cessation interventions may be insurmountable. Yet psychiatric nurses are increasingly recognizing the importance of sound physical health to recovery. With this realization, hopefully more will develop interest in understanding tobacco dependence and evaluating interventions to aid cessation in this clinical population.

Ample opportunities exist for nurses to contribute to tobacco dependence knowledge generation. Studies are needed to inform the neurophysiological underpinnings of tobacco dependence including the identification of mediators and moderators of cessation for those with mental illness and/or addictive disorders. There also is need for the testing of tobacco dependence intervention models (including various counseling strategies and pharmacotherapy) that are specifically tailored to meet the needs of this population. Perhaps more pressing, however, is the need for studies designed to facilitate understanding of the barriers and facilitators to implementing key tobacco dependence interventions in clinical practice. Efficacious and effective interventions are available but to date nurses have not integrated them widely into *good* nursing care (Sarna & Bialous, 2006). For psychiatric nurses, the research to date helps to explain that this may be due, in part, to the fact that nurses do not feel efficacious in delivering these interventions and they lack confidence in their clients' ability and motivation to stop smoking (Sharp, Blaakman, et al., 2009). Studies are needed that can help identify strategies for enhancing nurses' motivation and competence for delivering tobacco dependence interventions with their clients who smoke. Psychiatric nurses (in comparison to nurses in other specialties) have historically reported higher smoking rates (Trinkoff & Storr, 1998). Research indicates that health care professionals who smoke are less likely to intervene with their patients who smoke (Braun et al., 2004; Sarna, Wewers, Brown, Lillington, & Brecht, 2001; Slater, McElwee, Fleming, & McKenna, 2006). Evaluating effective strategies for intervening with nurses who smoke also could potentially enhance nurses' interventions with their clients who smoke. Additionally, research designed to assess the impact of stopping smoking on clients' quality of life and psychiatric symptoms also is needed.

Another focus of inquiry should be in the area of evaluating denormalizing and harm reduction strategies in this population. Although the culture in mental health and addiction treatment is beginning to change from tobacco dependent to tobacco free, more work is needed (Solway, 2009). Nurses need to explore how to improve the systematic implementation of tobacco free workplace initiatives (Williams, 2008) in mental health settings. Given the success of countermarketing strategies in the general population (Hu, Sung, & Keeler, 1995), research designed to evaluate the use of targeted countermarketing to aid denormalizing tobacco use among those with mental illnesses also is needed. The potential efficacy and effectiveness of telephone quitlines tailored to meet the needs of those with mental illnesses and addictive disorders needs development and evaluation as well (Morris, Tedeschi, et al., 2009).

With respect to public policy, advocacy initiatives are clearly needed to expand insurance coverage for counseling and pharmacotherapy to aid cessation in this population. Reimbursement structures in mental health settings frequently do not provide adequate coverage for tobacco dependence intervention despite the fact that this is an Axis I diagnosis per the fourth, text revision edition of the *Diagnostic and Statistical Manual* (*DSM–IV–TR*; American Psychiatric Association, 2000). Such constraints undermine the delivery of evidence-based interventions and inhibit clinicians in prescribing combination nicotine replacement medications (i.e., off label), which often is needed in this population to sustain cessation (Rigotti, 2009; Sharp, Bellush, Evinger, Blaakman, & Williams, 2009; Steinberg et al., 2006). Additionally, when prescribing FDA-approved cessation pharmacotherapy to patients with psychiatric diagnosis, clinicians need to be aware of both the issue of drug interactions as well as potential psychiatric side effects of some of these drugs. Nurses also should work with policy makers to secure funding for tobacco dependence research including studies designed to identify strategies for providing greater access to treatment for those with mental illnesses and/or addictive disorders (Bialous, 2006). Regulatory initiatives that support tobacco free health care settings including the requisite clinical training to support clinicians in aiding cessation is another policy avenue that would profit from the contributions of nurse researchers.

One promising initiative currently underway to support the work of psychiatric nurses is the prioritizing of tobacco dependence as part of the American Psychiatric Nurses Association (American Nurses Association, 2005) national agenda. Convinced that psychiatric nurses possess the requisite skills to effectively intervene with their clients who smoke, the board of the APNA in partnership with key representatives from the Smoking Cessation Leadership Center (a national program of the Robert Wood Johnson Foundation) drafted a national strategic plan that targets practice, education, research, and public policy initiatives designed to significantly advance the science of tobacco control and increase the reach and depth of psychiatric nurses intervention with their patients who smoke. In collaboration with the International Society on Addiction and the International Society for Psychiatric Nursing, the APNA developed a position statement that defines psychiatric nurses as champions for smoking cessation. The organization has committed to increase by 5% each year the number of psychiatric nurses who refer smokers to treatment and to increase by 5% each year the number of psychiatric nurses who provide best clinical practice in tobacco cessation interventions through the various methods described in the strategic plan (Naegle, Baird, & Stein, 2009). In addition to supporting research and policy initiatives, APNA has committed to advocating for expanding curricular content regarding tobacco dependence interventions in undergraduate and graduate psychiatric nursing education, based on results from a 2008 survey of APNA members in which less than half reported tobacco dependence content in either their undergraduate or graduate programs (Sharp, Blaakman, et al., 2009). The organization has committed to providing continuing education for nurses in practice to help fill knowledge gaps in evidence-based strategies for aiding cessation among those with mental illnesses and/or addictive disorders.

CONCLUSION

A highly vulnerable population, those with psychiatric and/or addictive disorders, is bearing a disproportionate health burden caused by tobacco dependence, yet psychiatric clinicians including nurses, have only recently began to address the issue of tobacco dependence. This review demonstrated that nursing research in this field is limited. Most research to date has been descriptive and largely focused on establishing smoking rates in this population as well as nurses' attitudes and beliefs about intervening with their clients who smoke. However, it is clear that nursing researchers can seize the opportunity to contribute to the advancement of new knowledge with regard to multifaceted tobacco dependence interventions with these patients. Psychiatric nurses have the skills to design, implement, and evaluate tobacco dependence interventions that will be most effective with the complex patients they serve. Consistent with other nursing specialties, evaluating nursing education with regard to tobacco-dependence interventions and outcomes is needed. The APNA argues that failure to act on tobacco dependence equals harm. The time to act to advance the science of tobacco dependence with this often stigmatized clinical population through research, policy, practice, and educational initiatives is now. The findings of this review provide direction for this vitally important work.

ACKNOWLEDGMENTS

This project was partially supported by a Ruth L. Kirschstein National Research Service Award (F31NR011266, Susan W. Blaakman, Principal Investigator) from the National Institute of Nursing Research. The content is solely the responsibility of the authors and does not necessarily represent the official views of the National Institute of Nursing Research or the National Institutes of Health.

REFERENCES

American Nurses Association (2005). Position statement: Tobacco use prevention, cessation and exposure to second-hand smoke. Retrieved October 22, 2009, from http://www.nurs ingworld.org/MainMenuCategories/HealthcareandPolicyIssues/ANAPositionState-ments/Archives/nfbtemp14495.aspx#

American Psychiatric Association. (2000). *Diagnostic and statistical manual of mental disorders: DSM–IV–TR* (text revision). Washington, DC: Author.

Benowitz, N. L. (2008a). Neurobiology of nicotine addiction: Implications for smoking cessation treatment. *The American Journal of Medicine, 121*(4A), S3–S10.

Benowitz, N. L. (2008b). Clinical pharmacology of nicotine: Implications for understanding, preventing, and treating tobacco addiction. *Clinical Pharmacology & Therapeutics, 83*, 531–541.

Bialous, S. A. (2006). Tobacco use cessation within the context of tobacco control policy: Opportunities for nursing research. *Nursing Research, 55*(4 Suppl.), S58–S63.

Braun, B. L., Fowles, J. B., Solberg, L. I., Kind, E. A., Lando, H., & Pine, D. (2004). Smoking-related attitudes and clinical practices of medical personnel in Minnesota. *American Journal of Preventive Medicine, 27*, 316–322.

Brimblecombe, N., Tingle, A., Tunmore, R., & Murrells, T. (2007). Implementing holistic practices in mental health nursing: A national consultation. *International Journal of Nursing Studies, 44*, 339–348.

Buchanan, C. R., Huffman, C., & Barbour, V. M. (1994). Smoking health risk: Counseling of psychiatric patients. *Journal of Psychosocial Nursing & Mental Health Services, 32,* 27–32.

Byrne, C., Brown, B., Voorberg, N., & Schofield, R. (1994). Wellness education for individuals with chronic mental illness living in the community. *Issues in Mental Health Nursing, 15,* 239–252.

Cataldo, J. K. (2001, June). The role of advanced practice psychiatric nurses in treating tobacco use and dependence. *Archives of Psychiatric Nursing, 15,* 107–119.

Cataldo, J. K., & Talley, S. (2001). Helping our clients with smoking cessation. *Journal of the American Psychiatric Nurses Association, 7,* 26–31.

Chou, K., Chen, R., Lee, J., Ku, C., & Lu, R. (2004). The effectiveness of nicotine-patch therapy for smoking cessation in patients with schizophrenia. *International Journal of Nursing Studies, 41,* 321–330.

Christakis, N. A., & Fowler, J. H. (2008). The collective dynamics of smoking in a large social network. *The New England Journal of Medicine, 358,* 2249–2258.

Currie, S. R., Karltyn, J., Lussier, D., de Denus, E., Brown, D., & el-Guebaly, N. (2008). Outcome from a community-based smoking cessation program for persons with serious mental illness. *Community Mental Health Journal, 44,* 187–194.

Dickens, G. L., Stubbs, J. H., & Haw, C. M. (2004). Smoking and mental health nurses: A survey of clinical staff in a psychiatric hospital. *Journal of Psychiatric and Mental Health Nursing, 11,* 445–451.

Doolan, D. M., & Froelicher, E. S. (2006). Efficacy of smoking cessation intervention among special populations: Review of the literature from 2000 to 2005. *Nursing Research, 55,* S29–S37.

Eastabrook, S., Krupa, T., Horgan, S., Gerber, G., Grant, R., Mayo, J., et al. (2003). Substance abuse in a Canadian population of assertive community treatment (ACT) clients: Implications for service planning and delivery. *Canadian Journal of Nursing Research, 35,* 44–51.

El-Guebaly, N., Cathcart, J., Currie, S., Brown, D., & Gloster, S. (2002). Smoking cessation approaches for persons with mental illness or addictive disorders. *Psychiatric Services (Washington, DC), 53,* 1166–1170.

Erwin, S., & Biordi, D. (1991). A smoke-free environment: Psychiatric nurses respond. *Journal of Psychosocial Nursing & Mental Health Services, 29,* 12.

Fiore, M. C., Jaen, C., Baker, T., Bailey, W., Benowitz, N., Curry, S., et al. (2008). *Treating tobacco use and dependence: 2008 update. Clinical practice guideline.* Retrieved May 22, 2008, from http://www.surgeongeneral.gov/tobacco/treating_tobacco_use08.pdf

Foulds, J. (2006). The neurobiological basis for partial agonist treatment of nicotine dependence: Varenicline. *International Journal of Clinical Practice, 60,* 571–576.

George, T. P., Termine, A., Sacco, K. A., Allen, T. M., Reutenauer, E., Vessicchio, J. C., et al. (2006). A preliminary study of the effects of cigarette smoking on prepulse inhibition in schizophrenia: Involvement of nicotinic receptor mechanisms. *Schizophrenia Research, 87*(1–3), 307–315.

Gerber, G. J., Krupa, T., Eastabrook, S., & Gargaro, J. (2003). Substance use among persons with serious mental illness in Eastern Ontario. *Canadian Journal of Community Mental Health, 22,* 113–128.

Grant, B. F., Hasin, D. S., Chou, S. P., Stinson, F. S., & Dawson, D. A. (2004). Nicotine dependence and psychiatric disorders in the United States. *Archives of General Psychiatry, 61,* 1107–1115.

Hall, S. M., Tsoh, J. Y., Prochaska, J. J., Eisendrath, S., Rossi, J. S., Redding, C. A., et al. (2006). Treatment for cigarette smoking among depressed mental health outpatients: A randomized clinical trial. *American Journal of Public Health, 96,* 1808–1814.

Hamera, E., Williams, G. J., Pelan, J. M., & Agnew, D. (1997). Variations in smoking policies on psychiatric units. *Journal of the American Psychiatric Nurses Association, 3,* 137–145.

Hanrahan, N. P., & Hartley, D. (2008). Employment of advanced-practice psychiatric nurses to stem rural mental health workforce shortages. *Psychiatric Services, 59,* 109–111.

Hitsman, B., Borrelli, B., McChargue, D. E., Spring, B., & Niaura, R. (2003). History of depression and smoking cessation outcome: A meta-analysis. *Journal of Consulting & Clinical Psychology, 71,* 657–663.

Hu, T. W., Sung, H. Y., & Keeler, T. E. (1995). Reducing cigarette consumption in California: Tobacco taxes vs. an anti-smoking media campaign. *American Journal of Public Health, 85,* 1218–1222.

Keltner, N. L., & Grant, J. S. (2006). Smoke, smoke, smoke that cigarette. *Perspectives in Psychiatric Care, 42,* 256–261.

Lasser, K., Boyd, J. W., Woolhandler, S., Himmelstein, D. U., McCormick, D., & Bor, D. H. (2000). Smoking and mental illness: A population-based prevalence study. *The Journal of the American Medical Association, 284,* 2606–2610.

Lawn, S., & Condon, J. (2006). Psychiatric nurses' ethical stance on cigarette smoking by patients: Determinants and dilemmas in their role in supporting cessation. *International Journal of Mental Health Nursing, 15,* 111–118.

McCloughen, A. (2003). The association between schizophrenia and cigarette smoking: A review of the literature and implications for mental health nursing. *International Journal of Mental Health Nursing, 12,* 119–129.

Modrcin-Talbott, M. A., Pullen, L., Ehrenberger, H., Zandstra, K., & Muenchen, B. (1998). Self-esteem in adolescents treated in an outpatient mental health setting. *Issues in Comprehensive Pediatric Nursing, 21,* 159–171.

Morris, C., Tedeschi, G., Waxmonsky, J., May, M., & Giese, A. (2009). Tobacco quitlines and persons with mental illnesses: Perspective, practice, and direction. *Journal of the American Psychiatric Nurses Association, 15,* 32–40.

Morris, C., Waxmonsky, J., Giese, A., Graves, M., & Turnbull, J. (2007). *Smoking cessation for persons with mental illnesses: A toolkit for mental health providers.* Denver, CO: State Tobacco Education and Prevention Partnership. Retrieved October 22, 2009, from http://www.tcln.org/bea/docs/Quit_MHToolkit.pdf

Murphy, L. N., Gass-Sternas, K., & Knight, K. (1995). Health of the chronically mentally ill who rejoin the community: A community assessment. *Issues in Mental Health Nursing, 16,* 239–256.

Naegle, M., Baird, C., Stein, K. F. (2009). Psychiatric nurses as champions for smoking cessation. *Journal of the American Psychiatric Nurses Association, 15,* 21–23.

National Association of State Mental Health Program Directors. (2007). *Tobacco-free living in psychiatric settings: A best-practices toolkit promoting wellness and recovery.* Retrieved October 22, 2009, from http://www.nasmhpd.org/general_files/publications/NASMHPD.toolkitfinalupdated90707.pdf

Ratschen, E., Britton, J., Doody, G. A., & McNeill, A. (2009). Smoke-free policy in acute mental health wards: Avoiding the pitfalls. *General Hospital Psychiatry, 31*, 131–136.

Rigotti, N. A. (2009). The future of tobacco treatment in the health care system. *Annals of Internal Medicine, 150*, 496–497.

Rosenberg, L. (2009, March 23). National council's Linda Rosenberg testifies before Congress about funding. *Behavioral Health Care* press release. Retrieved June 16, 2009, from http://www.behavioral.net

Roy, C. (1984). *Introduction to nursing: An adaptive model* (2nd ed.). Englewood Cliffs, NJ: Prentice Hall.

Sarna, L., & Bialous, S. A. (2006). Strategic directions for nursing research in tobacco dependence. *Nursing Research, 55*(Suppl. 4), 1–9.

Sarna, L., Bialous, S. A., Wells, M. J., & Kotlerman, J. (2009). Smoking among psychiatric nurses: Does it hinder tobacco dependence treatment? *Journal of the American Psychiatric Nurses Association, 15*(1), 59–67.

Sarna, L., Wewers, M. E., Brown, J. K., Lillington, L., & Brecht, M. L. (2001). Barriers to tobacco cessation in clinical practice: Report from a national survey of oncology nurses. *Nursing Outlook, 49*, 166–172.

Schroeder, S. A. (2007). The hidden epidemic. *The Washington Post.* Retrieved October 22, 2009, from http://smokingcessationleadership.ucsf.edu/Downloads/MH/Articles/AHiddnEpidc.htm

Schroeder, S. (2008). Stranded in the periphery—the increasing marginalization of smokers. *New England Journal of Medicine, 358*, 2249–2258.

Schroeder, S. A. (2009). A 51-year-old woman with bipolar disorder who wants to quit smoking. *Journal of the American Medical Association, 301*, 522–531.

Sharp, D., Bellush, N., Evinger, J., Blaakman, S., & Williams, G. (2009). *Intensive tobacco dependence intervention with persons challenged by mental illness: Manual for nurses.* Retrieved from http://www.apna.org/i4a/pages/Index.cfm?pageID=3645

Sharp, D., Blaakman, S., Cole, R., & Evinger, J. (2009). Report from a national tobacco dependence survey of psychiatric nurses. *Journal of the American Psychiatric Nurses Association, 15*(3), 172–181.

Slater, P. McElwee, G., Fleming, P., & McKenna, H. (2006). Nurses smoking behaviour related to cessation practice. *Nursing Times, 102*, 32–37.

Snyder, M., McDevitt, J., & Painter, S. (2008). Smoking cessation and serious mental illness. *Archives of Psychiatric Nursing, 22*, 297–304.

Solway, E. (2009). Windows of opportunity for culture change around tobacco use in mental health settings. *Journal of the American Psychiatric Nurses Association, 15*, 41–49.

Steinberg, M. B., Foulds, J., Richardson, D. L., Burke, M. V., & Shah, P. (2006). Pharmacotherapy and smoking cessation at a tobacco dependence clinic. *Preventive Medicine, 26*, 114–119.

Steinberg, M. B., Williams, J. M., & Ziedonis, D. M. (2004). Financial implications of cigarette smoking among individuals with schizophrenia. *Tobacco Control, 13*, 206–208.

Strasser, K. M. (2001). *Smoking reduction and cessation for people with schizophrenia: Guidelines for general practitioners.* South Melbourne: SANE Australia. Retrieved October 22, 2009, from http://www.health.vic.gov.au/mentalhealth/smoke/smoke.pdf

Tilley, S. (1987). Alcohol, other drugs and tobacco use and anxiolytic effectiveness: A comparison of anxious patients and psychiatric nurses. *British Journal of Psychiatry, 151*, 389–392.

Trinkoff, A. M., & Storr, C. L. (1998). Substance use among nurses: Differences between specialties. *American Journal of Public Health, 88,* 581–585.

Van Dongen, C., Kriz, P., Fox, K. A., & Haque, I. (1999). A quit smoking group pilot study. *Journal of Psychosocial Nursing & Mental Health Services, 37,* 26–34.

Williams, J. M. (2008). Eliminating tobacco use in mental health facilities: Patients' rights, public health and policy issues. *Journal of the American Medical Association, 299,* 571–573.

Williams, J. M., & Ziedonis, D. (2004). Addressing tobacco among individuals with a mental illness or an addiction. *Addictive Behaviors, 29,* 1067–1083.

Williams, J. M., & Ziedonis, D. M. (2006). Snuffing out tobacco dependence: Ten reasons behavioral health providers need to be involved. *Behavioral Healthcare, 26,* 27–31.

Ziedonis, D. M., Hobbs, M., Beckham, J. C., Zvolensky, M., Adler, L., Audrain-McGovern, J., et al. (2008). Tobacco use and cessation in psychiatric disorders: National institute of mental health report. *Nicotine & Tobacco Research, 10,* 1691–1715.

Ziedonis, D., Williams, J. M., & Smelson, D. (2003). Serious mental illness and tobacco addiction: A model program to address this common but neglected issue. *The American Journal of the Medical Sciences, 326,* 223–230.

Chapter 13

Nursing Research in Tobacco Use and Special Populations

Kristine K. Browning, Cathy J. Baker,
Gretchen A. McNally, and Mary Ellen Wewers

ABSTRACT

Smoking is responsible for approximately one in five deaths in the United States per year. The Surgeon General's 1964 report first linked smoking as a cause of cancer. Since then cigarette smoking has had a steady decline to its current estimate of 19.8%. There are, however, some special populations where smoking continues to occur at a higher prevalence than the general population. This chapter discusses tobacco dependence among the following special populations: low socioeconomic status including Medicaid, hard-core smokers, rural, and homeless; immigrants; and persons living with HIV. For each population, there is an overview of the disparities in tobacco use, special challenges unique to that population, and exploration of current research on tailoring of tobacco dependence treatment. Each of the special populations discussed present unique challenges with tobacco dependence treatment that will require careful examination before disparities will ultimately decrease. Eliminating disparities has been marked as an important research agenda item as noted in Healthy People 2010. Nurse researchers are well positioned to combine their clinical expertise and knowledge of

DOI: 10.1891/0739-6686.27.319

patient psychosocial needs with investigation of patient-focused research questions in each of these special populations.

Keywords: special populations; disparities; nicotine dependence; tobacco dependence treatment

Smoking is responsible for approximately one in five deaths in the United States per year (Centers for Disease Control and Prevention [CDC], 2008b). Cigarette consumption in the United States reached its peak in 1964, at the time of the Surgeon General's first report linking smoking as a cause of cancer, and then began to decline by 1974 (U.S. Department of Health and Human Services [U.S. DHHS], 1989; U.S. DHHS, 1988). Since that time, cigarette smoking has continued to have a steady decline to its current estimate of 19.8% (CDC, 2008a). There are, however, some special populations where smoking continues to occur at a higher prevalence than the general population.

This chapter discusses tobacco dependence among the following special populations: low socioeconomic status including Medicaid, hard-core smokers, rural, and homeless; immigrants; and persons living with human immunodeficiency virus (HIV). For each population, there is an overview of the disparities in tobacco use, special challenges unique to that population, and exploration of current research on tailoring of tobacco dependence treatment. Each section includes appropriate nursing research studies conducted within these populations. The method used for the literature review included a systematic review of research studies from 1993 to the present with the following search terms: culture, hardcore smoker, HIV, homeless, limited formal education, low income, Medicaid, rural, smoking, smoking cessation, and tobacco.

The prevalence of tobacco use among low-income smokers has been well documented. As such, a large number of research studies have examined this disparity. However, gaps in research are evident such as lack of treatment interventions with the homeless. Research studies among other special populations, such as immigrants and persons living with HIV, have not been as abundant. Studies about smoking prevalence have not received much attention in immigrant populations. Furthermore, there appears to be a relationship between acculturation and continued smoking after immigration to the United States that is not uniform across cultures or between genders. Within the last 15 years, HIV has evolved into a treatable chronic disease. Because of this, examining smoking behavior among persons living with HIV as well as investigating the high smoking prevalence within this population has become a high priority. Given their interest in behavioral interventions and clinical experience, nurse researchers are prepared to contribute a unique perspective when developing research questions and examining health disparities in each of these special populations.

LOW-INCOME SMOKERS

Socioeconomic Status and Smoking Behavior

Inequalities in smoking prevalence are apparent and include class-based disparities and higher proportions of smokers in the lower socioeconomic groups (Bobak, Jarvis, Skodova, & Marmot, 2000; Jarvis & Wardle, 1999). It is well documented that lower socioeconomic status (SES) is associated with having less information about the health risks of smoking, fewer social supports, and the least access to cessation services (Healton & Nelson, 2004; Sorensen, Barbeau, Hunt, & Emmons, 2004). Socioeconomic disadvantage is associated with persistent smoking, while higher rates of cessation are associated with higher SES (Fernandez et al., 2006; Jarvis & Wardle, 1999; Sorensen et al., 2004). Smoking prevalence is highest for those living below the poverty line (30.6%) while 46% of those with a General Educational Development (GED) diploma are categorized as current smokers. Those who are poor, less educated and marginalized have higher rates of smoking as compared to their more privileged counterparts. As such, they also suffer tobacco-attributable morbidity and mortality at significantly higher rates. The relationship between tobacco use and consequent disease burden has led health policy experts to view the association as an issue of social justice (Healton & Nelson, 2004).

Efforts to promote cessation and abstinence in these vulnerable groups have, to date, been relatively limited. Their lack of engagement in preventive health care services may, in part, be due to barriers to access and lack of information (Elnicki, Morris, & Shockcor, 1995). Knowledge about the consequences of tobacco use is lower among these current smokers, especially those of lower educational levels (Brownson et al., 1992). *Healthy People 2010* identified blue-collar smokers with low income, a high school education or less, and aged 25 and older, as a special population of tobacco users in need of interventions (U.S. DHHS, 2000). Poorer people lack not only sufficient income but material goods and the means for social connectedness (Marmot, 2001). Those who are disadvantaged often work in environments that lack strong indoor air regulations and are often exposed to tobacco smoke at work (Okuyemi et al., 2006).

According to the *Treating Tobacco Use and Dependence 2008 Update* (Fiore et al., 2008), patients with low SES and limited formal education have limited access to effective treatment (Connor, Cook, Herbert, Neal, & Williams, 2002; Murphy, Mahoney, Hyland, Higbee, & Cummings, 2005). As an example, using data from the 2001 National Health Interview Survey, Browning and others

(2008) observed that patients with higher education, higher income and health insurance were more likely to report assistance with quitting in the previous year during a health care provider visit. This finding is disappointing, as low-income smokers report the same interest in quitting, as compared to the general population (Wadland, Soffelmayr, & Ives, 2001). Another factor that has been noted among low-income smokers is the lack of accurate information about pharmacotherapy for tobacco dependence (Cummings et al., 2004). Presented below is information about specific subgroups of low-income smokers. Table 13.1 provides examples of clinical treatment trials in this vulnerable group of smokers, including examples of nurse-led trials.

Medicaid Smokers

Smoking among Medicaid enrollees is reported to be significantly higher compared to the general population, as well as those enrolled in commercial managed care organizations (CDC, 1997). As of 2005, a total of 38 state Medicaid programs offered coverage for some form of tobacco dependence treatment for all Medicaid enrollees (CDC, 2006). Four states covered only pregnant smokers. Oregon provided coverage for all medications and counseling treatments recommended in the 2000 U.S. PHS Clinical Practice Guideline, with six additional states offering coverage for medications and at least one form of counseling recommended in the Guideline. Jaen, Cummings, Shah, and Aungst (1997) examined the use and effectiveness of a free nicotine patch program among Medicaid and uninsured smokers and noted that the majority of participants, seen in urban family practice sites, used the program as intended and an overwhelming majority (90%) found the patch useful. The total supply included 6 weeks of patch therapy and 61% reported using the patch every day. Medication therapy was accompanied by either self-help materials or brief counseling at baseline by a nurse and other health care workers in the practice. According to self-report follow-up, using an intent-to-treat analysis, 10% of participants were abstinent from smoking at 6 months postenrollment. A randomized trial evaluating the effectiveness of a nurse-managed telephone counseling cessation approach delivered to very low-income smokers in Medicaid managed care determined that enhanced care (with automated telephone calls) improved outcomes (Wadland et al., 2001). Nurses and telephone counselors received special training in a computer-assisted counseling program that focused on relapse prevention. At 3 months, those smokers who received enhanced relapse prevention treatment were almost 3 times more likely to be biochemically confirmed as abstinent compared to usual care participants. Both groups had received a moderately intensive intervention that included brief advice by their provider to quit, a prescription of transdermal

TABLE 13.1 Examples of Tobacco Dependence Treatment Clinical Trials, Including Those Led by Nurse Researchers

Author/Year	Group	N	Design	Intervention	Results	Conclusion
Hahn et al., 2005[a]	Low-income rural	1006	2 group quasiexperimental	Quit and Win Contest versus control	Cotinine-validated (intervention vs. control): *3 months* 14.0% versus 1.0% $p < .0001$; *6 months* 10.1% versus 1.4% $p < .0001$; *12 months* 7.3% versus 0.6% $p < .0001$	The contest demonstrated a higher quit rate in low-income, rural smokers.
Lando et al., 1996	Hard-core smokers	1083	2 group quasiexperimental	Telephone support versus control after intensive intervention	Self-report at 34 months: Telephone support 17.1% versus control 11.8%; $p = ns$	Telephone support was not effective in preventing smoking relapse.
Murphy, Mahoney, Cummings et al., 2005	Low-income Medicaid	608	3 group RCT	Verbal information about medication benefit alone (Group 1) versus verbal information about medication benefit + pamphlet (Group II) versus case management to access medication (Group III)	CO-validated at 3 months: 1.0% Group I versus 2.0% Group II versus 2.4% Group III; $p = ns$	The intensive intervention, designed to promote pharmacotherapy use and smoking cessation among Medicaid users, was not more effective then less intensive interventions.

(Continued)

TABLE 13.1 Examples of Tobacco Dependence Treatment Clinical Trials, Including Those Led by Nurse Researchers (*Continued*)

Author/Year	Group	N	Design	Intervention	Results	Conclusion
Tønneson et al., 1996	Hard-core smokers	89	2 group quasiexperimental	Nicotine nasal spray: Ad libitum versus scheduled dosing	CO-validated at 12 months: Ad lib 7% versus scheduled dose 6%; $p = ns$	The long-term smoking cessation success rate with nicotine nasal spray use in hard-core smokers was low.
Wadland et al., 2001	Low-income Medicaid	233	2 group RCT	Relapse prevention (nurse telephone counseling) + usual care (physician advice, NRT, pamphlet) versus usual care alone	CO-validated at 3 months: 21% relapse prevention versus 8.1% usual care; $p < .01$	Individualized tele-phone counseling with a nurse improved smoking cessation rates with low-income Medicaid users.
Wewers et al., 2000[a]	HIV+	15 (pilot)	2 group quasiexperimental	Nurse-managed peer-counseling + NRT versus mailed print materials with advice to quit	CO-validated at 8 weeks and 8 months, nurse-managed versus print: 8 weeks: 62.5% versus 0% 8 months: 50% versus 0%	A nurse-managed, peer-led model of smoking cessation may be a promising intervention for HIV+ smokers.

Note. RCT = randomized controlled trial.
[a]Study conducted by a nurse researcher.

nicotine, a self-help pamphlet (*Clearing the Air*; NCI publication no. 95–1647), and a follow-up clinic visit.

More recently, a randomized trial to evaluate whether promoting pharmacotherapy use in a Medicaid population was effective, and failed to detect differences in quit rates when comparing minimal to intensive approaches (Murphy, Mahoney, Cummings, Hyland, & Lawvere, 2005). Medicaid clients were randomized to receive either: (1) verbal information on the Medicaid pharmacotherapy benefit; (2) verbal information about the benefit plus self-help quit materials; or (3) case management that included information, self-help materials, and assistance to facilitate access to the pharmacotherapy benefit.

Given the rising health care costs that state and federal agencies face, efforts to decrease tobacco-attributable morbidity and mortality among the Medicaid population are clearly cost effective. Enhancing tobacco dependence treatment through the use of trained nurse interventionists who provide relapse prevention strategies represents a scientifically valid approach to improving outcomes while addressing the significant health related and economic burden of tobacco dependence. Other novel approaches, such as media campaigns, which have demonstrated equivocal results, deserve further consideration and refinement. These campaigns have the capability of reaching large numbers of vulnerable disadvantaged smokers who intermittently lack access to preventive health care services (Niederdeppe, Kuang, Crock, & Skelton, 2008).

Hard-Core Smokers

A hard-core smoker (HCS), defined as being a daily smoker, with at least a 5 year history of the behavior, consuming at least 15 cigarettes a day and having never quit in the past with no intention of quitting in the future, is more likely to be of lower SES, as measured by both income and education (Augustson & Marcus, 2004; Emery, Gilpin, Ake, Farkas, & Pierce, 2000; Jarvis, Wardle, Waller, & Owen, 2003; MacIntosh & Coleman, 2006). Hard-core smokers are more likely to be male, non-Hispanic white, unmarried and no longer in the work force. Increased social isolation contributes to less contact with home and work smoking restrictions, and less exposure to potential sources of smoking cessation messages. Social contacts are more likely to be cigarette smokers (Augustson & Marcus, 2004; Emery et al., 2000). Only two studies have been conducted with HCS, although both studies included those motivated to quit, which calls into question whether the studies truly represented HCS. The first HCS study involved treatment with nicotine nasal spray and 8 to 9 behavioral counseling sessions during the first year. Biochemically confirmed abstinence at 12 months was low (6%), leading the authors to suggest that future treatment must involve more aggressive therapy (Tønneson, Mikkelsen, Nørregaard, & Jørgenson, 1996). A second study of HCS examined the effect of telephone support among those who had relapsed after an intensive intervention in a group clinic setting (Lando, Pirie, Roski, McGovern, & Schmid, 1996). At 34 months, 17.1% of participants receiving telephone support were abstinent, compared to 11.8% of the control group participants. This difference, although encouraging and perhaps useful among those prone to relapse, was not statistically significant.

As the current concept of HCS evolves, the characteristics of this group require further study. Patterns of previous quit attempts and future quit intentions, as well as the number of cigarettes smoked per day for specific subgroups (i.e., African Americans) may need reconsideration. Future research with subgroups of HCS may inform the development and testing of intensive cessation strategies, focusing on specific points of access. A nursing research perspective could enhance outcomes among this vulnerable population.

Rural Smokers

Rural smokers have increased estimates of tobacco prevalence compared to the general population (Bell et al., 2009; Doescher, Jackson, Jerant, & Hart, 2006). Data from 635 older adults (defined as $\geq$ 60 years of age) noted that approximately 70% were current or former users of any tobacco products, and about a third of the sample currently used at least one product. There is evidence that among rural groups the behavior often includes consumption of smokeless tobacco (ST) products, either instead of or in addition to cigarette use (Nelson et al., 2006). Smokeless tobacco use is especially apparent among white males residing in the rural south and Midwestern regions of the United States (Nelson et al., 2006). Coupled with higher prevalence estimates is decreased access to preventive services (Nelson et al., 2006). Focus group findings from studies conducted in Midwestern communities have reported three pertinent themes about cessation among smokers residing in rural areas (Hutcheson et al., 2008). Thematic areas included intrinsic, health-system resource and community or social factors. Intrinsic factors were person related and included facilitators of trying to quit (i.e., reducing one's health risk or saving money) and barriers to cessation such as an individual's low self-efficacy or concern about weight gain. Key health-system facilitators involved access to medication and medical care while barriers in the health system centered around infrequent utilization of the health care clinic visit and lack of preventive care locally, or lack of information about cessation services. While smokers noted that smoking was viewed negatively from a community or social perspective, the lack of alternative activities in rural communities, often in the presence of stress and exposure to other smokers, created a tension that made quitting difficult.

Appalachia is a rural population that is known for its high prevalence of smoking. It was originally defined as a physical and geographical region that included the Appalachian Highlands, which are a series of mountains that include the Piedmont, the Blue Ridge, the Ridge and Valley, and the Appalachian Plateaus (Raitz & Ulack, 1991). Initiated by the Appalachian Regional Development Act of 1965, the current Appalachian region includes 420 counties in 13 states from New York to Mississippi and contains three subregions (Appalachia Regional Commission, 2008).

Two cessation approaches have been designed to address the lack of tobacco control programs in rural communities, including Appalachia. First, A *Tobacco Cessation Project for Disadvantaged West Virginia Communities* was developed and tested in a quasiexperimental design for differences in success based on rural versus urban residence. The program was intensive and consisted of a medical examination, an eight-session educational and behavioral counseling program that included pharmacotherapy, and follow-up group meetings. When compared to urban residents, rural participants in the program were significantly less likely to quit at the end of the intervention ($OR = 0.58$; 95% CI 0.35, 0.94), after adjusting for characteristics known to influence cessation (Northridge et al., 2008). Second, Hahn and coworkers implemented a community-based approach to promote cessation among smokers residing in rural Kentucky (Hahn et al., 2005). Their approach implemented a Quit and Win contest that included large cash prizes, weekly mailings from a health care provider that encouraged quitting, online and telephone quit assistance, a media campaign, and community support. Compared to control group participants who received no treatment, Quit and Win contestants were greater than 5 times more likely to report abstinence at 12-month postintervention, as confirmed by urine cotinine analysis. This finding is encouraging and demonstrates that a novel, minimally intensive approach may be effective in underserved groups.

Unfortunately, systematic evaluation of tobacco dependence treatment approaches are lacking among rural smokers. Recently, several investigators have introduced a program of research to examine treatment in rural primary care practices in Kansas (Cox et al., 2008; Cupertino et al., 2007, 2008). To date, their work indicates that patients are willing to enroll in a disease-management approach to treat nicotine dependence. Of note, the authors reported that when offered free pharmacotherapy, the majority of patients (67%) were interested and requested either bupropion or nicotine replacement. These results are encouraging and support the need to implement and evaluate existing scientifically valid approaches among underserved groups.

Homeless Smokers

The prevalence of smoking among the homeless population is staggering. In a cross-sectional study by Connor and colleagues, approximately 70% of homeless persons reported current smoking (2002). About 37% wanted to quit in the next 6 months and those who had tried to quit in the past were more likely to be ready to try again. Homeless smokers were eager to try nicotine replacement therapy and expressed the need for social support to assist with the quitting process. Homeless respondents who recognized that assistance to quit was available reported significantly higher levels of self-efficacy to quit. In a study comparing inner-city homeless smokers to nonhomeless smokers, Butler and others (2002) observed that homeless smokers were more likely to be white, consume more cigarettes per day, start at a younger age, and have a longer history of smoking. Both groups recognized the risk of smoking but nonhomeless smokers were more likely to indicate plans for quitting, compared to the homeless. Very little research has been conducted to better understand persistent use and quitting patterns in this group.

Okuyemi and others (2006) have studied smoking attitudes, behaviors, psychosocial and environmental influences, and barriers to and interest in quitting, using focus group methods. The sample was recruited from homeless facilities and consisted primarily of African Americans (59%), males (69%) who were, on average, 41 years old and smoked 18 cigarettes per day. Findings from these groups indicated that most wanted to quit smoking but barriers prevented that from happening. The majority (76%) reported they planned to quit in the next 6 months. Unfortunately, the social norms and acceptance of smoking in homeless shelters were major deterrents to quitting. Not surprisingly, the stress of living in a shelter and lacking permanent housing, as well as the boredom experienced, served to promote persistent tobacco use. Other relevant factors included excessive alcohol consumption and illicit drug use. Participants were interested in pharmacotherapy during tobacco dependence treatment.

Future Research

From these reports, it is evident that treating homeless smokers presents significant challenges. Regardless, the barriers to cessation must be tackled among this vulnerable group who remain at high risk for tobacco-attributable diseases. It is critical that resources be made available to address tobacco control among the homeless. The lack of attention to treatment trials among the homeless is disappointing. The tobacco industry has clearly recognized the homeless market, as evidenced through the industry's efforts to influence homeless shelters and advocacy groups (Apollonio & Malone, 2005). Well-designed clinical trials that determine how best to treat homeless smokers are long overdue. While there have been some important contributions to this literature by nurse researchers thus far, additional nurse-led research teams are needed to contribute to the literature of smoking behavior in low-income populations.

IMMIGRANT POPULATIONS

The demographics of the United States are evolving, with immigrants and minorities becoming increasingly predominant groups. The U.S. Census Bureau estimates that by the year 2050, nearly half the U.S. population will be made up of ethnic minorities. Ethnic identity, both in individuals viewing themselves as belonging to a certain group and society categorizing them into that group, may help to create a unique cultural milieu around health behaviors such as tobacco use. Studies regarding smoking in first generation immigrants from areas with high smoking prevalence such as Southeast Asia (Jenkins et al., 1997; Wewers et al., 2000) have identified that their smoking rates in the United States continue to be similar to those of the native country. These rates have continued to be observed after a number of years postimmigration in some groups, such as in a nurse-led study of first generation Southeast Asian immigrants where smoking rates were similar to the native country among men who were in the United States an average of 7 years (Wewers et al., 1995). Cultural identification is an important influence on beliefs, habits, and values, which is known to impact health behaviors. Variations between ethnic groups in smoking prevalence and gender patterns of smoking underline the influence of culture on tobacco use (CDC, 2008a).

Acculturation and Smoking

Acculturation is the result of people of different cultures coming into continuous contact, which causes changes in the culture of one or both groups (Redfield, Linton, & Herskovits, 1936). Acculturation has come to be thought of as a *process* that an individual undergoes to adapt in a different cultural context (Berry, Poortinga, Segall, & Dasen, 2002) and is usually measured on a continuum, rather than as a dichotomous outcome. It is typically defined as multidimensional, incorporating factors such as food choices, interactions, language, and media use that reflect underlying values (Berry et al., 2002; Stephenson, 2000; Unger et al., 2003).

Level of acculturation has been found to be associated with smoking behavior in a number of studies with immigrants in the United States. Most results have shown that when acculturation level is higher toward the dominant culture, smoking behavior becomes more like the adopted U.S. culture. Studies among Asian immigrant groups, whose native countries have higher smoking prevalence among men and lower prevalence among women than in the United States, have upheld this trend. For example, higher linguistic acculturation was found to be associated with decreased smoking in Chinese American men (Fu, Ma, Tu, Siu, & Metlay, 2003) and Filipino American men (Maxwell, Garcia, & Berman, 2007).

Likewise, a survey of Korean Americans (n = 356) showed that higher acculturation to dominant U.S. culture was associated with more smoking in women and less smoking in men compared with those with lower acculturation levels (Lee, Sobal, & Frongillo, 2000). Investigations among Hispanic/Latino immigrants have shown similar patterns. A study of smoking behavior among Latino men and women in the United States (n = 8,882) found that high acculturation level was associated with more smoking in females and less smoking in males compared to the native country (Perez-Stable et al., 2001).

Therefore, in general, as acculturation level is higher toward the dominant culture, smoking behavior becomes more like the adopted U.S. culture. So, as immigrant women become more acculturated to American culture, their smoking rates have been shown to increase. A survey of Ethiopian immigrants in Toronto revealed that twice as many women reported initiating smoking since migration and a significantly higher proportion of males reported being former smokers than females (Hyman, Fenta, & Noh, 2008). Nurse researchers conducting a meta-analysis of studies among Asian Americans found that acculturated men were 53% less likely to smoke, while acculturated women were 5 times more likely to smoke (95% CI, 2.8–10.1; Choi, Rankin, Stewart, & Oka, 2008). These studies suggest that research examining more acculturated women among immigrant populations is warranted.

Prevalence and Challenges

There are likely many factors involved in smoking rates among immigrants. Rates in an ethnic group may vary widely according to their location, as found when comparing Chinese Americans in Chicago and California. There was significantly less smoking among those in California, where antismoking laws were stronger at the time (Yu, Chen, Kim, & Abdulrahim, 2002). In addition, the association between acculturation and smoking is not necessarily linear. A study among Mexican Americans in California (n = 767) did not show a linear increase with smoking prevalence, rather, those with a moderate level of acculturation were the most at risk for smoking (Wolff & Portis, 1996). Misclassification or misreporting of smoking status has been shown to be an issue among immigrants, such as Southeast Asians and Hispanics, with differences found between genders and acculturation levels (Everhart, Ferketich, Browning, & Wewers, 2009; Wewers et al., 1995).

Culturally Tailored Interventions

Cultural tailoring of interventions takes many forms, both superficial, such as translated content, as well as deeper changes, such as the involvement of family in collectivistic cultures. Intervention trial results with immigrant groups favor the use of some level of cultural adjustment of the standard intervention. For example, smoking cessation interventions in the native language have been shown to be more successful overall in Hispanic (Shea, Basch, Wechsler, & Lantigua, 1996; Wetter et al., 2007) and Asian groups (Shelley et al., 2008). Few interventions are adapted beyond language use. A small, randomized trial (n = 66) testing a cessation intervention for Chinese and Korean men consisting of a native language counseling session that addressed concerns such as cultural norms supporting smoking, acculturative issues, and the importance of familial support found that the intervention group had significantly higher self-efficacy and quit rates compared to controls at one-month follow-up (Fang et al., 2006). However, the effectiveness of these interventions may be influenced by level of acculturation, as Chen and others (1993) found with Asian Americans. In addition, the heterogeneity among the ethnic subgroups within racial categories underscores the need to tailor interventions with ethnic identification in mind (Chen & Tang, 2007; Perez-Stable et al., 2001). Setting can be used to increase success of interventions, such as a smoking cessation program integrated with worker health and safety training for Latino immigrants (Feldman, Christopher, Muniz, & Mejia, 2004). Furthermore, a nurse-led research team reported that cultural tailoring of recruitment and retention strategies among Chinese Americans improved enrollment and retention in a smoking cessation intervention trial (Wong et al., 2008).

Future Research

More research is needed regarding the factors that might influence efficacy in culturally tailored interventions, such as the extent of tailoring and acculturation level. Studies of interventions that incorporate deeper adaptations for immigrant groups such as specific psychosocial approaches are necessary. Research examining more acculturated women and less acculturated men among immigrant populations is also warranted. There have been some important contributions by nurse researchers in this emerging area of research. In the future, the nurse researcher perspective of more patient-centered care will be a valuable asset to further develop this research by addressing both the physical and psychosocial aspects of tobacco dependence.

SMOKING AND HIV

Adult smoking prevalence in the United States has significantly decreased over the past 40 years, with a current estimate of 19.8% (CDC, 2008a). However, smoking prevalence remains much higher for persons living with HIV. There is some disparity among smoking prevalence data estimates for this population with the estimated range being 47% to 80% (Gritz, Vidrine, Lazev, Amick, & Arduino, 2004; Mamary, Bahrs, & Martinez, 2002; Niaura et al., 2000; Tesoriero, Gieryic, Carrascal, & Lavigne, 2008). Table 13.1 includes a description of a clinical treatment trial for HIV+ smokers led by a nurse researcher (i.e., Wewers).

Little conclusive data is available to understand why smoking prevalence is elevated among persons living with HIV. Reports of higher rates of depression (Pence, Miller, Whetten, Eron, & Gaynes, 2006), patients' attempts to reduce symptoms of distress and improve overall well-being (Reynolds, Neidig, & Wewers, 2004), and the increased lack of social support (Tate, Van Den Berg, Hansen, Kochman, & Sikkema, 2006) may each relate to the increased prevalence of smoking among persons living with HIV. Additional factors that may contribute are increased alcohol and drug use (Galvan et al., 2002; Gritz et al., 2004; Lucas et al., 2006) as well as the increased prevalence (as compared to the general population) of smoking among men who have sex with men (Greenwood et al., 2005). A preliminary research study (n = 107) suggested that HIV/AIDS service providers may not take full advantage of addressing health-related needs, with 65% of HIV/AIDS service providers reported perceiving patient resistance as a barrier to providing smoking cessation services (Tesoriero et al., 2008).

Consequences of Smoking With HIV Infection

Increased risk of cancer, coronary artery disease, and pulmonary disease are just a few of the dangerous health effects of tobacco use. In combination with these health risks, HIV infection also predisposes the lungs to community-acquired and opportunistic infections (Wewers et al., 1998). When combining the ill effects of smoking with HIV infection, the HIV-infected person suffers additional poor outcomes. An accelerated form of emphysema has been shown to develop for this population of smokers as compared to non-HIV-infected persons with similar smoking history (Diaz et al., 2000). In a longitudinal study with HIV-positive persons (n = 327) with no history of AIDS-related pulmonary complications, respiratory symptoms (e.g., cough, dyspnea, and sputum production) were significantly more common than in an age- and smoking history-matched HIV-negative group. These findings suggest that HIV-positive smokers are more susceptible to respiratory symptoms prior to the onset of AIDS-related pulmonary complications (Diaz et al., 2003).

Additional health risks that are associated with smoking in HIV-positive persons include increased incidence and speed of progression to community-acquired pneumonia (Conley et al., 1996) and higher risk of bronchitis and hairy leukoplakia (Crothers et al., 2005; Moorman et al., 1999). Among HIV-positive pregnant women, smoking may increase the risk of transmission to the fetus (Burns et al.,

1996; Turner, Hauck, Fanning, & Markson, 1997). Daily tobacco use decreases the immune response to antiretroviral therapies by as much as 40% (Miguez-Burbano et al., 2003). The HIV-positive veterans who smoked had increased mortality (HR = 1.60, 95% CI, .03–3.86) and decreased quality of life (p < .001) as compared to former smokers and never smokers (Crothers et al., 2005).

Until the mid 1990s, HIV was considered a terminal illness. The advent of antiretroviral therapy (ART) and the use of highly active antiretroviral therapy (HAART) have made HIV a chronic disease that is medically managed (Patel et al., 2006). Now, the mortality rates of a person living with HIV (5 years after seroconversion) are similar to the general population (Bhaskaran et al., 2008). Thus, improving the health status and quality of life of the HIV-positive person by providing gold standard smoking cessation interventions is of great clinical importance. This area of research has been set as a high priority by the National Institutes of Health (U.S. DHHS, 2006).

Interest in Quitting

Although smoking prevalence is estimated to be high for this population of smokers, preliminary data suggests that HIV-positive patients are interested in quitting (Tesoriero et al., 2008). Among HIV-positive persons who were treated in a state-designated HIV/AIDS center (n = 1,094), two thirds (63.7%) reported they had stopped smoking for at least 1 day during the past 12 months and 74.5% indicated that they were interested in quitting. Eighty percent reported that they had been advised to quit smoking by their health care provider but only 41.2% reported assistance to quit with a recommendation or prescription for pharmacotherapy (Tesoriero et al., 2008). In an outpatient clinic setting, the majority of HIV-positive smokers reported they were currently considering quitting and were interested in both a group intervention and nicotine replacement (Mamary et al., 2002). These early research findings suggest that each clinical contact made with HIV-positive patients may be great teachable moments for smoking cessation interventions.

Tailored Smoking Cessation Interventions

A study that utilized an HIV positive ex-smoker as a peer educator for HIV-positive men who smoke (n = 15) consisting of an 8 week intervention with a nurse case manager, weekly counseling, nicotine patch and skills training found 50% of smokers were biochemically confirmed to be abstinent at 8 months as compared to 0% in the control group (Wewers, Neidig, & Kihm, 2000). The HIV-positive smokers treated at an inner-city clinic (n = 95) were randomized to receive either standard treatment (advice, self-help materials, and nicotine patch) or standard treatment plus eight counseling sessions via cell phone calls. Participants in the counseling group experienced significantly greater reductions in depression and increases in self-efficacy than those in the standard treatment group and were 3.6 times more likely (95% CI, 1.3–9.9) to be biochemically confirmed to have quit smoking as compared to the standard treatment group. Furthermore, a longer length of smoking abstinence was significantly associated with less HIV-related symptoms (p = .02; Vidrine, Arduino, & Gritz, 2007). Participants in this study were not actively seeking cessation treatment but 66.5% of those approached agreed to participate, suggesting that smokers living with HIV are willing to engage in smoking cessation attempts (Vidrine, Arduino, Lazev, & Gritz, 2006).

Barriers to Quitting Smoking

Some barriers do exist for HIV-positive persons who desire to successfully quit smoking. Illicit drug use, alcohol abuse, and comorbid psychiatric illness are known to be linked with unsuccessful quit attempts (Bing et al., 2001; Burkhalter, Springer, Chhabra, Ostroff, & Rapkin, 2005; Gritz et al., 2004). A study with low-income persons living with HIV (n = 428) found that most current smokers were more likely to use illicit drugs and perceive a lower health risk for continued smoking (Burkhalter et al., 2005). Among low income HIV/AIDS patients (n = 348), race–ethnicity, education level, age, and heavy drinking were significantly associated with smoking status (Gritz et al., 2004).

Future Research

Research that examines smoking prevalence among HIV-positive persons as well as barriers to quitting is warranted. Smokers who perceive a "greater health concern" are more likely to be intrinsically motivated to quit (Curry, Wagner, & Grothaus, 1990). Emphasizing health concerns related to smoking and identifying HIV-specific health benefits in cessation should be explored. As discussed, there is a lack of research with this population of smokers and very little has been conducted by nurse researchers. Nurse-led research teams could have an opportunity to contribute to this important gap in the literature.

CONCLUSION

Tobacco dependence research is an important topic that must continue to be examined. As the characteristics and dynamics of tobacco prevalence in the United States evolve, it is becoming evident that there are disparities among those who

TABLE 13.2 Summary of Research Needs for Reducing Tobacco Use Among Special Populations

Population	Research Needs
Socioeconomic status (SES); Medicaid	Determine the efficacy of novel treatment delivery approaches Test strategies to reduce barriers to intervention, including system and provider Test strategies to increase pharmacotherapy use for tobacco dependence among low-income smokers
Hard-core smokers (HCS)	Clarify conceptualization and defining characteristics of this group of smokers Investigate subgroups of HCS to inform the development and testing of intensive cessation strategies, focusing on specific points of access Patterns of previous quit attempts and future quit intentions of HCS
Rural	Test the efficacy of novel treatment delivery approaches
Homeless	Strategies to increase involvement in treatment trials Expand research to better understand persistent use and quitting patterns in this group
Immigrants	Test culturally tailored interventions: expanding interventions past just language use Increase efforts to target more acculturated women, less acculturated men
HIV	Test surveillance studies to document tobacco use prevalence in HIV+ subgroups Investigate barriers to quitting Identify HIV-specific health concerns and benefits related to smoking cessation

still use tobacco. These populations will subsequently have greater incidence of tobacco-attributable diseases, thus creating further disparity in disease burden. Due to lower accrual and smaller populations, large randomized clinical trials that have multisite accrual may be the most efficient manner to examine research questions. A summary of the research needs for each population is provided in Table 13.2.

Each of the special populations discussed in this chapter present unique challenges with tobacco dependence treatment and will require careful examination before disparities will improve. Eliminating disparities has been marked as an important research agenda item as noted in *Healthy People 2010* (U.S. DHHS, 2000). As this review demonstrates, few nurse researchers are conducting research in these important areas of research. Nurse researchers are well positioned to contribute to the science of tobacco dependence treatment by combining their clinical expertise and knowledge of patient psychosocial needs to investigate patient-focused research questions in each of these special populations.

REFERENCES

Apollonio, D. E., & Malone, R. E. (2005). Marketing to the marginalised: Tobacco industry targeting of the homeless and mentally ill. *Tobacco Control, 14,* 409–415.

Appalachia Regional Commission. (2008). *Sociodemographic, health and county economic status designation in the Appalachian region—fiscal year 2008.* Washington, DC: Author.

Augustson, E., & Marcus, S. (2004). Use of the current population survey to characterize subpopulations of continued smokers: A national perspective on the "hardcore" smoker phenomenon. *Nicotine & Tobacco Research, 6*(4), 621–629.

Bell, R. A., Arcury, T. A., Chen, H., Anderson, A. M., Savoca, M. R., Kohrman, T., et al. (2009). Use of tobacco products among rural older adults: Prevalence of ever use and cumulative lifetime use. *Addictive Behaviors, 34*(8), 662–667.

Berry, J. W., Poortinga, Y. H., Segall, M. H., & Dasen, P. R. (2002). *Cross-cultural psychology: Research and applications.* Cambridge, UK: Cambridge University Press.

Bhaskaran, K., Hamouda, O., Sannes, M., Boufassa, F., Johnson, A. M., Lambert, P. C., et al. (2008). Changes in the risk of death after HIV seroconversion compared with mortality in the general population. *The Journal of the American Medical Association, 300*(1), 51–59.

Bing, E. G., Burnam, M. A., Longshore, D., Fleishman, J. A., Sherbourne, C. D., London, A. S., et al. (2001). Psychiatric disorders and drug use among human immunodeficiency virus-infected adults in the United States. *Archives of General Psychiatry, 58*(8), 721–728.

Bobak, M., Jarvis, M. J., Skodova, Z., & Marmot, M. (2000). Smoke intake among smokers is higher in lower socioeconomic groups. *Tobacco Control, 9*(3), 310–312.

Browning, K. K., Ferketich, A. K., Salsberry, P. J., & Wewers, M. E. (2008). Socioeconomic disparity in provider-delivered assistance to quit smoking. *Nicotine & Tobacco Research, 10*(1), 55–61.

Brownson, R.C., Jackson-Thompson, J., Wilkerson, J.C., Davis, J.R., Owens, N.W., & Fisher, E.B., Jr. (1992). Demographic and socioeconomic differences in beliefs about the health effects of smoking. *American Journal of Public Health, 82*(1), 99–103.

Burkhalter, J.E., Springer, C.M., Chhabra, R., Ostroff, J.S., & Rapkin, B.D. (2005). Tobacco use and readiness to quit smoking in low-income HIV-infected persons. *Nicotine & Tobacco Research, 7*(4), 511–522.

Burns, D.N., Hillman, D., Neaton, J.D., Sherer, R., Mitchell, T., Capps, L., et al. (1996). Cigarette smoking, bacterial pneumonia, and other clinical outcomes in HIV-1 infection. Terry Beirn community programs for clinical research on AIDS. *Journal of Acquired Immune Deficiency Syndromes and Human Retrovirology, 13*(4), 374–383.

Butler, J., Okuyemi, K.S., Jean, S., Nazir, N., Ahluwalia, J.S., & Resnicow, K. (2002). Smoking characteristics of a homeless population. *Substance Abuse, 23*(4), 223–231.

Centers for Disease Control and Prevention. (1997). Health risk factor surveys of commercial plan- and medicaid-enrolled members of health-maintenance organizations—Michigan, 1995. *Morbidity and Mortality Weekly Report, 46*(39), 923–926.

Centers for Disease Control and Prevention. (2006). State Medicaid coverage for tobacco-dependence treatments: United States, 2005. *Morbidity and Mortality Weekly Report, 55*, 1194–1197.

Centers for Disease Control and Prevention. (2008a). Cigarette smoking among adults: United States, 2007. *Morbidity and Mortality Weekly Report, 57*(45), 1221–1226.

Centers for Disease Control and Prevention. (2008b). Smoking-attributable mortality, years of potential life lost, and productivity losses: United States, 2000–2004. *Morbidity and Mortality Weekly Report, 57*(45), 1226–1229.

Chen, M.S., & Tang, H. (2007). Review of smoking cessation research among Asian Americans: The state of the research. *Nicotine & Tobacco Research, 9*(Suppl. 3), 485–493.

Chen, M.S., Jr., Guthrie, R., Moeschberger, M., Wewers, M.E., Anderson, J., Kuun, P., et al. (1993). Lessons learned and baseline data from initiating smoking cessation research with southeast Asian adults. *Asian American and Pacific Islander Journal of Health, 1*(2), 194–214.

Choi, S., Rankin, S., Stewart, A., & Oka, R. (2008). Effects of acculturation on smoking behavior in Asian Americans: A meta-analysis. *The Journal of Cardiovascular Nursing, 23*(1), 67–73.

Conley, L.J., Bush, T.J., Buchbinder, S.P., Penley, K.A., Judson, F.N., & Holmberg, S.D. (1996). The association between cigarette smoking and selected HIV-related medical conditions. *AIDS* (London, England), *10*(10), 1121–1126.

Connor, S.E., Cook, R.L., Herbert, M.I., Neal, S.M., & Williams, J.T. (2002). Smoking cessation in a homeless population: There is a will, but is there a way? *Journal of General Internal Medicine, 17*(5), 369–372.

Cox, L.S., Cupertino, A.P., Mussulman, L.M., Nazir, N., Greiner, K.A., Mahnken, J.D., et al. (2008). Design and baseline characteristics from the KAN-QUIT disease management intervention for rural smokers in primary care. *Preventive Medicine, 47*(2), 200–205.

Crothers, K., Griffith, T.A., McGinnis, K.A., Rodriguez-Barradas, M.C., Leaf, D.A., Weissman, S., et al. (2005). The impact of cigarette smoking on mortality, quality of life, and comorbid illness among HIV-positive veterans. *Journal of General Internal Medicine, 20*(12), 1142–1145.

Cummings, K. M., Hyland, A., Giovino, G. A., Hastrup, J. L., Bauer, J. E., & Bansal, M. A. (2004). Are smokers adequately informed about the health risks of smoking and medicinal nicotine? *Nicotine & Tobacco Research, 6*(Suppl. 3), S333–S340.

Cupertino, A. P., Mahnken, J. D., Richter, K., Cox, L. S., Casey, G., Resnicow, K., et al. (2007). Long-term engagement in smoking cessation counseling among rural smokers. *Journal of Health Care for the Poor and Underserved, 18*(4 Suppl.), 39–51.

Cupertino, P. A., Richter, K. P., Cox, L. S., Nazir, N., Greiner, A. K., Ahluwalia, J. S., et al. (2008). Smoking cessation pharmacotherapy preferences in rural primary care. *Nicotine & Tobacco Research, 10*(2), 301–307.

Curry, S., Wagner, E. H., & Grothaus, L. C. (1990). Intrinsic and extrinsic motivation for smoking cessation. *Journal of Consulting and Clinical Psychology, 58*(3), 310–316.

Diaz, P. T., King, M. A., Pacht, E. R., Wewers, M. D., Gadek, J. E., Nagaraja, H. N., et al. (2000). Increased susceptibility to pulmonary emphysema among HIV-seropositive smokers. *Annals of Internal Medicine, 132,* 369–372.

Diaz, P. T., Wewers, M. D., Pacht, E., Drake, J., Nagaraja, H. N., & Clanton, T. L. (2003). Respiratory symptoms among HIV-seropositive individuals. *Chest, 123*(6), 1977–1982.

Doescher, M. P., Jackson, E. J., Jerant, A., & Hart, G. L. (2006). Prevalence and trends in smoking: A national rural study. *Journal of Rural Health, 22,* 112–118.

Elnicki, D. M., Morris, D. K., & Shockcor, W. T. (1995). Patient-perceived barriers to preventive health care among indigent, rural Appalachian patients. *Archives of Internal Medicine, 155*(4), 421–424.

Emery, S., Gilpin, E. A., Ake, C., Farkas, A. J., & Pierce, J. P. (2000). Characterizing and identifying "hard-core" smokers: Implications for further reducing smoking prevalence. *American Journal of Public Health, 90*(3), 387–394.

Everhart, J., Ferketich, A. K., Browning, K., & Wewers, M. E. (2009). Acculturation and misclassification of tobacco use status among Hispanic men and women in the United States. *Nicotine & Tobacco Research, 11*(3), 240–247.

Fang, C. Y., Ma, G. X., Miller, S. M., Tan, Y., Su, X., & Shive, S. (2006). A brief smoking cessation intervention for Chinese and Korean American smokers. *Preventive Medicine, 43,* 321–324.

Feldman, R. H., Christopher, B. W., Muniz, A. G., & Mejia, D. A. (2004). Integrating smoking cessation into worker training among Latino immigrant workers: Development of a program. *New Solutions, 14*(4), 349–355.

Fernandez, E., Schiaffino, A., Borrell, C., Benach, J., Ariza, C., Ramon, J. M., et al. (2006). Social class, education, and smoking cessation: Long-term follow-up of patients treated at a smoking cessation unit. *Nicotine & Tobacco Research, 8*(1), 29–36.

Fiore, M. C., Jaén, C. R., Baker, T. B., Bailey, W. C., Benowitz, N. L., Curry, S. J., et al. (2008). *Treating tobacco use and dependence: 2008 update. Clinical practice guideline.* Rockville, MD: U.S. Department of Health and Human Services. Public Health Service.

Fu, S. S., Ma, G. X., Tu, X. M., Siu, P. T., & Metlay, J. P. (2003). Cigarette smoking among Chinese Americans and the influence of linguistic acculturation. *Nicotine & Tobacco Research, 5*(6), 803–811.

Galvan, F. H., Bing, E. G., Fleishman, J. A., London, A. S., Caetano, R., Burnam, M. A., et al. (2002). The prevalence of alcohol consumption and heavy drinking among people with HIV in the United States: Results from the HIV cost and services utilization study. *Journal of Studies on Alcohol, 63*(2), 179–186.

Greenwood, G. L., Paul, J. P., Pollack, L. M., Binson, D., Catania, J. A., Chang, J., et al. (2005). Tobacco use and cessation among a household-based sample of US urban men who have sex with men. *American Journal of Public Health, 95*(1), 145–151.

Gritz, E. R., Vidrine, D. J., Lazev, A. B., Amick, B. C., 3rd, & Arduino, R. C. (2004). Smoking behavior in a low-income multiethnic HIV/AIDS population. *Nicotine & Tobacco Research, 6*(1), 71–77.

Hahn, E. J., Rayens, M. K., Warnick, T. A., Chirila, C., Rasnake, R. T., Paul, T. P., et al. (2005). A controlled trial of a quit and win contest. *American Journal of Health Promotion, 20*(2), 117–126.

Healton, C., & Nelson, K. (2004). Reversal of misfortune: Viewing tobacco as a social justice issue. *American Journal of Public Health, 94*(2), 186–191.

Hutcheson, T. D., Greiner, K. A., Ellerbeck, E. F., Jeffries, S. K., Mussulman, L. M., & Casey, G. N. (2008). Understanding smoking cessation in rural communities. *The Journal of Rural Health, 24*(2), 116–124.

Hyman, I., Fenta, H., & Noh, S. (2008). Gender and the smoking behaviour of Ethiopian immigrants in Toronto. *Chronic Diseases in Canada, 28*(4), 121–127.

Jaen, C. R., Cummings, K. M., Shah, D., & Aungst, W. (1997). Patterns of use of a free nicotine patch program for Medicaid and uninsured patients. *Journal of the National Medical Association, 89*(5), 325–328.

Jarvis, M. J., & Wardle, J. (1999). Social patterning of the individual health behaviours: The case of cigarette smoking. In M. Marmot, & R. G. Wilkinson (Eds.), *Social Determinants of Health* (pp. 240–255). Oxford: Oxford University Press.

Jarvis, M. J., Wardle, J., Waller, J., & Owen, L. (2003). Prevalence of hardcore smoking in England, and associated attitudes and beliefs: Cross sectional study. *British Medical Journal* (Clinical Research Ed.), *326*(7398), 1061.

Jenkins, C. N., McPhee, S. J., Le, A., Pham, G. Q., Ha, N. T., & Stewart, S. (1997). The effectiveness of a media-led intervention to reduce smoking among Vietnamese-American men. *American Journal of Public Health, 87*(6), 1031–1034.

Lando, H. A., Pirie, P. L., Roski, J., McGovern, P. G., & Schmid, L. A. (1996). Promoting abstinence among relapsed chronic smokers: The effect of telephone support. *American Journal of Public Health, 86*(12), 1786–1790.

Lee, S. K., Sobal, J., & Frongillo, E. A. (2000). Acculturation and health in Korean Americans. *Social Science & Medicine, 51*, 159–173.

Lucas, G. M., Griswold, M., Gebo, K. A., Keruly, J., Chaisson, R. E., & Moore, R. D. (2006). Illicit drug use and HIV-1 disease progression: A longitudinal study in the era of highly active antiretroviral therapy. *American Journal of Epidemiology, 163*(5), 412–420.

MacIntosh, H., & Coleman, T. (2006). Characteristics and prevalence of hardcore smokers attending UK general practitioners. *BMC Family Practice, 7*(24). Retrieved February 5, 2009, from http://www.biomedcentral.com/1471-2296/7/24

Mamary, E. M., Bahrs, D., & Martinez, S. (2002). Cigarette smoking and the desire to quit among individuals living with HIV. *AIDS Patient Care and STDs, 16*(1), 39–42.

Marmot, M. (2001). Inequalities in health. *New England Journal of Medicine, 345*(2), 134–136.

Maxwell, A. E., Garcia, G. M., & Berman, B. A. (2007). Understanding tobacco use among Filipino American men. *Nicotine & Tobacco Research, 9*(7), 769–776.

Miguez-Burbano, M. J., Burbano, X., Ashkin, D., Pitchenik, A., Allan, R., Pineda, L., et al. (2003). Impact of tobacco use on the development of opportunistic respiratory infections in HIV seropositive patients on antiretroviral therapy. *Addiction Biology*, 8(1), 39–43.

Moorman, A. C., Holmberg, S. D., Marlowe, S. I., Von Bargen, J. C., Yangco, B. G., Palella, F. J., et al. (1999). Changing conditions and treatments in a dynamic cohort of ambulatory HIV patients: The HIV outpatient study (HOPS). *Annals of Epidemiology*, 9(6), 349–357.

Murphy, J. M., Mahoney, M. C., Cummings, K. M., Hyland, A. J., & Lawvere, S. (2005). A randomized trial to promote pharmacotherapy use and smoking cessation in a Medicaid population (United States). *Cancer Causes & Control*, 16(4), 373–382.

Murphy, J. M., Mahoney, M. C., Hyland, A. J., Higbee, C., & Cummings, K. M. (2005). Disparity in the use of smoking cessation pharmacotherapy among Medicaid and general population smokers. *Journal of Public Health Management and Practice*, 11(4), 341–345.

Nelson, D. E., Mowery, P., Tomar, S., Marcus, S., Giovino, G., & Zhao, L. (2006). Smokeless tobacco use among adults and adolescents in the United States. *American Journal of Public Health*, 96, 897–905.

Niaura, R., Shadel, W. G., Morrow, K., Tashima, K., Flanigan, T., & Abrams, D. B. (2000). Human immunodeficiency virus infection, AIDS, and smoking cessation: The time is now. *Clinical Infectious Diseases*, 31(3), 808–812.

Niederdeppe, J., Kuang, X., Crock, B., & Skelton, A. (2008). Media campaigns to promote smoking cessation among socioeconomically disadvantaged populations: What do we know, what do we need to learn, and what should we do now? *Social Science & Medicine*, 67(9), 1343–1355.

Northridge, M. E., Vallone, D., Xiao, H., Green, M., Weikle Blackwood, J., Kemper, S. E., et al. (2008). The importance of location for tobacco cessation: Rural-urban disparities in quit success in underserved West Virginia counties. *The Journal of Rural Health*, 24(2), 106–115.

Okuyemi, K. S., Caldwell, A. R., Thomas, J. L., Born, W., Richter, K. P., Nollen, N., et al. (2006). Homelessness and smoking cessation: Insights from focus groups. *Nicotine & Tobacco Research*, 8(2), 287–296.

Patel, N., Talwar, A., Reichert, V. C., Brady, T., Jain, M., & Kaplan, M. H. (2006). Tobacco and HIV. *Clinics in Occupational and Environmental Medicine*, 5(1), 193–207.

Pence, B. W., Miller, W. C., Whetten, K., Eron, J. J., & Gaynes, B. N. (2006). Prevalence of DSM-IV-defined mood, anxiety, and substance use disorders in an HIV clinic in the southeastern United States. *Journal of Acquired Immune Deficiency Syndromes*, 42(3), 298–306.

Perez-Stable, E. J., Ramirez, A., Villareal, R., Talavera, G. A., Trapido, E., Suarez, L., et al. (2001). Cigarette smoking behavior among US Latino men and women from different countries of origin. *American Journal of Public Health*, 91(9), 1424–1430.

Raitz, K. B., & Ulack, R. (1991). *Regional definitions in Appalachia: Social context past and present* (pp. 10–26). Dubuque, IA: Kendall/Hunt Publishing.

Redfield, R., Linton, R., & Herskovits, M. J. (1936). Memorandum on the study of acculturation. *American Anthropologist*, 38, 149–152.

Reynolds, N. R., Neidig, J. L., & Wewers, M. E. (2004). Illness representation and smoking behavior: A focus group study of HIV-positive men. *Journal of Nurses in AIDS Care*, 15(4), 37–47.

Shea, S., Basch, C. E., Wechsler, H., & Lantigua, R. (1996). The Washington Heights-Inwood healthy heart program: A 6-year report from a disadvantaged urban setting. *American Journal of Public Health*, 86(2), 166–171.

Shelley, D., Fahs, M., Yerneni, R., Das, D., Nguyen, N., Hung, D., et al. (2008). Effectiveness of tobacco control among Chinese Americans: A comparative analysis of policy approaches versus community-based programs. *Preventive Medicine*, 47(5), 530–536.

Sorensen, G., Barbeau, E., Hunt, M. K., & Emmons, K. (2004). Reducing social disparities in tobacco use: A social-contextual model for reducing tobacco use among blue-collar workers. *American Journal of Public Health*, 94(2), 230–239.

Stephenson, M. (2000). Development and validation of the Stephenson multigroup acculturation scale (SMAS). *Psychological Assessment*, 12(1), 77–88.

Tate, D. C., Van Den Berg, J. J., Hansen, N. B., Kochman, A., & Sikkema, K. J. (2006). Race, social support, and coping strategies among HIV-positive gay and bisexual men. *Culture, Health & Sexuality*, 8(3), 235–249.

Tesoriero, J. M., Gieryic, S. M., Carrascal, A., & Lavigne, H. E. (2008). Smoking among HIV positive New Yorkers: Prevalence, frequency, and opportunities for cessation. *AIDS and Behavior*. doi: 10.1007/s10461-008-9449-2

Tønneson, P., Mikkelsen, K., Nørregaard, J., & Jørgenson, S. (1996). Recycling of hardcore smokers with nicotine nasal spray. *European Respiratory Journal*, 9, 1619–1623.

Turner, B. J., Hauck, W. W., Fanning, T. R., & Markson, L. E. (1997). Cigarette smoking and maternal-child HIV transmission. *Journal of Acquired Immune Deficiency Syndromes and Human Retrovirology*, 14(4), 327–337.

Unger, J. B., Cruz, T., Shakib, S., Mock, J., Shields, A., Baezconde-Garbanati, L., et al. (2003). Exploring the cultural context of tobacco use: A transdisciplinary framework. *Nicotine & Tobacco Research*, 5(Suppl. 1), S101–S117.

U.S. Department of Health and Human Services. (1988). *The health consequences of smoking, nicotine addiction: A report of the Surgeon General*. Rockville, MD: U.S. Department of Health and Human Services.

U.S. Department of Health and Human Services. (2000). *Healthy people 2010: Understanding and improving health* (2nd ed.). Washington, DC: U.S. Government Printing Office.

U.S. Department of Health and Human Services. (1989). Reducing the health consequences of smoking: 25 years of progress. A report of the Surgeon General. Rockville, MD: Public Health Service, Centers for Disease Control, Office on Smoking and Health, (DHHS publication No. (CDC) 89-8411)

U.S. Department of Health and Human Services. (2006). *Tobacco use: Prevention, cessation and control*. Washington DC: U.S. Department of Health and Human Services.

Vidrine, D. J., Arduino, R. C., & Gritz, E. R. (2007). The effects of smoking abstinence on symptom burden and quality of life among persons living with HIV/AIDS. *AIDS Patient Care and STDs*, 21(9), 659–666.

Vidrine, D. J., Arduino, R. C., Lazev, A. B., & Gritz, E. R. (2006). A randomized trial of a proactive cellular telephone intervention for smokers living with HIV/AIDS. *AIDS* (London, England), *20*(2), 253–260.

Wadland, W. C., Soffelmayr, B., & Ives, K. (2001). Enhancing smoking cessation of low-income smokers in managed care. *The Journal of Family Practice*, *50*(2), 138–144.

Wetter, D. W., Mazas, C., Daza, P., Nguyen, L., Fouladi, R. T., Li, Y., et al. (2007). Reaching and treating Spanish-speaking smokers through the national cancer institute's cancer information service. A randomized controlled trial. *Cancer*, *109*(2 Suppl.), 406–413.

Wewers, M. D., Diaz, P. T., Wewers, M. E., Lowe, M. P., Nagaraja, H. N., & Clanton, T. L. (1998). Cigarette smoking in HIV infection induces a suppressive inflammatory environment in the lung. *American Journal of Respiratory & Critical Care Medicine*, *158*(5 Pt. 1), 1543–1549.

Wewers, M. E., Ahijevych, K. L., Dhatt, R. K., Guthrie, R. M., Kuun, P., Mitchell, L., et al. (2000). Cotinine levels in Southeast Asian smokers. *Nicotine & Tobacco Research*, *2*(1), 85–91.

Wewers, M. E., Dhatt, R. K., Moeschberger, M. L., Guthrie, R. M., Kuun, P., & Chen, M. S. (1995). Misclassification of smoking status among Southeast Asian adult immigrants. *Journal of Respiratory & Critical Care Medicine*, *152*(6 Pt. 1), 1917–1921.

Wewers, M. E., Neidig, J. L., & Kihm, K. E. (2000). The feasibility of a nurse-managed, peer-led tobacco cessation intervention among HIV-positive smokers. *Journal of the Association of Nurses in AIDS Care*, *11*(6), 37–44.

Wolff, C. B., & Portis, M. (1996). Smoking, acculturation, and pregnancy outcome among Mexican Americans. *Health Care for Women International*, *17*(6), 563–573.

Wong, C. C., Tsoh, J. Y., Tong, E. K., Hom, F. B., Cooper, B., & Chow, E. A. (2008). The Chinese community smoking cessation project: A community sensitive intervention trial. *Journal of Community Health*, *33*(6), 363–373.

Yu, E. S., Chen, E. H., Kim, K. K., & Abdulrahim, S. (2002). Smoking among Chinese Americans: Behavior, knowledge, and beliefs. *American Journal of Public Health*, *92*(6), 1007–1012.

PART III

Tobacco Control
Nursing Research:
Systems, Community,
and Policy Approaches

Chapter 14

Systems Approaches to Tobacco Dependence Treatment

Anna M. McDaniel, Renee M. Stratton, and Maria Britain

ABSTRACT

Nurses have been at the forefront of initiatives to improve patient outcomes through systems change. Nursing research addressing systems approaches to treatment of tobacco dependence has demonstrated increased implementation of evidence-based practice guidelines. Existing health system research conducted by nurse scientists has focused on four strategies: tobacco use identification systems, education and training of nursing staff to deliver tobacco intervention, dedicated staff for tobacco dependence treatment in both acute and primary care settings, and institutional policies to support tobacco intervention. Nursing involvement in multidisciplinary health services research focusing on tobacco treatment has lagged behind advances in clinical nursing research of individual-focused smoking cessation interventions. Health information technology shows promise as part of an integrated approach to systems changes to support tobacco intervention, particularly in light of the current national emphasis on adoption and meaningful use of electronic health records. Future directions for translational research present unprecedented opportunity for nurse scientists to respond to the call for policy and systems changes to support tobacco treatment.

DOI: 10.1891/0739-6686.27.345

Keywords: health services research; systems change; health information technology; translational research

Nicotine addiction is a "chronic, relapsing condition" (Fiore et al., 2008) that leads to over 400,000 premature deaths each year (Centers for Disease Control and Prevention [CDC], 2009). The human and financial costs associated with tobacco use are staggering. The average smoking-attributable expenditures for health care in the United States total $96 billion annually, with an additional $97 billion in lost productivity due to smoking-related morbidity (CDC, 2008).

Tobacco use and concomitant nicotine addiction is prototypical of the complex interaction between cognitive, behavioral, biological, and social determinants of health (Warner, 2006). It should come as no surprise that to effectively combat the tobacco epidemic, a multidimensional, comprehensive approach is required (Bonnie, Stratton, & Wallace, 2007). Fiore and colleagues (2008) have called for a systematic approach to integrating effective, evidence-based tobacco interventions into existing health care delivery systems. Such systems integration has been identified as the "single most critical missing ingredient needed to maximize the as yet unrealized potential to significantly increase population cessation rates" (Abrams, 2007, p. 376). Unfortunately, traditional health care delivery system structures currently in place lack the capacity for widespread implementation of recommended tobacco cessation treatment due to technological concerns, lack of financial incentives, and the organizational culture of the system itself (Moolchan et al., 2007). Though these barriers may be well founded in the realities of the current system, the year 2009 will mark the beginning of unprecedented change as a result of long called-for health care reform. As the largest group of health care professionals (Sarna & Bialous, 2006; Sarna & Lillington, 2002), nurses will play an important leadership role in health care reform. Nowhere is this leadership more critical than in creating systems that ensure the adoption and implementation of evidence-based treatment of tobacco dependence across all health care settings (Bruce, 2004). The purpose of this chapter is to discuss the results of nursing research addressing systems approaches to treatment of tobacco dependence.

NURSING RESEARCH ON SYSTEM APPROACHES

Although considerable progress in the treatment of tobacco dependence has been noted (Fiore et al., 2008), universal delivery of effective intervention falls short of national goals (Moolchan et al., 2007; National Cancer Institute [NCI], 2007). For example, an estimated 70%–80% of smokers have contact with at least one health care professional, including nurses, yet in any year as few as 60% reported being advised to quit smoking (NCI, 2007). This figure represents a significant "missed opportunity" for reducing smoking prevalence in the U.S. population. A systematic approach to tobacco dependence identifies smokers within the care delivery setting and provides appropriate, effective intervention to *every* smoker (Fiore et al., 2008). The approach must include strategies to overcome the barriers to implementing universal tobacco treatment that are integrated into every level of a system (i.e., the individual smoker or clinician, the clinical microsystem or practice unit, the health care organization, and state or national policy-making bodies). The most recent U.S. PHS Clinical Practice Guideline identifies system-level, evidence-based strategies for delivery of tobacco dependence treatment based on the "5 A's" model: *Ask about tobacco use, Advise to quit, Assess willingness to quit, Assist in quitting process*, and *Arrange follow-up* (Fiore et al., 2008). In this chapter, we will review existing health system research conducted by nurse scientists that increase the likelihood that the 5 A's will be implemented.

METHODS

We conducted a search of the research literature using the Ovid and PubMed platforms. Using Ovid, we searched the CINAHL Plus with Full Text, Health Business FullTEXT, Health Source: Nursing/Academic Edition, and MEDLINE databases. Advanced search techniques that employed controlled terms mapping to Mesh Subject Headings (nursing research, systems change, health services research, nursing, organization innovation, smoking cessation, and tobacco), were used to identify relevant articles. Search results were further distilled by using a Boolean operator (and) and limiting the results to full text, English language, Ovid full text available, and review articles. Duplicate articles were removed. Article abstracts were reviewed for relevance and type of publication (i.e., research). In PubMed we employed a basic search strategy on the terms, electronic medical records, and nursing. The related articles feature was used to broaden the search to find related articles. Candidate articles were retrieved in full text format and reviewed by the authors for inclusion if meeting one of the following criteria: nurse/nurse scientist authorship or if nurses were the focus of the system change under study. To expand the search for additional articles that may have been omitted from general indexing terms, we also searched on specific nurse authors' names and by using the citing authors utility in Ovid to retrieve publications that cited relevant literature. No date limits were placed on the search.

RESULTS

We identified 38 articles that met our inclusion criteria. They have been organized under four categories, based on the U.S. PHS Guideline (Fiore et al.,

2008): tobacco use identification systems, education and training of nursing staff to deliver tobacco intervention, dedicated staff for tobacco dependence treatment, and institutional policies to support tobacco intervention are discussed below.

Tobacco User Identification Systems

Tobacco Use Vital Signs in the Acute Care Setting

The success of the 5 A's approach depends on accurately identifying all tobacco users. Thus, assessing tobacco status should be seen as a primary responsibility for nurses within their role in health promotion. To systematically identify all tobacco users requires a change in the workflow of a care delivery setting. Fiore and colleagues (2008) recommend screening every patient at each health care encounter by adding a question about tobacco use to the vital signs form. Evidence from clinical trials of such tobacco identification systems increases assessment and documentation of smoking status in the primary care setting (Ahluwalia, Gibson, Kenney, Wallace, & Resnicow, 1999; Fiore et al., 1995) and significantly increases the odds of physician intervention with patients who smoke (Fiore et al., 2008). McDaniel, Kristeller, and Hudson (1999) tested the effect of chart reminders on nurses' assessment of smoking status (i.e., ever smoker, current smoker, smoked within last 12 months, or smoked within last 2 months) among patients admitted to cardiovascular services in a tertiary care center. The study used an A_1-B-A_2 reversal design with a posted memo reminding nurses to assess smoking status and refer smokers for counseling (Condition A) versus a paper form with the same message placed in the front of each patient's chart (Condition B). The presence of the chart reminder significantly increased the identification and referral of smokers for tobacco intervention.

Even a simple "disruptive technology" (Bower & Christensen, 1995) like a chart sticker can trigger important change in clinical practice. Health information technology has become increasingly common in the health care system and is anticipated to reach an all but ubiquitous level of penetration with the signing of the American Recovery and Reinvestment Act (ARRA) of 2009 (Mandl & Kohane, 2009). The power of using health information technology to support tobacco dependence treatment has been recognized by several nurse scientists. Swallow and Dykes (2004) reported the results of the successful integration of a cessation program into a hospital's daily practice through the electronic health record (EHR). A system-wide tobacco intervention program was implemented where: (a) nurses assess tobacco use for each patient on admission and document smoking status in the EHR; (b) automated prompts for tobacco cessation intervention are delivered to nurses assigned to patients identified as smokers; and (c) at discharge the nurse documents tobacco treatment and outcomes in the EHR for follow-up with the patient's primary care provider. An evaluation of the automated system revealed a 15% increase in smoking cessation intervention by nurses. A year prior to implementation of the system, 85% of nurses were providing recommended advice and counseling; after implementation (in 2003), 100% of the nurses were doing so (Swallow & Dykes, 2004).

Tobacco User Identification Systems in Ambulatory Care

McDaniel, Benson, Roesener, and Martindale (2005) developed a clinical decision support system for identifying tobacco users and delivering brief tobacco dependence intervention in a primary care setting. The tobacco user identification system was designed to obtain smoking status information using interactive voice response technology (i.e., an automated telephone system). All patients scheduled for a clinic visit were called prior to their appointment and screened for current smoking status, readiness to quit smoking, and level of tobacco dependence. The tobacco use data were uploaded into the EHR to generate computer reminders to primary care physicians for tobacco cessation intervention. The content of the reminders was based on current national guidelines (Fiore et al., 2000) and tailored to the individual patient based on the self-reported data previously obtained (McDaniel, Benson, Roesener, & Martindale, 2005). In the pilot test of the system, 39% of the patients responding to the automated calling system reported current smoking (McDaniel, Benson, et al., 2005), which is higher than expected even for this low-income population. However, fewer than half (48.3%) of smokers reported that their providers discussed smoking cessation during the clinic visit. These results suggest that automated systems for tobacco use screening may be useful for identifying smokers in primary care, but a computer generated reminder alone may not be enough to change provider behavior in the demanding clinic environment.

Nurses are frequently the initial point of contact with patients in any given setting along the health care continuum. Nurse scientists have recommended implementing a tobacco user identification system consistent with national guidelines in various community-based settings. Albrecht and colleagues (2004) conducted a comprehensive literature review to develop the Association of Women's Health, Obstetric and Neonatal Nurse's (AWHONN) research-based practice project, Setting Universal Cessation Counseling, Education and Screening Standards (SUCCESS): Nursing Care of Pregnant Women Who Smoke. A protocol for assessing tobacco use in pregnant women was modified from existing evidence to incorporate the unique aspects of prenatal smoking cessation intervention. An ongoing study to evaluate the impact of the SUCCESS project in everyday clinical practice is underway among volunteers from the AWHONN membership.

Identifying Parental Smoking in the Pediatric
Setting to Address Secondhand Smoke

A multidisciplinary team, including physicians, nurses, and public health experts, used a similar strategy to develop evidence-based tobacco cessation interventions for the child health care setting (Winickoff et al., 2005). Pediatricians and child health care providers face barriers to addressing parental smoking, such as resistance to offering adult care, lack of time to offer cessation education during a clinic visit, and reimbursement issues. To this end, Winickoff and colleagues (2005) adapted the 5 A's framework to parent population for use by child health care providers. Based on review of available research, the authors suggest that child health care providers collect tobacco use data not only about the child but also about the parent(s)/guardian(s). This information can help child health care providers determine if the child is exposed to secondhand smoke within the home, thus enabling the provider to offer recommended tobacco treatment and promote healthy behaviors within the family unit.

With almost 50,000 deaths occurring in the United States each year as a result of secondhand smoke exposure (California Environmental Protection Agency, 2005) as well as increased rates of lower respiratory illness, middle ear disease, childhood asthma, and sudden infant death syndrome (Committee on Substance Abuse, 2001), nurses can play an important role on the multidisciplinary team by collecting information about tobacco use in the home. Turner-Henson, Kohler, Lyrene, and Johnston (1999) reported a program at Children's Hospital in Birmingham, Alabama that introduced smoking status of parent(s)/guardian(s) as a vital sign in routine nursing admission assessment. Approximately 55% of children with pulmonary disease at the institution were found to be exposed to passive smoke in the household. The authors conclude that identifying the presence of smokers is a first step for addressing needed tobacco cessation intervention in the pediatric setting. Adapting the 5 A's framework for child health care providers can yield significant benefits given that for parents without a primary care physician, a pediatric encounter for their child may be the only opportunity to receive cessation advice from a provider (Winickoff et al., 2005).

Tobacco Treatment Education and Training for Nurses

Most nurses want to provide cessation education to patients who smoke (Wewers, Kidd, Armbruster, & Sarna, 2004), but do not feel like they have the required skill set (Wetta-Hall et al., 2005). The most commonly cited barriers to implementation of the 5 A's model by nurses are: lack of knowledge, limited access to resources, doubts about effectiveness of brief advice, perceived patient reluctance, and hesitation by smoking nurses to provide education (Duffy, Reeves, Hermann,

Karvonen, & Smith, 2008; Grossman, Donaldson, Belton, & Oliver, 2008; McCarty, Hennrikus, Lando, & Vessey, 2001; Sarna & Bialous, 2005).

Academic nursing programs provide opportunities for educators to provide nurses with evidence-based tools to help them overcome these barriers to tobacco treatment. The National Action Plan for Tobacco Cessation (Fiore et al., 2004) recommends training and education to "ensure that all clinicians in the United States have the knowledge, skills and support systems necessary to help their patients quit tobacco use" (p. 208). However, national surveys in undergraduate and graduate nursing programs reveal insufficient content on tobacco use and clinical cessation strategies (Heath, Andrews, Thomas, Kelley, & Friedman, 2002; Wewers et al., 2004).

One possible explanation for the inadequate attention to tobacco intervention in nursing education is the lack of awareness of current evidence-based treatment guidelines among nursing faculty. Heath and colleagues (2007) report the findings of an intervention to increase tobacco treatment knowledge and skills for teaching tobacco content among acute care nurse practitioner faculty. Designed as a "train-the-trainer" program, participants completed measures of perceived effectiveness of teaching tobacco topics at baseline and 12 months after a 2-day teaching institute. Participants were provided with standardized educational materials (e.g., teacher "toolkit") to use at their home institution. At follow-up, perceived efficacy increased significantly for all areas of tobacco content. In addition, programs devoting three or more hours of content increased from 22% to 74% at 12 months among participating schools. These results suggest that providing nurse educators with the training and tools to teach tobacco cessation intervention can have a positive impact and sustainability.

All health care organizations should provide continuing nursing education and in-service opportunities in brief cessation intervention, particularly given the lack of content on tobacco treatment in preservice education (McCarty et al., 2001). Wetta-Hall and colleagues (2005) found that nurses who had received tobacco-related continuing education within the past 12 months were more likely to provide tobacco cessation counseling than those who had not. Randomized trials of continuing education interventions aimed at health care providers have shown to be cost-effective (Pinget, Martin, Wasserfallen, Humair, & Cornuz, 2007) and lead to increased rates of treatment (Fiore et al., 2008; Lancaster & Fowler, 2000), particularly when combined with a chart reminder system (Fiore et al., 2008).

Few studies have focused on tobacco treatment educational interventions for practicing nurses. In a recent study, a 2-day, face-to-face, tobacco education program specifically for advanced practice nurses and psychiatrists working in the mental health field was tested (Williams et al., 2009). The multidisciplinary educational program produced significant increases in knowledge and positive attitudes about tobacco intervention. The study was limited by the single group design using a convenience sample and the inability to determine whether program participants actually incorporated their new knowledge into practice. In a quasi-experimental study at Veterans Affairs Medical Center, Andrews, Tingen, Waller, and Harper (2001) found that an educational intervention for primary care physicians and nurse practitioners did not have an impact on adherence to the recommended 5 A's intervention, but written feedback on individual and team performance resulted in significant increases in advising patients to quit, offering assistance in the quitting process, and arranging follow-up contact after a quit attempt. Conversely, home care nurses who received training in cognitive and behavioral smoking cessation counseling strategies were more likely to ask about smoking status (pretraining = 34% vs. 6 months follow-up = 75%, $p < .01$), assess motivation to quit (pretraining = 13.7% vs. 6 months = 66.7%, $p < .001$), advise patients to quit (pretraining = 46.2% vs. 6 months = 85.7%, $p < .01$), assist patients with quitting (pretraining = 34% vs. 6 months = 83.3%, $p < .01$) and follow-up with patients who have quit smoking (pretraining = 0% vs. 6 months = 16.7%, $p < .01$) 6 months after the one-day educational session (Borrelli, Lee, & Novak, 2008). Perceived organizational support for smoking cessation intervention was strongly associated with counseling behaviors at 6 months.

Dedicated Tobacco Dependence Staff

Acute Care Settings

To overcome nurses' perceived time constraints and low self-efficacy for providing smoking cessation counseling, health care systems can develop an infrastructure to support smoking cessation intervention by designating staff that are responsible for the overall coordination of tobacco intervention activities. Mc Daniel (1999) assessed the feasibility of implementing a bedside counseling program for inpatients referred for cardiac rehabilitation at an academic medical center. Patients identified as smokers were referred to a specially trained smoking cessation counselor by the cardiac rehabilitation service staff. Twenty-eight smokers (80% of those who were eligible) were referred for counseling during the 5-week pilot study period, with 20 patients receiving guideline-based treatment (2 refused and 6 were discharged to the delivery of counseling). Hospital staff members were asked to rate feasibility of the program along six dimensions: (1) time, (2) patient accessibility, (3) coordination/collaboration with unit staff, (4) patient receptivity, (5) disruption of unit work routine, and (6) communication between staff and smoking cessation counselor. Cost to deliver the counseling and discharge telephone follow-up was estimated at $51.14 per patient. These results showed that inpatient smoking cessation intervention delivered by dedicated tobacco treatment staff was feasible in terms of cost and practicality in the acute care setting.

A multidisciplinary research team has studied the efficacy of nurse-managed tobacco treatment programs for hospitalized patients in a series of randomized clinical trials. Originally this multicomponent intervention model was tested in a postmyocardial infarction population, which resulted in a 12-month cessation rate of 71% in the intervention group as compared to 45% for the usual care group (Taylor et al., 1990). Subsequent clinical trials of the program were conducted in the general inpatient population (Houston-Miller, Smith, DeBusk, Sobel, & Taylor, 1997; Smith, Kraemer, Houston-Miller, DeBusk, & Taylor, 1999; Taylor et al., 1996), resulting in significantly increased biochemically validated 12-month cessation rates over usual care (27%–31% for treatment groups vs. 20%–21% for usual care). Central to the intervention was the delivery of bedside counseling by specially trained project nurses. Project nurses received 8 hours of standardized training on behavioral counseling techniques and a training reference manual to guide intervention. Study investigators conducted ongoing monitoring of the bedside counseling to insure treatment fidelity. The in-person counseling sessions lasted 30–60 minutes, followed by one to four brief nurse-initiated telephone calls focusing on relapse prevention.

The efficacy of nurse-delivered smoking cessation intervention for hospitalized patients has been demonstrated by translating the model to other research contexts. A team of researchers, led by a cardiovascular nurse scientist, adapted the in-patient intervention protocol to target the issues that women with cardiovascular disease have when quitting smoking (Martin, Froelicher, & Houston-Miller, 2000). The randomized clinical trial included 45 minutes of bedside counseling delivered by study nurses and five follow-up relapse prevention telephone calls (Froelicher & Christopherson, 2000). Survival analysis showed a significantly greater period of abstinence over time in the intervention group, although long-term cessation rates were not significantly different (Oka, Katapodi, Lim, Bacchetti, & Froelicher, 2006). Given that women are more likely than men to relapse after a cessation attempt (Monso, Campbell, Tonnesen, Gustavsson, & Morera, 2001), interventions to increase sustained abstinence may lead to increased self-efficacy for quitting and greater interest in "recycling" to another quit attempt.

Disseminating a structured research protocol into clinical practice can be challenging. Smith, Reilly, Houston-Miller, DeBusk, and Taylor (2002) report the results of a study of the effectiveness of a specially trained nurse-managed in-patient smoking cessation program in standard practice. The program adopted the same procedures as the clinical trial protocols (Houston-Miller et al., 1997; Smith et al., 1999) but showed sustained utilization (52% of eligible smokers enrolled in the program) and impact for 3 years (overall self-reported 12-month cessation rate was 35%). A two-phase dissemination study of the multicomponent Staying Free program was conducted in six heterogeneous hospital settings (Taylor, Houston-Miller, Cameron, Fagans, & Das, 2005). In the implementation phase the multidisciplinary research team assisted the institutions to identify and enact the system changes needed to support the program, including training for medical and nursing staff about how to help patients quit smoking as well as 4 hours of intensive training for specialized interventionists. In the institutionalization phase, responsibility for leadership of the program was transitioned to the individual hospitals, with research staff in a consultant role. Overall, 6-month cessation rates were 26.3% (range of 17.6%–52.8%) during the implementation phase but decreased to 22.7% (range from 12.9% to 48.2%) after institutionalization (Taylor et al., 2005).

Primary Care

Primary care nurses are uniquely qualified to deliver tobacco treatment, but nursing research using a systems approach in this setting is limited. An observational study in the primary care setting found that having an assigned smoking cessation nonphysician staff member increased the frequency of tobacco-related discussions during an encounter, although this was not a significant predictor (Ellerbeck, Ahluwalia, Jolicoeur, Gladden, & Mosier, 2001). It is important to note in the one practice where a nurse was designated to provide tobacco cessation intervention and follow-up, smoking behaviors were addressed in 90% of all patient encounters with smokers.

Pohl and Caplan (1998) designed a cessation program for low-income women at a county health clinic. The nurse-led, multisession group program focused on empowering the women to change by tobacco education, stress management counseling, and social support. Childcare and free nicotine replacement therapy were important to the success of the program in the targeted population. This study provides an innovative model for group-based intervention, but strategies for sustaining such a program once initiated were not addressed in the study. Although group cessation counseling is an effective treatment modality (Fiore et al., 2008), full integration within the clinical setting is key to a system's approach to tobacco treatment.

An example of a fully integrated primary care tobacco treatment was reported by Sidorov, Christensen, Girolami, and Wydra (1997). In this descriptive study, nurses and nurse practitioners in one managed care organization completed specialized training in smoking cessation counseling. The trained primary care nurses provided one-on-one counseling to patients who had been referred by their physicians after requesting nicotine replacement therapy or by self-referral. The program consisted of six visits with the nurse counselor, which was free to patients enrolled in the health maintenance organization (HMO) affiliated with the system. Patients on private insurance plans paid for the counseling out of pocket. Coverage for nicotine replacement therapy depended on the pharmacy benefit plan in which the patient was enrolled and participation in the program (i.e., HMO enrollees were required to attend four of the six counseling sessions to receive pharmacotherapy at no cost). Overall, the 12-month cessation rate for the HMO participants was 30.5% (20.5% by intent-to-treat). Even though this program was designed to provide dedicated tobacco control interventionists across a health care system, only 20 of the 67 clinic sites participated in the program. Of those 20 sites, referrals to the program varied from as low as 3 to as high as 230 patients over the 3-year project. This degree of variability in utilization underscores the need to create systems that are not dependent on busy clinicians as "gatekeepers" in order to deliver tobacco treatment to all smokers.

Institutional Policies to Support Tobacco Intervention

The current regulatory environment in health care focuses on documentation of care processes and outcomes that are consistent with scientific evidence and national practice guidelines. Public reporting of these data and administrative policies that tie reimbursement to achievement of quality indicators has tremendous financial implications for health care institutions. Nurses, who have been at the forefront of quality improvement initiatives in institutions, have the essential skills for shaping policies and changing the practice environment in response to the increasing demands for accountability in health care (Kurtzman, Dawson, & Johnson, 2008). Evidence of nursing's impact on improving quality of care delivery can be seen in tobacco intervention initiatives such as those reported by Zarling, Burke, Gaines, and Gauvin (2008) and Ginn, Cox, and Heath (2008).

The earliest quality indicator focusing on tobacco treatment was included in the Health Plan Employee Data and Information Set (HEDIS), developed by the National Committee on Quality Assurance, assessed whether health plan physicians advised smokers to quit (Davis, 1997). The Centers for Medicare and Medicaid Services (CMS) and Joint Commission (formally known as Joint Commission on Accreditation of Healthcare Organizations [JCAHO]) have designated tobacco cessation advice and counseling for all patients admitted with community-acquired pneumonia, myocardial infarction, or heart failure as core performance measures for hospitals. In 2004, the National Quality Forum endorsed these measures as voluntary standards for nurse-sensitive care (Kurtzman et al., 2008), although tobacco cessation counseling is not included in the American Nurses Association's National Database of Nursing Quality Indicators (NDNQI)®.

Although nurses have led systems changes in response to mandates to comply with evidence-based tobacco treatment guidelines, nursing research on the impact of these institutional policies is sparse. Lesho and colleagues (Lesho, Myers, Ott, Winslow, & Brown, 2005) examined the effect of mandated clinical practice guidelines for asthma, diabetes, and tobacco intervention on process and outcome indicators in a large managed care organization. Data were extracted from the electronic medical record and chart audits of written progress notes (smoking cessation counseling). After guideline implementation, tobacco screening and education increased significantly. The percentage of patients counseled to quit at least three times decreased, although the difference was not statistically significant.

The study by Lesho and others (2005) partially supported the hypothesis that institutional policies can influence the processes of care, but others have questioned the impact of quality measures on patient outcomes. A multidisciplinary research team analyzed the association between the hospital performance indicator for smoking cessation counseling for acute myocardial infarction (AMI) patients and self-reported abstinence at 12 months (Reeves et al., 2008). The Prospective Registry Evaluating Myocardial Infarction: Events and Recovery (PREMIER) study followed 889 AMI patients at 19 hospitals for a year after discharge. Documentation of smoking cessation counseling, a Joint Commission and CMS quality indicator, was obtained through medical record review. Telephone interviews were conducted at 1, 6, and 12 months postdischarge. Smoking cessation counseling was documented for 72% of the patients, although the rate of counseling varied across hospitals between 60% to 90%. The overall rate of self-reported cessation after AMI was 53%. An unanticipated finding was that there was a small, but statistically significant lower rate of smoking cessation in patients that had documented cessation counseling (50.1% vs. 60.7%, $P = .02$). At the hospital system level, there was no correlation between the rate of documented counseling and actual cessation ($r = -0.13$, $P = .45$; Reeves et al., 2008). These results indicate that even with a high rate of compliance with mandated performance indicators, which measure care *processes*, smoking cessation *outcomes* may still be lacking. One explanation for the lack of impact on outcomes could be due to shortcomings of the indicators themselves, which do not mandate rigorous, evidence-based smoking cessation intervention. Given the complex nature of tobacco dependence, it could be argued that documentation of smoking cessation counseling oversimplifies the problem of treating nicotine addiction in our current health care system.

GAPS IN THE NURSING RESEARCH LITERATURE

Historically, nursing has been essential in implementing changes in the practice setting for improving the quality of health care delivery, including efforts to systematically address tobacco treatment. Nursing involvement in health services research focusing on tobacco treatment has lagged behind advances in clinical nursing research of smoking cessation interentions (Wells, Sarna, & Bialous, 2006). Health services research is defined as

> The multidisciplinary field of scientific investigation that studies how social factors, financing systems, organizational structures and processes, health technologies, and

personal behaviors affect access to health care, the quality and cost of health care, and ultimately our health and well-being. Its research domains are individuals, families, organizations, institutions, communities, and populations. (Lohr & Steinwachs, 2002, p. 16)

Jones and Mark (2005) have called for advances in nursing-health services research by articulating an agenda that focuses on five key areas that "contribute to improved societal health and well-being: (a) access to and utilization of care; (b) health and health behaviors; (c) quality of care and patient safety; (d) cost and cost-effectiveness of care; and (e) organization and delivery of care" (p. 324). Clearly the problem of tobacco use and treatment touches on each of these foci.

ROLE OF TECHNOLOGY IN IMPROVING SYSTEMS APPROACHES TO TOBACCO TREATMENT

Implementing guidelines for systematic tobacco cessation intervention is complex. This complexity exists on two levels (Shiell, Hawe, & Gold, 2008). First, evidence-based tobacco treatment is a complex intervention because is consists of multiple interdependent components. On a second level, the health care delivery system, which is the setting for tobacco dependence intervention, is itself a complex system. "A complex system is one that is adaptive to changes in its local environment, is composed of other complex systems (for example, the human body), and behaves in a nonlinear fashion (change in outcome is not proportional to change in input"; Shiell et al., 2008, p. 1281). Information technology can reduce complexity on both levels in several ways, such as a standardized approach to documentation and treatment, customized cessation information through tailored cessation education printed "on the fly," aggregation of data for population trending and benchmarking, and relational databases that facilitate one-time data entry for system-wide use. The recently enacted American Recovery and Reinvestment Act of 2009 calls for a $19 billion stimulus package to invest in health information technology (Mandl & Kohane, 2009), including $17.2 billion for financial incentives to physicians and hospitals through Medicare and Medicaid to promote the use of EHRs (Steinbrook, 2009). This investment represents an unprecedented opportunity to the tobacco control research community to develop and test technologies to support evidence-based tobacco treatment.

Presently, it is estimated that only 17% of U.S. physicians and 8% to 10% of U.S. hospitals have a basic EHR system (Steinbrook, 2009). Even fewer have comprehensive systems that would allow health care professionals to use technology with higher computing potential. Implementation and usage of EHRs cannot deliver its promises of improved communication, outcomes, and safety if simply based on a paper process that is flawed or awkward in itself (Robles, 2009).

Rather than perpetuating the deficiencies of a paper system, an electronic system needs to be well designed—not only in terms of being user-friendly and decreasing documentation time and efforts, but in using computing to its full capabilities. Well-designed EHRs are crucial to whole system approaches in health care overall and for tobacco intervention in particular.

Electronic health records linked to automated clinical decision support systems can serve as a platform for standardized documentation of smoking status and prompting provider intervention across settings (McDaniel et al., 2005; Swallow & Dykes, 2004). In fact, the successful system interventions included in this review all included documentation of smoking status and some type of computer reminder as a component. The EHRs can also facilitate unbiased assessments of policy adherence and measurements of performance indicators. Automated capture of provider intervention through the EHR and advances in secure exchange of health information can facilitate reporting of quality indicators to regulatory agencies and third-party payers, thus increasing reimbursement and pay-for-performance incentives (Mandl & Kohane, 2009).

Systematic relapse prevention follow-up after initial cessation is difficult and can be costly. Technology can streamline the process by generating tobacco intervention history reports from automated queries of the hospital information system. Follow-up counseling can be scheduled with auto-prompts to nurses or dedicated tobacco cessation specialists. Interactive voice response (IVR) technology has been used to support relapse prevention counseling (McDaniel, 2004). Using a prerecorded set of questions designed to monitor risk for smoking relapse, the IVR system monitored progress and identified need for supplemental counseling. This use of technology can enhance the efficiency and cost-effectiveness of a comprehensive cessation program.

Time constraints in the busy clinical environment are frequently identified as a barrier to systematic tobacco intervention. Interactive multimedia technology can deliver tailored tobacco cessation education and motivational information as an adjunct to provider cessation counseling (McDaniel, Casper, Hutchison, & Stratton, 2005). Characterized as clinical encounters "in absentia" (Revere & Dunbar, 2001), interactive technology shows promise as part of an integrated approach to systems approaches to tobacco intervention.

SUMMARY AND IMPLICATIONS FOR FUTURE NURSING RESEARCH AND POLICY

Nursing research on the implementation of evidence-based tobacco treatment guidelines into practice demonstrates that changes in the health care delivery system and clinical workflow patterns can have a substantial effect on cessation rates. Pentz and colleagues (2006) described translation research in tobacco control and prevention. The National Action Plan for Tobacco Cessation (Fiore et al., 2004) recommends training and education to "ensure that all clinicians in the United States have the knowledge, skills and support systems necessary to help their patients quit tobacco use" (p. 208). Research that focuses on replicating, extending, and disseminating multicomponent interventions that have been shown to be efficacious is known as Type II translation (Pentz et al., 2006). Findings from Type II translation tobacco research by nurses are promising, albeit limited in scope. This dearth of research mirrors the relative lack of translational research by nurses in general. Nursing leaders have called for capacity building initiatives (Jones & Mark, 2005) and development of conceptual frameworks (Titler, Everett, & Adams, 2007) to guide research addressing needed changes in the health care delivery system. The Federal government has recognized the need to invest resources that support dissemination and implementation research in health through cross-institute funding programs, including the National Institute of Nursing Research.

Nurse scientists have an unprecedented opportunity to respond to the call for research in systems changes to support tobacco treatment. In 2003 the National Cancer Institute launched the Initiative on the Study and Implementation of Systems (ISIS). With tobacco control as the exemplar, the ISIS program proposes the use of systems thinking to advance transdisciplinary, team science (Leischow et al., 2008). The ISIS made four recommendations for tobacco researchers, practitioners, and policy makers: (1) develop and apply systems methods and processes, (2) build and maintain network relationships, (3) build system and knowledge capacity, and (4) encourage transformation to systems culture (NCI, 2007). These recommendations provide the needed direction for shaping the nursing research agenda in tobacco control.

REFERENCES

Abrams, D. B. (2007). A comprehensive smoking cessation policy for all smokers: Systems integration to save lives and money. In R. J. Bonnie, K. Stratton, & R. B. Wallace (Eds.), *Committee on reducing tobacco use: Strategies, barriers, and consequences, Ending the tobacco problem*. Washington, DC: The National Academies Press.

Ahluwalia, J. S., Gibson, C. A., Kenney, R. E., Wallace, D. D., & Resnicow, K. (1999). Smoking status as a vital sign. *Journal of General Internal Medicine, 14*, 402–408.

Albrecht, S. A., Maloni, J. A., Thomas, K. K., Jones, R., Halleran, J., & Osborne, J. (2004). Smoking cessation counseling for pregnant women who smoke: Scientific basis for practice for AWHONN's SUCCESS project. *Journal of Obstetric, Gynecologic, & Neonatal Nursing, 33*(3), 298–305.

Andrews, J. O., Tingen, M. S., Waller, J. L., & Harper, R. J. (2001). Provider feedback improves adherence with AHCPR smoking cessation guideline. *Preventive Medicine 33*(5), 415–421.

Bonnie, R. J., Stratton, K., & Wallace, R. B. (Eds.). (2007). *Committee on reducing tobacco use: Strategies, barriers, and consequences. Ending the tobacco problem.* Washington, DC: The National Academies Press.

Borrelli, B., Lee, C., & Novak, S. (2008). Is provider training effective? Changes in attitudes towards smoking cessation counseling and counseling behaviors of home health care nurses. *Preventive Medicine, 46*(4), 358–363.

Bower, J. L., & Christensen, C. M. (1995, January–February) Disruptive technologies: Catching the wave. *Harvard Business Review,* 43–53.

Bruce, S. (2004). Oncology nurses: On the frontlines of tobacco prevention and cessation. *Oncology Nursing Society, 19*(11), 1–6.

California Environmental Protection Agency. (2005). *Proposed identification of environmental tobacco smoke as a toxic air contaminant. Part B: Health effects.* Sacramento: California Environmental Protection Agency, Office of Environmental Health Hazard Assessment.

Committee on Substance Abuse, American Academy of Pediatrics (2001). Tobacco's toll: Implications for the pediatrician. *Pediatrics, 107,* 794–798.

Davis, R. M. (1997). Healthcare report cards and tobacco measures. *Tobacco Control, 6* (Suppl. 1), S70–S77.

Duffy, S. A., Reeves, P., Hermann, C., Karvonen C., & Smith, P. (2008). In-hospital smoking cessation programs: What do VA patients and staff want and need? *Applied Nursing Research, 21*(4), 199–206.

Ellerbeck, E. F., Ahluwalia, J. S., Jolicoeur, D. G., Gladden, J., & Mosier, M. C. (2001). Direct observation of smoking cessation activities in primary care practice. *Journal of Family Practice, 50*(8), 688–693.

Fiore, M. C., Bailey, W. C., Cohen, S. J., Dorfman, S., Goldstein, M., Gritz, E. R., et al. (2000). *Treating tobacco use and dependence: Clinical practice guideline.* Rockville, MD: United States Department of Health and Human Services, Public Health Service.

Fiore, M. C., Croyle, R. T., Curry, S. J., Cutler, C. M., Davis, R. M, Gordon C., et al. (2004). Preventing 3 million premature deaths and helping 5 million smokers quit: A national action plan for tobacco cessation. *American Journal of Public Health, 94,* 205–210.

Fiore, M. C., Jaén, C. R., Baker, T. B., Bailey, W. C., Benowitz, N. L., Curry, S. J., et al. (2008). *Treating tobacco use and dependence: 2008 update. Clinical practice guideline.* Rockville, MD: U.S. Department of Health and Human Services, Public Health Service.

Fiore, M. C., Jorenby, D. E., Schensky, A. E., Smith, S. S., Bauer, R. R., & Baker, T. B. (1995). Smoking status as the new vital sign: Effect on assessment and intervention with patients who smoke. *Mayo Clinic Proceedings, 70*(3), 209–213.

Froelicher, E. S., & Christopherson, D. J. (2000). Women's initiative for nonsmoking (WINS) I: Design and methods. *Heart & Lung, 29*(6), 429–437.

Ginn, M. B., Cox, G., & Heath, J. (2008). Evidence-based approach to an inpatient tobacco cessation protocol. *AACN Advanced Critical Care, 19*(3), 268–280.

Grossman, J., Donaldson, S., Belton, L., & Oliver, R. H. (2008). 5 A's Smoking cessation with recovering women in treatment. *Journal of Addictions Nursing, 19*(1), 1–8.

Heath, J., Andrews, J., Thomas, S. A., Kelley, F. J., & Friedman, E. (2002). Tobacco dependence curricula in acute care nurse practitioner education. *American Journal of Critical Care, 11*(1), 27–33.

Heath, J., Kelley, F. J., Andrews, J., Crowell, N., Corelli, R. L., & Hudmon, K. S. (2007). Evaluation of a tobacco cessation curricular intervention among acute care nurse practitioner faculty members. *American Journal of Critical Care*, *16*(3), 284–289.

Houston-Miller, N., Smith, P. M., DeBusk, R. F., Sobel, D. S., & Taylor, C. B. (1997). Smoking cessation in hospitalized patients: Results of a randomized trial. *Archives of Internal Medicine*, *157*(4), 409–415.

Jones, C. B., & Mark, B. A. (2005). The intersection of nursing and health services research: An agenda to guide future research. *Nursing Outlook*, *53*(6), 324–332.

Kurtzman, E. T., Dawson, E. M., & Johnson, J. E. (2008). The current state of nursing performance measurement, public reporting, and value-based purchasing. *Policy, Politics, & Nursing Practice*, *9*(3), 181–191.

Lancaster, T., & Fowler, G. (2000). Training health professionals in smoking cessation. *Cochrane Database of Systematic Reviews*, (3), CD000214. Doi:10.1002/14651858. CD000214

Leischow, S. J., Best, A., Trochim, W. M., Clark, P. I., Gallagher, R. S., Marcus, S. E., Matthews E. (2008). Systems thinking to improve the public's health. *American Journal of Preventive Medicine*. *35*(2 Suppl), S196–203.

Lesho, E. P., Myers, C. P., Ott, M., Winslow, C., & Brown, J. E. (2005). Do clinical practice guidelines improve processes or outcomes in primary care? *Military Medicine*, *170*(3), 243–246.

Lohr, K. N., & Steinwachs, D. M. (2002). Health services research: an evolving definition of the field. *Health Services Research*, *37*(1), 15–17.

Mandl, K. D., & Kohane, I. S. (2009). No small change for the health information economy [Electronic version]. *New England Journal of Medicine*, *360*(13), 1278–1281.

Martin, K., Froelicher, E. S., & Houston-Miller, N. (2000). Women's initiative for nonsmoking (WINS) II: The intervention. *Heart & Lung*, *29*(6), 438–445.

McCarty, M. C., Hennrikus, D. J., Lando, H. A., & Vessey, J. T. (2001). Nurses' attitudes concerning the delivery of brief cessation advice to hospitalized smokers. *Preventive Medicine*, *33*(6), 674–681.

McDaniel, A. M. (1999). Assessing the feasibility of a clinical practice guideline for inpatient smoking cessation intervention. *Clinical Nurse Specialist*, *13*, 228–235.

McDaniel, A. M. (2004). Interactive voice response technology for outcomes monitoring. *Clinical Nurse Specialist*, *18*, 5–6.

McDaniel, A. M., Benson, P., Roesener, G. H., & Martindale, J. (2005). An integrated computer-based system to support nicotine dependence treatment in primary care. *Nicotine and Tobacco Research*, *7*(S1), S57–S66.

McDaniel, A. M., Casper, G. R., Hutchison, S., & Stratton, R. (2005). Design and testing of an interactive smoking cessation intervention for inner-city women. *Health Education Research: Theory and Practice*, *20*, 379–384.

McDaniel, A. M., Kristeller, J. L., & Hudson, D. M. (1999). Chart reminders increase referrals for inpatient smoking cessation intervention. *Nicotine and Tobacco Research*, *1*, 175–180.

Monso, E., Campbell, J., Tonnesen, P., Gustavsson, G., & Morera, J. (2001). Sociodemographic predictors of success in smoking intervention. *Tobacco Control*, *10*(2), 165–169.

Moolchan, E. T, Fagan, P., Fernander, A. F., Velicer, W. F., Hayward, M. D., King, G., et al. (2007). Addressing tobacco-related health disparities. *Addiction, 102*(Suppl. 2), 30–42.

National Cancer Institute. (2007). *Cancer trends progress report—2007*. Retrieved June 1, 2009, from http://progressreport.cancer.gov/doc_detail.asp?pid=1&did=2007 &chid=71&coid=705&mid=#estimate

Oka, R. K., Katapodi, M. C., Lim, J. W., Bacchetti, P., & Froelicher, E. S. (2006). Quantifying smoking cessation outcomes: From the women's initiative for nonsmoking study (X): Methodological implications. *Nursing Research, 55*(4), 292–297.

Pentz, M. A., Jasuja, G. K., Rohrbach, L. A., Sussman, S., & Bardo, M. T. (2006). Translation in tobacco and drug abuse prevention research. *Evaluation & the Health Professions, 29*(2), 246–71.

Pinget, C., Martin, E., Wasserfallen, J., Humair, J., & Cornuz, J. (2007). Cost-effectiveness analysis of a European primary-care physician training in smoking cessation counseling. *European Journal of Cardiovascular Prevention & Rehabilitation, 14*, 451–455.

Pohl, J. M., & Caplan, D. (1998). Smoking cessation: Using group intervention methods to treat low-income women. *Nurse Practitioner, 23*(12), 13–39.

Reeves, G. R., Wang, T. Y., Reid, K. J., Alexander, K. P., Decker, C., Ahmad, H., et al. (2008). Dissociation between hospital performance of the smoking cessation counseling quality metric and cessation outcomes after myocardial infarction. *Archives of Internal Medicine, 168*(19), 2111–2117.

Revere, D., & Dunbar, P. J. (2001). Review of computer generated outpatient behavioral interventions: Clinical encounters 'in Absentia.' *Journal of the American Informatics Association, 8*, 62–79.

Robles, J. (2009). The effect of the electronic medical record on nurses' work. *Creative Nursing, 15*, 31–35.

Sarna, L., & Bialous, S. (2005). Tobacco control in the 21st century: A critical issue for the nursing profession. *Research and Theory for Nursing Practice, 19*(1), 15–24.

Sarna, L., & Bialous, S. A. (2006). Strategic directions for nursing research in tobacco dependence. *Nursing Research, 55*(Suppl. 4), S1–S9.

Sarna, L., & Lillington, L. (2002). Tobacco—An emerging topic in nursing research. *Nursing Research, 51*(4), 245–253.

Shiell, A., Hawe, P., & Gold, L. (2008). Complex interventions or complex systems? Implications for health economic evaluation. *British Medical Journal, 336*(7656), 1281–1283.

Sidorov, J., Christensen, M., Girolami, S., & Wydra, C. (1997). A successful tobacco cessation program led by primary care nurses in a managed care setting. *American Journal of Managed Care, 3*(2), 207–214.

Smith, D. P., & Jordan, H. S. (2008). Piloting nursing-sensitive hospital care measures in Massachusetts. *Journal of Nursing Care Quality, 23*(1), 23–33.

Smith, P. M., Kraemer, H. C., Houston-Miller, N., DeBusk, R. F., Taylor, C. B. (1999). In-hospital smoking cessation programs: who responds, who doesn't? *Journal of Consulting and Clinical Psychology, 1*(67), 19–27.

Smith, P. M., Reilly, K. R., Houston-Miller, N., DeBusk, R. F., & Taylor, C. B. (2002). Application of a nurse-managed inpatient smoking cessation program. *Nicotine & Tobacco Research, 4*(2), 211–222.

Steinbrook, R. (2009). Health care and the American recovery and reinvestment act. *New England Journal of Medicine, 360*, 1057–1060.

Swallow, A. D. & Dykes, P. C. (2004). Tobacco cessation at Greenwich hospital: One hospital integrates a cessation program into its daily practice. *The American Journal of Nursing, 104*(12), 61–62.

Taylor, C. B., Houston-Miller, N., Cameron, R. P., Fagans, E. W., & Das, S. (2005). Dissemination of an effective inpatient tobacco use cessation program. *Nicotine & Tobacco Research, 7*(1), 129–137.

Taylor, C. B., Houston-Miller N., Herman, S., Smith, P. M., Sobel, D., Fisher, L., et al. (1996). A nurse-managed smoking cessation program for hospitalized smokers. *American Journal of Public Health, 86*(11), 1557–1560.

Taylor, C. B., Houston-Miller, N., Killen, J. D., & DeBusk, R. F. (1990). Smoking cessation after acute myocardial infarction: Effects of a nurse managed intervention. *Annals of Internal Medicine, 113*, 118–123.

Titler, M. G., Everett, L. Q., & Adams, S. (2007). Implications for implementation science. *Nursing Research. 56*(4 Suppl), S53–9.

Turner-Henson, A., Kohler, C., Lyrene, R., & Johnston, J. (1999). Smoking status as a vital sign in pediatric settings. *Pediatrics, 103*, 1079–80.

U.S. Centers for Disease Control and Prevention (CDC). (2009). State-specific prevalence and trends in adult cigarette smoking—United States, 1998–2007. *Morbidity and Mortality Weekly Report, 58*, 221–226.

U.S. Centers for Disease Control and Prevention. (2008). Smoking-attributable mortality, years of potential life lost, and productivity losses—United States, 2000–2004. *Morbidity and Mortality Weekly Report, 57*, 1226–1228.

Warner, K. E. (Ed.). (2006). *Tobacco control policy.* San Francisco: Jossey-Bass.

Wells, M., Sarna, L., & Bialous, S. A. (2006). Nursing research in smoking cessation: A listing of the literature, 1996–2005. *Nursing Research, 55*(Suppl. 4), S16–S28.

Wetta-Hall, R., Ablah, E., Frazier, L. M., Molgaard, C. A., Berry, M., & Good, M. J. (2005). Factors influencing nurses' smoking cessation assessment and counseling practices. *Journal of Addictions Nursing, 16*, 131–135.

Wewers M. E., Kidd, K., Armbruster, D., & Sarna, L. (2004). Tobacco dependence curricula in U.S. baccalaureate and graduate nursing education. *Nursing Outlook, 52*, 95–101.

Williams, J. M., Steinberg, M. L., Hanos Zimmermann, M., Gandhi, K. K., Lucas, G. E., Gonsalves, D. A., et al. (2009). Training psychiatrists and advanced practice nurses to treat tobacco dependence. *Journal of the American Psychiatric Nurses Association, 15*, 50–58.

Winickoff, J. P., Berkowitz, A. B., Brooks, K., Tanski, S. E., Geller, A., Thomson, C., et al. (2005). State-of-the-art interventions for office-based parental tobacco control. *Pediatrics, 115*, 750–757.

Zarling, K. K., Burke, M. V., Gaines, K. A., & Gauvin, T. R. (2008). Registered nurse initiation of a tobacco intervention protocol—Leading quality care. *Journal of Cardiovascular Nursing, 23*(5), 443–448.

Chapter 15

Nursing Research in Community-Based Approaches to Reduce Exposure to Secondhand Smoke

Ellen J. Hahn, Kristin B. Ashford, Chizimuzo T. C. Okoli, Mary Kay Rayens, S. Lee Ridner, and Nancy L. York

ABSTRACT

Secondhand smoke (SHS) is the third leading cause of preventable death in the United States and a major source of indoor air pollution, accounting for an estimated 53,000 deaths per year among nonsmokers. Secondhand smoke exposure varies by gender, race/ethnicity, and socioeconomic status. The most effective public health intervention to reduce SHS exposure is to implement and enforce smoke-free workplace policies that protect entire populations including all workers regardless of occupation, race/ethnicity, gender, age, and socioeconomic status. This chapter summarizes community and population-based nursing research to reduce SHS exposure.

DOI: 10.1891/0739-6686.27.365

Most of the nursing research in this area has been policy outcome studies, documenting improvement in indoor air quality, worker's health, public opinion, and reduction in Emergency Department visits for asthma, acute myocardial infarction among women, and adult smoking prevalence. These findings suggest a differential health effect by strength of law. Further, smoke-free laws do not harm business or employee turnover, nor are revenues from charitable gaming affected. Additionally, smoke-free laws may eventually have a positive effect on cessation among adults. There is emerging nursing science exploring the link between SHS exposure to nicotine and tobacco dependence, suggesting one reason that SHS reduction is a quit smoking strategy. Other nursing research studies address community readiness for smoke-free policy, and examine factors that build capacity for smoke-free policy. Emerging trends in the field include tobacco free health care and college campuses. A growing body of nursing research provides an excellent opportunity to conduct and participate in community and population-based research to reduce SHS exposure for both vulnerable populations and society at large.

Keywords: secondhand smoke exposure; policy outcomes; community research; indoor air quality

Secondhand smoke (SHS) exposure is the third leading cause of preventable death in the United States and a major source of indoor air pollution, accounting for an estimated 53,000 deaths per year among nonsmokers from cardiovascular disease, lung cancer, chronic obstructive pulmonary disease and other lung diseases, and sudden infant death syndrome (U.S. Department of Health and Human Services [DHHS], 2006). Secondhand smoke is a mixture of the smoke from the burning end of tobacco products (sidestream smoke) and the smoke exhaled by smokers (mainstream smoke) and it contains at least 250 chemicals that are known to be toxic (National Toxicology Program, 2002; U.S. DHHS, 2006). Even short-term exposure to SHS (30 minutes) in relatively low doses places healthy nonsmokers at risk for developing heart disease by interrupting normal coronary circulation (Otsuka et al., 2001). There is no safe level of SHS exposure (U.S. DHHS, 2006). It is estimated that 46.4% of people in the United States have biological evidence of SHS exposure (Centers for Disease Control and Prevention [CDC], 2008). Current research suggests that exposure to SHS varies by gender, race/ethnicity, and socioeconomic status (Greaves & Hemsing, 2009), and smoking restrictions may have a differential impact on subpopulations such as low-income groups (Bell et al., 2009).

Community and population-based approaches are the most effective in reducing SHS exposure in workplaces and public places. Community-based approaches engage groups of people with diverse characteristics yet common interests who are linked by social and geographic ties (e.g., home smoking prevention programs for pregnant smokers). Population-based approaches target entire communities with macrolevel strategies such as media advocacy and policy change.

The most effective public health intervention to reduce exposure to SHS is to implement and enforce population-based comprehensive smoke-free workplace policies (CDC, 2000; U.S. DHHS, 2006) that protect entire populations including all workers regardless of occupation, race/ethnicity, gender, age, and socioeconomic status. Nonsmoking adults living in communities with strong smoke-free laws covering all workplaces, restaurants, and bars are less likely to be exposed to SHS, as evidenced by serum cotinine levels (Pickett, Schober, Brody, Curtin, & Giovino, 2006). As of July 1, 2009, over 121 million Americans were covered by local or state 100% smoke-free laws in workplaces, restaurants, and bars, protecting approximately 40.3% of the U.S. population (Americans for Nonsmokers' Rights [ANR], 2009a). Whether through state or local control, the gold standard for smoke-free policy is a law or regulation that covers all workplaces and enclosed public places, has no or very few exemptions, and protects all workers from SHS exposure.

Nurses are in an optimal position to conduct and participate in community and population-based research to reduce exposure to SHS for both vulnerable populations and society at large. Not only does community and population-based research contribute to the science of smoke-free policy and result in reductions in SHS exposure, it is also essential as advocates make the case for smoke-free policies in communities around the world (Bialous, Kaufman, & Sarna, 2003). Nurses can engage in policy research to make a case for enacting smoke-free legislation and maintaining the integrity of such laws. Unfortunately, few nurse researchers engage in community-based and policy research to reduce SHS exposure. Yet, the opportunities to contribute to this growing field of nursing research are endless. This chapter highlights the policy and community-based research conducted by nurses affiliated with the Tobacco Policy Research Program at the University of Kentucky College of Nursing as well as other nurse researchers in the United States and Canada.

PROPOSED MODEL TO GUIDE POLICY RESEARCH

We suggest a model to guide community and population-based research for policy change to reduce SHS exposure. The preponderance of nursing research to date has been outcome studies to document the health and economic impacts of smoke-free policy. These findings have been very useful to advocates as they make the case for smoke-free legislation (Greathouse, Hahn, Okoli, Warnick, & Riker, 2005) and maintain integrity of existing laws. To move the science forward, a model of policy change is needed to guide research into understanding community readiness for policy change as well as other factors that predict policy development. We suggest three major constructs in promoting policy change: (a) building capacity, (2) building demand, and (3) translating and disseminating science to policy makers and the public.

Building capacity involves coalition formation, development and enhancement, as well as building on existing organizational capacity for policy change. Further, identifying and growing legislative champions, or elected officials who favor the cause, is a critical element of building capacity for policy change. Leveraging funding and other resources also is an important part of building capacity, as is preparing advocates to understand the public policy process including basic legal/regulatory information. Research is needed to determine the influence of this construct on policy change.

Building demand involves media education, advocacy, and branding the campaign such that a tipping point is created. When elected officials say they have no choice but to vote in favor of a smoke-free law it reflects that the public has communicated demand for policy change. Research is needed to better understand how best to frame public health messages and market the health brand to elected officials, vulnerable population groups, and the public at large. Further, there is need for research on the role of the opposition in limiting demand for smoke-free policy. While identifying, anticipating, and exposing the opposition is a known advocacy strategy in smoke-free campaigns, there is little research on the efficacy of these strategies in changing public policy.

Translating and disseminating science is essential as policy makers attempt to make informed decisions. While it is widely known that information alone does not change opinion, research data presented in compelling ways can sway public and policymaker views toward smoke-free policy. Further research is needed to understand ways that scientific evidence is acquired and used by policy makers and what role science plays in smoke-free policy change.

PURPOSE AND METHODS

We aim to summarize the community and population-based research conducted by nurses to reduce SHS exposure. We conducted an exhaustive literature review of research papers using CINAHL from 1999 to 2009 and the search terms: nursing, policy, secondhand or passive smoke, and community. Authors with an affiliation with a college, school, or department of nursing and those with an obvious title (i.e., RN or DNS) were reviewed as nursing research studies, as well as those published in a nursing journal.

First, we discuss a series of 14 policy outcome studies conducted by nurses to document the health, public opinion, and economic impacts of smoke-free legislation. Second, we describe the use of the community readiness model to study the factors associated with the development of smoke-free policy. Third, we review studies focusing on the effects of SHS and smoke-free policy on disparate populations including rural communities, casino workers, and youth. Fourth, we discuss studies on the effects of smoke-free laws on tobacco industry marketing. Fifth, we summarize measurement studies to document levels of SHS exposure in vulnerable populations including hospitality workers, pregnant women, infants, and youth. Next, we describe SHS reduction as a quit smoking strategy and recent research evidence supporting the exposure to nicotine through SHS, making quitting more difficult when smokers are exposed to SHS. Last, we suggest emerging trends in community and population-based SHS and policy research.

RESULTS

We located 39 research studies that were authored by nurses. The studies on smoke-free policy outcomes by nurse researchers affiliated with the University of Kentucky are discussed first, followed by studies on community readiness, smoke-free policy and tobacco industry marketing, measurement issues, SHS as a quit strategy, and exposure to nicotine from SHS.

Smoke-Free Policy Studies

A series of 14 smoke-free policy outcome studies conducted at the University of Kentucky College of Nursing Tobacco Policy Research Program include those that document the effects of policy change on indoor air quality, worker health, asthma, heart attacks, public opinion, smoking prevalence and cessation behaviors, and economic indicators.

Air Quality Studies

A series of four prospective air quality monitoring studies showed that air quality significantly improves in indoor work environments after comprehensive smoke-free laws are implemented and the effect is immediate. Further, strength of smoke-free law is associated with indoor air quality. A TSI SidePak AM510 Personal Aerosol Monitor (TSI, Inc., St. Paul, MN) samples and records the levels of respirable suspended particles smaller than 2.5 μm in micrograms per cubic meter, or $PM_{2.5}$. Particle pollution, or particulate matter, is a combination of airborne liquid droplets and microscopic solid elements that when combined and inhaled, reach the distal regions of the lungs.

There was a 91% decrease in indoor air pollution (199 $μg/m^3$ prelaw to 18 $μg/m^3$ postlaw) after Lexington, Kentucky implemented a comprehensive smoke-free law (Hahn, Lee, Okoli, Troutman, & Powell, 2005). Average levels of indoor air pollution dropped from 86 $μg/m^3$ to 20 $μg/m^3$ after Georgetown, Kentucky implemented a comprehensive smoke-free law and the impact was immediate, within one day of implementation (Lee, Hahn, Riker, Head, & Seithers,

2007a). Two studies examined strength of law and indoor air quality. After a partial smoke-free law with significant exemptions was implemented in Louisville, Kentucky, the average $PM_{2.5}$ level rose slightly to 338 µg/m (Lee, Hahn, Okoli, Repace, & Troutman, 2008). Only 3 of the 10 venues were smoke free as a result of the ordinance that exempted most venues serving alcohol. After the law was strengthened including all workplaces and bars, the average $PM_{2.5}$ level dropped substantially to 9 µg/m³. Only comprehensive smoke-free laws protect workers and patrons from harmful indoor air pollution (Lee et al., 2008, 2009).

Hospitality Worker Studies

One study is among the very few nurse-led investigations of the effect of smoke-free policies on hospitality worker's health. This study assessed the effect of a smoke-free law on SHS exposure among 105 smoking and nonsmoking restaurant and bar workers from randomly selected establishments in Lexington, Kentucky (Hahn, Rayens, et al., 2006b). Hair nicotine samples, self-reported prevalence of upper respiratory symptoms (wheeze/whistle, dyspnea, cough in morning, cough during rest of the day, phlegm), and sensory symptoms (i.e., irritated eyes, runny nose, scratchy throat) were measured prelaw and 3 and 6 months postlaw. Controlling for cigarettes smoked per day, there was a significant decline in hair nicotine 3 months postlaw. Bar workers showed a significantly larger decline in hair nicotine compared with restaurant workers. The only significant decline in SHS exposure was in the workplace and other public places. Regardless of smoking status, respiratory symptoms declined significantly postlaw. The smoke-free law improved health status among hospitality workers. More research is needed to evaluate the differential effects of these laws by strength of law and subgroup of hospitality worker (e.g., women, minorities).

Health Outcome Studies

Studies have linked smoke-free workplace and public places legislation to significant declines in hospitalizations for acute myocardial infarction (AMI) in the general population (Glantz, 2008). Few studies have evaluated whether smoke-free laws that protect only some sectors of the workforce impact the incidence of AMI at the community level. Nurses at the University of Kentucky evaluated the effects of the smoke-free public places law on AMI and asthma. Data were collected on all discharges for asthma and heart attacks from the four Lexington hospitals and emergency departments before and after the smoke-free law covering all enclosed public places (all workplaces were not covered).

Among women, AMI hospitalizations declined 22% from pre- to postlaw (p = .01; 95% CI from 5% to 35%; Hahn, Rayens, Lee, Burkhart, & Moser, 2006a). The rate of AMI events among men did not change significantly from pre- to postlaw (p = .2). The overrepresentation of women in the hospitality industry in Fayette County combined with the disproportionate number of men work-ing in manufacturing facilities not covered by the smoke-free law, may partially explain why women may be more protected by the smoke-free law than men. Enacting comprehensive smoke-free laws that cover all places of employment and strengthening existing partial laws may extend protection against AMIs to both male and female workers. Further research is needed to evaluate the effects of smoke-free laws on populations that are disproportionately affected by SHS.

Adjusting for seasonality, secular trends, and demographic characteristics, Emergency Department (ED) visits for asthma declined 22% from pre- to post-law ($p < .0001$; 95% CI from 14% to 29%; Rayens, Burkhart, et al., 2008). The rate of decline was 24% in adults aged 20 years and older ($p < .0001$), while the decrease among children 19 or younger was 18% ($p = .01$). Though this study did not establish causation, the smoke-free law was associated with fewer asthma ED visits among both children and adults, with a more significant decline among adults. More research is needed to determine the effects of smoke-free laws on asthma outcomes.

Public Opinion Studies

Smoke-free laws are popular and well accepted by the public (McMillen, Win-ickoff, Klein, & Weitzman, 2003; Moore, 2005). Nurses have been involved in public opinion studies to assess attitudes toward smoke-free laws. As part of a community partnership to reduce the burden of cardiovascular disease, one Min-nesota study revealed that residents preferred smoke-free restaurants, bars, and nightclubs (Kottke et al., 2001).

While there has been an upward trend in smoke-free laws in countries, states, and municipalities in recent years, those living in certain regions of the United States (i.e., tobacco-producing states where smoking prevalence is generally higher than in nontobacco producing states) might be less likely to accept smoke-free laws. Given that smoke-free laws are more likely to be enacted in urban areas, there may be a differential level of acceptance in rural versus urban locales. Two nurse-led public opinion studies were conducted to assess change in public opin-ion toward smoke-free legislation over time in a tobacco-growing region and determine differences in public opinion between those living in rural versus urban areas.

A pre- and postlaw cohort study of noninstitutionalized adults ($N = 2,146$) living in Lexington-Fayette County, Kentucky assessed public support for the smoke-free law, perceived health risks from exposure to SHS, smoking behaviors, and frequency of visiting restaurants, bars, and entertainment venues (Rayens et al., 2007). Public support for the smoke-free law increased from 56% to 63%; respon-dents were 1.52 times more likely to support smoke-free policy postlaw ($p < .0001$; 95% CI: 1.24–1.86). Lexington adults favored the smoke-free legislation despite living in a traditionally protobacco climate. The smoke-free law acted as a public health intervention as it increased perceived risk of heart disease and cancer from SHS exposure.

A second public opinion study was a secondary analysis of a series of random-digit dialed phone surveys conducted in 2005–2006 with 3,672 adult Kentucky residents living in rural and urban communities without smoke-free laws (Rayens, Hahn, Langley, & Zhang, 2008). Respondents were asked whether they would support a local law prohibiting smoking in public places. More than half (59.6%) supported a local smoke-free law. Controlling for age, gender, ethnicity, education, and smoking status, there was a significant difference in level of support for a smoke-free law between rural and urban respondents. Compared to urban dwellers, rural residents were more likely to support these laws (odds ratio = 1.21; 95% CI: 1.03–1.42). This study suggests that smoke-free policy development in rural communities may be more acceptable and feasible than expected. This finding is important since rural dwellers are disproportionately affected by smoking and are less protected by smoke-free policy than their urban counterparts. Further research is needed on public opinion toward type and strength of smoke-free laws (i.e., smoke-free laws with exemptions).

Smoking Prevalence and Cessation Behavior Studies

While it is well known that voluntary smoke-free policies reduce tobacco consumption and smoking prevalence (Heloma & Jaakkola, 2003), far less is known about the effects of smoke-free legislation on adult smoking prevalence and smoking and cessation behaviors. Two nurse-led studies were conducted to determine the effects of smoke-free laws on adult smoking prevalence and cessation behaviors over time after these laws are implemented.

A secondary analysis of Behavioral Risk Factor Surveillance System (BRFSS) data from 2001–2005 ($N = 10,413$) determined whether smoking rates changed in Lexington-Fayette County before and after the smoke-free law relative to the change in 30 matched Kentucky counties (Hahn et al., 2008). There was a 31.9% decline in adult smoking in Fayette County (25.7% prelaw to 17.5% postlaw). In the group of 30 control counties, the rate was 28.4% prelaw and 27.6% postlaw. Controlling for seasonality, time trend, age, gender, ethnicity, education, marital status, and income, there was a significant time (pre- vs. postlaw) by group (Fayette vs. controls) interaction. There were an estimated 16,500 fewer smokers in Fayette County after the law took effect, resulting in an estimated $21 million per year in health care cost savings.

The second study analyzed smoking and cessation behaviors via brief telephone interviews with 295 randomly selected current and former smokers who had quit since a comprehensive smoke-free law took effect in their community (Hahn, Rayens, Langley, Darville, & Dignan, 2009). Compared with those living in communities with relatively new smoke-free laws (6–8 months), those in communities with more established laws (18 and 36 months) were more likely to be former smokers and report a longer time since smoking their last cigarette. Compared with the 6- to 8-month group, those in the 36-month group were more likely to have tried to quit since the law took effect. Smoke-free laws may have a delayed effect on cessation among adults. The longer a smoke-free law is in effect, the more likely adults will attempt to quit smoking and become former smokers. These findings have implications for policy advocacy in that maintaining integrity of smoke-free laws is a critical priority in protecting the public from exposure to SHS. Further research is needed to identify the effects of smoke-free laws on smoking prevalence in vulnerable populations including racial/ethnic minorities and those living in rural communities. In addition, research is needed to evaluate the differential impact of strength of smoke-free laws on cessation behaviors (e.g., comprehensive vs. laws with significant exemptions).

Economic Impact Studies

Nurses from University of Kentucky collaborated with economists to conduct three economic impact studies to assess the impact of smoke-free laws on employment in the hospitality industry, restaurant operating costs, and charitable gaming revenues (Pyles & Hahn, 2009; Pyles, Mullineaux, Okoi, & Hahn, 2007; Thompson et al., 2008). Given that the opposition typically perpetuates the myth that smoke-free laws harm business (Scollo, Lal, Hyland, & Glantz, 2003), research is critical to effectively advocate for the enactment and maintenance of comprehensive smoke-free laws with few or no exemptions. For example, some communities debate whether to exempt charitable gaming from smoke-free laws. Community organizations and school booster clubs with active fundraising in bingo halls may express fear that smoke-free laws may harm revenues from charitable gaming and negatively affect much needed income for extracurricular activities such as band or sports teams.

A time series study using fixed effects modeling analyzed charitable gaming revenues in 13 Kentucky communities with smoke-free laws compared to counties without such laws (Pyles & Hahn, 2009). When controlling for economic variables, county-specific effects, and time trends, there was no significant relationship between smoke-free laws and charitable gaming revenues. Municipal smoke-free legislation had no effect on charitable gaming revenues despite the fact that Kentucky is a tobacco-producing state with higher-than-average smoking rates.

A second economic impact study of Lexington, Kentucky's smoke-free law showed no economic harm after the law took effect (Pyles et al., 2007), similar to other economic studies (CDC, 2004; Scollo & Lal, 2008). There was a positive and significant relationship between the smoke-free legislation and restaurant employment, but no significant relationship with bar employment. No relationship was observed between the law's implementation and employment in contiguous counties nor between the smoke-free law and business openings or closures in alcohol-serving or nonalcohol-serving businesses.

A third economic study of one national restaurant chain showed that municipal smoke-free laws did not have a statistically significant effect on the probability of employee separation (Thompson et al., 2008). Over a 5-year period, there was no consistent pattern of either a decline or an increase in employee turnover after the implementation of a smoke-free law. The study examined payroll records of a franchisee of a national full-service restaurant chain that operates 23 restaurants in the state of Arizona. These results suggest that training costs associated with employee turnover would not rise for full-service restaurants in municipalities that adopt smoke-free laws.

A fourth nurse-led interdisciplinary team tracked economic data after the 2006 enactment of Nevada's voter-initiated clean indoor air act (NCIAA; York et al., 2009). Data were collected from 1999 through the first quarter of 2009 on restaurant and bar employment, openings, taxable sales, slot gaming revenues, and slot tax collections in one Nevada county. Controlling for seasonal effects and general economic trends, preliminary findings revealed no statistically significant downward economic trends in employment, bar, and restaurant openings, taxable sales or slot gaming revenues after the NCIAA. The results were presented to the Nevada Senate and Assembly in response to a proposal to weaken the NCIAA (York et al., 2009).

Community Readiness for Smoke-Free Policy

Nurses also have conducted research on community readiness for smoke-free policy. Nurse researchers from the University of Nebraska College of Nursing have evaluated the effectiveness of coalitions on policy change, attitudes, and public support for smoking restrictions using the Targeting Outcomes of Programs (TOP) evaluation model. The evaluation documented improved attitudes and knowledge about the harmfulness of SHS over time, leading to increased public support for smoke-free policies and significant changes in voluntary smoke-free restrictions in the home and workplace (Cramer, Roberts, & Xu, 2007). The University of Nebraska group has also conducted a formative evaluation study to guide coalition strategic planning on SHS risk reduction. Licensed child care facilities were the most ready for smoke-free policy change and residents were more interested in smoke-free restaurants than business owners perceived (Cramer, Mueller, & Harrop, 2003).

A nursing research study tested the effectiveness of an Internet media and capacity-building campaign on involvement in the political process and smoke-free bylaw development in Canada. Findings supported the utility of the Internet in mobilizing the community and building capacity for smoke-free policy development (Grierson, van Dijk, Dozois, & Mascher, 2006).

Four nurse-led studies assessed views of elected officials toward tobacco control policies in Kentucky. Elected state officials who had no affiliation with growing tobacco were more in favor of smoke-free policies, strong youth access laws, cigarette tax increases and local-level policy control than those who had affiliation with tobacco growing (Hahn & Rayens, 2000; Hahn, Toumey, Rayens, & McCoy, 1999). Elected officials with no personal or family history of tobacco use were also more supportive of tobacco control policies (York, Hahn, Rayens, & Talbert, 2008b). State officials who believe that SHS has a negative effect on health are more likely to support funding for smoking cessation programs (Hahn et al., 1999). Elected officials also report that contact with policy advocates and health groups increases their support for smoke-free law development while support from tobacco interests decrease officials' support (Hahn et al., 1999; York et al., 2008b).

Disparate Populations

There are a few nurse-led studies targeting readiness for smoke-free policy based on location (rural vs. urban) and population subgroup (i.e., casino workers, youth).

Rural Communities

As public support for smoke-free laws increases in the United States, a disparity in community readiness for smoke-free laws is evident between rural and urban communities. Using the Community Readiness model, one nurse-led study reported that smaller Kentucky communities were less ready than larger communities for smoke-free policy change (York, Hahn, Rayens, & Talbert, 2008a). A second nurse-led study evaluating rural smoke-free readiness in Kentucky found population size positively correlated with counties' capacity to implement tobacco control activities and antitobacco efforts (York et al., in press).

Casinos

Another disparate population in need of protection from SHS are casino workers and patrons. Casino employees face more severe exposure to SHS than other workforces due to weak or absent smoke-free laws covering gaming facilities (Berman & Post, 2007; CDC, 2009). Nonsmoking casino employees exposed to SHS have significantly higher levels of the tobacco metabolite cotinine in their urine and blood after their work shift (Trout, Decker, Mueller, Bernert, & Pirkle, 1998), significantly higher levels of NNAL, a tobacco specific carcinogen

(Anderson et al., 2003), and damage to the DNA, leading to an increased risk for cancer and heart disease (Collier, Dandge, Woodrow, & Pritsos, 2005). We identified one nurse-led research study examining the effect of Nevada's smoke-free policy exempting casino gaming areas on air quality in casinos. Nonsmoking restaurants in casino hotels had $PM_{2.5}$ levels between 5–102 µg/m³ ($M = 31$; $SD = 22.9$), while gaming areas in these same casino hotels ranged from 20 to 73 µg/m³ ($M = 48$; $SD = 15.9$; York & Lee, in press). There was also a strong correlation between $PM_{2.5}$ levels in nonsmoking restaurants and gaming areas ($r = .71$; $p = .005$). These findings indicate that $PM_{2.5}$ in hotel casinos is not restricted to the gaming floors with SHS drifting into nonsmoking areas, affecting employees and patrons who may consider themselves safe from SHS exposure. Even though 22 states have legalized gaming in casinos, only eight have enacted comprehensive laws protecting patrons and employees from SHS (ANR, 2009b). Further policy research is needed to evaluate the health and economic impact of these comprehensive laws and to determine effective advocacy strategies for enacting comprehensive smoke-free laws that include casinos.

Nursing research also is needed to determine the best cessation practices for casino employees who are continuously exposed to smoking cues and SHS during their work hours. Smoking casino employees believe their smoking behaviors are directly related to SHS exposure at work (Pilkington, Gray, Gilmore, & Daykin, 2006). These employees report widespread patron smoking throughout gaming areas; and their desire to quit smoking is hampered by watching others smoke throughout their workday (Pilkington et al., 2006; Shaffer, Eber, Hall, & Bilt, 1999; Trout et al., 1998). Examining this population is important as casino employees are rarely studied and represent an employee group with higher than typical health risks related to smoking and SHS exposure.

Youth

Few nurse-led investigations have assessed youth readiness for smoke-free policy. Youth who live in smoke-free communities are less likely to become established smokers than those who live in places that allow smoking (Siegel, Albers, Cheng, Hamilton, & Biener, 2008). Smoke-free laws may change the way youth view smoking and its social acceptability. One nurse-led study assessed the factors associated with SHS avoidance behavior among youth in Taiwan (Wang, Herting, & Tung, 2008). Secondhand smoke avoidance behaviors were predicted by individual characteristics (gender), interpersonal influence (family smoking behavior), cognition (knowledge), and affect (efficacy). Greater knowledge of and stronger attitudes opposed to SHS were predictors of youths' engagement in SHS avoidance behavior. Youth self-confidence and avoidance of SHS exposure was inversely related to the number of family members who smoke in the home and directly related to family discouragement of smoking among visitors (Wang et al., 2008).

Two nurse-led air quality studies revealed that SHS exposure in one rural Kentucky high school and at the State Capitol was dangerously high (Hahn, Lee, Riker, & Greenwell, 2005; Maggio, 2007). Nursing research is needed to evaluate the implementation and enforcement of school tobacco policies on SHS exposure in schools and health effects on youth and school personnel.

Smoke-Free Policy and Tobacco Industry Marketing

In 2005, tobacco companies spent over $13 billion marketing their products (Federal Trade Commission, 2007). Marketing practices include brand presence advertisements, promotional items, contests, and free trials of cigarettes (Sepe, Ling, & Glantz, 2002). These activities are aimed at moving the young adult from smoking experimentation to addiction (Ling & Glantz, 2002; Rigotti, Moran, & Wechsler, 2005).

Very few studies have examined the association between smoke-free policies and tobacco marketing. One study found that students who were protected by smoke-free policies had lower exposure to point-of-purchase marketing (Hammond, Costello, Fong, & Topham, 2006). One nurse-led pilot study of tobacco marketing in nightclubs and bars found that college students in a city with a comprehensive smoke-free policy reported less contact with tobacco marketer in nightclubs and bars compared to a city without a policy (Ridner, Walker, & Hahn, 2008). These small preliminary studies demonstrate the need for further research at the campus and community level to examine the relationship between policy protection and marketing exposure.

Measurement of Secondhand Smoke Exposure

Eight nurse-led studies, including three by the University of Kentucky group, reported measurement of SHS exposure in the community, using a variety of data sources from fine particulate air pollution to hair nicotine and self-report measures. Secondhand smoke exposure was documented in schools (Lee et al., 2007b), government buildings (Maggio, 2007), hospitality venues (Cramer et al., 2007; Hahn et al., 2006b; Lee et al., 2008; Okoli, Kelly, & Hahn, 2007), community mental health centers (Okoli, Johnson, & Malchy, 2009), and the general public (Okoli, Browning, Rayens, & Hahn, 2007).

Measuring SHS Exposure With Special Populations

Measuring SHS exposure in pregnant women and women during postpartum as well as in their infants present a unique challenge. Similar to smoking mothers, passive exposure to cigarette smoke damages the placenta by altering placental development (Genbacev, McMastera, Zdravkovic, & Fisher, 2003). Nicotine/cotinine is deposited in human amniotic fluid, fetal hair, meconium, placental tissue, and cord blood (Chan, Caprara, Blanchette, Klein, & Koren, 2004; Jauniaux, Gulbis, Acharya, Thiry, & Rodeck, 1999). Biomarkers for quantifying prenatal SHS exposure include salivary cotinine (Van't Hof, Wall, Dowler, & Stark, 2000), serum cotinine (Kharrazi, DeLorenze, Kaufman, Eskenazi, & Bernert, 2004), expired carbon monoxide (Hajek et al., 2001), urine cotinine (Webb, Boyd, Messina, & Windsor, 2003), hair cotinine (Klein & Koren, 1999), hair nicotine (Pichini et al., 2003), and personal or passive air monitors (Perera et al., 2004). Hair is one of the few biomarkers that provides a measure of chronic exposure to SHS in nonsmoking women (Pichini et al., 2003). Because human hair grows approximately 1 cm per month, hair offers an objective long-term measure for nonsmoking women exposed to SHS (Zahlsen & Nilsen, 1994).

One nurse-led study involved collection of hair samples from 209 postpartum women (within 48 hours of delivery) and 198 infants (Ashford et al., 2009). Maternal smoking status was the strongest predictor of nicotine consumption in both maternal and infant hair. Level of maternal and infant hair nicotine significantly correlated with one another, and maternal hair was a more valid measure of prenatal SHS exposure and smoking status. Mother–baby hair nicotine levels were also associated with urine cotinine levels.

Debate exists on the most objective measure of SHS in children. Urine cotinine levels, with a relatively short half-life (17 hours) decrease approximately 6% within 2 days of exposure (Repace, Al-Delaimy, & Bernert, 2006). Hair nicotine and urine cotinine levels in children have recently shown similar estimated values of air nicotine exposure (Repace et al., 2006). A mass biomarker screening program to identify children exposed to passive smoke reported urine cotinine was significantly higher if the mother smoked compared to if the father smoked (Ino, Shibuya, Saito, Ohshima, & Okada, 2006). Nursing research is needed to test measures of SHS exposure particularly in disparate populations such as pregnant women, infants, and children.

Measurement of Coalition Effectiveness in the Community

Nurse researchers from the University of Nebraska College of Nursing developed and tested the 30-item Internal Coalition Effectiveness (ICE) instrument to assess social vision, efficient coalition practices, knowledge and training relationships, participation, activities, and resources (Cramer, Atwood, & Stoner, 2006). The ICE was found to be a valid and reliable instrument for assessing internal effectiveness of coalition effectiveness. The ICE could be used to measure smoke-free coalition internal effectiveness in testing interventions to build capacity for smoke-free policy development.

Secondhand Smoke Reduction as a Population-Based Quit Smoking Strategy

Not only is eliminating exposure to SHS a public health priority, but it also is a known strategy to reduce tobacco consumption and promote tobacco cessation (CDC, 2000). One ongoing nurse-led evaluation study, GIFTS: Giving Infants and Families Tobacco-Free Starts, assists pregnant mothers to quit smoking and reduce their exposure to SHS during pregnancy (http://www.mc.uky.edu/KYgifts/index.htm). The GIFTS is a collaborative community engagement project with the Kentucky Department for Public Health, Kentucky Governor's Office of Wellness and Physical Activity, and the University of Kentucky College of Nursing. Key elements of the program include: (a) designation of a program coordinator and case managers; (b) identification of all pregnant women in the target area who smoke or who are exposed to secondhand (SHS) smoke; (c) individualized case management of women who smoke or are exposed to SHS during pregnancy; (d) proactive screening and referral for depression, social support, and domestic violence; and (e) development of a pregnancy and program specific database for outcome measures. In addition, participants are given an enrollment and delivery gift to enhance and acknowledge participation. Participants and their family members who are exposed to SHS are given the opportunity to track their CO levels and are referred to the local tobacco coordinator for additional counseling and community-based services.

There are very few studies of smoking cessation specifically among college students (Correia & Benson, 2006; Obermayer, Riley, Asif, & Jean-Mary, 2004; O'Neill, Gillispie, & Slobin, 2000; Ramsay & Hoffmann, 2004), and even fewer investigating population-based strategies with this group (Rooney, Silha, Gloyd, & Kreutz, 2005). Research that systematically examines SHS reduction and smoking cessation is lacking with the college population. However, a recent report by the American Lung Association (2008) documented decreases in smoking rates among college students with the introduction of smoke-free policies and comprehensive tobacco control efforts at several universities.

Exposure to Nicotine From SHS and Tobacco Dependence

While considerable research has examined the relationship between SHS exposure and health conditions and diseases, only recently have researchers begun to investigate the relationship between SHS exposure to nicotine and tobacco dependence. Secondhand smoke exposure can result in nicotine levels in nonsmokers comparable to that produced by active smoking (Al-Delaimy, Fraser, & Woodward, 2001; Dimlich-Ward, Gee, Brauer, & Leung, 1997). It has traditionally been believed that a person who does not smoke cigarettes cannot experience nicotine dependence. Yet, there is emerging evidence that a dose-response relation exists between SHS exposure and smoking behavior and symptoms of nicotine dependence. Two necessary conditions must be demonstrated for SHS to be pharmacologically linked to smoking behaviors: (1) environments of SHS must provide sufficient levels of exposure to nicotine, and (2) nicotine from such environments must be absorbed by nonsmokers in sufficient quantities known to have psychoactive effects among smokers.

In a nurse-led review (Okoli, Kelly, & Hahn, 2007), several studies assessing the quantity of SHS exposure (either from passive nicotine monitoring or self-report) and corresponding absorption (measured by biomarkers, i.e., cotinine) demonstrated that smoky environments can provide sufficient levels of exposure to nicotine at levels known to have psychoactive effects among smokers. This is consistent with studies reporting that SHS exposure in children (using salivary cotinine biomarkers) significantly predicted smoking initiation, even after controlling for demographic variables, number of siblings who smoke, and number of cigarettes smoked inside the home (Becklake, Ghezzo, & Ernst, 2005). Similarly, a nursing research study evaluated the relationship between SHS exposure in never-smoking fifth graders and perceived nicotine dependence (measured with items derived from the Nicotine Dependence Scale for Adolescents, Hooked on Nicotine Checklist, and ICD-10 criteria). The study found that 5% of never-smoking youth endorsed at least one symptom of nicotine dependence; and nicotine dependence symptoms were more likely to be endorsed with greater exposure to smoke in a car, after controlling for sibling and peer smoking, and smoking susceptibility (Bélanger et al., 2008). Further, a nursing research team demonstrated that the symptoms (i.e., cough, pleasure, nausea, sick, nervous, good, high, dizzy) experienced at initial smoking are associated with adolescents' exposure to smokers in their environment (Okoli, Richardson, & Johnson, 2008). Lastly, Okoli and colleagues (2007) examined the effects of SHS exposure on nonsmoking adult bar and restaurant employees and found a dose-response relationship between SHS exposure (measured by hair nicotine levels) and the number of withdrawal symptoms endorsed by nonsmoking bar and restaurant workers (Okoli, Rayens, & Hahn, 2007).

As a whole, these nursing research studies suggest there is a possible link between SHS exposure and tobacco dependence. Although the goal of smoke-free policies has been to limit the harm associated with the host of toxic contaminants in environmental tobacco smoke, the growing evidence of a link between SHS and tobacco dependence behaviors suggests that nurses need to advocate for smoke-free policies (particularly in homes and cars) to prevent potential uptake of smoking among susceptible youth and to enhance cessation among individuals who are motivated to quit smoking (Bélanger et al., 2008; Okoli, Browning, Rayens, & Hahn, 2007).

EMERGING TRENDS AND FUTURE RESEARCH OPPORTUNITIES

Research on exposure to SHS is an evolving field. As evidence grows about the harmful impact of exposure to SHS on health, new trends emerge about expanding protection against exposure at the community and population level. Thus, opportunities for research in this field abound. Below some of these trends and opportunities are discussed.

Outdoor Exposure to Secondhand Smoke

Although there is much evidence that tobacco smoke is a source of fine particulate indoor air pollution, few studies assess outdoor smoking areas as a point of source contaminants. A 1994 study in Los Angeles, California, estimated that tobacco smoke contributed to 1%–1.3% of the outdoor fine particle mass concentration (Rogge, Hildemann, Mazurek, & Cass, 1994). Recent studies document significant nicotine concentrations (California Air Resource Board, 2006), fine particle pollution (Boffi, Ruprecht, Mazza, Ketzel, & Invernizzi, 2006), respirable particles (RSP; Repace, 2005), and carcinogenic particulate polycyclic aromatic hydrocarbons (PPAH) from SHS in outdoor locations (Repace et al., 2006). In one experiment, diesel car exhaust doubled the outdoor fine particle pollution levels, whereas cigarette smoke produced 15 times the outdoor levels (Invernizzi et al., 2004). Most recently, Klepeis, Ott, & Switzer (2007) found that average outdoor tobacco smoke near active sources (i.e., during active smoking) are comparable to the average exposure from indoor SHS exposure; although average tobacco smoke levels drop almost immediately after active smoking ceases outdoors. Nursing research is needed to further assess the extent of SHS exposure in different outdoor venues and the health risk posed by such exposure.

Tobacco-Free Health Care Facilities

Smoke-free policies in hospital settings correspond with increases in tobacco cessation among workers (Longo, Johnson, Kruse, Brownson, & Hewett, 2001). It is recommended that smoke-free hospital initiatives be integrated into the health promoting hospitals initiative (Whitehead, 2005; World Health Organization, 1990, 1991, 1997) rather than being an isolated project. For example, smoke-free policies in psychiatric wards are often a result of broader tobacco control policies (Green & Hawranik, 2008). Although smoke-free policies in psychiatric wards do not produce adverse behavioral outcomes or noncompliance, these policies have not shown an effect on smoking cessation (el-Guebaly, Cathcart, Currie,

Brown, & Gloster, 2002). There are no nurse-led investigations of the impact of tobacco-free policies in health care facilities. Nursing research is needed to test withdrawal management interventions with smokers who experience forced abstinence (Zack, 2002), as well as the health outcomes and unintended consequences of tobacco-free health care facility policies.

Tobacco-Free Colleges and Universities

Colleges and universities have been slow to protect their students from SHS in campus buildings and residence halls. In a 1999 national survey of campus health and medical directors, only 27% reported that smoking was restricted in all campus buildings including residence halls (Wechsler, Kelley, Seibring, Kuo, & Rigotti, 2001). The American Nonsmokers' Rights Foundation (2009) reports that after a search of Internet Web sites, student handbooks, and documents from tobacco prevention agencies, over 1,200 college and university campuses had smoke-free policies in place. Of those with policies, more than 300 have 100% smoke-free environments restricting smoking both inside and outdoors. For college students who were not regular smokers in high school, living in a smoke-free residence hall is associated with a decrease in smoking initiation and progression to regular smoking (Wechsler, Lee, & Rigotti, 2001). Concerns frequently cited for colleges and universities not going smoke free include economic burden and concerns over student complaints. However, a study conducted at three universities in different states showed that enacting smoke-free residence hall policies did not affect the demand for university housing, student retention, or application rates (Gerson, Allard, & Towvim, 2005). There was a decrease in roommate conflict and the structural damage that buildings incur secondary to smoking. The benefits of smoke-free policies on campus far outweigh the barriers.

There is evidence that readiness for smoke-free policy on college and university campuses may be on the rise in recent years. In 1999, over one third of college students were interested in knowing more about the ill effects of SHS exposure (DeBernardo et al., 1999). More recently, Smith, Applegate, and Seo (2006) reported that 96% of college students agreed that exposure to SHS is harmful. In addition, several nurse-led studies have documented that support for smoke-free policies among nonsmoking and smoking college students is mounting (Ott, Cashin, & Altekruse, 2005; Ridner, Hahn, Staten, & Miller, 2006). Ridner and colleagues (2006) found that over 60% of college students were bothered by smoking at the entrances to buildings and nearly 30% of current smokers in that study agreed. Given that over 80% of college students are not current smokers (American College Health Association, 2009), protecting this population from the ill effects of SHS is paramount.

Future Research Opportunities

There is a need for nursing research on the differential effects of smoke-free policy on subpopulations who may be disproportionately affected by tobacco use; that is, low socioeconomic status, racial/ethnic groups, casino workers, youth, women, individuals with mental illness and substance use disorders (Bell et al., 2009). Further, more research is needed to understand how smoke-free policy influences tobacco industry marketing practices.

As smoke-free workplaces become the norm and health care/educational campuses go completely tobacco free, there is need for research on the unintended consequences of policy change. For example, how does the increased visibility of health care professionals smoking on the periphery of tobacco-free health care campuses affect societal perceptions and behaviors, especially among youth? Do tobacco-free campuses promote dual use of noncombustible tobacco products (i.e., snus and spit tobacco) and cigarettes/cigars? Do smokers and spit users switch to spitless products (i.e., snus) when there is a tobacco-free campus policy? What strategies are most effective in promoting compliance with tobacco-free campus policies? What is the association between community-wide smoke-free laws/regulations and compliance with tobacco-free health care campuses? How do smoke-free policies affect the most vulnerable subgroups including low-socioeconomic status, racial/ethnic groups, and women?

Further research is needed to examine SHS reduction as a quit smoking strategy. More population-based smoking cessation studies need to test the effects of SHS reduction as an intervention strategy. Three nursing research studies provide support for the role of SHS exposure in tobacco dependence among nonsmoking adults and youth. Further research is needed to examine the role of SHS exposure in preventing potential uptake of smoking among susceptible youth and enhancing cessation among individuals who are motivated to quit smoking.

In addition to studying the effects of policy change and SHS reduction as a quit strategy, nursing research is needed to better understand the dynamics of policy development, and how best to measure SHS exposure in vulnerable populations including hospitality workers, pregnant women, infants, youth, and individuals with mental illness and addictions. Studies by nurse researchers at the University of Nebraska provide data on how best to build capacity for smoke-free policy via coalition effectiveness. Four studies from the University of Kentucky-affiliated nurse scientist group sheds light on policy-maker views and characteristics that impact smoke-free policy development. No nursing research articles were found that study building demand for smoke-free policy. Research is needed to better understand how best to frame public health messages and market the health brand to elected officials, vulnerable population groups, and the public at large. Further, there is need for research on the role of the opposition in limiting demand for smoke-free policy. While identifying, anticipating, and exposing the opposition is a known advocacy strategy in smoke free campaigns, there is little research on the efficacy of these strategies in changing public policy. Lastly, nursing research is needed to understand ways that scientific evidence is acquired and used by policy makers and what role science plays in smoke-free policy change.

CONCLUSIONS

Given that nurses have a social obligation to be involved in public policy development (Bialous et al., 2003), the opportunities for community-based and policy research by nurses are infinite. This chapter highlights the policy and community-based research conducted by nurses to document the health and economic outcomes of smoke-free policy, as well as the studies designed to further understand readiness for smoke-free policy development through building capacity and demand for public policy.

Most of the nursing research in community-based approaches to reducing SHS exposure has been policy outcome studies, documenting the improvement of health outcomes and the lack of economic harm to business or charitable gaming revenues. There is emerging nursing science exploring the possible link between SHS exposure to nicotine and tobacco dependence in youth and non-smoking adults, suggesting one plausible explanation for SHS reduction as a quit smoking strategy. Another group of nursing research studies addresses community readiness for smoke-free policy, examining the factors that build capacity for smoke-free policy (i.e., coalition effectiveness, policymakers' views). This growing body of nursing research provides an excellent opportunity for nurses to conduct and participate in community and population-based research to reduce exposure to SHS for both vulnerable populations and society at large.

The opportunities for growing this critically important area of nursing research are endless. The benefits of conducting this type of population-based research are clear. Reducing exposure to SHS for entire populations will undoubtedly reduce the health and economic burden of tobacco use. The opportunities and challenges are many. Most of the authors of this chapter are public health nurses and policy development is an essential function of their practice. Public health nurses who conduct policy research studies need to be cognizant of the delicate balance between policy research and policy advocacy. One can be a scholar and an advocate but must have a deliberate plan to separate these goals for research and practice. For example, a nurse advocate may have to take a more behind-the-scenes role in the coalition when conducting policy research. Building an interdisciplinary team is critical, not only to provide needed expertise but also to provide separation between the role as advocate and scholar.

REFERENCES

Al-Delaimy, W. K., Fraser, T., & Woodward, A. (2001). Nicotine in hair of bar and restaurant staff. *New Zealand Medical Journal, 114*, 80–83.

American College Health Association. (2009). American college health association national college health assessment spring 2008 reference group data report (abridged). *Journal of American College Health, 57*(5), 477–488.

American Lung Association. (2008). *Big tobacco on campus: Ending the addiction.* Washington, D.C.: American Lung Association, 2008.

Americans for Nonsmokers' Rights. (2009a). *Percent of U.S. state populations covered by 100% smokefree air laws.* Retrieved July 9, 2009, from http://www.no-smoke.org/pdf/percentstatepops.pdf

Americans for Nonsmokers' Rights. (2009b). *Smoke-free gaming laws.* Retrieved June 20, 2009, from www.no-smoke.org/pdf/100smokefreecasinos.pdf

American Nonsmokers' Rights Foundation. (2009). *U.S. colleges and universities with smoke-free air policies.* Berkeley, CA.

Anderson, K., Kliris, J., Murphy, L., Carmella, S., Han, S., Link, C., et al. (2003). Metabolites of a tobacco-specific lung carcinogen in nonsmoking casino patrons. *Cancer Epidemiology, Biomarkers & Prevention, 12*(12), 1544–1546.

Ashford, K. B., Hahn, E. J., Hall, L. A., Rayens, M. K., Noland, M., & Collins, R. (2009). *Measuring prenatal secondhand smoke exposure in mother-baby couplets.* Manuscript submitted for publication.

Becklake, M. R., Ghezzo, H., & Ernst, P. (2005). Childhood predictors of smoking in adolescence: A follow-up study of Montreal schoolchildren. *Canadian Medical Association Journal, 173*, 377–379.

Bélanger, M., O'Loughlin, J., Okoli, C. T. C., McGrath, J. J., Setia, M., Guyon, L., et al. (2008). Nicotine dependence symptoms among young never-smokers exposed to secondhand tobacco smoke. *Addictive Behaviors, 33*, 1557–1563.

Bell, K., McCullough, L., Devries, K., Jategaonkar, N., Greaves, L., & Richardson, L. (2009). Location restrictions on smoking: Assessing their differential impacts and consequences in the workplace. *Canadian Journal of Public Health, 100*(1), 46–50.

Berman, M., & Post, C. (2007). *Secondhand smoke and casinos.* Retrieved January 22, 2009, from www.wmitchell.edu/tobaccoLaw/documents/casino.pdf

Bialous, S. A., Kaufman, N., & Sarna, L. (2003). Tobacco control policies. *Seminars in Oncology Nursing, 19*, 291–300.

Boffi, R., Ruprecht, A., Mazza, R., Ketzel, M., & Invernizzi, G. (2006). A day at the European respiratory society congress: Passive smoking influences both outdoor and indoor air quality. *European Respiratory Journal, 27*(4), 862–863.

California Air Resource Board. (2006, January 26). *Rulemaking to consider proposed identification of environmental tobacco smoke as a toxic air contaminant.* Retrieved May 18, 2006, from http://www.arb.ca.gov/regact/ets2006/ets2006.htm

Centers for Disease Control and Prevention. (2000). Strategies for reducing exposure to environmental tobacco smoke, increasing tobacco-use cessation, and reducing initiation in communities and health-care systems. *Morbidity and Mortality Weekly Report, 49*(RR12).

Centers for Disease Control and Prevention. (2004). Impact of a smoking ban on restaurant and bar revenues—El Paso, Texas, 2002. *Morbidity and Mortality Weekly Report*, 53(7), 150–152.

Centers for Disease Control and Prevention. (2008). Disparities in secondhand smoke exposure—United States, 1988–1994 and 1999–2004. *Morbidity and Mortality Weekly Report*, 57(27), 744–747.

Centers for Disease Control and Prevention. (2009). *Secondhand smoke and casino dealers*. Retrieved June 20, 2009, from www.cdc.gov/niosh/blog/

Chan, D., Caprara, D., Blanchette, P., Klein, J., & Koren, G. (2004). Recent developments in meconium and hair testing methods for the confirmation of gestational exposures to alcohol and tobacco smoke. *Clinical Biochemistry*, 37, 429–438.

Collier, A. C., Dandge, S. D., Woodrow, J. E., & Pritsos, C. A. (2005). Differences in DNA-damage in non-smoking men and women exposed to environmental tobacco smoke (ETS). *Toxicology Letters*, 158(1), 10–19.

Correia, C. J., & Benson, T. A. (2006). The use of contingency management to reduce cigarette smoking among college students. *Experimental and Clinical Psychopharmacology*, 14(2), 171–179.

Cramer, M., Atwood, J., & Stoner, J. (2006). Measuring community coalition effectiveness using the ICE instrument. *Public Health Nursing*, 23(1), 74–87.

Cramer, M., Roberts, S., & Xu, L. (2007). Evaluating community-based programs for eliminating secondhand smoke using evidence-based research for best practices. *Family and Community Health*, 30(2), 129–143.

Cramer, M. E., Mueller, K. J., & Harrop, D. (2003). Evaluation informs coalition programming for environmental tobacco smoke reduction. *Journal of Community Health Nursing*, 20(4), 245–258.

DeBernardo, R. L., Aldinger, C. E., Dawood, O. R., Hanson, R. E., Lee, S. J., & Rinaldi, S. R. (1999). An e-mail assessment of undergraduates' attitudes toward smoking. *Journal of American College Health*, 48, 61–66.

Dimlich-Ward, H., Gee, H., Brauer, M., & Leung, V. (1997). Analysis of nicotine and cotinine in the hair of hospitality workers exposed to environmental tobacco smoke. *Journal of Occupational and Environmental Medicine*, 39, 946–948.

el-Guebaly, N., Cathcart, J., Currie, S., Brown, D., & Gloster, S. (2002). Public health and therapeutic aspects of smoking bans in mental health and addiction settings. *Psychiatric Services*, 53(12), 1617–1622.

Federal Trade Commission. (2007). *Federal trade commission cigarette report for 2004 and 2005*. Washington, DC: Author.

Genbacev, O., McMastera, M. T., Zdravkovic, T., & Fisher, S. J. (2003). Disruption of oxygen-regulated responses underlies pathological changes in the placentas of women who smoke or who are passively exposed to smoke during pregnancy. *Reproductive Toxicology*, 17, 509–518.

Gerson, M., Allard, J. L., & Towvim, L. G. (2005). Impact of smoke-free residence hall policies: The views of administrators at 3 state universities. *Journal of American College Health*, 54(3), 157–165.

Glantz, S. A. (2008). Meta-analysis of the effects of smokefree laws on acute myocardial infarction: An update. *Preventive Medicine*, 47, 452–453.

Greathouse, L., Hahn, E., Okoli, C., Warnick, T., & Riker, C. (2005). Passing a smoke-free law in a pro-tobacco culture: A multiple streams approach. *Policy, Politics and Nursing Practice*, 6(3), 211–220.

Greaves, L. J., & Hemsing, M. J. (2009). Sex, gender, and secondhand smoke policies: Implications for disadvantaged women. *American Journal of Preventive Medicine*, 37, S131–S137.

Green, M. A., & Hawranik, P. G. (2008). Smoke-free policies in the psychiatric population on the ward and beyond: A discussion paper. *International Journal of Nursing Studies*, 45(10), 1543–1549.

Grierson, T., van Dijk, M. W., Dozois, E., & Mascher, J. (2006). Using the internet to build community capacity for healthy public policy. *Health Promotion Practice*, 7, 13–22.

Hahn, E., Lee, K., Okoli, C., Troutman, A., & Powell, R. (2005). Smoke-free laws and indoor air pollution in Lexington and Louisville. *Louisville Medicine*, 52(10), 391–394, 409, 415.

Hahn, E., Lee, K., Riker, C., & Greenwell, D. (2005). *Indoor air pollution from secondhand smoke in Monroe County*. Lexington: University of Kentucky.

Hahn, E. J., & Rayens, M. K. (2000). Public opinion and legislators' views on tobacco policy. *Journal of the Kentucky Medical Association*, 98(2), 67–73.

Hahn, E. J., Rayens, M. K., Butler, K. M., Zhang, M., Durbin, E., & Steinke, D. (2008). Smoke-free laws and adult smoking prevalence. *Preventive Medicine*, 47(2), 206–209.

Hahn, E., Rayens, M., Langley, R., Darville, A., & Dignan, M. (2009). Time since smoke-free law and smoking cessation behaviors. *Nicotine & Tobacco Research*. doi: 10.1093/ntr/ntp1086

Hahn, E. J., Rayens, M. K., Lee, S., Burkhart, P., & Moser, D. (2006, July). *Smoke-free laws and acute asthma and cardiac outcomes*. Paper presented at the Thirteenth World Conference on Tobacco or Health.

Hahn, E., Rayens, M., York, N., Okoli, C., Zhang, M., Dignan, M., et al. (2006). Effects of a smoke-free law on hair nicotine and respiratory symptoms in restaurant and bar workers. *Journal of Occupational and Environmental Medicine*, 48(9), 906–913.

Hahn, E. J., Toumey, C. P., Rayens, M. K., & McCoy, C. A. (1999). Kentucky legislators' views on tobacco policy. *American Journal of Preventive Medicine*, 16(2), 81–88.

Hajek, P., West, R., Lee, A., Foulds, J., Owen, L., Eiser, J. R., et al. (2001). Randomized controlled trial of a midwife-delivered brief smoking cessation intervention in pregnancy. *Addiction*, 96(3), 485–494.

Hammond, D., Costello, M. J., Fong, G. T., & Topham, J. (2006). Exposure to tobacco marketing and support for tobacco control policies. *American Journal of Health Behavior*, 30(6), 700–709.

Heloma, A., & Jaakkola, M. S. (2003). Four-year follow-up of smoke exposure, attitudes and smoking behaviour following enactment of Finland's national smoke-free workplace law. *Addiction*, 98(8), 1111–1117.

Ino, T., Shibuya, T., Saito, K., Ohshima, J., & Okada, R. (2006). A passive smoking screening program for children. *Preventive Medicine*, 42, 427–429.

Invernizzi, G., Ruprecht, A., Mazza, R., Rossetti, E., Sasco, A., Nardini, S., et al. (2004). Particulate matter from tobacco versus diesel car exhaust: An educational perspective. *Tobacco Control*, 13(3), 219–221.

Jauniaux, E., Gulbis, B., Acharya, G., Thiry, P., & Rodeck, C. (1999). Maternal tobacco exposure and cotinine levels in fetal fluids in the first half of pregnancy. *Obstretrics & Gynecology, 93*(1), 25–29.

Kharrazi, M., DeLorenze, G. N., Kaufman, F. L., Eskenazi, B., & Bernert, J. T. (2004). Environmental tobacco smoke and pregnancy outcome. *Epidemiology, 15*(6), 660–670.

Klein, J., & Koren, G. (1999). Hair analysis—a biological marker for passive smoking in pregnancy and childhood. *Human & Experimental Toxicology, 18*(4), 279–282.

Klepeis, N. E., Ott, W. R., & Switzer, P. (2007). Real-time measurement of outdoor tobacco smoke particles. *Journal of the Air & Waste Management Association, 57*(5), 522–534.

Kottke, T. E., Aase, L. A., Brandel, C. L., Brekke, M. J., Brekke, L. N., DeBoer, S. W., et al. (2001). Attitudes of Olmsted County, Minnesota, residents about tobacco smoke in restaurants and bars. *Mayo Clinic Proceedings, 76,* 134–137.

Lee, K., Hahn, E. J., Okoli, C. T. C., Repace, J., & Troutman, A. (2008). Differential impact of smoke-free laws on indoor air quality. *Journal of Environmental Health, 70*(8), 24–30.

Lee, K., Hahn, E. J., Riker, C., Head, S., & Seithers, P. (2007). Immediate impact of smoke-free laws on indoor air quality. *Southern Medical Journal, 100*(9), 885–889.

Lee, K., Hahn, E. J., Riker, C. A., Hoehne, A., White, A., & Thompson, D. (2007). Secondhand smoke exposure in a rural high school. *Journal of School Nursing, 23*(4), 222–228.

Lee, K., Hahn, E., Robertson, H., Lee, S., Vogel, S., & Travers, M. (2009). Strength of smoke-free laws and indoor air quality. *Nicotine & Tobacco Research.* doi:10.1093/ntr/ntp026

Ling, P. M., & Glantz, S. A. (2002). Why and how the tobacco industry sells cigarettes to young adults: Evidence from industry documents. *American Journal of Public Health, 92*(6), 908–916.

Longo, D. R., Johnson, J. C., Kruse, R. L., Brownson, R. C., & Hewett, J. E. (2001). A prospective investigation of the impact of smoking bans on tobacco cessation and relapse. *Tobacco Control, 10*(3), 267–272.

Maggio, L. (2007). *Secondhand smoke exposure at the Kentucky State Capitol.* Paper presented at the Southern Nursing Research Society.

McMillen, R. C., Winickoff, J. P., Klein, J. D., & Weitzman, M. (2003). U.S. adult attitudes and practices regarding smoking restrictions and child exposure to environmental tobacco smoke: Changes in the social climate from 2000–2001. *Pediatrics, 112*(1), 55–60.

Moore, D. W. (2005). *Increased support for smoking bans in public places.* Princeton, NJ: The Gallup Organization.

National Toxicology Program. (2002). *10th report on carcinogens.* Research Triangle Park, NC: U.S. Department of Health and Human Services, Public Health Service, National Toxicology Program.

Obermayer, J. L., Riley, W. T., Asif, O., & Jean-Mary, J. (2004). College smoking-cessation using cell phone text messaging. *Journal of American College Health, 53*(2), 71–78.

Okoli, C. T. C., Browning, S., Rayens, M. K., & Hahn, E. J. (2007). Secondhand tobacco smoke exposure, nicotine dependence, and smoking cessation. *Public Health Nursing, 25*(1), 46–56.

Okoli, C. T. C., Hall, L. A., Rayens, M. K., & Hahn, E. J. (2007). Measuring tobacco smoke exposure among smoking and nonsmoking bar and restaurant workers. *Biological Research for Nursing, 9*(1), 81–89.

Okoli, C. T. C., Johnson, J. L., & Malchy, L. (2009). Correlates of secondhand tobacco smoke exposure among persons with severe and persistent mental illness (SPMI) accessing community mental health services. *Community Mental Health Journal, 45*(3), 188–198.

Okoli, C. T. C., Kelly, T., & Hahn, E. J. (2007). Secondhand smoke and nicotine exposure: A brief review. *Addictive Behaviors, 32*, 1977–1988.

Okoli, C. T. C., Rayens, M. K., & Hahn, E. J. (2007). Behavioral effects of nicotine exposure from secondhand tobacco smoke among bar and restaurant workers. *Addictive Behaviors, 32*, 1922–1928.

Okoli, C. T. C., Richardson, C. G., & Johnson, J. L. (2008). An examination of the relationship between adolescents' initial smoking experience and their exposure to peer and family member smoking. *Addictive Behaviors, 33*(9), 1183–1191.

O'Neill, H. K., Gillispie, M. A., & Slobin, K. (2000). Stages of change and smoking cessation: A computer-administered intervention program for young adults. *American Journal of Health Promotion, 15*(2), 93–96, iii.

Otsuka, R., Watanabe, H., Hirata, K., Tokai, K., Muro, T., Yoshiyama, M., et al. (2001). Acute effects of passive smoking on the coronary circulation in healthy young adults. *Journal of the American Medical Association, 286*(4), 436–441.

Ott, C. H., Cashin, S. E., & Altekruse, M. (2005). Development and validation of the college tobacco survey. *Journal of American College Health, 53*(5), 231–238.

Perera, F. P., Rauh, V., Whyatt, R. M., Tsai, W. Y., Bernert, J. T., Tu, Y. H., et al. (2004). Molecular evidence of an interaction between prenatal environmental exposures and birth outcomes in a multiethnic population. *Environmental Health Perspectives, 112*(5), 626–630.

Pichini, S., Garcia-Algar, O., Munoz, L., Vall, O., Pacifici, R., Figueroa, C., et al. (2003). Assessment of chronic exposure to cigarette smoke and its change during pregnancy by segmental analysis of maternal hair nicotine. *Journal of Exposure Analysis and Environmental Epidemiology, 13*(2), 144–151.

Pickett, M. S., Schober, S. E., Brody, D. J., Curtin, L. R., & Giovino, G. A. (2006). Smoke-free laws and secondhand smoke exposure in U.S. non-smoking adults, 1999–2002. *Tobacco Control, 15*, 302–307.

Pilkington, P. A., Gray, S., Gilmore, A. B., & Daykin, N. (2006). Attitudes towards second hand smoke amongst a highly exposed workforce: Survey of London casino workers. *Journal of Public Health, 28*(2), 104–110.

Pyles, M. K., & Hahn, E. J. (2009). Smoke-free legislation and charitable gaming in Kentucky. *Tobacco Control, 18*, 60–62.

Pyles, M. K., Mullineaux, D. J., Okoi, C. T. C., & Hahn, E. J. (2007). Economic impact of a smoke-free law in a tobacco-growing community. *Tobacco Control, 16*, 66–68.

Ramsay, J., & Hoffmann, A. (2004). Smoking cessation and relapse prevention among undergraduate students: A pilot demonstration project. *Journal of American College Health, 53*(1), 11–18.

Rayens, M. K., Burkhart, P. V., Zhang, M., Lee, S., Moser, D. K., Mannino, D., et al. (2008). Reduction in asthma-related emergency department visits after implementation of a smoke-free law. *Journal of Allergy and Clinical Immunology, 122*(3), 537–541.

Rayens, M. K., Hahn, E. J., Langley, R. E., Hedgecock, S., Butler, K. M., & Greathouse-Maggio, L. (2007). Public opinion and smoke-free laws. *Policy, Politics, & Nursing Practice, 8*(4), 262–270.

Rayens, M.K., Hahn, E.J., Langley, R.E., & Zhang, M. (2008). Public support for smoke-free laws in rural communities. *American Journal of Preventive Medicine, 34*(6), 519–522.

Repace, J. (2005, June 1). *Measurements of outdoor air pollution from secondhand smoke on the UMBC campus.* Retrieved July 20, 2009, from www.repace.com/pdf/outdoorair.pdf

Repace, J., Al-Delaimy W. K., & Bernert, J. (2006). Correlating atmospheric markers in studies of secondhand tobacco smoke exposure and dose in children and adults. *Journal of Occupational & Environmental Medicine, 48*(2), 181–194.

Ridner, S.L., Hahn, E.J., Staten, R., & Miller, K. (2006). Attitudes toward secondhand smoke among college students. *Southern Online Journal of Nursing Research, 7*(1), 1–14.

Ridner, S.L., Walker, K. L., & Hahn, E.J. (2008). College students' knowledge, exposure, and the pervasiveness of tobacco marketing in two Kentucky cities. *Kentucky Journal of Communication, 27*(2), 107–124.

Rigotti, N.A., Moran, S.E., & Wechsler, H. (2005). US college students' exposure to tobacco promotions: Prevalence and association with tobacco use. *American Journal of Public Health, 95*(1), 138–144.

Rogge W. F., Hlldemann L. M., Mazurek M. A., & Cass G. R. (1994). Sources of fine organic aerosol. 6. Cigarette smoke in the urban atmosphere. *Environmental Science Technology, 28*(7), 1375–1388.

Rooney, B.L., Silha, P., Gloyd, J., & Kreutz, R. (2005). Quit and win smoking cessation contest for Wisconsin college students. *Wisconsin Medical Journal, 104*(4), 45–49.

Scollo, M., & Lal, A. (2008). *Summary of studies assessing the economic impact of smoke-free policies in the hospitality industry.* Melbourne, Australia: VicHealth Centre for Tobacco Control.

Scollo, M., Lal, A., Hyland, A., & Glantz, S. (2003). Review of the quality of studies on the economic effects of smoke-free policies on the hospitality industry. *Tobacco Control, 12*(1), 13–20.

Sepe, E., Ling, P. M., & Glantz, S.A. (2002). Smooth moves: Bar and nightclub tobacco promotions that target young adults. *American Journal of Public Health, 92*(3), 414–419.

Shaffer, H.J., Eber, G.B., Hall, M.N., & Bilt, J.V. (1999). Smoking behavior among casino employees: Self-report validation using plasma cotinine. *Addictive Behaviors, 25*(5), 693–704.

Siegel, M., Albers, A.B., Cheng, D.M., Hamilton, W.L., & Biener, L. (2008). Local restaurant smoking regulations and the adolescent smoking initiation process: Results of a multilevel contextual analysis among Massachusetts youth. *Archives of Pediatrics & Adolescent Medicine, 162*(5), 477–483.

Smith, M.L., Applegate, T., & Seo, D. C. (2006). A preliminary awareness study of tobacco issues among college students. *American Journal of Health Studies, 23*(1), 238–244.

Thompson, E., Hahn, E., Blomquist, G., Garen, J., Mullineaux, D., Ogunro, G., et al. (2008). Smoke-free laws and employee turnover. *Contemporary Economic Policy, 26*(3), 351–359.

Trout, D., Decker, J., Mueller, J., Bernert, J.T., & Pirkle, J. (1998). Exposure of casino employees: Self-report validation using plasma cotinine. *Journal of Occupational & Environmental Medicine, 40*, 270–276.

U.S. Department of Health and Human Services. (2006). *The health consequences of involuntary exposure to tobacco smoke: A report of the surgeon general.* Atlanta, GA: Department of Health and Human Services, Public Health Service, Centers for Disease Control and Prevention, National Center for Chronic Disease and Prevention and Promotion, Office of Smoking and Health.

Van't Hof, S. M., Wall, M. A., Dowler, D. W., & Stark, M. J. (2000). Randomised controlled trial of a postpartum relapse prevention intervention. *Tobacco Control, 9*(Suppl. 3), III64–III66.

Wang W., Herting J. R., & Tung Y. (2008). Adolescents' avoidance of secondhand smoke exposure: Model testing. *Western Journal of Nursing Research, 30*(7), 836–851.

Webb, D. A., Boyd, N. R., Messina, D., & Windsor, R. A. (2003). The discrepancy between self-reported smoking status and urine cotinine levels among women enrolled in prenatal care at four publicly funded clinical sites. *Journal of Public Health Management Practice, 9*(4), 322–325.

Wechsler, H., Kelley, K., Seibring, M., Kuo, M., & Rigotti, N. A. (2001). College smoking policies and smoking cessation programs: Results of a survey of college health center directors. *Journal of American College Health, 49*(5), 205–212.

Wechsler, H., Lee, J. E., & Rigotti, N. A. (2001). Cigarette use by college students in smoke-free housing: Results of a national study. *American Journal of Preventive Medicine, 20*(3), 202–207.

Whitehead, D. (2005). Health promoting hospitals: the role and function of nursing. *Journal of Clinical Nursing, 14*(1), 20–27.

World Health Organization. (1990). *Initiation of international network of health promoting hospitals at WHO-EURO workshop.* Paper presented at the World Health Organization, Vienna.

World Health Organization. (1991). *The Budapest declaration of health promoting hospitals.* Paper presented at the World Health Organization, Copenhagen.

World Health Organization. (1997). *The Vienna recommendations on health promoting hospitals.* Paper presented at the World Health Organization, Copenhagen.

York, N. L., Cochran, C., Shen, J., Schwer, K., Williams, D., & Azzrelli, M. (2009). *The economic impact of Nevada's clean indoor air act in Clark county.* Carson City: Nevada Assembly Judiciary Committee.

York, N. L., Hahn, E. J., Rayens, M. K., & Talbert, J. (2008a). Community readiness for local smoke-free policy change. *American Journal of Health Promotion, 23*, 112–120.

York, N. L., Hahn, E. J., Rayens, M. K., & Talbert, J. (2008b). Local elected officials' views on smoke-free policy in Kentucky. *Kentucky Journal of Communication, 27*(2), 125–146.

York, N. L., & Lee, K. (in press). Casino air quality after enactment of Nevada's clean indoor air act. *Public Health Nursing.*

York, N. L., Rayens, M. K., Zhang, M., Jones, L. G., Casey, B. R., & Hahn, E. J. (in press). Strength of tobacco control in rural communities. *Journal of Rural Health.*

Zack, E. (2002). Smoking withdrawal and prolonged hospitalization. *Clinical Journal of Oncology Nursing, 6*(1), 7–11.

Zahlsen, K., & Nilsen, O. G. (1994). Nicotine in hair of smokers and non-smokers: Sampling procedure and gas chromatographic/mass spectrometric analysis. *Pharmacology & Toxicology, 75*(3–4), 143–149.

Chapter 16

Opportunities for Nursing Research in Tobacco Control

Stella Aguinaga Bialous and Linda Sarna

ABSTRACT

Nurse scientists have made important contributions to evidence-based practice in tobacco control. This chapter will discuss recent tobacco control developments in the United States and globally, such as legislation giving the U.S. Food and Drug Administration regulatory authority over tobacco products manufacturing, marketing and sales, the World Health Organization Framework Convention on Tobacco Control, and a brief review of research that has guided policy advances and nursing research in tobacco control. Suggestions for future research based on the update of the U.S. Public Health Services Treating Tobacco Use and Dependence clinical practice guideline will be explored. These developments offer nursing researchers a wealth of opportunities and challenges to advance nursing and tobacco control knowledge, address research gaps, and bring a unique nursing perspective to tobacco use prevention, reduction of exposure to secondhand smoke, tobacco dependence treatment, and tobacco control policies. Additionally, we will address how nursing scholarship can and should be supported by academic and organizational leadership to support nurses in realizing their full potential in mitigating the global epidemic of tobacco-caused death and disease.

DOI: 10.1891/0739-6686.27.393

Keywords: tobacco control; policy; smoking; smoking cessation; research; nursing

The past decade has seen an increase in nurse-generated knowledge in tobacco control. Nurses are making a significant contribution in the areas of tobacco prevention, cessation, reduction of exposure to secondhand smoke (SHS), and tobacco control policy. Nurses have demonstrated their power to develop and implement evidence-based practices and to be crucial partners in local, national, and international initiatives to address the negative health and economic impact of the tobacco-related epidemic. Nonetheless, significant gaps remain. This chapter will discuss recent developments that offer nurse scientists the opportunity to address some of the research gaps, provide a brief overview of research that has guided policy advances and of current nursing research in tobacco control. We will discuss challenges for nursing involvement in tobacco research while also proposing strategies to overcome these challenges.

RECENT DEVELOPMENTS PROVIDING RESEARCH OPPORTUNITIES

Recent developments in tobacco control in the United States and internationally have opened up historic opportunities for scientists in this field, as discussed below.

The Family Smoking Prevention and Tobacco Control Act

On June 22, 2009, President Barack Obama signed into law the Family Smoking Prevention and Tobacco Control Act. This new law (H.R. 1256) gives the U.S. Food and Drug Administration authority to regulate the manufacturing, marketing, and sale of tobacco products (H.R. 1256 111th Cong., 2009), something that has been discussed among tobacco control advocates since 1996, when the FDA first attempted to regulate certain aspects of the tobacco business in the country (Koop, 2003; Food and Drug Administration [FDA], 1998).

The authority given to the FDA to regulate tobacco products is not without certain limitations, and although praised by many (Brown, 2009; Campaign for Tobacco Free Kids, 2009), it has also received some criticism (Glantz, Barnes, & Eubanks, 2009), particularly due to the fact that the final language of the legislation was negotiated with Philip Morris USA, the largest tobacco company operating in the United States. Additionally, some of the measures proposed by the new legislation do not yet have an adequate scientific-base and the legislation requires that proposed regulations consider "technical achievability" and economic impact on tobacco trade (Glantz et al., 2009). A discussion of the details of what the FDA is and isn't and able to regulate according to the new legislation is beyond the scope of this chapter and has been clearly outlined by others, for example, the Tobacco Control Legal Consortium (2009). Nonetheless, this new legislation includes a call and a need for additional research in tobacco control that presents a rich opportunity for nurses to not only address existing gaps in nursing and tobacco control knowledge, but to develop new pathways of knowledge. The research opportunities generated by the FDA legislation are discussed below.

Research Needs Highlighted by the Language of H.R. 1256

The ultimate goal of FDA regulation of the manufacturing, marketing, and sales of tobacco products is to decrease the prevalence of tobacco use and, subsequently, the death and suffering caused by tobacco use in society. The legislation calls for the involvement and input of scientists with expertise in tobacco control research in order to develop regulatory guidance and policies that are evidence-based. Researchers need to be involved in evaluating the actual impact of implementing these regulatory measures, whether the impact is intended or unintended. Some of the research needs will evolve as new tobacco products are developed and regulatory guidelines are implemented. For example, research will be needed to evaluate tobacco products' design, ingredients, impact on health and addictiveness, and the need to restrict or prohibit certain ingredients in tobacco products. Any marketing claims that tobacco companies propose will need to be evaluated to assess their health and market impact, including claims of "reduced harm" tobacco products, and standards will be necessary to determine what tobacco companies can and cannot say about their products. Health impact research will need to consider the impact on current users and on those who are considering quitting as well as on those who have not yet started to use tobacco.

The legislation requires the FDA to assess new tobacco dependence treatments, including current or new medications that could aid in cessation efforts and relapse prevention. Surveillance of consumer behavior and population impact will be integral to ascertain the success and need for modification of the regulatory framework developed by the FDA.

Another important area of research related to the FDA legislation is monitoring of the tobacco industry activities and the impact of industry representatives on the Tobacco Products Scientific Advisory Committee that the FDA is required to create. The committee will be charged to provide advice to the Secretary of Health and Human Services on matters related to implementation of the FDA regulatory guidelines, and will have an opportunity to review and comment on any regulation that will be promulgated. While tobacco interests representatives will have nonvoting status on the committee, it is unknown what impact their access to government regulatory plans will have on both tobacco industry behavior and the regulatory measures themselves. Thus, in addition to continued monitoring of tobacco companies' activities that interfere with tobacco control, researchers will need to study the impact of the industry's participation on the Advisory Committee.

Funding for the research that will be necessary to assure the proper implementation of FDA regulation of tobacco could come directly (since the law establishes annual fees that the tobacco companies are required to pay the FDA to create and maintain this regulatory framework) or through existing funding mechanisms, such as the National Institutes of Health (NIH). This is an unprecedented opportunity and call to action for scientists to critically evaluate tobacco-related science and policy outcomes and provide evidence on the impact of changes on public health in the United States and implications for global health.

The World Health Organization Framework Convention on Tobacco Control

Another opportunity for scientists in tobacco control is emerging because of developments at the World Health Organization. For the first time WHO assumed its prerogative to sponsor an international treaty and developed the Framework Convention on Tobacco Control (WHO FCTC), the first international public health treaty (World Health Organization [WHO], 2003). Evidence from surveillance, clinical trial, and community-based research at country and regional level led WHO to recognize tobacco use as having a worldwide negative impact that needed to be addressed not only through individual countries' efforts, but also through a major international collaboration. After a few years of global negotiations, the WHO FCTC entered into force in February of 2005 (after the 40th country's ratification) and as of July 2009, 166 countries are a party to the treaty. Countries that are a party to the treaty are legally bound to develop and implement the evidence-based tobacco control measures established by the treaty articles (Bialous, Kaufman, & Sarna, 2003). Although the United States signed the treaty in 2004, by July 2009 it had not ratified the WHO FCTC.

The WHO FCTC (WHO, 2003) offers various opportunities for nurse researchers to assist in the implementation of national tobacco control programs and to inform evidence-based practice. Research opportunities include reducing SHS exposure (Article 8 of the WHO FCTC), exposing tobacco industry attempts to interfere with tobacco control policy (Article 5.3), evaluating economic impact of price and taxation on consumption and consumers' behavior (Article 6), and determining the impact of restrictions on marketing of tobacco products and health warnings in tobacco packaging (Articles 11 and 13). Article 14 of the treaty, calling Parties to ensure that tobacco dependence treatment is integral to national tobacco control plans, creates a special opportunity for nurse researchers to demonstrate the impact of nursing involvement in the delivery of treatment. The article states specifically that Parties

Shall develop and disseminate appropriate, comprehensive and integrated guidelines based on scientific evidence and best practices, taking into account national circumstances and priorities, and shall take effective measures to promote cessation of tobacco use and adequate treatment for tobacco dependence. (WHO, 2003, p. 13)

Research in the provision of such "adequate treatment" is more urgently needed as only 5% of the world's population is covered by cessation programs, and only 9 countries in the world have a national quitline, as well as both nicotine replacement therapy (NRT) and some clinical cessation services (with either NRT or cessation services costs covered), while 77 countries have both NRT and counseling, but where costs for neither are covered (WHO, 2008). Nursing research could make an enormous contribution in evaluating strategies to engage nurses, over 17 million worldwide (WHO, 2009a), to provide the widest possible access to treatment for those most in need, particularly in countries where the population has a higher degree of access to nursing personnel than to physicians. Evidence-based nursing practice on tobacco dependence treatment will be essential to achieving the WHO FCTC goals.

The research needs for full implementation of Article 14 are similar to the needs previously identified both by the U.S. Public Health Services *Treating Tobacco Use and Dependence: 2008 Update Guideline* (Fiore et al., 2008; Table 16.1) and by nurse scholars (in this volume of the *Annual Review of Nursing Research*). These include theory development and testing, basic science and bio-behavioral approaches to nicotine addiction, optimal cessation interventions for subgroups of the population, for example, those with lower education and socioeconomic status, youth, those highly targeted by tobacco company marketing efforts, and people with comorbidities, such as psychiatric, cardiovascular, cancer, respiratory diagnoses, among others. In addition to investigating optimal tobacco dependence interventions, nursing research needs to address those policies that will facilitate and enhance population access to treatment and those that are not effective.

Importantly, the WHO FCTC calls for international collaboration and sharing of research (Articles 20, 21, and 22) to ensure that all parties benefit from evidence-based policy implementation and evaluation. This provides nursing with an opportunity to develop an international research network of nurse scientists working on tobacco control, and to engage in multicountry research endeavors and collaborations (Percival, Bialous, Chan, & Sarna, 2003). An example of this collaboration among nurses and nurse scientists were actions taken in a preconference workshop in Mumbai, India prior to the 14th World Conference on Tobacco OR Health, where nurses from several countries prioritized the need to create a global network to advance evidence-based nursing practice in tobacco control. The International Council of Nursing (ICN) and several nursing organizations have issued position statements and calls for action for nurses to do more in tobacco control (American Nurses Association, 2005; International Council of

TABLE 16.1 Examples of Opportunities for Nursing Scientists to Address Tobacco Dependence Research Gaps Identified in the Guideline

Area of Research Gaps	Examples of Research Needs
Improving access to, acceptability of, and demand for tobacco dependence treatment	Assess acceptability, feasibility, and compared efficacy of intensive treatment versus community-based approaches.
	Develop strategies to increase referrals to and utilization of quitlines (fax referrals, provider initiated call), evaluating effectiveness
	Address myths and misconceptions about cessation counseling and pharmacotherapy.
	Develop and assess impact of marketing tobacco dependence treatment.
	Develop and evaluate outreach to special populations.[a]
Assessing effectiveness of tobacco dependence treatment delivery methods	Assess impact of including social network on treatment on long-term abstinence rates (i.e., partners/family as target for intervention, smoke-free homes, etc.).
	Compare effectiveness of different combination of interventions, including newer treatment modalities (computer-based, texting, tailoring, Internet-based social networks, etc.), and comparing different formats and same content, different content and same format of intervention delivery.
	Assess utilization and effectiveness of intervention with medications and counseling treatments, including quitlines.
	Assess effectiveness of motivational interventions, physiological monitoring, and biological marker feedback and other techniques on cessation.
Assessing effectiveness by different providers and combinations thereof	Assess effectiveness of intervention by clinicians other than physicians, for example, quitline counselors, trained peer counselors, nurses, physician assistants, pharmacists, and social workers.
	Evaluate differences between combined and sole practitioner interventions, at the same level of intervention intensity.
Assessing effectiveness of intensity, duration, and timing/spacing of intervention	Assess the efficacy of different intensity (time and content per encounter), duration (number of weeks/months) and spacing (i.e., weekly, weekly to monthly) of interventions, including length of counseling and medication interventions.

Decreasing disparities in treatment access and effectiveness; addressing needs of specific groups[b]	Develop and evaluate strategies to reduce treatment disparities Evaluate effectiveness of different interventions (including pharmacotherapy), and tailored intervention, in special populations.[a] Assess gender differences in the effectiveness of interventions. Evaluate optimal timing and durations of weight control measures during cessation interventions.
Decreasing relapse rates/improving long-term abstinence rates	Strategies, methods, and timing for relapse prevention—maintain same method, combination, sequential (e.g., face to face to phone to text). Differences in efficacy of relapse prevention from brief to intensive intervention.
Assessing impact of policies on cessation/systems changes	Assess effectiveness of smoke-free policies and smoke-free homes on short- and long-term cessation. Evaluate interventions targeting family and social networks. Assess the effectiveness of training programs for other health care professionals, identifying successful elements of continuing education and basic training programs. Evaluate the impact of multiple systems changes (clinician training, reminder systems, incentive payments, etc.). Develop strategies to remove system-related barriers to delivery of cessation interventions. Assess the impact of using tobacco intervention performance measures on both clinician intervention and patient outcomes. Assess the effectiveness treatment delivery in alternative setting (e.g., community-based worksite).
Cost impact and cost-effective analysis	Assess the cost effectiveness of various treatments, treatment combinations and formats (e.g., telephone, face to face, medication) and short- and long-term cost-effectiveness. Assess the level of payment and reimbursement to enhance delivery of interventions, including economic incentives to promote quitting and sustained abstinence.

(Continued)

TABLE 16.1 Examples of Opportunities for Nursing Scientists to Address Tobacco Dependence Research Gaps Identified in the *Guideline* (*Continued*)

Area of Research Gaps	Examples of Research Needs
Pharmacotherapy	Continue to evaluate relative effectiveness and safety of the seven FDA-approved medications, in general and for specific subpopulations, as well as for long-term treatment.
	Evaluate the use and side effects of combined medications.
	Assess effectiveness of prequit nicotine replacement therapy use in increasing abstinence rates.
	Assess effectiveness of over-the-counter medications and extent of utilization.
	Assess impact of over-the-counter medication combined with counseling through quitline, computer, other counseling.
	Assess impact of OTC medication on access to treatment of special populations.

Note. From Fiore, M., Jaén, C., Baker, T., Bailey, W., Benowitz, N., Curry, S., et al., *Treating Tobacco Use and Dependence: 2008 Update, Clinical Practice Guideline*, Department of Health and Human Services. Public Health Service, Rockville, MD, 2008.

[a]Special populations as defined by the *Guideline* include but are not limited to: adolescents and youth; pregnant women; smokers who are lesbian, gay, bisexual, and transgender; smokers with low socioeconomic status or with limited formal education; older smokers; nontobacco chemical dependency; lighter smokers; racial and ethnic minorities; and patients with cancer, chronic obstructive pulmonary disease, psychiatric disorders, including substance use disorders, atherosclerosis, HIV-positive, postmyocardial infarction patients, and hospitalized patients in general.

[b]Research gaps identified by the *Guideline* emphasize the need to address disparities and how to improve access to treatment of several population subgroups. Displayed here is but a small sample of the identified research needs.

Nurses, 2006; Oncology Nursing Society, 2008). These organizations also need to commit the resources to ensure that these statements move from paper to practice.

Update of the Tobacco Dependence Treatment Guideline

As discussed by Sarna and Bialous (2009), the Guideline (Fiore et al., 2008) provides clinicians with evidence-based, state of the art interventions to help smokers quit. The Guideline panel also identified many areas where additional research on tobacco dependence treatment is needed, and provides a roadmap for nurse scientists to contribute to the knowledge base in this field. Table 16.1 provides examples of the research gaps identified in the Guideline—several of which have been previously identified by nurse researchers. Although there is overlap in the research gaps identified in the Guideline and by nurse scientists, the questions that nurse researchers seek to answer are driven by their experience in direct and indirect patient care and practice, bringing a unique perspective both to the type and breadth of research as well as to the specific knowledge contributed. However, unless we see the evolution of a critical mass of nurse scientists dedicated to developing evidence-based understanding of how tobacco dependence can be treated, many of the questions raised in the Guideline may remain unanswered. A meta-analysis on nursing intervention on smoking cessation showed some encouraging results of nursing effectiveness, but pointed to the need for additional clinical trials testing the efficacy of incorporating smoking cessation interventions into nurses' clinical practice (Rice & Stead, 2008).

Other Recent Developments

Another important development that could open additional opportunities for nursing research is the Department of Defense's commitment to gradually implement the findings of an Institute of Medicine report (Bondurant & Wedge, 2009) recommending a tobacco-free military (Garamone, 2009). Arvey and Malone (2008), Smith, Blackman, and Malone (2007), and Smith and Malone (2009) previously discussed how tobacco companies targeted the military and thwarted tobacco control efforts, suggesting policy changes are needed to support servicewomen and men in becoming tobacco free.

Additionally, President Barack Obama has announced his commitment to support legislation that would implement comprehensive reform in the health care system, including an investment in prevention and wellness (U.S. Department of Health and Human Services, n.d.). Although the final language of the legislation is not known, it is certain to offer nurse scientists additional opportunities to contribute research to translate evidence into tobacco control practice. Speaking at her nomination, U.S. Surgeon General-nominee, Dr. Regina Benjamin, supported the importance of tobacco control by highlighting the personal suffering causing by tobacco use in her family (White House, 2009).

RESEARCH AND TOBACCO CONTROL POLICIES

The U.S. has experienced a marked decline in the incidence and prevalence of tobacco use in the past four decades (Sarna & Bialous, 2009). Research has demonstrated that a significant portion of this decline is due to the implementation and enforcement of tobacco control policies that impact the demand and the social acceptability of tobacco use. For example, after initial success in the implementation of smoke-free workplaces in California, several other localities, states, and countries implemented smoke-free legislation that went beyond the earlier California efforts. Research confirming that smoking prevalence, as well as the incidence of lung cancer, heart disease and other tobacco-related illnesses, decreased subsequent to the implementation of smoke-free legislation lent credibility to smoke-free legislation as an effective tobacco control policy measure (Polednak, 2009a, 2009b; WHO, 2007). Research similarly demonstrated the positive impact of other measures such as tobacco products price and tax increases, marketing restrictions and countermarketing campaigns, among others, on decreasing tobacco use. The Centers for Disease Control and Prevention recommends comprehensive tobacco control policies as the most effective mechanism to achieve significant reduction in the current toll of tobacco use on the country's economy and on public's health (CDC, 2007).

However, the positive impact of tobacco control policies has not been felt by all segments of the population. As highlighted by several chapters in this volume of *Annual Review of Nursing Research*, there remain disparities in tobacco use, access to treatment, and exposure to SHS. For example, in addition to variance in the degree of SHS exposure protection from state to state, within a state or municipality, those in certain job categories, with lower socioeconomic status, living in rural areas, or from an ethnic minority, remain disproportionately exposed to SHS. Research is needed to understand and address these discrepancies, offering everyone the benefits of this evidence-based policy.

Tobacco dependence treatment interventions should also be an integral part of comprehensive tobacco control policy and, as with other evidence-based policies, additional research is needed to ensure that there is a better understanding on how access to, and effectiveness of, treatment can be enhanced and offered to those most in need, particularly to address the gap where the population subgroups that have been most affected by tobacco use are those least likely to be offered treatment (Fiore et al., 2008).

Another important area of tobacco policy research is studying the efforts of tobacco companies to obstruct the progress of tobacco control. Tobacco companies, and their affiliates, have a long history of influencing the public health process through several strategies such as direct and indirect lobbying and campaign contributions, funding of research, attempting to derail regulatory processes, disseminating misleading information about tobacco products' impact on health, among other tactics (WHO, 2009b). In May, 2009 the U.S. Court of Appeals in Washington, D.C. upheld the 2006 ruling that found several U.S. tobacco companies guilty of racketeering and fraud, misleading the American public about the harm of cigarettes (Scarcella, 2009). The Parties to the WHO FCTC approved Guidelines for implementation of Article 5.3 based on the "fundamental and irreconcilable conflict between the tobacco industry's interests and public health policy interests" (WHO, 2009c, p.2) and recommends, among other things, no partnerships with, or funding from, tobacco companies for any public health or research endeavor.

Nursing research has greatly contributed to better understanding of tobacco companies' behavior and how to counter their attempt to derail tobacco control (WHO, 2009b). In addition to research on the tobacco industry, nurse scientists also need to be aware that they might be unwilling targets in tobacco companies' efforts to present themselves as responsible corporations. Although the industry funding of research and the ethical implication of accepting industry funding for health-related research has been discussed (Chapman & Shatenstein, 2001; Hirschhorn, Bialous, & Shatenstein, 2006; Malone, 2006), less research has been devoted to industry funding of health prevention and other health promotion efforts. For example, tobacco companies fund youth smoking prevention programs (Mandel, Bialous, & Glantz, 2006) and other community-based health and social initiatives that have no positive impact on reducing the prevalence of tobacco use but have great impact in building alliances, and garnering positive public opinion for tobacco companies (WHO, 2009b). Recently, Philip Morris (PM) funded a university to recruit researchers to evaluate a PM-supported smoking cessation Web site. As Malone and Smith (2009) noted, researchers need to be aware that by lending their names to tobacco-funded research, they are advancing tobacco companies' public relations efforts but not necessarily advancing science.

Nurses need to continue to investigate the impact of policies on nursing practice and on the public's health. A search of publications in nursing journals and indexed on PubMed database, using the keywords tobacco control, policy, and nursing and limiting to studies from 1990 to 2009, yielded 43 papers, 16 of which were listed as reviews. Nurses scientists working on public health problems other than tobacco, for example obesity, could apply the lessons learned from research findings demonstrating the impact of policy implementation on decreasing tobacco-related morbidity and mortality to other fields, enhancing collaboration and networking among nurse scientists.

ADDRESSING CHALLENGES TO ENHANCING
NURSING SCHOLARSHIP IN TOBACCO CONTROL

Barriers remain to enhanced nursing involvement in tobacco control (Sarna & Bialous, 2009). However, these are not insurmountable and with leadership from nursing academia and professional organizations, nurse scientists can realize their full contribution to the development of new knowledge and evidence-based practice and policy.

Nursing scholarship in tobacco control is thriving, limitations in funding and other barriers notwithstanding (Sarna & Bialous, 2009). In order to estimate the juncture of nurse-specific tobacco control research and funding, we conducted a search, on July 2009, of the National Institutes of Health Computer Retrieval of Information on Scientific Projects (CRISP, http://crisp.cit.nih.gov/), looking at new research grants that were funded from 1990 to 2009, using either tobacco or smoking as keywords. Including all the institutes from the NIH we obtained 3825 new research project titles funded in that time period. While not surprising that the majority (1109) were funded by the National Cancer Institute (NCI), the number funded during that time period by the National Institute of Nursing Research (NINR) was approximately 60, of which 14 were randomized experimental studies that had tobacco use as either a primary or secondary outcome variable. To have an estimate of the relative numbers, we did a search using other keywords for new research projects funded by the NINR. During the same time period, NINR funded 161 new grants with the keyword cancer, four of which included the keyword tobacco or smoking; similarly, 64 new grant projects listed cardiovascular disorder as a keyword (125 using only cardiovascular), of which 13 also included either the keyword tobacco or smoking. It is important to note that while all research that advances evidence-base nursing practice is invaluable, there seems to be an inequity of funding for tobacco given the scope of the health and social problem that tobacco use generates (Sarna & Bialous, 2009).

Many nursing projects are funded through the NCI and other institutes and not all principal investigators funded by NINR are necessarily nurse scholars (to locate all nursing funded research projects is beyond the scope of this chapter, although a significant portion of this research has been covered in this volume of *Annual Review of Nursing Research*). The NINR also has a more limited budget than other institutes. Nonetheless, it is troubling that less than 2% of all tobacco-related research funded by the NIH is from NINR. It is also possible that NINR, and other funding agencies, are not receiving as many proposals from nurse scientists for research on tobacco-related topics as from other disciplines. As discussed in this volume of *Annual Review of Nursing Research*, there is not an adequate number of prepared nursing scholars to develop a program of research in tobacco control and efforts are needed to mentor and grow scholarship in this field. Other limitations include quality of the proposal and the expertise (or lack thereof) of the reviewers in the field of nursing research on tobacco control. Another barrier to identifying nursing research in tobacco control is that not only an unknown portion of the nursing research is funded by agencies other than NINR, but the results may not be published in the nursing literature (Wells, Sarna, & Bialous, 2006) or the authors may not be clearly identified as nurses.

The number of nurse-led studies in some specific areas, such as the metabolic and biologic processes of nicotine addiction, and with some populations such as those with mental illness is incipient. Nursing research in the evaluation of non-cigarette tobacco products (e.g., cigars, water pipes) and noncombustible tobacco products (e.g., snus, spit tobacco) is limited. As the range of tobacco products increase and the tobacco companies develop new products and marketing strategies, there is a growing need for nurses to be prepared to address and counter any negative impact these products may have through the application of evidence-based practices. The globalization of tobacco products, such as snus (a smokeless tobacco product that is sold in a small bag, thus different from spit or chew tobacco), and its impact has generated debated within the tobacco control community (Tomar, Fox, & Severson, 2009; Zeller, Hatsukami, & Strategic Dialogue on Tobacco Harm Reduction Group, 2009). Recently, electronic cigarettes have been launched in several countries without adequate safety data and efficacy as a cessation aid (FDA, 2009). Nurse scientists need to be prepared to assess and evaluate the impact of these and future changes.

SEIZING NURSING RESEARCH OPPORTUNITIES IN TOBACCO CONTROL

There is an urgent need to assess the status of doctoral and postdoctoral training of nurses to conduct tobacco-related research and to determine what needs to be done to prepare future scholars to address the current and future knowledge gaps in research (Sarna, Bialous, Rice, & Wewers, 2009). Nursing schools with master and doctoral programs need to evaluate their curricula and determine the best strategies to incorporate tobacco control into the preparation of nurse researchers. While there are many demands on curricula, not adequately preparing nurses to address the first preventable cause of illness, disability, and death is not acceptable. Research demonstrates that there are avenues to enhance teaching for the practice of tobacco control (Butler et al., 2009; Chan, So, Wong, & Lam, 2008; Heath et al., 2007). Academic leadership and commitment are essential to enhance teaching and to develop researchers. The limited training of nurses in tobacco control, leading to limited opportunities for research mentorship, should not discourage nursing scholars from exploring the wealth of research opportunities. Nursing leadership is imperative in supporting efforts to enhance research and training priorities to focus on exploring the full potential and value of nursing contributions to tobacco control research to help prevent death and disease, much as it has emphasized nurses' role in end-of-life care in the past. Additionally, there needs to be enhanced nursing presence both in multidisciplinary research and in research networks. Nurse scientists involved in tobacco-related scholarship often find themselves isolated within nursing scholarly venues, or not clearly identified as nurse scholars in tobacco research networks. This identity gap can be addressed with enhanced discussion of tobacco within nursing research networks and, conversely, enhanced nursing recognition and focus in tobacco control research groups. There is momentum to bridge this gap, as nurses' visibility within tobacco control grows (Sarna & Bialous, 2009).

Nursing scholars must continue to focus on translational research in order to improve evidence-based nursing practice in tobacco control. This chapter provides an overview of new opportunities in tobacco control research due to changing policies, legislation, and evolving science and offers many suggestions for future areas of study. The studies identified and discussed in this volume of *Annual Review of Nursing Research* demonstrate the pivotal contribution that nurse researchers make to nursing and to tobacco control. With appropriate levels of funding and stronger encouragement at the research training level, nurses will be perfectly positioned to address the research gaps and fulfill their potential in contributing to science-based solutions to counter the devastating impact of the tobacco epidemic on individuals and communities in the United States and globally.

REFERENCES

American Nurses Association. (2005). *Tobacco use prevention, cessation, and exposure to second-hand smoke* [position statement]. Retrieved from http://www.nursingworld.org/MainMenuCategories/HealthcareandPolicyIssues/ANAPositionStatements/social.aspx

Arvey, S., & Malone, R. (2008). Advance and retreat: Tobacco control policy in the U.S. military. *Military Medicine, 173*(10), 985–991.

Bialous, S., Kaufman, N., & Sarna, L. (2003). Tobacco control policies. *Seminars in Oncology Nursing, 19*(4), 291–300.

Bondurant, S., & Wedge, R. (Eds.). (2009). *Combating tobacco use in military and veteran populations*. Washington, DC: Institute of Medicine.

Brown, B. (2009, June 29). FDA unfiltered: Tobacco industry experts weigh in on the new law. *Los Angeles Times*. Retrieved from http://www.latimes.com/features/health/la-he-tobacco-viewpoints29-2009jun29,0,7981875,full.story

Butler, K., Rayens, M., Zhang, M., Maggio, L., Riker, C., & Hahn, E. (2009). Tobacco dependence treatment education for baccalaureate nursing students. *The Journal of Nursing Education, 48*(5), 249–254.

Campaign for Tobacco Free Kids. (2009, June 22). *President Obama delivers historic victory for America's kids and health over tobacco* [press release]. Retrieved from http://www.tobacco freekids.org/Script/DisplayPressRelease.php3?Display=1161

Centers for Disease Control and Prevention (CDC). (2007). *Best practices for comprehensive tobacco control programs*. Atlanta, GA: Centers for Disease Control and Prevention, National Center for Chronic Disease Prevention and Health Promotion, Office on Smoking and Health. Retrieved from http://www.cdc.gov/tobacco/stateandcommu nity/best_practices/pdfs/2007/BestPractices_Complete.pdf

Chan, S., So, W., Wong, D., & Lam, T. (2008). Building an integrated model of tobacco control education in the nursing curriculum: Findings of a students' survey. *The Journal of Nursing Education, 47*(5), 223–226.

Chapman, S., & Shatenstein, S. (2001). The ethics of the cash register: Taking tobacco research dollars. *Tobacco Control, 10*(1), 1–2.

Food and Drug Administration. (1998). *Proposals for comprehensive tobacco legislation, United States Senate*. Retrieved from http://www.fda.gov/NewsEvents/Testimony/ucm 115127.htm

Food and Drug Administration. (2009, July 22). *FDA and public health experts warn about electronic cigarettes* [press release]. Retrieved from http://www.fda.gov/NewsEvents/News room/PressAnnouncements/ucm173222.htm

Fiore, M., Jaén, C., Baker, T., Bailey, W., Benowitz, N., Curry, S., et al. (2008). *Treating tobacco use and dependence: 2008 update. Clinical practice guideline*. Rockville, MD: U.S. Department of Health and Human Services, Public Health Service.

Garamone, J. (2009, July 10). Report urges timeline for tobacco-free military. *American Forces Press Service*. Retrieved from http://www.defenselink.mil/news/newsarticle.aspx?id= 55085

Glantz, S., Barnes, R., & Eubanks, S. (2009). Compromise or capitulation? US Food and Drug Administration jurisdiction over tobacco products. *PLoS Medicine, 6*(7), e1000118.

Heath, J., Kelley, F., Andrews, J., Crowell, N., Corelli, R., & Hudmon, K. (2007). Evaluation of a tobacco cessation curricular intervention among acute care nurse practitioner faculty members. *American Journal of Critical Care, 16*(3), 284–289.

Hirschhorn, N., Bialous, S., & Shatenstein, S. (2006). The Philip Morris external research program: Results from the first round of projects. *Tobacco Control, 15*(3), 267–269.

H.R. 1256, 111th Cong. (2009). *Family smoking prevention and tobacco control act* (enacted). Retrieved from http://tclconline.org/documents/FDA-tobacco-regulation-final-bill.pdf

International Council of Nurses. (2006). *Tobacco use and health* [position statement]. Retrieved from http://www.icn.ch/policy.htm

Koop, C. (2003). Tobacco addiction: Accomplishments and challenges in science, health, and policy. *Nicotine and Tobacco Research, 5*(5), 613–619.

Malone, R. (2006). Nursing's involvement in tobacco control: Historical perspective and vision for the future. *Nursing Research, 55*(4 Suppl.), S51–S57.

Malone, R. E. & Smith, E. A. (2009). Contact me soon!!! Confidential, risk-free opportunity! *Tobacco Control, 18*(4), 249.

Mandel, L., Bialous, S., & Glantz, S. (2006). Avoiding "truth": Tobacco industry promotion of life skills training. *The Journal of Adolescent Health, 39*(6), 868–879.

Oncology Nursing Society. (2008). *Nursing leadership in global and domestic tobacco control* [position statement]. Retrieved from http://www.ons.org/publications/positions/ GlobalTobaccoUse.shtml

Percival, J., Bialous, S., Chan, S., & Sarna, L. (2003). International efforts in tobacco control. *Seminars in Oncology Nursing, 19*(4), 301–308.

Polednak, A. (2009a). Trends in death rates from tobacco-related cardiovascular diseases in selected US states differing in tobacco-control efforts. *Epidemiology, 20*(4), 542–546.

Polednak, A. (2009b). Trends in incidence rates of tobacco-related cancer, selected areas, SEER Program, United States, 1992–2004. *Preventing Chronic Diseases, 6*(1), A16.

Rice, V.H., & Stead, L.F. (2008). Nursing interventions for smoking cessation. *Cochrane Database of Systematic Reviews,* (1), CD001188.

Sarna, L., & Bialous, S. (2009). Nursing research in tobacco control. In L. Sarna & S. Bialous (Eds.), *Annual Review of Nursing Research* (Vol. 27). New York: Springer Publishing.

Sarna, L., Bialous, S.A., Rice, V.H., & Wewers, M.E. (2009). Promoting tobacco dependence treatment in nursing education. *Drug and Alcohol Review, 28*(Special issue), 507–516.

Scarcella, M. (2009). D.C. circuit upholds landmark RICO case against big tobacco. *The National Law Journal.* Retrieved from http://www.law.com/jsp/article.jsp?id=1202430952786

Smith, E., Blackman, V., & Malone, R. (2007). Death at a discount: How the tobacco industry thwarted tobacco control policies in US military commissaries. *Tobacco Control, 16*(1), 38–46.

Smith, E., & Malone, R. (2009, July 16). "Everywhere the soldier will be": Wartime tobacco promotion in the US military. *American Journal of Public Health* [Epub ahead of print].

Tobacco Control Legal Consortium. (2009). *Federal regulation of tobacco: A summary* [fact sheet]. Retrieved from http://www.tobaccolawcenter.org/FDA-fact-sheets.html

Tomar, S., Fox, B., & Severson, H. (2009). Is smokeless tobacco use an appropriate public health strategy for reducing societal harm from cigarette smoking? *International Journal of Environmental Research and Public Health, 6*(1), 10–24.

U. S. Department of Health and Human Services. (n.d.). *HealthReform.Gov.* Retrieved on July 30, 2009 from http://www.healthreform.gov/index.html

Wells, M., Sarna, L., & Bialous, S. (2006). Nursing research in smoking cessation: A listing of the literature, 1996–2005. *Nursing Research, 55*(4 Suppl.), S16–S28.

The White House, Office of the Press Secretary. (2009, July 13). *Remarks by the president in announcement of U.S. surgeon general* [press release]. Retrieved from http://www.whitehouse.gov/the_press_office/Remarks-By-The-President-In-Announcement-Of-US-Surgeon-General/

World Health Organization. (2003). *WHO framework convention on tobacco control.* Geneva, Switzerland: World Health Organization. Retrieved from http://whqlibdoc.who.int/publications/2003/9241591013.pdf

World Health Organization. (2007). *Protection from exposure to second-hand tobacco smoke. Policy recommendations* (Report No. HD 9130.6). Retrieved from http://whqlibdoc.who.int/publications/2007/9789241563413_eng.pdf

World Health Organization. (2008). *WHO report on the global tobacco epidemic, 2008: The MPOWER package* (ISBN 978 92 4 159628 2). Retrieved from http://www.who.int/tobacco/mpower/package/en/index.html

World Health Organization. (2009a). *Global health atlas, data query.* Retrieved from http://apps.who.int/globalatlas/default.asp

World Health Organization. (2009b). *Tobacco industry interference with tobacco control.* Geneva, Switzerland: World Health Organization. Retrieved from http://www.who.int/tobacco/resources/publications/9789241597340.pdf

World Health Organization. (2009c). *Guidelines for implementation of Article 5.3 of the WHO framework convention on tobacco control on the protection of public health policies with respect to tobacco control from commercial and other vested interests of the tobacco industry.* Retrieved from http://www.who.int/fctc/guidelines/article_5_3.pdf

Zeller, M., Hatsukami, D., & Strategic Dialogue on Tobacco Harm Reduction Group. (2009). The strategic dialogue on tobacco harm reduction: A vision and blueprint for action in the US. *Tobacco Control, 18*(4), 324–332.

Index

Abstinence, 263–264
Acceptability and feasibility, for
    intervention studies, for
    pregnancy and postpartum
    smoking, 206–207
Acculturation, smoking and, 329–330
ACS. *See* American Cancer Society
ACS CPS. *See* American Cancer Society
    Prevention Study
ACT. *See* Assertive Community
    Treatment
Acute care settings
    dedicated tobacco dependence staff
        relating to, 352–354
    hospital, tobacco dependence studies
        in, 281–282
    tobacco user identification systems in,
        348–349
Addiction. *See also* Genetics, tobacco
    addiction and
    of heroin, methadone treatment model
        for, 50
    of nicotine, concepts in, 16–21
Additives, to tobacco, 159–160
Adolescent smoking, 127, 129–130, 132,
    133–134, 155
Adult Tobacco Survey (ATS), 94, 97
Affect-model, 49
African Americans, 83, 85, 102, 103, 127,
    156, 162, 328
Agency for Healthcare Research and
    Quality, 257
Agent Working Group, report of,
    163
Air quality studies, 369–370

Ambulatory care, tobacco user
    identification systems in, 349
American Association of Critical-Care
    Nurses, 291
American Cancer Society (ACS), 108,
    110, 177, 237
American Cancer Society Prevention
    Study (ACS CPS), 94, 95–96
American Legacy Foundation, 24
American Lung Association, 237
American Nurses Association, 355
American Psychiatric Nurses Association
    (APNA), 313, 314
American Public Health Association, 24
American Recovery and Reinvestment
    Act (ARRA), of 2009, 348,
    357
American smokers, 162
American Thoracic Society, 291
Annual Review of Nursing Research, 402,
    404, 406
APNA. *See* American Psychiatric Nurses
    Association
Appalachia, smokers in, 326–327
    females, study of, 127
Appalachian Regional Development Act,
    of 1965, 327
Asian-Americans, 103, 162, 331
Assertive Community Treatment (ACT),
    309
Association of Women's Health,
    Obstetric and Neonatal Nurses
    (AWHONN), 349
Asthma, 274, 275, 276, 277, 281, 282,
    284, 289, 290, 292

413

22024268